Cam

This b
but m
by ar

Bc
i

KINGSLEY WOOD: SCENES FROM A POLITICAL LIFE
1925-1943

Hugh Gault

Gretton Books
Cambridge

First published in 2017 by Gretton Books

A CIP catalogue record for this title is available from the British Library.

ISBN   978-0-9562041-9-6 (hardback)

Set in 9/11 pt Arial

Printed and bound by 4edge in the UK

"There is nothing a government hates more than to be well-informed; for it makes the process of arriving at decisions much more complicated and difficult."

JM Keynes (1883-1946)

"There have been biographies of World War II figures whose importance ... rank far below" that of Wood.

BEV (Basil) Sabine (1914-)

Making the Heavens Hum
Overall Synopsis

Part 1: Kingsley Wood and the Art of the Possible 1881-1924
(published 2014)

Born in 1881 in Hull where his father was a Methodist minister, Kingsley Wood's family soon moved to London. Wood was imbued with the ethic of public service from an early age but was not a natural Conservative. Nor, unlike many other Conservative politicians, had he money behind him to smooth his path; initially dependent on his own efforts he soon accrued influential contacts and patronage, both Nonconformist and more widely.

A solicitor from 1903, Wood built a thriving practice in the City, provided free legal advice to the poor in various settlements and was the Methodists' legal adviser of choice. By 1906 he was the Conservative agent for Hoxton. Prominent as the acknowledged expert, already in the public eye, he represented various interests over the 1910 proposals for state insurance. Wood thought this a threat to individual thrift, as well as to business interests, clashing with Lloyd George, co-ordinating the response of Friendly Societies and securing amendments to the Bill. Wood was notable in the Nonconformist Unionist Association campaign against Home Rule and soon one of the leading opponents alongside Balfour, Carson and others. Risks to Empire, tariff reform, increasing socialism and world war might end civilisation as the western world knew it. Big city government, particularly the London County Council, was one of the battlegrounds and in 1911 Wood, out-flanking his Labour opponent, was elected as Municipal Reform representative for Woolwich. He was re-elected in 1913 ahead of Margaret Bondfield, subsequently one of Labour's first women MPs.

During World War I Wood chaired the LCC's Building Acts, Insurance and Old Age Pensions Committees, and was vice-chairman of the special committee established to administer separation allowances for the families of soldiers and sailors. He had campaigned against enemy aliens but he also fought for pension improvements so that people did not have to rely on the Poor Law and later against the scandal of short-weight bread. He kept the focus on tuberculosis, arguing for better access to sanatoria and improved housing to combat it.

Will Crooks, who had captured Woolwich from the Tories in a spectacular by-election, was the Labour MP from 1903 to 1918. In 1918 the seat was split in two, Crooks retaining Woolwich East while Wood won Woolwich West as a coalition Conservative with a majority over Labour of more than 5,000. Wood, now Sir Kingsley, had proposed a Ministry of Health to replace the Local Government Board and he was appointed as Parliamentary Private Secretary (PPS) there in Lloyd George's coalition government. Lloyd George and Wood shared similar backgrounds of nonconformity and law, but they were otherwise poles apart. Lloyd George was ruthless and ambitious, an orator, opportunist and self-publicist. Wood was understated, almost principled by contrast, yet a competent speaker and effective strategist nonetheless and, as with all natural politicians, quick to spot opportunities – for his geographical and religious constituents and consequently for himself as well.

In his early years in Parliament Wood oversaw the "homes for heroes" programme, helped the Ministry of Health into being and campaigned for allotments, earlier shop closing and continued employment at the Woolwich Arsenal. In 1923 he fought alongside Labour and Liberal MPs in opposing Irish deportations and his party's proposed limitations on the right to trial by jury, while in 1924 he was instrumental in the downfall of the first Labour government.

Part 2: Scenes from a Political Life 1925-1943

Neville Chamberlain's Parliamentary Secretary at Health throughout the five years of Baldwin's 1924-1929 government, Wood delivered major programmes of health, housing and local government reform. He was the Government's Civil Commissioner in Newcastle and the north-east during the 1926 General Strike.

In the 1929 general election Wood just retained his seat, becoming the chief parliamentary critic of the Labour government of 1929-1931. In the subsequent National Government he was Postmaster General for four years with responsibility for reforming the Post Office and for overseeing the BBC. He has been described as "... the best PMG in history ...", though Sir John Reith called him "a little bounder" when they were at odds over renewal of the BBC Charter. They reached a rapprochement in subsequent years, with Wood often the "giant autocrat's" advocate in the government. Dragging the Post Office into the twentieth century, Wood provided leadership for the Bridgeman reforms, raised employee morale and introduced public relations and advertising to promote the full range of services (savings bank, telegrams, telephones as well as letters and parcels). In doing so he resisted both the revival of the penny post and those people who wanted to see the Post Office sold off. As always there was a tension between those who thought it a public service and those who believed it should be a business.

Conservative Chief of Staff in the 1935 general election he then became Minister of Health, first under Baldwin then Chamberlain. He became Minister of Air from May 1938 when aircraft production vastly increased as Britain re-armed. In May 1940 he persuaded Neville Chamberlain to resign. Wood has been described as "the indispensable Judas" when he then immediately became Churchill's Chancellor of the Exchequer. As Chancellor he supported Keynes, the economic adviser Wood had appointed to the Treasury, giving him and the rest of a gifted team Wood had around him the political endorsement they required. Cato (Nye Bevan and others) identified Wood as one of "the guilty men" – not least over Dunkirk and appeasement, but the country faced increasing devastation and disaster on other fronts as well, not least how to pay for the war. Keynes described the budget that followed in April 1941 as "a revolution in public finance". In February 1943 Wood led Government opposition to early implementation of the Beveridge report, which he thought should be assessed alongside other social and physical reconstruction priorities after the war so that these were not pre-empted and - every Chancellor's refrain - the overall cost implications were tackled properly. When Wood died prematurely in September 1943, Churchill missed this "barometer of the Conservative party" – the consummate party politician with his "ear to the ground". "The keenest and most cunning of politicians," as Wood had been described.

Acknowledgements

Part 1 of Kingsley Wood's biography covering the years 1881-1924 was published in 2014. This second part covers the remaining nineteen years of his life, 1925 to 1943. A lot happened in this period and Wood was far from a bystander watching events unfold around him. To my delight, but also somewhat to my surprise and perhaps even more so to that of others, Wood was at the heart of much of this action, always engaged and frequently shaping the most striking moments.

Part 2 contains thirteen chapters and sixteen other episodes, or vignettes, outside the main stream of his story. A book of this length was necessary to do justice to the huge part that Wood played in Britain's history in the second quarter of the twentieth century. Every author makes such claims of course, and the sceptics are bound to dispute it, especially in the case of somebody like Wood who history has largely forgotten. But the test is in the text, so each reader must judge the veracity of this assertion for themselves.

Every biographer hopes, of course, for the personal papers that illuminate and provide the private counterpart to the public story. Wood's personal correspondence, diaries and other records have never turned up and probably never will. In all likelihood they were destroyed soon after he died. Despite Wood's political prominence then, the huge number of cartoons of him, only a very few of which are presented in this book, suggest that the background, his hinterland in current parlance, might prove as fertile as the foreground I have managed to disinter and write about. The biographer's role is often to unearth and in Wood's case there has turned out to have been much more than the skeleton that many accounts suggest. It is hoped that this book provides the flesh as well as the bones and that Wood is now more than just the silhouette he was before.

The Acknowledgements in Part 1 included tributes to the many people who had helped me prepare that volume since starting the research in September 2011. This section records the additional debts I have incurred in bringing Part 2 to publication.

Of the six people who read and commented on the draft of Part 1, four submitted to the ordeal again and were joined by another four who were also prepared to spend some of their summer in 2016 doing so. I have certainly benefitted from their inputs and I hope they can see the impact of their comments on the text that follows. In alphabetical order they were:

Robin Brothers, whose mother Marjorie went to live with Agnes and Kingsley Wood in 1914 aged 11 and was formally adopted by them in the late 1920s just before her own marriage. Robin is the closest living relative and one of the pleasures of research and biography is getting to know people you would not otherwise meet.

Peter Catterall, Professor of History and Policy at the University of Westminster and author of several acclaimed books on this era. His encyclopaedic knowledge has frequently put me right or pointed me in fresh and illuminating directions.

Martin Daunton, the economic historian and now Emeritus Professor at the University of Cambridge who also made me aware of new areas to explore.

Jane Gallagher, an archivist with University of Kent Special Collections who hold the twenty-five volumes of Kingsley Wood press cuttings (more details in Part 1). Her extensive comments have added greatly to the final outcome.

Leslie Griffiths, The Rev Lord Griffiths of Pembrey and Burry Port who has recently retired as superintendent of Wesley's Chapel. He initiated a housing debate in the House of Lords in November 2016 and mentioned Kingsley Wood in his opening speech. I have been conscious of his comments on simplicity and clarity, but at this length the book is unlikely to appeal to the wider readership he would prefer. Nevertheless, I hope it helps to remind people generally, as well as other historians, of Wood's contribution and the Methodist tenets of social reform to which he aspired.

Allen Packwood, Director of Churchill College Archives Centre, University of Cambridge, whose comments helped keep my assessment of Winston Churchill and his work with Wood in balance.

David Poole, originally a colleague in local government and still a friend despite being the only person who has read the drafts of all my books over the last eight years.

John Shepherd, Visiting Professor, University of Huddersfield whose knowledge of Labour Party history provided another perspective. Like me, he lives close enough to research in Cambridge University Library, an unparalleled resource and one of the world's great deposit libraries.

Many other people and organisations have helped with particular elements of Wood's story. In the order these appear in the text, they are:

- **Brighton, Rusthall, Tunbridge Wells, Westgate-on-Sea**
  Mark Bateson, Kent County Council archives, Maidstone
  Kathy Chaney, Curator, Salomons Museum
  Dawn Crouch, Westgate Heritage Centre
  Emma Leitch and Broomhill Bank School
  Shona Milton, Brighton History Centre
  Margate, Rusthall, Tunbridge Wells and Westgate-on-Sea
    Libraries

- **1926 General Strike**
  Simon Green, Gateshead Libraries
  Deborah Moffat and Northumberland Record Office
  Gail Robson and Tyne & Wear Archives and Museums
  Syndics of Cambridge University Library for permission to quote
    from the Baldwin Papers in Chapter 9

- **Post Office**
  Duncan Campbell-Smith
  Adrian Steel and Post Office archives
  News UK Information Services

- **BBC**
  Louise North, BBC Archives

- **The Athenaeum**
  Jennie De Protani, Archivist, The Athenaeum

- **Edward Campbell**
  Calista Lucy, Keeper of the Archive, Dulwich College

- **Conservative Party and Primrose League**
  Jeremy McIlwaine, Conservative Party Archive, Bodleian Library,
    Oxford University

- **Wood's Methodist connections**
  Peter Forsaith, Oxford Centre for Methodism and Church History,
    Oxford Brookes University

- **Wood's London homes**
  Alison Kenney and colleagues, Westminster Archives
  Nigel Hughes and Grosvenor
  London Metropolitan Archives

- **appeasement and fascism**
  Chris Low, Buckinghamshire County Council Archives
  University of Reading Special Collections

- **Air and Air Ministry**
  Professor John Ferris, University of Calgary

- **General Sikorski and Polish government in exile**
  Andrzej Suchcitz, Director/Keeper of the Archive, Polish
    Institute/Sikorski Museum

It would be misleading, however, to categorise everybody's help in this way. Several have assisted and advised with a number of elements, including:

Professor Stuart Ball, University of Leicester
Professor John Fair, University of Georgia
Joanna Baines, University of Kent Special Collections
Nick Hiley and University of Kent British Cartoon Archive
Ceri Humphries and other staff of Churchill College Archives
  Centre, Cambridge University
Eliza McKee, Parliamentary Archives
Professor Robert Self
Anne Taylor, Head of the Map Room, Cambridge University Library
Professor Philip Williamson, University of Durham

as well as the British Library; Cambridge University Library - particularly staff of the Commonwealth, Manuscripts and Map Rooms; and the National Archives at Kew.

This is a long list, but that reflects the huge range of Kingsley Wood's activities. He depended on the willingness of others to co-operate and exactly the same has been true in my case. I thank everybody for it for I could not have done it without their help.

Hugh Gault
Cambridge

January 2017

MAKING THE HEAVENS HUM

Contents - Part 1   **Page**
KINGSLEY WOOD AND THE ART OF THE POSSIBLE
1881-1924 (published 2014)

[From the death of Disraeli to the downfall of the 1924 Labour
government]

MAKING THE HEAVENS HUM

Contents - Part 2   **Page**
KINGSLEY WOOD: SCENES FROM A POLITICAL LIFE
1925-1943

Interspersed among the main stream of Wood's political life
are vignettes of other people and events important to him

Contents - Part 2
KINGSLEY WOOD: SCENES FROM A POLITICAL LIFE 1925-1943

Page

Abbreviations in text

ACN	Advisory Committee on Nutrition
BBC	British Broadcasting Corporation
BEF	British Expeditionary Force
BMJ	British Medical Journal
CAN	Committee Against Malnutrition
CAS	Chief of the Air Staff
CCEL	Central Council of Economic Leagues
CID	Committee of Imperial Defence
CRD	Conservative Research Department
DNB	Dictionary of National Biography
DPRC	Defence Policy and Requirements Committee
DRC	Defence Requirements Committee
EPT	Excess Profits Tax
ILP	Independent Labour Party
IMF	International Monetary Fund
LCC	London County Council
LRD	Labour Research Department
NI	National Insurance
NPB	National Publicity Bureau
NUDAW	National Union of Distributive and Allied Workers
NUR	National Union of Railwaymen
NUWM	National Unemployed Workers Movement
OMS	Organisation for the Maintenance of Supplies
PEP	Political and Economic Planning
PISM	Polish Institute/Sikorski Museum
PMG	Postmaster-General
PPS	Parliamentary Private Secretary
PR	Public relations
PS	Parliamentary Secretary
RACS	Royal Arsenal Co-operative Society
TGWU	Transport and General Workers Union
TUC	Trade Unions Congress
WWI	First World War
WWII	Second World War
£ s d	pounds, shillings and pence in pre-decimal currency where 6d = 2.5p, 1s = 5p and 20s = £1

Illustrations

Copyright permissions

8.   INTRODUCTION

Most politicians have a short shelf-life. Perhaps not as brief as yesterday's newspapers but once they have left office they rarely last long in the public memory. To die in September 1943 before the Second World War had turned decisively in the allies' favour, to be associated with Neville Chamberlain for large parts of your career and to have argued against the premature implementation of the Beveridge report (even if as Chancellor of the Exchequer you would be bound to), would consign most politicians to oblivion. To be remembered they had to be exceptional, either scandalous or very good. A solid record of achievement in various offices of State might not be enough, especially if they were eclipsed by colleagues, notably those who, in addition, wrote the history of their times. Such has been Kingsley Wood's fate.

Although rarely remembered today, Sir Kingsley Wood was nevertheless a leading Conservative politician, first elected to Parliament at the end of World War I and one of the most influential in the 1930s. But he was a man of many parts and this was only one of them. Then, as now, it is rare for private member's Bills to reach the statute book for they rarely receive the time or support they require, but in 1925 the measure Wood had introduced to make summer-time permanent did become law. Part 1 of this biography covered the first forty-three years of his life from 1881 to 1924;[1] this second volume continues the story to 1943 and his premature death aged sixty-two on the morning he was due to introduce a major income tax reform (Pay As You Earn, PAYE) in the House of Commons. Still Chancellor of the Exchequer, as he had been since Winston Churchill became Prime Minister in May 1940, this was the culmination of a career that had not just been confined to politics. He had started as a solicitor, often giving his services free as a poor man's lawyer to those who could not afford representation; had written articles and pamphlets to increase awareness of entitlement and rights (e.g., to old age pensions or for housing tenants); had been instrumental in the introduction of National Insurance in 1911 and the Ministry of Health in 1919; had been an active member of the London County Council (LCC) for over seven years and on other bodies during World War I; had campaigned for allotments and earlier shop closing; and would

---

[1] Hugh Gault, 'Making the Heavens Hum: Kingsley Wood and the Art of the Possible 1881-1924', 2014

become increasingly prominent both in the Conservative party organisation and as a Methodist.

Neither Nemesis Nor Nincompoop

In 1929 the *Northampton Evening Telegraph* quoted a Liberal MP to explain why Sir Kingsley Wood, then in opposition, was anathema to the Labour benches in the Commons:

> Behind his smiling, chubby face is indomitable perseverance and sleepless energy. I don't know any politician more feverishly active, more persistently tenacious, and more consistently partisan.[2]

According to the *Birmingham Daily Mail*, "Since Labour came into power he has been the Government's sharpest critic; he is quite the best-hated Unionist in the Commons".[3] Wood could irritate the Liberals too, as the *Star* reported of an incident in the House of Commons smokeroom at this time. When an ex-Liberal Minister gibed at the small number of Liberal MPs after the election, Wood replied: 'Yes ... but it is scarcely in good taste for Judas to sneer at a shortage among the Apostles'.[4]

The then Liberal MP Leslie Hore-Belisha (1893-1957)[5] wrote in his Speaker's Eye column in the *Daily Express* "An uninformed spectator of Parliament would assume at once that ... Wood was leading the Conservative party in the House",[6] while the *Saturday Review* judged him "as effective in opposition as he was efficient in office".[7] When the charismatic Labour MP David Kirkwood

---

[2] *Northampton Evening Telegraph* 20th November 1929, University of Kent archives KW17 143/6 (hereafter just KW..)
[3] *Birmingham Daily Mail* 22nd November 1929, KW17 149/7
[4] *Star* 25th November 1929, KW17 148/2
The Liberals had increased their number of MPs from 46 previously to 58 but this MP had expected them to do even better.
[5] Dates are given here unless the person also featured in Part 1, they are very minor characters or contemporary novelists who comment on, but do not otherwise feature, in Wood's story. All the major characters referred to in this volume are listed in the cast of characters on pp479-508
[6] *Daily Express* 21st February 1930, KW17 172/1
[7] *Saturday Review* 23rd February 1930, KW17 174/2

described him as a "nincompoop"[8] many must have thought this an accolade from an outspoken political opponent. Certainly it meant that Wood was noticed, and not being noticed must be an ambitious politician's worst nightmare. His assiduous homework and mastery of his brief meant that the opposition also feared him. Wood could dissect an argument, discard the inessentials and express his points convincingly; and though his legal background helped, it ultimately depended on long hours of study and the hard graft of a workaholic. A typical example was reported in the *Evening News*:

> Among the busy men who … returned to London from the South Coast last night was Sir Kingsley Wood …
> He boarded the train carrying two attaché cases, his arms full of Sunday papers which he had not had time to read. Lady [Agnes] Wood … told me. '… he has been poring over books and papers the whole of the weekend. Political husbands seem to have less time for their wives than golfing husbands'.[9]

The opinions of close colleagues, which in the case of politicians might mean MPs from other parties and the press, are often an excellent guide to the overall assessment of a person and their future prospects. Baldwin's popularity with the electorate was generally echoed by the perception of him in other quarters, including parliament. He was an electoral asset to the Conservative party, not least because of his "style of reconciliation and empathy with the values of labour",[10] but his common touch won him friends and admiration in the Commons and beyond too. One opponent judged that, while Baldwin "broke down the barrier between the Labour man and the rest of the House", he thought him "over-placed" as Prime Minister and that his "besetting sin was laziness";[11] another's assessment was that he "had not an enemy on our side of the House and … was trusted by all our Members. His weakness as a Leader of the Conservative Party was that he was incapable of political meanness".[12] At the other extreme the

---

[8] Hansard (HC Deb 5s unless stated otherwise), 6th May 1926, vol. 195, col. 480

[9] *Evening News* 25th November 1925, KW16 160/3

[10] Stuart Ball, 'Portrait of a Party: The Conservative Party in Britain 1918-1945, 2013, p85

[11] Percy Harris, 'Forty Years In and Out of Parliament', 1946, pp93-94

[12] Henry Snell, 'Men, Movements and Myself', 1936, p247

overwhelming judgement might be disdain, notoriety or, even worse perhaps, the humiliation of being ignored. Examples of all these types are not hard to find, people such as Pemberton Billing and Horatio Bottomley, while others move from one category to another (e.g., Oswald Mosley) as their fortunes fade or rise. Perhaps the most marked examples of changing political judgements are those typically exercised of Neville Chamberlain and Winston Churchill at different stages of their careers. At all times there have been MPs whose performance in the chamber reflected their limited abilities beyond it; they only had to get to their feet to speak for the House to empty. Some were poor speakers, though this would often be tolerated if the politician was believed to be sincere or their performance outside the Commons justified it, but others were too abstruse, pompous or shallow for their colleagues to stomach. Playing to the gallery for its own sake was greatly frowned upon, though oratory that had a purpose in conveying a message or ensuring it was remembered was viewed differently.

Cartoonists are often unforgiving and perceptive political commentators and their depiction of politicians, even in the more deferential inter-war years, generally reflect a view held more widely. It often gets at the heart of character too. So, while it might be expected that Conservative-supporting papers (such as the *Times*, *Morning Post*, *Daily Telegraph*, *Observer*, *Daily Mail* and *Daily Express*)[13] would tend to generosity if not eulogy in their appraisal of Wood, positive depictions in other papers must have overcome an instinctive opposition. Wood might be lampooned, but he was never humiliated and the over-riding image is of his geniality (a term often used of him) and the affection in which he was widely held. His lack of height did not go unremarked but he was not overlooked; his voice was not strong but he was heard nonetheless; in any event his arguments were usually thought through and compelling, and so people paid attention to what he was saying. The *Daily News* referred to him "mastering physical disadvantages

---

Henry Snell (1865-1944), Labour MP for Woolwich East from November 1922 to 1931, became Baron Snell of Plumstead in March 1931. Snell commented on various opposition MPs then, but not Kingsley Wood despite the Woolwich connection.

[13] Robert Graves and Alan Hodge include an assessment of the leading newspapers in 'The Long Week-End: A Social History of Great Britain 1918-1939', 1985 (orig. 1940), pp55-62.
More detail is provided in Francis Williams, 'Dangerous Estate: The Anatomy of Newspapers', 1984 (orig. 1957)

(he is dumpy and has a ladylike voice)" concluding that he had done "almost brilliantly",[14] while the *Evening Standard* went further:

> ... as a back-bencher, [Wood] was one of the most persistent people in the House at question time, and developed a natural faculty for the kind of guerrilla warfare that is the essence of successful opposition.
> When he came to answer instead of to ask questions he was much too experienced to be caught in the sort of booby traps which Labour members tried to bait for him. In debate, too, he knew his case inside out, and could put it. Moreover, he never loses his temper.[15]

He was often described as a "cherub", for example "All this makes him a veritable giant for work, but he smiles through it all so that he earns the nickname of the 'Cherub'",[16] but this did not imply that he should be disregarded or was intellectually flabby. In November 1925 a cartoon of Neville Chamberlain and Wood, the Minister and his deputy at Health, in the *Daily Chronicle*[17] shows Wood's notes on the floor, notes on which Chamberlain as well as Wood would have depended. The Rating and Valuation Bill that they had piloted through the Commons was nearing the end of its report stage (at the third reading on 4th December only fifty-eight votes were cast against it) and they had previously steered the Widows', Orphans' and Old Age Contributory Pensions Bill to royal assent on 7th August. On both counts they would be satisfied with the progress of these fundamental reforms.

Wood was a conscientious and respected constituency MP in Woolwich West, an area he had been associated with from the first decade of the twentieth century. Yet a cartoon in one of the more antagonistic local papers, the Independent Labour Party's (ILP) *Woolwich Pioneer*, the month before the Pensions Bill became law was headed 'Nemesis', and contrasted the claim on an election poster that "What Wood says in West Woolwich he says in Westminster" with a report in an anonymous daily paper that ascribed a worried look to Wood as he attempted to defend the

---

[14] *Daily News* 9th August 1926, KW16 228/2
[15] *Evening Standard* 6th August 1926, KW16 228/3
[16] *Manchester Evening News* 13th February 1925, KW16 117/8
[17] *Daily Chronicle* 26th November 1925, KW16 160/7

contributory scheme for widows' pensions.[18] The implication was that Wood had been found out and the Bill was his come-uppance. There might be difficulties in explaining and justifying the contributory principle, but Wood was certainly not the nemesis of the less fortunate in society and nor was the Bill his downfall either. He could be expedient and pragmatic, the givens of a life in politics but, as the succeeding pages show, he was far from a nincompoop and no more of a hypocrite than any other politician who lasted.

Health and Happiness.

Mr Neville Chamberlain,   Sir Kingsley Wood,

© Solo Syndication/Associated Newspapers Ltd.
Daily Chronicle 26th November 1925, KW16 160/7

1924 General Election

> All through the twenties … the stench from the trenches was gradually superseded by the smell of despair as the dole queues multiplied …[19]

---

[18] *Woolwich Pioneer* 3rd July 1925, KW16 139/3
[19] Ronald Blythe, 'The Age of Illusion: England in the Twenties and Thirties 1919-1940', 1963, p245

It had been the Conservative failure to stem unemployment after the 1921 slump that cost them the 1923 general election - called unnecessarily but courageously by Stanley Baldwin over trade protection, a matter of principle which he judged the critical remedy for unemployment but for which he thought he had no mandate. However, the minority administration that followed made little inroad either and on 8th October 1924 Labour's first government resigned after losing a Commons vote of confidence over their handling of the *Workers Weekly* prosecution. Kingsley Wood had been the first MP to ask searching questions about the curious withdrawal of the prosecution and had received from the Labour Prime Minister Ramsay MacDonald a misleading reply - to put it at its most charitable. Understandably, the Labour party perspective was that Ramsay MacDonald was "partly ... tricked - partly stumbled gratuitously over a silly irrelevant question",[20] but this belies the parliamentary record for MacDonald subsequently failed to correct his answer adequately when given the opportunity to do so. It had been Wood's questioning that instigated the subsequent censure debate, though he took no part in it himself as other, then more prominent, Conservative MPs weighed in.[21]

Labour's electoral prospects were further damaged during the campaign itself as a result of the Zinoviev letter. Allegedly from the President of the Third International Grigori Zinoviev (1883-1936) promoting the supposed Communist aspirations of army sedition and worker uprising, the *Daily Mail* ruthlessly exploited the Labour Party implications, a credible link given their government's attempted treaty with Russia. Although Zinoviev disclaimed responsibility two days before the general election, he was not believed and Labour scepticism about the letter was easily discounted as predictable. Some Labour MPs thought the letter too convenient for it reflected "all the arguments which the Conservatives had been using against the ratification of the Russian treaty".[22] For others, though, it was all too credible reflecting their worst fears, a view that the electorate endorsed.

After what inevitably came to be known as the "red letter" election, Stanley Baldwin became Prime Minister again on 4th

[20] Margaret Bondfield, 'A Life's Work', 1949, p260. She was briefly Labour MP for Northampton at this point.
[21] Hansard, 8th October 1924, vol. 177, cols.581-704
Chapter 7 in Part 1 provides further detail.
[22] For example, Frederick Pethick-Lawrence, 'Fate Has Been Kind', 1942, p138

November 1924 at the head of 413 Conservative MPs and with a majority of 211 over all other parties. Such were the number of Conservatives that they operated "a rota system for backbench MPs which allowed them certain nights each week absent from the House without need of a pair".[23] The Liberals had been trounced, reduced from 159 to 40 seats, while Labour had lost forty and with 151 MPs was now the official opposition. As the MP for North Southwark Leslie Haden Guest noted, this necessitated a measured approach for, as the alternative government in waiting, any wild and rash promises could no longer be made in the abstract for they might have to be fulfilled on return to office.[24] Baldwin must have felt triumphant, though it was neither in his nature to show it nor was he likely to ignore the emphasis King George V (1865-1936) had put on the need for social reform, stressing the improved housing and reduced unemployment that would be required to defuse class war,[25] views Baldwin shared for he "dwelt continually upon the legacy of Disraeli".[26] The first challenge was to form a government for, as the *Daily Express* had reported the previous day, seventy-seven applicants had to be squeezed into fifty-two posts.[27] A key consideration was what to do with Winston Churchill, the newly elected MP for Epping, returning to the Conservatives for the first time since crossing the floor in 1904 and having spent the previous two years out of Parliament since his defeat as a Liberal in Dundee. Neville Chamberlain, Baldwin's Chancellor of the Exchequer in late 1923, preferred to return to his previous position as Minister of Health and the opportunities for major reform it offered across housing and local government as well as health. This enabled Baldwin, though only after extensive consultation and much deliberation, to offer the Treasury to Churchill, thereby neutering the independent tendencies that Churchill might otherwise have shown

---

[23] Stuart Ball (ed.), 'Parliament and Politics in the Age of Baldwin and MacDonald: The Headlam Diaries 1923-1935',1992, p92
Ball, 2013, op cit, p368 explains that the Whips in the 1924-1929 Parliament divided Conservative MPs into ten rotating groups with seven of the groups designated to attend each day.
[24] Leslie Haden Guest, 'Where Is Labour Going? A Political Pamphlet', p83
[25] Keith Middlemas and John Barnes, 'Baldwin: A Biography', 1969, p277
[26] David Dilks, 'Neville Chamberlain - volume 1: Pioneering and Reform, 1869-1929', 1984, pp406-407
[27] *Daily Express* 3rd November 1924, KW16 89/3

in a spending department.[28] Churchill was both grateful, for such a senior post far exceeded his hopes, and relieved for he had feared that Baldwin might not offer him anything at all. Curzon, "after a short and tearful interview, was shunted into the Lord Presidency",[29] a post he had held seven years earlier when Lloyd George was Prime Minister, and a rehabilitated Austen Chamberlain was appointed Foreign Secretary instead, one of whose first decisions on 21st November 1924 was to declare the Zinoviev letter authentic.[30] AP Nicholson observed in his profile of Baldwin that "the appearance of not being too clever is an asset in a political leader",[31] but it might be more appropriate to remark that Baldwin was canny enough not to show how clever he was.[32] In this instance he had drawn Churchill and Austen Chamberlain back into the fold, apparently strengthening his and the government's position in the process.[33] His relaxed style may have been mistaken by many for negligence; it was sometimes, but not always.

The *Daily Express* expected that a post would also be found for Kingsley Wood for it judged that in the previous Parliament he "might often have been mistaken for Leader of the Opposition".[34] On 8th November Baldwin appointed him Neville Chamberlain's number two, Parliamentary Secretary at the Ministry of Health, thereby demonstrating that he intended to get to grips with the

---

[28] When Churchill returned to the Admiralty in 1939 at the outbreak of World War II he said that he preferred a Department to none at all no matter "however influential" the Minister. Martin Gilbert, 'Winston Churchill, vol.6 [sic]: The Prophet of Truth', 1977, p1113 [i.e., vol. 5 in the 1976 Heinemann edition] quoted in Leon J Waszak, 'Agreement in Principle: The Wartime Partnership of General Wladyslaw Sikorski and Winston Churchill', 1996, p18

[29] Iain Macleod, 'Neville Chamberlain', 1961, p110

[30] Lewis Chester, Stephen Fay & Hugo Young, 'The Zinoviev Letter', 1967, p42

[31] AP Nicholson, 'The Real Men in Public Life: Forces and Factors in the State', 1928, p9 Campbell-Bannerman and Attlee are other exemplars.

[32] According to Bossom, an MP for nearly thirty years, Baldwin "rather assumed the pose of a simple farmer type, but actually was one of the shrewdest occupants of Number 10 within living memory" (Alfred Bossom, 'Some Reminiscences', 1959, ch3 p1 - pages are not numbered in this reprint from the *Kent Messenger*).

[33] Though the gain would be short-term only, for events from 1925 on undermined the Government, starting with the return to the gold standard at the unrealistic rate Churchill preferred.

[34] As fn27 above *Daily Express* 3rd November 1924, KW16 89/3

housing issues.[35] Wood replied two days later from his Walbrook office thanking the Prime Minister for his confidence.

Neville Chamberlain's 'Diary Letters' refer to Wood many times and chart the development of their relationship from 8th July 1923 when they had clashed over Chamberlain's Rent Restrictions Bill. At that stage no longer at the Ministry of Health after three and a half years as PPS to Addison and Mond, Wood was free to speak his mind as a back-bencher when he disagreed with Chamberlain. Chamberlain had neglected the opportunity Wood gave him to drop the proposed "reference committees" (or rent courts as they were expected to be) at both the second reading and Committee stages so Wood introduced an amendment to this effect on third reading.[36] At this stage a haughty and superior Chamberlain described Wood as "out for self-advertisement".[37] At the start of 1924, when the first Labour government was in power, Chamberlain was unable to move an Amendment to their Rent Restrictions Bill owing to what he claimed were Wood's "dirty tricks".[38] A year later though, after Wood had been appointed his Parliamentary Secretary, Chamberlain was referring to him as "Kingsley" and their relationship had begun an upward course.[39] Chamberlain claimed Wood looked "solely at political expediency" at that point,[40] though whether this was a criticism or a compliment is not clear - an interesting view and far from correct (as Part 1 of this book demonstrated). They were still feeling their way into a better relationship for, as one of the papers noted that Christmas, Chamberlain was "forced into competition with the elegant wit of his understudy ... which makes civility difficult, if not impossible".[41] TP O'Connor, father of the House and Nationalist MP for the Scotland division of Liverpool since 1885, judged Wood "shrewd, well-informed, cool-tempered" and that, despite the disadvantages of

---

[35] *Times* 12th November 1924, KW16 94/1

[36] *Newcastle Daily Journal* 13th July 1923, KW15 37/1 See Part 1 for more detail.
Macleod, op cit, pp91-92 attributes Chamberlain's preservation of the Bill to "an adroit and meaningless concession on the Report Stage".

[37] Robert Self (ed.), 'The Neville Chamberlain Diary Letters: vol. II 1921-1927', 2000, 8th July 1923, p171

[38] Ibid, 23rd February 1924, p210

[39] Ibid, 7th March 1925, p274

[40] Ibid, 26th April 1925, p286

[41] *Daily Herald* in an article entitled "Christmas Crackers on the Treasury Bench" undated (but Christmas 1924), KW16 116/1

short stature and weak voice, "he'll get there all the same".[42] This was high praise indeed given O'Connor's encyclopaedic knowledge of people and personalities.[43]

Brighton

If London was the fulcrum of his and Lady Wood's lives, Kingsley Wood travelled widely throughout the UK even before this became part of his duties at the Ministry of Health. The Woods' main home in London was in Kensington at 111 Ladbroke Road from 1911 until they moved to Palace Mansions in Palace Street in the mid-1920s.[44] Perhaps predictably the place outside the capital that he and Agnes, Lady Wood, were attracted to most was Brighton. In addition to the strong emotional pull that it had exerted on Londoners since the days of the Prince Regent in the late eighteenth century, they had several other reasons for having a home there. Two of his friends Harry Preston and Lord Henry Dalziel lived in the town; the Sussex Downs immediately to the east of the town gave easy access to the countryside and, more importantly from Agnes' point of view, offered excellent horse riding; it was only fifty-four miles from London so far enough away to escape the city but near enough to reach when necessary; and it had fast road and rail links. Kingsley Wood did not drive but Agnes did and, if she was at best a carefree driver and at worst a reckless one,[45] she enjoyed it (though the same might not be true for her passengers or other drivers) - as enthusiastic about this as she was about everything. The Brighton Road itself was one of the main routes into the city and carried relatively little traffic when they first moved there.[46]

---

[42] KW16 51/3 and *Kentish Mercury* 23rd May 1925, KW16 162/3

[43] See FE Smith (Earl of Birkenhead), 'Contemporary Personalities', 1924 where TP O'Connor is profiled on pp259-266.

[44] The 1926 edition of Dod gives Wood's address as 7 Palace Mansions, Palace Street. This is nearby to, but north of, Buckingham Palace Mansions in Buckingham Palace Road, where he lived later. The latter is closer to Victoria Station but both would have been handy for the train to Brighton. London County Council, 'List of Streets and Places Within the Administrative County of London', 3rd edition, 1929, pp79 & 384

[45] Robin Brothers, personal communication, 17th December 2012

[46] Similarly, Bossom, op cit, ch2 p3 claimed that "in pre-traffic regulation days [he] could get from the Town Hall, Maidstone, to the House of

From 1921 until 1927/28 the Woods had a weekend home in Brighton, first at 2 King's Cliff Court at 88 Marine Parade until 1923 and finally at 3 Lewes Crescent on the eastern fringe of Brighton near Black Rock. Wood also owned a property in Westgate-on-Sea, Kent that he had acquired from a former client, though he seems to have used this only occasionally for holidays.[47] His friend Harry Preston, the "King of Brighton" as he styled himself, owned two of the best hotels in Brighton, the Royal York and the Royal Albion,[48] both on the front, a stroll along Marine Parade for the Woods or in winter a short ride on Volks electric railway from its terminus at the end of Marine Parade to the station by the pier. In 1922 Wood felt strongly enough to protest about Brighton Aquarium (next to the pier) being leased to a charabanc company, making it clear that he was doing so as a Brighton resident and not as Parliamentary Secretary to the Minister of Health.[49] Wood became a Brighton JP in March 1925, further evidence that he must have felt he was likely to remain part of the Brighton scene for some time. The Chairman of the Bench and former Mayor Sir John Blaker (1854-1926) introduced him by suggesting Wood "should attend when cross-summonses for assault and for abusive language were heard, as the atmosphere would then be familiar". Wood agreed that "after his experience in the House of Commons he would be equal to anything of that sort". His appointment was regarded as "an honour to Brighton".[50]

While horse-riding was Agnes' main leisure pursuit, not her only one for "… in her opinion, dancing is one of the healthiest recreations",[51] enthusiasms shared by Harry Preston.[52] In one

---

Commons in forty-eight minutes". Something that was soon "legally impossible".

[47] The 1927 edition of Dod identifies this as Ava Lodge, Westgate on Sea. He was on holiday there in 1921 when he spoke in Margate on housing. *Times* 30th August 1921, KW12 40/2

[48] Preston purchased the former in 1901 and the latter in 1913, restoring it to its former glory and making it "the haunt of many of the famous figures of the day". Brighton and Hove Corporation bought the Royal York after Preston's retirement in 1929 and converted it into offices. Tim Carder, 'The Encyclopaedia of Brighton', 1990, 160a and 163

[49] KW13 42/1-6; *Daily Telegraph* 17th August 1922, KW13 43/4; KW13 53/1-2

[50] *Star*, *Daily Telegraph* and *Brighton Gazette* 27th and 28th March 1925, KW16 121/2-4

[51] *Yorkshire Post* 1st May 1922, KW13 11/2

article, 'How Famous Men Diet and Train to Keep Thin', Preston was described as "the fittest man of over 70 I know" who "swears by horse-riding, missing lunch every now and then, and dancing". By contrast, it continued, "Kingsley Wood fights an increasing tendency to stoutness by incredibly rapid walking, by spells of riding, and by an annual cure from which he emerges seven pounds lighter and minus a chin". Somewhat enigmatically, the same report also described Agnes as spending a "good deal of time at Brighton" and it might reasonably be conjectured, therefore, perhaps rather more than Wood did. It might further be supposed that, as her intimate liaisons are known to later generations of her family, some of her relationships with dancing partners and riding companions developed further.[53] Preston was certainly aware of her charms, describing her in his books as "charming, vivacious and very good-looking" and "tall, charming, very good-looking, an accomplished musician".[54] Given that these observations were recorded for public consumption, his private opinion may have been even more laudatory, though possibly innocently so for Kingsley Wood was his friend first and a close one at that. Both Preston's books make this clear.[55] Wood and Preston often went to boxing matches together, sometimes in a larger party that Preston had arranged. On one occasion dinner at the Piccadilly Hotel was followed by boxing at the Albert Hall before going on to the New Princes night club. The all-male party included Sir Ronald Waterhouse (1878-1942), the Prime Minister's principal private secretary, and Mr Bertram Mills (1873-1938) ("King Circus" as Preston called him), as well as Wood and Preston. They were joined by the Prince of Wales for the boxing, but the future Edward VIII (1894-1972) declined to accompany them to the night club. The *Daily Sketch* reported that Preston "always works off the effort of sitting still for an hour or two by dancing vigorously till the small hours of the morning".[56]

---

[52] *Sunday Express* 23rd June 1929, KW17 133/1

[53] The same source also refers to Kingsley Wood's own, more guarded if not necessarily discrete, extra-marital affairs.

[54] Harry Preston, 'Memories', 1928, p158 and 'Leaves from My Unwritten Diary', 1936, p371

[55] For example: Preston, 1928, op cit, pp273 and 287; Preston, 1936, op cit, pp371-372

[56] *Daily Sketch* 1st April (probably1927), KW16 270/3 Other guests included Major Piers Legh (the Prince of Wales' equerry), Wing Commander Louis Greig (who won the RAF tennis doubles and competed at Wimbledon in 1926 with Prince George, the future George VI) and the

Perhaps HRH was wary of the publicity or had another engagement for he did not lack stamina and shared with Preston and Wood an eye for the opposite sex.

Wood began to accompany Agnes on horseback in 1925, though whether for his health, to share her interest or for other reasons is not clear. One newspaper confirmed that he was

> a comparatively recent convert to the saddle, having been persuaded to take up the exercise by Mr Harry Preston, who is a great believer in it. Lady Wood rides also, and is usually to be seen out on Sunday morning.[57]

But over the Christmas period that year he suffered a nasty fall when he was thrown from his horse.[58] Although he soon recovered, a salacious Sunday newspaper opted to wait until the following February before reporting it. This enabled them to add "His wife, an excellent horsewoman, rides side-saddle, and likes a spirited mount".[59] This might be, but is almost certainly not, an entirely innocent turn of phrase. Rather the double entendre would be understood by most readers, thereby confirming that Agnes, like her husband, was no different to many other people. Wood told a story against himself later that, similarly laced with innuendo, recalled a constituency supporter who had said "He is no ornament in the House of Commons, but he is a good hard-working Member".[60]

The *Daily Mirror* report had referred to Lewes Crescent as well:

> The Kingsley Woods live in town during the parliamentary session, but they spend every week-end at their delightful flat near Black Rock. At the back of this flat, and a kind of

---

barrister Mr St John Hutchinson, whose wife Mary was for several years the mistress of Clive Bell, husband of Vanessa Bell (a fact of which St John Hutchinson was aware as their son Jeremy, then in his ninety-ninth year, told R4's *Desert Island Discs* programme on 20th October 2013). St John Hutchinson was the Post Office Counsel until 1935 when, appointed KC, he had to relinquish the post and was replaced by John Maude (*Birmingham Daily Mail* 14th February 1935, KW19 279/8).

[57] *Daily Mirror* 29th December 1925, KW16 167/5

[58] *Reynolds, Daily News, Daily Express, Evening News & Sussex Daily News* 27th, 28th and 30th December 1925, KW16 167/2-4 & 167/7-8

[59] *Lloyds Sunday News* 14th February 1926, KW16 173/9

[60] *Yorkshire Observer* 5th November 1926, KW16 241/2

attachment to it, is a picturesque little smoking room, approached by an iron staircase from the mews outside. 'No need to trouble the front door,' says Sir Kingsley Wood when he asks his friends in for a cocktail after the exercise on the Downs.[61]

Wood addressed the Brighton Brotherhood, as he had done previously, at the London Road Congregational Church on 3rd January 1926 - a further demonstration perhaps that his roots in Brighton went beyond pleasure and leisure. This was a week after his horse had thrown him, so if his recovery was not yet complete it was at least sufficient for him to fulfil this commitment. Wood took as his text Abraham Lincoln's opinion after the American civil war "There is hope for any country where every man does something".[62] For both Wood and Lincoln (1809-1865) this reflected their belief in self-help and individual responsibility, but neither would dispute that society had a role in enabling this. Disraeli, Lincoln's contemporary, would have felt equally comfortable with the implications.

The impression gained is both of the Woods' relaxed time in Brighton (riding, mews, servant to open the front door, cocktails) but perhaps as importantly conveys their role in the life of the community itself. This makes it even more curious that by 1927 they should have abandoned it, moving to Tunbridge Wells instead.

It seems clear that at the start of 1926 Wood and Agnes were enjoying a full life in Brighton. They had a comfortable home into which they had moved just a couple of years earlier, a growing network of friends, a wide range of intellectual, cultural and leisure pursuits, and a community in which they were embedded. Wood's role at the Ministry of Health was increasingly arduous, but the post of Parliamentary Secretary had been demanding ever since Baldwin appointed him to it. It must be doubted therefore whether Wood's explanation for their move to Tunbridge Wells in late 1927 is entirely credible. That November he told the local paper that he would no longer reside in Brighton "to be nearer his constituency and his Department".[63] Traffic on the London-Brighton road had increased considerably since they first moved there and Agnes had been badly hurt in a car accident in November 1926 that prevented her

---

[61] *Daily Mirror* 29th December 1925, KW16 167/5
[62] *Sussex Daily News* 4th January 1926, KW16 170/1 Lincoln was often quoted by Conservative MPs at this time.
[63] *Sussex Daily News* 17th November 1927, KW17 6/12

riding again until the following spring. On the other hand, she had recovered enough within a month to open the Christmas bazaar at Woolwich, her first public engagement since the accident.[64] They may have had several reasons to take stock, especially as Agnes, more than four years older than her husband, had her fiftieth birthday earlier that year. But one characteristic that makes Agnes stand out above all others is her belief and constant demonstration that "life was for living". She would not have permitted age or accident to hamper her other than temporarily - and as she lived nearly another thirty years to 1955 it could not have been of lasting significance for her.

Tunbridge Wells is on the road between Brighton and Woolwich so they may have passed through it as they travelled between the two. It is seventeen miles nearer London than Brighton so only two-thirds of the distance, but a more tortuous car journey nevertheless. There was (and is) a railway station and the country around it would also have attracted them. Nevertheless, the over-riding impression is that there must have been substantial reasons for leaving Brighton beyond the obvious ones or those that Wood was prepared to concede. The home they bought, Broomhill Bank, is huge but it is also well out of Tunbridge Wells and somewhat isolated even today. Someone may have mentioned to them that it was available, perhaps even someone from the neighbouring David Salomons[65] house and estate, but it seems a curious choice nonetheless and very different to their home in Brighton on the front and surrounded by others. It was Salomons' daughter Vera (1888-1969) who had been left Broomhill Bank in his Will and sold it to Wood in 1927.[66] It is almost as though they were deliberately adopting a different course. Isolation can be an attraction of course, an antidote to a hectic life during the week, and it may be that the property enabled them to offer the country-house weekends that they experienced elsewhere, a marker if one was needed of their growing status. Certainly Agnes did hold parties there that are still remembered locally. This might mean that they were riotous or raucous or notorious for other reasons, but it might simply indicate that they were unusual in the area, one that is still

---

[64] KW16 256/3
[65] David Salomons (1851-1925) had inherited Broomhill from his uncle of the same name. The younger Salomons was predeceased by his one son and the estate then passed to his wife and four daughters.
[66] Item 9 in David Salomons' Will 7th August 1924, Salomons Museum.

thought a byword for its rectitude and "stiff upper lip". Not the
obvious place for someone such as Agnes to move to, or even it
must be said for someone like Wood who had always lived in towns
previously, unless there were also very good reasons for getting
away from Brighton and some of those who lived there.

Wood sold Ava Lodge in Westgate-on-Sea at much the
same time, either to release capital for other purposes or more likely
help fund the purchase of Broomhill Bank. Ava Lodge was (and is)
a very substantial property, having become a hotel in the 1930s and
flats today.[67] So, two homes on the coast of East Sussex and Kent
had become one inland.

It will become apparent that, while Wood's schedule was hectic
before 1924, it became increasingly frantic thereafter.
Consequently, Part 2 accords events space according to their
significance and omits some altogether so as not to obscure the
more important or overwhelm the reader. Partly for this reason the
following chapter, Chapter 9, covers Wood's role during the General
Strike of 1926. This is deliberately treated out of chronological
sequence because it provides insights into Wood's motivation and
character that only become apparent again in his time as
Postmaster-General from 1931 to 1935. One newspaper, referring
to his business ideas that had rejuvenated the Post Office and
describing him as an example of 'Push and Go' and a capable
speaker, argued in August 1934 that Wood should be retained as
the country's 'Lord High Booster'.[68] He and Chamberlain

---

[67] Although Wood is listed at Ava Lodge in the Kelly's Directories for
Westgate-on-Sea from 1920 to 1927, but not in either the previous
1916/17 one or the subsequent 1928 edition, he purchased it in 1908
(Dawn Crouch of Westgate Heritage Centre, personal communication, 10th
November 2016).
Ava Lodge Hotel is advertised in the 1937 Westgate-on-Sea Official Guide
issued by the Chamber of Commerce. The property looks the same today
and almost certainly did when Wood owned it in the 1920s. It won the
Margate Civic Pride Award in 2002.
Richard Hambridge, a resident of Westgate-on-Sea, recorded his
recollections of the period 1909-1969. This includes a paragraph on Ava
Lodge on p124, referring to Wood's ownership in the 1920s. In the mid-
1960s it was used as a home for foreign students.
[68] *Mirror* 20th August 1934, KW19 143/11 The report suggested that he
might have inherited his "gifts" from his maternal grandfather Daniel
Howard, "a well-known and much respected boiler-maker" of West

introduced several enlightened reforms at the Ministry of Health in the 1920s that served to decrease inequality and increase entitlement, for both individuals and deprived ("necessitous") areas, but Wood the man rather than the administrator is harder to discern. Furthermore, these reforms bracketed the General Strike, continuing afterwards in a much more cautious, yet heated and polarised, context, and for both reasons this forms the subsequent chapter, Chapter 10.

Wood was always a one-nation Tory in the Baldwin mould and like his mentor preferred co-operation and conciliation to confrontation. But he did not shy away from the latter when he felt it necessary. He was often ahead of his time in consulting and striving for consensus, characteristics that were apparent in several of his Ministerial roles. But he was also aware that views and actions sometimes had to be imposed to get the job done. Effective leadership depends on differentiating those occasions that require consultation first from those that demand action first. Public opinion can be ahead of political priority but it can also lag behind it; it can inform and influence but occasionally it has to be shaped, if not determined, first.

Interspersed among the scenes from Wood's political life are some vignettes of people and issues important to him. These are usually outside the main stream of Wood's story and throw other lights on the man. He was not only an aspiring politician though this was certainly his main motivation. These vignettes (or cameos or interludes if you prefer) illuminate his generosity, friendship and bias to action in other, complementary ways.

Bromwich and critically "a very clever business man of great constructive power".

Vignette

Woolwich and neighbouring constituencies in General Elections between the wars

After the overwhelming triumph of Lloyd George's Liberal/ Conservative coalition in 1918, there were another six general elections before the Second World War. The Conservatives won four of them in 1922, 1924, 1931[69] and 1935, with Labour forming a minority government in 1924 (after the 1923 election) and 1929. Wood was the MP for Woolwich West for twenty-five years but this was far from a natural Conservative seat, let alone an automatic one, so the fact that he managed to retain it (even in 1929) says much for his positive profile in Woolwich as well as in the country and parliament more generally.

Of the four constituencies on the eastern fringe of south London between the wars, two might appear solidly Conservative (Woolwich West and Lewisham East) and one solidly Labour (Woolwich East) in that they routinely returned MPs of these complexions at each election, but it was rarely as straightforward as that. The other seat (Greenwich) was more obviously volatile - as was Dartford, the neighbouring constituency in Kent. The Greenwich and Dartford constituencies mirrored the national results with Labour winning both seats in 1923 and 1929, but losing them to the Conservatives in the other four contests. Woolwich East always returned a Labour majority (with only a brief Conservative interlude in 1921-1922 after the long-standing Labour MP Will Crooks stood down because of ill-health), and Woolwich West and Lewisham East Conservative ones, but the latter two came close to changing hands in 1929. This was an election that most Conservatives were confident of winning after five years of reform,[70] but whether because of their unappealing slogan of 'Safety First', a

---

[69] Winning 471 seats as part of the National Government.

[70] KW17 120/2-20: The anticipated Conservative ministry after the general election was reported a number of times. This included, for example, the *Newcastle Daily Journal and North Star* 7th March 1929, KW17 104/8 which asserted that Stanley Baldwin would stop excluding women from Cabinet when he won, with the Duchess of Atholl to become President of the Board of Education and perhaps the Countess of Iveagh as Parliamentary Secretary to the Minister of Health "For it is a foregone conclusion that Sir Kingsley Wood ... will secure Cabinet rank".

"mistaken 'motto of the cemetery'" Ellen Wilkinson called it,[71] or the revised franchise that saw all women over twenty-one voting for the first time, they received a severe drubbing, losing over 150 seats from the heady days of 1924, down from 413 to 260. Assheton Pownall (1877-1953), the Conservative in Lewisham East,[72] saw his majority almost evaporate from over 10,000 to 402, while Wood just clung on in Woolwich West by 332 votes,[73] down from a comfortable 4200 in 1924. Yet at the outset of the election the *Kentish Independent* had predicted that, "having fulfilled his promises" the voters of West Woolwich "were hardly likely to exchange him for a disciple of 'Mr Lenin' Lloyd George or 'Mr Moscow' MacDonald".[74] Another local paper was of the view that Wood's parliamentary record had enhanced his chances of retaining the seat despite the new working-class housing estate that had been built in Woolwich.[75] They were right, but only just.

Although 1929 was the one year in which a Liberal candidate stood in either Lewisham East or Woolwich West, it was not this that resulted in hugely reduced Conservative majorities. Pownall's vote was almost as large as in 1924, and Wood's larger, but most of the additional and newly franchised voters split between the Labour and Liberal candidates.[76] Although the Liberal who stood against George Hume In Greenwich in 1923 and 1929 may have taken some votes from him, this was less obviously the case in Pownall's and Wood's constituencies (though the corollary is that very few of the new electors can have voted for them).

Two years later their fortunes had rebounded with Pownall's majority increased to nearly 21,000 and Wood's to almost 12,000. They were not alone: in Maidstone, for example, the Conservative vote almost doubled, with the majority for the new MP Alfred Bossom (1881-1965) increased from less than 4,000 for his

---

[71] *New Leader* 3rd May 1929. Her alternative was "Don't grin and bear it, vote Labour and change it". Quoted in Matt Perry, '"Red Ellen" Wilkinson: Her Ideas, Movements and World', 2014, p217

[72] MP from 1918-1945 Pownall was almost exactly Wood's parliamentary contemporary.

[73] The votes cast were 17296 for Wood, 16964 for William Barefoot (Lab) and 4140 for Phillips (Lib). *Times* 1st June 1929, KW17 129/3

[74] *Kentish Independent* 12th April 1929, KW17 113/3

[75] Though this was offset to some extent by more middle-class housing in Eltham. *Kentish Mercury* 12th April 1929, KW17 113/4

[76] 18,000 out of 26,000 in Lewisham East, 8,500 of 14,000 in Woolwich West

predecessor to over 20,000,[77] while a Labour majority of almost 8,000 in Willesden West in 1929 had become as large a Conservative one for Mavis Tate (1893-1947) in 1931. Even in the Labour bastion of Woolwich East the gap had closed to 608 votes.[78] Labour voters had either deserted the party or abstained.

---

[77] During Bossom's maiden speech in Parliament, Churchill is supposed to have said "[what] a very funny name, neither one thing nor the other!" Bossom, op cit, ch2 p1

[78] ES Shrapnell-Smith who contested Woolwich East for the Conservatives in these years was 8,500 votes behind Labour's Harry Snell in 1929 (*Times* 1st June 1929, KW17 129/3) and still almost 4,000 votes behind his successor in the by-election in April 1931 when Snell went to the Lords.

9.   GENERAL STRIKE 1926[79]

In his 1925 Budget speech Churchill proposed that Britain return to the gold standard at the pre-war level, a step "long regarded by the Bank of England and the bankers as the essential condition of a return to 'economic reality'"[80] and, after some delay and uncertainty, the Gold Standard Act received Royal Assent on 13th May 1925. The return to an exchange rate fixed by reference to gold was not necessarily a problem in itself, but the 1914 rate Churchill applied was too high, making sterling 10% less competitive overnight.[81] Keynes may have been virtually the only economist who criticised this, but the Labour MP for Leicester West Frederick Pethick-Lawrence (1871-1961), a specialist in finance, had long argued against it,[82] underlining the impact in a speech in the Commons that July:

> ... during the last twelve months the value of the £ in terms of the dollar has been pushed up 10 per cent. That is to say that, except in so far as there has been a fall in prices in this country, we are 10 per cent worse in our trading with the United States than we were a year ago. I think that fact is sufficient to account for the great fall in trade which has occurred in the last seven or eight months.[83]

Keynes had noted that in these circumstances the cost of living and prices could only be reduced by decreasing wages or increasing unemployment and, though politically unacceptable, unemployment was rising nonetheless. Pethick-Lawrence shared Keynes' view that it was being paid for "by changing over from being a lending country to being a borrowing one", "a disastrous course". The coal industry had been particularly hard hit with a small profit of 6d per ton turned into a loss of 1s 3d (1/3) per ton (i.e., from +2.5p to -6.5p in decimal money), so a reverse of almost four times. The coal owners' solution was to reduce miners' wages, thereby offering

---

[79] An earlier version of part of this chapter appeared in *The Historian* in November 2014.
[80] Alan Bullock, 'Ernest Bevin: A Biography', 2002, p67
[81] JM Keynes, 'The Economic Consequences of Mr Churchill', 1925, pp5-6 - originally a series of articles in the *Evening Standard*.
[82] Pethick-Lawrence, op cit, p141
[83] Hansard, 6th July 1925, vol. 186, col. 161

them "the choice between starvation and submission".[84]
Specifically, they demanded three concessions from the miners: an
extension of the seven-hour day, abolition of the minimum wage
and a guarantee of profits by reducing their wages.[85] It was
pegging the exchange rate to the gold standard that the miners
blamed for the slump in the coal trade and, once the owners
proposed increased hours and reduced pay, felt they had no
alternative but to strike. Families had only "just got off their knees"
after the three month strike of 1921,[86] with memories in
Northumberland still raw of begging trips to the posh houses of
Whitley Bay to cadge food,[87] so the prospect of another strike
showed their desperation. After saying that the country could not
afford to give in, at virtually the midnight hour on 31st July 1925
Baldwin agreed to provide a subsidy so that miners' wages could be
sustained for nine months while an inquiry into the options for the
industry was conducted by Herbert Samuel (1870-1963), a leading
Liberal politician out of Parliament since 1918 and most recently
High Commissioner of Palestine. In Keynes' judgement Baldwin
thereby "succeeded to the position in our affections formerly
occupied by Queen Victoria".[88] AJ Cook (1883-1931), the miners'
leader, may have believed that Baldwin's capitulation meant the
Government had been defeated[89] but it is at least as likely that,
realising the Government was unprepared for a strike at that point,
a pragmatic Baldwin was buying time to ensure he was better
prepared for the future. The Government updated its emergency
organisation in case it was needed: the Organisation for the
Maintenance of Supplies (OMS) was set up "by a number of
eminent ex-public servants" that September with funding from a few
patriotic citizens,[90] while in November the Ministry of Health issued
Circular 636, dividing England and Wales into ten Divisions and
appointing Civil Commissioners (junior Ministers) and their staff to
each so that, in the event of an emergency they could supplement
the work of local authorities and reach decisions on the

---

[84] Keynes, op cit, pp13,16, 20-24
[85] Jack Davison, 'Northumberland Miners 1919-1939', 1973, p54
[86] Reminiscences of J Allison, North Walbottle miner, Tyne and Wear
Archives and Museums DX201/2 (hereafter just T&W..)
[87] *The Journal* 6th November 1982, Northumberland Records Office NRO
08747/1 (hereafter just NRO..)
[88] Keynes, op cit, p26
[89] Michael Hughes, 'Cartoons from the General Strike', 1968, p18
[90] Ibid, p14

Government's behalf.[91] The Trade Unions on the other hand made no preparations at all[92] (at least before the start of May 1926), thereby demonstrating that they were not seeking to foment revolution, preferring and for the most part adhering to constitutional approaches.   Despite attempts by Churchill and others to characterise the General Strike as anarchy and revolution, the spirit in which it was conducted demonstrated this was hyperbole and largely inaccurate.[93] Or, as Ellen Wilkinson (1891-1947) put it in the opening chapter of 'Clash', her 1929 novel about the General Strike, "British revolutions are made by British churchwardens" not young Communists.[94]

When the Samuel Commission reported on 10th March the miners and the mine owners were both aggrieved by the recommendations, while even the Government was not pleased. Although the Commission thought longer hours would only produce more coal that could not be sold and lower wages only a temporary solution for an industry that required thorough re-organisation, they were trenchantly opposed to continuing the Government subsidy that had propped up wages. The Commission insisted that it should be withdrawn and, if pit closures were to be avoided, the miners would have to take a temporary pay cut while the industry was re-organised.   The mine owners were incensed by the proposals underpinning re-organisation (such as nationalisation of mineral rights, amalgamation of smaller pits and improvement of miners' working conditions and welfare). The Government took a fortnight to respond for it found some of the recommendations unpalatable and promised Government support only if the miners and the employers agreed to the report and worked to implement it. In other

---

[91] Wilfrid Harris Crook, 'The General Strike: A Study of Labor's Tragic Weapon in Theory and Practice', 1931, p308
George Glasgow, 'General Strikes and Road Transport', 1926 includes Circular 636 on pp102-112 and the main Divisional staff (the Northern Division is on p143).
[92] Anthony Mason,' The General Strike in the North East', 1970, p7
[93] Harris, op cit, p102 also states that most did not seek a revolution but only to support the miners.
[94] Ellen Wilkinson, 'Clash', 1989 (orig.1929), p9   She has William Royd continuing to her heroine Joan Craig "That's why they've been successful". Ellen Wilkinson, known as Red Ellen or the Fiery Atom (for she was under five feet tall), was Labour MP for Jarrow from 1935 until her death and at the head of the Jarrow march in 1936 walking much of the way and subsequently writing 'The Town That Was Murdered' (1939).

words, the miners should accept a pay cut immediately in the hope that the industry would be better organised in future. The Government had essentially abdicated responsibility and must have known, given the history of the industry, that there was almost no prospect of agreement between the two sides.[95] The mine owners, paying little heed to the re-organisation proposals, sought to impose district agreements and lower wages, thereby hardening the miners' position. When the miners refused to accept their proposals, the employers posted notices ending the existing terms and conditions from 30th April.[96] The miners would not accept that they should suffer a reduction first in the hope that the owners might keep their side of the bargain later and, when Baldwin was unable to get either side to unbend, the miners considered themselves locked out, the owners that they were on strike, the Trade Union Council that other workers should support the miners and the Government that there was a state of emergency. The slogan, first coined by AJ Cook, of "Not a minute on the day, not a penny off the pay" would remain the miners' battle cry. The dilatory and haphazard negotiations between the Government and the Trade Union Council then broke down, partly because the Government was tempted to call their bluff and right-wingers within the Cabinet thought it better to precipitate a general strike rather than seek to avoid it any longer,[97] finding a convenient pretext for calling off the negotiations when printers at the *Daily Mail* suppressed the paper because they took exception to a leading article.[98] The Government interpreted this as interfering with the freedom of the press.[99]

---

[95] DH Robertson, "A narrative of the General Strike of 1926", *Economic Journal*, 1926, 36, pp375-393; Bullock, op cit, pp86-91

[96] On Friday 30th April the coal owners held an emergency meeting at the Mining Association offices in London to discuss their ultimatum. The meeting confirmed a national uniform minimum based on the standard wage of July 1914 but on the basis of eight hours for all workers, regardless of whether they worked underground or on the surface - a decision endorsed by the Northumberland Coal Owners and the majority of their colleagues. NRO 263/B1: Northumberland Coal Owners' Association Minutes 1926, pp126-128

[97] Mason, op cit, p9 lists Churchill, Neville Chamberlain and Joynson-Hicks amongst the "Die-Hards".

[98] Hamilton Fyfe, 'Behind the Scenes of the Great Strike', 1926, pp22-23

[99] Hansard, 3rd May 1926, vol. 195, col. 69 in the Prime Minister's statement to the Commons on the failure of negotiations. The full debate occupies cols. 57-172.

Newcastle

John Moore-Brabazon (1884-1964), then Parliamentary Secretary to the Minister of Transport, was the original Civil Commissioner for Newcastle before being suddenly recalled at the beginning of May to oversee the London docks. He handed over the Northern Division command, covering Northumberland, Durham and some of north Yorkshire, to the genial Kingsley Wood (as Brabazon described him[100]) on Saturday 1st May 1926 at the Newcastle headquarters in St Mary's Place.[101] The other Northern Division officers were as in Circular 636, but whereas Moore-Brabazon had had time to prepare, Wood had to acquaint himself with the situation almost literally overnight. When the *Northern Echo* reported the handover it also gave some idea of the scale of the challenge: there were 210,000 miners in Durham and Northumberland (all of whom were entitled to unemployment pay so long as the miners' stoppage could be described as a lock-out rather than a strike) and, if there was no settlement in a few days, many thousands of men would be thrown out in shipbuilding and the iron and steel trades. The same day the Labour MP Joseph Batey (1867-1949) told the Durham miners that "Mr Baldwin had let them down and was as crooked as Mr Lloyd George". Batey's claim was to be the subject of Wood's first report, headed "Labour attitude to Premier", but by the time he made it on Monday 3rd May he was able to add that the President of the Northumberland Miners' Federation had told one of Wood's staff that Batey had no right to speak as he did. On the contrary, the Federation's executive "looked upon Mr Baldwin as an honest and kindly man who had done all he could for them".[102] An embattled Baldwin must have taken some satisfaction from Wood's note for he passed it on to his principal private secretary Sir Ronald Waterhouse for information.

When the General Strike was declared on 3rd May a million and a half front-line workers (primarily railways, transport and the docks) were called out initially by the Trade Union Council (i.e., the General Council of the Trades Union Congress). The Trade Unions had agreed to maintain sanitary, health and food services but trades other than those "employed definitely on housing and hospital"

---

[100] Lord Brabazon of Tara, 'The Brabazon Story', 1956, p158
[101] *Northern Echo* 3rd May 1926, KW16 188/3
[102] Report "General (1)", Baldwin Papers, vol. 23, 10

building were to cease.[103]   Food and building services would become particular issues of dispute. Meanwhile, the OMS had a thousand staff at its Newcastle headquarters in Lovaine Place and many more volunteers in outlying areas.

Bullock highlights the huge risk that people were taking:

> There were many men who ... risked secure jobs and pensions for which they had been paying for years. They did so with their eyes open, knowing that if the strike failed, they would have great difficulty in getting their jobs back; might see themselves replaced by younger men; might be left, in the dockers' phrase, 'on the stones' for months, reduced to the ranks of the unemployed. Working men do not go on strike lightly, least of all when unemployment is high, trade slack and there is no dispute in their own industry. Too much was at stake for them and the families dependent on them to indulge in gestures. The response to the call ... was a remarkable demonstration of working-class unity and of unselfish support for the miners.[104]

The Emergency Powers Act was still in force from October 1920 when it had been introduced to protect the State from exceptional threats once the wartime Defence of the Realm Act (DORA) had expired and, as the prospect of industrial crisis deepened, the Emergency Regulations were re-activated by an Order in Council on 30th April 1926.[105]   The Home Secretary laid them before the Commons on Monday 3rd May, as he was required to do, for they would lapse if not approved within seven days. They included section 33(1) the ability to arrest suspected persons without warrant and 33(3) the power of search. The debate continued into a second day as various MPs sought to have specific regulations excluded - for example, George Lansbury and David Kirkwood both spoke against Regulation 21, which covered, among other things, the

---

[103] Fyfe, op cit, p16

[104] Bullock, op cit, p106

[105] They were circulated to the Cabinet on that date. Baldwin Papers, vol.15, 223-225

Emergency Regulations had been used previously in 1921 and 1924, though on the latter occasion they omitted Regulations 21 and 22 (public meetings and processions).   They had to be renewed each month. KD Ewing and CA Gearty, 'The Struggle for Civil Liberties: Political Freedom and the Rule of Law in Britain, 1914-1945', 2000, p162

offences of sedition, interference with food, fuel or other necessary supplies or with transport unless these occurred as part of a strike or peaceful picketing.[106] They argued that they were attacks on the community and attempts to crush the workers. Kirkwood reminded the House of his deportation from the Clyde munitions area under DORA, adding that

> I say again, this Regulation 21 will place power in the hands of some nincompoop, for instance, the hon. Member for one of the Divisions of Woolwich - Sir Kingsley Wood, to make no mistake. He is away up in Newcastle to put Regulation 21 into operation there. He will miserably fail.[107]

Kirkwood was interrupted by Members shouting "He has failed" and by the Labour MP Robert Richardson (1862-1943), who like Batey had previously been a miner and now represented a Durham constituency, claiming over-optimistically that Wood had already been sent back. The Emergency Regulations were eventually agreed without a vote.

An account for the Plebs League, an independent working-class education movement originally founded at Ruskin College, Oxford in 1908, identifies the Northern Division as one of the strongest areas outside London, with innumerable unions involved and hardening attitudes on both sides.[108] On Saturday 1st May the Mines Department had issued an instruction that, with effect from the following Monday, coal was to be rationed. The unions interpreted this as the Government anticipating, even provoking, the breakdown of negotiations, while the Government countered that it was no more than prudent planning. Once the strike was underway the Ministry of Health repeated the call for rationing, though militant local authorities such as Blaydon Council chose to ignore it.[109] On 3rd May Wood in his capacity as Civil Commissioner wrote to all the Northern municipal authorities adding his appeal to that of the Government in Circular 636 "for the co-operation of your Authority in safeguarding the welfare of the community during the present

---

[106] Hansard, 5th May 1926, vol. 195, cols. 291-408; 6th May 1926, vol. 195, cols. 453-597
[107] Ibid, col. 480
[108] RW Postgate, Ellen Wilkinson and JF Horrabin, 'A Workers' History of the Great Strike', 1927, p65
[109] T&W DX 278/1: Blaydon Council 10th May 1926

emergency".[110] The Lord Mayor of Newcastle called for volunteers to act as special constables, to man the railways, tramways and food lorries, and to maintain public services such as gas, electricity and water. Other transport workers, messengers and clerical assistants would also be required. Wood saw his responsibility as preserving "the life of all sections of the community", a task which would require the "goodwill of every citizen". Whereas the Government and the TUC were now on opposing sides, Wood asserted that

> My object is not to take any side but so to act as to promote co-operation and goodwill in carrying on the services upon which the life of the community depends.[111]

The function of the Civil Commissioners was to maintain services and to do so without legitimising the strike.[112] But they had been appointed by the Government and circumstances in the North might prove this a difficult balancing act.

It took the Unions a further day until the 4th to set up a co-ordinating body.[113] The meeting agreed both a local General

---

[110] *Newcastle Journal* 4th May 1926, KW16 189/1

[111] *North Mail* 4th May 1926, KW16 188/5

[112] On 3rd June 1926 (after the strike was over) Winterton wrote to Irwin, the future Lord Halifax, about the wide range of powers available to Civil Commissioners. He continues "fortunately we did not have to put them into operation, and it is as well … not to state exactly what they were". Stuart Ball (ed.), 'Conservative Politics in National and Imperial Crisis: Letters from Britain to the Viceroy of India 1926-31', 2014, p41

[113] This comprised the Northumberland Miners Association, Northumberland Colliery Mechanics Association, National Union of Distributive and Allied Workers (NUDAW), Transport and General Workers Union (TGWU), National Union of Sailors and Firemen (though their national president Havelock Wilson ensured they were not on strike), Shop Assistants Union, National Union of General and Municipal Workers, Boilermakers' Union, Federation of Engineering and Shipbuilding Trades, Railway Clerks Association, National Union of Railwaymen (NUR) and the Builders Federation. The Gateshead Labour Party and Trades Council and the Newcastle Trades Council were also present, as were Will Lawther unofficially representing the Durham Miners and R Page Arnot, Director of the Labour Research Department (LRD). James White, Area Sec., TGWU was in the Chair with Charles R Flynn, Northern Division Officer, NUDAW the Secretary.

Council for the Northumberland and Durham area (which would convene daily at the offices of Northumberland Miners Association) and a Strike Committee, with the latter deciding that it would sit all day (rather than set up sub-committees) to sort out existing instructions from constituent Trade Unions and deal with permits.[114]

In contrast to their Durham counterparts, the Northumberland Miners Union were on the front foot immediately. As well as agreeing representatives on the Newcastle and District National Crisis Committee, they decided to open their office after hours to improve communication, to keep in touch with local collieries through the Executive and Wages Committee and to work with local stoppage committees. They made sure all branches were aware of these steps by circulating the minutes to them.[115] Their first Strike Bulletin was issued on Tuesday 4th May, including on its last page a notice to the 'Workers of Durham and Northumberland' which asserted that

> The Strike-breaking Organisations of Sir Kingsley Wood have proved feeble weapons against the united will and determination of hundreds of thousands of the working classes.[116]

According to Reid and Tolliday, Newcastle was one of only two places, along with Manchester, where there was a co-ordinated approach that went beyond local unions and independent action.[117]

Some newspapers continued to publish but many did not, and those that did were often briefer and more truncated than usual. Although Bullock states that the Government could rely on the BBC, and it could in the sense that it was the only widely available source of news,[118] the BBC had to fight hard to retain its independence, John Reith writing to Baldwin's close friend JCC Davidson (1889-

---

See also Emile Burns, 'The General Strike May 1926: Trades Councils in Action', 1926, pp152-153 and Postgate et al, op cit, p66. The latter add that the "lethargy of this society's [the Durham Miners' Association] headquarters was so great that no official Strike Committee was set up by it till two hours after the strike was over".

[114] *Labour Monthly*, KW16 204
[115] NRO Northumberland Miners Union Minutes, 4th May 1926, Minute 2
[116] NRO ZFO 3/8: *Strike Bulletin* 4th May 1926, pp1-4
[117] Alastair Reid and Simon Tolliday, "The General Strike 1926", *Historical Journal*, 1977, 20, pp1001-1012
[118] Bullock, op cit, p108

1970) that much as the Government, and Churchill in particular, might like to commandeer the BBC, censor the news and broadcast their own propaganda instead,[119] maintaining its independence was fundamental to restoring goodwill.[120] Although the BBC's struggle to remain impartial strained relations with the Government, Baldwin did write to thank them later for the "wonderful service" they had provided.[121]

The Civil Commissioners produced daily summaries for the government[122] while the Central Council of Economic Leagues (CCEL), set up during the 1924 Labour administration as a right-wing counter to "Red propaganda", produced seven Strike Bulletins of their own summarising the situation in major towns and cities around the country.[123] The CCEL Bulletins were one of the few sources of information providing the national picture, though no less partisan than the *British Worker* and *British Gazette* were to be (putting the Trade Union and Government viewpoints respectively). Newcastle featured in all but one of the CCEL bulletins, the first of which was datelined 4.00pm on that first Tuesday:

> All railways, docks and transport stopped. Only the privately-owned omnibuses are running. In the mining area everything is closed down, but all is quiet. In Newcastle all is quiet; there is an air of expectancy. Trade unions are permitting the removal of food at their instructions. The employers are working some lorries with voluntary labour.

---

[119] According to Fyfe, op cit, p47

[120] Baldwin Papers, vol. 23, p5: Reith letter to Davidson 6th May 1926. The battle for BBC independence features in Reith's autobiography 'Into the Wind', 1949, pp107-109 and on the latter page he mentions that it might have been better for him if the BBC had been commandeered.

[121] Baldwin Papers, vol. 23, pp6-9: Amery, Baldwin and Reith letters 17th and 18th May 1926

[122] The only summary to survive in the Baldwin Papers is no. 8 for 9th May 1926. The report from the Northern Division is included as a late item indicating everything was satisfactory and "signs of weakening in the Labour position". Baldwin Papers, vol. 22, pp69-72

[123] Baldwin Papers, vol. 22, pp21-43: Central Council of Economic Leagues (CCEL) Strike Bulletins 1-7, 4th-11th May 1926 An article in the *Daily Telegraph* on 10th June 1924 (repeated in the *Sydney Morning Herald* 17th June 1924) appealed for at least £100,000 for a war on socialism. It referred to the affiliation to CCEL of various groups opposed to Socialism including National Propaganda, British Empire Union and National Citizen's Union.

Newcastle was similar to the rest of the country at this stage with the strike being conducted in a very British fashion, low-key and in good humour. It began to change the following day.

A file in the Tyne and Wear Archives records the course of the strike at the Blaydon Benzol Works,[124] situated in the Blaydon Council area, one of the authorities that supported the strike most strongly. Benzol was routinely mixed with petrol in vehicles and was therefore fundamental to keeping the area moving. No problems were reported until mild picketing of the Blaydon depot began on Wednesday 5th May, the same day Blaydon and District Council of Action issued its 'Instructions to pickets'. On the 7th a notice was posted in the town seeking help to stop "blacklegs" moving petrol from the depot, and from the 8th an increasingly large and hostile crowd gathered, including a group from Chopwell (a village with a radical reputation) described as "a rough-looking party ... well-supplied with bludgeons", many of whom were "rattling pocketfuls of stones". On Thursday 6th the General Manager of the Newcastle Benzol Company wrote to Wood protesting about eight lorries that had been stopped by about two hundred men. Wood's office replied the same day to say that the Chief Constable had been consulted, confirming that "Blaydon Council has no authority to issue permits and no permits are necessary". Furthermore, police protection would be provided to lorries in future though the police would appreciate as much notice as possible in case reinforcements were required.

On Wednesday 5th the strike hardened as unscrupulous transport contractors and employers used 'Food Only' and 'Housing Materials Only' permits, the two categories that both sides had previously agreed could continue, to shift everything regardless of the actual contents. The response of the Joint Strike Committee was to withdraw all permits for the latter.[125] The second CCEL Strike Bulletin highlighted the worsening picture in the Northern Division:

> 11.30a.m. Things are reported to be quite quiet in the coal fields and in [Newcastle]. There was one ugly incident,

---

[124] T&W, DX 278/1: Miners and GS at Blaydon Benzol Works 30th April to 13th May 1926

[125] *Labour Monthly* June 1926, pp359-374: 'One Sector. An Account of the Proceedings of the Northumberland and Durham General Council and Joint Strike Committee' [text accepted by General Council on 20th May]

however, last night when hooligans held up some of the buses that are still running.

While in South Shields, "A destroyer and submarine have arrived in the Tyne. Trains and trams are at a standstill and shipping is held up. A curtailed ferry service is being run."[126]

The arrival of the navy in the Tyne exacerbated a major conflict, when dockers handling food refused to do so any longer for there were now OMS volunteers on the quayside as well, unloading ships and protected by the naval guns. Mason devotes ten pages to his account of the negotiations that followed and the later ramifications, while Crook accorded it six pages, the *Labour Monthly* four and Julian Symons an entire chapter entitled "What happened at Newcastle?".[127] In his history of the Northumberland miners between the wars Davison notes that the Newcastle and Durham General Council and Joint Strike Committee "protested against the naval contingent berthed on the Tyne",[128] while Postgate et al explain

> ... on Wednesday night, Sir Kingsley Wood, the Government's Commissioner, came to three representatives of the Strike Committee with what was in effect an appeal for aid and an offer of partial withdrawal. He retired to consult his assistants, the others to report to [their] colleagues, and the conversations were continued [the] next day. It then appeared that Sir Kingsley was offering at least a partial surrender; he was prepared to abandon any attempt to use non-union labour and to operate the docks 'under dual control' - himself and the union nominees. The Committee was faced with a delicate choice. Had it been a free agent it might have decided to take a revolutionary course: to force Wood to further concessions and in effect to take over his powers and use them in the interest of the workers (especially in the matter of food distribution). But the

---

[126] Baldwin Papers, vol. 22, p25: Central Council of Economic Leagues (CCEL) Strike Bulletin 2, 5th May 1926
[127] Mason, op cit, pp55-65 quotes extensively from Joint Strike Committee minutes and Wood's statement to Parliament on 20th May; Crook, op cit, pp406-411; *Labour Monthly* June 1926, pp366-369, KW16 206-208; Julian Symons, 'The General Strike: A Historical Portrait', 1959, pp127-136
[128] Davison, op cit, p62

intention of the TUC instructions was clearly opposed to this, and it was decided to refuse the offer and to withdraw all permits.[129]

Wood's approach might seem like a pragmatic, even conciliatory, one designed to get the ships unloaded again and the community fed as fast as possible, but Fyfe is among those who argued he had lost control and sought help in an attempt to recover it.[130] It was interpreted as a sign of weakness by the Unions at the time and by the Government as potentially undermining their hard-line and inflexible approach (though Hughes, remarkably and in contrast to the other accounts, went so far as to allege that "... in Newcastle strikers assisted the Civil Commissioner with unloading foodships until stopped by the Government").[131] On 6th May the Labour MP for Newcastle East Martin Connolly (1874-1945) stated in the Commons that essential services had broken down in Newcastle and that the Trade Unions had agreed to run them provided the extra police, the OMS and the military were withdrawn, an accusation denied by the Attorney-General on the basis of an assurance from the Chief Constable.[132] Wood was subsequently

---

[129] Postgate et al, op cit, pp67-68 See also Burns, op cit, p153
For Anne Perkins, 'A Very British Strike 3 May -12 May 1926', 2006, p133 "Sir Kingsley, rather daringly conciliatory, proposed some sort of dual authority, and there were two meetings to try to establish a modus operandi. The trade unionists refused to concede the principle of blacking volunteers, and talks broke down."
Just as the Joint Strike Committee did not agree to the shared control Wood had proposed so he had to follow his instructions over unloading.
GA Phillips, 'The General Strike: The Politics of Industrial Conflict', 1976, p199 also thinks Wood had "contemplated" some bargain such as dual control "though the assumption that, in its absence, the supply and transport agencies in Tyneside were rendered ineffective is much more disputable".
[130] Fyfe, op cit, p46
[131] Hughes, op cit, p54 Hughes seems to make this assertion on the basis of the similar statement in AJP Taylor, 'English History 1914-1945', 1965, pp245-246, one which Mason, op cit, p65 dismisses as "rather an astonishing summary in view of the evidence".
[132] Hansard, 6th May 1926, vol. 195, cols. 486-487 & 498-499
The issue was resurrected on 10th May when the Conservative MP for Newcastle North asked the Home Secretary whether there was any foundation to Connolly's allegations and, despite being assured that there

called to account in Parliament for his actions, an opportunity his opponents relished, not least because they hoped to embarrass the Government in the process,[133] but for the moment he dismissed the accusation that he had ever lost control of the situation or said he had; his visit to Burt Hall had been a friendly one and claims that "he had promised to withdraw troops [were] obviously absurd as no troops had been drafted into this district".[134]

The Newcastle Joint Strike Committee minutes for Friday 7th May claimed that, Union members having refused to work alongside the OMS on unloading the day before,

> ... the success of the General Strike appeared completely assured. It was clear to everyone that the OMS organisation was unable to cope with the task imposed upon it. The attitude of the population was favourable to the strikers and unfavourable to the Government. There were no disturbances, the Trade Unionists maintained an almost perfect discipline. There was no change from the ordinary except for the quietness in the streets and the absence of traffic.[135]

The Workers' Chronicle issued by the Newcastle Trades Council of Action adopted a more combative approach, highlighting the chaos on the Government side:

> The local Boss and Government press is making frantic efforts to keep up appearances, by printing statements in denial of the fact of Sir Kingsley Wood's request to the Council of Action for joint working, we can only repeat our statement that such an approach was made.
> What is the meaning of these developments? Firstly, it only means that the blackleg forces are failing the Government. Would Sir Kingsley have approached the Council of Action if he had not been in difficulties?
> This is confirmed by the City Council's telegram of appeal to Baldwin. Secondly, the withdrawal wipes out the widespread abuse of permits by the more unscrupulous

was not, Connolly continued to make them. Hansard, 10th May 1926, vol. 195, cols. 686-688 & 693-694
[133] Hansard, 20th May 1926, vol. 196, cols. 544-550
[134] *Newcastle Journal* 8th May 1926, KW16 190/2
[135] Davison, op cit, p64

employers. Thirdly, it places before the Civil Commissioner the question (bound to be reached sooner or later) of whether he will use soldiers (if they are available) and the military apparatus to the full in support of blacklegs, with the almost inevitable result of collisions with the workers on strike, or whether he will advise the Government that the attempt to break the strike has itself broken down.

NO COMPROMISE WITH THE ENEMY.[136]

Employers and strikers did not just have different views, they lived in different worlds. The third CCEL bulletin described the Joint Strike Committee as "largely composed of extremists and Communists" and *The Workers' Chronicle* as one of the main means by which it carried on its "antagonistic" work.[137] It continued "It is endeavouring to seduce the troops from loyalty to their oath by the subtle means of arranging sports between the soldiers and workers." There was little chance of finding any common ground.

CCEL's next bulletin reported at 4pm on Friday 7th that

There is a fair amount of rowdyism. The local Labour Party has issued a typed news-sheet containing revolutionary articles. The Strike Committee has formed Women's Committees, who are using motor-cycles to distribute the news-sheets over a wide area.[138]

Saturday 8th May opened with the *Daily Mail* repeating Sir John Simon's claim that the General Strike was illegal, a contentious view that, perhaps popular in the Government ranks,

---

[136] *The Workers' Chronicle No. 4* 7th May 1926 in Burns, op cit, p42
[137] Baldwin Papers, vol. 22, pp28-32: Central Council of Economic Leagues (CCEL) Strike Bulletin 3, 6th May 1926
The first issue of *The Workers' Chronicle* had described the situation as "an attack on the economic standards of the miners and all workers of this country", encouraging "Never has there been a greater need for workers to stand solid". This was accompanied by a cartoon in which "Your Master's Voice" demanded "It's your wages I want". Since it would mostly be men that were on strike, many of whom were already under pressure from their families, the women were urged to "analyse and try to understand the position". *Workers Chronicle No. 1* 6th May 1926, KW16 195/1
[138] Baldwin Papers, vol. 22, pp33-35: Central Council of Economic Leagues (CCEL) Strike Bulletin 4, 7th May 1926

was soon disputed by other lawyers.[139]   It might have been calculated to inflame trade unionists, and was bound to harden attitudes overall, for Simon was arguing that the General Strike was not a legitimate industrial dispute. In 1926 he asserted that it would be "the first and last attempt" to undermine the rule of law,[140] describing it in his 1952 autobiography as "the nine days blunder".[141]   However, Wood was among those who, perhaps conscious of the future, took a more emollient approach, reminding everybody that

> ... we have all got to live together, and we should not forget at any time we are all members of the British family, bound together by many mutual interests, obligations and duties.[142]

Two newspapers that had maintained production added that public order was generally good and, though the situation was improving throughout the district, Wood wished to use the unemployed to distribute food where possible.[143]   The reason he suggested this was that the food transport embargo had been so effective that there were fears of food shortages in mining villages. The Co-op, for example, was faced with the dilemma of closing down the food supply to comply with strike directives or applying for permits that would break the strike.[144]

However, by later on Saturday the situation in Newcastle had deteriorated - as it did generally in week two.[145] Police brutality

---

[139] NRO ZFO 3/12, *Daily Mail* 8th May 1926 As Ewing and Gearty point out (op cit, p213), this claim was not correct, or at any rate the Government was insufficiently confident that it was (which amounts to the same thing), otherwise they would not have had to pass the Trade Disputes and Trade Unions Act 1927 in retribution.
Simon, whose Liberal colleagues called him "a cold fish", had made this statement in the Commons and included it in his publication later that year 'Three Speeches on the General Strike', 1926.
[140] Simon, 1926, op cit, ppiv-xvi
[141] Sir John Simon, 'Retrospect: The Memoirs of the Rt Hon Viscount Simon', 1952, pp135-140
[142] In a typed, rather than printed, version of the *Newcastle Journal* 8th May 1926, KW16 190/2
[143] *Leeds Mercury* and *Yorkshire Post* 8th May 1926, KW16 189/4 & 189/2
[144] *Labour Monthly* pp371 & 373, KW16/210
[145] Though not everywhere: Glasgow, op cit, pp60-63 describes the Eastern Division centred on Cambridge as generally a backwater that ran very smoothly unless affected by London docks problems. The Civil

was reported in Newcastle on the Saturday afternoon and evening,[146] with baton charges continuing throughout the weekend to break down picketing by force and arrest several prominent people.[147] "There were hundreds of casualties when the police brutally charged a peaceful crowd"[148] and on Monday Blaydon Council protested "against the unprovoked and brutal attacks by the police", calling for an inquiry into their interference with lawful picketing.[149] The *Workers Chronicle* not only blamed Wood for his failure to handle the food problem appropriately by allowing OMS to operate under military protection, but suggested that the provocative tactics were deliberate in order to pave the way for Wood's next step (though it did not say what this might be).[150]

The CCEL bulletin on Monday 10th reported the midday situation in Newcastle:

> 12 noon. There has been a certain amount of rioting during the weekend, especially on Sunday night. Pickets are posted outside infirmaries and hospitals. Messrs Will Lawther and Bolton were arrested near Newcastle on Sunday night.[151]

It is most unlikely that those outside hospitals were pickets; much more probable that they were friends and family waiting for news of those injured in the riots and police charges. However, CCEL would have been keen to mislead and misinterpret in this way.

Will Lawther (1889-1976), a miner from the age of twelve, was the unofficial representative of the Durham Miners on the Joint Strike Committee, while Henry Bolton (1874-1953) was Chairman of Blaydon Council and a JP. They were accused of interfering with food supplies and although such things did happen (for example, there was an attack on a food waggon by fifty men near

---

Commissioner was Sir Philip Sassoon. Two thousand Cambridge University students volunteered and most were drafted to London.

[146] *Workers Chronicle No. 8* 8th May 1926, KW16 196/1

[147] *Labour Monthly* p371, KW16/210

[148] Hughes, op cit, p44

[149] T&W DX 278/1: Blaydon Council 10th May 1926

[150] *Workers Chronicle No. 8*, KW16 196/1

[151] Baldwin Papers, vol. 22, pp38-40: Central Council of Economic Leagues (CCEL) Strike Bulletin 6, 10th May 1926 Newcastle had not been mentioned in Bulletin 5 on Saturday 8th.

Gosforth),[152] this seems to have been a trumped-up charge in their case. According to Ewing and Gearty, they had stopped on their way home to investigate lorries parked outside a public house that were supposed to be carrying food for miners but were found to contain birdseed.[153] They were arrested on the spot when they refused to provide permits for the lorries,[154] appearing in court later that week, and were sentenced to three months in prison.[155] Baldwin then intervened on their behalf and the sentence was reduced to a £50 fine instead.[156] The Labour activist Ruth Dodds recorded in her diary that they refused to pay but then crossed out "rather than" and substituted "unable to" pay instead.[157] The upshot was that they went to prison anyway.[158]

Lawther was later on the TUC general council from 1935, elected President of the Miners Federation of Great Britain in 1939 then first president of the NUM, knighted in 1949 and became a magistrate in Whitley Bay after his retirement. By contrast, Bolton was removed as a JP and the Lord Chancellor refused to reinstate him.[159] On his release from prison, Bolton had compared communist Chopwell to the new Jerusalem, promising to destroy capitalism and "banish poverty, destitution, crime and all those things that were only by-products of capitalism".[160] He concentrated on Blaydon and County Durham, particularly education and Co-operative, matters for the remainder of his career and was a County Councillor into his seventies[161].

It was on Monday 10th that the LNER express from Edinburgh to London was derailed at Cramlington in Northumberland, the most notorious event of the General Strike in

---

[152] *Evening Chronicle* 10th May 1926, KW16 197/4; Davison, op cit, p75
[153] Ewing and Gearty, op cit, p172
[154] Hansard, 11th &12th May 1926, cols. 815-818 & 893-894; KW16 219/2 & 213/2
[155] *The New Leader* undated, KW16 221/1
[156] *North Mail and Newcastle Chronicle* 20th May; *Blaydon Courier* article 22nd May 1926
[157] T&W DF.DOD: Ruth Dodds 1926 diary entry for 14th May
[158] *North Mail* 14th May 1926, KW16 195/4; and were given a "wonderful reception" on their release, *Daily Herald* undated but November 1926, KW16 249/2.
[159] Hansard, 15th July 1926, vol.198, cols. 593-594
[160] Stuart Macintyre, 'Little Moscows: Communism and Working-Class Militancy in Inter-War Britain', 1980, p17
[161] Bolton's obituary in *The Blaydon Courier* 13th March 1953

the north-east. About twenty-five to thirty miners had removed a rail to stop blackleg coal trains when they saw that the next train was the Flying Scotsman, a passenger train. They flagged it down in an attempt to get it to stop but, according to William Muckle, one of eight men arrested some weeks later after one of their colleagues turned King's evidence, the drivers jumped off while the train carried on at about 20mph for 100 yards or so before derailing.[162] Fortunately, only one of the nearly three hundred passengers was slightly hurt. Muckle and another seven men were sentenced to between four and eight years in prison.[163] (One of Muckle's fellow inmates in Maidstone prison was Horatio Bottomley, then serving six years for fraud.[164]) The Northumberland Miners Union considered appealing against the sentence but decided that "such action would be inopportune and calculated to do more harm than good".[165] The men were not released until 1929 when they were greeted by Will Lawther on their return to Newcastle after a rally at Poplar Town Hall and a weekend in London.[166]

Also on 10th May Newcastle Council Transport sub-committee met a deputation about the tram stoppage in the hope of resuming the service, though in the event Councillors were irritated that the deputation would not answer questions and would only report back to the Council of Action, not the men themselves.[167] There was a police baton attack at Spennymoor the same day, though the local MP Batey and the Home Secretary were to dispute the circumstances, Batey claiming that it had been unprovoked, Joynson-Hicks that the police were responding to being stoned.[168] Blaydon Council, after protesting about police brutality over the weekend, allowed the Trades Council to use their typewriter to produce leaflets during the dispute.[169]

CCEL Bulletin 7 for Tuesday 11th reported that Newcastle had been quiet the day before:

---

[162] *Daily Graphic* 12th May 1926, KW16 200/2; William Muckle, 'No Regrets', 1981, p35
[163] *Journal and North Star* 2nd July 1926; also, *News of the World* July 1926, KW16 201/4; NRO 08747/1: *The Journal* 6th November 1982
[164] Muckle, op cit, pp53-55
[165] NRO Northumberland Miners Union Minutes 10th July 1926, Minute 10
[166] Muckle, op cit, p56
[167] T&W, MD,NC/268/8
[168] Hansard, 20th May 1926, vol. 196, cols. 417-419 & KW16 216/2
[169] Blaydon Council 10th May; the *North Mail and Newcastle Chronicle* 20th May 1926 reported this as "Blaydon Council Scandal".

Apparently, however, the revolutionaries are endeavouring to get forces together for an attack upon railway trains. There is, in fact, an organised attempt in this area to hold up railway trains and food supplies. The railway accident at Newcastle yesterday was due to sabotage. The situation in this area has developed; instead of gangs of men about the streets, the extremists are forming mass pickets with settled instructions to each picket not to be cowards and to be prepared to fight.[170]

Trade Unions and individual hooligans at the start of the Strike had now become extremists and revolutionaries a week later. While some of their actions might be illegal and described as unconstitutional, the workers were conscious that the authorities had previously defined the boundaries that best suited them - as authoritative and articulate lawyers such as Simon were once again attempting. As the *Workers Chronicle* put it, the Constitution ought to be subject to a "rapid and radical transformation" if workers were unable to protest legitimately against lock-outs.[171]

On Wednesday 12th May the TUC General Council told the Prime Minister shortly after noon that they were calling off the General Strike after Samuel had written to their President setting out the results of his negotiations, an initiative which he had taken himself and which did not commit the Government at all (as Samuel made clear).[172] Baldwin described it as a victory for common sense but failed to give any assurances about cancelling the mine lock-outs, though he did ensure there was no extreme reaction from "militant colleagues" such as Churchill. Winterton refers to Baldwin's moral courage in opposing the vindictiveness of right-wing Conservatives.[173] The miners had failed to agree the Samuel memoranda and their dispute continued.[174] In the Commons Baldwin argued that

---

[170] Baldwin Papers, vol. 22, pp41-43: Central Council of Economic Leagues (CCEL) Strike Bulletin 7, 11th May 1926

[171] *Workers Chronicle No. 12 11th* May 1926, KW16 197/1

[172] Baldwin Papers, vol. 21, pp158-161; Hughes, op cit, pp66-69

[173] Earl Winterton, 'Orders of the Day', 1953, p148

[174] Seebohm Rowntree was one of those who attempted to negotiate an end to the miners' strike once the General Strike had collapsed. He had previously been a conciliator in the 1919 rail strike. In Asa Briggs, 'A Study of the Work of Seebohm Rowntree 1871-1954', 1961, pp248-268

... it is of utmost importance at a moment like this that the whole British people should not look backwards, but forwards - that we should resume our work in a spirit of co-operation, putting behind us all malice and vindictiveness.[175]

Pressed by MacDonald, Baldwin agreed that a fuller statement would be required at a later date in order to reinforce this spirit of compromise and the tone of forgiveness, but in the meantime many employers proved less conciliatory than Baldwin, with some men treated as having broken their contract and, if they were re-engaged at all, on poorer terms and conditions than previously. Some employers saw it as an opportunity to remove unionisation from their workforce or to improve their margins by exploiting their workers.[176]

The miners largely blamed JH Thomas the railway leader for calling the strike off and mining villages thought him a traitor to the working-class for, if he hadn't called off the Strike himself, he had certainly persuaded the General Council to do so.[177] The *Workers Chronicle* concurred in describing the TUC's "unconditional withdrawal" (as the *British Gazette* had put it with a note of triumphalism[178]) as a betrayal of working class interests, not least because the TUC had responded to Samuel without even waiting for a Miners Federation (MFGB) delegate conference.[179] The counter-argument was that the miners had handed over responsibility for the conduct of the General Strike to the TUC.

On the 12th Ruth Dodds' initial concerns were how the miners would react, for as she confided to her diary,

I hope the miners will see possibilities in the new basis, for if they count themselves deserted they will fight on alone. Thank God it is over and pray God the government keep to their word.[180]

---

[175] Hansard, 12th May 1926, vol. 195, col. 878

[176] For example, Crook, op cit, pp425-446

[177] Muckle, op cit, p37; Davison, op cit, p68
In Margaret Bondfield's view though, Thomas "deeply imprinted the doctrine of constitutional methods upon the British Labour movement" and this might have been a further example of it. Bondfield, op cit, p242

[178] NRO ZFO 3/15: *British Gazette* 13th May 1926

[179] *Workers Chronicle* No. 14 14th May 1926, KW16 201/1

[180] T&W DF.DOD: Ruth Dodds 1926 diary entry for 12th May

Her apprehension for the future was accompanied by pride that

> Whatever may happen now our people have proved that the
> General Strike is a weapon of peace and can be so handled
> ... The workers stood together, they were very nearly solid -
> 75 to 80% I should say - they trusted their leaders, they
> preserved order, they were willing to carry on the vital
> services ...[181]

She particularly recalled "a great meat-boat, unloading opposite our
shop for two long warm days, by voluntary labour, and the dock-
labourers, the roughest class in the world, standing peacefully
watching". This captured the essence of the protest for her.

Volunteers and special constables were paraded at St
James Park on the 13th,[182] while Wood wrote to the papers to thank
volunteers and the press itself, the latter for upholding what he
called their "best traditions".[183] In a second letter thanking
volunteers he hoped that "we can look forward and not backward"
and so "quickly regain our national prosperity" - sentiments that he
attributed to Stanley Baldwin.[184]

Wood and his main Northern Division staff had their
photograph taken outside their St Mary's Place headquarters[185] and
a fortnight after the Strike began he left Newcastle by train.
Accompanied by Captain Derrick Gunston (1891-1985), who had
only recently become his PPS but had been with him throughout,
and given a civic send off by the Lord Mayor, Wood took the
opportunity once again to thank the citizens of Newcastle for their
support and the press for "disseminating reliable information in spite
of the handicaps to publication".[186]

But Baldwin's "fair promises" of no victimisation or revenge,
as Ruth Dodds described them, carried little weight outside
Parliament for "... employers are demanding a general reduction in
wages and prolonging the stoppage from their side until they get

---

[181] Ibid, 13th May
[182] *Newcastle Evening Chronicle* and *North Mail* 13th and 14th May 1926,
KW16 190/3 & 190/1
[183] *North Mail...* undated but May 1926, KW16 191/5; *Shields Daily News*
14th May 1926, KW16 191/6
[184] *Newcastle Daily Journal* 17th May 1926, KW16 192/1
[185] *North Mail* and *Northern Echo* 17th May 1926, KW16 191/1 & 200/1
[186] *Newcastle Evening Chronicle* 18th, *Shields Daily News* 19th and
Newcastle Chronicle 22nd May 1926, KW16 190/4, 190/5 & 192/10

it".[187] Workers' fury at the TUC might manifest itself in interference with Durham traffic and cutting telephone wires, as it had on the 12th,[188] or by the Annual Meeting of the Northumberland Miners failing to mention the General Strike at all,[189] but right-wingers such as Havelock Wilson wrote to fortify Baldwin, accusing the TUC of diabolical left-wing drift in case the risks to which the country had been exposed had not impressed themselves sufficiently or the Prime Minister should prove too accommodating.[190] A few weeks later Victor Spencer, 1st Viscount Churchill (1864-1934), a stalwart of the establishment, was one of those who proposed draconian measures to Baldwin, including the repeal of the 1906 Trade Disputes Act.[191]

The Northern Division had proved to be one of the most disturbed areas outside London with one-third of the cases of violence in English counties taking place in Durham (183 out of 583) and 103 proceedings being brought under the Emergency Regulations in Northumberland. In most of the country there were none.[192] The direct costs of the Strike to the Government had been £433,000 (about £13m now),[193] but the overall loss to the country was estimated at £30m or seventy times as much[194] and about £15m had been lost in wages.[195] According to Robertson, the number of people involuntarily unemployed (in other words, as a consequence of others going on Strike) had increased in the first week of the Strike by nearly 50% to 1.6m across the country.

---

[187] T&W DF.DOD: Ruth Dodds 1926 diary entry for 14th May
[188] NRO ZFO 3/15: *British Gazette* 13th May 1926 p3 reports from the Northern Division
[189] NRO Northumberland Miners Union Minutes, Annual Council meeting at Burt Hall 15th May 1926
[190] Baldwin Papers, vol. 21, pp246-251: 14th May letter from Havelock Wilson of the National Union of Sailors and Firemen
As an example of this "left-wing drift", the *Daily Telegraph* 3rd June 1926, KW16 191/9 reported that Tottenham District Council had told their staff to belong to Trade Unions or be dismissed.
[191] Baldwin Papers, vol. 23, pp16, 17-23
[192] Mason, op cit, p103; Hansard, 2nd June 1926, vol. 196, cols. 822-825
[193] Glasgow, op cit, p24; Robertson, op cit, p387 Earlier estimates had put this at £600,000 or more.
[194] 5th July 1926 Supplementary Estimate; Glasgow, op cit, p24; Robertson, op cit, p387
[195] Arthur Steel-Maitland (1876-1935), Minister of Labour, estimated this at between £14m and £16m; Hansard, 30th June 1926, vol. 197, col. 1125

Immediate Aftermath

Perhaps indicative of the breach that the General Strike had widened further, the Newcastle Benzol Company sent a cheque for ten guineas to the Chief Constable of Durham thanking him for the police action during the General Strike and asking that he donate it to the police charity of his choice.[196] To the Chief Constable's credit, he had still not banked it by late October and only did so when reminded forcefully by the Company. He explained that, though it had now been paid in, he had been waiting until the end of the miners' strike so as not to inflame the situation. But for every such example of even-handedness, there were contrasting illustrations. For example, a miner, charged under Regulation 21 with inciting disaffection, was sent to prison for three months with hard labour for distributing *Northern Light*, one of the worker bulletins. The chairman of magistrates added that he would have fined him £100 as well if "he had had his own way".[197]

The Northumberland Miners Union first decided that, rather than use branch money to pay fines for workmen summoned for preventing the proper use of the highway, they would be defended by the Union's solicitors instead. But, once the men had been convicted the Union agreed to loan money to branches to pay the fines.[198] On 18th May the Northumberland Coal Owners' Association rejected the Government (i.e., Samuel) proposals for settlement and indicated their preference for reverting to District negotiations.[199]

On 20th May, just over a week after the General Strike ended, Parliament debated the immediate issues and consequences. Arthur Henderson, Labour MP for Burnley, opened an adjournment debate by deploring the victimisation in which some Government departments as well as private employers had engaged, despite Baldwin's emphatic declarations. He singled out the Board of Admiralty and the War Office among the former, though he acknowledged that the situation had improved a little

[196] T&W, DX 278/1: 14th July 1926 letter
[197] T&W, DX 278/1: *Blaydon Courier* 22nd May 1926
[198] NRO Northumberland Miners Union Minutes: 17th May 1926, Minute 1 re Throckley Workmen Summoned; 25th May 1926, Minute 11 re Throckley Group and Montague
[199] NRO 263/B1: Northumberland Coal Owners' Association Minutes 1926, pp136-138 18th May 1926: General meeting at Coal Trade offices, Newcastle

since it first became clear that he would raise it.[200] Replying on the Prime Minister's behalf, Ronald McNeill (1861-1934), Conservative MP for Canterbury and Financial Secretary to the Treasury, pointed out that Baldwin had said on 14th May "I have given no pledge at all except one, and that is that those who have helped the Government shall not suffer for having done so". McNeill thought it entirely appropriate, therefore, that men who did not strike or returned early, or volunteers who wished to become permanent, should not be replaced by strikers. And in any case work had to exist and men had to be "able and efficient", not just long-standing employees, for them to be taken back. Though McNeill did not say so, Government departments were taking the opportunity, therefore, to weed out "trouble-makers" and any others whose popularity or performance fell short of the desired level. McNeill said that, of 125,000 men employed by the Government overall, 10% or 12,600 had joined the General Strike, with 9000 returning before it ended. All but 1000 of the 3,600 who saw the Strike through had since been re-employed, of whom 197 were in the Admiralty, 64 in the War Office and the remainder (about 740) in the Stationery Office.[201] The Ministers responsible for the Admiralty and the War Office, William Bridgeman and Laming Worthington-Evans respectively, gave examples justifying why some men had been dismissed and others yet to be taken back.[202] Reflecting the divisions in the country, the Labour MP Drummond Shiels (1881-1953) then highlighted cases of victimisation on the railways while a Conservative Gerald Hurst (1877-1957) asked about the steps that would be taken against the Union leaders who had called their men out on strike, often with misleading information, and had so far got off scot free.[203]

The debate then turned to the maintenance of supplies in Newcastle.[204] Connolly repeated his allegations of 6th and 10th May,[205] ones which he said were correct at the time and which he had taken some trouble to verify subsequently. He did acknowledge though that

---

[200] Hansard, 20th May 1926, vol. 196, cols. 513-518

[201] Ibid, cols. 519-526

[202] Ibid, cols. 526-530

[203] Ibid, cols. 530-534 & 535-538

[204] Ibid, cols. 538-550

[205] As above, that is to say "In Newcastle the OMS organisation has broken down, and the authorities have asked the trade unions to carry on the vital services, and they have consented, provided that the extra police and troops were withdrawn".

... eventually [Wood] made arrangements which carried on the services very well, indeed. Everyone in Newcastle is satisfied that the services were carried on magnificently ... [but] the information I have here proves absolutely that there was serious difficulty in Newcastle at the moment I was speaking ...

After the Under-Secretary at the Home Office had read out a letter from the Lord Mayor of Newcastle, asserting that Connolly's allegations were a "travesty of the actual position" and paying tribute to "the very great assistance" which Wood had rendered the people of Newcastle in his judicious handling of the Strike, Wood replied to the allegations at length:

The hon. Member's statement today is a very different one from that which I read [in the *Newcastle Chronicle*] ... There is not a word of truth in any of [the] allegations [that the services had broken down or that Wood had asked the Trade Unions to carry them on] ... from the time I reached Newcastle so far from there being any danger of the vital services failing they steadily improved.

Wood challenged anyone who had been in Newcastle to deny this. He continued that he had not initiated meetings with the Trade Unions but that "a very respected trade unionist in the district", the President of the Miners' Federation, had proposed it, suggesting that "if I saw the secretaries of the three trade unions concerned, he was confident that no further attempt would be made to interfere with the food supplies". Wood said that when he did indeed meet with them, unaware that they were representatives of the Strike Committee, he had not put forward the prospect of 'dual control'.

The only suggestion I made to them, and one which, on reflection, I should make again today, was this – that if they found there was any difficulty at the quay in relation to the employment of labour, they were to report it to my officer or me, and I would immediately deal with it.

Wood made it clear, however, that if the Government scheme for unloading food was unacceptable, he would

... see that the docks were properly protected, that all ill-disposed people were removed from the docks, and that if the men did not turn up the next morning, volunteers would take their places.

When Wood did then receive such a message, "Immediately ... I did what I said I should do" and "from that day to the end of the strike the whole of the work of the food supplies in that district was carried out by voluntary labour under police protection". Wood then turned to some of the other difficulties that had arisen in the Division, including the train derailment, an attempt to disrupt the supply of flour he had circumvented by the use of volunteers and the arrest of a member of Labour's National Executive, but his "spirited defence" had essentially disposed of Connolly's allegations.[206]

Demonstrating that there are (at least) two sides to every story, and that this clash of workers and employers was inevitable, Harold Macmillan was subsequently to conclude in 1938 that

Somebody decided in 1925 to return to the gold standard at a parity which ... it was impossible for us to support. The miners strike of 1926 and the General Strike which followed were a direct result of that decision. For years afterwards industry struggled under the burden which this decision imposed, and we endured all the consequences of unemployment and poverty associated with the effort of readjustment of costs and prices. We cannot escape the responsibilities of decisions upon which the welfare of an intricate and highly organised society depends.[207]

Trade Disputes Act 1927 and 1931 Labour Bill to repeal (Trade Unions and Trade Disputes Bill)

One, perhaps inevitable, outcome of the General Strike had been to polarise views further. In the immediate aftermath the collapse of the TUC might appear a victory for middle-class certainties, but only a short-lived and insubstantial one for, regardless of whether the General Strike had been revolutionary, it posed a threat to the

---

[206] *North Mail & Newcastle Chronicle* 21st May 1926, KW16 193/1
[207] Harold Macmillan, 'The Middle Way: A Study of the Problem of Economic and Social Progress in a Free and Democratic Society', 1938, p299

continuation of their expectations - even more so if such action was constitutional. In Mowat's estimation this realisation drove the government's legislative revenge in 1927, the Trade Disputes and Trade Unions Act, reinforcing working-class bitterness and rancour, and paving the way in turn for Labour's general election victory of 1929.[208]

The Bill took a year to finalise, with a Conservative majority of 368 to 171 on its third reading. In the Commons debate Baldwin explained that the events of the General Strike justified his move away from the conciliatory line he had taken previously in handling Macquisten's proposed political levy and the coal subsidy itself.[209] Nevertheless, he found the prospect distasteful, partly because he thought it reflected politics at its worst as each party "appealed to its mob".[210] Although the Act was intended to be restrictive and repressive, and did have an impact on relations with the TUC while it was being formulated,[211] it was never fully implemented and indeed some of the TUC came to welcome it: the TUC Chairman Ben Turner was supposed to have said that no Trade Unionist would willingly return to the days before the Act, even though its repeal was top of Labour's policy objectives.[212] Similarly, Wood had asserted in June 1926 that many Trade Unions and the moderate rank and file thought the General Strike a mistake and were "opposed to such methods".[213] He also noted that the Home Secretary's preparations might have failed had the community not backed them and hoped that there would now be an industrial truce for the next ten years.

---

[208] CL Mowat, 'Britain Between the Wars 1918-1940', 1955, pp229-230
[209] Middlemas and Barnes, op cit, pp449-451; see Part 1 p221.
[210] Ibid, p459
[211] GW McDonald and Howard F Gospel, "The Mond-Turner talks 1927-1933: A study in industrial co-operation", *Historical Journal*, 1973, 16, pp807-829
[212] JCC Davidson letter to Irwin on 3rd December 1928 in Ball (ed.), 2014, op cit, p254
In October 1930 Wood asserted that repeal was at the top of Labour's agenda even though, he claimed, the Conservative measure had given "freedom and dignity to the worker" and had been passed with general assent. *Kentish Independent* 24th October 1930, KW17 226/10 reporting a speech in Plumstead and *Sidcup Times* 31st October 1930, KW17 226/11 one at the Bridgeman Hall in New Eltham.
[213] *Yorkshire Post* and *Times* 4th June 1926, KW16 191/4 & 191/7 reporting Wood's speech at Studley Priory near Oxford.

According to Middlemas,[214] there was no demand from backbench Conservative MPs for legislative retribution after the General Strike until pressure from their constituency associations forced them to reconsider. He cites a survey by the whips to support this contention. Despite Baldwin's call for a spirit of conciliation and co-operation on 12th May 1926, reinforced by the King's message the following day,[215] it became clear within a week that some employers had taken matters into their own hands. By November the Government indicated that they would be introducing legislation to revise Trade Union law in the next session.[216]

In the Debate on the King's speech the following February, Oliver Stanley (1896-1950) asserted, as any Conservative starting the debate would, that the promised legislation amending and refining the law relating to industrial disputes would not "threaten any of the vital aims of trade unions" for everybody recognised that Unions "have an essential part to play in the modern industrialised state", particularly around collective bargaining.[217] Rather, while Labour MPs might think the legislation unnecessary, it would have to be seen as "fair and unbiased" and prevent abuses – by which he meant political strikes that undermined the authority of Parliament and threatened the community through the use of organised force (rather than peaceful picketing).

When the Conservative MP for Nottingham South asked the Prime Minister a few days later if he would first discuss with the Labour Party what changes were thought necessary, Baldwin replied "This matter was fully discussed in the Debate on the address and I have nothing to add to what was then said".[218] He was similarly dismissive when asked if the proposed legislation would require trade unionists to contract in to the political levy (rather than contract out as currently applied), advising his questioner to await the Bill.[219]

---

[214] Keith Middlemas, 'Politics in Industrial Society: The Experience of the British System since 1911', 1979, p203
[215] Hansard, 13th May 1926, vol. 195, col. 1043
[216] Hansard, 11th November 1926, vol. 199, col. 1251 (also 15th November, col. 1535; 16th November, col. 1681; 9th December, vol. 200, col. 2279)
[217] Hansard, 8th February 1927, vol. 202, col. 12
[218] Hansard, 21st February 1927, vol. 202, col. 1396 It had been discussed in both days of the Debate on 8th and 9th February cols. 11-256
[219] Hansard, 3rd March 1927, vol. 203, col. 577
This issue had already been broached several times by the Conservative MP and Lancashire cotton grandee Robert Waddington (1868-1941). He

The Bill was introduced on 4th April with its second reading on 2nd to 5th May.[220] The first day of debate proved very raucous, with Clynes characterising the Bill as "class hostility",[221] while on the 5th Ellen Wilkinson stressed the Bill's gender hostility and its deleterious effect on working women.[222] Nevertheless, the second reading resulted in 388 votes for and 168 against (in a Commons composed of 413 Conservatives and 202 others). The Committee stage took the rest of May and the Report stage much of June, with the third reading passed on 23rd June by 354 votes to 139.[223] It received Royal Assent on 29th July,[224] the last day before Parliament went into recess until 8th November.

Although the 1927 Act did outlaw sympathetic strikes and those of a purely political nature aimed at coercing the government, its main provision was the requirement that Trade Unions contract in to the political levy.[225] Yet the Act was badly drafted and largely symbolic. Lowe points out, as did Fraser, that it was just as noteworthy for what it did not include: compulsory arbitration, compulsory strike ballots, no extension of the criminal law and, most significantly, no repeal of the exemption granted to Trade Unions under the 1906 Act.[226] Baldwin had ruled out compulsory arbitration as impracticable when invited to consider it.[227]

The initial Mond-Turner talks between the employers and the Trade Unions had been called off by Ernest Bevin to demonstrate the Unions' displeasure and remained dormant from March to August 1927. But they had already divided opinion. For

---

had asked about it on 23rd and 24th February, and 2nd March (Hansard, vol. 202, cols. 1763, 1932-1934; vol. 203, cols. 366-367). He would do so again on 8th March (Hansard, vol. 203, 1038-1039) when he proposed that all Trade Unions that had balloted since the 1913 Act be required by the new legislation to do so again.

[220] Hansard, vol. 204, col. 1707; vol. 205, cols. 1305-1426, 1467-1584, 1639-1716, 1783-1902

[221] Middlemas and Barnes, op cit, p450

[222] Hansard, vol. 205, cols. 1822-1827

[223] Hansard, vol. 207, cols. 2077-2186

[224] Hansard, vol. 209, col. 1704

[225] W Hamish Fraser, 'A History of British Trade Unionism 1700-1998', 1999, pp169-170
The Act also strengthened the laws against intimidation and banned civil servants from joining Unions affiliated to the TUC.

[226] Rodney Lowe in Chris Wrigley (ed.), 'A History of British Industrial Relations 1914-1939', 1993 (orig. 1987), pp185-210

[227] Hansard, 21st June 1926, vol. 197, col. 23

the Minister of Labour Arthur Steel-Maitland,[228] who had tried but failed to get Baldwin to drop the Trade Disputes Bill, they represented the best chance for employers and the employed to thrash out their respective responsibilities. Ellen Wilkinson, however, for whom the General Strike had ended prematurely because the TUC's "nerve broke",[229] condemned the talks as indicative of the "collaborationist drift of the TUC" - especially at a time when victimisation by employers was apparent. Similarly, she called the Trade Disputes Act a "blackleg's charter".[230]

Wood had said very little during the passage of the Act and nothing at all before the Committee stage. This should not be surprising given that he had many other matters to attend to at the Ministry of Health and the Trade Disputes legislation was far from his ministerial brief. It would be different though when Labour returned to government and repeal was known to be one of their priorities.

The Labour Government elected at the start of June 1929 was faced with increasing unemployment even before the 1929 crash towards the end of October made a dire situation immeasurably worse. Consequently, the repeal of the Trade Disputes Act was not at the immediate forefront of their attention, an alteration that appealed to Wood, providing him with the opportunity to harass and embarrass the government. In April 1930 he challenged the Chancellor of the Exchequer Philip Snowden (1864-1937) as to whether his proposed Land Valuation Bill would have precedence over Trade Disputes and plans to increase the school leaving age to reduce the numbers of unemployed. Snowden replied that "The right honourable gentleman had better wait and see".[231] In June a Consumer Council Bill was dropped, giving Wood an opportunity to berate the government over whether they would still proceed with their Trade Disputes Bill, and if so when.[232] By early December, as the Daily Express reported, Wood had become a "one-idea man", especially since Arthur Henderson's announcement that the Bill would appear before Christmas. Wood redoubled his efforts to embarrass the Prime Minister:

[228] McDonald and Gospel, op cit, pp810-811

[229] Perry, op cit, p140

[230] Ibid, pp143-144

[231] Times 10th April 1930, KW17 190/8

[232] Evening Star & Yorkshire Evening Express both 26th June 1930, KW17 210/13 & 14

On every possible occasion he asks where the Bill is, and yesterday, when someone else by chance put the same question, all the Socialists cried 'Wood, Wood' and refused to listen.[233]

A week later, as *Punch* put it, Wood's "patience" was rewarded when Ramsay MacDonald himself said that the amending Bill would be published before Christmas:

Aware of the significance of this utterance Conservative leaders were observed to gaze at each other with a wild surmise. Visions of a pacific ocean of Lib-Lab co-operation swam before them.[234]

On 18th December the Attorney-General Sir William Jowitt[235] (1885-1957) formally presented the Government's Trade Disputes and Trade Unions (Amendment) Bill. Will Thorne (1857-1946), veteran Trade Unionist and Labour MP for Plaistow "led the cheers of thanksgiving which the Socialist back-benches raised". For their part the

Conservatives ... taunted the Government with their long delay. Sir Kingsley Wood, who has irritated the Prime Minister almost every day of the session with his polite inquiries for the Bill, drew howls of delight from the Socialists when he interjected 'At last!'

The Bill would be issued the following day for discussion when the House returned in the new year.[236]

The second reading began on 22nd January 1931, two days after the Commons reconvened, continuing into the following week.[237] The *Daily Herald* reported that

---

[233] *Daily Express* 3rd December 1930, KW17 233/6 (also 233/7-9)

[234] *Punch* 10th December 1930, KW17 236/10

[235] In 1929 he resigned as Liberal MP from his Preston seat, winning it back for Labour in the by-election. Following his friend Ramsay MacDonald into the National Government in 1931 as Attorney-General, he was expelled from the Labour Party. Re-admitted in 1939 he was unopposed in a 1939 by-election, remaining MP for Ashton under Lyne until he became Lord Chancellor after the 1945 general election.

[236] *Daily Express* 19th December 1930, KW17 238/2

[237] Hansard, 22nd January 1931, vol. 247, cols. 385-498

Thunderous cheers from the Labour benches greeted the Attorney-General when he rose in the House of Commons last night to move the second reading of the Trade Disputes Bill.

Equally enthusiastic applause rewarded him when he sat down after a brilliant speech ...[238]

Jowitt had called the 1927 measure "unjust to the workers of this country" and asserted that "By removing the causes of distrust which that Act implanted, the Government is making its contribution to the industrial peace which the nation so much needs". Wood contrasted the Liberal KC Jowitt who had described the General Strike as "indefensible" in the 1927 Yellow Book with his call now as Labour Attorney-General to "let us have better and bigger strikes".

If the minority Labour government were to get the Bill through they would depend on Liberal support. This was thought to be straightforward for "From the Liberal point of view, no difficulty arises ... as the Government is, in reality, resigned to its rejection by the House of Lords". The same report continued:

Sir Kingsley Wood has revealed that the TUC has been admonished on behalf of Mr. MacDonald for making the 'disastrous blunder' of forcing the Government to put the Bill in the forefront of its programme.

Some Ministers confess privately to a dislike of the Bill, which is only being brought forward at the dictation of the TUC.[239]

Other newspapers expected the same outcome for

Of the three major measures ... the Education Bill [has been] 'smashed to smithereens', the electoral reform scheme has been sentenced to dismemberment, and the course adopted in the name of the Liberal party yesterday suggests that [Labour's] Trade Disputes Act is good as dead.[240]

---

[238] *Daily Herald* 23rd January 1931, KW17 248/1

[239] *Evening News* 23rd January 1931, KW17 247/6

[240] *Northern Daily Telegraph* 23rd January 1931, KW17 247/7

The Bill resurfaced on the following Tuesday 27th January when the Conservatives attempted to kick it into the long grass by adopting the usual parliamentary formula and proposing the second reading be deferred for six months. At the end of the debate on the 28th it received 277 votes to 250 in favour of a second reading and even more comprehensively (306 votes to 244) that it be referred next to a Standing Committee rather than be considered by the whole House sitting in Committee.[241] The *Daily Herald* promised a 'Fight to the Finish'.[242]

Wood led for the Conservative Party on the Standing Committee, clashing on the 12th February with the Attorney-General who he accused of "prostituting his office".[243] This drew angry protests from the Labour side and a rebuke from the Labour Chair.[244] But Wood was undeterred, attempting the customary political gambit that "in the absence of a proper reply from the Attorney-General, he did not see how the Committee could proceed, and he moved that it should adjourn *sine die*". Matters became even more heated a fortnight later on a Liberal amendment defining an illegal strike or lock-out as one that put health and safety at risk by interfering with the supply or distribution of any of the necessities of life, such as essential food, water, fuel, light, medical or sanitary services.[245] The Attorney-General described this as "a wrecking amendment" for it would remove the right to withhold their labour from large sections of the Trade Union movement, effectively making them serfs rather than free labourers. It was "fundamentally unjust and they could never build any satisfactory system on an injustice". Labour were already antagonised, with one Labour MP suspended,[246] and so were in no mood to hear from Wood who, prevented from speaking, moved the amendment instead and the Government were defeated by 37 votes to 31.[247]

---

[241] Hansard, 27th and 28th January 1931, vol. 247,cols. 825-938 & 999-1112

[242] *Daily Herald* 29th January 1931, KW17 254/1

[243] Oxford, Bodleian Library, Conservative Party Archive (hereafter just CPA ...) NUA 3/1/2 Central Council Minutes 24th February 1931, p227

[244] John Scurr (1876-1932)
Reported by *Daily Telegraph*, *Daily Herald*, *News Chronicle* and *Times* all 13th February 1931, KW17 242/9, 243/1, 243/2 & 246/1

[245] *Times* 27th February 1931, p7

[246] W J Brown(1894-1960)

[247] *Yorkshire Post*, *News Chronicle*, *Daily Express*, *Times*, *Birmingham Post* all 27th February 1931, KW17 257/7, 257/8, 258/1, 258/3-5

On 2nd March MacDonald claimed that the Committee would finish its work,[248] but as one Nottingham newspaper put it, "The Trade Disputes Bill, to use Mr Churchill's lurid phraseology has 'had its dirty throat cut'".[249] A few days later another paper questioned

> Whether the slaughter of the Trade Disputes Bill has caused an irreparable breach between Labour and Liberals ..., for they are so much dependent upon one another for the continuance of their existence that they may find it better to forgive and forget than to indulge in the angry feelings which have been aroused during the Committee discussions of the measure.

It continued

> Kingsley Wood ... wished to place responsibility for the loss of the Bill upon the Executive of the TUC in forcing the Government to withdraw it at the moment it was discovered that the measure would deprive the unions of the weapon of the general strike. [250]

Many other newspapers reported on 4th March that the Bill had been abandoned,[251] with the *Morning Post* trailing Wood's question to MacDonald on the 9th as to "Whether he proposes to introduce any further proposals in relation to the repeal or

---

[248] Hansard, 2nd March 1931, vol. 249, cols. 34-36

[249] *Nottingham Evening Post* 27th February 1931, KW17 257/2

[250] *Nottingham Guardian* 4th March 1931, KW17 257/10
The *Sheffield Telegraph* 4th March 1931, KW17 258/2 reported Wood rubbing salt in the wound when he "said tonight that the first clause of the Trade Disputes Bill, if carried into law in the form the Government proposed, would enable a Soviet of Trade Unions to hold the nation to ransom. Some Parliamentarians say that Mr MacDonald's defeat by Mr [Arthur] Hayday [Lab Nottingham West] at the Labour Party meeting today and the subsequent public capitulation by the Attorney-General have the same effect."

[251] For example, *Morning Post, Birmingham Post* and *Times* all 4th March 1931, KW17 259/5, 259/6 & 259/2
In its report that day the *Liverpool Post* added "The Attorney-General, who is the most correct of Labour men, pronounced the doom of the Trade Disputes Bill. But he appears to have done so without regret. It was, no doubt, natural, however, that he should blame the Liberals for the fate of the measure." (KW17 258/7)

amendment of the Trade Disputes Act 1927".[252] The Prime Minister replied "Not at present". Wood then asked about the scope for a short Bill and whether the House would have an opportunity to debate the report of the Standing Committee. "No, Sir", replied MacDonald.[253]

MacDonald may have hoped to put this behind him and move on to other matters, but this is not the nature of politics and in any case Wood was not the sort of opponent to pass up an opportunity to harry him. Four months later on 20th July Wood asked MacDonald whether he had considered a recent NUR resolution urging repeal of certain sections of the Trade Disputes Act "at the earliest possible moment" and what action he proposed to take. The Prime Minister replied that "I have received no such resolution" and referred Wood back to the answer he gave him on 9th March. Wood then asked "Would the right honourable gentleman like to receive a copy ...?", to which MacDonald responded "I am always glad to receive anything which would be of value."[254]

---

[252] *Morning Post* 4th March 1931, KW17 257/5
[253] Hansard, 9th March 1931, vol. 249, col. 800
[254] Hansard, 20th July 1931, vol. 255, col. 1055

10.   AT HEALTH AGAIN 1925-1929

When he accepted the post of Minister of Health Chamberlain wrote to Baldwin on 7th November 1924 "I believe I may do something to improve the conditions for the less fortunate classes - and that's after all what one is in politics for".[255] His Parliamentary Secretary Wood may have concurred but was busy doing his homework and mastering the detail, exactly the characteristics that Chamberlain most respected. Without his own PPS until 1926 when Derrick Gunston, MP for Thornbury, filled this position,[256] Wood would have preferred to liaise with his parliamentary colleagues himself rather than through Chamberlain's PPS - confirming CFG Masterman's view that Wood "had more Parliamentary ability than half-a-dozen of his superiors ..."[257]

In the new year Wood received a congratulatory letter from the works committee at his uncle's firm, Edward Wood and Co. In addition to chairing the company's annual meetings in the difficult economic times of 1922 and 1923, he was well-known to the workforce and the mutual respect is clear from their letter:

> Although your views on political matters do not always coincide with those held by the workmen, we nevertheless appreciate to the full the active interest and consideration you have taken in the affairs of the company.[258]

Curiously it appeared in the company's local paper the *Manchester Guardian*, but whether this was the conduit chosen by the works committee, or just in addition to contacting Wood directly, is not clear. It is not beyond the bounds of possibility, given his talents for self-promotion, that Wood arranged its publication himself.

Much better-prepared than other members of the Cabinet, within a fortnight Neville Chamberlain set out a schedule of twenty-five Bills for the three years to 1927, which the Cabinet accepted - partly in the absence of any alternatives but also in agreement with

---

[255] Dilks, op cit, p405 Robert Self, 'Neville Chamberlain: A Biography', 2006, p105 cites this as Baldwin MSS 42/256 (i.e., Baldwin Papers, vol. 42, 256).

[256] Derrick Gunston was subsequently PPS to Neville Chamberlain at the Treasury 1931-1936 and to Sir Edward Grigg, the Under-Secretary for War, from 1940.

[257] *Westminster Gazette* 22nd November 1924, KW16 102/6

[258] *Manchester Guardian* 3rd January 1925, KW16 109/7

Chamberlain's analysis that "unless we leave our mark as social reformers, the country will take it out of us hereafter".[259] As well as housing and slum clearance, they included rating and valuation, Poor Law reform, pensions, health insurance and the re-organisation of medical services.[260] This huge programme across virtually every aspect of the Ministry of Health has rightly been described as the "link between the Liberal programme ... in 1906 and the Labour programme in 1945",[261] though strangely the same assessment does not mention at all Wood's role in generating and delivering it.[262]

The diagram on the following page sets out the overall programme and some of the policy and other elements that would contribute to delivery.

Realising this extensive Ministry programme, let alone delivering it in practice, would depend on key civil servants, particularly the Permanent Secretary Arthur Robinson (1874-1950),[263] the Chief Medical Officer Sir George Newman (1870-1948) and the large team of assistant secretaries, each of them responsible for one of the Ministry's discrete areas (housing, local government, Poor Law, hospital services, and so forth). Generally, either Chamberlain or Newman are credited with the Ministry programme,[264] but they were dependent on many others, not only for the roles they played in implementation but for contributing to the

---

[259] Middlemas and Barnes,op cit, p285

[260] Dilks, op cit, p415 also lists milk, dental services, wider public health education, larger hospitals as specialisms developed, the co-ordination of services across local authority boundaries, and the "integration" of local authorities, the voluntary sector and the State. Self, 2000, op cit, p21 adds smoke abatement to this list.
According to Dilks, Chamberlain set out a four-year programme of legislation that was agreed by the Cabinet before others had time to submit their programmes (p419). Keith Feiling, 'Life of Neville Chamberlain', 1946 includes an appendix that covers the three years 1925 to 1927.

[261] Macleod, op cit, p114

[262] Nor does Robert Self in his biography of Neville Chamberlain, 2006, op cit

[263] Robinson was subsequently Permanent Secretary at the Ministry of Supply after Neville Chamberlain transferred him there in 1940. His Minister Herbert Morrison recorded that the job did not suit Robinson - Herbert Morrison, 'An Autobiography', 1960, p178.

[264] For example, Ina Zweiniger-Bargielowska, 'Managing the Body: Beauty, Health and Fitness in Britain, 1880-1939', 2010, p155

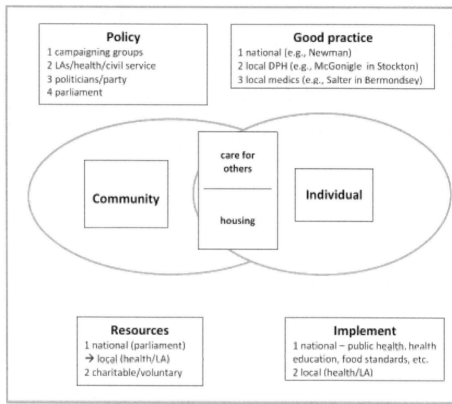

Ministry of Health programme 1925-1929

programme in the first place. In Wood's case this included his experience and his analytical and political skills. The staff might have been tempted to be insular and precious, as the Local Government Board had often been, but part of Robinson's co-ordinating task was to ensure that this was not the Ministry of Health culture. Gwilym Gibbon, for example, the Assistant Secretary responsible for town planning, had highlighted the inter-connections in a paper the year before.[265] That they worked well together depended in part on two other factors: Chamberlain and Wood favoured an approach based on logic and consistency, which helped others to anticipate and predict their likely response in other matters and, in turn, meant that the politicians themselves would not

_____

[265] IG Gibbon, "Town planning: It's place in social development", *Public Administration*, 1923, 1, pp333-342

be bogged down in minutiae any more than necessary;[266] and Robinson specifically encouraged the staff to mingle outside work, choosing his only known passion out of the office - golf.[267] An early example of team bonding perhaps, though Robinson would have thought it basic management, appreciating the benefits of good interpersonal relationships that went beyond work. For Dilks the upshot was that "…never in any office, even as Prime Minister, was [Chamberlain] better served than as Minister of Health".[268] That Wood enjoyed good relations with MPs of all parties was a further advantage.[269]

In a series of parliamentary profiles, Ellen Wilkinson included one of Neville Chamberlain who she said "would go to the stake to demonstrate his faith in a logical conclusion". She described Wood as "his round little Sancho Panza".[270] Sancho Panza usually did his master's bidding, or at least let Don Quixote believe he had, but in reality it was frequently his efforts that brought Don Quixote through his madder scrapes and saw him back on solid ground from his wilder flights of fancy.

This was echoed by James Johnston in his profile of Kingsley Wood:

> The Ministry of Health has undoubtedly been the busiest and most energetic of the Government departments during the lifetime of the present [1925-1929] Parliament. Its tale of legislation is an enormous one, and that legislation has … [called] for the most delicate and careful handling.
> When such a heavy task is laid upon a Ministry it is essential to success that there should be a harmony of understanding as between the Minister and his understudy. However exact the chief may be, and however efficient, his good qualities are neutralized if his subordinate is slipshod or ill-informed.

---

[266] Dilks, op cit, pp416-417
[267] William A Ross, "Local Government Board and after", *Public Administration*, 1956, 34, p21
[268] Dilks, op cit, p408
[269] Ibid, p415
[270] Ellen Wilkinson, 'Peeps At Politicians', 1930, p15
Wilkinson never married and in 1931 asked Beatrice Webb whether "a woman in public life should remain celibate if she had found a congenial friend with an uncongenial wife". (DNB entry) Webb assumed that she was referring to J F Horrabin (1884-1962) who had provided some of the illustrations for her 1930 profiles. However, this is far from certain.

That disaster has been completely avoided at the Ministry of Health. ... Sir Kingsley Wood has been a perfect second ... displaying on every occasion the exact knowledge which the efficient junior ought to possess. That these two Ministers have ... been perfectly mated has long been a matter of universal Parliamentary recognition.
... The place which [Wood] has acquired in the esteem of the House is the result of efficiency, of constant, painstaking study, of rapid grasp of complicated details.[271]

Housing

Parliament resumed on 9th December and Chamberlain's first substantial contribution was on the fourth day of debate on the King's address, a day given over to housing[272] - the issue which many MPs thought the most important social problem of the day[273] and the only one raised on the proposed Ministry of Health reforms. The amendment proposed by John Wheatley, Minister of Health in the previous Labour government, regretted that the Conservatives' preference for private sector solutions would do little to make available more rented housing at levels the working-class could afford or increase employment in building. Although Wheatley congratulated Chamberlain on his return to Health, "the post he has filled so well", he also warned him of the risks of his approach:

To my mind, housing reform is the Red Cross work of the class struggle. ...
There is at least one thing which I admit private enterprise can do much better than public enterprise. [It] can create slums.[274]

Continuing at some length, he noted that, if there were five to six million working-class houses in the country, each expected to last

---

[271] James Johnston, 'A Hundred Commoners', 1931, pp127-129 The profiles collected together in Johnston's book were written originally for the *Yorkshire Post* between 1925 and 1930.
[272] Hansard, 16th December 1924, vol. 179, cols.831-950
[273] For example, even Sir Samuel Chapman (1859-1947), who as Conservative MP for Edinburgh South represented one of the best-housed constituencies, avowed that he would support any practical scheme regardless of its political provenance.
[274] Hansard, 16th December 1924, vol. 179, cols. 832, 834

one hundred years, there must be 50,000 to 60,000 additional slums each year. But in 1923 only 1000 had been approved for clearance. The consequence was that the number of slums was greatly increasing, as were waiting lists for rented housing. Only a third of the 38,000 houses built during the first sixteen months of Chamberlain's 1923 Act were to let, while ten times as many people were forced to rent as could afford to buy. Wheatley therefore had two fundamental questions for Chamberlain: would he encourage local authorities to operate the 1924 Act (brought in by Wheatley to stimulate building by local authorities of housing to rent) or did he intend to "starve it into suicide?" and would he be persuading the building industry to co-operate or would he be threatening them with the same big stick that the Home Secretary Joynson-Hicks had already brandished?[275]

Chamberlain explained that his 1923 Act had been just a start towards solving the housing problems by encouraging private enterprise to build and assisting potential occupiers to obtain the capital they required to buy. In 1923 110,000 houses of all types had been completed under the various schemes, 15,000 by local authorities and 95,000 (86%) by the private sector. As this was not far short of the best ever annual figure of 129,000, Chamberlain argued that it vindicated his approach, though he agreed that there was still more to do.[276] Chamberlain then took the opportunity, one he relished, to bait Labour:

> I found a column headed 'Truth about Housing'. Well, when I see the word 'Truth' at the top of a column in the *Daily Herald*, I always make a trial boring. My experience tells me that generally I shall strike ore in the shape of demonstrable inaccuracies, and every now and then one comes across a rich patch of specially gross inexactitudes.[277]

---

[275] Ibid, cols. 835, 838, 839, 840-841, 842, 843 and 845-846
He added that Clitheroe Council had built six-room houses using direct labour at less than two-thirds of private sector tenders, asking Chamberlain how he planned to deal with local authorities that employed their own workforce. Chamberlain disputed the comparability of Wheatley's figures but stated that he had no intention of interfering with direct labour.
Clitheroe was the constituency of Chamberlain's PPS Captain William Brass which may explain why Wheatley selected this example.
[276] Hansard, 16th December 1924, vol. 179, cols. 846-847
[277] Ibid, col. 850

Nevertheless, he indicated that Wheatley's 1924 Act would "have a fair trial; it shall stand or fall by its own performance. But I cannot promise ... that, if it turns out to have failed, it will remain in its present condition ..."[278]

This was despite Chamberlain's view that

> ... the real greatness of [Wheatley's] Act lies in the variety and extent of the illusions which it has succeeded in creating.
> ... it is in fact an Act to apply certain financial provisions to housing. But it does not, and cannot and it never will, add one single house to the number which would have been provided if it had never been passed.[279]

However, he did consider Wheatley's scheme for augmenting building labour and materials, and better organising their distribution, "a statesmanlike piece of work" and he vowed to continue Wheatley's initiatives in this area "with every means in my power".[280] His conclusion was "not ... that the problem is solved, but that the goal at any rate is in sight".[281]

Chamberlain was followed by the Liberal MP Percy Harris (1876-1952) who gave some graphic descriptions of London slums. In one instance 100 people were living in five houses with one tap between them and, when he had asked LCC officers why nothing had been done, Harris was told that this was far from the worst. He reminded the House of the fanfare with which the Addison scheme had been launched, "as Kingsley Wood will remember", yet only one-third of the 29,000 houses planned for London had been built in the five years since. In Harris' opinion, Chamberlain needed to provide "homes for the ordinary weekly workers who live on wages paid by the hour" and not to pin all his hopes on owner-occupiers; more developments like Letchworth new town were required to encourage people out of London;[282] and the key advantage of the 1924 Act had been the certainty and continuity offered by a fifteen-year programme. Chamberlain's 1923 Act had only been a two-

---

[278] Ibid, col. 853
[279] Ibid, col. 852
[280] Ibid, col. 853
[281] Ibid, col. 861
[282] When Wood opened the Letchworth UDC offices in 1935 he praised the pioneering garden city (KW19 454/1-9, 455/1-16).

year scheme and this was insufficient to instil confidence in employers, potential workers or the materials manufacturers. The fluctuating number of LCC employees illustrated the problem.[283] Harris concluded that

> If the Minister of Health, with big battalions to back him and the promise of a long term of office to do his work, and with great experience of municipal government, will use his imagination on these lines, it may be that in five years' time he will be rewarded for his modesty in refusing higher office and being content to do great work as a Minister of Health.[284]

Six Scottish MPs, three Labour three Conservative, highlighted different aspects of the problem there. James Stewart (1863-1931), who had been Under-Secretary for Health in Scotland in the 1924 Labour government, warned how unaffordable a rent of even 13s (65p) a week was for the working-class and how badly Glasgow compared with Birmingham on various measures of housing quality and health, asking, as Wood had done previously,[285] why so little was spent on preventing TB and so much on treating it. He described Glasgow housing as "... the canker that is eating, and ever eating, deeper and deeper into the soul of the nation".[286] The Conservative Sir John Baird (1874-1941), soon to be appointed Governor-General of Australia as Lord Stonehaven the following June, spoke of the "supply of houses [as] the one thing that matters" and wanted housing treated as "an emergency problem", just as munitions and troops had been in the war.[287] Labour's George Buchanan (1890-1955) endorsed Stewart's speech on the Glasgow slums, adding that children in his constituency died at four times the rate of those in the neighbouring one - in large measure because of their extreme poverty and deplorable living conditions. For most people the six thousand houses built in Glasgow since 1919 might as well not have been for they could not afford them.[288] Sir Samuel Chapman promised that Chamberlain would have the support of all if "he can make any

---

[283] Hansard, 16th December 1924, vol. 179, cols. 861-869
[284] Ibid, col. 870
[285] For example, *Times* 13th January 1919, KW9 7/5
[286] Hansard, 16th December 1924, vol. 179, cols. 879-884
[287] Ibid, cols. 884-885
[288] Ibid, cols. 885-888

advance on this question of housing and the elimination of the slums in Scotland".[289] As might be expected from a Labour MP, Dr Drummond Shiels claimed that when Conservatives had done good things in the past this had not been "by allowing free rein to private enterprise". Had this been the approach to munitions during the war, he pointed out, "we should [have been] in very serious danger".[290]

The Scottish contributions were matched by the compelling illustration provided by the Labour MP for Southwark Central Colonel Harry Day (1880-1939). He was a theatre impresario and Houdini's manager at one time. When burglars broke into Day's flat in 1927 and "stole some thousands of pounds worth of jewellery", the joke was that they must have been seeking to re-distribute wealth.[291] But he was also a committed politician and the examples that drove his arguments were as vivid as Houdini's act. A quarter of the people in his constituency lived in slum tenements and a few days earlier a coroner's officer sent to inspect a dead child accidentally smothered in the over-crowded conditions had to go up the staircase sideways for it was too narrow for him to do otherwise in "this intolerable slum house". Yet the tenant had been forced to pay £5 10s in key money, while the one next door "in a miserable hovel" had to pay £6. In Day's view

Many of the houses in Southwark ... are little better than pigsties. I should not like to keep pigs in them. They are really death-breeding slums and the most appropriate name for them would be mortuaries.[292]

If a key duty of any government was to see that people were housed properly (a sentiment George V shared) and, since it would not hesitate to spend eight or nine million if attacked, it should spend the same on housing. John Pennefather (1856-1933), a Conservative MP reported on the fourteen different housing systems that Liverpool had tested. As there were even fewer plasterers than bricklayers, and traditional methods required both, the slab form of construction had much to recommend it. It would double the number of houses that could be built in a year, thereby

---

[289] Ibid, col. 897

[290] Ibid, col. 901

[291] CPA Pub 146/2 *The Elector* June 1924 - December 1934

[292] Hansard, 16th December 1924, vol. 179, cols. 905-907

increasing the work in allied trades and decreasing unemployment as a result.[293] The Liberal Trevelyan Thomson (1875-1928) argued that houses "are so needed it matters not" whether they come from private enterprise as the Conservatives preferred or from the public programmes Labour advocated.[294] It was now action rather than yet more legislation that was necessary, and up to the Ministry of Health to take a "risk ... in the national interests", with the £14 million currently spent on TB better deployed on the prevention that improved housing would provide. As Thomson pointed out, this was a

> ... grand field for [Kingsley Wood] the Parliamentary Secretary to exercise the powers he has and to put into practice some of the theories which he developed a few years ago. It is not a question of whether we can afford to deal with the slum problem, but whether we can afford to leave it alone.[295]

If the Government would tackle this question, they would get the support of the whole House and "a united country behind them". "... In this way they can do more to leave their mark on the pages of history than any other Government have done on this question."[296]

Given the chequered, stop-start record of housing since the war, the continuing gap between demand and supply, and the abominable conditions in which many people lived, it should not be surprising that it provided an early political test of the Ministry, particularly as the Labour opposition distrusted Chamberlain's assurance and assumed he would ditch the Wheatley reforms as soon as possible. Josiah Wedgwood, Labour MP for Newcastle under Lyme, made this point when confirming that the opposition would press their amendment to a vote.[297] Losing the vote (by 136 to 356) was inevitable given the scale of the Conservative majority; losing the arguments about replacing the slums and building more

---

[293] Ibid, cols. 907-912
[294] Ibid, col. 927
[295] Ibid, col. 930
[296] Ibid, col. 931
The opportunity the Ministry of Health offered to leave a "monument", whereas the Treasury did not, was soon a refrain and lament of Churchill's. See Self, 2006, op cit, p107
[297] Hansard, 16th December 1924, vol. 179, cols. 931-939

housing people could afford, the issues that mattered most, would be worse.

When a range of health-related questions were asked in Parliament later that day, it was Wood who answered them. In relation to housing they included

- the definition of slums and owners' responsibilities for repairing them: local authorities inspected housing against the definition in the Housing of the Working Classes Act 1890 (section 4) and if necessary could close them under the Housing Act 1909 (section 17). In the most recent year for which statistics existed, over 1.1 million houses had been inspected by medical officers of health and repairs secured in almost half, an indication of the scale of the problem - especially as repairs would only reflect the most extreme conditions.

- Wood's confirmation that the affordability of housing in rural areas by agricultural workers remained a difficult issue, despite the subsidy introduced under the 1924 Act. This assistance would be retained and Wood encouraged other suggestions that might improve the situation.

As well as the link to positive health outcomes, the quality of housing had the potential to breed social unrest: "Bad houses made Bolshevists and the slum bred Socialism", said Sir Kingsley Wood. Consequently, "The Government were not prepared to condemn the slum dweller to his miserable hovel for another generation."[298]

Housing would initially occupy much of Chamberlain's and Wood's parliamentary time once the Commons resumed in February, but rating reform was raised first. Trevelyan Thomson asked whether the Government intended a uniform system of valuation across local authorities so that charges for national services "shall be more equally borne than ... at present". Wood replied that the Minister of Health intended to bring in a Bill that session as this "uniformity ... is a necessary preliminary to any revision of ... local taxation". When Thomson pressed him as to how quickly rating uniformity would follow, Wood replied "I am afraid I cannot answer that. I must leave it to [your] imagination".[299]

The following day during a debate on supplementary estimates, including those of the Ministry of Health, Wood and his

---

[298] Quoted by Kevin Morgan in "Mass housing, 1918-1939", p72 in Stuart Ball and Ian Holliday (eds.), 'Mass Conservatism: The Conservatives and the Public since the 1880s', 2002.
[299] Hansard, 11th February 1925, vol. 180, cols. 176-177

law firm were accused by Joseph Compton (1881-1937), Labour MP for Manchester Gorton, of advising an injured workman to accept £20 compensation from an insurance company when another firm had subsequently obtained £175 for him.[300] Given Wood's background in insurance and workmen's compensation, this attack on his integrity must have stung, and indeed he immediately instituted a search of his company's records. He acknowledged that such a thing could happen, but nevertheless it must have been with some relief that he asked Compton for further details as his firm had been unable to trace the case.[301] If the information was forthcoming, it must have been handled outside the Commons for the issue did not re-surface in Parliament. No doubt Compton was aware that raising the matter would be sufficient to leave a question mark in some MPs' minds and confirm the doubts held by others.

It was Wood who, as the junior Minister, dealt with the first housing questions of the new session on 11th February.[302] He stated that there were nearly three times as many houses under construction at the beginning of 1925 (54,000) as a year earlier, an increase largely due to Chamberlain's 1923 Act, with another 28,000 sanctioned under the 1924 Act. The Labour MPs for Don Valley and Doncaster[303] asked about rising building costs for working class houses and whether any actions had been taken to limit these. Wood replied that local authorities had been advised to manage their local markets though they had not been discouraged from building themselves. In addition, local authorities had been circulated about allowing labourers of any age to become craftsmen after three years apprenticeship.[304] No new action had been taken to promote letting to working class tenants by either urban or rural councils.

Tasked with finding alternative forms of construction that could be completed more quickly than brick-built houses, the Moir Committee (set up by Wheatley) had considered various new methods of construction, including steel-clad houses (both Atholl

---

[300] Hansard, 12th February 1925, vol.180, cols. 491-493 Also KW16 119/4.

[301] Hansard, 13th February 1925, vol.180, col. 572

[302] Hansard, 11th February 1925, vol. 180, cols. 177-181

[303] Tom Williams (1888-1967) and Wilfred Paling (1883-1971) respectively

[304] In response to the Conservative MP for Kensington South Sir William Davison (1872-1953) who had asked about progress on dilution in the building trade.

and Weir types) and concrete ones.[305] Chamberlain had already viewed the Weir variety and, realising that people would be sceptical unless they saw them for themselves, had proposed a grant to local authorities prepared to build one as a demonstration house.[306] Even skyscrapers were a possibility, Wood had told the Chelsea Conservative and Unionist Association in a speech on slum clearance,[307] though the *Daily Graphic* claimed that this would increase congestion in London to unacceptable levels and the soil might not bear the weight anyway for even St Paul's Cathedral was in peril from subsidence, an issue first raised in the nineteenth century.[308] In their view expansion outwards would be better than upwards.[309]   In the supplementary estimates debate on 12th February, Wood sought authority for £10 grants to be paid to the twenty-five local authorities that had agreed to build the Weir, Wild and Telford types as demonstration houses.[310]   They would be permitted to dispose of them by sale or letting as they preferred.

Wheatley was opposed to the grant and to the promotion of the Weir steel houses at all (as was George Lansbury), despite having commissioned the Moir Committee, with George Hicks (1879-1954), the first General Secretary of the Amalgamated Union of Building Trade Operatives among its members. According to the March 1925 issue of the Conservative publication *The Elector*, Hicks was supportive of steel houses for "there is abundant evidence that houses made of steel on wooden framing [are] a reasonable   method   of   providing   immediate   housing

---

[305] The Moir Committee provided three reports: on steel (4th November 1924) and concrete houses (4th December 1924), and on the Wild and Telford types (29th January 1925).

[306] Hansard, 16th December 1924, vol. 179, col. 859

Weir houses had timber frames, steel panels on the outside and compressed wood and asbestos panels on the inside. Commonly described as "steel houses", most people were expected to resist living in them if this was all they had to go on.

One Atholl demonstration house was built in the East End and the Duke of Atholl, an engineer himself, conduced some of the guided tours incognito. Harris, op cit, p82

[307] *Morning Post, Daily Telegraph* and *Liverpool Post* 28th January 1925, KW16 113/1, 3 & 4

Commercial and office skyscrapers had been built in America since the 1880s, but there were no examples of residential buildings at this stage.

[308] The Cathedral was strengthened between 1913 and the 1930s.

[309] *Daily Graphic* 28th January 1925, KW16 113/2

[310] The concrete houses were not included.

accommodation".[311]   Wood mounted a spirited and combative rebuttal of the criticisms, pointing out that with so many more houses to build it was only through experiments such as this that progress could be made.   Nor were they the "dog-kennels" they were sometimes described as.[312]   But even after this, the Labour MP for Nelson and Colne Arthur Greenwood proposed that the grant be reduced to £5.[313]   There was a real danger of the political bun-fight preventing progress, for as one newspaper had reported, "The class war will not add a single dwelling, but in its worst aspect may burn some".[314]   On 13th February yet more Labour criticisms of the Weir houses led Wood to respond

> I should have thought they would have welcomed any effort made to get people out of the slums. What reasonable hope is there of people living, say, in the slums of Bethnal Green being rescued from those slums unless some effort in connection with supplementary buildings is made?   How much longer are you going to condemn these people to live there?[315]

It was during the course of this dispute that one newspaper, not entirely unsympathetically, noted of Wood:

> On Sundays he is converting Wesleyan Methodist brotherhoods to the new Disraeli policy of the Conservative party, and is holding up the bogey of Bolshevism.[316]

Wood would later be denounced as a Socialist by a peer who had never had a bathroom for suggesting they should be installed in workers' houses.[317]

---

[311] CPA Pub 146/2 *The Elector* June 1924 - December 1934
His DNB entry claims that his radical views moderated after the General Strike.
[312] Hansard, 12th February 1925, vol.180, cols. 477-481
[313] Ibid , cols. 481-484
[314] *Daily Sketch* 8th January 1925, KW16 108/5
[315] Hansard, 13th February 1925, vol.180, cols. 573-576
[316] *Manchester Evening News* 13th February 1925, KW16 117/8
[317] CPA Pub 210/3, January 1927, p3
During the Committee stage of Housing Rural Workers Bill (*Daily News* undated, KW16 250/2; *Glasgow Herald* 7th December 1926, KW16 250/3).

Steel houses (and the other alternative forms) never found public favour but this became less important over time as the number of houses built conventionally increased. In 1926 there were cuts in the subsidies under both the Wheatley and Chamberlain Acts, with a further cut in the former in 1928 and the latter abolished completely for houses completed after September 1929. They were no longer thought necessary to promote house-building whether for sale or rent.

Widows', Orphans' and Old Age Contributory Pensions

There were more than 1.6 million widows in England and Wales and nearly 50,000 orphans younger than fourteen at the time of the 1921 Census.[318] In addition, old age pensions were only available to those over seventy years of age, the same as they had been when Lloyd George first introduced them in 1908.[319] Pressure had been mounting for some time over the gaps in welfare provision, not least to advance women's economic equality and bring it into line with their political citizenship.[320] This was to be the first of the Ministry of Health's reforms and "perhaps the most popular of Neville Chamberlain's".[321] The Widows', Orphans' and Old Age Contributory Pensions Bill was introduced to the Commons on 29th April 1925, the same day as Churchill presented the Gold Standard Bill, and was to provide contributory pensions for widows, orphans and those aged between sixty-five and seventy.[322] In moving the second reading Chamberlain highlighted its significance:

> ... I do not think that any [of the Bills he had previously introduced in 1923] could be compared ... for the width of its range or for the permanence of the mark which it is likely to leave on the life of the nation, or for the intensity of its human interest.[323]

---

[318] Hansard, 9th April 1925, vol. 182, cols.2461-2462
[319] In 1908 Wood had written a series of articles letting people know how to obtain them.
[320] Pethick-Lawrence, op cit, pp106-7
[321] Self, 2000, op cit, p21; 2006, op cit, p106
[322] Hansard, 29th April 1925, vol. 183, col. 163 It would also amend the current statutes for health and unemployment insurance.
[323] Hansard, 18th May 1925, vol. 184, col. 73

Wood first became involved in the Bill when the financial and contributory aspects were considered on the 20th and 21st May,[324] and then at the detailed Committee stage from 30th June.[325] The following month he wrote an article on the "Conservative Widows Pensions Scheme - What it is and what it does",[326] setting out the benefits that would apply once the Act was in force from 1st January 1926. He would subsequently describe it as "one of the finest pieces of legislation ever put on the Statute Book", with 260,000 widows already being paid pensions by then and 600,000 to receive a pension at age 65 by January 1928.[327]

Rating and Valuation

The Rating and Valuation Bill was seen as a preliminary to wider Poor Law reform, the point Wood reiterated to the 1912 Club (a City network) after the Bill had completed its passage at the end of 1925.[328] It consolidated the number of rating authorities (i.e., reducing them by more than half in urban areas and by 95% in rural areas), simplifying assessment and combining the existing array of rates into one general one. In introducing the second reading,[329] Chamberlain stressed that it was another integral component of his programme of social reform that would help people to help themselves ("raise themselves to higher and better things"), as would the Poor Law reforms he hoped to introduce in 1926. As with his 1923 Housing Act the Rating and Valuation Bill would help establish the ability of local authorities to meet the standards required of them and better assess their need for state assistance to achieve these, while the contributory pensions and Poor Law reforms

> ... following on the two great schemes of insurance, combined with workmen's compensation and old age

---

[324] Hansard, 20th May, vol. 184, cols. 441-511 and 21st May 1925, cols. 839-848

[325] Hansard, 30th June 1925, vol. 185, cols. 2253-2490

[326] KW16 135/3

[327] *Kentish Mercury* and *Kentish Independent* October 1926, KW16 236/2 & 236/4

[328] *Morning Post* 13th January 1926, KW16 169/1

[329] Hansard, 13th May 1925, vol. 183, col. 1873

pensions under the existing Acts, complete the circle of security for the worker. [330]

Local government reform would mirror revised provision for the neediest in society and, within an overall framework of greater clarity and accountability than hitherto, it would be local government that had to deliver it - not surprising given Chamberlain's background in Birmingham.

Poor Law Reform

In March 1925 Wood answered a question addressed to the Prime Minister Baldwin from the Liberal MP for Middlesbrough West about the "unanimous desire of the last Parliament" for immediate legislation to reform the Poor Law system. He confirmed that this was under careful consideration by the government and a draft Bill would be discussed with local authorities and Boards of Guardians, but he could not be precise about the date when the Bill would come before parliament.[331] Wood was similarly non-committal a week later when answering the Labour MP for Barnsley.[332] Some preliminary proposals were subsequently circulated to local government associations (representing County and Borough Councils) to confidentially gauge their views on picking up the duties of Boards of Guardians on their abolition. However, it was only when he came under pressure in parliament to do so that Chamberlain agreed to circulate them to the Association of Poor Law Unions as well, thus making them public and available to MPs.[333] The West Ham Board of Guardians had already been subject to special action by the Ministry of Health,[334] "faced down" as Self describes it,[335] and Chamberlain's delay in circulating the proposals to their Association reflected his doubts about Boards of Guardians and their motives.

Such was the controversy surrounding Chamberlain's proposals that Baldwin was asked by Frank Briant, Liberal MP for Lambeth North and Chairman of the Lambeth Board of Guardians

---

[330] Hansard, 18th May 1925, vol. 184, col. 92

[331] Hansard, 24th March 1925, vol. 182, cols. 233-234; *Times* 25th March 1925, KW16 119/2

[332] Hansard, 31st March 1925, vol. 182, col. 1119

[333] Hansard, 26th November 1925, vol. 188, cols. 1596-1597

[334] Hansard, 19th November 1925, vol. 188, cols. 610-611

[335] Self, 2006, op cit, pp115-124

since 1910, to set up an all-party committee to consider them. Baldwin refused, for while everyone agreed an alternative to the existing approach to relief was required, there was unlikely to be unanimity about the form this should take. In the circumstances Baldwin thought Chamberlain's consultation the most efficient way of arriving at a majority view.[336]

Between 1st June 1924 and 26th June 1926 the numbers receiving Poor Law relief had more than doubled from 1.05 million people to 2.34 million.[337] That this was due in large measure, if not entirely, to the miner's strike and the aftermath of the General Strike was confirmed by the monthly figures Wood provided for the period from November 1924 to June 1926: an increase of 17% overall in the nineteen months to April 1926, almost doubling in May (+88%) and increasing marginally in June 1926 (+ 1%).[338] However, some Boards of Guardians operated more liberal scales of relief which, in the case of West Ham's ability to meet the costs, was compounded because they did not benefit from redistribution of London income under the Common Poor Fund.[339] They sought a grant of £434,000 from the Ministry of Health but this was made contingent on them adopting the scale of relief operated by the Greenwich Board of Guardians. The West Ham Board refused to do so and in the meantime the Greenwich Board reversed their decision as they judged the scale inhuman.[340] The Boards of Guardians (Default) Bill was the Ministry of Health response with Chamberlain introducing the second reading, and Wood winding up, on 5th July 1926.[341] It became law on 15th July 1926, two months after the General Strike, and enabled the West Ham guardians to be replaced by Ministry of Health nominees.[342]

On 15th November 1926 Chamberlain listed 101 Boards of Guardians that had been authorised to borrow money to set against outdoor relief.[343] West Ham, Bedwellty, Chester-le-Street and Sheffield were among them. Chester-le-Street and Bedwellty were also to have Ministry nominees imposed upon them but the others

---

[336] Hansard, 21st December 1925, vol. 189, col. 1946
[337] *Times* 22nd July 1926, KW16 210/4
[338] Hansard, 19th July 1926, vol. 198, col. 904
[339] MA Crowther, 'The Workhouse System 1834-1929', 1981, p104
[340] Hansard, 21st and 28th June 1926, vol. 197, cols. 28-29 & 827
[341] Hansard, 5th July 1926, vol. 197, cols. 1639-1766
[342] *Daily Telegraph* 27th July 1926, KW16 223/5: By this stage the West Ham Poor Law Union owed £2.275m to the Ministry of Health.
[343] Hansard, 15th November 1926, vol. 199, cols. 1555-1556

survived to abolition, which in Sheffield's case must have been due in part to their Conservative administration finding favour, for their problems had been known for some time.[344] The superseded Chester-le-Street guardians had sought an independent inquiry which Chamberlain refused on the grounds that he could no longer trust them,[345] Wood was accused of leaking a national document about Chester-le-Street for party purposes[346] and Labour moved a debate seeking the repeal of a "partisan and bureaucratic ... Act ... subversive of the principles of local self-government".[347] This was defeated by 297 votes to 119, but positions were hardening again and Wood was called a liar over the West Ham Guardians the following year.[348]

Chamberlain and Wood wanted to transfer the work of all Boards of Guardians to local authorities and introduce a block grant but this became bound up with Churchill's broader scheme of block grants for all local services and of rating relief. This delayed the next stage, the Local Government Bill, to 1928.

Local Government

A White Paper to reform the structure of local government was published in June 1928 and the second reading of the Bill itself started that November.[349] This included an exchequer block grant agreed for the next five years for each authority and a further sum distributed according to need. The able-bodied unemployed would become the responsibility of Public Assistance Committees while the Poor Law institutions (such as workhouses) would be transferred to local authorities with the intention that they become hospitals. Some of the original proposals for rating relief had been culled in the Chamberlain-Churchill discussions (railways for

---

[344] *Evening Standard* 13th January 1926, KW16 169/2 included the example of Sheffield Council's funding calculations being "upset by the activities of the Board of Guardians over which it has no control".
[345] Hansard, 29th March 1927, vol. 204, cols. 1056-1057
[346] *Labour Leader* March 1927, KW16 266/3
[347] Hansard, 29th March 1927, vol. 204, cols. 1155-1202
This followed a report of the Chester-le-Street Board's administration being published without the Guardians being given the opportunity to refute the allegations.
[348] KW17 33/1-19
[349] Hansard, 26th November 1928, vol. 223, cols. 65-194; Self, 2006, op cit, pp128-132

example) and others had been watered down (e.g., industrial rate relief at 75% rather than 100%). Total rate relief for agricultural land and buildings remained.[350]

The negotiations had been tortuous with the mutual antipathy between Chamberlain and Churchill much in evidence: Churchill thought Chamberlain would have been "a good lord mayor of Birmingham in a bad year", while Chamberlain judged Churchill's ambitious scheme would wreck the whole proposal. Daunton characterised their conflict as "tense and complicated, with mutual suspicion and dislike", the antagonism between Chamberlain's cautious but achievable scheme and Churchill's "characteristic preference" for a more expansive approach but one that might have unintended but deleterious consequences for older industries and the necessitous areas.[351]

As part of the government charm offensive to convince voters and local authorities about the changes, Wood had spoken at meetings and attended conferences around the country in the preceding months. These included the first conference in Gloucestershire and another in Oxford.[352] He also wrote articles that explained the reasons for local government reform and for relieving industry and agriculture from rates. He explained that the government would compensate local authorities for this loss of rates and add £8.5m on top. Local authorities would receive block grant based on needs and resources of each district (apart from police, education, main roads and a couple of other services), and this would be introduced in three stages over fifteen years with safeguards to make sure no local authority lost out initially. Wood concluded that to describe it as "a Bill for higher rates is sheer absurdity".[353]

---

[350] Farmers "don't need de-rating", thought Alfred Ezekiel Higgins, haulage contractor and Wesleyan Methodist lay preacher in Winifred Holtby, 'South Riding', 2011 (orig. 1935), p202

[351] Martin Daunton, 'Just Taxes: The Politics of Taxation in Britain, 1914-1979', 2002, pp340-348

[352] For example, *Gloucestershire Echo* 26th September 1928, KW17 55/1. Robert Self (ed.), 'The Neville Chamberlain Diary Letters: vol. III 1928-1933', 2002, p105 refers to an "extremely useful conference" with local authorities (including Guardians) in Gloucestershire over Poor Law reform on 6th October 1928.
Also, KW17 63/1-8 including Oxford conference.

[353] *Crystal Palace Advertiser* 23rd November 1928, KW17 72/1

It remained the case though that Chamberlain was as much interested in the administrative technicalities and arrangements as he was in the purpose of reform. Partly as a result of this, one newspaper thought the Bill dull and unintelligible, and that it might pose dangers for the government at the next election.[354]   For Headlam, Chamberlain's "progressive policy in local government may bring the Party into many awkward predicaments before he has done".[355]   The Commons spent virtually the whole of an eight-hour parliamentary day deciding how much time to allot to the stages after the second reading.[356]   When the *Spectator* reported in December that the 110-clause Local Government Bill would occupy much of the session, it also pointed out that Chamberlain was "fortunate in his enthusiastic and capable lieutenant, Sir Kingsley Wood".[357]   Ellen Wilkinson, on the other hand, accused Wood of ignoring the need for new money (for example, for the "very depressed area" of Middlesbrough, "one of the crucial tests of the Government's scheme"), not treating the issue seriously and preventing anyone else from getting a word in edgeways by behaving like Aunt Annie. In other words, "a lady who talks in a high voice, smiles all the time, gives nobody else a chance to put in a word, and then sends the children off to bed". At one point she told him not to pull faces.[358]   So bitter did the debate prove that the *Financial News* described Wood as "David" facing down the Goliath-like objections of Labour,[359] while the *Daily Sketch* thought him "The dulcet-voiced Sir Kingsley Wood, the stone-waller of the Government test team, ... taking a heavy part just now in the work on the Treasury Bench".[360]

When the third reading passed 292 to 113 on 18th February 1929 there was a sigh of relief on both sides that the Bill was finished at last, with Neville Chamberlain's speech including a most astounding tribute to Wood:

---

[354] *Evening Standard* 13th November 1928, KW17 66/3

[355] Ball (ed.), 1992, op cit, pp74-75 - Headlam diary entry 15th December 1925

[356] Hansard, 11th December 1928, vol. 223, cols. 1949-2080

[357] *Spectator* 10th December 1928, KW17 83/3

[358] Hansard, 14th December 1928, vol. 223, cols. 2539-2546; *Evening Standard*, *Daily News* and *Daily Mail* 14th & 15th December 1928, KW17 83/4, 81/3-4 & 82/3

[359] *Financial News* 15th December 1928, KW17 83/1

[360] *Daily Sketch* 17th December 1928, KW17 81/2

Without his indefatigable abilities and unfailing tact and good humour, his inexhaustible fertility of resource and his faultless loyalty, the task that I have imposed upon myself might well-nigh have been impossible. It is not the least of the satisfactions that I feel today that I have been associated throughout ... with a colleague ... who has so amply and so convincingly demonstrated his capacity for greater things.[361]

"The ingenious alacrity of his able lieutenant", as the *Times* put it.[362]

A wireless debate on de-rating held on 2LO between Wood, Arthur Greenwood and Ramsay Muir a month earlier had been reported in the *Daily Herald* and *Daily Mirror*, with the former, a Labour paper, judging Wood "child-like and bland", while the latter reported that "many listeners-in speak in glowing terms ... of the remarkable clearness of [his] voice". It continued that he was "one of the hardest-worked members of the Government"[363] with, for example, his articles on the Local Government Bill including ones on public health,[364] percentage v block grants,[365] and necessitous areas,[366] and a book on rating reform entitled 'Relief for the Ratepayer' with a foreword by the Prime Minister Stanley Baldwin and an introduction by Neville Chamberlain.[367] The book was in such demand that the first print run of 10,000 copies soon ran out and the publishers Ernest Benn had to produce a second impression just as large.[368]

The Local Government Act became law on 27th March 1929, just in time for people to receive rate demands ahead of the next general election. Exactly a month later, and a fortnight before the dissolution on 10th May, Conservative backbenchers hosted a dinner for Chamberlain and Wood to mark the achievement and "to congratulate us on our success".[369]

---

[361] Hansard, 18th February 1929, vol. 225, col. 814

[362] *Times* 19th February 1929, KW17 99/3

[363] *Daily Herald* 23rd & *Daily Mirror* 24th January 1929, KW17 89/3, 90/2
The debate had been keenly anticipated by many newspapers (KW17 84/3-6), including the *Sunday Express* 20th January 1929, KW17 88/1.

[364] *Burton Daily Mail* 7th February 1929, KW17 98/3

[365] *Burton Daily Mail* 14th February 1929, KW17 102/3

[366] *Brixton Free Press* 8th March 1929, KW17 107/6; *Leicester Mail* 6th April 1929, KW17 115/2

[367] *Lewisham Borough News* undated, KW17 115/3

[368] *Publisher's Circular* 23rd March 1929, KW17 110/15

[369] KW17 118/1-9; Self, 2002, op cit, p135

In the event the Act proved less significant than envisaged, though it did tackle the Poor Law, address issues of local government finance and enlarge local government authorities, thereby making them better able to plan and cater for the inequalities and differences in their area. However, there was little financial incentive for local authorities to be innovative or take risks and the advent of the depression choked off what little there was. Nevertheless, John Simon was one of those who thought the improvements in social legislation between the wars were mainly due to the work of Chamberlain and Wood.[370] For the *North London Recorder*

> The genius of the Prime Minister in getting the right man in the right place was never better evidenced than when he selected Sir Kingsley Wood to work in conjunction with Mr Neville Chamberlain at the Ministry of Health. Both are enthusiasts for the public weal; both are consumed with one ambition - the successful solution of problems which affect the lives of the people. And when the final record of the Government comes to be written, their joint work in the provision of decent homes for the workers will occupy a prominent and honoured place.[371]

In January 1928 the new year honours had included two new Privy Councillors, Wood and the chairman of the Conservative party JCC Davidson. It was not unknown for this honour to be bestowed on someone yet to be in the Cabinet, but it was unusual and even more unusual for this to be true of both Davidson and Wood, the only two such appointments then. It was ten years since Wood had been knighted on Lloyd George's recommendation over his promotion of a Ministry of Health and the same King, George V, was now elevating him further, again in relation to his health responsibilities. The *Times* report of the appointment was strictly factual, and most other papers confined themselves to the briefest praise,[372] but one report was particularly laudatory:

---

[370] Simon, 1952, op cit, p172
[371] *North London Recorder* 3rd May 1929, KW17 120/1
[372] *Times* 2nd January 1928, KW17 25/1-12

Of all the New Year honours, none is recognised in political circles as more deserved than the Privy Counsellorship [sic] conferred upon Sir Kingsley Wood, Mr Neville Chamberlain's understudy at the Ministry of Health. No-one among the under-secretaries is better informed, more painstaking, more diligent and more courteous ... It may be quite confidently stated that at no other Ministry are the Minister and Under-Secretary both so competent as at the Ministry of Health. [Wood] is as much master of all the details of the department as his chief, and he has a more placid and even temper, an asset which, from the Parliamentary point of view, is of great value. Sir Kingsley is not a mere expounder of departmental policies, but is also quite a skilful debater.[373]

Or, more bluntly, Neville Chamberlain and Wood are "the best parliamentary 'team' in the House".[374]

In recognition of the Privy Councillorship, Wood's friends paid for his portrait to be painted by AT Nowell, whose biographer calls him the "nonconformist painter" because of his links to Wesleyan Methodism. The portrait was presented to Wood the following October at the May Fair Hotel with both Sir Edward Carson and TP O'Connor making speeches.[375] In reply to O'Connor's presentation, Wood "paid a very timely tribute ... to the idealism that influences our parliamentary life, despite all assurances by soured critics to the contrary ..."[376] For his part O'Connor wrote at the end of that week that "I have rarely been at a pleasanter function ... I don't know any politician more feverishly active, more persistently tenacious, more consistently partisan than Wood".[377]

One does not need to search far for evidence of this in 1928:

---

[373] *Sussex Daily News* 3rd January 1928, KW17 26/3

[374] *Weekly Despatch* 3rd June 1928, KW17 41/1; to which the paper added "Sir Kingsley, by the way, is about to blossom out as a country squire. He has taken a large estate near Tunbridge Wells, and will soon be leaving the flat at Brighton which has been his favourite home for some years."

[375] *Evening News* and *Star* both 24th October 1928, KW17 57/3 & 58/8; *Morning Post* and *Times* 4th, *Daily Chronicle* 9th and *Evening Standard* 23rd October 1928, KW17 54/7-8 & 57/7-8

[376] *Liverpool Post* 24th October 1928, KW17 58/9

[377] *Sunday Times* 28th October 1928, KW17 60/3

... the star turn of the Ministerial Second Eleven is [Wood], so quiet and urbane. He sounds so reasonable and re-assuring. But attack him, and he shows himself possessed of the quickest brain and the sharpest tongue on the right hand side of ... Mr Speaker.[378]

The Labour MP for Hull Joseph Kenworthy (1886-1953)[379] even thought it possible that Wood would go on to lead the Conservative party, for he is a

... dapper little man ... he never gets rattled, is very quick-witted, and not only does well on the Ministerial bench but is absolutely first-rate in Opposition; and it is in Opposition that men really prove their mettle.[380]

Wood's tribute on the death of Asquith the previous February indicated that he was not overly-confined by party allegiance, able to think more flexibly when circumstances warranted. This is the first requirement of any statesman, able to distance himself from the shackles of ideology when necessary. Yet, as Wood put it four months later, evoking the sort of messages that we have become accustomed to hear from his political confreres of the twenty-first century,

This is an age when people are too apt to talk about their rights, rather than their duties.
Many people have got their wishbones where their backbones ought to be. We can do very little wishing but we can do a great deal of working.[381]

[378] *Reynolds* 13th May 1928, KW17 39/16
[379] A naval officer in WWI, among Kenworthy's books are 'Sailors, Statesmen and Others - An Autobiography', 1933 and 'Narvik and After: A Study of the Scandinavian Campaign',
[380] *The Sphere* 4th August 1928, KW17 52/1
[381] In a speech at Canterbury *Daily Mirror* 2nd June 1928, KW17 40/2

11.   LABOUR'S SCRUTINEER 1929-1931

1929 General Election

After five years of radical, and to some extent innovative, government the Conservatives were confident of winning the 1929 election, but then so were Labour - as Philip Snowden told Wood at the start of 1929.[382]   The outcome was not a foregone conclusion for either party and both sides had portents to encourage their expectations.   Although new rating demands would hit doorsteps that April, the Conservatives believed that the reforms they had introduced and the expansion of the franchise to include women between twenty-one and thirty would be enough to see them home. On the other hand, Labour could point to growing unemployment and the ill-will and contempt engendered by the 1927 Trade Disputes Act.   "The Conservative Government applies Socialism with one hand and knocks it down with the other ..."[383] argued MacDonald, contrasting those whose belief in the overall good had led them to pursue reform, such as Baldwin, Wood and Neville Chamberlain, with die-hards such as Winston Churchill always spoiling for a fight with those who challenged the establishment - as he had shown, not for the first time, during the General Strike and then whose insistence on the Trade Disputes Act confirmed it.

In 1928 the Liberals had set out proposals to tackle unemployment, with the regulation of private industry and constructive state schemes providing a middle course between the free-for-all of laissez-faire and the rigidity and state control of Communism.[384]   These were to be amplified in 1930 by Lloyd George and his colleagues[385] but some schemes for national development figured in the 1929 election.   It was all too easy to argue against them as "roadwork" for which, as Wood said, "physical condition alone debarred hundreds of men".   In his view the real solution was to train young men for industry, with 17,000 places a year already having been created by the Conservatives.[386]

---

[382] Self, 2002, op cit, 26th January 1929, p121

[383] Arthur Greenwood, 'The Labour Outlook', 1929, pvii

[384] 'Britain's Industrial Future, being the Report of the Liberal Industrial Inquiry 1928' (the Liberal Yellow Book), 1928, pxix

[385] David Lloyd George, Lord Lothian and Seebohm Rowntree, 'How to Tackle Unemployment: The Liberal Plans as Laid Before the Government and Nation', 1930

[386] *Kentish Independent* 12th April 1929, KW17 115/1

In Woolwich West Wood was opposed by William Barefoot for Labour, as he had been in 1924, with the addition in 1929 of a Liberal candidate AS Phillips. Derrick Gunston, his PPS from 1926 to 1929, thought the dissolution of Parliament on 10th May would only temporarily sever their relationship of four and a half years: "He looked upon Sir Kingsley with respect and great affection, and looked forward to being associated with him again in the near future".[387] In fact it was to prove the end of their partnership. Margaret Bondfield perhaps reflected the mood of the electorate when she claimed Lloyd George

> ... has had one of his nomination forms completely filled in by Tories; Sir Kingsley Wood has had one of his ... wholly signed by Liberals. Why shouldn't they? What is the difference between Tories and Liberals?[388]

In this view Labour was the antidote to both the other parties.

At the General Election on 30th May Wood only just survived in Woolwich West, his majority severely reduced to 332,[389] while nationally Labour was the largest party with 289 MPs, up from 162 previously. The Liberals gained twelve seats to return 58 MPs, but by contrast the Conservative ranks had been reduced by more than a third from 400 to 260.[390] This was a severe drubbing, even more severe for being so at odds with their hopes as well as their expectations, and one that Baldwin took very badly.

Facing a period out of office, with Labour sustained in government by Liberal acquiescence if not support, Wood was expected to take up appointments elsewhere, not least the Directorships that politicians relegated to the thankless wilderness of opposition often do. There was little doubt that he would "continue to give a great deal of his time and of his radiant and tireless energy to the work of the House, but the City attracts him

---

One of the public schemes proposed was for a Dartford tunnel. *Kentish Independent* undated, KW17 134/4

[387] *Western Daily Press* 9th May 1929, KW17 121/1 reporting Gunston's election meeting with Wood speaking in his support.

[388] *Daily Herald* 23rd May 1929, KW17 127/5

[389] This was the only election in which Wood won less than 50% of the vote.

[390] Eight MPs represented other parties, one more than previously, in the total of 615 MPs.

too".[391]   Yet the one Directorship that he is known to have acquired was of the Wesleyan Methodist Trust Assurance Company, a position he had occupied before becoming a Minister and which reflected his religious and insurance interests.[392]   In fact these years were to prove very significant for his future profile in the party, as well as in Parliament, as he was to establish himself as the main Conservative scrutineer of the Labour government, testing and harrying them at every opportunity.   But there was first a summer of recuperation for, though the House reconvened on 25th June, it was in recess for three months from late July to the end of October. Wood enjoyed an even longer hiatus with very little press attention paid to him between the election results at the start of June and the following November.   WS Sanders, Wood's opponent in his first election for the Woolwich seat on the LCC, had been elected for North Battersea and made his maiden speech on 5th July.[393] Wood's first intervention came ten days later in Committee on housing subsidy,[394] a matter he spoke on again a week later during its third reading.[395]   The following day Neville Chamberlain put forward a motion seeking to annul the orders Labour had recently made (on 27th June) under the 1927 Poor Law Act concerning the Bedwellty, Chester-le-Street and West Ham Poor Law Unions.[396] Wood objected to the attacks on the current regime at the West Ham Union[397] not least because he had appointed the Chairman of the Board of Guardians[398] and partly because the Chairman was unable to defend himself in Parliament.   According to Wood it was not the case that "all the virtue lies on one side of the House and ... all the wealth on the other"; rather "there is an equal amount of

---

[391] *Yorkshire Evening News* undated, KW17 130/3
[392] *Insurance Record* August 1929, KW17 139/10
[393] Hansard, 5th July 1929, vol.229, cols. 436-438
[394] Hansard, 15th July 1929, vol.230, cols. 118-125
[395] Hansard, 22nd July 1929, vol.230, cols. 953-961 & 996
[396] Orders by which the Labour government intended to replace the Guardians appointed by the Conservatives in 1926 when outdoor relief was far outstripping the resources available in these three Unions (Poplarism).
[397] By Valentine McEntee (1871-1953) and Fenner Brockway (1888-1988), Labour MPs for Walthamstow West and Leyton respectively, among others.
[398] Sir Alfred Woodgate (1860-1943), previously a Ministry of Health civil servant

sincerity and wealth on both sides at the present time".[399]   Ellen
Wilkinson accused him of lying: "You say what is not the truth" as
she put it in the stilted language acceptable in the House.
Subsequently, it was Susan Lawrence (1871-1947), Labour MP for
East Ham, and Wood's successor as Parliamentary Secretary to the
Minister of Health, whose magisterial contribution proved decisive.
Chamberlain's motion was defeated by 284 votes to 154 enabling
Labour to replace the Guardians they judged as biased with those
thought likely to administer the Poor Law more sympathetically.[400]

   After this encounter Wood restricted himself to some limited
observations on rents and radium.   When the House returned on
29th October, Wood was refreshed, re-invigorated and ready for
action.   By early December one newspaper described him as "the
cross-examiner in chief of the government"[401] while another noted
that he had spoken more in Parliament in the June to December
1929 period than all but Lloyd George and Arthur Greenwood.   In
Wood's case this referred mainly to the last two months of the
year.[402]

Foreign Issues

It may seem peculiar to start with foreign matters for, while Wood
had been interested in Ireland for a long time (initially with respect
to Home Rule proposals) and now took his holidays abroad, he
might be thought to have a mainly domestic focus.   However, he
was no little Englander, being vitally interested in the mutual
benefits and future of the Empire, having witnessed the impact of
the First World War and hoping the League of Nations would
prevent any future recurrence.   Furthermore, the next ten years
were to graphically illustrate how interlinked were Britain's
prospects with those of other countries.

   Britain still saw itself as the world's policeman - an image
that the declining influence of the League of Nations would

[399] Hansard, 23rd July 1929, vol.230, cols. 1230-1239
[400] In West Ham only for the period August 1929 to 31st March 1930 before
the Poor Law functions were taken over everywhere by Borough and
County Councils under the Local Government Act 1929.
[401] *The Graphic* 7th December 1929, KW17 160/4
[402] *Daily Express* 21st January 1930, KW17 172/3
Wood's 110 columns in Hansard compared with 128 for Lloyd George and
118 for Greenwood.

reinforce[403] - not just an administrator of Empire, never mind an island nation. Interestingly, when Labour's Foreign Secretary Arthur Henderson gave his initial assessment of the priorities to Parliament not many of them concerned the Empire. In the three weeks since he took office he had met representatives of between fifty and sixty countries and considered hundreds of documents.[404]

Ahead of the Wall Street crash, share prices soared as did other transactions powered by a similar irrational exuberance,[405] for example the sale of Jerome Kern's books and manuscripts in which Arnold Bennett was interested:

> While prices of shares on the New York Stock Exchange were shooting aloft in a manner to startle the entire world of speculators, the prices of books and manuscripts were outsoaring them, and some rose so high that it seems as if, being out of sight they could never come down.[406]

When the Wall Street market crashed in October 1929 the consequences would vividly demonstrate the international impact of the depression into the mid-1930s.

Russia was a provocation to any Conservative, not only because of Communist propaganda and its funding of that of the Comintern, but in Wood's case also because of religious persecution and its failure to pay its debts. It has been argued that some Christian Conservatives regarded Nazism and Fascism as less abhorrent than Communism in the early 1930s because they

---

[403] Russia eventually joined in 1934, by which point Conservatives such as Cecil judged "Communism a lesser threat than Fascism" with Spain subsequently putting democracy as well as Christianity on trial. Philip Williamson, "Christian Conservatives and the totalitarian challenge 1933-1940", *English Historical Review*, 2000, vol. 115, p613

[404] Hansard, 5th July 1929, vol. 229, cols. 410-422
Arthur Henderson was an eminent Wesleyan Methodist and President of the Brotherhood Movement. Another Methodist with whom Wood had been closely linked in the past, William Wedgwood Benn, was Labour's Secretary of State for India.

[405] The title of Robert Shiller's book on market volatility, initially in relation to the dotcom boom of 2000, and applied in later editions to the 2008 crash and sub-prime housing loans in the US.

[406] Arnold Bennett, *Evening Standard*, 14th February 1929 in Andrew Mylett (ed.), 'Arnold Bennett: The *Evening Standard* Years "Books and Persons 1926-1931"', 1974, p241

were "less directly anti-Christian in propaganda and policies". But leading Christian Conservatives such as Baldwin and Halifax soon saw all totalitarian regimes as a threat to freedom and therefore anti-Christian.[407]   Religious persecution in China would similarly exercise Wood, as did that country's attempts to renege on extraterritorial agreements that protected the rights of British citizens.   Germany sought to renegotiate the crippling reparations imposed on them at Versailles while a devastated Austria (all that remained of the Austro-Hungarian Empire) pursued a customs union with them.   France remained intransigent, setting its face against both and backing up its "non" with military might and financial blackmail. And all this preceded the rise of the Nazi party in Germany and pressure for independence in India, let alone Hitler coming to power and the Spanish Civil War.

Bridging foreign and domestic policy were the international financiers whose irregularities had been exposed by the financial crash.   Wood had two in his sights: Francis Lorang and John Gialdini, the latter implicated in the infamous Clarence Hatry (1888-1965) frauds.   JK Galbraith judged the collapse of Hatry's companies in September 1929 one of the key factors precipitating the fall in public confidence.[408]

In 1929 came the crash of the Hatry group. Clarence Hatry was not a picturesque figure ... and so newspapers blamed him more readily, though his crash affected comparatively few people.

Financial crashes became frequent - the Hatry case followed by the crash of the British shipowner, Lord Kylsant, and by the failure and suicide of the Swedish match-king, Kreuger.[409]

Hatry pleaded guilty at the Old Bailey in January 1931 and was sentenced to fourteen years in prison.[410]

On 17th December 1929 Wood asked about alien financiers who had absconded from England and what steps the Home

---

[407] Williamson, 2000, op cit, pp607-642

[408] JK Galbraith, 'The Great Crash 1929', 1929, pp88-89

[409] Graves and Hodge, op cit, pp222 & 255

[410] The barrister who led the Hatry defence was Norman Birkett (1883-1962), the future Lord Birkett. His supporting legal team included St John (Jack) Hutchinson - see Thomas Grant, 'Jeremy Hutchinson's Case Histories', 2015, pp5-6.

Secretary was taking to bring them back.[411]   Lorang, the only fugitive at that time, had been Chairman of four Bluebird companies, all now in compulsory liquidation, and was wanted for fraud.[412]   Wood was keen that he be pursued vigorously.[413]   A fortnight later he was arrested in Paris,[414] was eventually extradited to England six months later and after a year's trial at the Old Bailey was sentenced to seven years in jail in November 1931. As one newspaper reported

> Lorang's flight to the continent and his subsequent extradition from France provided one of the biggest sensations ever experienced in British financial circles. ... in imposing sentence, [the judge] said Lorang had been the cause of a terrible disaster to the companies and to numerous people interested in them. He declared commercial life in this city or any other community could not continue if men like Lorang were left.[415]

By contrast Gialdini, Hatry's Italian associate in his £20m frauds, was arrested in Italy (supposedly at Mussolini's behest but certainly at the British government's request) and tried in Milan. He was sentenced to almost six years in jail and a 10,000 lire fine, but one year of his prison term and the fine were remitted under a dispensation granted to celebrate the wedding of the Italian Crown Prince the previous year.[416]

Whereas the Conservative attitude to Russia had been one of boycott, the Labour government were keen to normalise diplomatic relations and resume trade. Yet they did so cautiously for MacDonald made it conditional on a parliamentary vote while Henderson required a Soviet guarantee that they would cease propaganda. In November 1929 the Commons agreed by 324 votes to 199 to exchange ambassadors, with other outstanding matters (including debts and propaganda) to be settled in accord with a protocol agreed a month earlier.[417]   However, relations

---

[411] Hansard, 17th December 1929, vol. 233, cols. 641, 1232

[412] *Financial Times* undated, KW17 163/1

[413] Hansard, 24th December 1929, vol. 233, col. 2108

[414] *Financial Times* 6th January 1930, KW17 165/1

[415] *Winnipeg Tribune* 25th November 1931

[416] *Glasgow Herald* 13th June 1931

[417] Hansard, 5th November 1929, vol. 231, cols. 895-1010; David Carlton, 'MacDonald versus Henderson: The Foreign Policy of the Second Labour

quickly deteriorated with anti-British propaganda increasingly obvious during 1930. Not surprisingly, the Russian provocations were raised frequently by Conservative MPs, for as well as being infuriating of themselves it was a stick with which to beat the government. Sometimes Henderson argued that the concerns were misplaced, or arose as a result of mistranslations, or that he had not heard of the matter referred to. On one occasion when pressed by Wood to explain what he was going to do, Henderson replied "I am going to follow the example of my predecessors",[418] which presumably meant that he intended to ignore it; a riposte to which even Wood had no answer. And if challenged, the Russians adopted a variety of strategies to explain it away. When one particularly extreme example of subversion was raised in Parliament in December 1930 Henderson asked the British ambassador in Moscow to protest.[419] The Soviet reply was that the broadcast came from a radio station not under their control. Wood asked whether Henderson was "going to swallow that fantastic statement?" with his colleague Ormsby-Gore adding "Is this the only example of private enterprise still allowed in Russia"?[420] Another MP suggested Henderson ensure the Admiralty blocked Soviet transmitters but he declined this proposal.

Ironically, a couple of years later the BBC was accused of bias by Poland, Italy and France who took exception to the way their armaments policies had been reported. Wood, then Postmaster-General, asked the BBC Chairman for an explanation. The Labour newspaper the *Daily Herald* took delight in suggesting that the Foreign Office explanation to their allies would be the same as the Russian response in 1930: i.e., the BBC was nothing to do with the Government![421]

Wood asked throughout 1930 about religious persecution and the prohibition against religious teaching in Russia, securing from Hugh Dalton (1887-1962)[422] a commitment that the Foreign Office would publish the Soviet Laws relating to religion as a White

---

Government', 1970, pp146-156 Although the House of Lords subsequently voted against this, Labour was able to ignore it as there was no new legislation required.

[418] Hansard, 5th November 1930, vol. 244, col. 829

[419] Hansard, 2nd December 1930, vol. 245, cols. 2195-2196

[420] Hansard, 8th December 1930, vol. 246, cols. 12-15; *Punch* 10th and 17th December 1930, KW17 236/10 & 238/1

[421] *Daily Herald* 6th January 1933, KW18 24/1

[422] Then Under-Secretary for Foreign Affairs

Paper during the summer recess.[423]   Religious teaching in all educational establishments offering a general education (whether State, public or private) had been banned in February 1918, though people could still teach religion, and be taught it, privately. Church ownership of property had been prohibited the same year, while Ministers of religion were banned from voting in June 1925. The separation of Church and State was a fundamental tenet of Communism and, needless to say, despite persistent questioning by Wood and others, there was no alteration in the Russian position.[424]   As a fellow Methodist, Henderson must also have wanted to do something but his advisers in the Foreign Office told him to ignore it.[425]   Wood had equally little impact on the negotiations between the British and Soviet governments over debts. In July 1931 he asked Dalton whether any time limit was to be imposed given that the issues had been under discussion for two years already. Dalton replied "No, Sir. I do not think that my right hon. Friend [Henderson] considered that that would be an effective way of handling the matter." To which Wood responded "Has the right hon. Gentleman any experience whatever of handling matters?"[426] It is difficult not to endorse the implication of Wood's comment for, with the exception of the League of Nations, Henderson had little impact in any arena as Foreign Secretary.[427] Apart from ideology, the reason for re-opening Russian relations, of course, was in the hope that increased trade would reduce unemployment. Carlton claims that it did, though he concedes not in comparison to 1925-1927.[428]   Wood was sceptical, despite the "very favourite device of the Soviet Russian authorities ... to go about the country talking about all the orders that they are going to give us".[429]

However, there is at least one sense in which Wood preferred the position in Russia at this time to that in China. He

---

[423] Hansard, 30th July 1930, vol. 242, cols. 461-462
'Certain Legislation respecting Religion in force in the Union of Soviet Socialist Republics', 1929-30, Cmd 3641
[424] Hansard, 13th May 1931, vol. 252, cols. 1162-1163
[425] Carlton, op cit, p161
[426] Hansard, 27th July 1931, vol. 255, cols. 1927-1928; *Punch* 5th August 1931, KW17 290/4
[427] Carlton concludes, for example, that improvements in Anglo-US relations and naval disarmament were due to MacDonald.
[428] Carlton, op cit, p161
[429] Hansard, 29th July 1930, vol. 242, cols. 398-401

might disagree with the politics and legislation of the former, making his distaste abundantly clear, but at least he could dispute them and as a politician he would have understood the necessity for, and benefits of, prevarication. In the case of China, however, the rule of law had broken down in some parts and was further undermined by a State seeking to renege on treaties or abrogate its responsibilities under them. The consequences for British subjects could be, and were, life-threatening - and for some life-ending.

Apart from the special cases of the two territories leased from China, Hong Kong and Kowloon, there were four areas (Shanghai, Tientsin, Canton and Hankow) where British citizens had been accorded the same extraterritorial privileges usually reserved for ambassadors - that is to say, they were subject to the civil and criminal laws of their home country rather than the one in which they lived. They enjoyed a correspondingly elevated and protected personal status because of it. China proposed to abolish this recognition, an issue Wood first raised as a supplementary question in January 1930, and which Henderson refused to answer then because he judged it not to arise from Wood's previous question about the general situation in China.[430] A few days later extraterritoriality was considered in its own right, with Wood's request for a statement from Henderson following questions from other MPs. Henderson replied that the Government had let China know that 1st January 1930 might be considered as the start of gradual abolition but only in principle until detailed negotiations between the governments resulted in an agreed and phased programme. The British Minister in China had begun those negotiations on 9th January but the Chinese government were already acting as though the rights had been abolished.[431] At the very least it appears that the Government understood the Chinese expectation of full sovereignty over everybody living in their area, a view that only changed in September 1931 when the National Government refused Chinese demands to renounce extraterritorial privilege on the outbreak of Sino-Japanese hostilities.[432]

While British subjects could be imprisoned for the flimsiest of reasons and mistreated in other countries as well (not least Russia),

---

[430] Hansard, 22nd January 1930, vol. 234, col. 185

[431] Hansard, 27th January 1930, vol. 234, cols. 591-593

[432] Carlton, op cit, p184
This remained the position until 11th January 1943 when both Britain and China were at war with Japan.

the situation in China outside the areas already referred to was particularly dangerous. In many areas the only British citizens were missionaries. In October 1930 two women caught up in fighting between Government forces and bandits in Fukien were brutally murdered.[433] Their killers had not been apprehended by the following March (as far as the Foreign Office was aware).[434] A couple of days later Wood asked about the safety of Father Tierney, superior of St Columbia's Mission in Keinchang [sic], who had been captured by Chinese bandits demanding a ransom.[435] This seems not to have been paid or at any rate did not prevent his death shortly afterwards, an outcome suspected in March but not confirmed until May 1931.[436] Wood then asked about the safety of British subjects generally given that in the previous two years fifteen had been captured, another eight had been murdered and one had died in captivity. Henderson replied that the Chinese government sought to discharge their responsibilities towards British subjects as best they could and "most of these outrages occurred in remote places" where bandits (often the Red Army) were in effective control. There was little the British government could do to prevent missionaries risking their lives by travelling to these conflict areas. As both Henderson and Wood appreciated, it was a matter of Christian conscience and any interference by the Government was resented by the missionary societies.

The London Naval Conference of 1930 was extensively debated by the Commons on 15th May 1930[437] with a Bill then going through all its stages in time for the London Naval Treaty Act to receive Royal Assent on the last day of that parliamentary session.[438] However, this was not the comprehensive measure hoped for because the mutual Anglo-American agreement to cease

---

[433] Hansard, 3rd November 1930, vol. 244, cols. 447-454
[434] Hansard, 2nd March 1931, vol. 249, cols. 15-16; *Times* 3rd March 1931, KW17 260/3
[435] Hansard, 4th March 1931, vol. 249, col. 366; *Times* 5th March 1931, KW17 259/4
[436] Hansard, 23rd March 1931, vol. 250, col. 9 and 6th May 1931, vol. 252, cols. 361-362
He had died of illness on 11th March. Father Tierney's "ill health and subsequent death were attributed to brutal and degrading treatment at the hands of the Red Army" according to http://aodhruadh.org/facilities/father_tierney.php.
[437] Hansard, 15th May 1930, vol. 238, cols. 2085-2204
[438] Hansard, 1st August, 1930, vol. 242, col. 1014

battleship construction themselves to 1936 was dependent on the Mediterranean powers of France and Italy agreeing likewise. When this did not prove possible, Britain and America activated an "accelerator clause" to reflect increased building by the Mediterranean powers. Indeed France, perhaps in response to the threatened Austro-German Customs Union or MacDonald spiking Henderson's efforts to meet the guarantees of military assistance the French had sought, adopted the curious interpretation that their arrangement with Italy allowed them to lay down new cruisers in 1935 and 1936 as long as they did not put to sea till 1937 or later.[439] Although Carlton says that this interpretation took Great Britain and Italy aback, and clearly it was "not playing the game", it is logical and demonstrates realpolitik.

Wood had kept out of this disarmament issue since April when MacDonald had been unwilling to reply to his question about the current position.[440] That November he asked "whether any further steps have been taken in relation to the outstanding differences left by the London Naval Treaty", to which Henderson replied by referring to "certain conversations" that continued to drag on with no definite outcome in sight.[441] Wood then pressed many times over the following months, re-phrasing the question so as to approach the naval agreement and armaments issue from different angles. For example, in March he asked in relation to Henderson's recent visits to Paris and Rome,[442] in June first whether a recent League of Nations meeting in Geneva had discussed it formally[443] and then three weeks later whether negotiations would now be renewed.[444] In July Wood repeated the question in the form he had put it the previous November. Henderson was unable to add to his previous answers, so Wood asked him whether he proposed "to take any further immediate steps in the matter". Henderson replied that the difficulty did not lie with the British Government, implying that France was the sticking-point. Wood continued "Did not

---

[439] Carlton, op cit, pp119-143
[440] Hansard, 29th April 1930, vol. 238, col. 29
[441] Hansard, 19th November 1930, vol. 245, col. 406
[442] Hansard, 4th March 1931, vol. 249, col. 366; *Times* 5th March 1931, KW17 261/5
[443] Hansard, 10th June 1931, vol. 253, col. 987; *Times* 11th June 1931, KW17 280/4
There had been no open discussion and no further action was proposed until a new French parliament was in place.
[444] Hansard, 29th June 1931, vol. 254, col. 872

[Henderson] claim a triumph for the results he had achieved?", to which Henderson replied

> Yes, and I was quite entitled to do so. The blame does not rest with the Government of this country, and I should have thought [Wood] would be the first to admit it.[445]

It is not certain what Henderson meant by this but he was probably accusing Wood of preferring party politics to common sense.

Although the possibility that Austria and Germany were considering closer union had first been questioned in Parliament in December 1929, the Government had no information at that time and the issue was not broached again until March 1931. Wood was just one of several MPs who asked then about the proposed customs union. Dalton replied that the Foreign Office had now received information from both countries which, though preliminary at that stage, might form the basis for treaty negotiations subsequently. They were currently examining it and in due course the legality of the proposals and the impact on existing treaties would be tested. The House should rest assured though that the Government would protect Britain's trading interests.[446] A few days later Wood asked Henderson whether he could now inform the House about the projected customs union and its impact on existing treaties. Henderson's statement was very extensive and for that reason he was given permission by the Speaker to defer it until the end of questions. In view of the issues raised by the proposals, particularly the legal compatibility with Austria's treaty obligations, Henderson explained that he would be taking the matter to the next League of Nations Council meeting. He described this as "the best, indeed the only proper, solution of an episode that has caused a regrettable perturbation in Europe".[447] The following day Wood asked William Graham (1887-1932) the President of the Board of Trade for, and received, an assurance that the impact on trade was being carefully considered.[448]

Although Wood periodically asked Henderson to update the House, the latter was unable to add to his end of March statement until early June. Henderson replied to Wood that the League of

---

[445] Hansard, 8th July 1931, vol. 254, col. 2063
[446] Hansard, 25th March 1931, vol. 250, cols. 317-320
[447] Hansard, 30th March 1931, vol. 250, cols. 715-725
[448] Hansard, 31st March 1931, vol. 250, col. 909

Nations Council had now referred the matter to the Permanent Court of International Justice for an advisory opinion.[449] The diplomatic screw was clearly being turned for, even in the unlikely event that the Court's opinion would fit Austria's and Germany's aspirations, it would take some time to arrive and the delay itself might prove fatal to their ambitions. On 5th September the Court announced its majority decision (by eight votes to seven) that the proposed customs union was incompatible with an existing treaty (the 1922 Geneva protocol) and was therefore illegal. No doubt forewarned of the impending decision, Austria and Germany had announced two days earlier that they would be abandoning the project[450] - but French pressure had also played a significant part in Austria's thinking.

In the meantime the Creditanstalt-Bank in Vienna had warned in May that it was about to fail. This was the start of an international financial crisis as foreign investors began to withdraw their holdings in Germany and Hungary as well. Austria sought a loan from France, which the latter made contingent on the end of the customs union proposal. The Bank of England came to Austria's rescue with a £4.3m loan instead but they had already succumbed to French demands to abandon the union. This gave France an inflated view of their strength, while Germany's "alarmist pronouncements" on the impact of reparations worsened as the financial crisis deepened. A vicious cycle had been set in motion that would reverberate throughout the world for the next fifteen years.[451]

There were divisive, often critical, issues in many other countries that received Britain's attention as well. For example: martial law had begun to be applied locally, but not yet generally, in Spain;[452] pressure for greater Indian legislative engagement and autonomy was mounting; Canada had been forced to call off the 1931 Imperial Economic conference due to take place in Ottawa because of Australia and New Zealand problems over representation, postponing it to 1932.[453] Wood asked questions about all of them and they are included both to demonstrate the

---

[449] Hansard, 8th June 1931, vol. 253, col. 601; *Times* 9th June 1931, KW17 279/3
[450] Hansard, 16th September 1931, vol. 256, cols. 812-813
[451] Carlton, op cit, pp191-195
[452] Hansard, 15th June 1931, vol. 253, col. 1410; *Times* 16th June and 2nd July 1931, KW17 281/11 & 278/4
[453] Hansard, 9th June 1931, vol. 253, cols. 786-787

extent and sweep of Wood's interests and provide the wider context against which the domestic issues should be considered. The one was not separable from the other, so treating them as if they were independent, as many have done, at best provides a partial understanding, at worst is misleading.[454] Politicians continue to demonstrate today that, no matter how well-articulated their vision and determined their intentions, their actions and attention ultimately depend on the events that swirl around them - and these are as likely to be international as national in the case of many countries, not least Britain.

National Concerns

The Thames had flooded in January 1928 and, indicative of the poverty and slum conditions in which many people existed, fourteen people drowned in the basements in which they lived along the river.[455] The then Conservative government had asked the LCC and other local authorities to establish what precautions could be taken to prevent this happening again. However, little had been done by December 1929 with the LCC claiming they were hamstrung by the powers resting in the hands of private owners.[456] When Wood stressed the urgency, "with his characteristic, gamin-like impudence", as the *Daily Herald* put it, for in the paper's view the Conservatives had done nothing,[457] the Lord Privy Seal JH Thomas explained that steps could not be taken before the necessary legislation was in place.[458] Both parties wanted action but in its absence blamed each other.

Yet as is usually the case the key differences between the Government and the opposition concerned the economy. The international aspects included, for example, the issue of free trade versus tariffs, as well as the Wall Street crash and the subsequent depression already alluded to, while domestically it was particularly evident in relation to poverty, poor law relief, unemployment and housing; in other words the social, welfare and political impact on people's lives.

---

[454] Not least because the Prime Minister continued to lead on aspects of foreign policy.
[455] *Annual Register*, 6th January 1928
[456] Hansard, 12th December 1929, vol. 233, cols. 668-670
[457] *Daily Herald* 11th December 1929, KW17 159/6
[458] Hansard, 10th December 1929, vol. 233, cols. 217-218

All parties covered a spectrum of views from those of the most left-wing Labour politicians (often members of the ILP) at one extreme to the Conservative die-hards at the other. Somewhere in the middle were the liberal Tories, the Fabians, other rationalists and the Liberals themselves. Position on this spectrum should not be confused with radicalism, for all were capable of this, nor should it be restricted to a particular issue, for differentiation might be better understood in terms of desire for change, the relative weight given to ideology over pragmatism and the speed with which change was sought. Revolutionary change was not openly pursued by many, but few on the left would align themselves with the gradualists of the centre ground, giving events a nudge from time to time but otherwise prepared to let them take their course. Both groups would resist those hardliners of the right who judged an evolutionary timescale fast enough.

Several of the issues that would animate Wood were already evident before 1929 was out: for example, housing, insurance, local government, pensions, Poor Law, unemployment and the effect of government policies in these and other areas on his Woolwich constituents. The first matter to arise had cropped up during the July 1929 debate on the Poor Law Unions when Labour had raised the issue of whether the Conservative aim had been to neuter local decision-making. Wood replied, according to the *Times*, that if the intention had been to smash up local government the Conservatives would not have stopped after three places: "The fact was that the three cases in question were a disgrace to local government and were ruining its administration in this country."[459] On 1st April 1930 Poor Law Guardians were replaced by local government Public Assistance Committees who would administer relief instead. In an article for the *Daily Mail* entitled 'The Vanishing of the Guardians of the Poor' Wood chose to highlight the compulsory inclusion of women on these Committees,[460] another reason in his estimation for judging it a significant advance on the old Boards of Guardians.

---

[459] *Times* 24th July 1929, KW17 132/1
The actual words Wood used in Parliament were slightly different: "If, as has been alleged, it was the intention of the Minister of Health to smash Poor Law administration or local government, **he would not have started with three cases**. [emphasis added] The fact of the matter is that these three cases [Bedwellty, Chester-le-Street and West Ham] were a disgrace to local government ..." Hansard, 23rd July 1929, vol. 230, cols. 1234-1235
[460] *Daily Mail* 1st April 1930, KW17 188/7

In the public mind, though, they continued to be thought of as Guardians, with all that implied about the harsh regime they administered in most places, not least the North-East.[461]

Another controversial measure was the Widows', Orphans' and Old Age Contributory Pensions Bill which began its second reading two days later.[462] Labour had included in their election pledges and the King's speech a commitment to immediately remedy injustices in the existing Act. This would precede urgent legislation to tackle unemployment before a wider review of existing pension schemes was undertaken with the aim of making them more inclusive and better co-ordinated. Wood and the Minister of Health Arthur Greenwood had engaged in an inconclusive exchange about the review earlier in the day:

Wood: "... can [the Minister of Health] now make any statement in relation to the co-ordination of schemes foreshadowed in the King's speech?"
Greenwood: "I intend to refer to the subject in my speech on the Second Reading of the Pensions Bill today."
Wood: "Can the [Minister] say how long this inquiry is proposed to last?"
Greenwood: "No, Sir."[463]

Greenwood's introduction to the second reading was extensive, occupying seventeen columns in Hansard, partly because he ranged over the whole issue of workers' insurance and the schemes that had been developed and operated independently of each other.[464] This first Bill would increase the number of widows receiving pensions and double the amount spent each year for, as Susan Lawrence later explained, the Bill added another 295,000 widows to the 362,000 already receiving a pension and increased the money spent from £4m in the following year to £8m, with annual

---

[461] See, for example, Keith Armstrong and Hugh Beynon (eds.), 'Hello, Are You Working? Memoirs of the Thirties in the North-East of England', 1977
[462] Hansard, 31st October 1929, vol. 231, cols. 365-472
[463] During oral answers: Hansard, 31st October 1929, vol. 231, col. 327.
[464] Neville Chamberlain welcomed the proposal to inject co-ordination if the review led to the sort of all-in insurance that he favoured, though he was conscious of the substantial difficulties that stood in its way. Greenwood rejected this as the likely conclusion or the outcome he sought.

increments of £1m thereafter.[465]   It was controversial for three reasons: firstly, Labour had said on many occasions previously that they would throw out a contributory scheme for widows' pensions and yet they were now maintaining this approach introduced by the Conservatives (though they did intend to tackle the issue later so that those whose husbands had not contributed, or were spinsters, would receive a pension); secondly, according to Wood it was "a gross betrayal of [Labour's] pledges" given during the General Election,[466] for many candidates, including some of the Party leaders other than Snowden, had made extravagant promises that every widow would receive a pension even though they knew this to be unaffordable;[467] and yet, thirdly and conversely, the Conservatives would not propose any amendment, and indeed would not vote against the Bill's second reading, despite their smears about Labour duplicity.   Lawrence said she had been expecting the Conservatives to propose an amendment but its omission demonstrated that much of their fury was feigned and a sham. She also advised them "not to try and ride two horses" at once:

> To say in the same speech that the country cannot afford the expenditure and that you ought to spend a great deal more is not a sensible or reasonable thing to do. I have tried to explain until the House is really weary that this is but the first instalment ...[468]

The necessary money was voted the following day by 206 votes to 64.[469]   On this occasion the Parliamentary Secretary explained the requirements to the House while the Minister of Health wrapped up the debate. This reversal of roles compared to the second reading resulted in a brief and succinct introduction from Lawrence that ensured a focussed debate, avoiding the all-encompassing, discursive and easily misinterpreted speech with which Greenwood had opened the second reading. He had of course chosen to explain the wider context, whereas Lawrence had

---

[465] Other people would also benefit who were presently excluded. Hansard, 31st October 1929, vol. 231, cols. 466-468

[466] Hansard, 31st October 1929, vol. 231, cols. 455-462

[467] A promise they would extend to the wives of men aged 65+ at the 1935 election.

[468] Hansard, 31st October 1929, vol. 231, cols. 468-469

[469] Hansard, 1st November 1929, vol.231, cols. 495-572

a much more constrained and circumscribed task, but her instinct was always towards brevity and concise statements that made it much more difficult for the House to pretend that it had misunderstood or been misled. Possibly with levity rather than sarcasm, Wood half-congratulated her:

> The difficulties, as I know, of explaining complicated matters of this kind are not inconsiderable, but most of us have been able to follow most of the statement she has just made.

Though, as he explained in some detail, this was not to say that he did not object to the impact on trade of the extra costs that businesses would have to bear.[470]

The Committee resolution was reported to the full House on the following Monday as the last item of business at 11pm.[471] Wood may not have been present,[472] though if he was he did not intervene. The Committee Stage of the Bill would begin that Thursday, but several of the newspapers had already reached conclusions about the relative merits of Wood and his Labour opponents at Health:

> [Wood is] especially happy just at present [for the Pensions Bill] affords him full opportunity for the 'gnat-biting' at which he is an adept. He seems even to enjoy the castigations he receives at the hands of his 'opposite number', Miss Susan Lawrence.[473]

Wood "is like a wasp, always ready to sting, and his favourite method of attack is to wait for an answer and then start 'But does not the right honourable gentleman [Mr Greenwood] remember what he said on that subject when he was in Opposition, how he ...' and he proceeds to quote earlier remarks. This must be most galling, for it is a difficult attack to counter."[474]

---

[470] Hansard, 1st November 1929, vol.231, cols. 503-11, 530-531

[471] Hansard, 4th November 1929, vol.231, cols. 770-800

[472] He had received a reply from Greenwood to a written question on housing completions earlier in the sitting. Hansard, 4th November 1929, vol.231, col. 654

[473] *Star* 5th November 1929, KW17 152/9

[474] *Daily Mail* undated, KW17 181/14 in a report entitled 'The Battle of the Words' about Wood's questions to Greenwood.

Fortunately Mr Greenwood has in Miss Susan Lawrence as competent a colleague as Neville Chamberlain had in [Wood].[475]

Wood's waspish tendencies were to the fore on 5th November when he asked about the implications of the Government's disarmament policies for unemployment in the dockyards. His Liberal colleague Leslie Hore-Belisha, MP for Plymouth Devonport,[476] had challenged AV Alexander (1885-1965), the First Lord of the Admiralty about this the previous day[477] and Wood, perhaps not to be outdone and perhaps in an attempt to embarrass the Government, now made the same enquiry of the Lord Privy Seal. JH Thomas was no more forthcoming and promised to send Wood a copy of Alexander's reply. This might be taken to imply that Wood had not been present, but more likely Thomas was indicating that either Wood had not been paying attention or Thomas was alive to his tricks.[478] This would not be the first time their interactions enlivened proceedings, nor would it be the last; indeed, they were friends and both were close to Harry Preston.[479] For his part Wood then asked whether Thomas had consulted the Prime Minister and whether he knew that "when [MacDonald] was a candidate for East Woolwich [in 1921] he was full of schemes of this kind". Thomas did not reply but made it clear that it was the Admiralty rather than his Department that was responsible for alternative work in the dockyards. Wood then asked about schemes for land colonisation for the unemployed, eliciting from Thomas the information that the Forestry Commission

---

[475] *Eastern Daily Express* undated, KW17 186/2

[476] After Hore-Belisha lost his seat as an Independent in the 1945 General Election (having been a Liberal National from 1931 to 1940) he became a Conservative, but failed to win Coventry South in 1950. He was elevated to the House of Lords as a Baron in 1954.

[477] Hansard, 4th November 1929, vol.231, col. 619

[478] Wood had been present at the start of the sitting on 4th November for he had asked Wedgwood-Benn about India, though he did not speak thereafter with just five or six written questions after that. On the following Monday 11th November Wood spoke often in the Committee session on the Widows', Orphans' and Old Age Contributory Pensions Bill, voting at the end. He did not routinely absent himself from Parliament on Mondays or indeed ever.

[479] For example, a reporter joined all three for lunch at the Ritz in 1934: *Sunday Graphic and Sunday News* 4th March 1934, KW19 72/17

programme had been expanded from £5.5m to £9m thereby enabling increased numbers of married miners to settle on forestry holdings. In this instance Wood impishly asked whether he had consulted George Lansbury, the First Commissioner of Works, who had "devoted a great deal of time to this matter". Thomas was stung into replying that "I also have devoted a considerable time to it, and this is the practical result of that consideration".[480]

But if the *Daily Mail* compared Wood to a wasp, the *Daily Express* judged him capable of inflicting more severe and lasting wounds. In his column, Hore-Belisha's assessment of Wood was that

> He is restless and agile on the Front Bench, and regards the Ministers opposite, I feel sure, as whales. There he is in his much-tossed little boat, flinging harpoons at one after another. The whales sometimes survive to beat back against the craft, but though they shake it mercilessly they have not yet succeeded in capsizing it.
> Sir Kingsley Wood's activities give zest to the session.[481]

Needless to say Labour, or in this instance Ellen Wilkinson in her column in the *Daily Herald* on the week in Parliament, had a different view altogether, shrugging off Wood's barbs and drawing attention instead to his "waspish whinings". She noted with approval Herbert Morrison's reply that

> The honourable gentleman spends half his time demanding the production of Bills by the Government, and the other half obstructing the Bills that have been introduced.[482]

On 7th November prior to the Committee Stage of the Widows', Orphans' and Old Age Contributory Pensions Bill Wood asked whether the Government proposed to discontinue test work for able-bodied men as a condition of outdoor relief. Greenwood replied that test work would remain available to Poor Law Guardians but that it would be targeted where possible on education and training that would make men better able to get a job

---

[480] Hansard, 5th November 1929, vol.231, cols. 803-804
[481] *Daily Express* 21st February 1930, KW17 172/1
[482] *Daily Herald* 31st March 1930, KW17 188/3

in the future.[483]   Three weeks later, having made it clear to the Gateshead Guardians that they could not give unconditional outdoor relief to able-bodied men without an adequate labour test, Greenwood resisted Wood's suggestion that he should communicate this to Poor Law authorities generally.[484]   Wood had also asked whether necessitous areas would be receiving further assistance from national sources, to which Greenwood's reply had been that he was still considering representations on additional aid for mining areas.[485]   Their next exchange on this subject was more testy:

Wood: "... [does the Minister of Health propose] to introduce any Measure ... that relief due to unemployment should be borne nationally?"[486]
Greenwood: "I am not at present in a position to make any statement on this matter."
Wood: "Is [the Minister] in a position to make any Parliamentary proposals at the moment; has he thought this matter over and come to any conclusions about it?"
Greenwood: "I have replied to this question before and said: 'Not at this stage'."[487]

Within a month of Parliament resuming after the summer recess, therefore, Wood was irritating Greenwood and clearly nettling him. This was a pattern that he hoped to extend to other Labour Ministers. But some were more impervious to Wood's barbs than others - with JH Thomas a case in point. When Wood had asked him about schemes to bring new industries into distressed areas to reduce unemployment, Thomas "was exploring every avenue" but it

---

[483] Hansard, 7th November 1929, vol. 231, col. 1240
The Committee debate was delayed by the statement Baldwin was forced to make on India and whether the Viceroy Lord Irwin's suggestion of Dominion status for India pre-empted the conclusions of the Simon Commission. Hansard, 7th November 1929, vol. 231, cols. 1303-1339 It certainly went further than many Conservatives wanted. Ball (ed.), 2014, op cit, p274
[484] Hansard, 28th November 1929, vol. 232, col. 1608
[485] Hansard, 7th November 1929, vol. 231, cols. 1241-1242
[486] In 1935 Wood in his turn was to be asked the same question about Special Areas.
[487] Hansard, 28th November 1929, vol. 232, col. 1590

was up to industry itself to decide where to locate.[488] In effect, like Greenwood, he had yet to decide what help the Government might be able to give but, unlike Greenwood, he had seen off Wood for the moment. If, or more likely when, Wood returned to question Thomas he would do so more warily and have to put his questions more cannily. Greenwood, on the other hand, had shown himself to be an inviting and rewarding target.

Part of Wood's frustration in relation to the Ministry of Health, of course, was that its responsibilities were now out of his hands. While Labour might not be strong enough politically to overturn the reforms he and Chamberlain had introduced, other than in some specific areas, changed priorities combined with economic factors and inertia might have the same effect. Wood had left office with a series of steps in mind that appeared to him both necessary and logical in terms of further implementation. But there was little he could do about this in the immediate future other than keep watch and he was a shrewd enough politician to concentrate on those anomalies that gave Labour the greatest difficulties. One such was the link to co-operative society chemists and the gifts and inducements they could offer doctors in relation to National Health Insurance prescriptions. When Wood asked about this, Greenwood replied that he was considering the matter, to which Wood responded "Surely we must have real business done ..."[489] Wood was not just tackling particular issues though but creating an atmosphere of doubt around the Government's competence in general and Greenwood's in particular. This was a large part of the reason why he infuriated the opposition and they in turn, Liberals as well as Labour, hated him. His dogged persistence compounded the matter. In late November and then two months later he followed up his previous question to Greenwood about the progress of the pensions schemes review. Greenwood was no more forthcoming on either occasion with Wood provoked in

---

[488] Hansard, 28th November 1929, vol. 232, col. 1188
In some senses though, Thomas was in a stronger position having amended the conditions of Unemployment Grants to make these available to local authorities with 10% rather than 15% unemployment for twelve months, with authorities receiving grants then having "to speed up" for three rather than five years. Schemes already approved by the Committee amounted to £7m, with another £20m under review. Hansard, 4th November 1929, vol. 231, cols. 660-664
[489] Hansard, 14th November 1929, vol. 231, col. 2207

January to ask "Is this a Government of action, or is it a farce?"[490] Similarly, he may have been genuinely interested in the gender balance of jurors but he was also keen to expose any gap between legal practice and Labour's determination to uphold the will of Parliament. In a recent case at the Old Bailey jurors had been challenged, as defence lawyers could, but in this instance the challenges had continued until no women were left on the jury. Wood asked the Attorney-General whether he proposed to amend the law to prevent this, so requiring that a replacement juror was of the same sex as the one displaced.[491] Alfred Short (1882-1938), Under-Secretary for Home Affairs, replied, thereby downgrading the importance of Wood's question. Short did not rise to the bait, holding to the line that he was not aware of any difficulty. Wood had failed to embarrass the Government on this occasion, indeed his strategy was undermined by another Conservative, Frederick Macquisten, suggesting Wood must know that as some defendants preferred female jurors things balanced out over time.

But, as the saying goes, a week is a long time in politics and the following Monday a gilt-edged opportunity arose when the Prime Minister announced the members of the Ullswater Committee on Electoral Reform. The Committee was supposed to be political only but the first name MacDonald read out was that of the Lord Chief Justice Gordon Hewart (1870-1943). Baldwin objected very strongly as soon as MacDonald sat down and Wood asked how it would be possible for Hewart to "carry out his duties properly and serve on a committee of this kind representative of the different political parties".[492] Baldwin initiated a debate later that day and by the early evening Hewart had resigned. He had previously been a Liberal MP and it transpired that his good friend Lloyd George had nominated him. Lloyd George claimed he had understood the inquiry to be non-party but took responsibility for the error - though he also blamed MacDonald and Baldwin for not clarifying the position sooner.[493]

Wood had asked previously about aspects of unemployment and schemes for alleviating it, and he continued this oblique

[490] Hansard, 21st November 1929, vol. 232, col. 693 and 23rd January 1930, vol. 234, col. 332
[491] Hansard, 25th November 1929, vol. 232, cols. 990-991; *Woman's Leader and Common Cause* 6th December 1929, KW17 159/16
[492] Hansard, 2nd December 1929, vol. 232, cols. 1921-1923
[493] Ibid, cols. 2019-2025; *Daily News* 8th December 1929, KW17 158/1; *Punch* 11th December 1929, KW17 161/2

approach before targeting the issue directly. On 19th November he questioned JH Thomas about local authorities whose low rates of unemployment (less than six per cent) might enable them to develop schemes that, by drawing in workers, would reduce unemployment in the distressed areas, and about the impact on male and female unemployment. On neither point was Thomas able to enlighten him.[494] According to Asa Briggs, MacDonald was too weak and distracted to tackle unemployment, while JH Thomas was not prepared to put in the hard work required.[495] Margaret Bondfield, the Minister of Labour, had recently introduced the Unemployment Insurance (No. 2) Bill, the twentieth Bill on unemployment insurance that Parliament had considered since 1920, to "remedy the outstanding defects of the present system, ... provide money [for the scheme to be carried on]" and enable it to continue beyond April 1931 pending the outcome of the Government's review of all pension and insurance schemes.[496] The second reading was completed on 25th November with 299 votes in favour and 213 against. Wood had not yet spoken and barely did so during the debate that immediately followed on the increased funding that would be necessary. This raised the fund to £12.5m (more than £420m today) allowing 1.2m people to receive insurance payments. The House approved this Money Resolution by 243 votes to 130.[497] Wood, like Baldwin and many other Conservatives, voted against both.

The Bill began its Committee stage later that week and, curiously, Wood took no active part in the clause by clause examination. This might appear remarkable in terms of his legal and analytical skills, especially of an issue with which he was so closely identified, but he may have realised that any interventions he made were only likely to goad the opposition and prove self-defeating. His silence, however, did not prevent him voting against those clauses with which he disagreed (for example, clause 1 reducing minimum age for insurance to 15, and clause 2 the rates of benefit). When these rates of benefit were discussed on 3rd December, Ellen Wilkinson pressed Bondfield to concede an extra

---

[494] Hansard, 19th and 26th November 1929, vol. 232, cols. 262, 263-264, 1187-1188
[495] Briggs, 1961, op cit, pp208-209
[496] Hansard, 21st and 25th November 1929, vol. 232, cols. 737-851, 1027-1099
[497] Ibid, cols. 1099-1172

shilling a week for the wives of unemployed men, allowing them ten rather than nine shillings, for

> These wives of the unemployed men have been through hell these last few years. No women have had to put up with what they have had to face. They have had the whole burden of the children on their shoulders during this trying time. They have sacrificed themselves; they have starved themselves for their children, very often. Although it is only 1s [1 shilling] for which we are pleading, it is the amount that was put forward by the Trades Union Congress.[498]

Despite this direct appeal, her Labour colleague Bondfield replied with regret that this apparently modest concession would cost £1.65m and was unaffordable. When the amendment was pressed to a vote 229 MPs voted for a rate of 9s, but 28 voted against. The latter were mainly left-wing Labour MPs who wanted the rate increased to 10s and included people such as Joseph Batey, Fenner Brockway, Joseph Devlin, Percy Harris, Frank Horrabin, Frederick Jowett, David Kirkwood, James Maxton and John Wheatley, most of whom were well-known and many of whom have already featured in Wood's story. Ellen Wilkinson was among them and was particularly fortunate that she was not forced to resign as PPS to Susan Lawrence at Health as would be customary for a member of any government (even an unpaid one) voting against it. Apparently, Wilkinson had previously quipped that other parties were "redundant as Labour was now providing both the government and the opposition", though whether she saw Bondfield as the "scapegoat for Snowden's parsimony" or the victim of it is open to question.[499] She was not prepared to subordinate her principles, even in an instance such as this when personal and party considerations had to be carefully weighed against feminist ones.

The Bill eventually received its third reading on 16th December, but it had monopolised three more parliamentary days in the meantime and almost did the 16th as well. The Lords amendments were considered at the end of January with some taking a further week before the Commons and Lords could agree - or at least agree to differ. The following day 6th February 1930 the

---

[498] Hansard, 3rd December 1929, vol. 232, cols. 2220-2221
Ten shillings in 1930 is the equivalent of about £20 today.
[499] Perry, op cit, p221

Unemployment Insurance Act 1930, as it was now called, was enacted.[500] However, as the numbers of unemployed continued to increase and the demands on the insurance fund mounted accordingly, Bondfield was forced to seek further rises to the borrowing powers in order for the fund to remain solvent. The No. 3 Act introduced in mid-April increased these from £40m to £50m[501] and the No. 4 Act, introduced in mid-July, to £60m.[502] This Bill received assent on 1st August 1930, the day the House rose for the summer recess. In less than six months the financial pressures on the fund had increased by 50% in effect.

It had been known as early as mid-June, as Bondfield had confirmed to Wood, that this next instalment increasing the borrowing powers would be required before the recess.[503] So, in mid-July Wood asked the Prime Minister whether he would be introducing any proposals to mitigate unemployment before the summer recess. MacDonald said not, apart from the Public Works Facilities Bill, the Unemployment Insurance (No. 3) Bill and the vote on especially necessitous areas already planned or before the House. Another MP asked what the last Labour party meeting had said about that. MacDonald did not reply but in the *Morning Post* account the question had been greeted with laughter.[504]

The process increasing the borrowing powers was to be repeated a further four times in the 1930-31 session, so that by July 1931 they stood at £115m, almost twice as high as a year earlier and almost three times as high as when the 1930 Act had come into effect fifteen months earlier. Although there was now some attempt to reduce the increasing demands by tackling "anomalies", it must have been apparent to all that this escalation could not continue indefinitely.

---

[500] Hansard, 6th February 1930, vol. 234, col. 2159

[501] Technically this was simply seeking statutory endorsement for the resolution that the Commons had passed on 28th March and 31st March. Hansard, vol. 237, cols. 783-864, 1034-1035, 1659-1735, 2197-2226, 2803

[502] Hansard, vol. 241, cols. 1627-1707, 1903-1904, 2179-2288; vol. 242, cols. 225-228, 1014

[503] Hansard, 19th June 1930, vol. 240, col. 555; *Times* 20th June 1930, KW17 208/3

[504] Hansard, 14th July 1930, vol.241, col. 922; *Morning Post* 12th July 1930, KW17 216/7

The latter, almost certainly as a dig at Lloyd George, reported the Public Works Facilities Bill as the Wales Facilities Bill.

While this financial summary helps illustrate the deteriorating situation, on its own it either might indicate an approach that was inappropriately generous, insofar as it was unaffordable and distorted other priorities, or it might reflect a rapidly increasing number of unemployed people themselves. In reality it mirrored both, but mainly the latter. National unemployment had never been less than one million since 1923 (about one-tenth of the workforce) and had crept up to 1.14m by April 1928.[505] But the nation's economy declined rapidly after 1929 as Britain's exports reduced in the face of the American collapse and unemployment increased. By July 1930 it had risen to 2m and by December 1930 stood at 2.5m. Another way of conceiving this is in terms of the days lost by insured people through unemployment: 424m in the year to 26th May 1930 compared to 397m the previous year.[506] Unemployment would remain above 2m from 1932 to 1935.[507] Yet, according to Keith Middlemas' summation of Thomas Jones' diary for 1930, "... there was not, at this stage, either an acute balance of payments problem or a budgetary deficit (other than the bankruptcy of the Unemployment Fund)..."[508] In January 1930 the Labour MP for Smethwick Oswald Mosley had put forward proposals for tackling unemployment to the Cabinet as alternatives to the Government's approach. When these were finally rejected in May, he resigned as Chancellor of the Duchy of Lancaster.[509] Though re-elected to Labour's National Executive Committee in October 1930, he was expelled by the party the following March and soon afterwards began his long march into opprobrium and ultimately contempt and imprisonment.[510]

---

[505] JM Keynes and Hubert Henderson, 'Can Lloyd George Do It? An Examination of the Liberal Pledge', 1929, p12

[506] Margaret Bondfield reply to Assheton Pownall, Wood's neighbouring MP for Lewisham East. Hansard, 3rd July 1930, vol. 240, col. 2116; *Times* 4th July 1930, KW17 216/4

[507] Armstrong and Beynon, op cit, p5

[508] Keith Middlemas (ed.), 'Thomas Jones: Whitehall Diary vol. II 1926-1930', 1969, p230

AJ Youngson, 'The British Economy 1920-1957', 1960 provides a very clear explanation of why the Fund was bankrupt.

[509] Hansard, 21st May 1930, vol. 239, cols. 404-405 On 28th May he gave a detailed analysis of the unemployment position and an explanation of the proposals he had submitted to the Cabinet to relieve it.

[510] He formed the New Party on 28th February 1931 and then, after its mauling at the 1931 General Election, disbanded it in April 1932 and set

At the local level, as Bondfield informed Wood, there were 50% more people unemployed in Woolwich in March 1930 compared to nine months earlier when Labour first held office.[511] By October 1930 another 900 people had joined them making the increase 2000 in total "since the Socialists took office".[512] Wood painted the picture for his constituents a few months later:

> ... at no time in history had the country been in so serious a position as it was today. The ship of State was rudderless, and nobody knew under the present Administration where we were drifting. Mr MacDonald, who boasted and promised so much at the last election, stood helpless and hopeless before the rising tide of unemployment. The Government was blind to the situation, and blind to the fact that even advanced Cobdenites and members of the TUC were in favour of protecting British industries against foreign competition.[513]

In July 1931 Wood sought the April, May and June figures for Woolwich for the years from 1928 to 1931. At June 1931 5246 insured people were out of work in total, with the steepest increase during the previous twelve months, and while the numbers of men and juveniles had begun to decrease from their highs in April 1931, the number of women unemployed had carried on increasing. By then one in four (23%) of the unemployed were women whereas two years earlier in June 1929 they had comprised about one in eight (13%).

In many ways the Government's reaction was predictable, for the political and bureaucratic reflex until it went out of fashion recently was to set up a Royal Commission on any issue that politicians found particularly perplexing or too difficult. This had a number of beneficial effects from a government's point of view: it gave the impression that something was being done, in other words the illusion of action; it provided cover under which to dismiss opposition questions for they could be told to "wait and see"; it

---

up the British Union of Fascists instead. Matthew Worley, 'Oswald Mosley and the New Party', 2010, pp1-3, 9-10

[511] *Kentish Mercury* undated, KW17 186/5: 3266 at 17th March 1930 compared to 2104 at 3rd June 1929

[512] *Kentish Independent* 24th & 31st October, *Kentish Mercury* 31st October 1930, KW17 226/8, 226/9 & 226/14

[513] *Times* and *Kentish Mercury* both 3rd October 1930, KW17 223/7& 223/9

reduced uproar and alarm to the status of disquiet, thereby raising morale on the backbenches; and of course it was always possible that a solution would be identified, which might also be timely and practicable (as it sometimes was). Accordingly in December 1930 MacDonald announced the seven members who would comprise the new Royal Commission on Unemployment Insurance.[514] Despite the headline 'Yet Another Commission', it seemed to have achieved its first purpose for it was reported to have met with general satisfaction.[515]   However, the *Daily Mirror* did refer to Wood's letter to the *Times* the previous day which pointed out that there seemed "no end to the spending of Government".[516]   There was another view of course and, in defending the "wonderful record" of the government at an Eltham meeting, Stafford Cripps (1889-1952)[517] put it. After reading out Wood's letter of protest at £135m spent on unemployment relief and £104m on benefit, Cripps went on to remind his audience that

> ... a thing often forgotten was that the only way to decrease unemployment was to increase the buying power of the public. At least half that £135m would be spent in wages, buying power would increase, trade would expand and unemployment would be reduced.[518]

All fair points, except there was little evidence that the rapid increase in benefits had had such an effect thus far.

---

[514] Hansard, 9th December 1930, vol. 246, cols. 222-223; *Evening News* 10th December 1930, KW17 236/9

[515] *Daily Mirror* 11th December 1930, KW17 236/11

[516] *Times* 10th December 1930, KW17 236/12

[517] Stafford Cripps was the Labour candidate for Woolwich West until he was appointed Solicitor-General in October 1930 and a safe seat had to be found for him - as it was in Bristol East in early 1931. This soon left Wood unopposed as the Liberal candidate AS Phillips withdrew at the end of February. *Times* 27th February 1931, KW17 258/6; *Kentish Independent* 6th March 1931, KW17 261/6

When Herbert Morrison first introduced Cripps as the Labour candidate at Woolwich Town Hall, Cripps had said of Wood "He is not useful, not even amusing, except to himself; he is one of the ablest obstructors and best mischief-makers in the House of Commons." *Kentish Mercury* undated, KW17 176/4

[518] *Kentish Mercury* 12th December 1930, KW17 237/9

A month later at a meeting of North Woolwich Women's Polling Committee Wood said that he "did not think he had ever spoken in North Woolwich when times had been so bad or so depressing".[519] Not only had unemployment increased by 1.5m since Labour took office, Margaret Bondfield had told him in the House of Commons that Government schemes had provided employment for only 86,000 people. This had cost millions.[520] Wood had gone on to ask MacDonald, as he had six months earlier, whether he had any further proposals to mitigate unemployment. When MacDonald said that he had not, Wood suggested the time had now come for him either to "bring forward fresh proposals or resign his post".[521] "No wonder," Wood told his Woolwich audience, "that the Conservatives and even the Liberals had had enough of this Government".

The following week Wood brought together the lack of any fresh Government ideas with the alarm with which Lloyd George was viewed by the Conservatives[522] in a dispute with Snowden over the Government's unemployment policy. Wood's fellow Conservative Daniel Somerville (1879-1938) had asked Snowden whether, given that new Ministerial arrangements "have not in any way improved the position, would the Prime Minister himself not concentrate on this question [unemployment] ...".[523] Snowden had assured him that the "Prime Minister is concentrating on it" when Wood jumped in with the suggestion "Cannot he invite the right hon. Member for Carnarvon Boroughs (Mr Lloyd George) to do

---

[519] *Kentish Independent* 23rd January 1931, KW17 249/5
[520] Hansard, 20th January 1931, vol. 247, col. 18
Although the numbers employed on work schemes was a snapshot in December 1930 (rather than the numbers ever employed), the schemes sanctioned since June 1929 cost £77m in total. Wood, like any politician, was bound to interpret the figures in the way that best suited him and unlikely to report the distinction accurately.
[521] Ibid, cols. 19-20
[522] On 29th May 1930, for example, Churchill had warned MacDonald in a letter to the *Times* to be very careful before inviting Mr Lloyd George to take charge of the Labour government. Briggs, 1961, op cit, pp208-209 In this instance Lloyd George was being castigated for proposing a loan for relief - in other words, yet more spending - before there were specific proposals for deploying it.
[523] The "new Ministerial arrangements" referred to Vernon Hartshorn (1872-1931) replacing JH Thomas as Lord Privy Seal in June 1930 when the latter became Secretary of State for the Dominions. Hartshorn died two months after this debate.

something?" Snowden did not give Wood the satisfaction of responding to this and the dispute continued:

Wood: "... in view of the increase in unemployment, what is the attitude of the Government towards the proposal for a national loan for reconstruction and development purposes in connection with the mitigation of unemployment?"
Snowden: "I would refer ... to the reply which I gave him [Wood] on 11th November last, to which I can add nothing."[524]
Wood: "Does [Snowden] still adhere to his statement that it is not the policy of the Government to promote a public loan and then try to devise some means of spending it."
Snowden: "Most emphatically."[525]

On the same day that this exchange was taking place, the *Daily Mail* reported that the Lloyd George "deal" (i.e., a national loan for schemes of national development to tackle unemployment) had given the Government a new lease of life.[526] If not entirely spurious, it was certainly not new, and Wood may well have prompted the *Daily Mail* to resurrect the slur at this time in order to further undermine the Government.

In early May Bondfield confirmed that she still expected the Royal Commission's interim report by the end of the month,[527] though she was increasingly uncertain of the timescale when Wood asked a fortnight later, promising then to "look into the matter".[528] In between these two dates Neville Chamberlain had arranged a Party Business Committee to clarify the Conservative position on transitional benefit, for he was opposed to the Commission's likely recommendation that it be administered on a scale more generous than that of any Public Assistance Committee. Permitted to take anyone he liked to the Business Committee, he had decided on "Hilton Young and Betterton who can be relied on to stand firm and

---

[524] They had had an equally inconclusive altercation then too, though on this occasion Wood referred to the "national loan for reconstruction as has been so graphically described by" Lloyd George. Hansard, 11th November 1930, vol. 244, cols. 1468-1469
[525] Hansard, 27th January 1931, vol. 247, cols.792-793
[526] *Daily Mail* 27th January 1931, KW17 251/6
[527] Margaret Bondfield reply to Assheton Pownall. Hansard, 7th May 1931, vol. 252, cols. 533-534
[528] Hansard, 22nd May 1931, vol. 252, cols. 2387-2388

Walter Elliott [sic] and Kingsley who can't".[529] At first sight this seems a very odd comment on Wood for Chamberlain was particularly concerned that the Conservatives oppose the Commission's expected conclusion and Labour and Liberal automatic acceptance of it. It must mean that Wood would not toe the party line regardless of other considerations. Yet, given his repeated questioning (more frequent than Chamberlain's) over the indebtedness of the Insurance Fund and the deteriorating position on unemployment, it still seems curious. It may reflect Wood's preference for consensus when people's lives were affected rather than just scoring party political points.

In the event the Royal Commission presented its interim report in early June 1931, though only after much pressing,[530] and in mid-July MacDonald understood that they hoped to produce their final report by the end of the year, though he could not guarantee it. MacDonald assured the House that, as had happened with their interim report, they had been made aware of "the great importance of expediting their work" yet many had long since begun to doubt its value.[531] Some Conservative MPs sought a three-party conference to discuss the interim report, while others wanted to hear the Government's views and at least one thought it "another chance for the Government to waste time".[532] Although Bondfield said that her Unemployment Insurance (No. 3) Bill was a response to some of the matters covered in the interim report,[533] this was giving their work a gloss that it did not warrant. The Commission's first conclusion was that, despite being asked to come up with ways in which the Insurance Fund could be made solvent,

> ... this appears to us to be an objective which cannot be fully realised without much greater changes in the provisions of the Scheme than we are prepared to recommend. Nor do

---

[529] Self, 2002, op cit, 9th May 1931, pp258-259
As Minister of Labour in the National Government from August 1931, Betterton opposed Chamberlain's proposals that unemployment relief be administered nationally rather than by local government.
[530] Hansard, 4th June 1931, vol. 253, cols. 329-330; 22nd June 1931, vol. 254, cols. 34-35
[531] Hansard, 16th July 1931, vol. 255, col. 745
[532] Hansard, 11th June 1931, vol. 253, col. 1176; *Times* 12th June 1931, KW17 280/6
[533] Hansard, 18th June 1931, vol. 253, col. 1960

we think that its attainment is the sole or even principal consideration to which we should have regard.[534]

Inevitably, therefore, they focussed on the margins and Bondfield did likewise. The Commission were hampered by disagreement among themselves and neither they nor the Minister of Labour were prepared to take the extreme action that, in the absence of economic growth and reduced unemployment, would be required to bring the Fund under control.

During May and June six radio talks on unemployment were given by William Beveridge,[535] then Director of the LSE but already prominent in Liberal circles. By contrast on 25th July Wood was the principal speaker at a major Conservative demonstration at Burghley House, Stamford. With a mixture of hindsight and foresight, Wood argued

> ... the nation must exercise strict economy, reduce taxation and protect its own markets. We should have to face a grim winter and we had the running sore of a bankrupt unemployment insurance fund. The Socialist government stood hopeless and helpless before the advancing tide of unemployment. We needed above everything a modern and scientific fiscal policy.[536]

Wood clearly felt that the time for pulling one's punches had long since passed and his alarmist message would not surprise a sympathetic audience who, if not yet fully converted, he hoped soon would be. He had recently warned that Health Insurance might go the same way as Unemployment Insurance for there were "too many" insurance claims, particularly in the north.[537] This might not be too surprising given the link between unemployment and ill-health, but Wood argued against this explanation and the May Economy Committee was not convinced, or at least chose to ignore

---

[534] 'First Report of the Royal Commission on Unemployment Insurance', Cmd 3872, para 72

[535] Asa Briggs, 'The History of Broadcasting in the UK: Vol. II –The Golden Age of Wireless, 1927-1939', 1995, p40 These were subsequently published as 'Causes and Cures of Unemployment', 1931.

[536] *Observer* 26th July 1931, *Peterborough Standard* and *Lincoln & Stamford Independent* both 31st July 1931, KW17 284/4, 289/1 & 290/1

[537] *Liverpool Post and Mercury, Manchester Guardian, Times* & *Scotsman* all 30th July 1931, KW17 287/3, 287/4, 287/5 & 288/1

the connection, for one of its suggested savings was £1m (more than £35m today) in National Health Insurance, including a reduction in doctors' fees. In Wood's view,

> The rapid increase in expenditure on sickness and disablement cannot be explained by deteriorating health of the population [but is due to the] growing laxity in the granting of benefits to people not really entitled to them.[538]

To justify his argument, Wood cited the estimate of the Insurance Controller that 12% of those getting benefits were able to work, as he had told the Association of Trade Union Approved Societies at a recent conference - so not necessarily the message this group had wanted or hoped to hear.

---

[538] *Truth* 5th August 1931, KW17 289/3

Vignettes

Municipal trading

In February 1930 the Commons gave a second reading to a private Member's Bill on municipal trading.[539] The aim of the Bill was to permit local authorities the same powers as companies to trade generally, though the Labour proposer McShane thought the priorities coal, meat, milk, bread and, as already happened in Birmingham, municipal banking.[540] This is a list, of course, of the basic commodities of life on which most depend and, therefore, also one on which the poorest are most vulnerable to private sector exploitation. In introducing the Bill, McShane referred extensively to the positive impact of local authorities in almost every area of life over the previous hundred years, particularly health, housing and transport. He contrasted local authority charges for electricity with those in the private sector: in London the latter could be 70% higher, while in Margate (a town Wood knew well) the price was the highest in the country for a town of that size (47,000 people) and nearly three times as much as London local authorities charged. He also used a similar cliff analogy to the one Wood had used a decade earlier in arguing that a Ministry of Health should be established.[541] McShane's formulation was:

> It is equivalent almost to placing an ambulance at the foot of a cliff and waiting until people fall over ... one by one ... instead of putting up a fence to prevent them falling over the cliff at all.[542]

McShane then used the analogy to highlight the risks of adulterated food, particularly milk, an issue that Wood had sought to tackle himself at the Ministry of Health. Many companies worked to the highest standards of course, but many did not and the LCC spent

---

[539] Hansard, 14th February 1930, vol. 235, cols. 803-892

[540] The Birmingham Municipal Savings Bank was the only one of its kind in the country, though with sixty branches serving one-third of the City's households; in other words, social reform through local government could be indistinguishable from socialism. In Kevin Morgan, "Mass housing, 1918-1939" chapter in Ball & Holliday (eds.), op cit, p66

[541] *Times* 13th January 1919, KW9 7/5 See Gault, 2014, op cit, p112

[542] Hansard, 14th February 1930, vol. 235, col. 808

£100,000 a year on inspectors in an attempt to safeguard the public (against, for example, milk infected with tuberculosis).

In terms of party politics, municipal trading was anathema to the Conservatives, and to Wood in particular, but there might be practical benefits - though these boiled down to the impact of regulation and the balance between purpose and profit. When McShane sat down, Wood asked him to "... kindly repeat what he said that the local authorities ought to do? Did he say meat, milk, coal, bread, and municipal banking?" McShane confirmed that these were the areas he wanted to see initially, drawing attention to Neville Chamberlain's comment when he had inaugurated the municipal bank in Birmingham:

> You may call this Socialism if you like. I have never been frightened by a name. I do not care whether it is good Socialism or not, so long as it is a good thing.[543]

Wood must have been in two minds whether or not to support the Bill, his party loyalty in conflict with his principles.

This dilemma may have deepened when Alfred Salter seconded the Bill.[544] Salter and Wood had both given their services free to the Bermondsey settlement nearly thirty years before and their shared history went back almost to the turn of the century.[545] Salter compared the restrictions on local authorities in Britain with the wider powers enjoyed by comparable bodies in Europe to act on behalf of their people. This was at the nub of the issue for Salter for he thought "municipalities should possess the power of supplying communal necessities".[546] When Wood asked him whether this might include a municipal medical service, Salter said that he would prefer a State service.[547]

Derrick Gunston was one of the Conservative MPs who opposed the Bill as a whole, and particular clauses within it, while ED Simon was among those who supported it. Arthur Greenwood, the Labour Minister of Health, was also positive about greater freedom for local authorities and his remarks might have been designed to infuriate the opposition. He started by observing that

---

[543] Ibid, col. 811

[544] Ibid, cols. 812-824

[545] Gault, 2014, op cit, pp26-27

[546] Hansard, 14th February 1930, vol. 235, col. 815

[547] Ibid, col. 823

Whenever the subject of municipal Socialism is raised in the House you may be quite sure that hon. Members opposite will disclose their minds in the froth of their own oratory,

referred to the "offensive epithets" they had voiced in an attempt to characterise this "relatively innocent Measure", and closed by stating that the Conservatives were

afraid of the trend of local government ... frightened by the developments for which [they were themselves] responsible, and [are] trying now to stem the free progress of local authorities. That will never be done. The tide which brought us here [i.e., Labour into government] is a tide which is still flowing strongly.[548]

Had Wood still harboured doubts, this speech would have resolved them, for not only was it provocative, his particular bete-noire Greenwood had delivered it. But as it happened Greenwood had also argued that a major step such as this in the role of local government should be a Government measure not a private motion and as Minister of Health he would hope to put this forward "one day". Wood's reaction was immediate and powerful, dripping with irony only when he felt he had overdone the sarcasm:

We have had a most interesting and illuminating speech from [Greenwood]. I desire to acquit him ... of deliberately endeavouring to sneak this Bill through the House. ... He said that he was a Socialist. He reminds me of the case of the boy who was asked whether his father was a Christian, and he replied; 'Yes, Sir, but he does not do much of it'.
... the Minister of Health says that ... many more safeguards must be inserted. In fact, he wishes it to be talked out.

Wood ended by hoping that a vote would take place in order to "condemn this Bill", which opposed the interests of co-operative societies as well as private traders.[549] One report described his intervention as

---

[548] Ibid, cols. 865-870
[549] Ibid, cols. 870-874 Also, CPA PUB 220/71 Gleanings and Memoranda, vol. LXXI, January - June 1930, pp316-317

... a quite excellent speech by Sir Kingsley Wood, who is as effective in opposition as he was efficient in office. His chaff of the co-operative members for supporting a Bill which, if passed, would be the prime enemy of their own movement, could not have been bettered.[550]

The point Wood was making, and the *Saturday Review* had pounced on, was that municipal trading would be meeting similar objectives to those the Co-op Societies already did. In effect, therefore, they would be competing for the same parts of the market. In the Co-op's case any profits were returned as a dividend to their members, while local authorities would have an additional source of funding for services and thereby could reduce rates. It might appear that Wood was highlighting the unintended consequences of local authority trading, throwing the impact of their socialism back at Labour members, but he may also have been espousing a regulated rather than completely free market and conscious of the long-standing Conservative aim to make everybody a small capitalist (at least as a member of their local Co-op). Regulation of the market was of a piece with protection, tariffs and Imperial Preference, while the latter was reminiscent of the drive for property ownership and other ways of giving people a stake in a capitalist society as co-partners.[551]

Gunston was one of the tellers when the Bill passed its second reading by 150 votes to 124 and was then forwarded to a Standing Committee (rather than being considered by the whole House) by 144 votes to 119. Greenwood had been in the majority on both occasions, Wood in the minority.

A fortnight later Wood asked Greenwood whether he would be introducing a municipal trading Bill himself. Greenwood said he had no such intention at present and it was likely that the pressure of other parliamentary business would prevent it. It must have been with particular relish that Wood responded:

Was not this Bill promised in 'Labour and the Nation' [the manifesto] and cannot the right hon. Gentleman be a little more enthusiastic about it?[552]

---

[550] *Saturday Review* 23rd February 1930, KW17 174/2
[551] For example, Noel Skelton, 'Constructive Conservatism', 1924 is discussed in Gault, 2014, op cit, pp220-221
[552] Hansard, 27th February 1930, vol. 235, col. 2416

There was no comeback from Greenwood and Wood had once again got the better of his parliamentary opponent. Wood the golfer must have thought it the equivalent of a hole in one. Many others seem to have shared this view for the archives of the West Woolwich Conservative and Unionist Association record that "Sir Kingsley Wood has just been specially commended by the Political Correspondents of all parties for his parliamentary work in the past [1929-1930] session ...". This refers specifically to his performances on the Municipal Trading Bill.[553]

---

[553] Greenwich Heritage Centre, West Woolwich Conservative & Unionist Association folder, undated item 5 - accessed 30th January 2013

Housing

Housing construction, the obligations on rural authorities and slum clearance were priority issues throughout this period both for the Labour government and the Conservative opposition, with Wood at the forefront of the latter. The Minister of Health Arthur Greenwood had told the Commons in July 1929 that legislation on slum clearance would be introduced as soon as possible[554] but, provocatively or perhaps just because they were tired of waiting, eleven Conservatives and one Independent introduced a private members' Bill four months later.[555] This was withdrawn when the Government did eventually bring forward their own Bill at the end of March 1930, ten months after they had been elected.[556] This received its second reading in early April without a vote,[557] being immediately followed by a debate on the money required to put it into effect. The debate on 8th April had opened with a lengthy peroration from Wood explaining why he viewed "some of the proposals … with particular apprehension" and he also expressed substantial doubts about the lack of detail in the financial resolution.[558] At least one newspaper thought him

> … one of the most belligerent men on the front Opposition bench, [who] never misses an opportunity by question or speech of paying back the Minister of Health for all that he and his chief endured in office. But if Miss Lawrence, who has succeeded him, knows as much about housing as she showed she knew about rating, she will be very useful in dealing with detail when the Slum Clearance Bill gets into Committee. Her speeches display the industry with which she gets up her facts, and … the keenness of her cultivated intellect.[559]

---

[554] Hansard, 11th July 1929, vol. 229, cols. 1113-1114

[555] Hansard, 11th November 1929, vol. 231, col. 1537

[556] Hansard, 27th March 1930, vol. 237, col. 612
Wood was later to ask Greenwood why there had been such a long delay (Hansard, 26th June 1930, vol. 240, col. 1336). He did not receive a reply.

[557] Hansard, 7th and 8th April 1930, vol. 237, cols. 1801-1860, 1864-1917, 1999-2059

[558] Hansard, 8th April 1930, vol. 237, cols. 1999-2011 & 2086-2092

[559] *Eastern Daily Express* undated, KW17 186/2

At the end of June 1930, on a day when Greenwood was receiving an honorary degree from Leeds University, "a public engagement which none of us desire him to forgo" as Wood put it, a consideration of Ministry of Health estimates gave Wood the opportunity to criticise the Government's policy on housing.[560] As well as the *Times* report the following day,[561] Ellen Wilkinson made it a centrepiece of her column in the *Daily Herald* the following week:

> [Wood,] ... the late Parliamentary Secretary to the Minister of Health, who might have been thought to know better, bleated in his curious high voice that 'the great contribution of the Conservative Party to the housing situation was their revival of private enterprise in house building'.
> That just means that enough semi-detached villas and luxury flats were built at a profit to swell his figures of the number of houses provided under a Conservative government.[562]

Ernest Simon, a housing expert and, among other things, ex-chairman of Manchester's Housing Committee (and again a Liberal MP) clashed with Wood in the pages of the journal *The Nineteenth century and After* over housing subsidies and the effect on affordable rents.[563] Simon had written that demolishing slums was not the key problem but rather building new homes for the two million children now living in slum conditions, the same number as at the end of the First World War. Simon acknowledged that 1.5m homes had been built since then but that this had barely touched the slum problem, not least because the houses were too expensive for former slum-dwellers to rent. In other words, the house-building programme had been largely directed towards the needs of the better-off rather than to those of the working-class.

This sparked a response from Wood, perhaps written at the request of the editor, but inevitable since his responsibilities at the Ministry of Health had included housing between 1918 and 1929 (apart from the brief interlude of the first Labour government in 1924). Wood's overall argument was that building 1.5m homes was

---

[560] Hansard, 30th June 1930, vol. 240, cols. 1617-1625
[561] *Times* 1st July 1930, KW17 212/1
[562] *Daily Herald* 7th July 1930, KW17 214/3
[563] ED Simon, "Slum clearance", *The Nineteenth Century and After*, 1930, 107, pp331-338; Kingsley Wood, "Slum clearance: A reply", *The Nineteenth Century and After*, 1930, 107, pp480-483

"undeniably right". Simon had advocated subsidies, particularly for slum-dwelling families, but Wood demonstrated that subsidies inflated building prices and therefore the rents charged by showing how the costs of building houses had moved in line with increases and decreases in subsidies ever since the Addison Act of 1921. In addition, he argued, the number of houses being built had reduced by 25% between the final quarter of 1928 and the same months in 1929. The consequence was that nearly 150,000 insured building workers were unemployed. These latter effects might have been due both to the international depression and the consequent reduction in house-building as the numbers unemployed increased and moving home became less of a priority than retaining the existing one. This, though, was not the point Wood wished to make - even had he accepted it. In support of his position, Wood quoted a speech by the recognised housing authority and Liberal MP Sir John Tudor Walters. Walters had said the previous month that

> ... he did not believe in any form of State subsidy; that the cost of building was still ridiculously high; [and that] 'The non-parlour house of the three-bedroom type ought not to cost more than ... £265 a house. If you reckon that out, you could get a 6s a week basis for your rent.'

This weekly rent of six shillings equates to the spending power of about £12 today and therefore within range of even the poorest, at between a third and a quarter of Poor Law rates for an average family. The critical conclusion is that, while Wood may have been riled by the middle-class jibes of Simon (and Wilkinson), and although he might have been expected to support subsidies, he was arguing for an affordable rent.

When Ministry of Health estimates were again up for consideration in April 1931, Wood and Simon both attacked the Government over housing. Wood laid out the facts, describing it as "half-hearted and timorous";[564] Simon "entirely agreed" with Wood's figures, decrying "a deplorable position not only from the point of view of housing, but also from the point of view of employment".[565] He concluded

---

[564] Hansard, 14th April 1931, vol. 251, cols. 55-65
[565] Ibid, cols. 65-72; *News Chronicle* 15th April 1931, KW17 268/6

> ... the Greenwood Act stands condemned as a failure [and] I ask [Greenwood] to deal with this question with all the energy which he possesses - both with the question of the houses to be built and the rents to be charged.

This should not be taken to imply, though, that Wood was any the less passionate for being analytical. He retained his combative edge as his initial comments about Greenwood's opening speech and his leadership at the Ministry of Health had confirmed:

> ... I have seldom heard a more apologetic and dispirited speech than that which we have heard this afternoon. As far as I can make out, [Greenwood] described a year of easy-going jog trot along the old and well-worn paths, varied by an occasional leap into the thorns and rocks of Socialism, following the application of the stick to the Government's hindquarters by its impatient supporters.

There was much more, with Wood ascribing an "inferiority complex" to Greenwood and assuming he had now withdrawn his statement of the previous year that the expenditure the "nation could afford depended on how much it desired it". He went on to compare Greenwood to a Slipper Limpet which, as an article in that week's *Spectator* had explained,

> [if] attached to the shell of a more mature and stabler species it passes through the most robust and vigorous state of its existence ... [but] ... when it leaves the shell - in this case I suppose it is the Ministry of Health - it reverts and becomes one of the weaker and less dependable animals.

Wood was delighting in Greenwood's volte face over the administration of the Poor Law by local authorities under the Conservative Local Government Act that Wood and Neville Chamberlain had introduced. In November 1928 Greenwood told the Commons that the Act "perpetrated the evils of the Poor Law system" whereas he had spoken recently of his pride in being "associated with so great a change, carried out with such success". Wood underlined the Slipper Limpet's "great capacity for repeated functional changes".[566]

---

[566] Hansard, 14th April 1931, vol. 251, cols. 52-55

Wood was a difficult opponent for Greenwood across the despatch box:

> Mr Greenwood has discovered that Sir Kingsley Wood has only to get up and fix him with his glittering eyeglass, like the Ancient Mariner, and the House chuckles in anticipation.[567]

Although another newspaper had judged Arthur Greenwood brilliant at baiting Tory Ministers when in opposition, in an article "Politicians in the Pillory" it commented that his "lustre [had] dimmed" as Minister of Health, continuing

> There are few men who seem capable of doing well both in office and out of it. Mr Lloyd George, Mr Winston Churchill and Sir Kingsley Wood are, perhaps, the three outstanding exceptions.[568]

However, whether for reasons of courtesy or uncertainty, Wood was less dominant when opposed by competent women.[569] He did not necessarily restrict his criticisms, nor was ever reticent about expressing them, yet he was less rude and more careful how he phrased them. They for their part were less fazed by his bluster. In a series of altercations during the passage of the Housing (Rural Authorities) Bill that July, Susan Lawrence accused him of "pompous solemnity" while he referred to her "impertinent and insulting observations". Wood had undertaken to support the Bill but thought Lawrence was not going about it the right way. This disconcerted her as little as it would have him.[570]

---

[567] *Evening News* 14th November 1930, KW17 229/5
[568] *Star* 4th March 1931, KW17 260/2
[569] Brian Harrison, "Women in a men's house: The women MPs, 1919-1945", *Historical Journal*, 1986, 29, pp623-654
[570] *Star* 17th July 1931, KW17 286/3; Hansard, 16th July 1931, vol. 255, cols. 917-962; also *Times* 17th July 1931, KW17 286/4

Electoral reform

In July 1930 James Lowther (1855-1949), 1st Viscount Ullswater, wrote to Ramsay MacDonald to tell him that the work of the committee on electoral reform had foundered.[571] The committee, or 'conference', had met on ten occasions mainly to debate the merits of proportional representation and it became clear that the three parties on the committee were not going to agree on a new electoral system to replace the existing one. The Conservatives and some Labour members would not agree the Liberal proposals at any price while the remaining Labour members would only do so if other matters of electoral reform were adopted at the same time. Ullswater decided to bring the conference to an end. The proceedings had taken place in private and they had agreed that only the information in Ullswater's letter to MacDonald should be published. The Prime Minister adhered to this even when the Labour Member for Hull asked him to publish the evidence submitted.[572]

Given this stalemate, it seemed unlikely that an Electoral Reform Bill of any significance could proceed. Yet the Government maintained the fiction that it might into December 1930, even allowing MPs to believe that the text of the Bill would be available by Christmas. Wood asked about this on 10th December with Snowden admitting he was doubtful it would appear before the recess.[573] A few days later Arthur Henderson re-iterated that the Bill would be introduced before Christmas though he did not know as yet when the text would be available. Wood asked him "... who thought of this Bill first? Was it the right hon. Member for Carnarvon Boroughs (Mr Lloyd George)?" To which Henderson replied "I am quite certain that it was not the right hon. Member for West Woolwich."[574]

This was good knock-about stuff and it got even better the following day when JH Thomas was standing in for the Prime Minister. Thomas and Wood clearly enjoyed their verbal sparring, "returning jest for jest" as the *Evening Standard* reported,[575] and the

[571] 'Conference on Electoral Reform. Letter from Viscount Ullswater to the Prime Minister', Cmd 3636
Lowther had been Speaker of the House of Commons from 1905 to 1921 and Deputy Speaker for the ten years before that.
[572] Hansard, 6th November 1930, vol. 244, cols 1026-1027
[573] Hansard, 10th December 1930, vol. 246, col. 399
[574] Hansard, 15th December 1930, vol. 246, col. 814
[575] *Evening Standard* 17th December 1930, KW17 237/11

opportunity to lighten House of Commons proceedings. Once again Wood had started by asking whether the text would be available before Christmas. He continued "Is there any hitch about this Bill? Is everything proceeding satisfactorily?"

Thomas: "The last inquiries that I made indicated that things were going well. I am sure that [Wood's] anxiety is caused by his feeling that this Bill might impede his progress from that side of the House to this side."

Wood: "Is it not a fact that certain Labour Members are beginning to think that someone has tried to sell them a pup?"

Thomas: "I am sure that no one wants to put himself up for auction."[576]

The *Evening Standard* report concluded

> Sir Kingsley Wood has set himself up as the chief interrogator of the Government on two subjects - the Trade Disputes Bill and the Electoral Reform Bill. The Government's intentions regarding both measures provide many opportunities for sly digs, and [Wood] is an adept in putting bland and simple-looking questions which have their sting. It is all taken in good part, but occasionally the Prime Minister shows himself a trifle impatient.

The latter was evident on 19th December when Wood was questioning MacDonald's assertion that he had a mandate for electoral reform from the country. In that case, asked Wood, why had the Labour Party been asked to vote on the issue, dividing 133 to 29. MacDonald bridled at a further question about the mandate being that of Lloyd George: "The mandate was given to stop the abuse of a situation such as that which held good between 1924 and 1929 [i.e., when the Conservatives were in office]."[577] Thomas, on the other hand, could be relied on to give as good as he got and, if Wood ever riled him, would be determined not to show it.

The Bill remained a carrot to dangle before the Liberals, one which Neville Chamberlain exploited in 1931 in seeking to get rid of the Labour government. In the spring he "induced Sir Edward Grigg (1879-1955) to organise a 'Liberal Unionist' wing to act in alliance

---

[576] Hansard, 16th December 1930, vol. 246, col. 1045
[577] Hansard, 19th December 1930, vol. 246, col. 1629

with the Conservatives", while in July he even went so far as to authorise negotiations with Lloyd George, offering him a limited measure of electoral reform in return for defeating the government.[578]   Moreover, as might be expected when Lloyd George was involved, the plotting was not just one-way round:

> Which leads me to a humorous incident. [Wood] has been following up his talks with Lloyd George about a deal over the Electoral Reform Bill but has reported that he thinks his mind is now set upon a reconstruction of the Government which would enable him to slip in. The little man however has been keeping K.W. on the string always saying he would see him again so that it was with some surprise that we heard that the Liberals had concerted a plot to get the Bill through the Commons on Monday.
>
> Truly, as Adam Smith said, the politician is a cunning and crafty animal.[579]

Proportional representation re-surfaced at the 1935 general election when the Cabinet's Emergency Business Committee considered it as one of fifty-seven questions of policy about which National Government candidates were to be briefed. Attractive as the principle of proportional representation might be, the formula they proposed was to refer to the difficulty experienced by the Ullswater Conference in finding an acceptable alternative to the existing system.[580]

---

[578] Self, 2006, op cit, p151
[579] Self, 2002, op cit, 25th July 1931, pp270-271
[580] CPA, CRD 1/7/21 Cabinet Emergency Business Committee 1935 General Election questions of policy 11 and CRD 1/7/18 5th November 1935 item 3, EBC(35)6

Woolwich[581]

Herbert Morrison, who had introduced Stafford Cripps to the West Woolwich voters in October 1930, had previously been on the LCC for East Woolwich and lived in Woolwich West. Wood was already "a power in the Conservative Party and ... earmarked for high office in the next Unionist administration", while Ramsay MacDonald had stood for Woolwich East in 1921. The area's connections at the highest levels of both parties were extensive.[582] Tongue-in-cheek, Wood noted the following March "[as] Mr Morrison is one of [my] constituents ... I have no doubt he voted for me"; adding "My neighbour Mr Snell has become a Baron. My constituent Mr Morrison has become a Cabinet Minister. I wonder what fate holds for me."[583] Another recently created Socialist peer was George Marks (1858-1938), senior partner of an engineering company that had offices in Birmingham, Manchester and New York as well as London. Although Marks did not live in Woolwich he had been to school there, and when ennobled as the 1st Baron in 1929 had chosen the title Lord Marks of Woolwich. In March 1930 the Woolwich Chamber of Commerce had held a dinner for him in the Victoria Hotel. Wood spoke, with Lord Marks observing that "You cannot walk through Woolwich without feeling that you are walking through British history – if you keep your eyes open."[584]

In addition to the growing numbers unemployed, local issues in Woolwich included the roads (both their upkeep and traffic jams), short-time at the Arsenal, an increase in the rates of 10d, and the absence of pensions for workers at the Arsenal. It has been asserted that poor housing conditions were to be found in all working-class areas throughout South London from Woolwich in the east to Battersea in the west.[585] In 1930 Wood's book 'Relief for the

---

[581] More detail on Woolwich's history can be found in Part 1, particularly pp66-67 & 104-105.
[582] In a report entitled "Are Woolwich and success in politics synonymous?" *Kentish Independent* 24th October 1930, KW17 225/10
[583] *Star* 24th March 1931, KW17 264/3
Snell was elected chairman of the link committee between Labour's backbenchers and the Cabinet from 1929, a role made increasingly difficult by the disruptive ILP members. Snell, op cit, pp229-232
[584] *Kentish Independent* 21st March 1930, KW17 185/1
[585] Allen Hutt, 'The Condition of the Working Class in Britain', 1933, p141
The same author notes the low level of infant mortality in Woolwich in 1930

Ratepayer' was published, with a preface by Neville Chamberlain. The local and national issues combined led Wood to conclude at a Woolwich Primrose League meeting that there was "very little merrie England today": ten months of disastrous Labour rule had resulted in increases in unemployment, cost of living, national expenditure, coal prices and taxes, while national revenue and wages were down.[586] Twelve months later he repeated his indictment of the Government.[587]

Needless to say, this did not stop Wood enjoying himself: the Annual Building Societies lunch, for example, which Lord Riddell had finally induced him to attend, or dinners at the House of Commons. One of the latter was held by Wesleyan MPs for the President of the Wesleyan Conference at which Wood was

> twitted ... with being the only Conservative Wesleyan to eight Liberals and four Labour men of that faith. He retorted that, of course, this only meant that one Conservative was equal to that number of his opponents.[588]

But just as Wood wanted to see off the Labour Government, so many in Woolwich wanted to see the back of him. 'Get Rid of Sir Kingsley Wood' was the co-operators war cry in June 1931 because he and Neville Chamberlain had previously made it illegal for the Co-op to make profits on medicines or distribute profits on medicines to members.[589] It would seem, however, that the local Labour Party was in disarray at this time or, if it was not, it was reported as such in order to even matters up. 'Discord' was the headline of an article the following week covering a Labour Party meeting at the Old Town Hall, Woolwich. The grievances mainly,

---

and 1931, below the London average as it had been before WWI too (see Gault, 2014, op cit, pp104-105).
[586] *Manchester Guardian* 24th April 1930, KW17 190/10
[587] In a speech to Woolwich Primrose League habitation annual dinner at New Shakespeare Hotel as part of East Woolwich by-election: *Kentish Independent* 3rd April 1931, KW17 266/1
[588] *The Star* 13th May 1930, KW17 197/6
Ellen Wilkinson was the only woman there which presumably made her the equivalent of more than a dozen men.
[589] At the 7th annual meeting for those serving the Co-op movement and Labour in elected positions in London; Susan Lawrence and Alfred Barnes (1887-1974), MP and Chair of the Co-operative Party were among those present. *South Eastern Mercury* 9th June 1931, KW17 280/3

though not exclusively, concerned the continuing non-appointment of a Labour candidate to oppose Wood in West Woolwich.[590] Although their significance was dismissed by Lord Snell, Cllr William Barefoot (the Party secretary) and Alderman Berry of the LCC, many readers must have assumed that something must lie behind the report. Rebuttals are more effective than silence but many discount them and few will recall them.

The following month one constituent pointed out that Wood may have asked 569 questions in the last parliamentary session (the most), but how much did the preparation of answers cost Government departments? He asked Wood to explain in relation to the Local Government Act (a) what the benefits of de-rating had been to Woolwich ratepayers (other than manufacturers/brewers), (b) the effect on the numbers of unemployed locally, and (c) whether Wood had any support from ratepayers who have had to pay more because of the de-rating clauses.[591] The following week's paper had three letters in support of Wood, though not a direct response from him. One from 'Fair Play' of Eltham ended

Woolwich ... is proud of [Wood], its one Member who speaks in the House, and we know he will occupy a prominent Ministerial position in the next Government. But wherever great men are to be found, there are bound to be puppies to snap at their feet. Woolwich is unfortunate in not being able to have the one without the other.[592]

---

[590] *Woolwich Gazette* 16th June 1931, KW 281/10
[591] Letter from 'Observer' of Woolwich dated 22nd July in *Kentish Independent* 31st July 1931, KW17 287/6
[592] *Kentish Independent* 7th August 1931, KW17 290/6

12.   NATIONAL CRISIS 1931

When the R101 airship crashed in flames in October 1930 on its maiden voyage to India, killing all but six of the fifty-four people on board, it signalled the end of this form of aviation in Britain and provided an omen for the year ahead. Within twelve months the downward spiral of the economy had led Ramsay MacDonald to abandon the Labour government and form the National Government instead. Initially conceived to tackle the crisis of confidence in August 1931 with the intention that it would be disbanded once equilibrium had been restored, it was still in place in October long after the immediate danger had passed, and at the end of that month fought and won the 1931 general election with a massive majority.

Yet the year in Britain had started in another mode, for in February 1931 the world-famous film star Charlie Chaplin (1889-1977) provided an antidote to people's immediate concerns when he visited the country of his birth. Most people would have heard of him, even if they had not seen him on the screen themselves, and while it is not certain that the Government had orchestrated the visit to distract people from the daily grind, they must have welcomed it and were certainly complicit in aspects of it. However, it was not entirely light relief for Chaplin had survived an impoverished childhood in south London, some of which was spent in a workhouse, and though he had long left these days behind him, continued to empathise with those for whom poverty was ever-present. After meeting MacDonald at Chequers, he attended the House of Commons on 23rd February and heard Wood speak on George Lansbury's estimates for Labour exchanges.[593] This was not the purpose of his visit though, for it was Ellen Wilkinson that he asked to meet in particular, the reason being, explained one newspaper, that "Red Ellen's outspoken speeches ... are still fresh in his memory".[594] In sharp contrast, eight months later the Chairman of the Covent Garden Opera Syndicate (formed in 1930 with the BBC as a shareholder) was blaming its financial difficulties on "the great National Crisis, the abandonment of the gold standard,

---

[593] Hansard, 23rd February 1931, vol. 248, cols. 1797, 1798, 1822-1826
This was also the day on which the Unemployment Insurance (No. 2) Bill received its third reading. Ibid, cols. 1896-1922
Glasgow Evening Citizen, East Anglian Times & Manchester Guardian all 24th February 1931, KW17 256/10, 256/12 & 257/1
[594] *Sheffield Independent* 24th February 1931, KW17 256/11

the formation of the National Government and the general election".[595] If even Covent Garden was feeling the economic chill, how much colder it must have been for most people.

Trade and Tariffs

A belief in Free Trade was one of the defining features of Liberalism and reason enough, Dingle Foot (1905-1978)[596] argued, for supporting Labour against the Conservative Party pursuit of tariff reform and protectionism. The Conservatives had re-adopted this stance in 1927 (having taken it previously in 1923) and Ball describes it as one of the three major policy crises confronting the Party in the 1930s (along with India and appeasement).[597] Churchill retained his belief in Free Trade and, combined with his opposition to the Party's policy on India, found himself isolated during this period:

> In the early 1930s Churchill was still widely mistrusted by members of all Parties. ... It was still true, as was said of him by the Tory leaders in 1916, that 'There is no man who has more admirers and fewer followers'.[598]

There were many reasons for this mistrust, among which Gallipoli, the gold standard and the General Strike were just specific examples of faulty judgement and a predisposition for action. There were also doubts over his personal as well as Party loyalty. As Wood was to say in 1935, Churchill "as a boy was hurt by a bad fall while playing 'follow my leader' - a contingency, [he] added, from which Mr Churchill seemed quite safe today".[599] Wood was referring to the position Churchill had taken, in opposition to his

---

[595] Briggs, 1995, op cit, p168

[596] Dingle Foot, 'British Political Crises', 1976, pp120
As Liberal MP for Dundee, Foot retained the constituency in the 1935 general election but lost it in the Labour landslide of 1945. After joining the Labour Party he became MP for Ipswich from 1957-1970.
One of his brothers Michael Foot (1913-2010) was a Labour MP for nearly fifty years and the main author of 'Guilty Men' in 1940.
Their father Isaac Foot (1880-1960) was a Liberal MP.

[597] Ball, 2013, op cit, pp477-497

[598] Foot, op cit, pp119-120

[599] *NA* undated but April 1935, KW19 352/3, reporting Wood's speech to the 72nd annual dinner of the Newspaper Press Fund.

party leaders, over Indian independence. Churchill would adopt a contrary line again in 1936 over Edward VIII's abdication, though the one he is mainly known for is agitation for speedier re-armament.

Countries across the world deployed tariffs as a way of protecting their own markets, an approach that became increasingly prevalent as the economic downturn worsened, but also one that was internationally short-sighted and globally hazardous. In September 1929 the League of Nations identified the need for a tariff truce, drawing up a preliminary draft convention for debate.[600] Although Britain agreed to participate in the forthcoming conference, India, Australia and South Africa refused, making the necessity for trade agreements within the Empire even more of a priority for the Conservative Party while Labour sought to maintain the country's global profile as well.[601] "Tariff truce" was not just a colloquial term but the description given to, and recorded in, parliamentary debates, thereby demonstrating that it was thought of as economic war. Wood had asked the President of the Board of Trade William Graham about this, seeking confirmation that ratification would be subject to parliamentary debate.[602] Graham, an MP since 1918 and therefore Wood's parliamentary contemporary, subsequently referred to a Command Paper laid before Parliament on 8th April.[603] The convention had been signed by eighteen countries by mid-April, fourteen of which were in Europe (the others being Colombia, Japan, Peru and Turkey). Graham accepted that the convention was just the beginning,[604] but given the omissions from the list (all of the Empire apart from Britain, and of course the United States and Russia who were outside the League of Nations) and that it required further work from the few signatories, it was soon branded a failure that could only have a cosmetic impact. Philip Cunliffe-Lister (1884-1972), Graham's Conservative predecessor as President of the Board of Trade and another 1918 entrant to Parliament, pointed out that Canada had "refused to have anything to do with this Tariff Truce",

---

[600] Hansard, 9th December 1929, vol. 233, cols. 16-17
[601] Hansard, 24th December 1929, vol. 233, cols. 2091-2093
[602] Hansard, 1st April 1930, vol. 237, col. 1057
[603] Hansard, 15th April 1930, vol. 237, cols. 2759-2760
'Preliminary Conference With a View to Concerted Economic Action. Commercial Convention and Protocol, Protocol Regarding Future Negotiations, and Final Act', Cmd 3539
[604] Hansard, 29th April 1930, vol. 238, col. 19

indeed had "warned [Graham about it] in advance", but was reducing its tariffs of its own accord. Cunliffe-Lister concluded:

> If the President of the Board of Trade [Graham] would seek the interests of British industry, he would turn his mind away from the Tariff truce, he would cease to make gestures at Geneva, but would make them to his own people - he would make offers to his own countrymen here and in the Empire.[605]

During a by-election that April in the midst of a tariff dispute with the United States, Neville Chamberlain recorded Wood saying that "the canvas [sic] of the back streets shows that the new policy [of protectionism] has not caught on". However, Chamberlain continued "But then [Wood] is very lukewarm himself and I rather discount his information on that account".[606] Not surprisingly, the Woolwich United Empire Party wanted to know Wood's position in relation to protective tariffs, with their Honorary Secretary seeking clarity through one of the local papers.[607] Wood's response, confirming his endorsement of trade within the Empire, came two months later:

> Surely it is the height of folly to say today that because Cobden laid down a policy many years ago Free Trade is going to prevent us evolving a policy that will help business now. Soon we will find the Imperial conference a failure. Unless we are very careful the chance of trade with the Dominions will be too late.[608]

Wood expressed this view the day after a specially convened meeting of Conservative party peers, MPs and candidates at Caxton Hall, ostensibly to hear Baldwin set out Party policy but actually to vote on his leadership. The motion put forward by Colonel John Gretton (1867-1947)[609] that the unity of the Party depended on a Leader other than Baldwin was overwhelmingly

---

[605] Hansard, 14th May 1930, vol. 238, col. 2007

[606] Self, 2002, op cit, 4th April 1930, p175

[607] *Kentish Independent* 15th August 1930, KW17 220/4

[608] *Kentish Mercury* 31st October 1930, KW17 226/15

[609] He would stand alongside Churchill in opposing the Government of India Bill 1931-1935.

defeated by 462 votes to 116.[610] Later that day a meeting was held in Woolwich, one that in all likelihood Wood had arranged in advance either so that his constituents could receive speedy feedback on the Caxton Hall meeting or perhaps so that Wood could put his hat in the ring had Baldwin been defeated for the leadership. Wood argued that "no leader of any party had been subjected to a more severe test, and Mr Baldwin had come out of the ordeal triumphantly". Wood believed the minority who had voted against Baldwin would show themselves loyal to the Party and most of them "would ... accept the verdict of the meeting".[611]

The Liberal and Labour parties were also showing signs of strain. Although Liberal acquiescence had bolstered the Labour government, and three-quarters of the Liberal MPs wanted to keep them in power as a check against protection, some (including Sir John Simon) were keen to end the Socialist government immediately.[612] The Liberal leader Lloyd George continued to plot, as he was constitutionally predisposed and certainly accustomed to do, while the Liberal Chief Whip Sir Robert Hutchison (1873-1950) resigned - though not necessarily to join the Conservatives.[613] Within the Labour Party, tension between the leadership and the left-wing Independent Labour Party members who wanted more far-reaching and faster change[614] was amplified by that between the leaders themselves. Wood went so far as to ask Philip Snowden if the "Chancellor of the Exchequer and the Prime Minister were on speaking terms", to which he got the reply he deserved when Snowden responded that "Both our personal and our official relationships appear to be much more harmonious than those of the leaders of the party opposite".[615]

At the end of that month a meeting of the Conservative National Council was held at the Kingsway Hall, with the *Times* announcing that the business would include "uncompromising opposition" to amendment of the Trades Disputes Act and the

---

[610] *Manchester Guardian* 31st October 1930, KW17 228/1

[611] Ibid

[612] *Daily Express* 6th November 1930, KW17 227/4

[613] He would become a Liberal National under Simon's leadership in 1931. Foot, op cit, p124 refers to Walter Runciman (1870-1949) and Leslie Hore-Belisha as other leading members, as was Ernest Brown (1881-1962).

[614] Snell, op cit, pp230-232 judged their attempts to bring about "Socialism in our time" ineffective.

[615] *The Star* 10th November 1930, KW17 226/12

prospect of a Shadow Cabinet comprising "new men".[616]   Eight hundred delegates heard Wood move the Executive Committee report, agreeing that the next annual conference be held in Birmingham as proposed. Wood referred to the huge loss to the Party that the recent deaths of Arthur Balfour and Lord Birkenhead[617] represented before a newly fortified Baldwin responded to Lord Bayford's motion that

> ... the Council expresses its implicit and unabated confidence in Mr Stanley Baldwin as Leader of the Conservative and Unionist Party, and its grateful appreciation of the eminent services he has rendered to the Party at all times.

This was carried unanimously and Baldwin was not only cheered to the rafters but accompanied by "musical honours" as he got up to speak. Wood had clearly been correct that the majority of the Party would, and had, put their doubts behind them.

Baldwin opened by remarking that the Conservatives were now "the only united party in the country" (more cheers) before going on to say that

> We meet today at a moment of unparalleled national depression. The clouds lying over the country have never been so thick, so heavy and so dark. ... The party has had two very difficult years, difficult at the end of our time in office, difficult in opposition. While we were struggling with the aftermath of that disastrous year of 1926 the Socialists were working up and down the country ... building, on shifting sands as they will find, a marvellous palace of promises.

---

[616] *Times* 24th November 1930
In the event, however, Baldwin made it clear in his speech that it was up to him as Party leader who he invited to join the Shadow Cabinet and people should stop grousing.
[617] Balfour was 81 when he died in March, whereas Birkenhead, his brilliance squandered, was struck down by pneumonia at the age of 58. The day after Birkenhead's death eight weeks earlier Wood had said at the Junior Constitutional Club, Piccadilly that Birkenhead "would be remembered by members of the club as a great advocate, a keen party man, an outstanding Lord Chancellor, and a wise counsellor". This harked back to Birkenhead's career a decade earlier. *Times* 2nd October 1930, KW17 223/1

... and from the moment the Socialists came in, and when they had to leave the land of promise for the land of performance - from that moment their fate was sealed and their doom was written.[618]

Baldwin then described the recent Imperial Conference at which the Dominions urged on Britain the need to form an economic union that would provide mutual protection in the face of global trade depression:[619]

They warned this country of the dangers of delay; they warned it that an opportunity not seized might not arise again; and they have been sent home empty-handed, with merely an undertaking that some of these subjects might be discussed within a year at Ottawa [though in the event this was postponed]; and that is the only good thing that has come out of this Conference, because they will be discussed at Ottawa, and they will be discussed by our party [i.e., by then we will be back in government]. (Cheers) The Government had no policy at the Conference, and, indeed ... they could not have because ... the Government is controlled, and absolutely controlled, by the knot of bigoted and fanatical free-traders led by the Chancellor of the Exchequer, who nevertheless at last has made his great contribution to the solution of the unemployment problem by subsidizing Covent Garden Opera. (Laughter)
[Whereas the Conservatives would have put the Dominions' proposal to the country as if their 1924 pledges still applied, there] has been a want of courage, a want of imagination, in the Socialist party that is disastrous. I made an offer only in July, and I made it in all sincerity ... if [the Government] would promote any steps that they chose to take in the way of tariffs or preference with the Dominions, we would support them; and the Chancellor of the Exchequer laughed at me. But he laughs best who laughs last. (Cheers)

---

[618] *Times* 26th November 1930
[619] The Imperial Economic Conference had taken place on 8th October 1930 in London when Canada had led the way in proposing imperial preference.

Baldwin was not just rallying the faithful but re-energising them, rehearsing the motion censuring the Government he would put before the Commons the following day and re-motivating the most active workers for the battle ahead. In the Commons Baldwin's motion, accusing Labour of not taking steps to extend Empire trade or consider the offers made by the Dominions, received more than six hours of debate, before being defeated by 299 votes to 234 along party lines, with enough Liberals supporting Labour to see the Government through.[620] Wood had voted but he did not speak. In addition to the report in the *Times* the following day, a leading article described it as 'A Disappointing Debate'.[621] Although it acknowledged that the Government had "failed lamentably to take advantage of the great opportunity presented by the Imperial Conference", the debate was "not illuminating" and Baldwin was "not inspiring". MacDonald was absent as he was attending the Round-Table Conference on India and JH Thomas who replied for the Government instead was "even more disappointing" than Baldwin. The Government had failed to set out, let alone clarify, its plans and intentions so everybody's hopes were thwarted. The article concluded that "The whole debate was an opportunity wasted," a "lost chance" as another *Times* article put it.

The following day in Cardiff Austen Chamberlain repeated the indictment that the Government had failed to appreciate "the real gravity of the unemployment problem" and squandered the opportunity of the Imperial Conference,[622] but there was an absolute distaste for protection on the Labour and Liberal benches and a fear that tariffs meant more expensive food. Furthermore, the Conservatives had yet to convince enough waverers of the force of their argument for imperial preference. There was insufficient impetus to put aside party ideology and therefore no agreement as yet on how best to serve the public interest or, as is often the case in adversarial politics, no solution acceptable to both sides presented itself. Circumstances would soon change that.

National Economy

In his book on the 1931 financial crisis, Robert (now Lord) Skidelsky writes that "The real story of the domestic politics of the inter-war

---

[620] Hansard, 27th November 1930, vol. 245, cols. 1539-1662
[621] *Times* 28th November 1930
[622] *Times* 29th November 1930

period is the defeat of the economic radicals by the economic conservatives",[623] with business opposed to government intervention to benefit the working-class but not when it was in their interests - in other words, against socialism but in this instance for tariff reform to protect them against foreign competition.[624] In practical terms, therefore, *laissez faire* was acceptable only when businesses benefitted and in circumstances that favoured them.[625] To the arguments the Conservatives made for protectionism to reduce unemployment, therefore, should be added the business perspective based mainly on considerations of profit - though they would of course argue that continuing employment depended on their survival.

Three days before he died in February 1931, Laming Worthington-Evans, the Conservative MP for St George's Westminster, opened a debate on national economy by censuring the Government

> ...for its policy of continuous additions to the public expenditure at a time when the avoidance of all new charges and strict economy in the existing services are necessary to restore confidence and promote employment.[626]

Wood spoke briefly only once and, though the motion was defeated by 310 to 235 votes, the Commons did agree overwhelmingly (by 468 votes to 21) an amendment to establish "a small and independent committee" to advise the Chancellor of the Exchequer on "all practicable and legitimate reductions in the national expenditure consistent with the efficiency of the services". This was the May Committee, set up to restore confidence given "the effect of the present burden of taxation in restricting industry and employment".[627]

---

[623] Robert Skidelsky, 'Politicians and the Slump: The Labour Government of 1929-1931', 1967, pxi

[624] Ibid, p12

[625] This is reminiscent of the distinction applied to the 2008 financial crash between the privatisation of profit and the nationalisation of losses.

[626] Hansard, 11th February 1931, vol. 248, col. 427; *Times* 12th February 1931, KW17 245/8

Worthington-Evans' death on 14th February led to the by-election on 19th March 1931 won by Duff Cooper.

[627] Hansard, 11th February 1931, vol. 248, cols. 549-550

Wood grasped a further opportunity to nettle Snowden at questions the following week when he not only asked about Government proposals to tackle the financial crisis but suggested that Cabinet members might wish to contribute directly. Snowden initially replied that he could not add to his comments in the national economy debate. Wood pressed him:

"As the right hon. Gentleman then stated that the national situation was so grave that it demanded temporary sacrifices from us all, does he not think that an early statement of the proposals is urgent?"
Snowden: "I congratulate the right hon. Gentleman on the tenacity of his memory."
Wood: "Will the right hon. Gentleman say something about the latter part of my question with reference to the contribution from Members of the Cabinet; is it not a fact that gifts which are given quickly are given doubly?"
Snowden: "I have nothing at present to add to the observations I have made."[628]

Wood had had no instant result but it was an issue that he was not prepared to drop, for even if Cabinet ministers such as the impervious Snowden could not be seen on the outside to squirm, they might be doing so within. And, more importantly, the hypocrisy would not be lost on a country whose standard of living was at risk (through unemployment, the international depression and cuts to public expenditure).

In April he asked the Financial Secretary to the Treasury Frederick Pethick-Lawrence about Law Officer salaries and fees in the nine months to the end of March (actually 10th June 1929 to 31st March 1931). In addition to the Attorney-General's £12,654 salary, Jowitt had received £26,564 in fees, making over £39,000 in total. The two Solicitors-General (Stafford Cripps from 27th October 1930 and his predecessor) had received £18,500 between them. These huge sums are equivalent to about £1.5m and £650,000 today. Wood continued provocatively "May I ask if this is Socialism in our time?", a rhetorical question that received no answer.[629] In Wood's

---

[628] Hansard, 16th February 1931, vol. 248, cols. 879-880
[629] Referring to the title of the 1926 ILP manifesto and possibly Snell's judgement on it. Hansard, 15th April 1931, vol. 251, col. 182; *Times* 16th April 1931, KW17 268/4

favour it might be argued that he was making a moral point rather than just engaging in political needling.

Two weeks later Wood and Pethick-Lawrence clashed again, first about the Law Officers and then on the more general point:

Wood: "[What is] the proposal that the Law Officers have made for a reduction of their emoluments; what is the estimated amount of the proposed annual reduction; ... is [this] retrospective and also a free gift to the Exchequer for the forthcoming year, or ... permanent ...?"
Pethick-Lawrence: "I am not in a position at present to make any further announcement on the subject."
Wood: "Seeing that the Chancellor of the Exchequer informed us that this offer had been made, why is there any secrecy concerning it?"
Pethick-Lawrence: "Seeing that the English Law Officers have, on their own initiative, made an offer to forgo part of their emoluments, I think it would be more seemly if hon. Gentlemen opposite would curb their impatience until the details are available."
Wood: "Will the hon. Gentleman, at any rate, state whether the Chancellor of the Exchequer has closed with the offer?"
Pethick-Lawrence: "I have nothing further to add at present."
Wood: "[Can he now state what] contributions ... are to be made by Members of the Cabinet to assist the national financial situation; and whether the same will be made by way of deduction from Ministerial salaries and be retrospective?"
Pethick-Lawrence: "I am not at present in a position to add anything to what my right hon. Friend [i.e., Snowden] has said on this subject."
"Wood: "What is the secrecy about this matter? Has anything gone wrong? Is anybody backing out of it?"[630]

Although this might appear tangential, even a side issue, in the context of the overall crisis, it was a powerful symbol of a Government coming under increasing pressure on many fronts. The *Morning Post* gleefully reported,[631] for example, that the Government had been defeated six times in the previous year:

| 11th March 1930 | Coal Mines Bill | lost by 8 |
| 31st March 1930 | Eleven o'clock Rule | lost by 4 |

[630] Hansard, 4th May 1931, vol. 252, cols. 35-36
[631] *Morning Post* 17th March 1931, KW17 263/1

21st January 1931	Education Bill	lost by 32
26th February 1931	Trade Disputes Bill	lost by 6
26th February 1931	Agricultural Marketing Bill	lost by 3

and most recently by four votes (246 to 242) over electoral reform (the Representation of the People No. 2 Bill) when, on the third day in Committee, eleven Liberals (including Sir John Simon) voted against the Government over a clause that would abolish University constituencies.[632]   Overall, the Government must have felt increasingly helpless, even impotent, if not yet fear and panic. However, after a couple of days reflection MacDonald indicated that the Government would bring the Bill back after the Easter recess, the "pressure of financial business" preventing them from doing so before then.[633] It did reappear on 22nd April for its fourth day in Committee, monopolizing much of the Commons time on this and subsequent days.[634]   Eventually, the third reading on 2nd June passed by 278 votes to 228 but it was not enacted.[635]

In early March, ten days before his speech that clinched a Conservative victory in the St George's by-election, Baldwin had already assured Wood "that he did not intend to go till he was kicked out!"[636]

When Snowden presented his Budget speech on 27th April, he started by taking the unprecedented step of referring MPs to a

---

[632] Hansard, 16th March 1931, vol. 249, cols. 1695-1811
It had been considered previously by the House in Committee on 4th and 5th March (Ibid, cols. 415-538 on Clause 2 and cols. 623-732). Wood voted in every division but only contributed the very occasional barbed aside.
The second reading on 2nd and 3rd February had passed by 295 votes to 230 (Ibid, vol. 247, cols. 1467-1588, 1653-1774). Wood did not speak but had done so previously on 22nd January when he asked why the title of the revised Bill seemed to be at odds with its contents: "Have these lost Clauses yet been discovered? Where is the Clause relating to the funds of political associations?" (Ibid, vol. 247, col.345) and on 29th January when the opportunity for two barbs at the price of one proved too much for him: "Why should we not have an extra day for the Electoral Reform Bill, instead of this mock battle between the Prime Minister and the right hon. Gentleman the Member for Carnarvon Boroughs (Mr. Lloyd George)?" (Ibid, vol. 247, col. 1150).
[633] Hansard, 18th March 1931, vol. 249, col. 2038
[634] Hansard, 22nd April 1931, vol. 251, cols. 985-1116, 1177-1286; vol. 252, cols. 1013-1134
[635] Hansard, 2nd June 1931, vol. 253, cols. 43-166
[636] Self, 2002, op cit, 7th March 1931, p244

printed statement of income and expenditure for the previous year (1930-31).[637] This showed revenue undershooting by £13.5m, supplementary estimates of £14.9m (£10.5m of which had been for the Ministry of Labour "arising from exceptional unemployment") and an overall shortfall of £23m. Turning to 1931-32, Snowden proposed to raise an additional £37.5m in order to balance the Budget - partly by increasing the oil duty (a tax that in other circumstances he would wish to remove altogether) but mainly by bringing forward some income tax payments. He had made no provision for supplementary expenditure even though it "would be contrary to all experience if no item should arise during the year". Any such requirements could be met from increased taxation in the unlikely event that "prosperity should return", but otherwise the gap

> should be met by economy, and for that reason I shall anxiously await the recommendations of the [May] committee which is at the moment examining the field of national expenditure on the instruction of all parties in the House of Commons. [638]

In summarising the outlook the Chancellor was candid:

No one [a year ago] had foreseen the full extent of the crisis, financial and industrial, through which the world was about to pass or had realised how slow recovery would be. When much later the position had become clear, there was of course no lack of prophecies of complete ruin and disaster to our finances. ... [T]he position continues to be grave and ... the finances of next year may present difficult problems. Indeed, if the world depression fails meanwhile to lift, reduction of expenditure will be the only alternative to increased taxation. For these reasons ... the proposals ... from the Economy Committee and the Unemployment Commission [will be critical].
... If we can effect substantial economies during the year, and if there is some improvement in trade, I do not think next year's Budget will be unduly alarming, but failing this a

[637] It was made clear to Snowden that this was acceptable on this occasion, but in future an oral report would be expected as usual. Hansard, 27th April 1931, vol. 251, cols. 1391-1395
[638] Hansard, 27th April 1931, vol. 251, col. 1408

heavy increase of taxation will be inevitable ... which I have this year happily been able to avert.[639]

This enabled Snowden to confirm that the main feature of the Budget would be the re-introduction of the Land Valuation Bill, trailed a year earlier but dropped then because of the pressure of other business.   Valuation would be the first step, a process expected to take two years, enabling tax to be raised from 1933-34. This would start initially at one penny in the £ on (i.e., 1/240th of) the capital value.   Snowden did not say at this stage how much he expected the tax to raise, but even at this modest starting-point (0.4% in effect) the amount would be substantial.   A special Resolution would be required of the Commons in order for this future taxation to be included in the Finance Bill.   Snowden was clear about the justification:

> The proposals ... will, I am convinced, be heartily welcomed and supported by the great majority of the House ... and the country.   The scandal of the private appropriation of land values created by the enterprise and industry of the people and by the expenditure of public money has been tolerated far too long.   In asserting the right of the community to a share in what has been created by the community, we are taking a step which will be approved not only by the Labour and Liberal parties, which have long advocated this reform, but also by a large number of Conservatives, whose sense of justice is outraged by glaring examples of the exploitation of the public by private land monopolists.   The present system stands in the way of social and economic progress, inflicts crushing burdens on industry and hinders municipal development.[640]

The following day Neville Chamberlain asked the Prime Minister what the procedure for the land tax Resolution would be, with MacDonald confirming that it would come before the House two days later and, if approved, would then go before the Committee of Ways and Means[641] the following Monday, when the Chancellor

---

[639] Ibid, cols. 1408-1409

[640] Ibid, col. 1411

[641] The House of Commons sitting as a Committee to consider the 'ways and means' or taxation needed to raise revenue for the Government.

would make a full statement of his proposals.[642] When Snowden then brought the Resolution before the House it was speedily passed to the Committee without a vote,[643] but this belied the lengthy discussions that would follow. Snowden's motion occupied nearly all of Monday's business and another seven hours on Wednesday 6th before eventually being agreed by 289 votes to 230 along party lines. Wood had remained silent but voted with his fellow Conservatives against it.[644] The Report stage took another six hours on Thursday 7th and three divisions before the Resolution was finally passed at 1.00am on Thursday 8th by a depleted 166 votes to 94.[645] The attrition of parliamentary debate had seen off all but the hard core, with even MacDonald, Snowden, Clynes, Henderson, Attlee, Lloyd George and Churchill having paired off. But Baldwin, Wood and both Chamberlains remained on the Conservative bench, as did Greenwood, Lansbury, Bondfield, Lawrence and Pethick-Lawrence on the Labour side. Sir John Simon spoke briefly but did not vote in any of the divisions.

The Finance Bill's second reading on 19th May[646] was agreed by 270 votes to 230 and the Committee stage started on 8th June,[647] six weeks after Snowden had sat down at the end of his Budget speech and only seven weeks before the end of July, by which time MPs would have expected the summer recess to start. It was still in Committee on 24th June, eventually receiving royal assent on 31st July. When the Committee Chairman had moved closure on the third day of its discussion (10th June), there had been cries of "shame" and "gag", and when "Conservatives had shouted 'Send for the Speaker', the Socialists retorted 'Send for the nursemaid'".[648] The following day, the Bill's fourth in Committee, started with Wood questioning Stafford Cripps, the Solicitor-General, about the technicalities of recording and registering land values and the places where the valuation register would be held. Wood was concerned that, if local authorities held the register, land values would eventually become the basis for rating. Cripps confirmed that this might well be the long-term intention, in accordance with the wishes of many local authorities, but the initial

---

[642] Hansard, 28th April 1931, vol. 251, col. 1452
[643] Hansard, 30th April 1931, vol. 251, cols. 1853-1863
[644] Hansard, 4th and 6th May 1931, vol. 252, cols. 47-169 & 405-528
[645] Hansard, 7th May 1931, vol. 252, cols. 659-748
[646] Hansard, 19th May 1931, vol. 252, cols. 1801-1944
[647] Hansard, 8th June 1931, vol. 253, cols. 635-778
[648] *Daily Express* 11th June 1931, KW17 280/2

purpose was taxation and rating would remain tied to improvement values for the moment.[649]

A Conservative MP[650] had asked the Chancellor twice at the end of April why the Government was not permitting commemorative Empire Day medals to be struck by the Royal Mint that year. Pethick-Lawrence replied that, though they had been distributed to children for the last three years, the Government thought this should be left to a private contractor, thereby neatly side-stepping the link to the Empire Union and imperial preference (and possibly cost) that the question was code for, and teasing the opposition at the same time.[651] In other words, if the Empire was of such importance that children should receive these commemorative medals, surely the private sector ought to step in to provide them.

Empire Day was officially 24th May but, whether it was not possible to hold all the events on the one day or because its supporters wanted to drag out the celebrations for as long as possible, it was still being marked in mid-June. Consequently, and curiously enough, the determination to maintain free trade that Snowden represented, and the passage of his Finance Bill through parliament, coincided with some of the events involving Wood, a link that he was bound to exploit. For example, he and Duff Cooper spoke at the Great Empire Festival at Eltham Parish Hall, including a message from Agnes to the women of Woolwich about her "many happy years [spent] in Australia".[652] Wood and his fellow MP Harold Balfour (1897-1988)[653] addressed the West Woolwich Conservative

---

[649] Hansard, 11th June 1931, vol. 253, cols. 1215-1216; *Times* 12th June 1931, KW17 281/2
The distinction was between domestic, agricultural, business or industrial improvements (i.e., added value, often through buildings) and "unimproved" land (whether agricultural, sporting or waste) which accounted for much of the overall capital value (i.e., wealth).
[650] Sir William Davison, MP for South Kensington 1918-1945
[651] Hansard, 21st and 28th April 1931, vol. 251, cols. 799-800 & 1444-1445
[652] Greenwich Heritage Centre, West Woolwich Conservative & Unionist Association folder, item 10 5th June 1931 - accessed 30th January 2013
This was in line with appeals to women voters more generally. See, for example, Laura Beers. "A model MP? Ellen Wilkinson, gender, politics and celebrity culture in inter-war Britain", *Cultural and Social History*, 2013, 10, pp231-250 (p237).
[653] Under-Secretary to Wood at the Air Ministry 1938-1940. Balfour remained at the Air Ministry until 1944 and, out of loyalty to the RAF (according to his DNB entry) turned down Churchill's offers that he

Association Empire Day Festival at Woolwich Town Hall.[654]   On both occasions Wood argued that the depression would be even worse without trade with the Empire, and said that when a Conservative Government was returned it would

> immediately enter into a conference with the Dominions to secure mutual commercial and economic development on a free and unrestricted basis.   Our aim will be mutual advantages for all. It is a policy worth fighting for and worth working for.

His wife added: "I believe much British business could be recovered if there is closer co-operation between Great Britain and Australia, and more can be done by mutual preferences".

At the end of June Wood returned to his question about voluntary reductions in the emoluments of Cabinet Ministers and Law Officers. This time he asked it of the Prime Minister, with Clynes answering on MacDonald's behalf that there was no further information on either. Wood continued as six weeks before: "What is the difficulty? The Chancellor of the Exchequer announced this three months ago. Is anybody backing out?" Clynes responded that Snowden had been urging "the necessity of general sacrifices being made, and said that the Cabinet were prepared to make a substantial contribution". He continued

> I appreciate the lofty motives which have prompted the right hon. Gentleman to press now for a reduction in his own future salary, but I can add nothing to my former reply.

A lesser, or at any rate less politically-attuned, man than Wood might have been distracted by the personal flattery in Clynes' response, as Clynes may have intended, and even in Wood's case there must have been a temptation to opt for a purely humorous rejoinder. Even if Wood judged that Clynes was only being realistic, his response maximised both the party political opportunity and the parliamentary levity when he then asked "Will interest be charged on the amount contemplated, so that we shall not lose over the

---

become Financial Secretary to Wood at the Treasury and then head up a civil Department of State of his own.
[654] *Sidcup Times* and *Kentish Independent* both 12th June 1931, KW17 281/1 & 283/1

matter?"[655]   As a supplementary question this can hardly be bettered in the hurly-burly of parliamentary procedure, particularly given the continuing crises that assailed the Government.

National Crisis

Although the ever-assiduous Wood continued to harry the Government in the Commons on a wide range of domestic issues during July, speaking extensively on the Housing (Rural Authorities) Bill for example,[656] unemployment and the consequent Government spend exercised him greatly (as to a lesser extent did the international financial crisis).   On 16th July the Prime Minister assured him that, if the report of the Economy Committee[657] was not available before the summer recess, it would be sent on to MPs. Wood continued: "May we assume that action will not be taken on the report before the House has had an opportunity of considering it?" To which MacDonald gave the non-committal reply: "I would like to have an opportunity of considering it first myself".[658]   On 20th July Wood asked the Chancellor for "the total amount of extra financial commitments incurred by the present Government since its accession to office".   Pethick-Lawrence, the Treasury Financial Secretary, said it was between £14m and £15m in the current year (over £500m today) "apart from transitional benefit". Wood pressed him for the grand total but, when Pethick-Lawrence asked him to put this down as a question, Wood commented "The hon. Gentleman ought to be able to tell us".[659]   Subsequently, Wood's formal question did receive a response on 31st July:

Pethick-Lawrence: "The total cost of transitional benefit in the current year was estimated at £35m [about £1.2bn today] in Command Paper 3890.[660] It is impossible to say what is the extra

---

[655] Hansard, 25th June 1931, vol. 254, col. 612; *Kentish Independent* 3rd July 1931, KW17 278/9

[656] Hansard, 10th July 1931, vol. 254, cols. 2444-2453 at second reading; 14th to 16th July 1931, vol. 255, during the Committee stage

[657] Following on from Assheton Pownall's similar query about the final Royal Commission report.

[658] Hansard, 16th July 1931, vol. 255, col. 758

[659] Hansard, 20th July 1931, vol. 255, col. 1066

[660] Margaret Bondfield, the Minister of Labour, had presented this 'Memorandum on the financial resolution to be proposed relative to unemployment insurance' to Parliament in June.

financial commitment incurred by the present Government. Transitional benefit was being paid before the Government took office, although its cost was not met by the late Government out of the Budget but out of the Unemployment Fund which was supported by loans. The growth of the charge is due largely to the increase in unemployment."

Wood: "Has not transitional benefit been very largely extended in its operation during the present Administration?"

Pethick-Lawrence: "The increased charge is due largely to increased unemployment."[661]

At which point another Conservative MP observed "Then really the Treasury know nothing whatever about what expenditure they have incurred", saving Wood the trouble of making this comment.

The situation was then made immeasurably worse when the May Committee Report was published on this last day before the summer recess.[662] Delaying its publication may have avoided an immediate schism in the Labour Party but it achieved little else for this was an incredibly crass decision and extraordinarily inept politics, especially when MPs had complained the day before that they were being asked to consider the Consolidated Fund (Appropriation) Bill in the absence of the Report.[663] Even though the Bank of England took in more gold that day than it paid out for the first time since 14th July,[664] the possibility of stability was immediately undermined and balancing the Budget again became the key issue.[665] The May Committee predicted a budget deficit of £120m which required an immediate retrenchment (reduction) of £100m, with two-thirds of this to come from Unemployment Insurance (£66.5m).[666] A "nation living beyond its means".[667]

---

[661] Hansard, 31st July 1931, vol. 255, col. 2623

[662] 'Report of Committee on National Expenditure', Cmd 3920
The Committee was established by a Treasury minute of 17th March 1931, with Lord Plender one of six members under Sir George May's chairmanship. Plender would later be one of the three members of the committee Wood set up in 1932 to examine the Post Office.

[663] Hansard, 30th July 1931, vol. 255, cols 2497-2620, the Bill's second reading. It passed all subsequent stages the following day 31st July.

[664] Hansard, 14th July 1931, vol. 255, col. 229; Youngson, op cit, p83

[665] Carlton op cit, p215

[666] Also, *Times* 1st August 1931 report (p10) and detailed analysis (p15). The latter refers to the May Committee Report having been published "last night", i.e., after the House rose, as does Harold Macmillan in 'Winds of

Baldwin asked the Prime Minister how the Government intended to tackle the Report and was told that a Cabinet Committee had been set up to consider it during the recess. MacDonald and Snowden were to be joined on the Committee by Arthur Henderson and JH Thomas, Secretaries for Foreign and Dominion Affairs respectively, and by William Graham, President of the Board of Trade.[668] On the face of it this was a very high-powered Committee, comprising four of the Government's most senior members, and with trade well-represented. Significantly, however, none of the Ministers responsible for domestic affairs, particularly Clynes and Bondfield, would be present even though they had a huge stake in the outcome and excellent links to the backbenches. Mischievously, and misleadingly, the *Evening Standard* reported that Wood had missed the opportunity to ask questions about the Report in the Commons because, it claimed, he was not there but presiding at the Conservative Central Council.[669] He may have been later but, given that Baldwin's question to MacDonald had immediately followed Wood's about financial commitments, the article was inaccurate and perhaps designed to deflect attention from the Report itself.

As might be expected in August, high summer and often a government's "high noon" as well, things heated up almost immediately. On Monday 3rd August the report of a Cabinet split over the Committee's proposals was denied, while questions already tabled included one from Wood asking whether the Chancellor had any early actions in mind to address the Committee's recommendations and how spend was to be curtailed over the summer.[670]

On Tuesday the *Times* leader, entitled 'End of a Chapter', began

The rising of Parliament last Friday [with the intention that it not re-assemble until Tuesday 20th October[671]] was

---

Change 1914-1939', 1966, p267. Macmillan also makes the point that "... the wish to avoid Parliamentary debate might equally be due to the desire to preserve the Labour Government as to destroy it during the recess".
[667] As the May Committee had revealed, according to CPA PUB 146/2 *The Elector*, September 1931, p1
[668] Hansard, 31st July 1931, vol. 255, cols. 2623-2624
[669] *Evening Standard* 31st July 1931, KW17 277/3
[670] *Times* 3rd August 1931
[671] Hansard, 31st July 1931, vol. 255, cols. 2638 & 2734

technically an adjournment, but in reality it was the end of the session that began last October. The King's speech then ... recognized no probability of a crisis in international affairs, and the domestic measures which it foreshadowed recognized no special intensification of economic and industrial problems at home. ... There were traces of uneasiness in the document, but no sign of alarm. Even six months later the Budget was framed on much the same assumption that fundamental difficulties could be postponed in the hope that they might disappear. Today both the King's speech and the Budget are admittedly irrelevant to the actual situation. The onset of the international economic crisis ... [has] shown that a policy of drift at home and abroad ... is quite inadequate. ... Time has seldom brought a revenge so rapid ...

Its final sentence was:

Lack of leadership is the essential fault of this Parliament, and the lesson of the Session is that resolute leadership is necessary to re-establish both the faith of the nation in Parliament and the power of the nation to save itself.[672]

Its views of leading MPs included, among the Conservatives: Baldwin "not at his best as an Opposition leader", whereas Neville Chamberlain's "freedom from the cares of organising his party has been the nation's gain". Wood it thought "pertinacious at pertinent criticism" while Churchill "has resumed his proper place as an individualist. His party has not suffered and the House has gained".

The following week MacDonald returned to London as the crisis deepened, "a welcome sign" the *Times* leader reported "that he, at least, knows that neither decision nor action can be safely postponed" until the Commons reconvenes in two months time. In the newspaper's view "He has not returned a day too soon".[673] By the end of the week the Cabinet Economy Committee had met and Samuel, Baldwin and Chamberlain had been summoned to Downing Street to meet with MacDonald. The Cabinet was to meet the following Wednesday. The crisis then intensified the following week as different views within the Cabinet, both of what was

---

[672] *Times* 4th August 1931, KW17 290/3
[673] *Times* 12th August 1931

required and what was politically acceptable, were magnified by an increasing fault line within the Labour Party itself. According to Self, Neville Chamberlain's strategy was to keep the focus on the £100m retrenchment so that MacDonald's options narrowed down to jettisoning either Snowden or Henderson. In Chamberlain's assessment the latter would necessitate a National Government with the Conservatives in order to restore confidence abroad and re-assure both bankers and other countries.[674]

Events then developed speedily and the National Government was formed on 24th August 1931.[675] As the *Times* reported, Conservative ex-ministers (including Neville Chamberlain, Cunliffe-Lister and Wood) had been in daily touch throughout the crises of the previous week, as had Baldwin once he arrived back from his holiday on the Saturday night. The Liberal delegates to the three-party discussions (Samuel and Maclean) and Lloyd George had also liaised closely, with an "immense amount of work at Buckingham Palace [having] fallen on Sir Clive Wigram" who had succeeded Stamfordham as the King's secretary a few months earlier.[676] Snell, with his ear to the ground, remarked that junior Ministers had no information on why the National Government had been formed, "They were simply the tragic orphans of the storm". The reason, Snell thought, was "known only to the Prime Minister himself and his Cabinet colleagues".[677]

---

[674] Self, 2006, op cit, pp154-157

[675] Retold, for example, in Philip Williamson, 'National Crisis and National Government: British Politics, the Economy and Empire, 1926-1932', 1992 and Stuart Ball, 'Baldwin and the Conservative Party: The Crisis of 1929-1931', 1988 in addition to those referred to already.
Also, John D Fair, "The Conservative basis for the formation of the National Government of 1931", *Journal of British Studies*, 1980, 19, pp142-164; John D Fair and John Hutcheson "British Conservatism in the twentieth century: An emerging ideological tradition" *Albion* 1987, 19, pp 549-578
CPA CRD 1/13/3 includes a financial diary of the crisis 15th July to 5th September 1931 as well as various publications produced in September 1931 to explain the crisis and the consequences.

[676] *Times* 25th August 1931, KW17 293/2

[677] Snell, op cit, p251
Snell had previously judged (p226) that Lloyd George was prepared to "... tolerate the Government for just so long as it did nothing in particular; but should it ever attempt to carry out its own party programme he would at once butcher it to make a Liberal holiday".

A full report of Monday's machinations appeared in the *Times* on Tuesday 25th August, though this did not get much nearer to explaining them:

> The Prime Minister yesterday tendered the resignation of the Ministry to the King, who entrusted Mr MacDonald with the task of forming a National Government for the sole purpose of meeting the present financial emergency. Mr Ramsay MacDonald accepted the commission, and is now in conference with Mr Stanley Baldwin and Sir Herbert Samuel, who are co-operating with him in the constitution of such an Administration.

The official statement confirmed that

> It will not be a Coalition Government in the usual sense of the term, but a Government of Cooperation for this one purpose.
> When that purpose is achieved the political parties will resume their respective positions.

To that end Parliament was expected

> ... to meet on September 8, when proposals [would] be submitted ... for a very large reduction of expenditure ... As the commerce and well-being, not only of the British nation, but of a large part of the civilised world, has been built up and rests upon a well-founded confidence in sterling, the new Government will take whatever steps may be deemed by them to be necessary to justify the maintenance of that confidence unimpaired.[678]

On the Sunday (23rd August) MacDonald had concluded at first that he would have to resign as the Labour Cabinet was "hopelessly divided". However, George V asked him to sleep on it before seeing the three party leaders the following (Monday) morning and then leaving them alone to hammer out a solution. All the party leaders agreed that the old Cabinet of twenty-one Ministers was too large and that one of ten would be more appropriate to the task: four Labour, four Conservative and two

---

[678] *Times* article 'A National Cabinet' 25th August 1931

Liberal. Snowden would remain at the Treasury and Thomas at Dominions, while Baldwin preferred not to have a Department but assist MacDonald either as Lord President or Lord Privy Seal.[679] Although MacDonald's resignation was thought superfluous, it was done partly because

> ... a new Government was in effect being formed, partly the need for a free hand in dropping or retaining his old colleagues, and partly no doubt to provide a formal covering for the deep rift in the Labour ranks.

Then, once a "programme of retrenchment ... [had been agreed] to balance the Budget", the National Government was to be brought to an end, Parliament dissolved and "all who [had] taken part ... entitled to return to their old political allegiances". In the meantime the usual Conservative/Liberal hostilities were suspended, the first sign of which was the Liberal candidate standing down in the forthcoming Guildford by-election.[680]

Aware that Labour backbenchers thought he and Snowden had "committed political suicide", and that they were likely to replace him as quickly as possible as Labour party leader with Henderson, MacDonald went on BBC radio that day to appeal for confidence in the National Government.[681] Similarly, Baldwin immediately called a meeting of Conservative MPs and candidates for the coming Friday (28th August) to explain his position. With Wood presiding, Baldwin's ally, the Lancashire grandee and consummate political operator Edward George Villiers Stanley (1865-1948), 17th Earl of Derby, proposed that "This meeting supports the Leader of the party in his decision to take part in the formation of a National Government to deal with the present

---

[679] Sankey was the fourth Labour Minister. Neville Chamberlain, Hoare and Cunliffe-Lister were the other three Conservatives. Herbert Samuel and Donald Maclean had represented the Liberals in the negotiations, but the Marquess of Reading would be the second Liberal in the Cabinet as Financial Secretary to the Treasury. Wood was appointed PS to Maclean at the Board of Education.

[680] It was intended that no General Election would be held before the new electoral register was available in mid-October - actually held on 27th October 1931.

[681] Briggs, 1995, op cit, p129
Henderson became Labour Party leader two days later on 27th August 1931.

financial emergency".[682] No Liberal meeting had been called as yet though they were expected to endorse the outcome Samuel and Maclean had negotiated.

What was widely considered MacDonald's treachery within the Labour Party was remembered fifty years later when Dickie Beavis recalled an old Welsh miner telling him MacDonald "should have been hung on the back of the Brockwell [pit] cage and sent to coal work". Beavis added "And those words are as true today [the 1970s] as ever they were".[683]

The formation of the National Government satisfied America's criterion for the financial backing that they had previously withheld from the Labour government - indeed this had been a major part of the rationale for it in order to steady the nerves of investors and bankers - and the US President Herbert Hoover (1874-1964) officially sanctioned a credit of £80m on the 27th August. To the extent that this restored confidence in sterling and the Government's financial equilibrium if not quite its credibility, it helped smooth their intended spending reductions.   However, organisations like the TUC disputed the necessity for the savage welfare retrenchment, effectively declaring war on the Government's economy plans. A manifesto was issued jointly by the TUC General Council, the Labour Party's National Executive Committee and the Parliamentary Labour Party Consultative Committee explaining that

> The justification offered ... is the existence of a financial crisis which has been aggravated beyond measure by deliberately alarmist statements in sections of the Press, and by the fact that a protracted campaign has created the impression abroad that Great Britain is on the verge of bankruptcy. Nothing could be further from the truth.

On the contrary, it argued, £4000m of British capital (the equivalent of about £140bn today) was invested abroad and therefore Britain

[682] *Daily Telegraph* 29th August 1931, KW17 293/4
CPA NUA 4/2/1 Reports of the Executive Committee to the Central Council: An emergency meeting of the Executive Committee was briefed by Neville Chamberlain, also on the 28th August. This was reported to the Central Council on 8th March 1932. Further detail of the meeting is provided in CPA NUA 4/1/5 National Union Executive Minute Book pp468-470.
[683] See Armstrong and Beynon (eds.), op cit, pp16-23

remained "one of the greatest creditor countries".[684] In the view of one economic historian today:

> The device of a national government was a superb political ploy, neutering both right and left, in the classic style of Whig statecraft. Yoked together, MacDonald and Baldwin could now do what they had done separately in the 1920s, which was to crowd out extremism.[685]

Nevertheless, this symbolised Britain's move from the creditor nation it had been before WWI to the debtor one that it was subsequently.

In the middle of the crisis Lord Hailsham, who as Douglas Hogg had been Attorney-General and then (from 1928) Lord Chancellor in Baldwin's administrations in the 1920s, and was to be Lord Chancellor again when Baldwin was once more Prime Minister after 1935, had issued 'A clarion call to the country' (as one newspaper described it) in his speech as guest of honour at the West Woolwich Conservative Association fete.[686] "There was a good collection of MPs there," another newspaper reported,

> ... prominent amongst them the indefatigable Sir Kingsley Wood, who has been described as the model MP, and his faithful henchwoman, Lady Wood, a political campaigner who combines skill with affability. Blessed is the candidate or member who has a good-looking and tactful wife.[687]

At the end of the month Wood explained to Woolwich residents that the National Government had been formed:

> ... to deal with an urgent national emergency - an emergency comparable in many respects to war.
> It is a Government of National Safety.
> It has been formed in response to the urgent demand for national unity.

---

[684] *Daily Mail* 28th August 1931, KW17 294/3

[685] Robert Skidelsky, 'Britain Since 1900: A Success Story?', 2014, p211

[686] *South Eastern Mercury* 18th August 1931, KW17 292/1; also *Kentish Independent and Kentish Mail* 21st August 1931, KW17 293/1

[687] *South Eastern Mercury* 18th August 1931, KW17 288/11

It has been constituted without thought of political advantage or party precedent.

It is a complete refutation that the urgent steps that will have to be taken are inspired either by class prejudice or 'reactionary' policy.

Our first and only consideration must be the good of the nation and the financial stability of the country.

... The formation of the National Government shows also that Great Britain realises the grave character of the economic situation, and that the country will 'face up' to it and, I believe, will 'back' it.

The nation has only to be told the truth and when that has been done there has always been a full response by rich and poor. It once again demonstrates to the world that the British people will face their difficulties in good heart and spirit.

There is an urgent need for immediate action, and amongst the employed and the unemployed the spirit of self-sacrifice will not be absent.

The National Government has been formed to carry out an urgent national task. I appeal to every one of my constituents to help them in their great work.[688]

This oratory, some of which is reminiscent of Churchill's call to arms in World War II, must have been compelling at a time when political appeals and justifications are less common than they are now. Explaining the need for the National Government was one thing, perhaps difficult, but not nearly so complex as conveying the rationale for joining it yourself - especially when you had spent much of your political career thus far denigrating the Labour Party and particularly MacDonald. Explaining and justifying his membership of the National Government was the task facing Wood when he agreed to be Parliamentary Secretary at the Board of Education, in other words deputy to the Liberal Maclean.[689] Wood's long letter, nominally addressed to his constituency chairman FT Halse but essentially for his constituents, which to his credit did not duck the issue of his apparent hypocrisy, appeared in the *Kentish Independent*:

---

[688] *Kentish Mercury* 28th August 1931, KW17 293/3
[689] *Bristol Times and Mirror* 5th September 1931, KW17 294/4

... I have felt it my duty to accept the invitation to become a Minister in the new National Government, believing as I do that at this grave and difficult time that each one of us should be prepared to act in any capacity and in any post that may be deemed best to serve our country.

During the last ten days of crisis I have been in close touch with the situation, and at Mr Baldwin's request served with my Conservative colleagues in helping to advise him as to the best course our party should take in the national interests. We have been animated by no other object than to rescue the nation from [the] immediate financial peril that confronted it and ... we have no thought of party or political advantage. We have in no way sacrificed our principles ...

Critic as I have always been of Mr MacDonald, it is to the knowledge of the great majority of the country that he has with Mr Snowden and Mr Thomas taken a great and patriotic course, in company with Mr Lloyd George, Sir John Simon and others, and our own leaders ... we determined to take immediate and effective steps to rescue Great Britain from the real and imminent danger of a serious depreciation of British credit.

Few will believe that such patriotic men would, as has already been so wildly and foolishly alleged, 'humbug' our people into needless sacrifices. Labour men and women will not accept the slanderous suggestion that Mr MacDonald and Mr Snowden have been the tools of foreign financiers, or that the crisis is a 'ramp' so that the Government will be made to impose unfair or needless sacrifices.[690] As representative of this great constituency [i.e., Woolwich], I would not be party to any proposals that economise at the cost of the poor and let off the rich. ...

It was indeed only cowardice and incompetence in the face of a great national danger that caused the Labour Government to fail the nation in its hour of need and abandon its post.

---

[690] This is the same issue raised by Self, 2006, op cit, p152: The "principal remaining controversy" over 1931 events is whether it was a Conservative ramp with Neville Chamberlain exploiting the financial situation to ensure the National Government was under Conservative control; but even if this was not the outcome he sought, "it was the logical outcome of the strategy he had pursued throughout the preceding year".

You may have read recently the dangerous proposals just issued by the Labour Party under the leadership of Mr Arthur Henderson. ... If this country was mad or foolish enough to adopt them we should soon find ourselves in the unhappy and disastrous condition recently experienced by the people in Germany and Austria.[691]

The National Government has been formed to deal with the immediate crisis, but there will remain that other task to accomplish, the desperate position of our national trade and industry. We supported more than we could pay for, and so our unemployment figure reached catastrophic dimensions. This can only be dealt with by tariffs. This is the constructive side of our Conservative policy and programme. The steps we must now take are necessary expedients and temporary sacrifices, but we have got to restore our credit and trade, the first largely destroyed by the late Socialist Government, and the second seriously jeopardised by our effete and outworn Free Trade system. The next election will be fought on this issue. We shall fight to win, and we can only win by hard work and constant endeavour in making the truth known and the facts plain.

It is the duty of each one of us to support the National Government in its urgent, difficult, but temporary task, and, above all, to work unceasingly to bring about that change in the fiscal system which is the only alternative to further drift and disaster.[692]

Halse's reply was published later that month, drawing attention to what it called Wood's "right and courageous course".[693]

Although the naval mutiny at Invergordon in mid-September when reductions in service pay were believed to be imminent raised the prospect of revolution, as did the furore over unemployment benefit restrictions, the National Government deflected the immediate implications of the financial crisis. Nevertheless, the Means Test was particularly reviled for the genuine hardship it created:

---

[691] Though this had not stopped Wood going to Karlsbad in 1928. This is in Czechoslovakia, but only just.
[692] *Kentish Independent* undated, KW17 294/5
[693] *Kentish Mercury* 18th September 1931, KW17 297/3

The Means Test broke up many homes. After twenty-six weeks on unemployment pay one had to apply to this dreaded court ...
We had the brutal, vile Means Test. It was the birth-child of the 1929-1931 Labour Government ..." but implemented in full by the National Government
The Means Test lives in memory, / A scar upon their soul. / The land they'd fought for ... / Had put them on the Dole.[694]

On 21st September Britain was forced off the gold standard with slight improvements in the country's competitiveness as a result. This relieved some of the immediate pressure but the longer term remained uncertain. By the start of 1933 thirty million people were unemployed worldwide and forty countries had raised tariffs or put on import controls.[695] Britain was not, and could not, be immune to the consequences.

General Election

One immediate effect was that, rather than the National Government stabilising matters in the short-term and then disbanding in favour of a return to party allegiances, it continued on to fight the general election on 27th October 1931 when the Conservative part of the National Government won 470 of the 615 seats. Some commentators argue that, while the National Government might have been justified in continuing to the end of the financial year in March 1932 to demonstrate the budget was balanced and "to separate uninsured unemployment from insured unemployment", the Conservatives were determined to have an early election and impose tariffs thereafter as the only way the budget could really be "balanced".[696]

The National Government won a total of 556 seats at the 1931 general election, with seventy-four Liberal and twelve National Labour victories in addition to the Conservatives. Wood appreciated that the National Government's credibility depended on a high turn-out as well as on the size of the parliamentary victory:

---

[694] Charles Graham, John Bell and Mary Louise Walker de Medici in Armstrong and Beynon (eds.), op cit, pp27, 29 and 71
[695] Skidelsky, op cit, p384; Youngson, op cit
[696] Ramsay Muir, 'The Record of the National Government', 1936, pp35-36

If there is one man I would despise, it would be the man who does not do his duty and go to the polling both. I would sooner that man faced up to his responsibility to vote Socialist, detrimental as it is to the country, rather than he should not vote at all.[697]

He had made this point at an electoral rally in Sittingbourne, Kent for his position on the Conservative Party Executive required this prominent national profile. Wood was used to travelling widely so doing so on the stump was no hardship, though it must have meant that he was sufficiently confident of his constituency to be able to afford the time elsewhere. In the event he was rewarded on both counts: 21m people voted nationally out of just under 30m on the register, while the West Woolwich figure was even better at 79% (41,000 out of an electorate of 52,000); and, whereas Wood's majority in West Woolwich had been a slender 332 in 1929, it was now almost 12,000.[698]

The "opposition" comprised a Labour rump of fifty-two MPs and seven representing other parties. Many of the Labour party casualties were major party figures, including Henderson, Clynes, Greenwood, Addison, Pethick-Lawrence, Morrison, Graham, Alexander and Dalton, all of whom lost by less than 1000 votes, enabling Attlee and Cripps to leapfrog their seniors into the party leadership in parliament, alongside an increasingly symbolic Lansbury.[699] Dalton, though claiming not to be bitter, clearly was. He resented the positions in the party that Attlee and Cripps secured for the future, asserting that, had he not lost in this anomalous election, he would have been ahead of Attlee in the leadership pecking-order.[700]

---

[697] *Times* 19th October 1931, KW17 301/5

[698] Wood (C) 26,441, Reeves (Lab) 14,520. Majority 11,921 Also, *Times* 29th October 1931, KW17 307/4. Having contested several elections, William Barefoot had stepped aside as the Labour candidate to be replaced by Joseph Reeves, a member of Deptford Borough Council and secretary of the Royal Arsenal Co-operative Society (RACS) Education Department.

[699] Hugh Dalton, 'The Fateful Years: Memoirs 1931-1945', 1957, pp19-20 Lansbury was the designated leader but the leadership increasingly came from others.

[700] Dalton assesses his party colleagues on pp24-25, particularly remarking on the influence that Attlee and Cripps exerted over Lansbury.

Conservative-led though the National Government was, MacDonald remained as Prime Minister. His first dilemma, summed up in the cartoon on the next page, was to decide on the Cabinet from his home at Lossiemouth. It took him until 10th November to do so for, though Snowden had retired from the Commons, deciding on his successor at the Treasury was just one of the difficulties MacDonald had to resolve; Baldwin's position another. In the event Baldwin remained as Lord President ("the power behind the throne", to coin a phrase) and Neville Chamberlain became Chancellor of the Exchequer once again (the power behind the power), while John Simon and Herbert Samuel were "rewarded" with the Foreign and Home Office briefs respectively. The major surprise perhaps was that Hailsham went to the War Office, while the entirely inappropriate Charley Londonderry went to Air.[701] In a Cabinet doubled in size to twenty members, and split as expected twelve Conservative, four National Labour and four National Liberal,[702] Snowden became Lord Privy Seal, with Sankey remaining Lord Chancellor and JH Thomas retained at Dominions. Wood was appointed Postmaster-General, outside the Cabinet but a post with plenty of scope to advance or not as the incumbent chose.

In February 1932, a resolution to impose tariffs was carried in the Commons by 452 votes to 76. Even though seven Liberal Ministers were among the 'Noes', as were another twenty-one Liberals grimly hanging on to Cobden's free trade admonition,[703] the Conservative party had finally imposed its view.

---

[701] Charles Stewart Henry Vane-Tempest-Stewart (1878-1949), 7th Marquis of Londonderry was in the Lords (as was Viscount Hailsham). He was the husband of MacDonald's close friend and confidante, the society hostess Edith Stewart (1878-1959).
One of his ancestors was Robert Stewart (1769-1822), the 2nd Marquis and better known as Castlereagh, a hugely influential and hard-working Cabinet Minister at the start of the nineteenth century. (See Hugh Gault, '1809: Between Hope and History', 2009) Any resemblance to Londonderry was purely coincidental.
[702] *Daily Telegraph* 2nd November 1931, KW17 314/2
[703] *Daily Express* 10th February 1932, KW17 338/4

from *Yorkshire Observer* 5th November 1931, KW17 314/1

caption: "At a Lossie-Mouth" - Knowall: What about these Cabinet fireworks; don't you know it's the Fifth? Ramsay: Yes, but I am having a bit of trouble with the labels. You see I'm not quite sure **which of these things are bangers and which are not.**"

13.   POSTMASTER-GENERAL 1931-1935

Post Office[704]

Kingsley Wood was the nineteenth person to hold the office of Postmaster-General (PMG) in the twentieth century. Traditionally, it had been rare for people to stay in the post for more than a year or two and indeed only four of his recent predecessors had done so (Sidney Buxton, Herbert Samuel, Albert Illingworth and William Mitchell-Thomson[705]). Sometimes the post was a proving-ground for those on the way up (such as Austen and Neville Chamberlain[706]) and sometimes it was a sinecure reserved for those on their way out of government to ease their passage. There were opportunities for an outstanding politician to make their mark given the wide-ranging responsibilities (savings bank,[707] telegrams, parcels, letters and counter services, such as pension payments and licences for example, and subsequently telephones and the BBC), but the services depended for their effective operation on the competence of the Post Office staff who administered them. A PMG could stand aside, leave them alone and just be a political figurehead if he preferred and, while he might be questioned in Parliament, this was a limp form of accountability, often more theoretical than actual.

The structure of the Post Office was hierarchical, old-fashioned and Victorian, with all the authority for day-to-day

---

[704] An article based in part on this section was published in *History Today* in March 2015.

[705] Mitchell-Thomson (1877-1938) was Chief Civil Commissioner during the General Strike and PMG throughout the 1924 to 1929 Conservative government.

[706] Respectively, Balfour's PMG for sixteen months in 1902/03 and Bonar Law's for five months in 1922/23.

Martin Daunton describes the latter's as "a post of comfortable security" in 'Royal Mail: The Post Office Since 1840', 1985, p310.

[707] Created in 1861, when Palmerston was Prime Minister and Gladstone the Minister responsible, as a way of safeguarding the poor (Howard Robinson, 'Britain's Post Office: A History of Developments from the Beginnings to the Present Day', 1953).

Henry Fawcett, PMG from May 1880 to November 1884 and probably the best-known (coincidentally sharing the same name as Agnes Wood's father), encouraged the bank's growth during the 1880s so that it became a fundamental part of the "social economy of the nation". (p193).

Robinson's official history was superseded in 1985 by Daunton's.

functions residing in the Secretary. His power resembled that of a colonial viceroy, his decisions generally unchallenged and effectively enjoying the force of law. The Secretary was a career civil servant and at the turn of the century Sir George Herbert Murray (1849-1936) was in the middle of a six-year stint, knighted for his services in 1899 before moving on to the Treasury in 1903 for the remaining eight years of his career. His son (George) Evelyn Pemberton Murray (1880-1947) was appointed Secretary in 1914 and was to stay there for the next twenty years. His position endowed him with a natural prestige, an oracular command that encompassed all aspects of the service, cemented by his knighthood in 1919, and it was not long before his length of office gave him an unrivalled authority with his political "masters" as well. They would be as likely to defer to his opinion as did his subordinates.

This was not to say, though, that the service was badly run. There were gripes about the cost of a letter rising by 50% from 1d in Rowland Hill's day (the "penny post") to 1½d in the 1920s, but most of the public understood that this was effectively a tax imposed by the Treasury with some justification at a time of national austerity. Much of the service was exemplary, though concern was growing about the diminishing returns on telegrams and the increasing number of complaints from the public about the telephone service.

Yet, even given the background and political vagaries of the office, 1931 was exceptional with Kingsley Wood the fourth PMG that year. The Labour government's original appointee in 1929 Hastings (Bertie) Lees-Smith (1878-1941) had been promoted in March to the Board of Education and was replaced by Clement Attlee (1883-1967), elevated to his first Ministerial post at the head of a Department employing a quarter of a million people. After five months of typically assiduous study Attlee had just got to grips with his brief, was beginning to make some changes and propose others, when MacDonald ended the Labour government in 1931 in favour of the National one. Attlee remained in the Labour party and, understandably furious (though in his inimitable and under-stated way), was replaced as PMG in September by the National Government's nominee, William Ormsby-Gore. Two months later he in turn was removed, shuffled into the Cabinet as first commissioner of works, and Wood, whose tenure as Parliamentary Secretary at the Board of Education had been equally brief, took his place. If this is reminiscent of "pass the parcel", it should not be surprising that the National government sought a safe pair of hands it could rely on.   Neither MacDonald nor Snowden would have chosen Wood though for he had often deliberately clashed with them in Parliament, questioning their explanations and attempted justifications as much as the government's policies, but Baldwin and Chamberlain knew him well and respected his steadiness and reliability.   They were already exerting a significant influence in the National Government and the upshot was that Wood was left holding the parcel.

In November 1931, perhaps partly to assuage his fury, Attlee set out in the *New Statesman and Athenaeum* his views on the changes he thought vital for the future of the Post Office.[708] Describing it as "the outstanding example of collective capitalism", he argued that its contribution to the Treasury should be restricted to an agreed amount (rather than the indefinite sum depending on profitability that had resulted in an increase of £5m over the previous five years).   He judged the civil service-type structure too rigid and inflexible for the active campaigning that was needed to promote the savings and telephone services, in other words advocating a public relations (PR) approach that went beyond just information alone.   He also wanted to reduce parliamentary control, introduce a Whitley Council and consider the user/employee balance between amenities and wages.

These were substantial proposals, several of which would have been anathema to the rigid and inflexible Secretary Evelyn Murray[709] who had a particular distaste, hatred even, for public relations.   Nevertheless, they were not as radical as the claims Attlee made in his 1954 autobiography,[710] asserting that it was he who introduced public relations, appointed Stephen Tallents (1884-1958) (then at the Empire Marketing Board and later the Post Office's first PR officer), adopted advertising and improved the telephone service.   These are very striking claims, especially for someone who was only in the post for five months and was generally so modest, not to say deprecatory, about his own achievements.   It is the case that he set up an advisory committee on public relations and invited Tallents to join it, but it had got no

---

[708] Clement Attlee, "Post Office reform", *New Statesman and Athenaeum*, 7th November 1931, pp565-566

[709] Duncan Campbell-Smith, 'Masters of the Post: The Authorised History of the Royal Mail', 2011 is not alone in describing him as autocratic. Martin Daunton characterises him as "aloof and patrician" in Murray's DNB entry.

[710] Clement Attlee, 'As It Happened', 1954, pp70-71

further than that. With regard to the telephone service he only received the report setting out proposals the day he left office. That these claims are both over-blown and at odds with Attlee's customary style demands an explanation. There seem to be three possibilities: his memory was faulty, perhaps prompted by the circumstances of his early removal as PMG when the National Government came into being; he recalled his intentions as having happened, partly because his analysis was similar to others', including Wood's, but it was Wood who implemented the consequent changes; and in 1954 Attlee was still Leader of the Labour Party and was perhaps hoping to become Prime Minister again. In the latter case the more positive public perception of the Post Office compared to twenty years earlier would have been an advantage to the extent that he was seen as responsible for it. It is also conceivable that he was simply repeating what he had told Roy Jenkins six years earlier. In 1948 Jenkins had published an interim biography of Attlee, based in part on Attlee's "powers of recollection" and "hitherto unpublished writings". This referred to Attlee's five-month period as PMG seventeen years before and clarified that the *New Statesman and Athenaeum* article was based on Attlee's analysis of what he thought should happen.[711] This was not very different to the views of many others but it was Wood who brought the main changes about.

Also in November 1931, but by contrast from the Conservative standpoint, Lord Selborne's oldest son Roundell Cecil Palmer (1887-1971), better known as Lord Wolmer, stepped up his campaign for reform. He had been Assistant Postmaster-General from 1924 to 1929 but had only begun to agitate for reform thereafter.[712] His campaign was conducted initially through proposals to Mitchell-Thomson and Baldwin, then in articles in the *Times* and other newspapers, culminating in a parliamentary offensive that was capped by a memorial to the Prime Minister MacDonald signed by 320 MPs in November 1931.[713] As early as March 1931 when Attlee had only recently become PMG, Wolmer informed him in a supply debate on Post Office funding for 1931/32 that

---

[711] Roy Jenkins, 'Mr Attlee: An Interim Biography', 1948, pp134-140
[712] In 'Post Office Reform: Its Importance and Practicability', 1932, Wolmer argued that his operational responsibilities in support of the PMG William Mitchell-Thomson had prevented him from raising the issues earlier (p13).
[713] Ibid, pp23-25

> The action I want to take is to remove the Post Office altogether out of the hands of politicians and the Civil Service, and to put it in the hands of a statutory authority ... controlled by the ablest business brains we can find, in a position to raise its own capital ... and to run this great concern as a business.[714]

This was now the substance of Wolmer's proposals. The reform bandwagon had been rolling for some time but was rapidly increasing momentum; Wood was directly in its path, but would he also be in its way?

It might be expected that Wood would find Wolmer's prescription appealing. He too had often railed against increasing public expenditure falling on taxpayers who had no effective redress between elections. However, now a more experienced politician who had seen the benefits and helped deliver them, he could separate a political stance which saw increased spending per se as automatically objectionable (in other words a knee-jerk reaction of "more equals worse") from a response that depended on the values and purpose of, and therefore the justification for, the spend. So, he could write to the *Times* in December 1930 objecting to £40m (5.5%) growth from Churchill's budget for 1929/30 to Snowden's for 1930/31:

> Mr Lloyd George, I believe, last week described the Labour government as 'the most incompetent' he had known, and he might well have added 'the most reckless' so far as our national finances are concerned.[715]

This was quite apart, as Wood identified, from the as yet unknown burden of unemployment relief schemes. However, the public service that was the Post Office was quite a different matter, particularly if increased spending initially resulted in savings in the long run - i.e., an invest to save model.

In a leading article on 4th January 1932 the *Times* summarised Wolmer's reform proposals and the memorial from MPs that encapsulated them.[716] Written the same day but

---

[714] Hansard, 19th March 1931, vol. 249, col. 2221

[715] *Times* letter dated 9th December and printed 10th December 1930

[716] 'Post Office reform', *Times* 4th January 1932; also, *Daily Mail* 8th January 1932, KW17 329/1 reported the MPs' petition.

appearing in the *Times* on the 8th was an anonymous letter from "OUTIS" challenging several of Wolmer's assumptions. Campbell-Smith points out how pertinent were the eight questions asked in the letter and therefore how timely it was in slowing down the Wolmer bandwagon. He claims Wood was the author and it would be typical of Wood's prescience if he were.[717] Wood frequently wrote letters to the newspapers but never anonymously and, while it might have been anomalous for a Minister to comment publicly, it would have been even more unusual for him to do so anonymously. Both would have been inappropriate, the latter perhaps more so, but anonymity was in any case not Wood's style. He expected to be held accountable and was aware of, and would not willingly breach, the larger collective responsibility of which he was a part. Indeed it transpires that the letter was written by Sir George Murray,[718] Evelyn Murray's father, then living at 15 Cadogan Square.[719] This makes its provenance even more intriguing for the author had retired twenty years earlier and had left the Post Office in 1903. He obviously maintained more than a passing interest though, for the questions anticipated uncannily some of the conclusions of the committee of enquiry Wolmer had sought and which Wood was about to announce.

Five of the questions in the OUTIS letter were particularly problematic for Wolmer's arguments:

2: "How is Parliament to be persuaded to surrender its control over a service which has so many points of contact with our everyday life?"
3: "Who is to prescribe the policy of the new body? Will it be allowed, like any other concern run on business lines, to select its own business?"
"Much of the present business … is probably unremunerative. Will the emancipated Post Office be allowed to jettison this?"
4: "Will the new body be compelled to undertake gratuitously such work as the payment of pensions, the issue of licences, etc?"
5: "How is the staff to be dealt with? They are now Civil Servants, and would probably be unwilling to surrender the advantages which accrue from their dual position as electors and employees."

---

[717] Campbell-Smith, op cit, p294
[718] Personal communication from News UK Information Services 13th August 2014
[719] Kelly's Post Office Directory for London 1930

8: "Would the international activities of the Post Office ... be capable of management by a commercial concern?" [720]

The committee of enquiry Wood established comprised three Lords,[721] chaired by the politician William Bridgeman accompanied by the industrialist John Cadman (1877-1941) and the accountant William Plender (1861-1946). Plender and Cadman were leaders in their fields, known for their philanthropy and "good works" as well as for their experience, while Bridgeman was one of Baldwin's closest confidantes, had been Home Secretary and First Lord of the Admiralty in the 1920s, and was a leading layman in the Church of England. In less than six months the Committee produced a short, but pithy and extremely sophisticated, report to the terms of reference Wood had given them:

To enquire and report as to whether any changes in the constitution, status or system of organisation of the Post Office would be in the public interest.[722]

---

[720] Indeed, three remain relevant to the Royal Mail sell-off in 2013: Question 2 is similar to the issue of "why was a public service owned by all sold to the few?" To facilitate the sell-off, pension liabilities remained with the government rather than passing to the purchasers. In other words, short-term financial advantage trumped long-term costs, while ideology and the appearance of adhering to values were thought more important than the actual effect.

Question 3 evokes the arguments about the parcels/letters distinction, cherry-picking by other private delivery organisations and whether rural services are uncommercial. The upshot would be that the Universal Service Obligation (USO) dating from Queen Victoria's jubilee in 1897 was no longer realistic or appropriate.

There are fewer staff today so their potency as electors is reduced, but question 5 raises issues as to why protests by Trade Unions and citizens were ignored, how the 2013 coalition government was able to force through the sale, and how staff were "bought off" with a share allocation (or at least the pill of privatisation sweetened for them) – though it has to be said that they had little option, with a long-term agreement on pay reached soon after privatisation.

[721] *Daily Herald* 18th February 1932, KW17 341/7

[722] The composition of the Committee reflected careful thought from Wood for this and their arguments and conclusions required respect, even (or perhaps especially) from Wolmer.

Wood did not sit back to await the outcomes though for, even as the Bridgeman Committee began its work, he was already "winning the loyalty of all grades of the [Post Office] staff" as he sought to make it more efficient,[723] instituting improvements to the postal service[724] and advertising telephones in the newspapers under the strapline 'You Are Wanted On the Phone ... A Message from the Postmaster General'.[725] Later, and once Tallents had been appointed as PR officer, there would be a Pathe advertising campaign, the use of motorcycles as motorised billboards and a telephone week. The latter was a gift to cartoonists of course (as the example on the next page shows).

The Bridgeman Committee reported in August 1932, summarising in 137 paragraphs, 37 pages of text, its assessment of the current provision and the overall service.[726] Meeting twenty-five times (weekly in effect), it had taken evidence from witnesses (Attlee and Wolmer among them), as well as receiving written submissions. The report distinguished the Post Office communications services from its other functions on behalf of the State (for example, the savings bank and pension payments). It was very positive about the efficiency and effectiveness of the latter, and indeed about the postal service itself. It was more critical of the telegram and telephone systems (as Wolmer had been), but it was most concerned about the dead hand of the current administration, and Murray's excessive authority as Secretary, judging, and in reality condemning, it as old-fashioned and stifling initiative. It rejected the transfer of some services to a public utility company or another statutory body and damned Wolmer's private sector option as well, concluding that this would result in the development of the "more remunerative business of the denser areas to the detriment of more remote and sparsely populated districts",[727] a direct riposte to the issue raised in question 3 of the OUTIS letter. It recommended a new relationship with the Treasury, whereby the Post Office would contribute an agreed, but fixed, amount each year and 50% of any profits above this figure, retaining the other 50% for the

---

[723] *Sunday Chronicle* 6th March 1932, KW17 345/1

[724] *Daily Mail* 16th February 1932, KW17 340/1

[725] *Kent Independent* January 1932, for example, KW17 331/1

[726] Committee of Enquiry on the Post Office, 'Report', Cmd 4149, 1932

[727] Ibid, para 54, p20

"We'd love to Sir Kingsley - when?"
Will Dyson (1880-1938), *Daily Herald* 5th October 1934, KW19 191/4

development of services.[728] It rejected Wolmer's assumption that public criticism was always justified: "... the public will come to learn that it cannot demand luxuries at the same price which it pays for necessities".[729] The PMG's role was seen as entirely appropriate in order to separate policy from operation and maintain Parliamentary control,[730] something which it averred remained in the public

---

[728] Ibid, para 56, p21 On the basis of its calculations, the Committee suggested £11.5m but expected the exact figure to be negotiated between the Treasury and the Post Office subsequently (para 68, p25).
[729] Ibid, para 58, p22
[730] It had been proposed that either the PMG should be in the Cabinet or the emoluments of the post increased so that it was not just viewed as a stepping-stone to higher office, but the Bridgeman Committee remained unconvinced.

interest,[731] but modern management demanded a Board chaired by the PMG, led by a Director-General and comprising other executives charged with regional and/or specialist functions. The Secretary's post would no longer be required in this new structure.

The carefully thought through, and judiciously worded, recommendations for re-organisation were presented in twenty-one paragraphs, with the final eleven paragraphs given over to some general but nevertheless subtle conclusions that moved the arguments about the future on to another plane. Amounting to almost a quarter of the total report, the Committee ably demonstrated that public and staff confidence was vital to the future of the service. It concluded that

> The criticisms, so far as we find them to be justified, in our opinion point to defects in the present organization which can be remedied without ... a complete change of status.[732]

> ... we wish to place on record our opinion that on the whole the Post Office performs the services for which it is responsible with remarkable efficiency.[733]

> No organization can fail to be adversely affected when on the one hand it is denied credit that is its due, and on the other, is subjected to continuous and often unfair and un-informed criticism.

> ... the staff as a whole are genuinely anxious to give their best service to the public ...[734]

The Post Office establishment book for 1935 indicates that Wood received a basic £2312 10s which he could increase to £2500 if he earned a bonus. The new Director-General was paid £3000 that year. These compare with an MP's salary of £400pa in 1936 (House of Commons Information Office, Members pay, pensions and allowances, Factsheet M5 Members series, revised May 2009, Appendix A, p12). In other words, Wood's salary was six times that of a backbench MP (today's equivalents are about £14,000 and £84,000).

[731] Bridgeman Committee report (Cmd 4149), op cit, para 127, page 40
[732] Ibid, para 127, p40
[733] Ibid, para 133, pp41-42
[734] Ibid, para 134, p42

The presentation was subtle but the recommendations were radical as well as sophisticated and, in management terms, ahead of their time. The report gave Wood the vision he required; it would now be up to him to implement it.

When the Committee report was published in late August 1932 the *Times* devoted almost two pages to it.[735] A full and factual report of the proposals was accompanied by a positive leading article that concluded:

> If, as is to be hoped, it secures the approval of the Government, Sir Kingsley Wood will have before him a great opportunity of giving to the country a Postal, Telegraph and Telephone service far better than it now enjoys.

Not surprisingly, Wood responded favourably, taking the opportunity to further improve staff morale:

> ... few comparable organizations today ... would wish for a more favourable verdict. All ranks of the service are justly entitled to full credit in securing this impartial testimony to the British Post Office.

The *Times* also reported Attlee's reaction from the Labour benches:

> From the general summary I have received ... I think the Committee's recommendations are on the right lines. I agree that there should be a great deal more decentralization and that the functions of the secretariat should be revised in the way suggested. The suggestion of an advisory council is very good. I put forward a plan on the same lines when I was at the Post Office.

The tide had begun to turn for the same issue included a letter from a satisfied customer whose telephone had been fitted the day after his wife ordered it.[736]

Even Wolmer was fulsome in his praise, for in a letter written a week later he told the *Times*

---

[735] *Times* 23rd August 1932, pp11 & 12
[736] Ibid, p6

Those who have advocated Post Office reform must welcome the important changes recommended. They amount to no less than an entire recasting of the headquarters and provincial organization of the department.
...
These are very far-reaching reforms. ...
[They] are no mere tinkering. [The Committee] recognise that the shortcomings of the Post Office are due to the present system and seek to alter it radically. ...
While I regret that the Committee have rejected the proposal to transfer the Communications Services to a statutory authority, it seems to me that Lord Bridgeman's proposals go as far as possible in the direction of organizing the Department in its present status as a business ...
I suggest, therefore, that the efforts of Post Office reformers should be concentrated on endeavouring to secure that the recommendations ... be carried out to the full and not whittled down. ... It is of vital importance that they should be applied by men who are whole-hearted supporters of the proposals, and not by those who are wedded to the *ancien regime*. In this we can, I feel sure, look to the present Postmaster-General to give us a square deal.[737]

Wolmer would have continued to agitate had he had reason to do so, but the authoritative report was well-judged and the Committee itself beyond reproach. Furthermore, he had given Wood his whole-hearted endorsement and, with the sternest critic disarmed, lukewarm Labour support (but support nonetheless) and a set of credible proposals with which he was entirely in accord, Wood must have felt not only motivated to see them through but mandated to do so.

In the October 1932 issue of the Post Office magazine *St Martins le Grand*, Wood wrote to staff to let them know the next steps to implementation and to congratulate them on the overall conclusion.[738]

Wood had no sympathy when Murray attempted in January 1933 to rubbish the regional directorates that would give more autonomy to those who delivered the services, changing their relationship to the centre, though not necessarily diluting its

---

[737] *Times* 3rd September 1932, p11
[738] *St Martins le Grand*, 1932, vol. XLII, p311

authority.[739] So, once Wood had secured Cabinet approval to the recommendations, he removed Murray in 1934[740] and appointed Donald Banks (1891-1975) as the first Director-General of the revitalised Post Office instead. Banks had previously run the savings bank, about which the Bridgeman Committee had been particularly favourable.[741] The other proposals were also seen through, with Wood chairing the new Board, the financial arrangement with the Treasury re-negotiated, public relations and advertising to the fore once Tallents was appointed in October 1933,[742] an advisory council in place and the service re-organised.[743]

Wood was a firm believer in the power of advertising and publicity to promote goods, and services such as telephones and the Post Office were no different. In June 1934 he spoke at the banquet of the Advertising Convention in Leicester, arguing that the use of newspaper advertising had contributed significantly to the

---

[739] Campbell-Smith, op cit, pp301-302

[740] To Customs and Excise, his civil service berth before joining the Post Office twenty years before.
The quarterly *St Martins le Grand* ceased at the end of 1933 to be replaced by a monthly magazine from January 1934. To underline the symbolism of the new start the April 1934 issue carried both Murray's leaving letter (p151) and details of the new Board from 27th February (p154).

[741] Robinson, op cit, p285 indicates that between 1930 and 1935 the number of savings bank accounts increased from 9.2m to 9.7m (+5.4%), while the amount saved rose by over a third from £290m to £390m.

[742] Tallents had been one of Beveridge's Labour Exchange civil servants (William Beveridge, 'Power and Influence', 1953, p78) and Secretary of the Cabinet Sub-Committee for Supply and Transport Organisation at the time of the General Strike (Middlemas, 1969, op cit, pp27-28). He was picked by Wood out of the wreck of the Empire Marketing Board. Also, KW19 7/1-2 *Post* 16th and '*Supervisory*' 15th July 1933
The Empire Marketing Board, of which Tallents was the Secretary, had been established as "the principal organ of non-tariff preference" but fell foul of the Treasury and and was "disbanded in 1933 as an outmoded failure". It remains best known for the publicity campaign that was Tallents' direct responsibility. See Robert Self, "Treasury control and the Empire Marketing Board: The rise and fall of non-tariff preference in Britain, 1924-1933", *Twentieth Century British History*, 1994, 5, pp153-182

[743] Daunton, 1985, op cit, p302 includes the revised structure of Banks' headquarters that took effect from 1934, but it was 1936 before the first two regions (Scotland and North-East England) were fully operative.

'Post Office Advance' (as the *Leicester Evening Mail* headlined its report).[744]   The same month Wood was photographed at the 'Pictures in Advertising' exhibition sponsored by Shell-Mex and BP at the Burlington Galleries.[745] Such was Wood's commitment that the President of the Advertising Association in 1935[746] told the House of Commons that he thought Wood should succeed him: "I shall certainly suggest that, in his spare time, the PMG" should be the next President.[747]

One indicator of Wood's success is that MacDonald brought him into the Cabinet in December 1933, the first PMG to be elevated to this rank since 1915,[748] thereby recognising his achievements thus far and reinforcing his impetus for the future as well; another the improvement in Post Office finances.[749] He was the fourteenth Conservative Minister in a Cabinet of twenty, and one that had comprised only twelve Conservatives when it was formed two years before. In June 1934 Wood invited two hundred MPs to a display of new Post Office films at a London theatre, while the 150th anniversary since mail coaches started in 1784 was marked that August.[750] The public relations drive would include the "Brighter Post Office" and "You're Wanted on the Telephone" campaigns, the Pathe films, and with Wood's full endorsement Tallents rescued

---

[744] *Leicester Evening Mail* 13th June 1934, KW19 119/1

[745] *Bystander* 26th June 1934, KW19 133/3

[746] Sir John Pybus (1880-1935) whose father was a Hull Alderman.

[747] *World's Press News* 21st March 1935, KW19 294/4
In the event Lord Iliffe was likely to be Pybus' successor as Advertising Association President, given that Wood was unable to accept once he had been appointed Minister of Health. *World's Press News* 24th June 1935, KW19 403/4

[748] For example, *Express* 21st December 1933, KW19 6/19; also, KW19 8/1, 8/6 & 20/9 *Yorkshire Post*, *Daily Telegraph*, and *Daily Herald* all 21st December 1933

[749] Net revenue of £62.3m and a surplus of £9.4m in 1930 on the post, money orders, telegraphs and telephones compares with revenue of £76.4m and a net surplus of £11.9m in 1935 (Robinson, op cit, p284). In other words, revenue had increased by 22%, the surplus by almost 27%. Less well-paid staff received an increase in their wages from 1935. Similarly, Daunton, 1985, op cit, pp328-331 sets out the postal profits between 1837 and 1967, showing that the profit margin peaked between the wars in 1933/34 at 34.5% declining to 25.7% in 1938/39. By then profits were no longer being handed over in their entirety to the Treasury but were being used to develop the service and pay staff better.

[750] Post Office magazine July 1934, p295 and August 1934

Grierson's documentary film unit just before it imploded, turning them into the Post Office film unit that is best remembered for the film 'Night Mail' in 1936, with a WH Auden script and Benjamin Britten score.[751]

A surplus of £9.4m in 1930 had increased to £11m in 1933 and would increase again in 1934.[752] Wood's contribution was widely recognised with the *Sunday Times* reporting the Commons debate of 24th July when Wood reported the improvement:

> There is no more respected and popular Member of the House of Commons than the PMG, and his account of his stewardship last week produced much applause and little criticism. He had a good story to tell with an optimistic moral, but the tribute was as much to his personality as to his work.[753]

Alongside this though were headlines such as 'Starvation Pay in the Post Office' for part-time workers[754], while the *Daily Herald* drew attention to low paid jobs such as the caretaker/phone operator who was paid 11/3 for a 96-hour week and ancillary postmen outside London paid 24/-.[755] Not surprisingly, low paid employees at the Post Office expected that they should also benefit. However, one report of the Commons debate made clear Wood's resistance:

[751] BBC Radio 4 programme 9th June 2013
[752] *Daily Telegraph, Evening News,* 21st July and *Manchester Guardian* 25th July 1933, KW18 142/1-3 Also, *Leeds Mercury* 22nd July 1933, KW18 133/3 cartoon of Wood carrying bag of Post Office profits for 1932/33; *Spectator* 28th July 1933, KW18 145/1 including Wolmer praise for Wood's handling of the Post Office.
[753] *Sidcup Times* 4th August 1933, KW19 1/10 quoting Atticus in the *Sunday Times* and continuing "[He] is the type of man who, thirty years ago, was generally found on the Liberal benches - an authority on local government, a loyal Free Churchman, a practical man who never says a foolish word. He was one of the original advocates of the Ministry of Health, and he did admirable work during his five years as Under-Secretary to that Ministry under Neville Chamberlain.
"In debate his manner is at once confident and modest - always friendly, humorous and imperturbable. I have heard Labour Members say that he was as difficult to catch out as Lord Bridgeman when he sat in the Commons, and that is a high tribute. Most consider that he is next in succession to Cabinet honours."
[754] *Daily Express* 22nd July 1933, KW18 141/2
[755] *Daily Herald* 16th August 1933, KW19 4/7-10

> When ... the PMG presented to the House of Commons the kind of annual report which would at once send up the shares in any private company and announced the highest Post Office surplus on record - £10.792m - a lot of MPs naturally asked whether, in view of this huge profit, he would restore the cuts in the wages of the employees.
> Sir Kingsley Woodn't.[756]

For their part Post Office Supervising Officers appealed directly to the PMG for a seven-hour day.[757] The Postmistress interviewed by Walter Greenwood thought six hours a day appropriate for counter staff given the range and complexity of their tasks. In fact ten hours a day was common, especially on Fridays when health and insurance stamps, pensions and football pools came on top of the ordinary business.[758]

Staff expected to share in this turnaround to profit but there was no immediate response from Wood and the long-suppressed discontent continued to be evident throughout 1934. At their conference in Southport that May the Union of Post Office workers made it clear both that they would be pressing on with their claim and that they were dissatisfied with Wood's response asking for evidence of hardship. The General Secretary and his Assistant asserted that not only are "Men employed by the PMG ... in dire straits to maintain themselves" but that Wood was "not only perpetuating poverty but was whipping the backs of their people".[759] In response to the claim for a 40-hour week Walter Citrine of the TUC pointed out that this would provide 10%+ more employment.

At the beginning of November it was reported that Wood wanted to raise the wages of the lower-paid workers by Christmas[760] and in the middle of the month he explained to the Commons how this would be achieved.[761] This would cost

---

[756] *People* 30th July 1933, KW19 1/11

[757] 'Supervising' [sic] 1st September 1933, KW19 11/14

[758] Walter Greenwood, 'How the Other Man Lives', undated but 1938/39, pp65-70

[759] *News Chronicle* 10th May 1934, KW19 94/8

[760] *Daily Sketch* 1st November 1934, KW19 218/7

[761] *Morning Post* 14th November 1934, KW19 243/7 referring to Wood's announcement in the Commons the day before that pay for Post Office workers would be increased by up to 4s 10d (or 24p) per week and backdated to 1st November 1934. Also, *Manchester Guardian* 14th November 1934, KW19 243/8

£275,000 in the first year and £500,000 thereafter. The *Morning Post* report took the opportunity to summarise the reforms Wood had instigated in the previous three years:

Jan 1932	Newspaper advertising campaign for telephone services
Jan 1933	Post Office Advisory Council appointed
Sep 1933	Tallents appointed as first Public Relations Officer
Feb 1934	Appointment of Post Office Board and committee of business men to advise on telephone and telegraph services
Aug 1934	First inland air mails; new 1.5d stamps
Oct 1934	Substantial decreases in telephone rentals and trunk call charges; flat (and lower) rates for Empire air mail service
Oct-Nov 1934	Record 70,000 new telephone subscribers in six weeks
Dec 1934	Start of Australian air mails

The report also identified, though without ascribing dates: completion of Empire radio telephone links; start of Post Office teleprinter service; gradual conversion of telegraph service to teleprinter system of transmission; and introduction of 'on demand' telephone services between principal cities both in the UK and on the continent. To this might be added the rescue of the Empire Marketing Board film library,[762] as well as Grierson's film unit. The writer Arthur Quiller Couch was among those who put pen to paper to thank Wood publicly.[763]

At the start of 1934 the readers of *Pearson's Weekly* had voted Wood the most popular MP,[764] while in December 1934 Alan Pitt-Robbins (1888-1967), then the *Times* Parliamentary Correspondent,[765] assessed the impact of the changes up to that point. In a column headed 'The Modernised Post Office: Period of Progress' he was enthusiastic about Wood's impact in the previous three years:

---

[762] *Birmingham Post* 23rd September and *Kentish Mercury* 29th September 1933, KW19 5/15 & 5/13

[763] *Yorkshire Herald* (?) undated, KW19 5/14

[764] *Pearson's Weekly* 20th January 1934, KW19 20/11

[765] He attended Wood's memorial service, both in his own right and as the representative of the Institute of Journalists.

There has been ... an almost unprecedented number of new ... services and reduction of charges. But what may well be regarded as much more important so far as the history of Government offices is concerned has been the orderly development of a great State Department on bold and progressive lines to meet the needs of our time. Some three years ago a considerable majority of the House of Commons were so dissatisfied with Post Office policy and administration that, irrespective of party, they presented a formidable indictment of its policy and methods to the Prime Minister. Today no Department stands higher with the House of Commons and the public, and the reason is not far to seek ...

All this has been accomplished in a comparatively short time. Sir Kingsley Wood has had considerable advantages. He has had practically a free hand, the help of the Bridgeman Committee, such support and confidence from the Chancellor of the Exchequer as few [PMGs] have received, and he has managed to carry the great body of ... employees with him, as well as his political opponents. ... In days when so many men of all parties are thinking of national planning and reconstruction ... a careful study of recent Post Office developments is well worth while.[766]

Or, as the *Edinburgh Evening News* put it, Wood is

not only a remarkably good organiser and a man of business, but he also has 'ideas'.

The Post Office is his pet and his pride. For three years he has watched it rise from contempt to respect, and from respect to admiration.[767]

Attlee may have "sown a few seeds" in his brief tenure, as Jenkins claimed in his 1948 biography, but it was Wood who sowed others, made sure they all germinated, plucked out the weeds, brought in the harvest and dried it out. By then it could be sold to the public and they were ready to buy it. His thoughtful management was accompanied by a skilled approach that depended on a great deal of hard work.

---

[766] *Times* 18th December 1934, p11
[767] *Edinburgh Evening News* 22nd December 1934, KW19 251/4

New "Ondemand" Telephone Exchange at G.P.O.

Opening Hull Corporation telephone exchange 21st March 1935, KW30[768]

Not surprisingly, in his 1946 autobiography Banks wrote of Wood

> He was an ideal Minister from the standpoint of a Chief Executive. He said in effect: 'It is your job to run the show. I will tell you what is the policy and back you to the limit of carrying it out.'[769]

---

[768] Hull was the last municipally-owned telephone service and although the Council had sold its stake by 2007 it remains independent of BT. The white phone boxes could still be seen at the start of the twenty-first century.

Wood was also alive to the needs of rural areas, promising a public telephone to every village that had a Post Office so that the isolation of villages would end (*Sussex Daily News* 1st May 1935, KW19 356/3).

In addition, Wood opened many modernised and enlarged Post Offices in urban areas, including the Cambridge one (*Cambridge Daily News* 21st April 1934, KW19 91/3).

[769] Donald Banks, 'Flame Over Britain: A Personal Narrative of Petroleum Warfare', 1946, p3 The title reflects Banks' role in World War II.

BBC

However, John Reith at the BBC had a very different view. For example, in his autobiography Reith writes that Wood wanted to take Banks with him in 1935 as civil head of the Ministry of Health, but Warren Fisher (1879-1948), Head of the Civil Service and Permanent Secretary at the Treasury, objected.[770] Reith continues: "Wood had a cynical disregard of civil service principles ... There was no need for me to say anything about Kingsley Wood when Fisher was around". Yet Reith had an exaggerated view of his own importance, "a swelled head" as Crawford described it,[771] while Henry Pownall recorded in his diary in February 1934 that "Fisher, in [the Cabinet Secretary Maurice] Hankey's opinion, is rather mad", his judgement affected by a nervous disorder.[772] Banks went to the Air Ministry in 1936 instead, where he and Wood were re-united later.

Although the PMG did not have the same day-to-day functions with the BBC as he did with the Post Office, he still exercised strategic, operational and financial oversight on behalf of Parliament, with wavelengths allocated and licence fees collected through the Post Office. As he would be the person held accountable if things went wrong, and as the politician responsible for negotiating the BBC's Charter renewal, this was still a very significant role. And one that Reith would be likely to find irksome unless the PMG was hands-off and allowed Reith and the BBC the independence he sought and which he thought justified.

It is worth noting that Wood's impact on his colleagues at the Post Office must have been lasting as a decade later Tallents also attended Wood's memorial service while Banks ensured he was represented.

[770] John Reith, 'Into the Wind', 1949, p223

[771] Crawford chaired the 1925-1926 committee on the BBC and was in a position to know. He subsequently declined Baldwin's proposal that he be the Corporation's first chairman.
John Vincent (ed.), 'The Crawford Papers: The Journal of David Lindsay 27th Earl of Crawford and 10th Earl of Balcarres 1871-1940 during the years 1892-1940', 1984, p504

[772] Brian Bond (ed.), 'Chief of Staff: The Diaries of Lt Gen Sir Henry Pownall, vol. 1: 1933-1940', 1972, p36
Also, Stephen Roskill, 'Hankey: Man of Secrets - vol. III 1931-1963', 1974 p122 where, in a letter to Baldwin 23rd August 1934, Hankey (1877-1963) wrote "I don't think [Fisher] is a fit man or that his judgement is at its best". He and Fisher were friends but had different views on the Navy and defence in the Pacific.

The British Broadcasting Corporation was created in 1927, as recommended by the report of the 1926 Crawford committee

> ... [whose] main task was to give a constitutional form to principles already generally accepted. 'Monopoly' and 'unified control' were an accomplished fact, as was a dislike of the American [private sector] system of broadcasting. Politicians were anxious not to see broadcasting go the way of the popular press.[773]

Replacing the Company that had operated from 1923, it was still required to avoid controversy. The BBC had fought hard to maintain its neutrality during the General Strike, though some thought it had not been neutral enough, but a prescribed blandness soon proved unrealistic and the Post Office ban on controversial items was withdrawn at the BBC's request, a year after the new Corporation had been formed.[774] By that November one speaker in the House of Commons called for the BBC to publicise Chamberlain's and Wood's Local Government Bill, this "Magna Carta of public health and local government".[775] In other circumstances this might be thought apolitical public information, but the legislation had proved controversial.

However, being permitted to raise and debate controversial matters is not the same as an absence of oversight, regulation or even censorship. In February 1931, for example, Churchill was not allowed to broadcast on India[776] (even offering Reith and the BBC £100 to let him). It was pointed out to him that this was not censorship of the people's view but of a private individual seeking to over-turn the Government's position. The ban was confirmed again two years later when Wood defended the BBC's position in Parliament.[777] In November 1933 Wood and Stephen Tallents

---

[773] Vincent, op cit, pp504-506

[774] Briggs, 1995, op cit, p120

[775] The speaker was Lt-Col Francis Fremantle (1872-1943). Hansard, 27th November 1928, vol. 223, cols. 270-271 Also, *BMJ* 1st December 1928

[776] Briggs, 1995, op cit, p128

[777] *Daily Mail* 23rd February 1933, KW18 40/4
Although the report in the *News Chronicle* 23rd February 1933, KW18 45/1 was headlined 'MPs Attack the BBC', the *Times* stressed the votes cast on a motion that the BBC not be subject to any further Government control beyond the licence and Charter: 203 yes, 27 no (*Times* 23rd February 1933, KW18 48/3).

visited the BBC in order to prepare "to defend [it] against [yet more] threatened attacks in the House of Commons".[778] It would be 1935 before Churchill was eventually allowed to broadcast his views on India.[779] In another instance, this time in September 1933, Austen Chamberlain, Lloyd George and Churchill, all of whom were out of favour with their parties, were not included in a series of political talks on the radio. In a letter to the BBC Chairman John Whitley (1866-1935),[780] published in the *Times*, they accused Kingsley Wood of bias. Whitley's reply was also printed, to which the trio responded that their exclusion, even if it was not actually biased, set a worrying precedent: political censorship of views that were not approved by the mainstream parties.[781] It might be thought, however, that they would be unlikely to support such a stance when they were in office.

On the last day before the Christmas recess in December 1931, Clement Attlee (briefly Postmaster-General earlier that year) opened an adjournment debate on the issue of balance in party political radio broadcasts on the BBC.[782] Attlee was concerned that broadcasts during the recent General Election campaign had split eight to National Government parties and three to the opposition. He argued that this was bias, despite the BBC's best efforts, and a template ought to be agreed for the future because all political arrangements, including the National Government, were inherently unstable. He argued that this should be important not only to any government and opposition, but would have to take account of issues such as the Independent Labour Party versus the Labour Party, extremists like Sir Oswald Mosley, and mavericks such as Winston Churchill, "a semi-detached Member of the Conservative Party and ... so to speak, on the transfer list".[783] For his part Wood pointed out that it was up to the Governors to decide on political

---

[778] *Popular Wireless* 11th November 1933, KW19 22/1
The report continued "Mr Churchill can be counted on to rally the forces that are hostile to Broadcasting House. The Labour Opposition is restless because of the feeling of insufficient microphone time compared with the Government."
[779] Briggs, 1995, op cit, p135
[780] Appointed Chairman of the BBC by Ramsay MacDonald in 1930, he retained this position until his death in 1935. His DNB entry refers to the "impartiality and imperturbability" that made him well-suited to this role.
[781] *Times* 11th September 1933, KW19 11/5; Briggs, 1995, op cit, p135
[782] Hansard, 11th December 1931, vol. 260, cols. 2307-2315
[783] Ibid, col. 2312

balance as regards broadcasts and he assured Attlee that, as far as he was aware, they had not been given any direction otherwise in this instance.[784] He went on to counter Attlee by claiming that, had the BBC given Labour more radio time at the General Election, they "would have [been] wiped out entirely".[785]

One newspaper report the next day described Attlee as complaining that the BBC was too middle-aged,[786] though what he actually said was that it must remain fresh by appealing to the young (even at the risk of scandalising the old) and leave room for the unorthodox. In his view the BBC's governing body should include younger people to ensure this. The sister paper on Sunday alleged that the acronym BBC stood for "Bad, Boring, Cranky" and that "If the BBC were not a Government Department it would have to entertain the public or get out of business".[787] No doubt many agreed with this, while many others (Herbert Morrison, for example) took the opposite view: 'Hands Off the BBC' was the title of his article in the *Daily Herald* later that month.[788]

The BBC was rapidly becoming as prevalent a medium for the news as newspapers and word of mouth. In 1927 there were about 2.2m licence-holders but over four times as many, more than 9m, by the start of World War II.[789] As nearly half the licence-holders in 1939 (4.2m) had incomes of less than £4 per week, radio was fast becoming a necessity for even the poorest; newspapers remained a luxury by comparison. Whereas many newspapers took an overtly party political line, the BBC's credibility and authority depended on independence and impartiality, though this did not preclude, indeed in some instances required, more than one perspective. Whereas the default position was a patriotic and imperial tone and perspective, the Corporation's rationale ultimately was to inform listeners - though most of the audience would expect this to be filtered through a British perspective. Yet in 1932 Lord Stonehaven the Conservative party chair wrote to Baldwin to complain about the BBC's left-wing bias,[790] a criticism that would be repeated during WWII over JB Priestley's talks. Many other people,

---

[784] Hansard, 11th December 1931, vol. 260, cols. 2316-2319

[785] Ibid, col. 2319; Briggs, 1995, op cit, pp130-131; *Times* 12th December 1931

[786] *News Chronicle* 12th December 1931, KW17 321/3

[787] *Sunday Chronicle* 13th December 1931, KW17 322/1

[788] *Daily Herald* 31st December 1931, KW17 332/2

[789] Briggs, 1995, op cit, p235

[790] Ball, 2013, op cit, p101

however, applauded Priestley's candour and his talks remained very popular. As today, the BBC could argue that its independence was demonstrated by criticism from both sides. Wood himself noted that "Such critics as there have been have come from opposing political forces, a tribute to, rather than a condemnation of, the freedom from political bias of the corporation".[791]

However, one example when the BBC was thought to have gone too far in the pursuit of balance concerned the Hashagen case in 1932. Hashagen, a U-boat commander in WWI, had been invited by the BBC to broadcast his experiences. As this would include the sinking of allied shipping,[792] it was thought inappropriate both in terms of relatives' distress and the disarmament negotiations then taking place. On 6th July 1932 the Cabinet discussed it in the context of a Commons question that was to be put the following day about preventing Hashagen from entering the UK. Rather than prohibit the broadcast outright, Baldwin briefed Wood to make it clear to Reith the Cabinet's "unanimous view ... that the talk must be cancelled".[793] However, Reith refused to cancel without Whitley's authority as BBC Chairman and according to Briggs, who covers the controversy in detail,[794] added that the political intervention was "monstrous" and Wood's interference unwelcome. The next day Reith and his Chairman met Wood at his office and Whitley,

> ... perhaps worried by threats that the King's imminent visit to the BBC's new headquarters at Broadcasting House might be cancelled - was less resolute, and he agreed to stop the broadcast.[795]

Later that day when Arthur Marsden[796] did ask in the Commons

---

[791] Hansard, 22nd February 1933, vol. 274, col. 1843

[792] Gordon Campbell, the brother of Wood's PPS Edward Campbell won the VC as a commander of a decoy Q-ship used to lure German submarines.

[793] Asa Briggs, 'Governing the BBC', 1979, p191

[794] Ibid, pp191-194

[795] http://www.bbc.co.uk/historyofthebbc/research/culture/bbc-and-gov/hashagen The BBC history continues: "He [Whitley] was very unhappy about it ... as were the press and many MPs."

[796] Cdr Arthur Marsden (1883-1960) was the newly-elected Conservative MP for North Battersea where in 1931 he had defeated both the Labour incumbent WS Sanders, Wood's opponent for the LCC seat in Woolwich in

... if he will refuse to grant a permit to Captain Ernst Hashagen to land in this country for the purpose of broadcasting his experiences of sinking British and Allied merchant shipping during the last War while in command of a German U-boat?

Wood was able to answer on behalf of the Minister of Labour

I understand from the British Broadcasting Corporation that the talk was planned as a serious contribution towards the elimination of this method of warfare, and would have been so expressed. In view, however, of international discussions now proceeding at Geneva, I have been informed that it has been decided not to proceed with the talk. The question of a permit does not therefore arise.[797]

Both a ban on Hashagen entering the country and outright Government prohibition of the broadcast had been avoided but, after the BBC Governors discussed it on 13th July,[798] Whitley protested to the Cabinet

... the Corporation feels that an incident so contrary to the spirit and intention of the Royal Charter should not pass without protest. The Governors venture to assume that it will not form a precedent.[799]

Wood replied, but neither this reply nor the subsequent correspondence were considered by the Governors until their first meeting after the summer in late September.[800] By then the

---

1911 and 1913, and Shapurji Saklatvala (1874-1936), the first Communist MP. Sanders regained the North Battersea seat in 1935.

[797] Hansard, 7th July 1932, vol. 268, cols. 593-594
Reported for example by the *Daily Mail* 8th July 1932, KW 17 364/4

[798] BBC archives R1/2/1, BBC Board of Governors Minute 86 (1932) 'Cabinet intervention'

[799] The BBC Board of Governors had approved Whitley's letter at their meeting on 27th July 1932. BBC archives R1/2/1, Minute 102 (1932) Briggs, 1979, op cit, pp192-193 includes Whitley's protest in full (copies of which Whitley asked Hankey to circulate to the Cabinet) and notes the "measured terms" in which it was couched.

[800] BBC archives R1/2/1, BBC Board of Governors Minute 114 (21st September 1932)

immediate issue had been overtaken by the formation of a Parliamentary Advisory Committee[801] that would assess political talks outside general elections - perhaps partly in response to the issues Attlee had raised the previous December. This was just after Bridgeman had delivered his report on Post Office reform but before Wood appointed him a BBC Governor the following January. Bridgeman had been Whitley's choice to chair the Advisory Committee but Bridgeman informed Dawson, the editor of the *Times*, in a letter that December he had refused to join Whitley's "shock-absorber".[802]   In February 1933 his memorandum about political talks was discussed by the BBC Governors and the role of the Parliamentary Advisory Committee explained.[803]

Reith downplays the Hashagen incident in his autobiography, somewhat surprisingly given the implications of the BBC's about-turn in the face of Cabinet pressure.[804]   The BBC history prefers to describe it as "persuasion" but the controversy raised constitutional issues, for the BBC felt that the Royal Charter granted in 1927 only gave the PMG powers to intervene at times of national emergency. With this exception BBC autonomy should be exercised through the Governors.   Wood disputed this interpretation, setting out for the Cabinet his understanding that the PMG had "complete power to prohibit any broadcast" and not just at times of national emergency (as the BBC maintained they had been promised by a previous PMG in 1927).

This was a further reason for Reith to dislike Wood, even ahead of the Charter renewal negotiations in 1934. Reith "felt that Wood had given the BBC insufficient protection from [the] pressure", while "Wood, for his part, was less inclined than his

---

[801] BBC archives R1/2/1, BBC Board of Governors Minute 115 (21st September 1932)
Briggs, 1995, op cit, p105 lists five members of the Committee though the Labour one never attended because of the Labour leader Lansbury's disapproval.
[802] Philip Williamson (ed.), 'The Modernisation of Conservative Politics: The Diaries and Letters of William Bridgeman 1904-1935', 1988, p255
[803] BBC archives R1/3/1, BBC Board of Governors Minute 21 (22nd February 1933)
Bridgeman's memo was discussed again on 8th March (Minute 31) and on 22nd March the Board noted the Parliamentary Advisory Committee recommendation that no talks on the India White Paper were to be broadcast before the Select Committee reported (Minute 44).
[804] Reith, op cit, pp160-161

predecessors to agree with the Director-General on every question".[805] Perhaps in an attempt at conciliation, Wood told Reith that he would not have used his veto in any case.[806] But as Reith must have interpreted this as an invitation to resist government pressure in the future, it perhaps only served to add to the acrimony between them.

Reith and Wood were frequently in dispute, as they were almost bound to be from their different perspectives, with Wood exercising the oversight that Reith resented. This manifested itself in three ways in particular: BBC contributions to the Treasury, the role of wireless exchanges and the Ullswater report on Charter renewal and political responsibility for the BBC.[807] Reith's autobiography takes the view that Wood was a bureaucratic restraint on his vision. Not surprisingly, historians who rely almost entirely on this source interpret it as a clash of wills, with Reith seeking to counter Wood's excessive and unreasonable demands. The material in the BBC written archives, however, provides examples of Reith's neurotic petulance. He could be the autocrat clashing with another strong and determined character in Wood, but he was also overly, indeed unnecessarily, defensive. On the membership of the Ullswater Committee, for example, Reith thought it too Post Office, reflecting Wood's interests and designed to ensure he retained his existing powers. Reith objected in particular to the inclusion of Mitchell-Thomson who, when Postmaster-General himself in the 1920s, was supposed to have caused Reith "trouble", as he put it.[808] However now Lord Selsdon, Mitchell-Thomson had just reported on the development of television, advocating that it be entrusted to the BBC.[809] The Selsdon Committee had been established by Wood to advise him on television,[810] including the financial aspects and rival TV systems

---

[805] Wood's DNB entry written by George Peden.

[806] Briggs, 1995, op cit, pp121-122

[807] 'Report of the Broadcasting Committee 1935', Cmd 5091, 1936

[808] BBC archives R4/69/1, Letter to Donald Banks 26th April 1935. Also, Reith, op cit, p105

[809] BBC archives TV 16/214/1 31st January 1935

[810] *Daily Herald* 23rd April 1934, KW19 91/14: PMG expected to set up a technical committee to decide best system for TV among four competing possibilities; *Daily Mail* 1st May 1934, KW19 84/3: on 30th April Wood had announced in Parliament that he would "set up a committee to consider the development of TV and to advise on the conditions under which a public TV service should be provided".

(Baird, EMI and others), and after visits to Germany and America[811] the Committee concluded that it should be the BBC that was given the authority to take this forward - especially as the overlaps between sound and picture broadcasting were huge and it would not be sensible to try to separate them. On both counts the BBC stood out.[812] As this had not been a foregone conclusion even a few months earlier,[813] Selsdon/Mitchell-Thomson could hardly be considered automatically hostile to Reith or the Corporation.

With the growth in the number of licence-holders, the BBC was in surplus at a time when the country was experiencing severe economic hardship. Like many other individuals and organisations, the BBC was asked to make voluntary contributions to the Treasury to help alleviate the May Committee cuts: £50,000 from the licence fee income in 1931/32 and £150,000 in 1932/33.[814] In October 1932 Whitley reported to the Governors his conversations with Wood about a 1933/34 contribution. The Board agreed a figure of £200,000 which, four times that of two years before, gives some indication of the BBC's growing popularity.[815] But after further discussions, Wood over-ruled the Board and the BBC eventually paid across £250,000 for 1933/34.[816] This is the equivalent of about £10m today. The discrepancy for 1934/35 was to be even more marked. Perhaps anticipating a difficult round, conversations

---

[811] *Daily Express* 5th November 1934, KW19 215/11: Some of the Committee were about to visit Germany, while others had already gone to the USA (including Lord Selsdon himself on 24th October).

[812] On 30th December 1934 *Reynolds News*, under the over-optimistic headline 'Television for All in 1935', reported that the Selsdon Committee was expected to recommend that the BBC be given the powers to develop television (KW19 256/1). The *Daily Express* reported on 18th December 1934, KW19 258/3 that Wood was preparing a TV Bill on the basis of the Committee's outline report, probably giving control to the BBC. One of the popular concerns that had to be overcome was that TV could look into people's homes, another that it would kill off cinema.

[813] *Popular Wireless* had reported 5th May 1934 that the Post Office might take over TV directly (KW19 95/7).

[814] 'British Broadcasting Corporation Sixth Annual Report 1932', Cmd 4277, 1933

[815] BBC archives R1/2/1, BBC Board of Governors Minute 123 (12th October 1932)

[816] BBC archives R1/2/1, BBC Board of Governors Minute 27 (22nd February 1933)

between Reith and Wood had begun as early as February 1934,[817] and after a letter from Wood the BBC offered £150,000. Warren Fisher, Permanent Secretary at the Treasury, and Reith already knew each other well and, in the hope that Fisher might prove more amenable, Reith sought his advice in advance, with the final decision to be taken by Reith and the BBC vice-chairman (in Whitley's absence because of ill-health).[818] It is perhaps an indication of Reith's naivete, however, that he thought Fisher able to exercise the influence over Wood that he might over other less capable and confident PMGs. To the extent that Wood thought Reith's tactic unauthorised, unjustified and underhand, his response would more likely be annoyance and irritation rather than acceptance.

After discussion with Fisher, however, the BBC was to "acquiesce" in £250,000 again for 1934/35. On this occasion the BBC Governors also wrote a formal letter so that their displeasure was evident in both the Treasury and Post Office files.[819] The following year the Post Office and the Treasury seem to have taken the money without any discussion with the BBC let alone their approval. The BBC protested vigorously and the Treasury and Post Office were forced to apologise, with Donald Banks writing from the Post Office to explain what had happened. In the end the BBC agreed a reduced contribution for 1935/36 of £125,000 to cover the quarter to the end of June.[820] As they had also agreed by this stage to meet half the costs of the TV experiment (£90,000 to the end of 1936),[821] this seems to have been an end of the matter for 1935/36 as the issue did not re-appear at Governors' meetings.

Wireless exchanges enabled listeners who could not afford a receiving set to listen via a loudspeaker wired to a local exchange. Such listeners paid a subscription to the exchange, which was permitted to carry programmes from anywhere, not just the BBC.

---

[817] BBC archives R1/2/1, BBC Board of Governors Minute 29 (14th February 1934)

[818] BBC archives R1/2/1, BBC Board of Governors Minute 36 (28th February 1934)

[819] BBC archives R1/2/1, BBC Board of Governors Minute 38 (14th March 1934) The text of the letter was agreed by the Governors on 11th April 1934 (Minute 46).

[820] BBC archives R1/2/1, BBC Board of Governors Minute 75 (22nd May 1935)

[821] BBC archives R1/2/1, BBC Board of Governors Minute 15 (30th January 1935)

What the exchanges were not allowed to do was originate their own. It was Wood's contention that poorer listeners who received a service through exchanges should not be disadvantaged compared to those with their own radio who could listen to transmissions from anywhere they chose. By 1933, however, the BBC were growing increasingly concerned that exchanges might threaten the BBC service by concentrating on light entertainment and music programmes from other networks.[822] At their meeting on 24th May 1933 the Board were informed that there were 207 wireless exchanges at the end of March, the largest of which in Hull had more than 10,000 of the total of 94,000 subscribers.[823] The BBC and the Post Office had been discussing the scope and development of wireless exchanges for some time and in August 1933 Reith was particularly put out when the Postmaster-General permitted one such exchange, Nottingham Rediffusion, to broadcast the opening of their new control room. Reith protested that this set an unhelpful precedent and Wood should adhere to the "no origination" rule that prevented exchanges from generating their own programmes. The Post Office replied confirming that Nottingham Rediffusion had been allowed to carry the programme but it had been re-iterated to them that no programme could be originated at the exchange. Reith continued to express concern, quoting Tennyson that "freedom slowly broadens down from precedent to precedent".[824]

The BBC hoped that the Ullswater Committee would resolve the issue by putting exchanges under Post Office control and by giving the BBC authority for programmes. This was the Committee recommendation (paras 134-136), but the Government response shelved it. Although exchanges that carried two programmes had in future to ensure one of them was a BBC programme when the BBC was broadcasting, they otherwise sided with Wood's view that the private sector should not be constrained or poorer listeners disadvantaged. It may be significant that the Cabinet Sub-

---

[822] The *Daily Herald* had reported the previous year (27th April 1932, KW17 350/1) that the BBC and Post Office disagreed vehemently over the merit of the exchanges, with Reith opposing them as a threat to the BBC.

[823] BBC archives R1/69/2, Director-General Reports to BBC Board of Governors Two years later the Ullswater Committee report referred to 340 exchanges with 200,000 subscribers.

[824] BBC archives R1/69/2, Director-General Reports to BBC Board of Governors referring to Post Office communications of 3rd and 15th August and Reith's replies of 10th and 23rd August 1933.

Committee which formulated the Government response included Wood, though he had long since moved to Health.[825]

A related issue concerned advertising on continental radio stations. One of the questions asked by the League of Freedom of 1935 general election candidates was whether they would support British manufacturers being allowed to advertise on stations that could be heard in Britain and, unlike the BBC, were funded through advertising. The Cabinet's Emergency Business Committee endorsed the suggested Post Office reply that they await the report of the Ullswater Committee. National Government candidates were briefed accordingly.[826]

The existing, indeed the first, BBC Charter expired at the end of 1936 (ten years after it had been granted) and Reith's hope and expectation was that the new one would take account of the formidable progress that the Corporation had made since then. The BBC had become an integral part of the country's life with even the BBC's weekly magazine, the *Listener*, celebrating its fifth anniversary at the start of 1934. The 31st January issue carried a twelve-page supplement to mark the occasion, noting that there had been a ten-fold growth in wireless licences from 600,000 at 1st January 1924 to 6m ten years later.[827] One role of the *Listener* was to augment the BBC's educational function by printing broadcast talks: for example, HG Wells on 10th January, Winston Churchill on 17th January and George Bernard Shaw on 7th February 1934, all in a 'Whither Britain?' series.[828] Another function was to provide public information, with Wood setting out Post Office plans for 1934 in an article culled from a fifteen-minute talk.[829] *Popular Wireless* judged Wood's talk "the most outstanding one of recent weeks", adding inaccurately but nonetheless impressively that

... the PMG was making his debut at the microphone too! It says very little for the difficulty of the art of broadcasting

---

[825] In Reith's view "... it looked as if Kingsley Wood were still in virtual control". Reith, op cit, pp247-248

[826] CPA CRD 1/7/18 Cabinet Emergency Business Committee 11th November 1935 item 8, EBC(35)29

[827] *Listener* 31st January 1934, twelve page supplement on BBC constitution

[828] A talk by Keynes' on 'Roosevelt's economic experiments' appeared shortly afterwards (p93).

[829] *Listener* 3rd January 1934, KW19 81/2; BBC archives RCont1, 27th December 1933

when a novice can master it at once. Perhaps broadcasters are born not made.[830]

The reduction in charges to telephone users with the aim of increasing the number of subscribers was reported in June.[831] The BBC archives refer to a five-minute News Reel item at this time on 'Changes in the Post Office service', and it is likely that this covered the same ground.[832]

At the beginning of January the *Listener* magazine had carried an article by Professor Ernest Barker comparing the broadcasting systems of France, Germany and America with the BBC.[833] The USA was entirely private, funded through advertising, product placement and wealthy (though rarely disinterested) benefactors, Germany entirely State, France a mix of private and State, and only the British approach independent (though with a responsibility to Parliament through the PMG). The risks to editorial integrity in other countries were clear, with the power of broadcasting to disseminate propaganda increasingly apparent in Germany through the 1930s.[834]

It was being suggested as early as February 1934 that the Charter negotiation should start, though Wood made it clear in reply to a question in Parliament that he considered this premature given

---

[830] *Popular Wireless* 13th January 1934, KW19 38/12
Inaccurately, because a year earlier Wood had set out the Post Office's plans for 1933 (*Radio Times* 30th December 1932, KW18 13/2; BBC archives RCont1 2nd January 1933). BBC archives list two earlier talks in 1932, though without any detail on either.

[831] KW19 179/3; *Listener* p992

[832] BBC archives RCont1, 6th June 1934

[833] *Listener* 3rd January 1934, p10 reporting Professor Ernest Barker's analysis the previous month for a weekend course at Bonar Law College. Ernest Barker (1874-1960), a historian and political theorist, was by then Professor of Political Science at Cambridge University.

[834] Hitler had become Chancellor in January 1933 and by May the persecution of the Jews was already known outside the country. For example, the *Jewish Chronicle* on 5th May 1933 sought League of Nations intervention given that the Jewish race was considered a nation under Article 22 (KW18 94/1).
Over the weekend of 1st/2nd July 1934 between 77 and 400 political assassinations would be carried out on Hitler's orders in the "night of the long knives" (Bond, op cit, p48). According to Harold Macmillan, however, "It is now believed that between 5000 and 7000 persons were 'liquidated'" (1966, op cit, p394).

that the existing Charter still had nearly three years to run.[835] Nevertheless, Reith was soon agitating for discussions to begin, suggesting people for a Committee that July. Briggs refers to a meeting in June 1934 with Wood which Reith thought "most unsatisfactory" because of Wood's "political expediency" and assumption that the new Charter should not be very different from the existing one. In which case, Reith thought, why bother to have a Committee at all?[836] Wood, however, was in the driving seat and was determined that Reith should understand this. On 14th August Reith wrote to Warren Fisher that Wood had made it clear that he would not be doing more before the next Cabinet meeting, having consulted Baldwin since their last meeting but not Neville Chamberlain as yet.[837]

Three months later Reith again wrote to Fisher reporting a further conversation with Wood about Committee members. Reith's preference had been for the Committee to be chaired by Reginald McKenna, a possibility Wood did not discuss and one that the Prime Minister MacDonald had dismissed as inappropriate (according to Briggs).[838] Having failed to interest two people in the position, Wood was next to approach another former Speaker of the House of Commons, James Lowther now aged 79 and far too old in Reith's view. Wood may have done this deliberately to counter-balance Whitley or the latter may even have suggested it. Wood added, as a further demonstration that he was in charge, that he had now decided not to appoint the Committee before the new year.[839] By the start of 1935 Wood made it clear that the Committee, now called the Ullswater Committee, might assemble before Easter but would not begin work until afterwards. Reith suggested that, in order to avoid lobbying, there should not be a gap between announcing the Committee and it starting work. Wood agreed to this, and that he would not confirm the three party representatives to serve on the Committee (the MPs WS Morrison, Attlee and Graham White[840])

---

[835] *Manchester Guardian* 20th February 1934, KW19 76/4 Also KW19 75/5-7 *Daily Telegraph, Daily Mirror* and *Manchester Guardian* all 20th February 1934

[836] Briggs, 1995, op cit, p442

[837] BBC archives R4/69/1, 14th August 1934

[838] Briggs, 1995, op cit, p443

[839] BBC archives R4/69/1, 26th November 1934

[840] Conservative, Labour and Liberal MPs respectively. Graham White was Assistant PMG from August 1931 to September 1932 and had therefore worked with Wood at the Post Office for a while.

until nearer the time in order to avoid leaks. Wood told Reith that he hoped the report and its recommendations would be through the Cabinet and the House of Commons before the summer recess as he remained of the view that "the fewer changes [to the existing Charter] the better".[841]

In April Banks sent draft terms of reference to Reith's holiday address in Scotland.[842] These were exactly the same as for the Crawford Committee a decade before and Reith proposed various amendments three days later, particularly the addition that the Committee should "indicate what changes in the law, if any, are desirable in the interests of the service".[843] Reith would have had in mind both the position of the wireless exchanges and his preference for the BBC to report to a senior member of the Cabinet, ideally the Lord President of the Council, rather than through a junior Minister such as the Postmaster-General. Banks replied the same day, writing that, after consulting Wood and Warren Fisher, the Committee's terms of reference would be:

> To consider the constitution, control and finance of the broadcasting service in this country and advise generally on the conditions under which the service, including broadcasting to the Empire, television broadcasting and system of wireless exchanges, should be conducted after December 1936.[844]

Given the speed with which Banks replied, it is possible that these had been settled before Reith's comments were received but Reith would hardly have objected to them in any case. What he did object to was being sent them on holiday when they could have been decided long before, an irritation that increased when Wood announced them publicly while he was still away.

Reith's anxiety that he was being marginalised was soon apparent with Banks doing his best to convince him that his worries might be understandable but were unnecessary. Ullswater had assured Banks he had no wish to cause any upheaval and was keen to keep the inquiry as short as possible.[845] Nevertheless,

---

[841] BBC archives R4/69/1, 3rd January 1935
[842] BBC archives R4/69/1, 12th April 1935
[843] BBC archives R4/69/1, 15th April 1935
[844] Ibid
[845] BBC archives R4/69/1, Banks handwritten letter to Reith 17th April 1935

Reith continued to express disquiet about the composition of the Committee (ten members rather than the seven he had expected with, to make matters worse, a Welshman to look after Welsh interests as well as Mitchell-Thomson) and what he perceived as Wood's changed attitude to him.[846] Even though Wood, perhaps prompted by Banks, had written to Reith to re-assure him that his fears were unjustified, Reith believed the PMG had been friendly before but no longer[847] - "the most unfriendly PMG there had ever been," as Reith put it in his autobiography.[848] Discounting the hyperbole that Reith automatically applied to Wood, another way of putting this would be that Wood was prepared to stand up to him.

A few days later Reith found out that, as the Ullswater Committee would be meeting in private, the papers and evidence would not automatically be available to the Corporation. Reith argued that the BBC could only correct inaccuracies and rebut improper assertions if they saw the material, but it still might be thought inappropriate that they should do so if witnesses were to be encouraged to express their views openly. It should be up to the Committee to decide what was fair and accurate and what was not. Although Ullswater was prepared to put Reith's request before the Committee if he submitted it in writing,[849] this suggests either that Reith had a lack of confidence in the BBC or that he was becoming increasingly neurotic, even paranoid, that he and/or the Corporation would be stitched up. It would not have defused Reith's belief that Wood was underhand and expedient, traits he was eager to ascribe to him, when he endured a "thoroughly unpleasant twenty minutes" with him on 30th April, with Wood asking him to prepare a paper on broadcasting in war for a Committee Wood was to chair. Reith asked Wood if the BBC were to be represented on the Committee, to which the response was emphatically negative.[850] This was a sub-committee of the Committee of Imperial Defence (CID) and, as Maurice Hankey subsequently explained, there were never outsiders on such bodies. Yet Reith told Banks that this was further

---

[846] Wood had been asked in the Commons if he would appoint a Wales representative. He said he would bear the suggestion in mind. (*North Wales Observer* 1st November 1934, KW19 218/9)
[847] BBC archives R4/69/1, Reith letter to Banks 26th April 1935
[848] Reith, op cit, p219
[849] BBC archives R4/70/1, Reith letter to Banks 30th April 1935 and Banks reply 2nd May 1935
[850] Reith, op cit, pp220-221

evidence that Wood's attitude to him had changed for it had been "different in every respect from any meeting I have had with him".[851]

The BBC were sent an advance copy of the Ullswater report by the new Postmaster-General George Tryon (1871-1940)[852] in January 1936 and asked for their observations on the recommendations. Tryon's covering letter noted

> the general approval of the work of the BBC expressed by the Committee, and [their unanimous endorsement] of the broad policy which has characterised its operations.[853]

The report was issued on 16th March accompanied by the BBC's "self-satisfied" statement to the press (as Briggs describes it). The report endorsed the BBC view that, while technical control should remain with the PMG, the responsibility for the Corporation's policy and culture should be transferred to a senior member of the Government free from heavy departmental responsibilities (i.e., the Lord President of the Council without actually naming him).[854] However, like their recommendation on wireless exchanges, this was never enacted - though Baldwin's reluctance to take on the task may have been at least as responsible as Wood's disagreement with the proposal. In his autobiography Reith claims that his dispute with Wood over this point, and the support he had received from both Warren Fisher and Donald Banks over it, was one of the main reasons he and Wood fell out. Reith asserted that he "would not sacrifice BBC interests to suit [Wood's] ideas of political expediency".[855] Unfortunately, there is no record of Wood's view but it might be assumed that, like Attlee and Cripps,[856] he bridled at Reith's dictatorial and autocratic stance, and consequently was prepared to challenge Reith's views rather than just accept them as the "sermons from the mount" that Reith thought them.

---

[851] BBC archives R4/70/1, Reith letter to Banks 30th April 1935
[852] Although Tryon was never in the Cabinet, he had been Minister of Pensions 1924-1929 and 1931-1935. He would have worked with Wood in the latter capacity and it is inconceivable that they did not know each other in Brighton.
[853] BBC archives R4/70/2, Tryon letter to Chairman of BBC 2nd January 1936
[854] Ullswater Committee report (Cmd 5091), paras 53-57
[855] Reith, op cit, p251
[856] Hansard, 29th April 1936, vol. 311, col. 974

When Wood left the Post Office to become Minister of Health, the General Secretary of the Union of Post Office Workers, JW Bowen, wrote an article in the in-house publication *The Post* praising Wood as "one of the best Postmaster-Generals who ever held the office".[857] This might be thought unduly sycophantic in what was still an age of deference, but it is difficult to see what Bowen would get out of it if he was not expressing the general view of his members. His "generous tribute", as it was described, did not blind Bowen to those occasions when the Union and Wood had been at odds, but nevertheless "we found ourselves pleased in many things he has done for our service". Bowen's respect and affection led him to send Wood a copy, to which he added a handwritten note:

> I am sorry you have left us but I hope it is for the good health of your new Department. Many thanks for many courtesies
>
> …

---

[857] *The Post* 15th June 1935, KW21 24/9

Vignettes

Robert Williamson

In the Kingsley Wood archive at the University of Kent there is a curious handwritten letter to Wood from a Robert Williamson:[858]

> Dear Sir Kingsley Wood, It delighted me very much to read that my benefactor had been promoted to Cabinet rank. Time's revenge indeed![859]

It may be that "revenge" refers to Wood's harrying of Ramsay MacDonald in 1924, contributing to the downfall of the first Labour government, and/or his continual baiting of him during Labour's second period of office. The words are also a reminder of those used by the *Times* at the beginning of August 1931 as the international crisis began to bite: "Time has seldom brought a revenge so rapid". Three weeks later MacDonald had resigned as Labour Prime Minister and the National Government was formed.

Yet why Williamson refers to Wood as his benefactor is not entirely clear but may be of even more interest.

Williamson was a publicity journalist[860] who shared his Adam Street premises with the (unrelated) Robert and John Refreshment Rooms. The latter were still there in 1945 but Williamson had been replaced by an architect. It is likely, therefore, that these were the offices from which he ran his public relations company (though other buildings in the same street were occupied as flats).[861] In 1932 and 1935, for example, Williamson was employed by the Department of Overseas Trade to handle news from their British Industries Fair, which on each occasion had both London and

---

[858] Williamson's dates of birth and death have not been found.

[859] Letter dated 28th December 1933 from 10 Adam Street, Adelphi, London WC2 in KW33 (a box of unsorted press cuttings from various years and other ephemera).

[860] Though he is not listed in the Institute of Journalists 'Grey Book' for 1923 or 1928-1930, this is hardly conclusive (British Library 4th and 11th September 2014).

[861] Kelly's Post Office Directory 1930 and 1945
The Diamond Press was at this address in 1927 while Hore-Belisha and a male friend survived a fire at their flat (number 5) in 1925.

Birmingham sites.[862] The Fair had been preceded in 1931 by the Business Efficiency Exhibition at the White City, possibly an earlier publicity commission in which Williamson was involved. This exhibition, opened by Wood on 17th March, had been staged to help foster a revival in business optimism, under the slogan 'Get ready for big business', with one report claiming that "Recent events indicate that the spirit of optimism and confidence is returning to the ranks of industry and business".[863] At the opening Wood pointed out that "The average man spends about a third of his life in an office and some of the offices are more like prison cells or lumber rooms than anything else",[864] while another evening paper reported his call for "not only more efficient, but brighter and better offices".[865] Although Wood was never in need of an intermediary to ensure his words appeared in print, he may have appreciated Williamson's assistance at this time. With the Labour Government in retreat in the face of unemployment and political crises, there were other priorities for the press and, while everybody likes good news, it still has to be publicised. A grateful Wood in 1931 may well have proved Williamson's benefactor subsequently.

In later years Williamson was to be closely connected with cycling, including as Honorary Secretary to the National Committee on Cycling, in which capacity he wrote letters to a variety of newspapers in 1937 on road safety, particularly with regard to child cyclists.[800] Wood may have been persuaded to take up riding, but only on horses not bicycles. His connection to Williamson must have another genesis therefore and is more likely to have arisen through business efficiency, putting work Williamson's way and thereby becoming in effect his "benefactor".

---

[862] Williamson's responsibilities were announced well in advance in the *Western Daily Press* 26th June 1931 and the *Aberdeen Journal* 30th August 1934.

[863] *Western News and Mercury* 26th February 1931, KW17 257/3
Also, *Financial Times* 9th March 1931, KW17 261/7; *Star, Glasgow Herald* and *Northampton Echo* all 11th March 1931, KW17 262/5-6, 262/12

[864] *Evening Standard* 17th March 1931, KW17 262/10

[865] *Evening News* 17th March 1931, KW17 262/3

[866] For example, *North Devon Journal* 2nd August and *Yorkshire Post and Leeds Intelligencer* 2nd November 1937

The Athenaeum

In March 1934 Wood, already a member of the Carlton and Constitutional Clubs, was elected to the Athenaeum. The Carlton was inevitable for a leading Conservative politician but the Athenaeum Club drew its membership from a wider spectrum, encompassing the arts and literature as well as politics. Membership was highly coveted, a recognition of impact on society whatever the field of endeavour. No more than nine people were invited to join each year on the basis of their eminent public service (Keynes in 1942, for example),[867] but even the slightly larger handful elected by the Committee each year had first to be nominated by two existing members. Wood's nomination was proposed by the extraordinarily colourful mountaineer and first Director-General of the Imperial War Museum[868] Martin Conway (1856-1937), Lord Conway of Allington, and seconded by Stanley Baldwin,[869] one of the three Trustees elected by Athenaeum members, a position he held from 1930 until his death in 1947.[870] Baldwin, Wood's friend, political colleague and mentor, would be a natural choice but the connection to Conway and the reason for his support is far from obvious.

Ten years earlier in 1924, when Conway was already sixty-eight, he had begun a six-year affair with a divorcee of twenty-four, an affair that only ended (though not completely) when she re-married. In November 1934, slightly less than a year after his own wife's death, he married Iva Lawson, the widowed owner of Saltwood, another Kent castle like Allington.[871] She was five years

---

[867] FR Cowell, 'The Athenaeum: Club and Social Life in London, 1824-1974', 1975, p167

[868] Adrian Tinniswood, 'The Long Weekend: Life in the English Country House Between the Wars', 2016, p69

[869] Personal communication 7th August 2014 from Athenaeum Club archivist

[870] Cowell, op cit, p160

[871] Conway's DNB entry and Joan Evans, 'The Conways: A History of Three Generations', 1966

Saltwood Castle was later bought by Sir Kenneth Clark (1903-1983), famed as Director of the National Gallery and for the seminal TV series "Civilization", and subsequently passed to his son the notorious Conservative MP and diarist Alan Clark (1928-1999).

Sir Kenneth Clark opened the 'Pictures in Advertising' exhibition sponsored by Shell-Mex and BP at the Burlington Galleries in June 1934

younger than Conway's daughter, the Delphi archaeologist Agnes Conway. Martin Conway and Wood were Kent neighbours in the loose sense that Allington was north of Maidstone, with the Castle nestling in a bend of the River Medway, but it is not on the direct route between Woolwich and Tunbridge Wells. It is twenty miles from Broomhill Bank, thirty from Woolwich. Conway was the Unionist MP for combined universities from 1918 to 1931 so he and Wood would have known each other in the Commons, held similar views against Irish Home Rule and their fathers had both been church ministers, Wood's a Wesleyan Methodist and Conway's the Canon of Westminster. Yet it may have been their independent views that drew them together initially. In Conway's case, James Johnston described him as a man who "thinks things out for himself, [and] views questions from angles quite unfamiliar to other Members". On the other hand, his "wayward and dreamy" mind was very different to Wood's hard-nosed, practical bent. Johnston's profile of Wood is far removed from his description of Conway's "idea-laden sentences ... like the palm-trees of an oasis"; "refreshing" perhaps, but also unsuited to, and unrealistic in, Commons debate.[872]

About twenty Athenaeum members would attend Wood's memorial service in 1943, with the Club formally represented by the Conservative MP Sir Edmund Brocklebank (1882-1949). Bridgeman's colleagues on the Post Office inquiry, Plender and Cadman, were both members (as was the Committee Secretary Austin Earl), though Bridgeman himself was not.

---

at which Wood, the fervent advocate of publicity and advertising, was photographed viewing the posters in *Bystander* 26th June 1934, KW19 133/3.

Martin Conway wrote many books himself and though his autobiography ('Episodes In A Varied Life', 1932) gives little hint of his extra-marital affairs, it does refer to the death in 1931 of a mountaineer with the same name as the youthful divorcee.

[872] Johnston, op cit, pp61-63

Edward Taswell Campbell, PPS

Derrick Gunston, Wood's PPS from 1926 to 1929, joined Neville Chamberlain as his PPS at the Treasury in 1931. Gunston retained this position until January 1936 when "he could stand [Chamberlain's] policies no longer".[873]

Edward Taswell Campbell (1879-1945), Conservative MP for North West Camberwell from 1924 to 1929 had been defeated in the 1929 general election but was re-elected in a 1930 by-election as MP for Bromley. In November 1931 he became PPS to Wood as Postmaster-General, continuing as his PPS (at Health, Air, Lord Privy Seal, the Treasury) until Wood's death in 1943. This is an extraordinary record of association, especially as Campbell was more than two years older than Wood and held many other posts outside politics during this time. His Bromley seat was close to Wood's at Woolwich, but they may have become acquainted first through less formal routes than the London Conservative Committee.

Harold Balfour, Wood's PS at Air, refers to Campbell as "Captain of the 'Bores Eleven'" in the 1931 parliament,

> Invariably loquacious, with eyes that gleamed kindly through round glasses, he kept [this] place of honour until, by popular acclaim, he was superseded by the Liberal Sir Percy Harris.[874]

A report in the *Daily Mail* highlights Campbell's easy-going attitude and ability to see both sides when, in early 1934, he was contacted by a woman who had received a letter from her husband postmarked Brighton even though he was supposed to be on business in Nottingham. Campbell told the woman that he had been particularly busy at the Post Office when the letter came in

---

[873] Ronald Tree, 'When the Moon Was High: Memoirs of Peace and War 1897-1942', 1975, p75.
Tree (1897-1976), on the Eden wing of the Conservative Party, claims in his biography (op cit, p76) that in 1940 his phone was tapped by Sir Joseph Ball, then Minister of Information and still Chamberlain's henchman. This would almost certainly have been because of Tree's criticisms of appeasement.
Gunston exacted his revenge when he voted against the Chamberlain government in the Norway debate in May 1940.
[874] Harold Balfour, 'Wings Over Westminster', 1973, p84

and had put the wrong postmark on. A couple of days later Campbell received a gold cigarette case from the husband to thank him for his discretion.[875]

Balfour's assessment of Campbell described him as Wood's

Jagger ... a member appendage to some Minister or ex-Minister. If in Office the Minister might make the Jagger his PPS but not necessarily so. Out of office the Jagger just did his jiggering without trimmings. The Jagger was a faithful friend, not unlike a master's faithful hound. He was seen constantly with his master. You could scarcely walk into the Lobby without meeting both, arm-in-arm, in close conversation. ...

... Dear old Sir Edward Campbell was Kingsley's disciple in and out of Office, as well as being his loyal and earnest PPS [876] ...

As Balfour points out, Eden, Churchill and Cunliffe-Lister also had their "Jaggers", making Campbell as important to Wood as Bracken was to Churchill.

In later 1934 a group was formed to ginger up the National Government as it ran out of steam. One of those supposed to be involved was Campbell, but as the *Northern Whig* reported:

I am surprised ... to see Sir Edward Campbell, Sir Kingsley Wood's energetic PPS, among them, for he has been such a model PPS to Sir Kingsley that I should think his association with any 'ginger group' might have its repercussions on his own chief's head.[877]

Campbell was one of sixteen children, eleven of whom survived to adulthood. His younger brother Gordon (1886-1953), a naval officer and winner of the Victoria Cross in 1917 as a commander of a decoy Q-ship used to lure German submarines,

---

[875] *Daily Mail* 17th February 1934, KW19 61/3 The woman seemed to have remained innocent on both counts: how the Post Office worked as well as her husband's "business".

[876] Balfour, op cit, pp94-95
Similarly, Campbell described himself as Wood's "fag ... and in that capacity had a great deal of work to do". *Beckenham Journal* 24th October 1936, KW21 72/4

[877] *Northern Whig*, 24th August 1934, KW19 166/3

stood for the National Government in 1931, defeating Labour's Arthur Henderson in Burnley. Bridgeman and Churchill were among those who had spoken for him, presumably because of the Admiralty connections. Gordon Campbell subsequently lost to Labour there in 1935, an outcome for which he may have been grateful as the country's crisis was increasingly military rather than financial and he never considered himself a professional politician.[878]

Edward Campbell attended Dulwich College, as did all seven of his brothers. He left at sixteen to join James Finlay and Co., East India merchants in the City of London, a post he held from 1895 to 1899. In 1900 he went out to Sumatra as a tobacco planter, became a partner in the firm of Maclaine Watson and Co., served as British Vice-Consul in Java from 1914 to 1920 and for some of that time as French and Russian Consul as well. Back in England from 1921 he was LCC member for Lewisham from 1922 to 1925 before beginning his parliamentary career, and (among other things) was a governor of Dulwich College from 1922 until his death, President of the National Association of Boys' Clubs, on the Boy Scouts Council and the executive of the National Playing Fields Association, and Vice-President of the Kent Association of Boys' Clubs.[879] He won the 1945 general election in Bromley but died before the result could be declared.[880] At the Alleyn Club dinner for Dulwich College Old Boys three days later (the first since before the war) several of the speakers inserted brief tributes into their speeches. His *Alleynian* obituary refers to his "faithful and assiduous service" to Kingsley Wood. Campbell's knighthood in 1933 and baronetcy in 1939 must have been due in large measure to his efforts on Wood's behalf.

---

[878] Gordon Campbell, 'Number Thirteen', 1932

[879] 'Who Was Who' entry and obituary in the *Alleynian*, vol. LXXIII, No. 509, November 1945 The latter was provided by the Dulwich College archivist on 4th June 2014.
Much of this information is also included in a report headlined 'Knight and Rubber Expert' in the *Evening Star* 9th February 1934, KW19 59/9 and up to 1925 in CPA PUB 210/1 'Man in the Street', February 1925, p17.

[880] The future Prime Minister Harold Macmillan who had been defeated heavily in Stockton won the subsequent by-election in November 1945 and represented Bromley for the remainder of his parliamentary career.

14.   CONSERVATIVE BAROMETER

In 1935 the *Times* judged Wood, then the newly-appointed Minister of Health, both a "competent administrator" and a "master of publicity",[881] skills that were as much in demand within the Conservative party as they were in his ministerial posts. Earlier that year another newspaper had profiled him, still Postmaster-General at that point, as their 'Man of the Week', characterising him as the "live wire of the Cabinet",

> ... reminiscent of a rubber ball - alike in appearance and resilience ... extremely able speaker in House and on platform - a terror at question time - very popular, always smiling, always friendly and always approachable.[882]

Three days earlier the Conservative Party's National Publicity Bureau had been established with Wood at its head and in effect he had become Director of Propaganda and Publicity to the entire National Government as well, their election supremo. It was not just his competence and efficiency that had carried him this far, for they were augmented by an amiable and genial nature that many remarked upon over the years. For all these reasons, as well as his knowledge of local government and health, he had been picked to put some vim into housing and slum clearance after his many successes at the Post Office, and his co-operative approach would later make him ideal for the Air Ministry as war became inevitable.[883] But they were also the skills the party sought and that made his policy and propaganda talents even more attractive to them. Wood had begun his ascent of the Party hierarchy when he joined the Executive Committee in March 1927. Little more than

---

[881] *Times* 8th June 1935, KW19 395/7

[882] *Sunday Referee* 14th March 1935, KW19 320/5
It continued "in spare time is enthusiastic film fan - when duties permit is to be seen at film premieres - a possible PM of the future".

[883] For example, an article by Harold Laski in the *Listener* (22nd February 1933, KW18 43/1) on the 'Hows and Whys of Running the State' singled out the Advisory Council Wood had established at the Post Office as an example of good practice that would help keep any Minister in touch with ordinary opinion.

three years later he would be the Chair.[884] In a tribute in Parliament the day after Wood's death in September 1943 the Prime Minister Winston Churchill described him as, among other things, a "good party man".[885]

Executive Committee

After the Conservative election defeat in 1929 pressure had mounted on the Party Chairman JCC Davidson as well as on Baldwin.[886] The Executive Committee post-mortem included questionnaires to all constituencies to establish their views[887] and eight months later the sub-committee appointed to consider their replies proposed that in future it should be provincial divisions (rather than constituencies) that the Party looked to for the revival of local interest and the dissemination of Conservative principles.[888] It was during Wood's time as Chair of the Executive Committee between October 1930 and March 1932 that representatives of these provincial areas were elected to the Executive for the first time.[889]

Eventually, Davidson resigned on 29th May 1930, Neville Chamberlain having "told [him] bluntly ... that he had to go",[890] and the following month new rules for the National Union were ratified by a special Party conference. According to Self, Austen Chamberlain thought Wood "the best man to succeed as Party Chairman",[891] perhaps because Austen wanted his half-brother Neville to be free to challenge Baldwin for the leadership. If so, Baldwin anticipated the risk and was strong enough to rule out Wood and others[892] so that it was Neville Chamberlain who became

---

[884] CPA NUA 4/1/4 Executive Committee minutes 1922-1930: first meeting 15th March 1927 (pp212-218) when JCC Davidson was still Chair; elected Chair 14th October 1930 (p403)

[885] Hansard, 22nd September 1943, vol. 392, col. 215

[886] Davidson's wife Mimi (1894-1985) succeeded him as MP for Hemel Hempstead. He was a long-standing ally of Baldwin, whose PPS he had been in 1921-1922, while his wife was often Baldwin's walking companion.

[887] CPA NUA 4/2/1 Report of Executive Committee to Central Council 2nd July 1929.

[888] Ibid 4th March 1930.

[889] Ibid 24th February 1931.

[890] Stuart Ball in Davidson's DNB entry.

[891] Self, 2002, op cit, 21st June 1930, p190: "Wood was also recommended by Bridgeman when [the latter] refused it."

[892] Ibid, p191

Party Chairman. Under new rules from 1st September 1930 the Executive Committee elected its own chairman instead of this devolving *ex officio* to the Chairman of the Party Organisation, thereby separating the two roles that Davidson had held previously. The Party Chairman was now an ordinary member of the Executive and Kingsley Wood their first chairman, elected in October 1930, "a respected moderate MP on the verge of Cabinet rank" as Ball describes him, and of course close to Neville Chamberlain.[893] The Executive agreed that there would be no annual conference in 1930, but a special meeting of the Central Council of the National Union should be held instead. It was Wood who defined the two roles of the Executive as suggesting policies to the Leader and dealing with organisational matters,[894] while only the Party Leader could formulate and finalise policy.[895]

A few months later in February 1931 Mosley formed the New Party, the Labour Government's attempt to repeal the 1927 Trade Disputes Act was defeated, the official Tory candidate in the St George's, Westminster by-election (John Moore-Brabazon) resigned and Baldwin came close to giving up the Party leadership. Neville Chamberlain stood down as Party Chairman in order to be free to succeed Baldwin - in accordance with Austen Chamberlain's analysis and preference, if not at his behest.[896] At this point, therefore, not only were the Liberals out of touch with their roots and Labour focussed on ideology, while unemployment continued to

---

[893] Ball, 2013, op cit, p263
Also, *Telegraph* and *Nottingham Journal* both 15th October 1930, *Portsmouth Evening News* 16th October 1930, KW17 225/3, 225/5 & 225/8: Wood unanimously elected Chairman of Executive Committee of National Union of Conservative and Unionist Associations for the rest of the year to 28th February 1931; Ken Young, 'Local Politics and the Rise of Party: The London Municipal Society and the Conservative Intervention in Local Elections 1894-1963', 1975, pp27 & 151; Robert Rhodes James, 'Memoirs of a Conservative: JCC Davidson's Memoirs and Papers 1910-1937', 1969, pp269-270
[894] CPA NUA 4/1/5 Executive Committee minutes 16th June 1931
Also, Ball, 2013, op cit, p265
[895] Ibid, p513 - referring to the National Union Executive 29th June 1931 (and 12th July 1927).
[896] Self, 2006, op cit, p150; *Guardian* 10th April 1931, KW17 265/2 reports Chamberlain's decision to retire as Chair of the Conservative Party. Self describes the Chamberlain and Tory Party machinations in more detail on pp147-151, as do many others, including Middlemas and Barnes, op cit, pp588-598 and Ball, 2014, op cit, pp403 & 406.

increase and the Unemployment Fund got further out of control, but Beaverbrook was pressing for Empire economic union and Baldwin was at his lowest ebb, fighting for his position as leader of the Conservatives against continuing disquiet over the 1929 general election result and growing disaffection over his policy towards India, fuelled by the Beaverbrook and Rothermere press. In the event, though, Baldwin recovered to easily face down Beaverbrook and Rothermere, the "insolent and irresponsible plutocracy" as Self describes them. Eventually persuaded by Bridgeman and Davidson not to resign, Baldwin's speech in the St George's, Westminster by-election included the memorable barb against Beaverbrook and Rothermere and their papers: "power without responsibility - the prerogative of the harlot throughout the ages".[897] The by-election, brought about by the death of Laming Worthington-Evans, was expected to be won by Beaverbrook's candidate until the Conservative fightback, exemplified by Baldwin's speech, and two days later the Conservative candidate Duff Cooper (1890-1954) romped home with a majority of more than 5000. His wife Diana Cooper (1892-1986) recorded how the American heiress Emerald Cunard (1872-1948) was in the audience when Baldwin spoke at the Queen's Hall and would look up from reading the *Star* or *Telegraph* (both Baldwin-supporting papers) whenever Beaverbrook or Rothermere were mentioned and mutter audibly: "Degenerates; they're both degenerates!"[898]

In the week before the by-election Wood had been re-appointed Chairman of the Executive Committee,[899] which would not have happened had his loyalty to Baldwin been at odds with his ambition. With his position strengthened, Baldwin followed up with a Shadow Cabinet re-shuffle to demonstrate that he was back in control of the Party. Chamberlain became Shadow Chancellor and Chair of the Finance Committee, with Wood replacing him at Health and as Chair of the Conservative Health and Housing Committee.[900] Churchill's disloyalty over India (and his advocacy of free trade) ensured he was dropped altogether.[901]

---

[897] Middlemas and Barnes, op cit, pp580, 586 & 600

[898] Diana Cooper, 'The Light of Common Day', 1959, pp98-101

[899] CPA NUA 4/1/5 Executive Committee minutes 10th March 1931 Wood unanimously re-elected Chair (p437); *Morning Post* 12th March 1931, KW17 262/7

[900] CPA NUA 4/1/5 Executive Committee minutes 12th May 1931 approved proposal to set up Conservative Health Committee.

[901] *Times* 6th May and *People* 10th May 1931, KW17 274/9 & 275/6

At the end of June the half-yearly meeting of the National Union of Conservative and Unionist Associations took place at Kingsway Hall in London. Six hundred and fifty delegates from England, Wales, Scotland and Northern Ireland unanimously adopted the report of the Executive Committee that Wood presented as Chairman. Lord Stonehaven (Chamberlain's replacement as Party Chairman) warned that, "... however attractive the name 'Labour' sounded, nothing could be worse for the young working man and working woman than for the country to adopt Socialism"; Australia had "turned the corner" when it "turned against Socialism" and Britain should do the same. The *Birmingham Post* headed its report 'Socialism v Sanity',[902] while from the other side of the fence the *Daily Herald* concentrated on Conservative demands for pledges from the Prime Minister before they would take part in further proceedings of the India Round-Table Conference.[903]

Lloyd George had not given up on the possibility of electoral reform and in 1931 drew on his links with Wood to re-establish a committee with the Conservatives. Lloyd George proposed that the Conservatives should concede the alternative vote option in the House of Lords and he would then turn out the Labour Government immediately. Neville Chamberlain accepted this offer and Lloyd George undertook to have the Government out by the following April. However, the economic crisis intervened before electoral reform could be considered, let alone the Lloyd George deal pursued. The upshot was that this fitted Ramsay McDonald's shift to a National Government.[904] Subsequently, Lloyd George claimed in his diary (on 21st February 1934) that Wood was dissatisfied with the government and had suggested Lloyd George as Prime Minister instead.[905] No matter how disgruntled Wood was with MacDonald - and, it should be remembered, MacDonald had been sufficiently impressed by Wood's performance as PMG to bring him into the Cabinet only two months before - it is most unlikely that Wood would have thought Lloyd George the best alternative at this time.

---

[902] *Birmingham Post* 1st July 1931, KW17 278/1 (also *Times* 1st July 1931, KW17 278/5)

[903] *Daily Herald* 1st July 1931, KW17 278/2

[904] John D Fair, "The second Labour government and the politics of electoral reform", *Albion*, 1981, 13, pp276-301

[905] Frances Stephenson, 'Lloyd George: A Diary', 1971, p256

Wood certainly admired Lloyd George,[906] having written only a couple of months before to thank him for his support, recalling that it was Lloyd George who had first appointed him to a Government committee (the National Insurance Advisory Council in 1912): "So in some sense you are responsible for me in public life".[907] But it is a considerable leap from Wood's letter to Lloyd George's diary entry. This only makes sense as a tongue-in-cheek, off-the-cuff comment that Lloyd George noted for his own amusement or for the purpose of making mischief in the future: his "friends were often pawns in the game of power politics", as Koss put it.[908] Possibly it relates to Lloyd George's disgust at this time that the Liberal stance on issues including housing had been stolen by the Labour Party and progressive Conservatives (among whom he would have included Wood).

Lloyd George's diary entry the following January asserted that Beaverbrook and Rothermere had approached Wood to discuss the scope for destroying the government. It further claimed that they did so together so that Wood could not "persuade Rothermere to toe the line, as has happened before".[909] It is difficult to know what to make of this. Rothermere did not need a minder to stand firm, though he and Beaverbrook did sometimes hunt as a pair, not so much as "good cop-bad cop" but the better to corner their prey. Even if Beaverbrook and Rothermere did approach Wood together, it is unlikely they thought his status and influence so exalted that he could bring an end to the government; only that he was somebody they would prefer on their side. He might have been

---

[906] It was mutual to some extent, for in early 1935 Lloyd George included in the opening speech of his New Deal campaign at Bangor "I have a great opinion of him [Wood], and I only wish they were all up to his sample". (*NA* undated, KW21 24/12)

[907] Parliamentary archives LG/G/19/22 item 5: handwritten note from Wood dated 27th December 1933

Earlier that year a lunch had been held to mark the twenty-first anniversary of National Health Insurance, "The unwanted child" as the *Manchester Guardian* put it in their report (18th July 1933, KW18 134/1). Among those who attended were Lloyd George, the "parent", and Wood among the "god-parents" (others being Lord Reading, Churchill and JH Thomas). Three of those involved were already dead (Masterman, Morant, Worthington-Evans); Addison was not mentioned.

[908] Stephen Koss, 'Fleet Street Radical: AG Gardiner and the *Daily News*', 1973, p132

[909] Stephenson, op cit, 10th January 1935, p297

only one of those approached, and there were more likely candidates with the position and power to remove MacDonald and create difficulties for Baldwin, but Lloyd George does not mention them. Taken at face value this seems a mis-reading of Wood's loyalty to Baldwin and, if it was Wood who told Lloyd George, he almost certainly told others too to make it apparent that his hands were clean.

Within days of the National Government's formation Wood convened an emergency meeting of the Executive Committee to explain the Party's decision to participate in it,[910] and soon after the General Election at the end of October Baldwin attended to stress that, rather than rest on their laurels, the large Conservative majority was an opportunity to press home their advantage. In particular, he wanted MPs and the Party generally to concentrate on "political education" in those constituencies that they would not normally expect to win on party lines.[911]

In the event Wood was not Chair of the Executive Committee for much longer. After less than eighteen months in the role he was replaced by George Herbert in March 1932. Herbert remained Chair for five years to 1937 (as would Eugene Ramsden from 1938 to 1943)[912] and, given their longevity in the post and Wood's increasing workload at the Post Office, it may be that he had chosen to stand down. Perhaps indicative of this, Wood attended only six times between May 1932 and April 1938.[913] Had this been pique or otherwise unjustified it is unlikely that he would have become such a fundamental component of the Party organisation in other respects. Among other things he was soon one of the London representatives on the Executive. Clearly, his profile was such that non-attendance at the Executive Committee was no barrier.[914]

---

[910] CPA NUA 4/1/5 Executive Committee minutes 28th August 1931 (pp468-470)
[911] Ibid 4th November 1931 (p477)
[912] CPA NUA 4/2/1
[913] CPA NUA 4/1/5 Executive Committee minutes 1931-1937, NUA 4/1/6 Executive Committee minutes 1938-1948
By September 1939 many constituencies had decided to close down their activities during the Second World War.
[914] CPA NUA 4/2/1 As reported to the Party's Central Council meeting on 28th March 1934.

Conservative Research Department

One of JCC Davidson's innovations after the 1929 election defeat was to establish the Conservative Research Department (CRD) in 1930 under Joseph Ball (1885-1961), previously the Party's Director of Publicity. The CRD was designed to clarify the Party's policies and help resolve the policy disputes that had followed the election result.[915] Its first chairman (briefly) was Eustace Percy but he was soon replaced by Neville Chamberlain, the Party Chairman. He and Ball became good friends and would remain so, with Chamberlain retaining control of the CRD until his death.[916]

By October 1931 there were eleven Committees, each charged with exploring a particular issue, such as imperial affairs, reform of the House of Lords, tariffs, with CRD staff providing the secretariat. The 'Industrial Foundations' Committee, for example, was "to inquire into and report upon the economic and social needs, habits and aspirations of the wage-earning classes". Chaired by WS Morrison it was typical in having only a few Members (in this case four others, usually MPs or peers). The most important of the Committees, and the one that had an overarching rather than a specific investigative role, was the Policy Committee. In October 1931 this was chaired by Lord Hailsham with only three other members: Cunliffe-Lister, Hoare and Kingsley Wood. Joseph Ball, the Director of the CRD, also attended and his second in command Brooke was the Secretary.[917]

A year later the National Co-ordinating Committee was formed to eliminate duplication of essential tasks

> common to all three parties [in the National Government], and to review National propaganda for by-elections in conformity with the views of the three component parts.[918]

This initiative was intended to calm Simon and his Liberal Nationals, for the Samuelite Liberals had departed the National Government a couple of weeks earlier (over the adoption of tariffs, particularly after the Ottawa conference that summer)[919] and with the Conservative

---

[915] Ball, 2013, op cit, p442-444 and 448
[916] Self, 2006, op cit, p150
[917] CPA CRD 1/25/1, Organisation of Conservative Research Department 1930-1939
[918] Stannage, op cit, p37
[919] Ibid, p90

conference in early October having endorsed the National Government, Simon was alarmed that he might be the bystander in a Conservative take-over. Baldwin was happy to re-assure Simon and his colleagues that the three parties would retain their own identity within the overall National Government.[920]

Party Policy and Election Supremo

Perhaps as much because of his role on the CRD's Policy Committee as for his success at the Post Office, press speculation was soon mounting that Wood might become the Party's Director of Propaganda.[921] There were several reasons why Wood was a leading candidate for this role. Apart from his use of advertising and publicity at the Post Office, he was a natural conciliator and co-operator. This had got him into trouble during the General Strike, and could infuriate his opponents in parliament, but his ability to re-assure people, Conservative diehards as much as those in other parties, was second to none. He was as capable as the next politician of emollient words, but his actions backed him up and would convince many in any case. His work alongside people as different as Lloyd George and Baldwin, not to mention the evolution of his relationship with Neville Chamberlain from a fractious, even hostile, start to mutual approbation, meant that he was trusted. And in those instances when he was not trusted, his genial character went a long way towards deflecting anxiety and dislike.

A few months later Wood's elevation to policy supremo had become reality. The *Morning Post* reported a meeting Baldwin held at 11 Downing Street on 27th September 1934 for Conservative Party chiefs at which it was agreed that Wood be given responsibility for preparing Conservative General Election policy "relying on his energy and political flair to produce one which will capture the public imagination".[922] Consequently, Wood's new role in the inner councils of the Conservative Party would ensure that "His influence ... will be considerable."[923] Baldwin was to announce

---

Roskill, op cit, p95 adds that, despite Free Trade Liberal and Labour Ministers resigning over the Ottawa agreements in 1932 (Samuel, Snowden and Sinclair, for example) everything was generally stable on the home political front in 1933.
[920] Stannage, op cit, p90
[921] *Daily Mail* 28th February 1934, KW19 63/4
[922] *Morning Post* 28th September 1934, KW19 188/1
[923] *Evening Standard* 28th September 1934, KW19 180/11

this to the party conference at Bristol the following week[924] in a speech which asserted "I am Leader and I am going to lead".[925]

The Conservative Party conference took place a fortnight after the horror of the Gresford colliery disaster in which two hundred and twenty-six miners were killed - still one of the worst peacetime tragedies in Britain in terms of death toll. This was one of those rare occasions when a mining tragedy made the national newspapers. In the year 1937, for example, in total 859 miners would be killed and almost 3,500 seriously injured, but their deaths were never mentioned for they "were killed singly or in twos or threes".[926] Such was the grief nationally that a country-wide collection for their dependants raised over half a million pounds.[927] The Conservative Party conference showed their respects too, a short silence followed by a collection among the 1100 delegates which raised £49 12s 6d - i.e., about £2000 today - or less than a shilling each on average. Little more than a gesture in effect but it was this, as much as the amount raised, that was important.

The London County Council (LCC) election in March that year had resulted in Labour control for the first time in twenty-seven years and it had been Wood as a prominent London Conservative who had opened the Municipal Reform campaign [928] But the first measure of his party role was to come the following November when each of the twenty-eight Borough Councils within London also went to the polls. The leader of the LCC, and Wood's constituent in Woolwich, Herbert Morrison gleefully anticipated

> To our delight ... [Wood] will bring Labour luck. We remember that he opened the Tory LCC campaign and that the result was the defeat of the Municipal 'Reformers' for the first time in twenty-seven years.[929]

Morrison continued "We are also encouraged by the fact that Lord Beaverbrook has brought his newspapers blundering into the campaign with characteristic irresponsibility". Morrison had told the

[924] CPA Annual Conference minutes NUA 2/1/49, 4th and 5th October 1934 at Colston Hall, Bristol
[925] *Manchester Guardian* 6th October 1934, cited by Stannage, op cit, p49
[926] Greenwood, 1938/9, op cit, p30
[927] www.wrexham.gov.uk/english/heritage/gresford_disaster/nations reaction.htm - accessed 29th July 2015
[928] *Islington Gazette* 31st January 1934, KW19 58/2
[929] *Star* 31st October 1934, KW19 215/8

Daily Herald a few days earlier "Sir Kingsley Wood is a joke; he ought to be preserved".[930] Despite a four-page election supplement in Beaverbrook's *Evening Standard*[931] headed 'Vote for Prosperity: Tomorrow Decides London's Fate: Big Anti-Socialist Poll Essential',[932] and Wood's warning that Tory apathy and failure to vote would let the Socialists in, just as he claimed it had in the earlier LCC result, it was the Labour Party that enjoyed success. They added 457 Councillors to the 257 they had before the election, winning control of another eleven Councils to add to the four they already held (Bermondsey, Deptford, Greenwich and Poplar). A disastrous outcome for the Tories, with more than half London now Labour, and Wood pulled no punches when he told the East Leyton Conservative Association dinner the following week that there were "some hard lessons to be learned by the supporters of the National Government". Only "constant work, education and propaganda by the anti-Socialist forces" would be sufficient.[933] On the other hand there was only one way for Wood's leadership to go after the scale of this defeat and by speaking in East Leyton, previously the constituency of ILP activist Fenner Brockway, he was sending a clear message to Labour opponents as well.

The London Borough Council elections had come too soon after Wood's appointment to test his role or reflect on his performance, but they must have caused MacDonald and his ex-Labour Party colleagues some concern for by December Wood had become election co-ordinator and Director of Propaganda for the National Government as a whole.[934] On 20th December the *Morning Post* and *Manchester Guardian* were among the papers that announced Wood was to be the link between the Prime Minister and the national organisation formed for running candidates.[935]

---

[930] *Daily Herald* 26th October 1934, KW19 214/6

[931] Wood had written to Beaverbrook on 23rd October 1934 to thank him for his help in Woolwich at these elections. Beaverbrook replied on the 25th glad that the *Evening Standard* could help. Parliamentary archives, BBK/C/330, Correspondence between Wood and Beaverbrook 1931-1940

[932] *Evening Standard* 31st October 1934, KW19 216/3

[933] *Kentish Mercury* 9th November 1934, KW19 218/5

[934] *World's Press News* 13th December 1934, KW19 244/8: 'Poster and Film Campaign for Government Launched; Sir Kingsley Wood Controlling All Propaganda'; *Morning Post* 20th December 1934, KW19 251/3

[935] Also, *Evening Standard* 20th December 1934, KW19 263/10; *Star* and *Daily Telegraph* both 21st December 1934, KW19 257/5 & 260/5; *Morning*

According to the *Daily Herald*, Wood had "been told to get everything ready for [an Election] ... either next autumn or the following spring" (i.e., late 1935 or early 1936).[936]   The *News Chronicle* assured their readers that this would not make him Britain's Goebbels,[937] but nevertheless Wood was to be the "guiding genius", with Sir Patrick Gower (1887-1964), chief propaganda officer of the Conservative Party, as his right-hand man.

Low's cartoon (on the next page) depicted Christmas 1934 arriving with Wood at the reins. However, the National Government link caused considerable disquiet within the Conservative Party who feared both the loss of focus and the dissipation and dilution of funds,[938] while there was perceived to be a conflict of interest between Wood's PMG and election roles. On 11th March 1935 David Grenfell, Labour MP for the Gower in south Wales, asked Baldwin whether it was appropriate for the man in control of broadcasting also to hold this party post as organiser of propaganda. Baldwin was dismissive, replying that

> Responsibility for broadcast programmes rests entirely with the British Broadcasting Corporation. The Postmaster-General, as has been frequently stated in this House, takes no part in the compilation of these programmes, and exercises no censorship over them in any way. I can see, therefore, no reason why the ... Postmaster-General should alone be debarred from party activities, and such a condition has never been made in connection with the office. The hon. Gentleman may rest assured that my right hon. Friend, as always, will in any political or other work he may undertake have due regard to the duties and responsibilities of his office.

Grenfell continued:

Post 31st December 1934, KW19 250/7; *National Review* January 1935, KW19 267/14

[936] *Daily Herald* 29th December 1934, KW19 256/5: 'All Set for General Election'

[937] *News Chronicle* 28th December 1934, KW19 256/7: 'No Goebbels for Britain'

[938] *Star* 21st December 1934, KW19 257/5; *Edinburgh Evening News* 22nd December 1934, KW19 251/4

I do not desire to challenge the ability of the right hon. Gentleman, but is it not a temptation to officials who are responsible for broadcasting to consider the susceptibilities of the right hon. Gentleman?

To which Baldwin replied "The greater the temptation, the greater the opportunity to resist it."[939]

© Solo Syndication/Associated Newspapers Ltd.
Evening Standard 24th December 1934, KW19 253/2
David Low (1891-1963) 'Christmas arrives' cartoon with Wood driving
reindeer of National Government

Yet whatever the parliamentary reaction, and Grenfell was sowing doubt even if he stopped short of accusing Wood outright, Wood's treatment in the press continued to be generally positive. In an alphabetical guide to the Cabinet published in the *Saturday Review*

---

[939] Hansard, 11th March 1935, vol. 299, col.27; *Daily Herald* 11th March 1935, KW19 321/2

Wood escaped relatively unscathed compared to many of his colleagues, some of whom he would eventually succeed (not least at Health and Air). The poem included the following:

> A's for the Air Force - inadequate, very-
> Mismanaged at present by Lord Londonderry.
> B is for Baldwin, who gives satisfaction
> As Acting Prime Minister - minus the action.
> C's for Conservative. Inskips and such
> May know what it means. It has ceased to mean much.
> …
> K is Sir Kingsley, the telephone gent,
> L is the pound he has knocked off the rent.
> M is the money we toil for all day.
> N is for Neville, who takes it away.
> …
> P's the Prime Minister, Maundering Mac;
> Q is the question 'Why did he come back?'
> …
> Y is for Young. I refer to Sir Hilton.
> Z are the slums that have still to be built on.[940]

The breadth of Wood's interests far exceeded that of many politicians, making him ideal for the party post. In Woolwich he did not shy away from issues that, on the face of it, were well outside his brief. In December 1934 he told constituents that Britain stood for stability and peace whereas "the insecure character of foreign Governments is responsible for the state of the world today".[941] This might appear automatic, insofar as most MPs would adopt this panoptic stance in their constituencies, but the early timing is significant. This says much about both Wood's confidence and his knowledge and understanding of the events around him. It is one thing to follow the herd, another to lead it. This was both a function of Wood's prominence in the Party and a reason for it.

[940] *Saturday Review* 27th October 1934, KW19 218/1 'Letters of Mark' by Hamadryad
Graves & Hodge, op cit, p270 describe the *Saturday Review* as "filled … with extravagantly jingo articles, poems and news-items, a great many written by" the owner 'Fanny' Houston, who they allege was "'psychic', not to say 'slightly touched'".
[941] At a meeting in Eltham Parish Hall reported in the *Kentish Independent* 14th December 1934, KW19 247/5

Four days earlier he had railed against the prospect of a future Labour government at a nation-wide demonstration in Plymouth:

> If a Socialist government is returned [at the next General Election] there is no doubt that all the sacrifices this country has made will be in vain, and that its advent to power will be followed by the deliberate precipitation of both a constitutional and a financial crisis.[942]

The local constituency paper was significantly and evocatively called the *Woolwich and Eltham Searchlight*, a title which, if Wood did not think of it himself, he would certainly have agreed and have to be comfortable with. The first issue had appeared not long before,[943] and the issue that December carried two articles by Wood, one on slavery and another on peace and war and the work of the new House of Commons session in the face of foreign provocation and belligerence.[944]

Even before Hitler came to power in 1933 the rising tension in Germany was evident, prompting the novelist Storm Jameson to record her impressions of a visit in 1932. She described Hitler as Germany's "wish-fulfilment" after years of weakness, and though she did not know whether he "would succeed" and whether Germany would recover or fall into all-too-easily imagined ruin, there was much that she found alarming:

> It is from them [students, with universities called 'waiting rooms for the workless'], and from the small, ruined shopkeepers, and from the women, that Hitler draws his support.
> [The German people] are too tough to be finished by anything less than violence or catastrophe.[945]

In November 1933 Germany withdrew from the League of Nations and one reaction in Britain to the growing international problems

---

[942] *Western Morning Press* 11th December 1934, KW19 248/1 referring to Wood's speech at the National Government demonstration at Plymouth Guildhall.

[943] KW19 134/1 June 1934

[944] *Woolwich and Eltham Searchlight* December 1934, KW19 246/1

[945] Storm Jameson, 'Civil Journey', 1939 including chapter "City to Let - Berlin 1932", pp36-52

was the peace ballot that by June 1935 had received responses from 11.6m people, with 95% for Britain to remain a member of the League of Nations and 91% for international disarmament.[946] Another illuminating response was Baldwin's warning to Conservatives in July 1934 not to join the Fascists.[947] The January 1935 issue of the *Woolwich and Eltham Searchlight* included the answers that people such as Shaw, Keynes, Lansbury and AA Milne had given to the peace ballot.[948]

With this increasing uncertainty, press speculation grew about possible Prime Ministers in the future, with Wood now listed as one of the potential candidates.[949] For Hannen Swaffer (1879-1962)[950] in the *Daily News* Wood was possible "if there is [ever] going to be another" Tory Prime Minister because "He makes the best broadcast speeches of all the lot of them. He sounds as friendly as Franklin Roosevelt".[951] The *Glasgow News* agreed:

> [His] veritable triumph as PMG automatically marks him out for promotion - once he starts climbing there is no saying where Sir Kingsley will stop. He has high administrative abilities, is personally popular, secretly ambitious and he is one man who has every reason to look forward to 1935 with great hope and confidence.[952]

A competition in the *Sunday Dispatch* had five journalists and the public agreeing that Lloyd George was the greatest politician of the twenty choices they were given, with Churchill second and Cripps twentieth in both lists. Wood came sixth in the public poll with almost 200,000 votes (more than 29,000 behind Lloyd George), but 2,500 votes ahead of Baldwin in eighth and 13,000 ahead of MacDonald in eleventh.[953] By contrast the journalists judged Baldwin fourth behind Snowden (as well as Lloyd George and

---

[946] CPA CRD 1/8/1: *Guardian* 10th November 1934; also, Stannage, op cit, p130 fn48 includes the six questions on the ballot.

[947] CPA Pub 146/2 *The Elector* June 1924 - December 1934

[948] *Woolwich and Eltham Searchlight* January 1935, KW19 304/1

[949] For example, *Good Housekeeping* July 1934, KW19 138/1

[950] Swaffer was to become one of the best-known journalists of his time. See his DNB entry for further details.

[951] *Daily News* 12th November 1934, KW19 219/3

[952] *Glasgow News* 27th December 1934, KW19 257/1: 'Men to Watch in 1935'

[953] *Sunday Dispatch* 4th November 1934, KW19 219/1

Churchill) and placed Wood halfway down the list at tenth. Their view was less favourable than the public's, therefore, but Neville Chamberlain had an even more marked reverse being placed third by the public but seventeenth by the journalists. The theme was continued in Hannen Swaffer's column in the *Daily Herald*:

> They tell me that Neville's stock as potential Premier has fallen heavily in the last few months, and that now it is Sir Henry [sic] Kingsley Wood, the anti-nationaliser, who boasts of the success of his nationalised Post Office, who fancies himself as Tory leader.
>
> Well, Kingsley has humour and humanness - he is a young man on a flying trapeze - and I wish him well. But no Tory leader could explain away, today, the plight in which the Government finds itself because of its starving of the very poorest.[954]

Swaffer had identified an apparent dilemma that others soon latched on to for, in their view, Wood had to decide whether he was the "anti-nationaliser of the anti-Socialist crusade" or proud of the nationalisation at the Post Office he had undertaken as PMG.[955] This dilemma was more apparent than real, though, for Wood saw it not as an either/or choice but dependent on the circumstances. Yet inevitably the press sought to create controversy and discord, for even if there was no ideological reason, and there certainly was for the Labour-supporting *Daily Herald*, this was what sold newspapers.

Although the timing might be coincidental, ten days later the *Morning Post* published a "Test vote form" of thirty-nine questions for return by their readers.[956] On the day after the deadline for returning forms, the paper presented an initial analysis but had received so many responses (45,182) that it would be another fortnight before the results were fully analysed, and only then after extra staff had been employed to help. Although the leading article published alongside the final results stated it was not just sectional, the majority of those replying must have been Conservative Party voters given the nature of the paper.[957] It is not surprising,

---

[954] *Daily Herald* 14th February 1935, KW19 298/7

[955] KW19 324/1-10

[956] *Morning Post* 23rd February 1935, KW19 303/1

[957] For, as Graves and Hodge, op cit, p57 put it, "Usually the *Morning Post* was more die-hard than the Government ...".

therefore, that only a quarter (27.6%) wanted to see the National Government continue in its present form, but striking that not many more (30.7%) wanted to return to the party system, with almost two-thirds (61.3%) preferring to see the National Government re-constructed. Even more remarkable were the responses readers gave to the six choices as leader of the Conservative Party in either a Conservative or National Government.[958] Neville Chamberlain topped the poll with almost 30% of the vote (29.4%), with Baldwin 5% behind him (24.4%). The three men who had only recently opposed the India Bill, and therefore the Party leadership, mustered only a third of the votes between them: Churchill 17.3%, Lord Lloyd[959] 11.2% and Lord Salisbury 4.9%. Kingsley Wood came in fifth with 6% of the vote. This was a resounding endorsement of the existing leadership for between them Baldwin, Chamberlain and Wood had carried just under 60% of the vote.

Wood could hold his own in this company, as is evident from a report in the *Times* that commented on the Government's excessively "cautious approach to public works, particularly in the north, and especially on housing". However, "Sir Kingsley Wood obviously believes in and practises constructive expenditure. [Neville Chamberlain] does not."[960] Another article was even more explicit:

> The PMG has made great strides since 1931. A few years ago he was definitely not news in Fleet Street.
> His personality seemed unprojectable, and even when he fell off his horse at Brighton it was not a spectacular fall, nor did the newsreels feel any necessity of showing it in slow motion to ascertain the facts of the mishap.

---

[958] They were also given the option to write in somebody else, with 192 people being named but only accounting for 6.8% of the vote in total. *Morning Post* 18th March 1935

[959] George Lloyd (1879-1941) was a favourite of "die-hard *Morning Post* readers" (according to his DNB entry). Like Churchill a proponent of rearmament and therefore on this count, as well as their opposition to the India Bill, alien to Baldwin's brand of conservatism. Lloyd's "concerns amounted to a sweeping critique of the National Government".
The principle of rearmament had been accepted in 1934, and there was some speeding up from 1935, but it would be March 1938 and the Anschluss before rearmament became the Government's priority and the 'normal trade' principle was revoked.

[960] *Times* 15th January 1935

Now he is definitely front page. He carries himself with the alertness of a man who knows where he is going and the modesty of a man who no longer has to try to attract public attention.

He is obviously in good physical condition and today there is little room in politics for the unfit. If there were such things as political shares, I would say 'Buy KW Deferreds'.[961]

National Publicity Bureau

In March 1935 the campaigning journalist Hannen Swaffer reported that Kingsley Wood was to be appointed the "chief Government propagandist" in readiness for the general election,[962] adding, as he was almost bound to do given the political allegiance of the *Daily Herald*, that no matter how much Wood might attempt to praise it, the National Government was held in contempt by the masses. The National Publicity Bureau secretary was to be Lt Col EG Davidson (a member of Northcliffe's propaganda committee in World War I)[963] with Lord Hutchinson and Malcolm MacDonald on the Committee along with Wood,[964] thereby reflecting the tripartite composition of the National Government for Hutchinson was head of the Liberal National Council and Malcolm MacDonald a member of the National Labour Committee as well as the son of the Prime Minister. Subsequently, Sir Patrick Gower was co-opted to link the work of the NPB with that of Conservative Central Office.

A week later it was reported that Wood had displaced David Margesson, the Chief Whip, and Lord Stonehaven, the Party Chairman, as the representative of the Conservative Party on the propaganda co-ordinating committee.[965] At the end of March a meeting of the Conservative Central Council at Friends House in Euston Road crystallised the disquiet that was already being voiced about the relations between the National Government and the Conservatives, between the National Publicity Bureau and Conservative Central Office, and regarding the selection and financing of Conservative candidates.[966] According to the *Times*

---

[961] *Sunday Referee* 7th April 1935, KW19 350/1

[962] *Daily Herald* 7th March 1935, KW19 313/7

[963] Stannage, op cit, p52

[964] Ibid

[965] *Birmingham Gazette* 14th March 1935, KW19 330/4

[966] *Morning Post* and *Times* both 28th March 1935, KW19 339/1 & 340/1; also Stannage, op cit, pp52-53

report, Lord Stonehaven responded in detail to the mistaken and misleading views some had formed:

> Sir Kingsley Wood explained [to me] that [the NPB] was purely temporary and that its activities would cease at the General Election. It was not concerned with any single political party, but it desired to work as far as possible in close collaboration with the organisations of all three parties which supported the National Government. Accordingly, he invited the co-operation of the Conservative Party organisation.
>
> 'I decided at once,' Lord Stonehaven said, 'that since the policy of our party was to support the National Government, I would welcome the assistance which this committee was able to afford. (Cheers.) When it came to discussing ways and means, Sir Kingsley Wood asked me to appoint a liaison officer to act between him and the central office, and I appointed Sir Patrick Gower.'[967]

Stonehaven continued:

> 'The campaign ... will be carried out, so far as the central office is concerned, on the same lines as the successful campaign carried out by us in support of the National Government last year, but on a larger scale. The films, broadsheets, posters, etc., will be approved by the Bureau just as the propaganda was approved by all three parties ... in last year's campaign. The Bureau will have no authority whatever over the central office, and our propaganda office will remain completely free to issue any propaganda it requires ...' (Cheers.)

The implication of this, damping down Conservative disquiet, was that the entire publicity and propaganda effort pivoted around Kingsley Wood. He had been selected for the role because of his instinct, and indeed preference, for co-operation and he could be relied on to follow this approach. It would be naïve, however, to expect any gifted operator, and Wood was a politician to his

---

[967] *Times* 28th March 1935 article 'Unionist Party Publicity: Lord Stonehaven's assurance'

fingertips, to adhere to this slavishly. He would clear his lines when he needed to, but for all day-to-day purposes the authority was his.

One editor recalls the Downing Street press officer George Steward telling him that he was

> very contemptuous of [Wood] as a propagandist [saying,] rightly enough, that the art of propaganda is not to let anyone know it is being done, whereas Wood began with a great burst of trumpets and thus aroused a mental resistance complex in everybody.[968]

However, this describes the sort of propaganda that, if not underhand, at least involves sleight of hand and depends on partiality or bias to convince. Needless to say, Wood's role required this approach at times but usually what was needed was publicity and information. Propaganda might benefit from subtle and insidious tactics but effective publicity does depend on trumpets on the rooftop.

Baldwin and others in the National Government trusted Wood not to abuse the position. As one newspaper put it, Wood as NPB head was "expected to mollify public opinion because Sir Kingsley is held up to us as a model Conservative".[969] This was something of a backhanded compliment, however, and not the accolade it might appear, for the newspaper continued that Wood's good work at the Post Office stood out because he followed "a succession of duffers". More starkly, it argued, Wood "slavishly followed [MacDonald and Baldwin] in all their policies. He has no independent outlook ..." However, this assertion must have been dictated by the proprietor of the *Saturday Review*, the die-hard Tory Lucy Houston. She hated Ramsay MacDonald and spent much of her time, and even more of her money, castigating him - in pamphlets and articles elsewhere, as well as in her own magazine.[970] She would have bracketed Baldwin alongside him and may have viewed Wood as their poodle, or at any rate in this instance it suited her to do so.

---

[968] NJ Crowson (ed.), 'Fleet Street, Press Barons and Politics: The Journals of Collin Brooks, 1932-1940', 1998, p133 - diary entry for 18th October 1935

[969] *Saturday Review* 30th March 1935, KW19 346/1

[970] Crowson, 1998, op cit, pp77-80

J Wentworth Day, 'Lady Houston DBE: The Woman Who Won the War', 1958

It could be countered from a less jaundiced, and certainly less partisan, perspective though that to follow both Baldwin and MacDonald was quite an achievement; for example, it was MacDonald who had sought to resist Bridgeman's appointment as head of the Post Office inquiry, but Wood had not given way. It might also be pointed out that this was exactly the stance required of a junior Cabinet Minister in a National Government, following the leader(s) and keeping any independent opinions out of the public view.

The *Punch* cartoon on the following page provides an alternative image, capturing Wood's geniality as well as his decisiveness, purposiveness and competence. "A man on a mission" might be another way of putting it, with the track record to justify his position. Between then and the general election in November, the NPB spent nearly £67,000 on posters, the equivalent of almost £3m today. By any measure this is a huge number of posters but, while there were other ways of reaching the electorate of 31 million people, few would be so striking or economical.

Ramsay MacDonald's health had been deteriorating for some time and, both ailing and failing,[971] he resigned as Prime Minister in June 1935, swapping posts with Baldwin. Now premier for a third time, Baldwin gave a speech on the radio the following day, in which he stressed the continuing importance of the National Government as "men of goodwill from all three parties ... working together for national benefit".[972] This captures much of Baldwin's appeal: fellowship, an ability to co-operate and a focus on the public good. Duty and service were the key words in Baldwin's lexicon,[973] or, as Williamson put it later in the same assessment, quoting Baldwin himself "Use men as ends and never merely as means; and live for the brotherhood of man ..."[974] Concerned with political atmosphere and culture, Baldwin left the specifics of particular programmes to his colleagues; hence giving them their head, or, as it would be called today, "hands-off management" rather than always just the indolence it was taken for. Like Disraeli, Baldwin

---

[971] Arthur Salter refers to MacDonald's deterioration first in spring 1933 in 'Memoirs of a Public Servant', 1961, p234.

[972] Graham Tayar (ed.), 'Personality and Power: Studies in Political Achievement', 1971, p9

[973] Philip Williamson, "The doctrinal politics of Stanley Baldwin", pp181-208 in Michael Bentley (ed.), 'Public and Private Doctrine: Essays in British History presented to Maurice Cowling', 1993, p196

[974] Ibid, pp188 & 207

was concerned with "the sanitation of the soul", with moral values, for in his view it was "more important to form good habits than to frame good laws". It should not be surprising, therefore, that Wood,

Punch 13th March 1935, KW19 328/1
Wood as Director of Propaganda about to post bills
'The Postermaster General'

who shared many of the same values, should admire Baldwin and trust him implicitly - as did many others. A few days later in a speech to the Primrose League Baldwin congratulated Wood on the "universal popularity he enjoyed", but warned him that it was in the nature of politics that it should not last:

He himself [Baldwin] had been popular for a week after the General Strike but told his wife 'These roses are all very fine, but they will turn to cabbages in a fortnight'.

I say that lest Sir Kingsley, who is young in years but old in cunning, should think it is going to be roses, roses all the way. It is not.[975]

That Baldwin was significant in Wood's career was not a negligible consideration but the admiration was mutual, for Wood supplied the perspiration and hard work that Baldwin generally left to his subordinates. The potential conflict of interest between his PMG and propaganda roles had been raised previously, but Wood was by now Minister of Health, a larger and more high profile portfolio - particularly in the circumstances of the 1930s.[976] Even though the propaganda role was time-limited, many might have sought to reduce their commitments or at least phase them. This does not seem to have been Wood's approach, however, for he remained Chairman of the NPB, "chief of the boosting department" as the *Daily Despatch* called him,[977] while taking a vigorous approach to his responsibilities as Minister of Health.

It must have helped that Wood was already familiar with the workings of the Ministry from his previous positions there and his wider party brief, but nevertheless many might be tempted to concur with the advice Baldwin was receiving from Hoare, Eden and others to delay the general election to 1936.[978] Yet, even with the particular slant that the *Daily Herald* gossip column brought to its report, it is clear that this was not Wood's position (nor, perhaps coincidentally, Neville Chamberlain's):

Sir Kingsley Wood is another strong influence for an early general election.

---

[975] 3rd May 1935 speech to Primrose League, KW19 366/2

[976] With this elevation Wood was no longer the junior member of the Cabinet. The Minister of Labour (Ernest Brown) and the First Commissioner of Works (Ormsby-Gore then Earl Stanhope) were below him, with the junior member subsequently Hore-Belisha when he was added as Minister of Transport in December 1936. (Vacher's Parliamentary Companion for 1935 and 1936)

[977] *Daily Despatch* 13th June 1935, KW19 388/2

[978] For example, Stannage, op cit, p120 says that a Gower memo to Baldwin in August 1935 advocated an election in January 1936 rather than November 1935.

> As chief campaign organiser for the 'National Government',
> Sir Kingsley is keenly alive to the danger of over-training.
> It is costing, so I am informed, something like £5000 every
> week to keep the Government propaganda going. Sir
> Kingsley wants to increase this as the general election
> approaches, but if the date is postponed too long both
> money and enthusiasm may peter out.
> 'Let's get it over quickly,' are the last words which Mr
> Baldwin will carry with him when he departs to Aix-les-Bains
> to think it over.[979]

"Getting it over quickly" might be an alternative strategy if Wood
was to keep his workload manageable.

The Conservative Party archive includes the NPB accounts
that Wood received each month from the accountants Maxwell
Hicks. These have a number of interesting features, only some of
which concern the obvious expenditure. Between the start of the
NPB on 11th March and the general election in November, the NPB
spent £172,000 (the equivalent of about £7m today). The main
items, in addition to £67,000 on posters, were £25,000 on a
broadsheet publication, £23,000 on film propaganda, nearly £9000
on "missioners", over £4000 on pamphlets, and more than another
£16,000 on the election itself (broadsheet and pamphlets).[980]

The eight-page broadsheet publication was called 'Popular
Illustrated', number 1 of which appeared for May and June 1935
(shown on the following page).[981] The captions under the four
pictures reinforce the message of 'Peace, Progress and Security'.
The "olde world" cottages speak for themselves; the others show
children "enjoying" school milk, the Chancellor Neville Chamberlain
who had reduced taxation by £60m in three years and, illustrating
the country's economic recovery, a passenger liner and tramp
steamer on the high seas.

Among the material prepared for prospective candidates, the
NPB produced five pamphlets: 'Working for Peace', 'Britain and
World Peace', 'Re-building Britain', 'A Better Way to Better Times'
and 'As Safe as the Bank'.[982] As well as these positive messages,

---

[979] *Daily Herald* 5th August 1935, KW19 462/2
[980] CPA FIN42: Monthly NPB Statements to Kingsley Wood
[981] KW19 opp 373
[982] CPA CRD 1/7/28a Miscellaneous candidate material for 1935 General
Election - item 1 letter from Ball to Hailsham 28th October 1935

the CRD were also on the look-out for opportunities to take their opponents to task, and therefore fastening on one such in GDH Cole's book 'The Simple Case for Socialism',[983] which contemplated

"an intervening period of mass starvation and civil war before Socialism can really come into its own".[984]   Referring to this

---

[983] GDH Cole, 'The Simple Case for Socialism', 1935, pp286-287
[984] CPA CRD 1/7/28a Miscellaneous candidate material for 1935 GE - item 2 letter from Ball to Hailsham 6th November 1935

inevitably became a routine component of National Government campaigning against the Socialist alternative.

The monthly accounts were sometimes sent to Wood at the NPB offices at 3 Central Buildings but always to his flat at 23 Buckingham Palace Mansions. The accounts to April 1936 refer to "certain payments of a private nature" to Joseph Ball and Maxwell Hicks totalling £26,301. These were not the usual monthly payments that they, and others such as Gower, received for their NPB responsibilities. Rather the entry in the accounts is deliberately oblique and, while it is not possible to do more than speculate eighty years on, it is at least possible that it refers in part to the purchase of the magazine *Truth*. According to Cockett, Ball bought *Truth* for the benefit of the Neville Chamberlain wing of the Party using National Publicity Bureau funds. Cockett further asserts that other members of the NPB business committee (including Wood) never knew anything about it, which may or may not be correct, but this might be one of those occasions when "ignorance was bliss".[985] Crowson confirms that *Truth* was "effectively owned by the Conservative Party since 1936 without anyone knowing".[986]

Another file in the Conservative Party archive largely duplicates the record of NPB accounts, but covers a longer period from March 1935 to November 1938, when Wood was still involved.[987] This raises some further points of interest: Firstly, a handwritten and confidential note to Maxwell Hicks from Wood on 29th July 1935 asked that "Major Ball and Sir P Gower [be paid] the sum of fifty guineas each and [that this be charged] to the joint account in the names of yourself and Ball as special fee". Secondly, at a time when Maxwell Hicks himself was away, a letter from Hicks & Co to Wood on 13th November 1936 referred to the August 1936 NPB balance sheet and accounts, checking Wood had authorised three payments for:
- £1500 (about £60,000 today) to the Metropolitan Area for canvassing in the LCC election. It is not clear whether this was a very late payment for 1934 or a down-payment on the next one.

---

[985] RB Cockett, "Ball, Chamberlain and *Truth*", *Historical Journal,* 1990, 33, pp131-142 (p134)
Also, Richard Cockett, 'Twilight of *Truth*: Chamberlain, Appeasement and the Manipulation of the Press', 1989, pp10-11
[986] Crowson, 1998, op cit, p9
[987] CPA FIN43: Monthly NPB Statements March 1935-Nov 1938

- £20 to somebody called "Markham", possibly but not necessarily Wood's Woolwich agent, for special publicity on a National Government demonstration.
- salaries for Ball and Gower at £500 each (£20,000 each today) compared to the usual £41 per month. Perhaps this was a reward or performance-related payment in relation to the previous election result.

Wood confirmed the following week (19th November 1936) that he had authorised all three.

Film propaganda had been an essential part of Conservative campaigning since the mid-1920s, one area in which it remained ahead of the Labour Party for the next twenty years. During the 1935 election "an estimated 1.5 million people watched films from Conservative Party touring vans".[988] This was an invaluable addition to radio broadcasts, especially when cinemas banned National Government publicity films, restricting them to "touring talkie vans, barns, halls and public squares".[989] A Conservative and Unionist Film Association had been set up in May 1930 by Gower, with British Films Ltd. formed to maintain and run the vans (and hire them out for commercial purposes between election campaigns). The NPB built on this in 1935 by forming its own film department,[990] with fourteen outdoor film units and seventeen vans carrying indoor film equipment. Not surprisingly, these proved popular in areas of high unemployment and isolated rural communities, in both of which alternative forms of information were either unavailable or out of reach financially.[991]

1935 General Election

According to Stannage,[992] Baldwin only fastened on the election date on 18th October, delaying the announcement in Parliament until the last possible moment (23rd October) that it was to be held

[988] Sian Nicholas, 'The construction of a national identity: Stanley Baldwin, Englishness and the mass media in inter-war Britain", pp127-146 in Martin Francis and Ina Zweiniger-Bargielowska (eds.), 'The Conservatives and British Society, 1880-1990', 1996
[989] *Daily Express* 22nd May 1935, KW19 373/2
[990] TJ Hollins, "The Conservative Party and film propaganda between the wars", *English Historical Review*, 1981, 96, pp359-369
[991] Stannage, op cit, pp175-177
[992] Ibid, p126

three weeks later on 14th November.[993] Despite the different views as to timing in the Conservative Party, the autumn date was of little surprise to anybody. All the main party manifestos were ready to be published, with the *Times* reporting on the Liberal one on the 25th, Labour's on the 26th and the National Government's on the 29th.[994] Collin Brooks confirms that it was Wood's team who had drawn up the National Government manifesto, sending it to Baldwin, Mac-Donald and Simon for their approval.[995] The *Times* report was immediately followed by a brief item on the Communist Party (CPGB) manifesto, subtly linking it with Labour's. The National Government manifesto claimed that if the Labour opposition came to power it would "inevitably be followed by a collapse of confidence". Furthermore, the well-being of the country's economy depended on a period "in which stability will be assured and confidence remain undisturbed". It concluded:

> In present circumstances it is more than ever necessary that the British government should not only be united among themselves, but that they should represent that spirit of national co-operation which will best secure the confidence and respect of the world.

For its part the 1935 Labour manifesto was equally combative and refreshingly frank. Entitled 'Call to Power' it was only two pages long and did not dilute the force of its arguments, accusing the National Government of having gained "a swollen majority on a campaign of fraud, misrepresentation and panic".[996]

Although the campaign did not get underway until late October, Wood was well-placed as Minister of Health to make substantial speeches in advance and one of the first of these was to the annual meeting of the Church Congress in Bournemouth on 11th October. Extensively reported in the *Times* the following day[997] under the headline 'Fight Against the Slums', he spoke about the Government's record on building new homes and clearing slums but also about the Housing Act passed earlier that summer and the

---

[993] Collin Brooks and Rothermere made the same point in their joint diary entry 23rd October 1935. Crowson, 1998, op cit, p134
[994] CPA CRD 1/7/29
[995] Crowson, 1998, op cit, p134 - diary entry for 26th October 1935
[996] CPA CRD 1/7/19 EBC35(2) - National Government manifesto and 1/7/29 - Liberal and Labour manifestoes
[997] *Times* 12th October 1935, KW20 10/10

house-to-house survey of overcrowding that was about to start. On the 28th Wood spoke in Leyton to all MPs and prospective candidates in the area, "the first large scale National Government demonstration to be held in the East End of London".[998] On the 29th the *Times* reported Baldwin's speech in Wolverhampton on the Government's policy on arms, MacDonald's in London on the coal industry and Wood's in Leyton on plans to improve health and social services, including maternity care.[999] It also reported the first Labour radio broadcast, this one by Attlee, which questioned whether the National Government could be trusted on the country's security and the League of Nations. MacDonald was already disputing the "callous and reckless" expectations that Labour was raising, a theme Wood would amplify in relation to claims about more generous pensions in the Labour manifesto. At Doncaster on the 31st he said their statement favouring the extension of pensions to wives of men aged 65+ was "not particularly honest [and] likely to deceive many people".[1000] Baldwin thought the cost to the country of £6.5m unaffordable.[1001]

As in the four previous General Elections the Cabinet established an Emergency Business Committee (EBC) to handle ordinary Cabinet business, unless matters arose that were so important that a full Cabinet was required.[1002] This left Ministers free to concentrate on campaigning, though the EBC could if necessary comprise the Prime Minister, the Lord President of the Council, Lord Chancellor, Chancellor of the Exchequer, the Secretaries of State for the Home, Foreign Affairs and India Offices, the First Lord of the Admiralty and the President of the Board of Trade, "together with any other members of the Cabinet who might be available, and other Ministers according to the nature of the business". But in fact it was only the Lord Chancellor Hailsham and Wood who attended all three (on 5th, 8th and 11th November). Wood was either thought to be indispensable or his energy was making him so. At any rate he clearly preferred to attend these than the Party Executive Committee from which he was often absent.

---

[998] KW20 1/10

[999] *Times* 29th October 1935, KW20 16/6

[1000] *Times* 1st November 1935; also Stannage, op cit, p142

[1001] CPA CRD 1/7/23 General Election 1935 Correspondence - item 17 re pensions 11th November 1935; also see CRD 1/7/28b item 3 Ministry of Health note 28th October 1935

[1002] CPA CRD 1/7/19 Cabinet Emergency Business Committee 1935

In his radio broadcast for Labour Arthur Greenwood accused Wood of misleading pronouncements:

> [He] has tried hard to convince you that most of the new houses have gone to the more lowly paid people. I think you know better. It is not true. No more than a fourth of all the houses built has been built to let.[1003]

Claim and counter-claim are in the nature of political dispute but ignoring the balance to be struck between criticising their opponents and setting out Labour Party policies, Clynes and Attlee spent more time in their speeches criticising the National Government.[1004]

There was no love lost between Lloyd George and Samuel. Indeed, one of Lloyd George's many memorable sayings was his assertion about his then deputy that "When they circumcised Herbert Samuel they threw away the wrong bit!"[1005] So the former Prime Minister was most surprised to be asked by Samuel to deliver the first broadcast for the Samuelite Liberals. It is probable that this was in an attempt to associate their campaign with the Council of Action (on Peace and Reconstruction) that the ever-independent Lloyd George had generated separately, the focus of his talk.[1006] Their third broadcast was by Snowden who, having resigned from Labour and castigated his erstwhile colleagues previously, also had a distinctive slant.

Baldwin, the consummate radio performer, opened and closed the National Government radio campaign with Neville Chamberlain, Ramsay MacDonald and John Simon providing those in between. Wood helped Baldwin prepare for his second broadcast on 8th November, with a CRD draft amplified by information received by Wood and Baldwin.[1007] In their view Labour would concentrate on industrial issues as they believed the masses generally understood these better than international affairs. Wood suggested Baldwin concentrate on the Government's record on industry too and on the importance of voting, for it was not just everybody's "right" to vote but their "duty". Stannage describes Baldwin's broadcast as statesmanlike, elevating the general

---

[1003] CPA CRD 1/7/28b Opposition misrepresentations

[1004] Stannage, op cit, p142

[1005] Foot, op cit, p122

[1006] Stannage, op cit,, p181

[1007] CPA CRD 1/7/22 Cabinet Emergency Business Committee 1935

election above petty party considerations for "in this election democracy itself is on trial".[1008]   This was an appeal to people's higher values but what underlay it was the perennial and more basic concern of the party in power about voter apathy.   Baldwin, contrasting his personal sense of honour with the misleading claims Labour had made (notably about pensions), stated that "I would sooner go out of office than deceive the elector with promises incapable of fulfilment".[1009]

The *Daily Herald* had claimed in January that, as Wood faced a hard fight to retain West Woolwich, a safer berth was to be found for him because he would "be so busy supervising the 'National' Government propaganda that he will not have time to nurse this dangerous seat".[1010]   In March the paper attacked his Leyton speech, claiming that Wood was "fighting a desperate battle for his political life" and that he had "made so many promises that his speech became an apology for the Government rather than a championship of it".[1011]   The *Daily Worker* went even further, calling the "much-boosted meeting ... a complete flop" despite the good write-ups in the Tory press.[1012]

Wood's sole constituency opponent, selected that March to fight the seat for Labour, was George Wansborough,[1013] a Marylebone Councillor, educated at Eton and Cambridge University and employed as a merchant banker - hardly the sort of Socialist likely to appeal to the Woolwich electorate or challenge Wood's popularity.   Indeed, though Wansborough might have had a headstart as a member of Lloyd George's Council of Action, the Council "did not see its way clear to support an upstart Labour candidate against one of the nation's most prominent Methodists and a respected statesman".[1014]   Council of Action support was not

---

[1008] Stannage, op cit, p149

[1009] Nicholas, op cit, p131
Interestingly, Nicholas makes no mention of Wood's role in crafting the speech, but asserts that Reith allegedly contributed many of the best lines, and was even re-writing the speech as Baldwin spoke (p136). This sounds most unlikely and the only source is Reith himself.

[1010] *Daily Herald* 14th January 1935, KW19 267/9

[1011] *Daily Herald* 29th October 1935, KW20 5/1

[1012] *Daily Worker* 31st October 1935, KW20 26/5

[1013] *Evening Standard* 2nd March 1935, KW19 314/3

[1014] Stephen Koss, "Lloyd George and Nonconformity: The last rally", *English Historical Review*, 1974, 89, pp77-108 (pp101-102)

automatic, therefore.[1015] Nor was this the end of his troubles, for Wansborough also resigned from his merchant bank during the campaign, though denying that this resulted from his candidacy or that there had been any rift with his employers.[1016]

At Wood's adoption meeting at the Old Town Hall, Woolwich in late October 1935, Alderman Halse drew attention to Wood's work over seventeen years as the constituency MP, adding "From a national point of view he had made a name for himself, and would go down in history as one of the greatest Postmasters General". Lord Marks of Woolwich in his first venture on to a political platform noted Wood's "untiring energy" and that Labour were asking the people of Woolwich to "turn out a general and put a private in his place".[1017] For his part Wood asked that people not return to the situation that "brought so much misery and unhappiness four or five years ago" by electing a Socialist government. Furthermore, he claimed that the National Government was not divided like the Labour party in the face of momentous and troubling events abroad. Yet despite the advantages that the successful incumbent had, Wood was not immune to the national revival in Labour's fortunes and Wansborough reduced his majority by nearly 5000 compared to 1931, polling 2800 more votes than had his Labour counterpart four years earlier while Wood secured 1800 less. This was to be Wood's last election (and indeed the country's for ten years) and, though much reduced, his majority of over 7000 remained substantial, one-sixth of the 42,000 who had voted.

Across the country, the Conservatives with 387 seats had lost 83, while Labour increased their representation by over 100 MPs to 154. Overall, while the opposition increased from 59 to 184 and the National Government was reduced to 431, 125 less than four years before, it still had a substantial majority of almost 250. Furthermore, if proportional representation had been in place, an issue that worried the CRD as electoral reform was again under

---

[1015] The Council gave approval to Ellen Wilkinson at Jarrow, but her speeches during the campaign caused the Council to strike her off their list.
Partly as a result of the Council of Action proposals, the National Publicity Bureau produced a 63 page pamphlet 'A Better Way to Better Times' in July 1935, comprising nine sections all of which had been discussed with Lloyd George. CPA CRD 1/67/1
[1016] *Daily Express* 27th September 1935, KW19 488/3
[1017] *Kentish Independent* 1st November 1935, KW20 22/6

discussion,[1018] the National Government majority would have been slashed to 53 (334 v 281) with 297 Conservative MPs and 230 Labour ones.

No doubt Wood had been hoping for a more resounding success than this, but like his personal vote it was more than enough. Nor was it as disastrous as the London elections had been a year earlier. The test of his role, needless to say, is not the comparison with four years before but with the outcome that might have occurred otherwise. The latter can never be known, of course, but at a time of huge anxiety, with Attlee having only recently replaced Lansbury as Labour leader, and in the face of German re-armament[1019] and Italy's invasion of Abyssinia a month earlier, the Conservatives must have hoped to do better. Labour had increased its vote by 1.7m[1020] a national swing in their favour of 9.9% (12% in London),[1021] while the Conservative vote had reduced by 1.5m. Even allowing for a degree of Labour recovery after 1931, the electorate must have had doubts about the National Government's handling of matters at home as well as abroad and perhaps like the *Morning Post* voters thought it should have been restructured. Wood, however, remained bullish: "The country has shown in no uncertain fashion its trust and confidence in the National Government and in our policy of peace, security and progress."[1022]

National Labour retained eight seats but Ramsay MacDonald had been defeated at Seaham Harbour by Manny Shinwell (1884-1986) and JH Thomas, though re-elected, was but "a pale shadow of his formerly ebullient self".[1023] George Lansbury thought that Thomas would be a "wonderful leader ... if only he wasn't such an awful man",[1024] and as if to demonstrate the force of Lansbury's view, Thomas would resign in 1936, first from the Government and then as an MP, when he was censored by an

[1018] CPA CRD 1/72/1 Electoral Reform 1935-1938: Brooke note on proportional representation 17th December 1935
[1019] Germany would not re-occupy the Rhineland until March 1936, the moment at which decisive action might have deterred Hitler, but German conscription had been ordered in March 1935, against which the British Government's protest was ineffective.
[1020] Morrison, op cit, p163
[1021] Stannage, op cit, p229
[1022] *Times* 16th November 1935, KW20 4/16
[1023] Morrison, op cit, p163
[1024] Cited in Kingsley Martin, 'Harold Laski (1893-1950): A Biographic Memoir', 1953, pp67-68

inquiry tribunal for disclosing budget secrets from which others profited (though he did not).[1025] His one consolation, Thomas told the diarist and Conservative MP Chips Channon,[1026] was that his great friend King George V had died before his disgrace. A second must have been that not all his friends deserted him, for a few months after the inquiry reported in May 1936, Wood and Agnes met JH Thomas and his wife in Brighton for a long lunch:

> Mr JH Thomas is not altogether forgotten.
> Earlier in the week he interrupted his task of writing his life story to motor to Brighton with Mrs Thomas. They had luncheon with Sir Kingsley Wood ... and Lady Wood.
> The meal and the reunion chat lasted over three hours.[1027]

Thomas' book, somewhat unimaginatively entitled 'My Story', was published the following year and Wood does not feature in it.[1028] If this was for reasons of discretion, Thomas was capable of being sensitive about his friends if not about the disclosure of budget secrets.

Wood's party and political skills were in evidence again in 1938 when he chaired the committee tasked with reforming the Conservative Party organisation in London to counter their poor performance in recent elections. In May 1938 it was reported that the committee was "finding difficulty in reaching unanimous conclusions", notably over the proposal that there should be a single, uniform body for all election campaigns.[1029] A week later the *Daily Telegraph* claimed that the report was now unanimous but could still only speculate about the proposals that would be sent to Neville Chamberlain.[1030] The following month the *Evening Standard* asserted that the report was now with Chamberlain but that he was unlikely to accept the recommendation that London constituencies be put in the charge of a new body independent of Conservative Party headquarters. Headlam records how Wood's report was

---

[1025] Budget Disclosure Inquiry, 'Report of the Tribunal Appointed Under the Tribunals of Inquiry (Evidence) Act, 1921', Cmd 5184, 1936
[1026] Robert Rhodes James (ed.), 'Chips: The Diaries of Sir Henry Channon', 1967, p66
[1027] *The Star* 25th September 1936, KW21 35/7
[1028] JH Thomas, 'My Story', 1937
[1029] *Evening Standard* 17th May 1938, KW23 178/7
[1030] *Daily Telegraph* 24th May 1938, KW23 199/5

considered by the Executive Committee on 15th June 1938.[1031] There was said to be strong opposition in both constituencies and Central Office to this proposal and the *Evening Standard* claimed that it was not even clear if Wood supported the recommendations himself.[1032] So much for the *Daily Telegraph* supposition of unanimity, though it was likely that the *Evening Standard* report was no more authoritative. The proposals were eventually submitted to the Party's Central Council for a decision the following year,[1033] but by then there were more pressing matters to tackle.

[1031] Stuart Ball (ed.), 'Parliament and Politics in the Age of Churchill and Attlee: The Headlam Diaries 1935-1951', 1999, pp131-132
[1032] *Evening Standard* 20th June 1938, KW23 216/2
[1033] *Times* 22nd April 1939, KW23 240/3

Vignettes

Distressed (Special) Areas

Unemployment in Woolwich was certainly grim during the first half of the 1930s but the position was considerably worse in those parts of the country that had been dependent on a single industry. The coal, iron and steel, shipbuilding and textile industries had been hard hit by unemployment since 1921 and in many areas in which these predominated any competitive advantage had been lost to cheaper imports, the region had failed to keep pace with the market or there was little call for the products during a slump. Some contemporary observers, Wal Hannington (1896-1966) of the National Unemployed Workers Movement (NUWM),[1034] for example, concluded that "the crisis within capitalism is deep and fundamental".[1035] He contrasted this with the Indian company Tata that in 1922 had issued a prospectus aimed at attracting another £7.25m of British capital, and offered huge dividends to Indian shareholders while shutting their Cumberland mine.[1036]

As Denys Blakeway has noted, "The poverty of the ... 'distressed' areas was a constant running sore on the face of plenty".[1037] The four most depressed, suffering mass long-term unemployment among the nearly 4m people who lived there, were South Wales, north-east England, Cumberland and central Scotland and at the end of 1934 the National Government brought in a measure to cover these regions.[1038] Eventually, this was called the Special Areas (Development and Improvement) Act 1934 for the House of Lords deprecated the use of 'depressed' or 'distressed' and had changed it to 'Special Areas' as the Bill worked its way through Parliament.[1039] Commissioners for the distressed areas

[1034] From 1921 Hannington was national organiser of the National Unemployed Workers' Committee Movement (NUWCM), which later as the NUWM brought about the suspension of the National Government's Unemployment Assistance Board scheme in 1935. See Hannington's DNB entry for further details.
[1035] Wal Hannington, 'The Problem of the Distressed Areas', 1937, p31
[1036] Ibid, p34
[1037] Denys Blakeway, 'The Last Dance - 1936: The Year of Change', 2010, p12
[1038] Graves and Hodge, op cit, pp308-310
[1039] It received Royal Assent on 21st December 1934. Hansard, vol. 296, col. 1544

were appointed and sections created within the civil service to support them. "But from the start Whitehall in-fighting and economic orthodoxy hampered their work."[1040] In addition, as early as November 1934 Harold Macmillan was among those who criticised the Commissioners' terms of reference for they advocated yet more research rather than galvanising and promoting the solutions that were needed.[1041] The Commissioners had been allotted £2m initially, a sum that Lloyd George and others derided as effectively zero when, in their view, the problems necessitated at least £100m per year if they were to be tackled effectively.[1042] At the third reading on 13th December George Lansbury had explained that the Labour Party would be voting against the Bill because "we consider it to be mean and miserable and feel it will have no practical effect".[1043] Two years later Hannington's view echoed Lansbury's for, he argued, not only was there no economic development in these depressed areas, but there had been no effective social improvement either.[1044]

The National Government always claimed that the Act had been introduced as an experiment and while initially this might have been to help them decide whether to continue it,[1045] by the time of the 1935 General Election their manifesto explained that, though the initial £2m was exhausted, "financial considerations will not be allowed to stand in the way of any practical and reasonable scheme". Improved selling arrangements for coal were to be pursued and new industries encouraged into the Special Areas by, for example, building trading estates and ready-made factories. Defence orders would be directed towards these areas where feasible to increase employment, but if necessary labour would be transferred to other areas.[1046]

[1040] Blakeway, op cit, p53
[1041] Hannington, op cit, p25
[1042] Ibid, p26
Hansard, 6th December 1934, vol. 295, cols. 1868-1872 sets out the Lloyd George criticisms (father David and son Gwilym) during the Committee stage.
[1043] Hansard, 13th December 1934, vol. 296, col. 674
[1044] Hannington, op cit, p30
[1045] For example, the Minister of Labour's Parliamentary Secretary Lt-Col. Anthony Muirhead (1890-1939). Hansard, 26th June 1935, vol. 303, col. 1101
[1046] CPA CRD 1/7/19 EBC35(2) - National Government manifesto point 8 re Special Areas and the Coal Mining Industry

As Blakeway explains,

Britain in 1936 was still a class-bound and divided nation, split between a rapidly modernising and growing south and the impoverished outer regions ...
For the long-term unemployed the only way to get assistance in 1936 was to undergo the Means Test. Introduced five years earlier by the National Government to reduce public spending, it was the most hated of all the government's measures to deal with unemployment.[1047]

When the Means Test had been introduced in 1931, the weekly rates of unemployment benefit were reduced by about 10%[1048] from 17s (or 85p in decimal money) to 15s 3d (the equivalent of about £30 today[1049]) for men over 21 and from 15s to 13s 6d for women over 21. There were three bands of age-related rates for those aged between 16 and 21, each of which was reduced by a similar proportion. In addition, these rates were restricted to twenty-six weeks in a year after which everybody was required to undergo the means test before transitional benefit was paid. With 2.7m unemployed in August 1931 (almost 23%, with only 9.2m in work),[1050] GK Chesterton wrote "For the first time within mortal memory the Government and the nation has set out on a definite and deliberate campaign to make the poor poorer".[1051]

The savings that had to be made from cuts in wages and welfare were £22m in 1931/32 and £70m in 1932/33, with increased taxes bringing in a further £40m and £81m in each year respectively. The Means Test, administered by the Public Assistance Boards Wood and Chamberlain had introduced, took overall household resources into account in calculating transitional benefit, causing great hardship and were consequently detested.[1052] For example, in 'Love on the Dole' one of the characters overheard at the Labour Exchange "The Public Assistance Committee have

---

[1047] Blakeway, op cit, pp53 & 65
[1048] And "rounded off to the nearest 3d". Labour Research Department, 'Why It Happened: Capitalism in Crisis', 1934, pp14-15
[1049] In other words, about 75% of the weekly benefit rate for single migrants of £37 in 2015.
[1050] Labour Research Department, op cit, p13
[1051] Hannington, op cit, p48
[1052] Armstrong and Beynon, op cit and Hannington, op cit, pp46-48 provide case examples.

ruled your household's aggregate income sufficient for your needs; therefore your claim for transitional benefit is disallowed".[1053] Knowing that he would be told the same, Walter Greenwood's main protagonist Hardcastle did not bother to query it. Or, as Winifred Holtby describes the people coming before a Public Assistance Committee,

> Here were the men and women who had fallen a little lower even than those on transitional benefit, the disallowed, the uninsured, the destitute. The Means Test was no new humiliation to them. Since the days of Queen Elizabeth those who had become dependent on their neighbours had to submit to inquiry and suggestion. What was new was the type of person who came to ask for outdoor relief. The middle-class worker fallen on evil times, the professional man, the ruined investment holder.[1054]

Wood said nothing during the Act's passage through Parliament, but in December 1935 he was asked as Minister of Health whether the local authority rates that helped fund unemployment relief were adding to hardship in these areas. Wood explained that, since the Local Government Act 1929, "abnormal unemployment" was already a factor in the formula for determining central government grant distribution to local authorities and this allocation was currently being reviewed.[1055] A few days later he confirmed that there was no definition of a Special Area but the seven county boroughs listed in the Act were Gateshead, Merthyr Tydfil, Newcastle-upon-Tyne, South Shields, Sunderland, Tynemouth and West Hartlepool.[1056] On 16th December Sir William Jenkins (Labour MP for Neath since 1922) asked Wood whether he intended the country as a whole to bear the cost of unemployment rather than this being funded out of local rates and whether local authorities in distressed areas would get further grant to alleviate the pressures on their rates. Wood's written answer confirmed that no such national legislation was planned. With regard to additional

[1053] Walter Greenwood, 'Love on the Dole', 1993 (orig. 1933), p195
[1054] Holtby, op cit, p300
[1055] Hansard, 9th December 1935, vol. 307, cols. 555-556
[1056] Hansard, 12th December 1935, vol. 307, col. 1131

grant to distressed areas, he was unable to say more than his reply the previous week.[1057]

The following March the Labour Party initiated a censure debate, with Hugh Dalton's motion asking the Commons to note the Commissioners' reports on the Special Areas and express

> ... its profound regret at the inability of His Majesty's Government to produce any effective policy for dealing with the fundamental causes ... or for bringing any substantial measure of relief to the victims of these economic circumstances.[1058]

Ironically, but pointedly, it was Ramsay MacDonald who, now Lord President, largely bore the responsibility for replying on behalf of the National Government. Wood responded to the Labour MP for Blaydon[1059] who raised the issues of overcrowding and housing rents,[1060] giving Wood the opportunity to take a wider view, adopt a conciliatory tone and advocate a co-operative approach, in this case between the local authorities whose very real difficulties he said he appreciated, and the association established by the Commissioners on behalf of central government. The censure motion was eventually defeated along party lines by 357 votes to 154.[1061]

Wood was nevertheless blunt and unforthcoming when Whiteley proposed further rate relief later that month (this time to meet the interest charges arising on capital expenditure to build more houses and tackle unemployment). "No, Sir," Wood replied, arguing that such costs were "already largely met out of Exchequer subsidies".[1062] He was equally forthright when asked in July by another radical Labour MP, Thomas Johnston (1881-1965),[1063] what

---

[1057] Hansard, 16th December 1935, vol. 307, col. 1420

[1058] Hansard, 2nd March 1936, vol. 309, col. 1023

Dalton had returned to the Commons the previous November for Bishop Auckland after four years without a seat.

[1059] William Whiteley (1881-1955) had been MP for Blaydon between 1922 and 1931, and he and Wood would have known each other during the General Strike, given Blaydon's prominence. Like Dalton, Whiteley had just returned to Parliament at the 1935 General Election.

[1060] Hansard, 2nd March 1936, vol. 309, cols. 1067-1070

[1061] Ibid, cols. 1140-1142

[1062] Hansard, 19th March 1936, vol. 310, col. 603

[1063] Secretary of State for Scotland in the wartime government from 1941 until he retired from politics in 1945 and refused a peerage.

steps he would be taking "in view of the distressing physical condition of ... children in the Special Areas as revealed in the annual report of the National Council of Social Service". Wood replied that he was "unable to trace this reference in any recent report".[1064] Like Whiteley, Johnston was as canny a politician as Wood and both were demonstrating it in this exchange. However, Wood could respond positively to political opponents in certain circumstances. Jenkins, the Neath MP, raised the provision of playing fields in depressed areas on 13th July, asking whether such areas would get special treatment. Wood replied, "Yes, Sir. I am always willing to communicate to local authorities on ... playing field provision in their areas".[1065] Wood had long accepted that the opportunity for physical exercise was fundamental to individual and community health, and had gone further during the First World War by encouraging the provision of allotments and then the establishment of the Ministry of Health itself to take this broader, preventive view. This was of a piece with his work on the prevention and cure of tuberculosis (e.g., through better housing and village settlements). Wood added that Jenkins should also question the Minister of Labour on the financial assistance available to Special Areas if only to get further information.

Another example of Wood's conciliatory approach is provided by Thomas Johnston himself. In his 1952 autobiography, Johnston writes:

> I should like to pay tribute to Kingsley Wood, the Chancellor of the Exchequer, who not only allowed his name to go on the back of the [Hydro] Bill, but, despite some Treasury hesitations, insisted upon supporting the provision under which Hydro Board stock to the extent of £30m was guaranteed by the Treasury on demand by the Hydro Board.[1066]

Admittedly, this was during the war when Johnston was a Cabinet colleague as Secretary of State for Scotland, but perhaps precisely for that reason Wood's response was even more enlightened. It would have been all too easy to follow the Treasury line and prevent this quality of life development in the Scottish highlands at a time

---

[1064] Hansard, 2nd July 1936, vol. 314, cols. 626-627
[1065] Ibid, cols. 1683-1684
[1066] Thomas Johnston, 'Memories', 1952, p150

when even a Treasury guarantee risked removing resources from other priorities.

In April 1937 Wood was asked, again by a Labour MP,[1067] about the block grant allocations to the seven counties "scheduled, partly or wholly, as Special Areas" and changes from the previous year.[1068] Wood's written answer demonstrated that it was the four Welsh counties that had benefitted the most in percentage terms, while Durham's allocation remained the largest (about £70m today).[1069]

Later that year the recently elected Labour MP for Clay Cross[1070] asked Wood for the numbers of people receiving public assistance between 1931 and 1937 in the Special Areas.[1071] The September figures provided by Wood showed that:
- of the seven counties, Durham and Glamorgan were much the highest (about 50,000 people each) and both had increased to peaks in 1935 and 1936 respectively before reducing in 1936/37. Nevertheless, they were still higher in 1937 than in 1931. Monmouth was the third worst and again a reduction only came in 1936/37. Although it had only a third as many people unemployed

---

[1067] William Mainwaring (1884-1971), Labour MP for East Rhondda 1933-1959

[1068] Hansard, 16th April 1937, vol. 322, col. 1318

[1069] Wood explained that, although the 1937-38 figures were provisional at that time, all seven counties benefited in addition from the ending of "contributions which up to 1st April 1937 were payable by them under the Unemployment Act 1934". In other words, the review Wood had referred to in December 1935 had delivered a year later.
The full details were:

| | £ | | |
	1936–37	1937–38	% Change
Cumberland	414,206	473,694	14.36
Durham	1,555,649	1,726,326	10.97
Northumberland	591,764	641,753	8.45
Brecknock	99,316	118,559	19.38
Glamorgan	1,295,150	1,524,696	17.72
Monmouth	526,717	674,816	28.12
Pembroke	155,435	184,457	18.67

For comparison £1m in 1937 equates to about £40m today.

[1070] George Ridley (1886-1944) elected November 1936

[1071] Hansard, 15th November 1937, vol. 329, cols. 36-38

as Durham and Glamorgan, it was more than twice as high as anywhere else.
- among the seven county boroughs entirely in the Special Areas,[1072] Newcastle and Sunderland had the most people unemployed: Newcastle increased from over 14,000 in 1931 to nearly 23,000 in 1934 and then decreased to just over 12,000 in 1937; in Sunderland 9000 in 1931 had increased to nearly 16,000 in 1936 before reducing by a quarter to 12,000 in 1937. But whereas Newcastle's unemployed figure in 1937 was 2000 down on that for 1931, Sunderland's remained higher.

Wood's final Commons answer on the Special Areas, again in writing, came in December 1937 when he batted away a question from a fellow Conservative, the MP for Cardiff East, Owen Morris (1896-1985) who had asked whether the transference of workers had impeded the operation, or reform, of public health. Wood may have been genuinely perplexed by the question for his non-reply was

> I shall be glad if my hon. Friend will let me know more precisely what he has in mind, and if he will furnish me with particulars of any case affecting the matter, I shall be glad to inquire into it.[1073]

These details were not forthcoming either before or after Wood became Minister of Air in May 1938. Possibly the Cardiff East MP was warned not to press the issue by the party whips, or even that there was no real issue to pursue. Perhaps Morris had looked at other South Wales MPs asking questions of Wood and thought he had better do so too. They were mostly Labour MPs, of course, representing deprived communities in south Wales whereas Cardiff East was comparatively prosperous.[1074] It is striking though that it was these MPs who raised health concerns regarding the Special

---

[1072] Only Merthyr was not in the north-east of England.

[1073] Hansard, 2nd December 1937, vol. 329, cols. 2277-2278

[1074] Owen Morris was a barrister from 1925, a judge in Merthyr Tydfil from 1936, MP for Cardiff East from 1931 to 1942 and a prominent lay member of the Church in Wales. His middle name, appropriately enough as it captured both aspects, was Temple, and he was later knighted as Sir Owen Temple-Morris, QC. His father had been a Cardiff physician but Morris was essentially a Conservative placeman who could be relied on to toe the party line. This may explain why he did not respond to Wood's invitation to provide further information.

Areas. By contrast, Labour MPs in the North East focussed on the structural problems caused by unemployment and poverty, as well as on the immediate day-to-day issues, and so directed their questions towards Ministers with these briefs rather than the health one.

However, Wood's party responsibilities and roles ensured that he had further involvement in the issues around the Special Areas outside the Commons. The report from the Party's Central Council to the October 1935 Annual Conference noted that, though the general employment situation had continued to improve, "the position in the Special Areas still gives cause for anxiety".[1075] The following month the matter was considered at one of the three meetings of the Emergency Business Committee (EBC) set up by the Cabinet to deal with any urgent business that might arise during the run-up to the 1935 general election. Only Hailsham the Lord Chancellor as Chairman and Wood in his Cabinet role as Minister of Health, but no doubt in reality as election supremo, attended all three. On the 8th a Distressed Areas Questionnaire was considered, to which it was agreed that the response should point out that the State now bore more than 95% of the cost, with less than 5% coming from local authorities, and that, as relief cost the Treasury £5.56m per annum, local authority budgets were already cushioned; but if necessary the position would be reviewed.[1076] This was similar to the replies Wood gave in Parliament subsequently, though the Conference of Distressed Areas, headed up by Wal Hannington the leader of the unemployed, sought 100% Government support for the able-bodied unemployed.[1077] The pressure in parliament had the same genesis.

At its 8th November meeting the EBC took a related item concerning the hours of work of young people. The Factory Act permitted up to sixty hours a week for under 18s but, not only did the excessive employment of youngsters increase adult unemployment, it was morally abhorrent in any case. The EBC noted that the Home Secretary had decided this was excessive and had been investigating 'unregulated occupations' (i.e., outside the Factory Act regulations) since July. In addition, he and Malcolm MacDonald

[1075] CPA Annual Conference minutes 1930, 1932-1937 NUA 2/1/50, 3rd and 4th October 1935 at Bournemouth
[1076] CPA EBC (35)16
[1077] CPA CRD 1/7/21 Cabinet Emergency Business Committee 1935 - Questions of Policy 1-57 item 27

$(1901-1981)^{1078}$ planned to introduce legislation to reduce the sixty-hour limit when possible.[1079] The conflict between the interests of employer, employee and the unemployed was tangible, particularly in the run-up to an election.

Unemployment in the Special Areas began to decline substantially only in the immediate years before the Second World War. In December 1938 Inskip reported in the Commons that in the two and a half years between April 1936 and September 1938 contracts worth £112m (mainly for rearmaments) had been placed in these areas against £405m elsewhere.[1080] This reflected the government's deliberate policy and by May 1939 the impact was clear for in four of the areas (Durham & Tyneside, West Cumberland, South Wales & Monmouth, South West Scotland) unemployment had fallen by almost one-half from 480,623 at September 1931 to 255,496 at May 1939.[1081]

[1078] Son of Ramsay MacDonald and at this point in a junior post at the Dominions Office; like Wood he was a theatre aficionado.
[1079] CPA EBC (35) 20
[1080] CPA CRD 1/78/2 Points for Propaganda January to July 1939 - Item 107 13th December 1938
[1081] Ibid - Item 127 15th June 1939

George V

In February 1934 King George V sent Wood a signed photograph of himself. The King's private secretary Clive Wigram wrote

> Dear Postmaster-General,
> I have received the King's instructions to send you the enclosed signed photograph with His Majesty's best wishes.

The photograph (on the following page), sent 22nd February 1934, belongs to Kingsley Wood's grandson. It may be that Wood had already been to Balmoral (not necessarily as the Minister on duty but simply to brief the King) and the photograph was a memento of the occasion, or it may have been recognition of Wood's impact at Health and the Post Office. It seems less likely to have been a routine acknowledgement to a Privy Councillor for Wood had become one six years earlier in 1928. What is indisputable though is that Wood was the Minister on duty at Balmoral in September 1935 and on this occasion he kept some of the Balmoral menu cards.[1082]

It is said that

> Ministers abhorred having to go to Balmoral, not only because they wasted so much time travelling there ... but also because they were so uncomfortable when they did get there.[1083]

This was supposed to be Disraeli's view of visiting Queen Victoria there, which might be understandable given the regularity with which they saw each other in any case, but matters may have improved fifty years later. No doubt Wood's view was that it would be as well to enjoy it if one could. A duty perhaps, but not one he found tedious, rather an opportunity to be part of history that was given to few people. Wood's natural inclination was always a "glass half full".

[1082] KW33/9-11
[1083] Christopher Hibbert, 'Disraeli: A Personal History', 2004, p313

Subsequently, one newspaper reported

The King is paying a high compliment to Sir Kingsley Wood in having him at Balmoral Castle. The Sovereign is always interested in a Minister of exceptional energy and resources, and Sir Kingsley Wood certainly has claim to that description,[1084]

while another explained that he had been Minister-in-Attendance for four days and was to be followed by Neville Chamberlain and John Simon.[1085]

Baldwin hugely admired the King's sense of duty and conscientious commitment to public service,[1086] and it is likely that Wood was of the same mind. George V reciprocated Baldwin's respect and Wood's performance as a Minister would have brought him to the King's attention for similar reasons. That the public generally thought of George V affectionately was apparent from the overwhelming response to his silver jubilee in 1935.

[1084] *Citizen* 13th September 1935, KW19 464/10. The report noted the King's interest in housing for the working-classes and Wood would have briefed him about this.
[1085] *Truth* 18th September 1935, KW19 482/5
[1086] Middlemas and Barnes, op cit, p811

Primrose League

Baldwin had intended to stand down as Prime Minister and Leader of the Conservative Party in 1936 but various crises, not least the death of George V at the start of the year and the abdication of Edward VIII at the end, prevented him from doing so before May 1937. According to the respected editor of the *Sunday Times* WW Hadley, so resolute was Baldwin that he would resign as soon as circumstances permitted that he insisted Neville Chamberlain select the Ministers in a Cabinet re-shuffle more than six months earlier.[1087] However, when Baldwin's ill-health prevented him from addressing the 1936 Party conference for the first time since he had become Leader and Chamberlain deputised for him,[1088] the CRD advised Chamberlain not to go beyond what either Baldwin or the Cabinet had already said, so that it could not be claimed that he was already acting as if he were the Leader.[1089] What was acceptable privately was not yet for public consumption.

Wood first came to the attention of the Primrose League[1090] on 3rd May 1935 when he moved the main resolution at the annual Albert Hall demonstration. This was to the effect that the financial and industrial recovery that had taken place under the National Government would be imperilled if the Socialists were re-elected. The Grand Master Baldwin had introduced him:

> I rejoice to think that we are to be addressed by my friend Sir Kingsley Wood, the Postmaster General. (Applause) He is a man of proved administrative capacity and he enjoys something rarer at the moment than that reputation - he enjoys at the moment universal popularity. (Laughter) I once enjoyed universal popularity for a week. (Laughter) It was immediately after the General Strike ...[1091]

As might be expected, the Primrose League played a substantial role at the November 1935 general election, with a pamphlet

---

[1087] WW Hadley,'Munich: Before and After', 1944, p27

[1088] CPA NUA 4/2/1

[1089] CPA CRD 1/24/2 Brooke letter 23rd Sept 1936

[1090] The primrose was Disrael's favourite flower and the Primrose League was set up by his admirers in 1883 to honour his memory. Alistair Cooke, 'A Gift from the Churchills: The Primrose League 1883-2004', 2010 provides further detail.

[1091] *Primrose League Gazette* June 1935, p15

'Preparations for Election Work' available to Habitations (as the local branches were called) at 2s 6d (12.5p) per 100.[1092] The following month's magazine trumpeted 'A Resounding Victory' with a round-up of some constituency results including Wood

> ... subjected to a fierce attack from Mr George Wansborough, the Old Blue [but] Sir Kingsley Wood had two trump cards, his twenty-five years association with the Division [since he had first stood in Woolwich for the LCC] and his personal record as a Cabinet Minister.[1093]

Nevertheless, the Woolwich Habitation seems not to have been one of the more active, featuring only once in the four years 1935-1938 in the monthly summaries of programmes, and Wood himself was never a member of the League's Grand Council until he took over from Baldwin as Grand Master in spring 1938. Baldwin had been replaced as Prime Minister by Neville Chamberlain almost a year earlier (on 24th May 1937), but his resignation as Grand Master was reported in April 1938 and the Grand Council chose Wood to replace him.[1094] The May issue of the magazine, the first in a vibrant primrose colour,[1095] continued to list Baldwin, but now as the Ex-Grand Master, while his wife Lucy Baldwin (1869-1945) was still the Grand Dame.[1096] Lucy Baldwin was accorded this accolade but Wood's wife was not (nor it would seem was Churchill's subsequently). It may have been in recognition of her campaigning over many years for women's rights.

Wood's first set-piece speech as Grand Master to the Albert Hall demonstration on 6th May was reported in the same edition. He started with Disraeli's legacy, moved on to describe the ways in which the Prime Ministers Baldwin and now Neville Chamberlain had kept this alive, stressed the importance of securing world peace as the storm clouds gathered,[1097] and concluded by quoting at length from Disraeli whose 1876 views Wood argued were relevant

---

[1092] *Primrose League Gazette* November 1935, p5

[1093] *Primrose League Gazette* December 1935, pp1, 9-12

[1094] *Primrose League Gazette* April 1938, p5 This had taken place in February 1938 according to Wood's obituary in the October 1943 issue.

[1095] The magazine reverted to a faded primrose colour in April 1939.

[1096] *Primrose League Gazette* May 1938, p3

[1097] The Italian-Abyssinian crisis had been reported in the *Primrose League Gazette* for October 1935 (p8), while the issue a year later included the Spanish Civil War (October 1936, p8).

to the current situation.[1098]   Chamberlain's missions to Berchtesgarden and Godesberg over the Czechoslovakian crisis were reported that autumn, as was the text of the Munich agreement. The former included a map of Czechoslovakia with the Sudeten German regions marked where they accounted for more than 50% of the population, while the latter added extracts from speeches that were made in Parliament and elsewhere applauding Chamberlain for the Munich agreement.[1099]

Wood's first new year message to the Primrose League appeared in the January 1939 issue. After Munich the future looked more positive than it had a year earlier:

> We have had many anxieties during the past year, and the maintenance of the peace of Europe has been in the balance, but it has been manifest that it has been the desire of the people of every country to avoid war ... Peace will not come to the world by 'sitting still and waiting for it to come', but ... we must continue to actively pursue every approach open to us to remove hostility and differences between nations.[1100]

Now Air Minister, he advocated negotiating from strength, judging that re-armament made peace more, not less, likely. But he did not omit "further efforts to improve the conditions of the people", a message that was important for morale, even if the expectation proved impossible to realise in practice.   These included early treatment for cancer and continuing slum clearance.

All parties had thought a general election likely in autumn 1939,[1101] but once war was declared this was abandoned and the Primrose League ceased its political propaganda, turning its attention to "patriotic service".   Symbolic of this, the League's headquarters in Victoria Street were transferred to the Red Cross for their Comforts and Collections Committee.[1102] In November the magazine scaled down in size by a quarter, from sixteen pages to twelve, but Habitations were advised not to disband, rather keeping "their members in touch with one another, ready when the time

---

[1098] *Primrose League Gazette* June 1938, pp12-13
[1099] *Primrose League Gazette* October 1938, p9 and November 1938, p9 respectively
[1100] *Primrose League Gazette* January 1939, p8
[1101] *Primrose League Gazette* July 1939, p8
[1102] *Primrose League Gazette* October 1939, p3

comes to renew [their] normal work".[1103]   In May 1940 Wood's Grand Habitation speech (at the Westminster Palace Rooms rather than the Albert Hall as in previous years) included

It is now too evident that ... this great war was inevitable unless we were prepared to submit to tyranny and barbarism, to give up our freedom and our rights and to see civilisation perish.[1104]

In his 1942 new year address Wood was able to contrast November 1940 when "Britain still stood alone, 'the sole champion of freedom in arms'" with the improving situation at the end of 1941: "This may still be a long and hard war, but we do not doubt the outcome".[1105] During 1942 the *Gazette* was reduced in size by a further four pages, not returning to twelve pages until after the war. This austerity was augmented in April when the Grosvenor House luncheon was cancelled following consultation between Wood and Lord Woolton, the Minister of Food.[1106]   On 15th April an official announcement had discouraged lunches and dinners that attracted "large numbers of people and the consequent travelling", and the Primrose League would have been keen to set an example.[1107]   By January 1943 the optimistic gloss to boost morale at the start of 1942 was becoming more substantial. In that new year message Wood asserted

During the last few months there has been a considerable turn of the tide in favour of the cause of .... The Allies [who] have now assumed the offensive ...[1108]

[1103] *Primrose League Gazette* January 1940, p3

[1104] *Primrose League Gazette* June 1940, p4

[1105] *Primrose League Gazette* January 1942, pp3-4
Japan had declared war on the USA and bombed Pearl Harbour in December 1941. This precipitated America's entry into the war and the assumption that this would result ultimately in a victory for the Allies.

[1106] As Frederick Marquis (1883-1964), a businessman who often worked with government, he had been a member of the Post Office advisory council Wood had established.
When Beaverbrook advised Wood to get to know Marquis, Wood was able to reply that he already did. Parliamentary archives, BBK/C/330, 8th March letter and 9th March 1935 reply.

[1107] *Primrose League Gazette* May 1942, p2

[1108] *Primrose League Gazette* January 1943, p1

The victory at El Alamein in November 1942 had prompted Churchill to refer to "the end of the beginning" and it would be this that Wood had in mind.

The Beveridge report had just been published and Parliament debated it in February 1943. Only one of the twenty-three proposals were rejected outright but there were concerns about the costs, the possible distraction of social security ahead of national security and that it was being considered in advance of other post-war priorities. As Chancellor of the Exchequer Wood had adopted the cautious position that went with the finance role, but while he was concerned to curb over-exuberance and inject reality, others thought he was damping down legitimate aspirations unreasonably. Wood recognised this when he addressed the annual meeting of the Primrose League at Caxton Hall in April 1943: "It is very kind of you to give a welcome to the Chancellor of the Exchequer. It is not everybody who is so kind to me. (Laughter)" He went on to say that people were mistaken when they argued that, because the country could afford a war, it could automatically afford Beveridge. A more appropriate analogy might be paying as much as necessary for an emergency operation but having to compensate afterwards by reining in your spending.[1109]

This was to be the last time Wood featured in the *Gazette* before the obituary they published in October 1943. His predecessor as Grand Master had been Baldwin, his successor another Prime Minister Winston Churchill. This is indicative of the esteem in which Wood was held for

> The League requires for this position a man whose name carries weight, who inspires confidence and whose experience and judgement and foresight are assets.
> ... [Wood] was in full sympathy with the people and their aspirations; he understood how politics touch the lives of the people and affect their very existence ...[1110]

This was affection for the man as well as admiration for his "enterprise and initiative".

[1109] *Primrose League Gazette* May 1943, p1
[1110] *Primrose League Gazette* October 1943, p3

15.   FAMILY, FRIENDS AND LIFE BEYOND POLITICS

Wesleyan Methodism

Kingsley Wood's father, the Reverend Arthur Wood, was a leading Methodist Minister based at Wesley's Chapel in City Road, London from 1891 and worked in London for over thirty years, his ministry to the poor referred to in Charles Booth's 'Life and Labour in London'.[1111]   He died in 1919 and in 1935 Wood and his sister Dorothy Weaver gifted a window to Wesley's Chapel in memory of their parents.   The dedication service was conducted on 24th October by the Reverend Scott Lidgett, one of the best-known Methodist preachers of his time[1112] and a prominent supporter of Lloyd George's Council of Action[1113] until a week before the 1935 general election when Scott Lidgett changed his mind, urging people "to vote for the National Government and against the Socialists".[1114]

The London correspondent of the *Toronto Evening Telegram* reported that

> By this act on the part of Kingsley Wood and his sister, a debt of gratitude is acknowledged, though ([Kingsley] would admit) not paid off.   The present writer [probably WT Cranfield] remembers the Reverend Arthur Wood as a father more than usually devoted to the welfare of his son.   It may be that he had no more than a father's pride in his boy; it may be that he had premonitions of that boy's public gifts and coming eminence.   In any case he eclipsed his own interests in the service of his son, preparing him educatively and socially for whatever serious destiny lay ahead.   What Sir Kingsley Wood is today - and what he may be tomorrow - and there are those who see in him a future prime minister - he owes in rich measure to his father's love and devotion.[1115]

[1111] Further details in Gault, 2014, op cit, p11ff

[1112] Alan Turberfield, 'John Scott Lidgett', 2003

[1113] As were other Methodists such as the editor of the *Methodist Times*.

[1114] Stannage, op cit, p149

[1115] *Toronto Evening Telegram* 2nd November 1935, KW21 23/2
The London office of this newspaper was 2 Adam Street and it was from here that WT Cranfield sent his report.   It was therefore just four doors away from Robert Williamson's office and virtually opposite the flat that Hore-Belisha had occupied.

The headline 'Gives Memorial Window to "Mecca" of Methodists' must have appealed to the paper's sub-editor because of the alliteration rather than its appropriateness or accuracy.

The lower part of the window (below) depicts Charles Wesley writing a hymn, while the upper half "illustrates one of the great moments in [his] life … in May 1738, when he sang the hymn 'Where shall my wondering soul begin?'" with friends in Aldersgate Street.[1116]   Dorothy's husband was also a Methodist Minister, the Rev Edward Weaver, and Wood was one of the most prominent Methodist laymen. As one paper put it, Wood, a fourth generation Methodist, "preserves the tradition, for he is still on the plan of local preachers".[1117]

Part of memorial window donated by Wood and his sister Dorothy Weaver to Wesley's Chapel, City Road, London - Reproduced with the permission of the Trustees of Wesley's Chapel, City Road

---

[1116] *Times*, 25th October 1935
Also, *Methodist Times and Leader* 14th October, *Methodist Recorder* 1st November 1935, KW20 6/1 & 6/14
[1117] *Birmingham Daily Mail* 1st November 1935, KW20 17/14

Wood's paternal grandfather Thomas S Wood had joined the Methodist church in his home town of Canterbury, having heard one of their services while sheltering from a storm in the chapel porch. He subsequently became a Minister and less than fifteen years later, aged only 45, was in a horrendous railway accident at Chilham in Kent in 1858, dying from his injuries in Kent County Hospital.[1118]

In September 1934 Wesley's house on the City Road site had been re-opened after refurbishment with Wood, the treasurer of the Friends of Wesley's Chapel, accepting a new portrait of Wesley they had commissioned.[1119] That December Wood chaired the National Children's Home and Orphanage (NCHO) Christmas festival at Queen's Hall,[1120] with an article on him in the NCHO Christmas magazine by his friend Reverend GH McNeal calling him "a genial, generous, fascinating man". When McNeal died unexpectedly a few days later, Wood and Arthur Henderson were among the mourners at his funeral at Highgate cemetery.[1121]

Personal Life

An admiring 1935 profile, 'A Man of Action Stirs Up Whitehall',[1122] by the journalist and author Sidney Campion concentrated on a typical day for Wood as Minister of Health, including the travelling he chose to undertake throughout the country to find out the situation on the ground. Campion was told by one of Wood's friends that Wood worked twenty hours a day and had little time for leisure. It was certainly the case that Wood's life revolved around his political and Ministerial activities, but it was not the case that he found no time for recreation. He was President of Shooters Hill Golf Club and the annual Sir Kingsley Wood Trophy remains part of the

---

[1118] *NA* undated, KW19 467/7: Talbot Brierley article in Methodist publication pp517-519
[1119] *Methodist Recorder* 27th September 1934, KW19 170/1
[1120] *Methodist Recorder* 20th December 1934, KW19 252/1
[1121] *Daily Independent* 21st December 1934, KW19 253/6
[1122] KW20 55/9
Although the press cuttings book does not record either the date of the article or the newspaper in which it appeared, Campion worked for Lord Kemsley at this stage of his career so the paper was the *Sunday Chronicle*, *Sunday Graphic* or *Daily Sketch*, most likely the latter. (The other Kemsley nationals, the *Sunday Times* and *Empire News*, are less probable.)

Club's calendar in 2015. He was still attending boxing matches in 1936 with his friend Sir Harry Preston, the Brighton hotel owner,[1123] and often lunched with Preston and JH Thomas, usually at the Ritz Hotel in Piccadilly where Preston was an even more regular customer.[1124] As Kingsley Martin put it in his biography of Harold Laski, referring explicitly to the bibulous JH Thomas,[1125] some 1929 "Labour ministers [were] defeated not by force or fraud, but by being asked out to dine".

On an official visit to Brighton in 1936 the longest slot in Wood's timetable was for a lunch hosted by Preston at his Royal Albion Hotel. He attended parties too, one of which was given at the Ritz by another well-known figure in the hotel world for the return of a daughter and son-in-law from honeymoon. A reporter was talking to the Prestons when Kingsley Wood joined them:

> He was greeted by Sir Harry with one of those graceful little speeches - impromptu poems in prose - a Prestonian speciality.
> Without a word the PMG [as Wood then was] pressed half-a-crown into Sir Harry's palm. Would Mr Neville Chamberlain have done this? I doubt it. But Sir Kingsley is so justifiably proud of that Post Office surplus that it imparts a lavishness to all his gestures.
> He did not get the half-crown back. 'This is going into my collection of illustrious coins,' said Sir Harry.[1126]

TP O'Connor was another of his friends and it was Wood who made the arrangements for a presentation on the Commons terrace overlooking the Thames of a trust deed making financial provision for O'Connor the year after his 80th birthday.[1127] When her telephone was out of order in January 1935, Emerald Cunard contacted the PMG himself rather than her local exchange. She

---

[1123] *Sunday Dispatch* 26th April 1936, KW20 119/1 They had been to the British heavyweight title fight between Petersen and McAvoy.
[1124] *Sunday Graphic and Sunday News* 4th March 1934, KW19 72/17; *Bystander* 2nd October 1934, KW19 188/7
[1125] Kingsley Martin, op cit, pp76-77
[1126] *Daily Sketch* 1st November 1934, KW19 218/10
[1127] *Cork Examiner* 15th July 1929, KW17 133/2; *Daily Telegraph* 16th July 1929, KW17 133/3; *Times* 19th July 1929

was never short on over-confidence but must have felt sufficiently connected to Wood to ring him up directly.[1128]

On 1st July 1938 Wood opened Salomons House as a Kent County Council convalescent home.[1129] It had been donated by Vera Salomons, the woman who had sold the neighbouring Broomhill Bank to Wood over ten years before and he had decided to fulfil the engagement even though it had been agreed when he was Minister of Health and, by then Minister of Air, he no longer needed to. Wood was not only a neighbour but may have wanted to demonstrate his appreciation to Vera Salomons for the donation, given his previous involvements with health and social services in Kent. Additionally, the ceremony took place on a Friday afternoon and a cynic might say that his attendance enabled Wood to be home sooner than otherwise (had he been at the Air Ministry in London). However, there may have been a further more laudable reason. The Salomons were pillars of the Jewish community in Britain and had been for well over a hundred years. An article in the *Sunday Pictorial* the week after he opened Salomons House had Wood telling a Jewish gathering that it was "unhappily and tragically true" that Jews were facing persecution and ignominy in many countries but not in Britain where "The Jewish community ... has made many contributions to our common life".[1130] Keeping the invitation to open Salomons House would have provided a very public demonstration of Wood's solidarity with the Jewish community, putting his head above the parapet at a very difficult time.

Wood regularly attended first nights at the theatre for he was one of thirty-four people Gitano chose to caricature in *Nash's Magazine* in June 1935 (half of which is on the following page) as those whose "nightly devotion to drama makes every theatre season a perennial jubilee".[1131] Anthony Eden, JH Thomas and Philip Sassoon are the only other politicians depicted, but many of those portrayed are well-known: JB Priestley, Ivor Novello, Noel Coward, John Gielgud, James Agate, Douglas Fairbanks, Charles B Cochran and Gordon Selfridge. Gertrude Lawrence, Gladys Cooper, Emerald Cunard and two Guinness sisters, Maureen

---

[1128] Robert Rhodes James (ed.), 1967, op cit, p23
[1129] *The Courier* 8th July 1938, *BMJ* 30th July 1938; also *NA* 8th July 1938, KW23 255/1
[1130] *Sunday Pictorial* 10th July 1938, KW23 254/1
[1131] 'First Nights', *Nash's Magazine* June 1935, KW19 373/1

(Marchioness of Dufferin and Ava) and Aileen (Hon Mrs Brinsley Plunket), are among the sixteen women.[1132]   The journalist Valentine Kenmare (better known as Lord Castlerosse) is also pictured, as are Sheila Chisholm who had recently become Lady Milbanke and Jeanne Stourton, soon to become Lady Camoys.

Gitano caricature (part): *Nash's Magazine* June 1935

Kenmare, by all accounts a close friend of Beaverbrook, would die on the same day as Wood (21st September 1943).[1133]   The cartoonist David Low worked with Castlerosse, concluding that "he knew the idle rich from the inside. But he was a dislocating chap to

---

[1132] Their cousin Honor Guinness was the wife of Chips Channon.
[1133] Robert Rhodes James (ed.), 1967, op cit, p375

work with [even though] the liveliest social columnist of his generation."[1134]

Agnes, Lady Wood, is not shown though some couples (such as Lord and Lady Plunket) are, nor is she referred to in any of the Ritz reports, so while she and Wood went on holiday each year[1135] and to the cinema together, he pursued some interests without her. His compartmentalised life extended beyond politics to his time in London but, refreshingly, he recognised that the world was opening up for women as well:

'The young woman of today,' said Sir Kingsley, 'is no longer a clinging vine or the mental inferior and the dutiful handmaid of a mere man. But she is self-reliant, tenacious and courageous, and is taking her part more than ever in the world's work.'[1136]

Little Joe

In his diaries John Colville, one of the Prime Minister's private secretaries, recalls Lord Beaverbrook and Brendan Bracken referring to Wood as "Little Joe".[1137] This might be thought a slur on his diminutive height or possibly some link between Wood's character and either that of Stalin or the cartoon character GI Joe. However, the correct attribution emerges from a postscript Beaverbrook had added a month earlier in a letter to Wood: "Did you ever hear the song 'Little Joe' in [the film] 'Destry Rides

---

[1134] David Low, 'Low's Autobiography', 1956, p290

[1135] Often to a spa at Harrogate (*Bystander* 14th September 1932, KW17 371/6; *Yorkshire Post* 27th September 1933, KW19 7/3-4; KW20 103/1-9 in March 1936) or Karlsbad (*Yorkshire Evening News* 16th August 1927, KW17 5/6; *Northern Echo* 14th September 1927, KW17 5/4; Self, 2002, vol. 3, op cit, p100: 5th August 1928; *Star* 26th June 1931, KW17 283/12), and often Wood's annual cure for excess weight. In 1930 they went to the Black Forest (*North Eastern Daily Gazette* 6th August 1930, KW17 222/2) and in 1933 to Sweden (KW18 143/7; *Daily Telegraph* 22nd August 1933, KW19 4/6).
When the Woods were at Harrogate for ten days in 1938 while Agnes was "undergoing treatment," the *Yorkshire Evening News* commented "... isn't it a terrific compliment to Harrogate when the Minister of Health and his wife stay there for the good of **their's**?" (29th April 1938, KW23 147/4)

[1136] *Queen* 20th December 1933, KW19 1/12

[1137] John Colville, 'The Fringes of Power: Downing Street Diaries 1939-1955', 1985, entry for 4th February 1941, p352

Again'?"[1138] Wood and Beaverbrook had corresponded since 1931 and at various stages over the next ten years were clearly friends as well as close colleagues. However, at the time of this letter they were in dispute about Beaverbrook's suggestion that £1m of public funds be transferred to the RAF Benevolent Fund (in remembrance of the Battle of Britain), a proposal about which Wood as Chancellor of the Exchequer had not been consulted. When Wood had asked "My dear Max" about this, Beaverbrook replied

> But why should I consult you?
> You would probably oppose me.
> Everything I have put forward so far has been opposed by you. Yet everything that I put forward cannot be wrong. That would be quite inconceivable.

Beaverbrook's postscript followed what must have been intended as a threat "... my first act [as Minister] was to help you. I hope that my last act will have the same character". Beaverbrook was not so crass as to refer explicitly to his intimate relationship with Churchill (the Prime Minister) but this may have been what he had in mind.

However, Wood was capable of giving as good as he got and, unlike some of his government colleagues, was never cowed by Beaverbrook. He replied two days later that he had "not yet been able to get the text of 'Little Joe'. I will come and have a talk with you when you are better."[1139] Whether Wood did have access to the words or not is unclear, though as a film enthusiast he may have had some idea of the lyrics, especially as the film from a couple of years before had been very popular and Marlene Dietrich had sung 'Little Joe'. The three verses are

> Little Joe, Little Joe
> Oh, whatever become of him, I don't know
> Oh, he sure did like his liquor
> And it would have got his ticker
> But the sheriff got him quicker - yeeha!
>
> Little Joe, Little Joe
> Oh, wherever his body lies, I don't know

[1138] Parliamentary archives, BBK/D/336, 5th January 1941 Beaverbrook letter
[1139] Parliamentary archives, BBK/D/336, 7th January 1941 Wood reply

When the yellow moon was beamin'
He could wrangle like a demon
And you'd always hear him screamin' - yeeha!

Little Joe, Little Joe
Oh, whatever he's doing now, I don't know
He had women by the dozen
And he swore they woz his cousins
Till he met up with their husbands - yeeha!

Although Beaverbrook may have been thinking of the first verse, seeing himself as the sheriff who would expose Wood, or possibly equating him with the argumentative wrangler[1140] of the second verse, it is much more likely that it is the third verse and Wood's womanising that he was alluding to. There is other apparent evidence for this, as in the 1935 story that Preston told a newspaper:

It was at a big reception, and as he turned to greet a friend, the point of an Order Sir Kingsley Wood was wearing got caught in the lace of his wife's gown.
'Ah, entangled with the ladies again, I see,' chided the friend.
'Yes, but I never got clear so easily before!' retorted Sir Kingsley, as with his laughing wife's help he stepped clear.[1141]

Agnes may have been genuinely amused but possibly found it ironic as well.

Preston died in August 1936 at the age of 76. An operation that June appeared to have been successful and he returned to Brighton in mid-July. A fortnight later though his condition deteriorated and he received a blood transfusion from a boxing friend. This also appeared to go well at first but in early August he had a relapse and died on 13th August.[1142] Three days later the friend who had given blood, an amateur heavyweight boxing

---

[1140] In the US west of the film "wrangle" is to take charge of a string of horses, although it can also mean argue noisily, wrestle and herd. Any or all of these may have been intended.
[1141] KW19 456/13
[1142] *Times* 14th August 1936

champion, died from an infection he had contracted during the procedure and another three days after that this man's brother collapsed and died on hearing the news.[1143] The loss of his friend Preston, particularly in such tragic circumstances, must have had a profound impact on Wood.

Preston's funeral at Cuckfield in Sussex was widely reported, including in the *Morning Post* among the national papers,[1144] with Wood, JH Thomas and the Chief Constable of Brighton listed among the mourners. Wood, "for many years a friend of Sir Harry's" as another paper recorded, had already paid his respects to Lady Preston "to express sympathy with her in her grievous loss". Not surprisingly given Harry Preston's reputation as a bon viveur and his legendary sociability, many people sent her condolence messages, including the music hall stars Flanagan and Allen. One of Preston's last wishes had been that his widow should carry on with the Royal Albion Hotel, and this she intended to do.[1145]

Married Life

Agnes and Kingsley had married in 1905[1146] and while they remained a couple they also spent much time apart. From 1927 their main home was Broomhill Bank outside Tunbridge Wells but there was a series of properties in London that enabled Wood to attend to his work there during the week. In 1926 there was a flat at 7 Palace Mansions with a move across the way to number 10 by 1928, and he had moved again by 1930.[1147] (The Post Office Directories for 1933 and 1934 indicate that Wood was then living at 66 St George's Square in Pimlico, but this address is not referred to anywhere else.) By 1935 he was living at 23 Buckingham Palace Mansions and by 1941 at number 12, the flat in which he died in September 1943. In between his address was sometimes given as 15 Walbrook, sometimes as the Athenaeum or Carlton Clubs. While the former, his law firm's office, was presumably an address to which to send his post, the Post Office itself would have fulfilled this function between 1931 and 1935. He must either have stayed from time to time at the Athenaeum or Carlton Clubs in these years

---

[1143] *Times* 17th and 20th August 1936
[1144] *Morning Post* 19th August 1936, KW21 28/12
[1145] *NA* undated, KW21 28/15
[1146] Gault, 2014, op cit, pp32-38
[1147] Dod's and Post Office Directories respectively.

or done so routinely. In December 1932 an article entitled 'Sir Santa Claus' stated that Wood was only at Tunbridge Wells at weekends, otherwise being at a small flat at Westminster and "Lady Wood often stays there too".[1148] Either there was another flat between 10 Palace Mansions and 23 Buckingham Palace Mansions (possibly at St George's Square) or it is deliberate obfuscation since Agnes would not have been able to stay at one of the Clubs. If she was in London during the week it must have been a lonely life for, when not travelling the country, the article claims that Wood "usually dines at the House of Commons (one of his few luxuries) and works late". In December 1939 the front page of the *Primrose League Gazette* referred to "fifteen evacuee children from Woolwich ... in the care of Lady Wood" at Broomhill Bank.[1149] Although she would not have had much day-to-day responsibility for their care, more than her husband who "occasionally finds time to visit his pleasant Kentish home".[1150] The implication is that they were apart for much of the time.

According to Wood's grandson, his mother told him that Wood had many affairs.[1151] Wood's humour and personality would have made him attractive to women, as would his power and achievements, for as one newspaper put it in a 1937 profile, he was the "Real power behind Baldwin", "Could have any job he wants in Cabinet", but "Prefers to be Minister of Health and in control of party machine". It concluded "Kingsley Could - If Kingsley Wood!"[1152] As not even an appointments book has been discovered, any firm evidence for his extramarital liaisons is hard to find. Indeed, Wood was one of those politicians whose allegedly stable home life was contrasted with the convoluted crisis that Edward VIII was putting the country through in 1936:

[1148] *The Passing Show* 3rd December 1932, KW18 13/1
The article adds that, until recently, he had played cricket, an enthusiasm he shared with his PPS Edward Campbell, was a pipe-smoker, a film buff and "an excellent raconteur".
[1149] Agnes' obituary in the *Kent and West Sussex Courier* recorded that after Kingsley Wood's death she looked after twenty-five evacuees at Broomhill Bank (21st October 1955, p8).
[1150] *Primrose League Gazette* December 1939, p1
The accompanying picture, now in the possession of Wood's grandson Robin Brothers, had first been published in the *Daily Sketch*.
[1151] Robin Brothers, personal communications
[1152] *Sunday Referee* 14th February 1937, KW21 146/3

Because business keeps him so much in town he can only live at his home at Tunbridge Wells at the week-ends, so he has a small flat in Westminster.

This is furnished in the soft blues and greys that he and Lady Wood both like, and Lady Wood is nearly always there to see that slippers and a bright fire, with a pile of magazines on the nearest table, are waiting to welcome this pocket Cabinet Minister. ...

Sometimes after a busy day at the House of Commons you see him hurrying for his hat. She is waiting.

They go to the cinema just like any of their constituents. They are agreed that a good plot with a thrill is better than a galaxy of stars.[1153]

This portrait was published on the day that Edward VIII's abdication was expected to be announced. Appearing alongside other 'Romances of the King's Advisers', it was intended to reassure the public that their King's emotional circumstances were not representative of the establishment generally. In Wood's case, though, it might have fostered the image he wished to project as a home body rather than the bon viveur and "man of the world" that family legend suggests.

Nor was Agnes the subservient wife waiting at home that this article implies. In 1926, for example, she had been involved in a motor accident at 3am on the way back from a party. The Woods had yet to move to Tunbridge Wells, dividing their time between London and Brighton, and it might even be supposed that this played some part in precipitating the move. The accident was extensively covered by the London and national papers with the *Daily Mirror* reporting 'Knight's Wife Injured in Motor-Car Crash in London'.[1154] The *Evening Standard* explained that on the way back from a party, or in some reports a dinner party, in St John's Wood, a car driven by a Thomas Comins swerved to avoid a taxicab in Edgware Road, hit a street refuge, overturned and threw out the three passengers.[1155] Thomas Comins and Marjorie Henry, the Woods' adopted daughter, had only superficial cuts but Agnes had

---

[1153] *Daily Sketch* 10th December 1936, KW21 105/6 (b)
Two years later another profile of Agnes was so similar that it may just have been copied verbatim (*Sunday Referee* 22nd May 1938, KW23 284/1).
[1154] *Daily Mirror* 10th November 1926, KW16 245/3
[1155] *Evening Standard* 9th November 1926, KW16 242/1

to be treated at St Mary's Hospital for severe cuts and bruises before returning home to Palace Mansions. Agnes' companion in the back seat was alleged to be Mrs Comins who, despite also being thrown out of the car, was uninjured. The *Evening News* added that "Soon after the occupants had been released there was an explosion. It was caused by a light getting too near the escaping gas". It quoted Thomas Comins as "very glad indeed when I saw that none of the women was killed or seriously injured" and Marjorie Henry's recollection that

> ... we had no time to shriek, and the next thing I knew we three women were struggling in the hood of the car. We were not there many minutes before we were pulled out somehow by someone.[1156]

It may be apparent, however, that the three stories are not completely consistent, the discrepancies rather more than just differences of emphasis.

Agnes was still convalescing the following January and would be unable to ride before Easter,[1157] though she did manage to open the Christmas bazaar in Woolwich Town Hall, her first public engagement since the accident.[1158]

The Woods were listed among those attending the London premiere in 1937 of 'Wings of the Morning' starring Annabella and Henry Fonda "the first film to be made in England in Technicolor".[1159] Towards the end of that year they attended the premiere of 'Lo Squadrone Bianco', a 1936 Italian film about the Libyan Camel Corps that had won the Coppa Mussolini at the Venice film festival.[1160] It is worth noting that the British premiere took place more than a year later, but significantly was also two years after Mussolini's invasion of Abyssinia and the subsequent Hoare-Laval pact; further evidence that the British government were still trying to forge an alliance with Italy and keep Mussolini out of Hitler's grasp, a strategy that they would continue to pursue for some time yet.

[1156] *Evening News* 9th November 1926, KW16 242/7
Marjorie later married FH Brothers, their engagement announced in April 1930 (*Times* 10th April 1930, KW17 185/5).
[1157] *Daily Mirror* 4th January 1927, KW16 256/6
[1158] NA December 1926, KW16 256/3
[1159] *Today's Cinema* undated, KW22 44/3
[1160] *Tatler* 1st December 1937, KW23 104/9

The picture of Agnes below was taken by the society photographer Bassano in 1925, and is one of eight in the National Portrait Gallery collection.[1161] She claimed to be 44 or 45 then, just a few months older than Kingsley, for she had been knocking four years off her age since their marriage and had to stick to it. This is

Agnes, Lady Wood by Bassano Ltd
whole-plate glass negative, 26 June 1925
© National Portrait Gallery, London

a confident and assertive, if not provocative, pose and perhaps Agnes is simply keen to demonstrate her continuing charms at 48

[1161] The NPG also has many Bassano portraits of Wood but none of them are from this date.

and that she is an emancipated woman of the 1920s. Certainly, it is not the picture of a shrinking violet for whom sex was anathema. Like her husband, Agnes extolled the virtues of women's advance,[1162] but only a few years earlier she had been aware that women had little independence, their future dependent on marriage. In a 1922 article 'To Every Bride Elect', Agnes wrote, ostensibly on the subject of cooking, that "Every girl who contemplates matrimony should acquire a working knowledge of 'how things are done downstairs'."[1163] The latter rather reinforces the point noted by Jarvis in his celebrated article 'Mrs Maggs and Betty', to the effect that all in the Conservative Party were agreed in the 1920s that "Conservatism could offer women many things, but nothing so vulgar as feminism".[1164] Agnes' pose for the photographer, however, suggests that emancipation and individuation were available to women as well as men in the 1920s even if they did not associate (or confuse it) at the time with the feminism that would come much later.

When Agnes and Kingsley celebrated their silver wedding anniversary in November 1930 they received congratulations from as far afield as Newcastle,[1165] but most significant perhaps was the report in the *Evening Standard*. To Wood's assertion that

> The secret of my own happiness is that my wife has put up with a great deal from me and has discovered how to get on with me. To a large extent life is a gamble - so is matrimony, and my best luck has been my wife.[1166]

it added his joke that "Marriages are always happy, but it is the living together that causes all the trouble". As with all personal jokes there may have been more than a grain of truth in this.

[1162] *Sunday Herald* 2nd January 1927, KW16 259/1

[1163] *Weekly Despatch* 22nd October 1922, KW14 16/1

[1164] David Jarvis, "Mrs Maggs and Betty: The Conservative appeal to women voters in the 1920s", *Twentieth Century British History*, 1994, 5, pp129-152 (p137)
I am grateful to Martin Daunton for bringing this article to my attention.

[1165] *North Mail and Newcastle Chronicle* 15th November 1930, KW17 229/13
Also, *Morning Post* 4th November 1930, KW17 226/19; *Kentish Independent* 14th November 1930, KW17 229/4; *Kentish Mercury* 21st November 1930, KW17 230/10

[1166] *Evening Standard* 14th November 1930, KW17 229/2

On 27th May 1936 the Queen Mary sailed on its maiden voyage from Southampton to New York via Cherbourg.[1167] Agnes was among the passengers, accompanied by Marjorie, as were many Cabinet Ministers but Wood was too busy to go. The Queen Mary had been completed after two years rotting in a Clyde dockyard at the height of the depression,[1168] and it may be this Hannnington was thinking of when he contrasted £33.8m subsidies to the "Capitalist class" in two years, including £4.5m to the Cunard Line for the Queen Mary, compared to the niggardly £2m Neville Chamberlain allowed Commissioners for the Special Areas.[1169]

Marguerite Eveleigh-de-Moleyns

When Wood moved to 23 Buckingham Palace Mansions in 1935,[1170] Lady Conan Doyle was living at number 15, as she and her husband Sir Arthur Conan Doyle had before his death in 1930. In later years number 15 would be occupied by Sir Stanley Woodwark (1879-1945) and his wife,[1171] a member of the Athenaeum Club like Wood and the doctor who signed Wood's death certificate. The Woodwarks were the only residents of the mansion block to attend Wood's memorial service.

Number 23 was a ground floor flat with a rateable value of £93, reduced two years later to £75 when the flat was recorded In the rate book as being an entrance one.[1172] In 1941 Wood moved to a larger second floor flat number 12 with a rateable value of £147,[1173] perhaps because a five-year lease on number 23 had expired in 1940 and rather than renew it he decided that, by then Chancellor of the Exchequer, a larger flat above the ground floor would be more appropriate. This would be entirely unremarkable except that the person who succeeded him at number 23 was a

---

[1167] CWR Winter, 'Queen Mary: Her Early Years Recalled', 1986, pp 69-79
[1168] Gault, 2014, op cit, p197
[1169] Hannington, op cit, p21
[1170] Buckingham Palace Mansions had been built in 1883 and in 1974 was replaced by an office block Belgrave House.
[1171] Post Office directories 1928-1945
[1172] Rate books 1935-1943, Westminster Archives; accessed 19th August 2015
[1173] The rateable values of all the flats were reduced when the block was affected by blast damage from a bomb in the Second World War. Anne Saunders (ed.), 'London County Council Bomb Damage Maps 1939-1945', 2005, map 75

widow Marguerite Eveleigh-de-Moleyns (1879-1982), and a symbol in the rate book links the two of them. This symbol is not used elsewhere in the rate books, so is unlikely to mean that Wood was sub-letting the flat to her, nor does it indicate a move mid-way through the year since this is recorded separately. It is a deliberate entry between the left-hand margin and the name of the occupants.

A twenty-year old Marguerite Noon had married the Honourable John Gilbert Eveleigh-de Moleyns (1878-1928), the fifth son of the 4th Baron Ventry, in 1899 and by 1912 they had two sons and a daughter. Their oldest child was also called John but in 1945 changed his surname by deed poll to Wauchope of Niddrie Marischal. Wauchope was the family name of his paternal grandmother and Niddrie Marischal the Wauchope home on the south-east outskirts of Edinburgh since 1390. The family became major coal owners, with fifteen pits on the land by 1895, but in 1944 the house and land was purchased by Edinburgh corporation to extend a housing estate. Changing his name would have been one way of preserving the links.

After her husband's death Marguerite lived at 66 Cornwall Gardens, a five-storey Georgian house in Kensington. Arthur Salter (1881-1975) had a flat in the house in the early 1930s between his return from the League of Nations and his appointment as a philosophy professor at Oxford University.[1174] He still had a flat there in 1939, but Marguerite had moved to 58 Cheyne Court in Chelsea[1175] before Buckingham Palace Mansions in 1941. She was still at number 23 when her second son Frederick and his wife came from the United States to visit her there in 1950.

Although there are many other Eveleigh-de-Moleyns, Ventry and Wauchope citations between the late nineteenth and mid-twentieth centuries, there is no other mention of Marguerite. Although she did not attend Wood's memorial service, this is hardly evidence either way of a link between them. However, the 7th Lord Ventry (1898-1987) did, not because of any family connection but as a member of the Balloon Command that covered Woolwich in the Second World War.

[1174] Post Office Directories for 1933 and 1934; Salter, op cit, p233
[1175] Post Office Directories for 1939 to 1941

Dorothy and Edward Weaver

Wood's surviving sibling, his sister Dorothy, was born three years after him in 1884 and lived until 1966, dying in Weymouth at the age of 82. Wood had married in 1905 but Dorothy was still living with their parents in 1911 and did not marry until several years later. Her husband Edward was thirteen years older than her and they had no children. He attended Wood's memorial service in September 1943 but she did not, and neither of them attended the funeral service at Wesley's Chapel earlier that day. It might have been difficult for her to attend during the war, or she may been too upset to do so, but it is possible that she and her brother had fallen out. Wood's Will, dated 1941, left everything to his wife Agnes, and only in the event of her pre-deceasing him was Dorothy to receive anything. In this case she and Agnes' sister, Wood's sister-in-law, were to share equally in the estate (£64,000 in 1943 or about £2m today).

Mary Thurston

Agnes' sister Mary was ten years younger than her, having been born in 1888 In Australia. She married HP Thurston who captained three ships for the Shaw-Savill Line. His first ship the 8,000 ton steamer the Matakana was built in 1921 and he was captain as early as 1928 when the ship called at Pitcairn Island on its way from Liverpool to Auckland.[1176] In May 1940 it was wrecked in the Bahamas, with only part of the cargo salvaged before the ship broke up.[1177] His second, another 8,000 ton steamer the Maimoa had been built a year earlier in 1920[1178] and in November 1940 this ship was captured by the Germans and sunk. His third ship, the Ionic II had been built in 1902 and was larger at over 12,000 tons. It had been used as a New Zealand troopship during the First World War and was bought by Shaw-Savill in 1934 on the merger of White Star with Cunard. This ship was broken up in Japan in 1937 and may have marked the end of Thurston's career.[1179] As early as 1888 the *Launceston Examiner* reported a Captain Thurston whose

---

[1176] Herbert Ford, 'Pitcairn Island as a Port of Call', 2012, p129
[1177] Duncan Haws, 'Merchant Fleets 10: Shaw, Savill and Albion', 1987, p58
[1178] Ibid, p57
[1179] Ibid, p52

schooner had been beached.[1180] This was probably his father or another relative, so bad luck with ships was not confined to HP himself.

In 1939 Mary left Australia on her own, perhaps because her husband had died, and spent the Second World War with Agnes at Broomhill Bank. This made it more likely both that Wood was at Buckingham Palace Mansions on his own during these years and that Mary Thurston was on hand when Wood died in 1943. She is thought to have spirited away many objects from the house, perhaps when she accompanied Agnes to Australia once the war was over for a six month holiday. They were to stay with their cousin Mrs M Prideaux at her house in Katoomba.[1181]

According to the *Times* (5th January 1956), Agnes left £42,257 net or rather less than £1m today. In other words, half the estate Wood left had disappeared or been spent by the time Agnes died twelve years later. It would be Mary Thurston to whom Agnes left the bulk of her estate rather than her daughter Marjorie. It may be that Agnes judged her sister more in need of the money than her married daughter, but her grandson believes that Mary had exerted a pernicious influence on Agnes.

[1180] *Launceston Examiner* 11th June 1888
[1181] *Melbourne Argus* 18th November 1946

16.   MINISTER OF HEALTH 1935-1938

In his novel 'Scoop' Evelyn Waugh had the reporter Wenlock Jakes type "The dominant member of the new Cabinet was colourful Kingsley Wood …".[1182] As Waugh's book was published in 1938, this probably refers to Baldwin's 1935 Cabinet rather than the one Neville Chamberlain took over in 1937. In both cases though Wood was Minister of Health, a post to which Ramsay MacDonald had been expected to appoint him in 1934 so that slum clearance was "in the shop window"[1183] and indeed a change of this sort had been planned as early as March 1933.[1184] In the event, however, Wood only attained this post once Baldwin became Prime Minister in June 1935.

As the *New Statesman and Nation* put it, Wood "stands out from the new appointments. We shall at least have a live Minister in charge of health and housing",[1185] a reference to the outrageously blinkered and over-optimistic, not to say self-satisfied, approach that the previous Minister Sir Edward Hilton Young and his Chief Medical Officer Sir George Newman had shown.[1186] Hilton Young became Baron Kennet on MacDonald's resignation (taking no further part in politics, according to his DNB entry) and by November Newman had retired, to be replaced by Arthur MacNalty (1880-1969). The positive opinion of Wood in the *New Statesman* was shared elsewhere in the press:

> Discontent with the Government's conduct of the housing programme may bring a more energetic Minister - perhaps Sir Kingsley Wood, who has done excellently well at the Post Office - to the Ministry of Health …[1187]

[1182] Evelyn Waugh, 'Scoop', 1938, p87
[1183] *People* 30th September 1934, KW19 192/6
[1184] Wood would have replaced Hilton Young, with Housing "a new semi-autonomous Department … not in the Cabinet". Only six people knew of MacDonald's plan before it was leaked to the *Daily Mail*.
[1185] *New Statesman and Nation* 15th June 1935, KW19 410/5
[1186] For example, Ina Zweiniger-Bargielowska, op cit, p287 and Richard Titmuss, 'Poverty and Population: A Factual Study of Contemporary Social Waste', 1938, p155. According to Charles Webster, "Healthy or hungry Thirties?", *History Workshop Journal*, 1982, 13, pp110-129 the Ministry of Health was more realistic after MacNalty succeeded Newman (p122).
[1187] *Economist* 1st June 1935, KW19 391/12

[Wood is] One of the most popular of the new Ministers ... Making his name in the first place as a parliamentary sniper from a corner seat, he became an Under-Secretary and later the PMG. In that position he made a striking success of what is usually regarded as a very secondary office. He has now become Minister of Health ...[1188]

While the Campion article referred to in the previous chapter gives a flavour of Wood's daily routine:

It may not be generally realised that the Ministry deals with more than health - the whole range of local government comes within its purview. ...

Sir Kingsley arrives at the Ministry every morning with an attaché case full of Government papers. He begins work after breakfast, and between then and reaching Whitehall, he loses not a moment. ...

A vast amount of correspondence naturally awaits the Minister and this must receive early attention ...

[His] morning passes on with an almost endless succession of conferences, consultations ... meeting deputations, studying Cabinet documents, attending Cabinet meetings and meetings of several Cabinet sub-committees. Urgent messages are constantly being received ...

During the Parliamentary session [he] must frequently appear on the Government Front Bench to answer questions. ... The 'supplementaries' call for extensive knowledge and resourcefulness ...

[Then there are] more deputations, consultations, the scrutiny of Department documents [back at the Ministry, then opposite Parliament]

If [he] finds that it is not possible for him to go back to his office after questions, he continues his work in a room at the House, breaking off only to vote ... when the division bell rings.[1189]

In addition to steering legislation through Parliament, Wood "insists on seeing for himself the progress that is being made", for example with housing schemes and slum clearance, and "[He] regards the

---

[1188] *Walthamstow Guardian* 2nd August 1935, KW19 458/7
[1189] Probably *Daily Sketch* undated, KW20 55/9

whole country as his parish and deems it part of his task to visit his parishioners. Few Ministers tour the country on business so frequently as he does". Early examples included his visits to Kent in September 1935, covering both local government and social services in the county,[1190] and to hop-pickers following the concerns that had been raised in the Commons in August about their living conditions.[1191] Wood was to praise the improvements the growers had made[1192] and the following year it was reported that the Minister

> ... seems to enjoy September holidays with the hop-pickers. Last year he spent some days in Kent during the hopping season.
> Next week he is going to Worcester ... Part of his object is to study the conditions under which hop-pickers live and to see what improvements could be made. He was impressed last year with the arrangements made in Kent for the comfort of the London workers who go down for the picking season.[1193]

Yet George Orwell gives a compelling description of the harsh living conditions and circumstances that then faced Kent hop-pickers, whether tramps and the unemployed for whom this might be the only paid work in the year; families, often from the East End, for whom this was their annual holiday; and gypsies, who picked hops every September between harvesting earlier in the summer and then lifting potatoes in Lincolnshire in the autumn.[1194]

[1190] *Kent Messenger* 14th & 21st September 1935, KW19 479/3, 485/1, 486/1
The Centre for Kentish Studies in Maidstone (now the Kent History and Library Centre archives) holds the programme and correspondence about the visit: "At the Minister's request, arrangements were made for him to make a tour of certain establishments of interest to him such as housing estates for miners and mental hospitals, on 17-19 September 1935."
[1191] Hansard, 1st August 1935, vol. 304, cols. 2838-2389
[1192] *Times* 5th September 1935, KW19 462/5
[1193] *Daily Telegraph* 3rd September 1936, KW21 22/2
[1194] George Orwell, 'A Clergyman's Daughter', 1935, pp108-128
All three groups mixed together, their common enemies the hop farmers who would try to reduce their piece rate, the foremen and measurers who oversaw their work, and the police who might prevent raids on neighbouring fruit orchards.

In 1937 Wood issued

> revised model by-laws for receiving decent lodging and accommodation for hop-pickers. ... [which] have been agreed so far as practicable with representatives of local authorities and hop-growers.[1195]

Campion's article also set out Wood's stance on the Ministry:

> [He] insists that it is the duty of public departments to establish and maintain cordial relations with the public. The basis of good relations, he contends, is not a mere willingness to furnish information, but an eagerness to let the public know what the department is doing and why; and he also sees that the main channel of information between the department and the public must be the Press. He therefore insists that the Ministry ... should be freely accessible to the Press and to anyone else who is genuinely seeking information.
> I don't think I am very wide of the mark when I say that one of [his] tests of whether a job is worth doing is whether it is worth letting the public know you have done it when it has been done - not a bad test for a department, the purpose of whose very existence is to serve the public in such vital matters as health, housing and so on...

The difference between Wood and some other politicians, however, was that as well as expressing such sentiments he followed them through. His use of advertising at the Post Office had revolutionised people's understanding of what was available and how to access it. The advisory council he had established had helped promote services and ensured that public concerns were addressed. He adopted the latter approach at Health, setting up a twenty-five member Central Housing Advisory Committee which he chaired. The members were drawn from local government, different political parties and various interest groups.[1196]   On 11th December 1935

[1195] *Observer* 16th May 1937, KW22 34/2 The by-laws also applied to fruit and veg. pickers.

[1196] *Daily Mail* & *Times* 19th November 1935, KW20 35/1 & 35/3; *Derby Evening Telegraph* 25th October 1935, KW20 14/13

Balcarres (representing the Council for the Protection of Rural England) recorded his assessment of Wood at the inaugural meeting:

> I was interested in the way he handled us. I have always looked upon this rubicund little solicitor as the most astute man in the party, as the cleverest propagandist and the master mind of political publicity. He sat at the end of the table, addressed us in mellifluous tones, purred compliments at the Socialists, told us what he wanted and got his way without apparent effort, surprise or pleasure - it all came so naturally, so inevitably to his conclusion. A very shrewd little person this rosy persuasive knight bachelor and they say that when he wishes to be acid he can be quite tart.[1197]

Two years later Balcarres' view continued to be positive:

> I admire the skill and geniality with which [Wood] conducts these meetings [housing conferences at the Ministry of Health] which are largely packed with his opponents who watch every movement in hope of tripping him up - but he knows a great deal more than the socialist critics.[1198]

an opinion echoed by Churchill in a 1938 parliamentary debate

> As to the Minister of Health ...he is absolutely necessary where he is. The fact is that we never begin to realise how good these Ministers are in their jobs until we begin to think of them for some other job.[1199]

When Wood had been Chamberlain's number two at the Ministry of Health between 1925 and 1929, housing and slum clearance, local government, Poor Law reform, pensions, health insurance and the re-organisation of medical services were among the most significant matters they tackled. Not surprisingly, given the huge sweep of the Ministry's responsibilities, these continued to exercise Wood as Minister as well. However, with the exception of housing and slum clearance, issues that consumed even more time

---

[1197] Vincent (ed.), op cit, p566
[1198] 28th October 1937 in Vincent, op cit, p584
[1199] Martin Gilbert and Richard Gott, 'The Appeasers', 1963, pp72-73

in the 1930s than they had in the 1920s, they are not addressed in any detail in this chapter in order to avoid repetition; though it is worth noting what the Liberal MP Geoffrey Shakespeare (1893-1980) wrote in his memoirs about the extension of voluntary insurance during these years.

> When, later, I became [PS] at the Ministry of Health, nothing gave me greater pleasure than to help my chief, Sir Kingsley Wood ... put into operation the scheme for the extension of voluntary insurance, so that professional men of humble means ... could, as voluntary contributors, receive a small pension at the end of their life's work.[1200]

Instead the focus in this chapter is on some of the other major challenges then facing the Minister and his department, such as maternal and child welfare (particularly maternal mortality), nutrition and physique, all of which relate in one form or another to the wider aim of improving public health. In 1927 Wood had singled out the infant death rate as "one of the best tests of health progress",[1201] already a truism but no less significant for that. It remains a litmus test of a country's development and indeed its civilisation.

In Wood's view the health of the people should be the first concern of the statesman - as it had been for Disraeli, he told the Conservative Party's in-house magazine shortly after he had been appointed Minister of Health.[1202] Underlining his broad view of public health Wood pointed out that:
- while there were many measures of ill-health there were almost none of positive health, by which he meant an individual physical abundance of life; though he intended to tackle this, he failed to do so.[1203]
- the focus in the twentieth century on individual hygiene complemented the progress that had been made in the previous century on environmental factors, such as sanitation and clean water; continuing vigilance on both fronts was required
- the National Health Insurance Act 1911 had confirmed GPs as the first line of defence enabling the poor to access medical advice

---

[1200] Geoffrey Shakespeare, 'Let Candles Be Brought In', 1949, p347
[1201] Titmuss, 1938, op cit, p82
[1202] *NA* 11th October 1935, KW20 1/4 refers to this article 'Health of the people' in *Politics in Review*
[1203] Conservative government intentions to measure happiness in Britain in the twenty-first century have also fallen away.

without resort to the Poor Law; 16.5m people were now insured, but recent unemployment had threatened to undermine this success; the introduction of the 1935 Act meant that, so long as people had ten years insurance, their rights were preserved regardless of unemployment[1204]
- in 1934/35 £2.3m had been allocated for public open spaces and playing fields; access to both was fundamental to people's health and well-being.[1205]

Among Wood's other early articles as Minister ahead of the 1936 Public Health Act were 'My Work and Your Health', 'We Have Added Ten Years To Your Life', 'Building Up An A1 People' and 'Help Me to Help You',[1206] all of which, but particularly the latter, stressed that health was a State matter not just a personal one. Individuals necessarily bore the ultimate responsibility (and most had little choice then anyway) but, by setting the overall conditions for society as a whole, the State could assist everybody not just those dependent on interventions. Twelve months on, Labour's Arthur Greenwood and Wood would reiterate these themes in the Commons debate on the King's address that autumn, thereby reinforcing the priorities for Wood's tenure. These had been summarised as

> ... the need for more comprehensive efforts to improve the physical condition of the nation, especially among the younger members of the community, ... [and] the development of the existing public health services. Vigorous action for the provision of housing accommodation to replace slum dwellings and abate overcrowding will be maintained.[1207]

[1204] There was in effect two years free insurance after unemployment, though Wood had resisted at Committee stage the restoration of lost maternity benefit. *Manchester Guardian* 9th July 1935 KW19 427/1

[1205] CPA CRD 220/80 '*Politics in Review*', 1935, vol. 2, opening article to quarter 3 pp3-7

[1206] *Sunday Express* 21st July 1935, KW19 443/1; *Tit-Bits* 28th September 1935, KW19 477/1; *Home and Empire* September 1935, KW19 474/1; *The Passing Show* 5th October 1935, KW19 496/1

[1207] Hansard, 3rd November 1936, vol. 317, cols. 12-13

According to Smart, improving the health of the nation, including the promotion of physical fitness, would be one of the few achievements of the National Government.[1208]

In between the King's Speech and the debate, Ellen Wilkinson had presented Jarrow's petition in parliament:

> During the last 15 years Jarrow has passed through a period of industrial depression without parallel in the town's history. Its shipyard is closed. Its steelworks have been denied the right to re-open. Where formerly 8,000 people, many of them skilled workers, were employed, only 100 men are now employed on a temporary scheme. The town cannot be left derelict and therefore your Petitioners humbly pray that His Majesty's Government and this honourable House should realise the urgent need that work should be provided for the town without further delay.[1209]

The petition had been brought to London by the Jarrow marchers who, unlike the other national hunger marchers of this time, were bound together by geography rather than by any political or class motivation,[1210] making their appeal much more difficult for the Government to ignore. The Jarrow petition was immediately followed in the Commons by a separate one on the town's behalf signed by 68,000 people on Tyneside. The same week a national hunger march organised by Wal Hannington and the NUWM reached London on 8th November with a rally in Hyde Park.[1211] This was timed to encourage the Government to withdraw the Unemployment Assistance Board regulations that were due to come into force a week later, but their petition was ignored. Three days later Clement Attlee called an adjournment debate to draw attention to the Prime Minister's refusal "to grant any facilities for the unemployed hunger marchers to voice their grievances to him, to the Cabinet, or to the House".[1212] Accepting that it was not "possible or allowable ... to raise the whole question of the means test or the whole question of the depressed areas", Attlee did ask, but to no avail, that "the people who come from the depressed

---

[1208] Nick Smart, 'The National Government 1931-1940', 1999, p4

[1209] Hansard, 4th November 1936, vol. 317, cols. 75-77

[1210] Peter Kingsford, 'The Hunger Marchers in Britain 1920-1939', 1982, pp200-222

[1211] Ibid, p208

[1212] Hansard, 11th November 1936, vol. 317, cols. 957-1011

areas should themselves be able to state their case to the Prime Minister, to the Cabinet, or to the House".

This was the context in which Greenwood introduced Labour's amendment to the King's address regretting the Government's failure to appreciate

> ... that under the existing capitalist system the present improvement in trade and industry, largely stimulated by the world race in armaments,[1213] can only be temporary; that, whilst making tardy acknowledgment of the deterioration in the physical fitness of the nation, due mainly to long-continued unemployment, low wages, and consequent malnutrition, they are continuing to enforce a means test which intensifies this deterioration and to neglect the problems of those areas which have been most severely affected; and that they have no proposals for making the fundamental changes in the basis of society ... in which the full resources of the nation shall be utilised for the benefit of the community as a whole.[1214]

As well as drawing attention to the lack of recovery in distressed areas (though a revival of shipbuilding as well as rearmament was underway in a few, such as Clydeside and Tyneside), Greenwood highlighted the malnutrition identified by inquiries by the BMA and Sir John Boyd Orr, the cost of an adequate diet unaffordable by millions of people. He continued:

> What contribution are the Government making to the solution of this problem? Not more food for school children, not more milk for school children, not an attack on the problems of maternal mortality. No, it is physical exercise. ... But open spaces, exercises, gymnasia ... come a very long way after good food, good clothing and good housing. There will be no permanent improvement in the national physique as the result of exercising distorted and stunted bodies. The whole energy of the Government ought to be

---

[1213] By making this accusation in 1936 Greenwood was rather giving the lie to those who accuse Baldwin of a failure to re-arm. "Re-armament began in 1934", according to Basil Collier, 'The Defence of the United Kingdom', 1957, p49. Contemporary historians confirm this.

[1214] Hansard, 6th November 1936, vol. 317, col. 397

directed to the fundamental problem. Until the income of the people is raised to that level which will enable them to spend money to get that efficiency which right hon. Gentlemen suggest and desire, mere physical training will not have any serious influence on the situation.[1215]

Whether this was just rhetoric and party political posturing, or Greenwood hoped to spur Wood to redouble his efforts, is unclear. Three months earlier the *People* had reported that Wood was preparing a scheme to supply cheap milk to mothers and young children as "... part of his plan for reducing the maternal and infantile death rate. It will really be an extension of the cheap milk scheme which is working so well in schools."[1216] To the extent that the report was accurate, and much of it proved to be, Greenwood either did not know about it or was determined to make his points anyway.[1217]

In Greenwood's estimation the position could not change "as long as [the overpowering] motive in production is that of private profit", for the resulting inequality,

> ... heavy aggregations of wealth in a few hands at one end of the scale and ... malnutrition and semi-starvation at the other, ... is not good economically for the country, and it certainly is bad morally for every section of society, whether they enjoy the wealth or whether they suffer the poverty.

Public ownership and a living wage were vital, by which Greenwood meant specifically that "It ought to be a crime for any employer to employ an adult at wages less than are necessary to enable him to carry out his duty as a citizen". He concluded that the current system should be changed by making public service the motive rather than private profit.[1218]

In replying Wood referred to the many occasions he had followed Greenwood in the Commons, and "as he knows, I have

---

[1215] Ibid, cols. 401-402

[1216] *People* 2nd August 1936, KW21 23/7

[1217] A scheme for extending cheap milk to children under school age and expectant mothers had been considered as early as February 1935 (CPA CRD 1/33/4). *News World* reported in mid-August 1936 that Wood was considering expanding the scheme despite take-up by only half those eligible. (16th August 1936, KW21 29/1)

[1218] Hansard, 6th November 1936, vol. 317, col. 405-406

always closely watched his efforts with a great measure of personal sympathy and even with commiseration". Wood thought the Labour party was not only going through an "intellectual crisis on foreign policy and armaments", as Herbert Morrison had stated, but on "industrial, social and health conditions" too.[1219] Wood was more acerbic than Greenwood for he had earlier dismissed him as a slipper limpet clinging on to office, while Greenwood could only refer to Wood as "a benign mosquito" and, as he admitted, that was "after years of thought".[1220] Whereas previous disputes had reflected personal as well as party animosity, they had clearly moved on to more friendly territory by this point. In July 1936 they had visited Manchester slum clearance areas together, Wood opening "Arthur Greenwood House" at Kirkhamshulme Lane, while Greenwood laid the foundation block for "Kingsley Wood House" at Collyhurst.[1221] So striking was this rapprochement that it was widely reported, with the *News Chronicle* characterising it as "A delightful vindication of the British system of democratic government".[1222] For the *Manchester Guardian*

> Manchester's re-housing programme was carried two stages farther yesterday by the visit of Sir Kingsley Wood, the Minister of Health, and Arthur Greenwood, a former Minister. They had declared a 'political amnesty' for the day and showed their good fellowship by naming blocks of flats after each other. The truce was nearly broken at lunch, however, when the two indulged in partisan witticisms at each other's expense.[1223]

Wood then concentrated in the Commons debate on the health and physical condition of the nation, asserting, as he often did,[1224] that "We are not a C3 nation. The reverse is true, and ... our

---

[1219] Ibid, cols. 406-407

[1220] *Star* 17th July 1936, KW21 8/12
Geoffrey Shakespeare used the 'mosquito' analogy thirteen years later after Wood's death.

[1221] *Times* 25th July 1936, KW21 4/10

[1222] *News Chronicle* 22nd July 1936, KW21 7/10 Also, KW21 13/7, 13/11, 14/7, 14/8, 17/4, 18/4, 18/10

[1223] *Manchester Guardian* 25th July 1936, KW21 20/2

[1224] In an article 'Comradeship in search of physical efficiency' for the *Daily Telegraph* Fitter Britain supplement 7th December 1936, Wood wrote "We are not a C3 nation. Nor have we cause to be ashamed of our public

national health is improving, not merely steadily, but remarkably". In support of this he cited the Registrar-General's figures showing that life expectancy at birth had increased by seven years in the last twenty, while infant mortality was the lowest on record in 1935 at 57 per 1000 live births.[1225] As recently as 1929 it had been 74/1000, and after a slight increase in 1936 and 1937, it reduced further to a new low of 53 per 1000 in 1938 and 1939.[1226] On 25th January 1939 the Conservatives singled out the 1938 figure in the party's Points for Propaganda,[1227] with the *Daily Herald* describing it as a milestone in the country's development. The 1935 figure enabled Wood to claim that the Government's concentration on physical education was not because the condition of the country was so poor (as Labour's amendment alleged), but because they wanted "to achieve still greater results". A positive focus on promoting good health, as he put it, part of which depended on exercise, would augment their existing record on preventing and curing disease.

Maternal Mortality

Nearly fifty years later a front-bench Labour party politician would write in his memoirs that "'To govern is to choose' ... a fundamental political truth long before Nye Bevan said that 'the language of priorities is the religion of socialism'".[1228] This stricture applied as much to Wood as to anyone else and, while it might have been feasible for him to continue the relaxed, not to say lackadaisical,

---

health services: they are second to none." CPA CRD 1/60/6 Physical Training Oct 1936 to Aug 1938, item 36

[1225] Hansard, 6th November 1936, vol. 317, cols. 407 & 408
Despite the poor quality of housing in West Ham, for example, the infant mortality rate there had decreased from 149/1000 in 1886 (five years after Wood's birth) to below the national average at 45.3 per 1000 in 1935. E Doreen Idle, 'War Over West Ham: A Study of Community Adjustment', 1943, p42

[1226] Arthur MacNalty (ed.), 'The Civilian Health and Medical Services, vol. I', 1953, pp3 & 4

[1227] No. 110 CPA, CRD 1/78/2
However, the conclusions to be drawn from statistics depend on the particular ones selected. For example, Webster argued that the 1930s was a drag on the downward incidence of infant mortality by focussing on the following figures: 1921 - 83/1000; 1931 - 66/1000; 1941 - 60/1000; 1946 - 43/1000, and thereby being able to claim that decline was most rapid (28%) between 1918-1923 and 1941-1946 (op cit, p123).

[1228] Denis Healey, 'The Time of My Life', 1990 (orig. 1989), p271

regime of Hilton Young and Newman, the expectations of the public, the press and his colleagues were that he would not. Furthermore, it was not in his nature to mark time and having been one of those instrumental in bringing the Ministry of Health into being after the First World War he was particularly unlikely to adopt such a stance in this post. No doubt Wood was soon assisted by Newman's retirement and his replacement by MacNalty for it was at the annual dinner of the Society of Medical Officers of Health, at which Newman was the guest of honour, that Wood noted that "... there was still a great deal to do. The problem of maternal mortality had shown no decline since the beginning of the century ..."[1229] This was a scourge of which the Ministry had long been aware[1230] and Wood was determined to tackle. Indeed in the 'Health of the people' article with which he had first announced himself as Minister of Health, Wood had pointed out that in 1934, the year before, one in every 200 mothers had died in childbirth, or more than 3000 women a year. Not only was this rate of 4.41 maternal deaths per 1000 live births worse than in 1931 or 1932,[1231] the Ministry of Health's 1933/34 report put the figure in each of the two previous decades at 4.07/1000. One had to go back to the nineteenth century to find a higher rate.[1232] A Departmental Committee had been set up as long ago as 1928, when Neville Chamberlain was Minister of Health, but it had then taken four years to report, Its results inconclusive, and yet the figures were so alarming that even Hilton Young had been galvanised into establishing another investigation in October 1934. It would not report until April 1937 and Wood was not prepared to wait that long.

There were several reasons why giving birth was such a hazardous procedure for mothers. According to Blakeway,

> Many were unable to pay [for a doctor] because their right to some limited maternity benefit had lapsed when their

[1229] *Municipal Journal* 29th November 1935, KW20 55/2
[1230] Jane Lewis, 'The Politics of Motherhood: Child and Maternal Welfare in England, 1900-1939', 1980, pp26-29 regarding Ministry surveys from 1924 of maternity in problem areas.
[1231] As n24 above, i.e., CPA CRD 220/80 'Politics in Review', vol. 2, opening article to quarter 3 pp3-7
[1232] Fifteenth Annual Report of the Ministry of Health 1933-34, 1934, Cmd 4664, p44

husbands lost their jobs and ceased to pay NI [National Insurance] contributions.[1233]

But even if they could afford one, the maternity services were "disparate, ill-organised and often [offered a] poor standard of maternal care in the first thirty years" of the twentieth century.[1234] There was a lack of trained midwives and deliveries at home would be undertaken by GPs, for whom this was not necessarily a regular event and sometimes beyond their competence. The use of forceps to hurry the process along was routine, with more weight being given to GP convenience than either the baby or the mother.

In July 1935 in an article for the *Daily Herald* Wood explained that, as 'Motherhood is the Nation's Business', immediate steps were required to reduce the high rate of maternal mortality.[1235] It was bound up with issues such as overcrowding and slums, both of which should be substantially reduced even if they could not be removed entirely, and the MacNalty investigation (the one Hilton Young had established) would examine these issues as well as compare parts of the country where the death rate was well above the average with those where it was well below. Unfortunately, however, it would not address other indicators of poverty such as diet and nutrition. In advance of the report, though, it was appreciated that a good maternity service was vital throughout the country, as Wood proposed in Sheffield that October.[1236] Later that month it was reported that Wood was "enquiring into the question of better pay for midwives",[1237] something he confirmed at the end of the month when he expanded on the social reform programme in the National Government manifesto, making it clear that it would include a salaried midwifery service.[1238] One of the first steps was to be the Midwives Act, enacted in 1936. Its adoption made good

---

[1233] Blakeway, op cit, p162

[1234] Irvine Loudon, "The transformation of maternal mortality", *BMJ*, 1992, 305, pp1557-1560

[1235] *Daily Herald* 11th July 1935, KW19 425/3

[1236] *NA* 5th October 1935, KW20 1/9 in a speech at Sheffield City Hall to mark the local government centenary.

[1237] *John Bull* 26th October 1935, KW20 11/1

[1238] *Daily Telegraph* 29th October 1935, KW20 7/4

sense and was an issue on which Lucy Baldwin (the Prime Minister's wife) had long campaigned.[1239]

In introducing the Bill's second reading in April 1936, Wood explained that the main purpose was

> ... to establish an adequate service of salaried and trained midwives, so as to ensure that every expectant mother, whatever her circumstances, will be able to obtain the services of a qualified midwife; and ... to raise the status of the midwifery profession by providing adequate salaries and sure prospects; and also ... to ensure further facilities for their instruction.[1240]

He continued:

> Few ... matters exceed in importance the necessity of providing a safe and healthy motherhood, especially when we remember the large amount of suffering, incapacity and ill-health, as well as death, which occurs as a result of complications arising from childbirth.[1241]

The Bill amended the Midwives Acts of 1902 to 1926 but went further. The second reading was unopposed for the House as a whole was supportive, though Arthur Greenwood argued that Wood should have gone further still. Nevertheless, Greenwood acknowledged that it was a positive step towards tackling "the most dangerous of occupations" and a problem that had proved intractable for some time. The Committee stage was considered by the House as a whole and the third reading passed, also without a vote, on 7th July.[1242] The Lords agreed it without further amendment.[1243] As Wood told one newspaper:

> Within the next twelve months most of the local authorities who will be in control, under the Ministry of Health, of the

---

[1239] Blakeway, op cit, pp162 & 169 describes her as in her own way "a quiet revolutionary", part of which was her long campaign to improve women's experience of childbirth.

[1240] Hansard, 30th April 1936, vol. 311, col. 1117

[1241] Ibid

Titmuss, 1938, op cit, pp155-156 also quoted this statement from Wood.

[1242] Hansard, 7th July 1936, vol. 314, cols. 1047-1086 & 1120-1153

[1243] Hansard, 27th July 1936, vol. 315, col. 1102

new arrangements will have established a service of salaried midwives.

Thus every expectant mother, rich or poor, will be able to have a qualified person to attend her, and for a fortnight [instead of ten days] afterwards. If she engages a doctor, a qualified midwife will be available for the maternity nursing.[1244]

Wood was also able to report to the Commons the same month that putting the issue in the spotlight had already begun to have an effect, with maternal mortality at last decreasing - if only slightly as yet.[1245] Two days later the *Sunday Times* asserted that Wood had been rightly praised, for he was now repeating his previous success at the Post Office at the Ministry of Health. It added "Sir Kingsley is particularly liked in the House for his imperturbable manner and jovial good humour".[1246]

On 10th December 1936, four months before the MacNalty report appeared, Wood was asked in the Commons about the other steps being taken to reduce maternal mortality. He replied:

I would refer the hon. Member to the annual report for 1935[1247] of the Chief Medical Officer of my Department ... which contains, in the section relating to maternity and child welfare, a summary of the action taken by my Department both by way of investigation into this problem and by way of administrative action for the improvement of maternity services. Further measures it may be desirable to take will be reviewed when I have before me the report, now in course of preparation, of the special investigations recently made into maternal mortality in various parts of the country.[1248]

[1244] *Daily Mail* 31st July 1936, KW21 21/13

[1245] Hansard, 16th July 1936, vol. 314, col. 2281
Daily Express and *Times* both 17th July 1936, KW21 11/1 & 12/1

[1246] *Sunday Times* 19th July 1936, KW21 14/12

[1247] Sixteenth Annual Report of the Ministry of Health 1934-35, 1935, Cmd 4978, pp129-130, 281-282 &291-293
Also referred to in the "Official organ of the National Council for Maternity and Child Welfare", *Mother and Child* October 1935, KW21 loose

[1248] Hansard, 10th December 1936, vol. 318, col. 2156

The measures included self-assessments by local authorities of the effectiveness of services within their areas and, where necessary, special visits by Medical Officers identified for the task by the Ministry of Health. In 1934 such visits had been made to Plymouth, Wakefield, Barnsley, Preston, Blackpool and Wigan, with another to Portsmouth to see what might be learnt from its low rate. In addition, Wood had sent a circular to local authorities encouraging them to open gynaecological clinics where possible.

He was also quizzed in the House about the action being taken to ensure that "a fully qualified midwife is at hand for every expectant mother in the country" as the Midwives Act required. Wood replied

> Each local supervising authority has been sent a circular, explaining the provisions of the Act and containing suggestions and advice as to how the objects of the Act can best be secured.[1249]

The Act required that local authorities submit their proposals to the Ministry by the end of January and implement them by July 1937. They were already consulting on these with voluntary associations in their areas.

In April 1937 the MacNalty investigation was published. It concluded that, after investigating areas of England and Wales where the maternal mortality rate in 1924-1933 was more than 20% above or below that of the country as a whole, there was no association overall with overcrowding and no clear association with unemployment. Nevertheless, as the north and west tended to have higher rates than the south and east, there were likely to be a combination of these and other poverty factors at work. Yet the most critical issue was the health and care of the mother, particularly during her first birth when she was most at risk. As well as recommending ways in which the quality of the existing services could be improved, they proposed new ones were required and underlined the overarching importance of medical teamwork between nurses, midwives, GPs and hospitals.[1250]

This was far from the end of the matter but, to adopt Churchill's quote about another horror that faced the country a few

---

[1249] Ibid
[1250] Ministry of Health, 'Report of an Investigation into Maternal Mortality', 1937, Cmd 5422

years later, it was the end of the beginning. In 1937 the maternal mortality rate had reduced by almost 30% to 3.13/1000 and in 1938 to 2.97/1000, a third down on the 1934 figure, with both rates the lowest then recorded.[1251] The 1938 figure meant 2000 women rather than 3000 died in childbirth, a significant reduction, but equally clearly not a position about which an advanced country could be complacent. Indeed, as Loudon subsequently described it for the *BMJ*,

> From 1935 ... there was a dramatic change. Maternal mortality began its steep and sustained decline until, by the 1980s, it had fallen to less than nine deaths per 100,000 births: roughly one-fiftieth of the rate in 1934.[1252]

In May 1937 Wood was questioned about the "abnormally high rate" in Wales, particularly in rural areas, by Jim Griffiths (1890-1975) the Labour MP for Llanelli,[1253] but was able to assure him that, where further information was required from local areas about their plans under the Midwives Act, it was being requested. Nancy Astor (1879-1964) ascribed the situation in Wales to abortion and the lack of birth control clinics, a point Wood ignored then though he had already told the House that he and the Home Secretary had

> ...appointed a committee to inquire into the prevalence of abortion and to consider what steps can be taken, by more effective enforcement of the law or otherwise, to secure the reduction of maternal mortality and morbidity arising from this cause.[1254]

Eighteen months earlier a ten-strong deputation from the National Council of Women of Great Britain, led by Nancy Astor and including three other MPs (Eleanor Rathbone, Mavis Tate and Irene

---

[1251] MacNalty, op cit, p4 Also, CPA CRD 1/78/1 Points for Propaganda No. 100 2nd November 1938 and *Daily Herald* 31st October 1938: deaths of mothers in childbirth dropped below 2000 in 1937/38 for the first time ever; and the rate of 3.13/1000 births was the lowest since 1911.
[1252] Loudon, op cit, p1557
[1253] Griffiths had been elected a year earlier in 1936, having previously been the agent in Llanelli 1922-1925, and since 1934 the President, of the South Wales Miners Federation.
[1254] *BMJ*, 22nd February 1936, p378

Ward) had asked Wood to establish such an inquiry. He promised to consider what action could be taken (as he clearly did), but pointed out that abortion was only one factor in maternal mortality, with social factors such as housing overcrowding and slums, the quality of the midwifery, maternal and child welfare services, and particularly "adequate ante-natal care", also critical. He was "determined to press on" with all of these. To this end, Wood had circulated

> ...all the maternity and child welfare authorities ... setting out the recommendations made for securing a complete and effective maternity service in each area, and requesting those authorities to take such steps as are necessary to extend and improve the services already available in their areas.[1255]

He was also exploring with the Medical Research Council questions recommended for further research, such as diet and nutrition.

Indeed, a month earlier, he had been depicted in *Punch* as the owner of a 'Nutrition Shop'.[1256] This image might imply that as access to vitamins was dependent on the ability to pay for them, Wood was gate-keeping their availability, ensuring they did not reach those who could not afford them. Equally, though, it might mean that he was acting like a chemist, ready to dispense them to those in need. Either way, though, he was clearly aware of the importance of nutrition - despite the accusations Boyd Orr would level at him.

In the supply debate on Ministry of Health estimates the following month, Wood was able to confirm that

> We are doing much, and I hope that we shall do more in the coming year, to make motherhood safer still in this country. The fight to reduce maternal mortality is a particularly stern and difficult one. It is true that in comparison with other countries our rate is not a specially high one, but we are faced with the fact that for a long period the rate has not substantially varied. [Following] a recent report from our investigators ... I have come to the conclusion that a

---

[1255] Hansard, 27th May 1937, vol. 324, cols. 417-418
[1256] *Punch* 21st April 1937, KW22 18/17

proportion of the deaths that take place in this country are preventible.

... The ... report shows that the main line of attack on maternal mortality must be the continuous improvement of the local maternity services, the keynote of which is the necessity of team work. The new Midwives Act will come into operation a few weeks hence, and from the proposals which have been submitted by the local authorities it can be said that satisfactory arrangements are being made in the greater part of the country. Important steps are being taken in regard to the training of midwives, and it is also satisfactory to know that the number of antenatal clinics has increased by 76 [with] an increasing number of mothers attending these clinics during the year.[1257]

Wood was then asked how the average for working-class districts differed from that for middle-class ones. For many MPs the link to poverty and inadequate diet that the question implied was at the nub of the problem, but conversely it might be argued that this made the quality of services and their accessibility even more fundamental. As if to demonstrate his ability to stonewall and deflect attention, Wood referred the questioner to the Ministry's annual report (which "I think" contained that information), adding "but if he has any district specially in mind, I will try to supply him with the information he desires".

Maternal mortality was a concern in its own right but also part of the wider question of public health, bound up with the issue of child welfare generally and particularly the gap between services for infants and those of school age. Wood continued:

I am glad to report that there is a steady increase of children under one year of age who are brought to the infant welfare centres. ... I have urged on local authorities the importance of the fullest supervision over the health of children between the ages of 18 months and five years, and ... during the past year there has been a substantial increase in the number of visits paid by health visitors to such children. As a result of my representation at least 47 authorities have established special clinics for toddlers, and 53 have arranged for the school medical services to be available for the younger

---

[1257] Hansard, 8th June 1937, vol. 324, cols. 1623-1624

children, while 64 have appointed additional health visitors.[1258]

He had not contented himself with a flow of memoranda from the Ministry, however, for administrative fiat would never be sufficient, and with his belief in the importance of publicity and advertising to change attitudes and behaviour, he had also written articles and ensured items appeared elsewhere, for example in *School Governor Review*, stressing the importance of paying attention to the health of this age-group between infancy and school. In this way reductions in maternal and infant mortality could be built on to reduce morbidity in the pre-school years.[1259]

This reflected Wood's view that the publicity policy at Health had to be different to, and more subtle than, the one he had adopted at the Post Office, for "the latter has goods to sell".[1260] Consequently, more aggressive and commercial tactics could be justified at the Post Office that would not be appropriate for the awareness-raising and marketing in which the Ministry of Health was engaged.

Nutrition/malnutrition

Nutrition is "perhaps the chief fertiliser of health", as Walter Elliot remarked in 1938,[1261] but just a few years earlier the significance of nutrition to health had been much more obscure. In 1931 Newman had convened a Ministry of Health Advisory Committee on Nutrition (ACN) which only grudgingly acknowledged the existence of vitamins A to D and either failed to recognise their significance or, perhaps more likely, resisted the implications for an affordable and healthy diet, concentrating instead on a minimum nutritional standard of 3000 calories per man per day and 37gm protein.[1262]

[1258] Ibid
[1259] CPA CRD 1/60/3 item 1(2) and *School Governor Review* undated but 1936, KW21 9/2
[1260] Wood to Secretary 12th July 1935, MH 78/147 cited in Mariel Grant, 'Propaganda and the Role of the State in Inter-War Britain', 1994, p163
[1261] Shortly after Elliot succeeded Wood as Minister of Health, according to Colin Coote, 'A Companion of Honour: The Story of Walter Elliot', 1965, p185.
[1262] James Vernon, 'Hunger: A Modern History', 2007, p124

Even this was judged unaffordable on unemployment relief,[1263] and was in any case soon overtaken by the BMA recommendation for a healthy diet of 3400 calories per man per day and 50gm protein.[1264] As Vernon points out, the issue of nutrition in the context of the depression and distressed areas was becoming increasingly politicised, with the Committee Against Malnutrition (CAN) and the Children's Minimum Council both established in 1934, and "the classic texts of the 'hungry thirties'" published in 1936, all of which estimated that half the population (20m+) was malnourished.[1265] Political and Economic Planning (PEP), a think-tank which had already produced authoritative analyses of British society, and would produce similar reports on Social Services and the health services the following year, judged that nobody need go hungry but could still suffer "a serious deficiency of one or more protective food elements, such as various vitamins, calcium or iodine".[1266] What this meant was that families would resort to bulk products to satisfy their hunger regardless of their calorie content or vitamins. In some instances it was argued that this reflected ignorance, incompetence or laziness, but Hannington was clear that it was poverty that caused hunger and malnutrition, **not** any deficiencies in people's knowledge of food values or in the art of cooking. He reported on a CAN meeting in November 1936 which included the wife of a Greenock shipbuilder and a miner's wife from Chopwell.[1267] The shipbuilder had worked nine months in the previous twelve years and the budget to feed their family of four children was 38s per week, while the miner had not worked at all in that time and his family with two children, having exhausted statutory benefits, were subsisting on the niggardly Unemployment Assistance Board scale. Similarly, the Bowley inquiry in *Week-End Review* summarised the letters the magazine had received responding to the case of a woman who died of pneumonia compounded by voluntary starvation so that her husband and seven children could be fed on

---

[1263] *The Week-End Review*, April 1933, pp357-360, the Bowley inquiry report and summary
[1264] Vernon, op cit, p125
[1265] GCM McGonigle and J Kirby, 'Poverty and Public Health', 1936; John Boyd Orr, 'Food, Health and Income: Report on a Survey of Adequacy of Diet in Relation to Income', 1936; Robert McCarrison, 'Nutrition and National Health', 1936
[1266] PEP, "The malnutrition controversy", *Planning*, 1936, No. 88, p2
[1267] Hannington, op cit, pp63-64

48s per week. It was widely agreed that it was impossible to feed nine people on this amount.

A few months later Hilton Young made the same point, understandable if lamentable, that any mother would deprive herself of adequate food "for the sake of her children".[1268]   Eleanor Rathbone (1872-1946), the Independent MP for Combined English Universities since 1929, was one of those who subsequently drew attention to this:

> It is the natural thing, where the mother is the administrator of the family income and wants to make the income go as far as possible, that, if somebody has to go short, she goes short herself as any normal, unselfish person would do in her place.[1269]

At first glance Hannington's assessment is at odds with the conclusion John Burnett reached after comparing the Boyd Orr and Crawford surveys of income and diet:

> For many millions the problem was not so much a financial as an educational one: a nutritionally adequate diet was probably possible in the 1930s for five-sixths of the population, but because of ignorance or prejudice, lack of time or lack of facilities, only half the population was able to receive it.[1270]

However, both Hannington and Burnett would concur that "a nutritionally adequate diet" was impossible for the other one-sixth. They, not just the "submerged tenth", simply could not afford it.

Part of the Kingsley Wood myth is that he disbelieved, even denied, that people lived in such extreme and impoverished circumstances. However, this is most unlikely given his background as a Poor Man's lawyer before entering parliament, let alone the work he undertook subsequently (for example, to improve people's housing circumstances and well-being) which involved him seeing people's situation for himself, thereby underlining his position as a

---

[1268] Hansard, 7th July 1933, vol. 280, col.657

[1269] Hansard, 25th March 1935, vol. 299, col. 1648

[1270] John Burnett, 'Plenty and Want: A Social History of Diet in England from 1815 to the Present Day', 1979 (orig. 1966), p317

one-nation Conservative. But there is also direct evidence that some of it is inaccurate too.

The myth may have started with John Boyd Orr's (1880-1971) recollection in his autobiography that

> Mr Kingsley Wood, the Minister of Health, asked me to come and see him. He wanted to know why I was making such a fuss about poverty when, with old age pensions and unemployment insurance, there was no poverty in the country. This extraordinary illusion was genuinely believed by Mr Wood, who held the out-of-date opinion that if people were not actually dying of starvation there could be no food deficiency. He knew nothing about the results of the research on vitamins and protein requirements, and had never visited the slums to see things for himself.[1271]

This encounter is sometimes repeated uncritically, for example by Gilbert,[1272] and in the case of one recent author gives rise to the remarkable judgement that "despite [his] unusual background for a senior Tory, Kingsley Wood was clearly as ill-informed as most of his colleagues".[1273] However some others, such as Branson and Heinemann, are more discerning. They point out that "Orr ... was not merely a detached investigator, but a keen propagandist for a new policy".[1274] In other words, he would not let the facts spoil a good story or dilute his argument. Orr may have been right that Wood did not fully appreciate the difference between food deficiency and starvation, though this is doubtful given that, in his robust response in the Labour censure debate on malnutrition in the Commons on 8th July 1936, Wood clarified that Orr's focus was on the optimum, which necessitated changes far beyond diet, referred to McGonigle's different perspective, and drew attention to Orr's own conclusion that further research and discussion were required given that his work was based on the budgets of a small sample of

---

[1271] John Boyd Orr, 'As I Recall', 1966, pp115-116

[1272] Bentley Gilbert, 'British Social Policy 1914-1939', 1970, p190

[1273] AJ Davies, 'We, The Nation: The Conservative Party and the Pursuit of Power', 1995, p313
Davies' only other reference to Wood is to his time at the National Publicity Bureau, describing him as "the driving force behind the GPO Film Unit in the 1930s" (p207).

[1274] Noreen Branson and Margot Heinemann, 'Britain in the Nineteen Thirties', 1971, p210

1152 families.[1275] Furthermore, in one article about this time Wood declared 'Malnutrition Must Be Fought',[1276] and had also recently published an article arguing for more nourishing food, headlined 'Diets That Nourish'.[1277]

Nevertheless, information is often filtered to fit preconceptions, and Mary Sutherland, Chief Woman Officer of the Labour Party, reported that

> The Minister of Health tried to repudiate [in the debate on malnutrition] Sir John Orr and Dr McGonigle by quoting experts like Professor Cathcart, who has said that ignorance of cookery and food values rather than poverty is the cause of malnutrition.
>
> But he did not dare to tell the House how a healthy diet can be obtained on four shillings per head per week or less. It is, of course, significant that none of the experts who attribute malnutrition to the ignorance and inefficiency of the mother instead of her lack of income, have told us how to maintain a high standard of health, say, on unemployment benefit, or its equivalent. They have not told us because they know it can't be done.[1278]

Wood did not repudiate Orr nor even imply that he did. Rather he accepted and soon promoted the further research Orr had advocated by inviting local authorities to co-operate with the dietary surveys suggested by the Advisory Committee on Nutrition (of which Orr was a member).[1279]

[1275] Hansard, 8th July 1936, vol. 314, cols. 1240-1253, particularly cols. 1241-1243

Chips Channon records in his diary for 8th July 1936 that Wood and Walter Elliot were "our brilliant defenders" against the Socialist vote of censure over malnutrition (Robert Rhodes James (ed.), 1967, op cit, p69), with Wood's speech quoted in the *Daily Mail* on 9th July 1936 (KW21 3/1).

[1276] *Morning Post* undated, KW21 1/3

[1277] *Sunday Despatch* 2nd August 1936, KW21 23/6

[1278] *Forward* 8th August 1936, KW21 27/10 reprinting Mary Sutherland's August article from 'Labour Women'.

Mary Sutherland would later lead a deputation to Wood from the Standing Joint Committee of Industrial Women's Organisations that October (*Daily Herald* 23rd October 1936, KW21 78/6; *Times* 24th October 1936, KW21 64/6).

[1279] *Times* 3rd October 1936, KW21 57/5

But, regardless of this, the other justification Orr gives for his argument is patently wrong. Not only are there many articles, such as that of Campion which attest to Wood's determination to see things for himself,[1280] there is photographic and other documentary evidence to demonstrate that this is incorrect in relation to slums (e.g., 1935 visits to Manchester and Birmingham below). This in turn raises questions about Orr's objectivity and interpretation, for he was clearly not an entirely candid witness or rapporteur in this instance. It may be relevant that, ten years later when Director-General at the newly formed Food and Agriculture Organisation after the Second World War, Orr's world food plan was rejected in September 1947 and his attempt to set up a supra-national body to tackle under-nutrition was spurned.[1281] He resigned shortly afterwards, his idealism at odds with the political realities. This might have been a principled approach but it was also naïve. Whereas politics entails, even depends on, knowing when to compromise, the campaigning activist and scientist abhors any such accommodation.

In an early television programme in March 1937 Wood discussed food and health with John Hilton who had made his name as a radio interviewer previously. One report the following day included

Professor John Hilton, *News Chronicle* adviser, put Sir Kingsley Wood through the hoop at Alexandra Palace and persuaded him to produce some interesting charts and food demonstrations.

The Minister of Health came prepared with bottles of milk, bread, baskets of eggs, spinach and one herring, all measured up in units of 100 according to their calorific value.

[1280] Wood visited many local areas at this time, including Bath, Plymouth, Hull, Bristol and Portsmouth. Indeed, on 18th September 1936 the *Bath Chronicle and Herald* used these very words when it reported "The Minister of Health, Sir Kingsley Wood, who believes in seeing things for himself …" (KW21 45/1).

[1281] Boyd Orr's DNB entry

Martin Daunton shared an advance copy of his chapter on the 1943 Hot Springs Conference, the food equivalent of the Bretton Woods conference the following year. Entitled "Nutrition: Food, agriculture and the world economy", it will appear in a book edited by Ian Shapiro and Naomi Lamoreaux in 2017.

'To get his daily 3000 calories a man has to eat 30 herrings, then,' reasoned Hilton.

But the Minister, who seemed to enjoy having his leg pulled, suggested a balanced diet and drew public attention to his beloved milk, which he said contains five vitamins.

This sort of screen interview at least convinces you that there are human beings in the Cabinet.[1282]

Nevertheless, Wood's position as Minister at a time of depression, unemployment and impoverishment made him an automatic target and one that views such as Orr's made more likely. In August 1936, for example, the topical magazine *GK's Weekly* printed a poem that encapsulated many of these issues around diet, poverty and health. Entitled 'A Ballade of Prosperity', it lampooned society's inequalities, ending with a reference to the future Prince of Wales and the contrast between his opulent lifestyle and that of many of his subjects:

> The world is fit for heroes, the machine
> Does all our work, while science points the way;
> There is no need for us to intervene,
> Leisure and cultured ease have come to stay.
> Our millionaires are buying shares that pay
> And line their coats with more expensive fur;
> And yet a woman said the other day,
> 'Of course we never eat on Thursdays, sir.'
>
> The great unwashed are getting nice and clean;
> The unemployed are learning how to play;
> Perry has won at Wimbledon; 'the Queen

[1282] *NA* 12th March 1937, KW22 6/9; *Radio Times* listing at KW22 2/9
Pictures from the programme appeared the following day: Wood and Hilton, and Wood and milk bottles, in KW22 9/3 and 9/4 respectively. The *News Chronicle* headlined their report 'John Hilton Pulls Sir Kingsley's Leg' (KW22 14/2)
In April the *Daily Herald* reported Jim Griffiths telling the House of Commons "Give the mother the money and she will provide the vitamins." The paper continued "With that one simple sentence, thrown passionately across the House of Commons last night, a Welsh miner dramatically brought the problem of malnutrition down from the incomprehensible heaven of percentages to the ordinary earth terms of insufficient food." (KW22 32/1, 14th April 1937)

Mary' Will yet be garlanded with bay.
England directs with undisputed sway
The happy nations that depend on her.
With everything so prosperous and gay
Of course we never eat on Thursdays, sir.

We know the secrets of the vitamin,
And how the growth of science can allay
The risk of malnutrition; we have seen
Dietaries sponsored by the B.M.A.
How could such experts ever go astray?
And can we doubt the word of Westminster?
Sir Kingsley Wood is satisfied. Hooray!
Of course we never eat on Thursdays, sir.[1283]

Other investigations into poor diet around this time included those at Peckham Pioneer Health Centre and earlier in the Rhondda in 1934.[1284] Robert Graves brought together many of the threads across a decade, telescoping events in his analysis that

The Pioneer Health Centre at Peckham ... reported that 86% of those examined were found to be suffering from some disorder, only 20% were aware of it, and only 7% receiving treatment. It was to remedy this state of affairs that the National Fitness Campaign was begun [in 1937], but Low in a cartoon pointed out the absurdity of recommending physical jerks to citizens suffering from malnutrition and the effects of living in dilapidated houses in Special Areas.[1285]

[1283] *GK's Weekly* 13th August 1936, KW21 23/11 The poet signed as RDJ.
[1284] Burnett, op cit, pp303, 305-307
S Mervyn Herbert, 'Britain's Health', 1939, a condensed and updated version of the 1937 PEP report, includes Peckham Pioneer Health Centre and its survey of 500 families (pp170-172), and a section on nutrition initiatives taken by the Government (pp173-178).
When, in August 1942, Mass Observation asked for views on post-war organisation of medical services, Olivia Cockett's reply included the Peckham Centre as a model for the future. Robert Malcolmson (ed.), 'Love and War in London: The Mass Observation Wartime Diary of Olivia Cockett', 2008, p214
[1285] Graves and Hodge, op cit, pp399-400

McGonigle's 1936 study showed the unintended consequences of treating social initiatives independently for, as part of slum clearance, some Stockton residents had been decanted to new housing but rather than their move resulting in improved health it deteriorated. The reason was that rents were higher in the better housing and, as incomes did not increase, families had less to spend on food. As Burnett puts it, McGonigle found that

> ... the death-rate in the new housing estate went up while in the town as a whole, including the slum areas which still existed, it went down. Malnutrition could be found in council houses as well as slum tenements.[1286]

Burnett concluded, in contrast to Orr's dismissive treatment of Wood, that "For the first time in the thirties the subject seriously occupied the attention of government departments, local authorities and the press, both serious and popular". Burnett was not referring just to Wood of course, but he and the Ministry of Health were certainly amongst those who responded.

In April 1935, even before Wood became Minister, a report had been received on the impact of poverty and unemployment on health in Durham and Sunderland [1287] MacNalty drew on it in his 1935 annual report, particularly in the sections on maternal welfare and unemployment, where he included quotations on the connections between unemployment and health. CAN also referred to the Durham report in July 1935 and January 1936, on the second occasion taking MacNalty to task and arguing that, while it was a step forward to see details of nutrition and regional variations in food intake considered, MacNalty was either ignorant of, or ignoring, recent evidence (e.g., on vitamins or Boyd Orr's research).[1288] It was the role of CAN to keep the pressure on, but there was a risk that a pursuit of the best could drive out the good. The Ministry was having some impact within the constraints it faced, but for CAN this remained inadequate and insufficient.

[1286] Burnett, op cit, p304

[1287] Ministry of Health, 'Report of an inquiry into the effects of existing economic circumstances on the health of the community in the county borough of Sunderland and certain districts of County Durham', 1935, Cmd 4886

[1288] Committee Against Malnutrition, Bulletin 9 'Economic depression and health'; Bulletin 12 'The state of the public health', CPA CRD 1/60/4

Yet when the first ACN report had been published on 1st April 1937 Wood described it as "the most valuable document on nutrition yet issued". He told a press conference that he would implement the Committee's conclusions immediately:

> He had that day communicated with all the maternity and child welfare authorities in the country asking them to review at an early date their arrangements for the supply of milk and other foods.[1289]

Underlining this rapid response, the newspaper report had five headlines:

> 'Minister's Prompt Actions on Food Report', 'Milk Consumption Key to Proper Nutrition', 'Big Increase Best Step Towards Better Health', 'Authorities to Review Supply Arrangements', 'More Vegetables and Fruit Should Be Eaten'.

A few months later in November 1937 the Ministry of Health took a full page in the newspapers to explain 'New Ways of Putting Milk on the Menu', advertising it as "The key to national fitness: the extra pint".[1290] Consequently, neither Wood's actions nor the speed with which he took them accord with Boyd Orr's negative judgement.

Individual Physique and the Environment

The Durham inquiry had been sparked by a letter to the *Times* on 11th December 1934 regarding "a substantial and progressive deterioration in public health" in the distressed area between the Tyne and the Tees. The letter was from a local doctor with extensive experience in the area, having worked in the community, in four hospitals in Darlington and Sunderland, and with local authorities. Despite the considerable statutory, voluntary and philanthropic effort that had been put in across the region, the writer considered that there were six main indicators of decline, not least increasing anaemia due to malnutrition, horrific cases of rickets and

---

[1289] *Western Mail and South Wales News* 2nd April 1937, KW22 22/1
Also, *Leeds Mercury* 2nd April 1937, KW22 28/1: 'Swift Action by Minister on Food Report'.
[1290] *Daily Mail* 5th November 1937, KW23 67/1

"decrepitude and bodily dilapidation" more generally. In his view recent public health reports from the Ministry (several over Newman's name) had been wildly optimistic and he concluded:

> I therefore make a very earnest plea for more consideration for the ailing and impoverished. There is, I fear, a certain complacency growing up in national feeling about the distressed areas. People in the South of England ... seem to think that things are somehow coming right. My object in writing is to combat this complacency with the utmost vigour.[1291]

That Dr Walker's letter precipitated an inquiry points to the Ministry's heightened concern, whereas had there been any lingering defensiveness from the previous regime it might have ignored it altogether. Nevertheless, the inquiry conclusions were mixed, arguing that Dr Walker's claims were exaggerated, with little evidence that disease had increased and "none of increased mortality".[1292] But this was in comparison to a very low base and there was "considerable incidence of subnormal nutrition and some incidence of malnutrition", with almost a quarter of people under-nourished in Durham and about three-tenths in Sunderland. Health in Sunderland was generally poorer than in Durham due to "the less favourable housing conditions and environment",[1293] yet things might have been much worse given "the long continued economic stress to which this population has been subjected".[1294]

Titmuss, in an analysis using 1936 data, separated the 2.22 million people in Durham and Sunderland from the rest of the north, for it was clear how extreme was the situation in this area let alone compared to the rest of the country or the south-east. For example, infant mortality was 65% above, and maternal mortality 120% above, the corresponding positions in Greater London; indeed, maternal mortality was higher than it had been for the country as a whole in "**1896 and every subsequent year**" [emphasis added]. Unemployment was 200% above (i.e., treble) that in the south-east and long unemployment 1325% above (i.e., more than fourteen times greater). Yet poor relief was only 162% higher in Sunderland

[1291] *Times* 11th December 1934
[1292] Ministry of Health, 1935, Cmd 4886, op cit, p43
[1293] Ibid, p42
[1294] Ibid, p43

and 594% in Durham. In other words, the north-east was markedly more disadvantaged but public assistance did not appear to be dispensed commensurately.[1295]

In July 1936 a deputation from Durham County Council and eleven MPs for the county had attempted to put their case to the Prime Minister Stanley Baldwin. However, he pleaded a heavy workload at the end of the parliamentary session and diverted them to Wood instead. With 70,000 less people working in the mining industry than in 1924, the deputation asked for new industries to be started and for Treasury help. Wood informed them that the county's plight would be taken into account in the review of the block grant to local authorities that was in progress, promised to pass on their views to Baldwin and to confer with other members of the Cabinet regarding the specific points they had raised.[1296] Wood was clearly in a difficult position and no doubt thought his response as positive as possible in the circumstances. Some of the deputation saw it differently for, as the *Northern Echo* reported, 'We Asked for Bread and They Gave Us A Stone'. But, as is often the case when the press is involved, the eye-catching headline proved more strident than the report:

> The Minister was very sympathetic ... he told us that the matter had caused him much personal thought. But he promised nothing except that he would report our appeal to the Cabinet. It is most disappointing.[1297]

Even if "disappointment" was political code for "angry", this may appear unduly restrained and unnecessarily deferential, though it might also indicate that Wood had given them a full hearing and they appreciated that his room for manoeuvre was limited. Wood was not just feigning interest though, for it was reported later that year that the Government expected to announce before Christmas its revision of block grant tranches to relieve authorities in the Special Areas of the "heavy additional burdens they have been carrying".[1298] The promise was made good just before Christmas

---

[1295] Titmuss, 1938, op cit, pp304-305
[1296] *Times* 28th July 1936, KW21 10/2; *Durham Chronicle* 31st July 1936, KW21 25/1
[1297] *Northern Echo* 29th July 1936, KW21 18/11
[1298] *Morning Post* 27th November 1936, KW21 108/3

when it was announced that Wood would bring in a Bill in the new year; Beaverbrook's *Evening Standard* trumpeted this as 'New Government Relief for the Distressed Areas'.[1299]   The *Times* reported the outcomes on 18th February 1937 with the distressed areas receiving much of an annual £5m addition to the existing Treasury grant of £44m overall, comprising £2.25m extra grant each year and a reduction in contributions to support the able-bodied unemployed.   In the case of Merthyr Tydfil, for example, "the estimated gain is equivalent to a rate of 5s in the pound".[1300]

The debilitating impact of poverty on health and physique had been apparent since a large number of potential recruits had been rejected in both the Boer and First World Wars. As late as 1936 one newspaper reported that just as public school pupils were about six inches taller than those in publicly-provided schools so a crowd watching varsity rugby at Twickenham would be taller by the same amount than one watching a football match.[1301]   But according to Burnett,

> By 1939 ... the results of ... policies [such as 3000 Infant Welfare Centres] were already impressive. Twelve-year-old boys attending elementary schools in London were three inches taller and eleven pounds heavier than their fathers had been twenty years earlier ...[1302]

Not all the discrepancy had been erased, but the deficiency had been reduced. Some of this was due to enlightened policies such as free milk, school meals and improved health care, but much to fuller employment and higher wages as the country re-armed.

Another significant factor was the development of health and social services. Herbert Morrison had told the House of Commons in May 1936 that Britain was fifty years ahead of the United States in this respect and more than fifty years ahead of France. Not surprisingly Kingsley Wood drew attention to Morrison's statement in an article for *Politics in Review*, subsequently re-printed as a

---

The report also noted that the distress in Durham had shocked the new commissioner, former Labour MP for Finsbury Sir George Gillett (1870-1939), who had replaced Sir Malcolm Stewart.

[1299] *Evening Standard* 23rd December 1936, KW21 119/2

[1300] *Times* 18th February 1937, KW21 144/10, 145/1, 145/3

[1301] *Hertfordshire Hemel Hempstead Gazette* 22nd February 1936, KW20 86/3

[1302] Burnett, op cit, p321

twelve page pamphlet 'Our Social Services' in August 1936.[1303] Wood added:

> Long ago Disraeli laid it down that the health and well-being of the people should be a fundamental part of national policy, and now on all sides it is accepted as a national duty that we should ensure to our working population social conditions conducive to good health and the highest possible standard of life which our national resources will allow.

This encompassed education, housing and the preventive services as well as treatment and intervention. Wood pointed out that a hundred years earlier the Poor Law had been the only form of Social Services[1304] whereas it then extended from National Health Insurance via housing to Workmen's Compensation. Similarly, fifty years earlier expenditure was £50m whereas in 1936 it was ten times as great at £500m, while the population had only increased by 50%. The upshot was that spend per head was then about seven times what it had been in 1911, twenty-five years earlier, when health insurance had first been introduced.

Contrary to what the Socialists claimed, therefore, it was Wood's contention that the National Government had not starved social services, a position substantiated by the 1937 PEP reports on the country's health and Social Services.[1305] It might be argued, of course, that much of any increased spend was due to the high levels of unemployment in the depression. This was certainly part of it where Social Services was concerned, but far from the full story. PEP had surveyed provision in 1935, dividing individual Social Services into three groups: Community, Social Insurance and

---

[1303] CPA PUB/B, pamphlet reprinted from 'Politics in Review' April-June 1936

[1304] Indeed, when Wood addressed the silver jubilee conference of the National Association of Relieving Officers in May 1937 about humanising the Poor Law, he argued that the "Poor Law ... now a social service, a humanitarian spirit animated its administration and the human and personal touch had superseded old mechanical methods and routine. The tramp was going from the road, young men were being persuaded to enter hostels and train themselves for a useful life and many were obtaining regular work." KW22/1-2 loose NA 15th May 1937

[1305] PEP, 'Report on the British Social Services', 1937 and 'Report on the British Health Services', 1937

Social Assistance services. In 1934 total spend on these services accounted for one-tenth of national income (£400.8m), with another £11m for Workmen's Compensation. Since 1900, gross spend had increased eleven-fold and spend per head nine-fold. In 1934 poor relief (public assistance) was given to 1.5m people at a cost of £46m, or less than one-sixth of the total net spend of £286m.[1306] Most telling, perhaps, was PEP's conclusion that one-seventh of central government and local authority budgets had been used for Social Services in 1900, whereas they accounted for one-third in 1934. Much had been developed by the reforming Liberal Government between 1906 and 1914 and some since 1919, both philosophies reflecting the cultural and intellectual shift away from the nineteenth century view that State support undermined individual independence, self-reliance and initiative to the twentieth century perspective that the over-riding responsibility of any civilised state and advanced economy was to tackle individual welfare and deal with community poverty. Harold Macmillan's vision for the future, 'The Middle Way' published in 1938, endorsed this stance, as did those of the Coles[1307] and the 'Five Years On' group from different political traditions. Exploring the implications in greater detail, they all subscribed to planning as the critical cornerstone of a coherent and rational way forward. Or, as Burnett was to put it:

> Council housing rescued millions from the misery of industrial slums; medical services and insurance benefits gave a hope of better health and greater security, while the development of public utilities and recreational amenities was beginning to add to the richness of enjoyment of life.

[1306] The detailed cash figures on p12 of the Social Services report were (excluding housing and war pensions):

	1900	1934	Increase
Spend per head of population	19s 2d	£8 16s	x9
Total gross spend	£35.5m	£400.8m	x11
Total net spend	£34m	£286m	x8

Total net spend represented the additional burden falling on the taxpayer/ratepayer, with almost £115m coming from other sources by 1934 (compared to less than £2m at the turn of the century).
Details on the three groups of Social Services and diagrams of the coverage of each can be found on pp13-29 & 34-35 of the PEP report.
[1307] GDH Cole and Margaret Cole, 'The Condition of Britain', 1937

The State was at last coming to provide for the working classes the conditions of civilised life which the middle classes had provided for themselves.[1308]

Smoke abatement and other health issues

PEP's report on the health services made many of the same points that Wood had elsewhere, particularly the implications of protective services (such as housing and sanitation) that might not ordinarily be associated with "health" in a narrow medical sense. Although the recent Public Health Act 1935-36 had consolidated smoke nuisance legislation, the PEP report was critical of both river and atmospheric pollution. The Act re-affirmed local authority inspection and bye-law functions, with fines and Ministerial abatement powers as further sanctions,[1309] but did not go far enough in the view of some opposition MPs, both Labour and Liberal, as well as of PEP.[1310] Manny Shinwell, the Labour MP who had defeated Ramsay MacDonald in Seaham, asked Wood in November 1936 what further steps were being taken to abate smoke nuisance. Wood replied cautiously that

> … many steps with my encouragement are being taken by local authorities, industrial interests and voluntary organisations who are co-operating in the matter, and smokeless methods of using coal are being increasingly developed both for domestic and industrial purpose[s].

However, Wood resisted the proposal that the use of raw coal be prohibited, arguing that such a step would require additional legislation and there was already a "very heavy Parliamentary programme before the House".[1311] Nor did he consider it a

---

[1308] Burnett, op cit, p320

[1309] Sections 101-106, Public Health Act 1935-36 consolidating legislation in the 1875 and 1926 Acts and adding further clauses.

[1310] See also Stephen Mosley, 'A network of trust: Measuring and monitoring air pollution in British cities, 1912-1960', *Environment and History*, 2009, 15, pp273-302. An attempt by the Glasgow representative to get up a deputation to Wood to press for tougher anti-smoke legislation in May 1936 is referred to on p278.

[1311] Hansard, 26th November 1936, vol. 318, cols. 546-547 Wood took a similar line three months later (Hansard, 4th March 1937, vol. 321, col. 557).

sufficient priority when the consequences for industry might be costly and insufficient stocks of smokeless fuel were available.[1312]

An exhibition on smoke abatement had been held at the Science Museum in Kensington throughout October 1936, and although Wood had opened it, it was not explicitly referred to in the Commons exchanges - though it may have been what prompted Shinwell to raise the issue at that time. The exhibition was trailed in several newspapers, which among other things highlighted that Londoners breathed twenty million tons of soot a year and "a thousand tons of sulphuric acid descends on London every day".[1313] According to the *Engineer*, Wood pointed out in his opening speech that

> ... proclamations forbidding the use of coal in London were made in Queen Elizabeth's reign, and ... in spite of the fact that there were now 4,250,000 more dwelling-houses in London than in 1601, conditions were considerably improved.[1314]

Wood further claimed that "Industrial smoke had largely been eliminated, and the greater part of the problem today was the control or elimination of domestic smoke".[1315] As one hundred local authorities attended, there may be some justification for Wood's belief that he was encouraging co-operation. In addition, the annual four-day conference of the National Smoke Abatement Society took place at the Science Museum during the exhibition, opened by Wood's colleague Harry Crookshank (1893-1961), Parliamentary Secretary of Mines at the Board of Trade.[1316]

Wood was pressed again at the beginning of December 1937 after an extensive fog over London the previous week was described as "a disgrace to London and his Department"[1317] by Sir Percy Harris, a prominent LCC Liberal for many years. Harris pursued Wood further three weeks later, forcing him to concede that there had only been two prosecutions in London in 1936, though Wood looked forward to the formation of the Joint Smoke

---

[1312] Hansard, 1st December 1937, vol. 329, cols. 2089-2090
[1313] *Liverpool Daily Post* 24th August 1936, KW21 31/14; *Evening Standard* 21st September 1936, KW21 33/20
[1314] *Engineer* 9th October 1936, KW21 68/11
[1315] Ibid
[1316] *Nature* and *Times* 19th and 22nd September 1936, KW21 34/15 & 34/16
[1317] Hansard, 2nd December 1937, vol. 329, cols. 2253-2254

Abatement Committee for London that would bring the metropolitan borough councils (the authorities with day-to-day responsibility) together with the LCC and its default powers. He thought this should have some impact[1318] - though not much until the Clean Air Act 1956.

It is perhaps significant that Wood was harried most when pollution and fog in London brought the issue home for MPs, inconveniencing them on their own doorstep as it were. Much the same had been true in the middle of the nineteenth century when the Thames was an open sewer flowing, or rather sliding, past the Commons. The stench then had forced them to act. As long as pollution remained in the industrial districts "up north", the sub-text for many being that this was a natural if not an acceptable state of affairs, they were much less likely to do so. Yet despite this, Walter Elliot, Wood's successor, judged smoke abatement as one of the achievements of the previous twenty-five years in his 1938-39 review of the Ministry of Health.[1319]

The PEP report was also critical of the hospital system, split between public and voluntary provision 3:1 since 1929, with bed shortages at times, an ineffective use of resources, uneven provision across areas and a lack of co-ordination.[1320] This was doubly significant for Wood since the 1929 date referred to the Local Government Act he and Neville Chamberlain had introduced, while as Minister he now bore sole responsibility for a service that, as today, was struggling to keep up with demand. In 'The Citadel', first published in 1937, AJ Cronin underlines the inequities in the system:

> Many of [the] cases were urgent - surgical emergencies which cried aloud for immediate admission to hospital. And here Andrew [Manson, then a London GP] encountered his greatest difficulty. It was the hardest thing in the world to secure admission, even for the worst, the most dangerous case. ...
> ...'They're not full up. They've plenty of beds at St John's, for their own men. If they don't know you they freeze you stiff. ... And this is London! This is the heart of the bloody

---

[1318] Hansard, 23rd December 1937, vol. 330, cols. 2142-2143
[1319] Coote, op cit, p196
[1320] PEP, 'Report on the British Health Services', op cit, pp16-18 See p23 for Peckham Pioneer Health Centre

British Empire. This is our voluntary hospital system. And some banqueting bastard of a philanthropist got up the other day and said it was the most marvellous in the world. It means the workhouse again for the poor devil [Manson's patient] ... and him with peritonitis.'[1321]

The deficiencies were later laid bare by the Second World War for an overall shortage of 98,000 acute beds, with about 100,000 people waiting on any particular day, was much worse in many of the specialisms that would become most important in wartime.[1322]
Similarly, the evacuation of mothers and children from urban areas in September 1939 proved a national revelation in many ways, not least the realisation that "... the standard in quality and quantity of the social services in the rural areas was inferior to that in London and other big cities".[1323] The same was true of health services outside London. The condition of the evacuees was often alarming to people in the rural reception areas for, while poverty existed in the countryside as well, there was at least access to fresh air, decent food and vegetables. Not all the 1.5m official evacuees (there were another 2m voluntary ones) lived in "squalor reminiscent of the 1890s" of course, but according to Titmuss the public shock rivalled that "after the Boer War [at] sickness and low physical standards".[1324] This was the challenge Wood had been set, and set himself, even before he returned to the Ministry of Health.

National fitness

While still at the Post Office in 1934, Wood was one of thirteen people circulated with a War Office memo on the physical condition of army recruits in the year to September 1933.[1325] Of 95,000 who had applied, a quarter were rejected at the first examination and less than a third, only 29,000, were finally recruited for the regular army. In other words, 70% were unsuitable or fell out of the process for other reasons. Wood and Joseph Ball exchanged

---

[1321] AJ Cronin, 'The Citadel', 1937, p218
[1322] Richard Titmuss, 'Problems of Social Policy', 1950, pp72 & 73
[1323] Ibid, p111
[1324] Ibid, pp131 & 133
[1325] CPA CRD Cabinet Conservative Committee 1934-1935 1/64/1- 7/1 item: War Office 2nd May 1934 memo

letters on the physical condition of Post Office workers,[1326] most of whom were in much better shape - as Wood's chief medical officer was able to testify.[1327] Though Wood could hardly claim the credit for this, it was agreed that he should preside over a sub-committee to improve the national physique and consider "a ... policy with regard to national health".[1328] The latter helped make him a leading candidate for Minister of Health the following year, and at the Sub-Committee's first meeting on 11th July it was agreed unanimously that the gap in health services for 14 to 16 year olds should be closed by providing some medical benefit between these ages and the fullest possible extension of physical training in elementary and secondary schools.[1329]   Subsequently,   the   Sub-Committee concentrated on how "the present urge for physical exercise could be turned to account by the Party organisation".[1330] The example of the Hitler Youth in Nazi Germany, combining physical health and aptitude with political allegiance, had clearly made an impression on politicians in Britain (as it had in France and elsewhere[1331]) and one

---

[1326] CPA 1/60/8 Physical Condition of Potential Recruits for Regular Army 1933 - item 2 4th and 6th June 1934

[1327] CPA CRD Cabinet Conservative Committee 1934-1935 1/64/1 - 7/3 item: 8th June 1934 generally positive assessment of physical condition of Post Office employees in note from HH Bashford, Chief Medical Officer

[1328] CPA CRD Cabinet Conservative Committee 1934-1935 1/64/3 - meeting 7 6th July 1934; CPA CRD Health and physique of the nation – Physical training 1/60/2 - item 21: Joseph Ball note 21st March 1935 re the composition of this Sub-Committee A (Hoare, Lloyd, Topping, Gower, Ball with Wood as Chair).

[1329] CPA CRD Health and physique of the nation – General 1/60/3 - item 1: Notes of meeting 11th July 1934

[1330] CPA CRD Health and physique of the nation – Physical training 1/60/2 Item 22: 25th March 1935 - SCA7 'Health and Physique of the Nation memorandum'; Item 23: 29th March 1935 – CRD report on actions from Sub-Committee A re gymnasia construction; Item 24: Preliminary report by Sub-Committee A on SCA7

[1331] *Daily Worker* 9th October 1936, KW21 73/2
Referring to efforts to raise the level of sports and physical recreation in France, the article continued: "A similar move is mentioned in this country. [Wood] has been reported to have said that a 'forward drive will be undertaken to improve the physique of the nation'. Many people have commented when returning from abroad upon the well-conditioned looks of the people in comparison with the mass of people here." One observer judged 5 out of 5 people fit in Germany against only 1 out of 5 in Britain, as he said at a lunch to inaugurate the National Sporting Club. But the *Daily*

suggestion was that the Junior Imps League should be re-organised along those lines. However, the principal Party agent Sir Robert Topping (1877-1952) objected, arguing that the attraction was the social side rather than "political duties" and that there should be a new National Government organisation aimed at those aged twenty to thirty-five. Wood's view was that it "should be non-political in appearance and, in consequence, no persons prominently identified with politics should be on the council or executive"; rather this should consist of people such as athletes and social workers. Topping and Lloyd were to sketch out a plan of organisation, while Wood and Ball would draft principles

> ... to foster real patriotism and social service, combined with physical fitness, and at the same time to make it impossible for persons with socialist leanings or sympathies to become members.[1332]

The 'League of Good Companions', as it would have been called, with healthy minds in healthy bodies the rationale for its formation, never came into being and once the General Election in November 1935 was out of the way, Wood concluded that

> It will be possible now to carry into effect the plans which have already been made by the Government for expanding our national health services and improving the health and physique of the nation.[1333]

Neville Chamberlain, standing in for Baldwin at the 1936 Conservative Party conference at Margate, promoted the national fitness programme to the top of the country's agenda. This was Chamberlain's personal project[1334] in the sense that he was putting

---

Worker view was that long hours, low wages and "wretched conditions" made 1 out of 100 more likely.

[1332] CPA CRD Health and physique of the nation – General 1/60/3 - item 1: Notes of meeting 11th July 1934

Ball added a postscript to the notes that, as this new organisation was unlikely to get going before the next General Election, it might therefore be necessary to fall back on a "drastic reorganisation" of Junior Imps League and "a big recruiting drive to get into it the people who are staying out today".

[1333] *Times* 16th November 1935, KW20 4/16

[1334] Zweiniger-Bargielowska, op cit, p309

his prestige behind it and rousing the nation with a patriotic appeal, but it was also at the heart of the "progressive welfare agenda", associating the National Government with national fitness, while at the same time demonstrating an unthreatening physical and moral "re-armament" that went alongside the aim of preserving peace but readied the country for worse.[1335]   People did not have to understand any of this, of course, for their participation would be enough: partly in response to Britain's poor performance at the Berlin Olympic Games that summer, but driven as much by the fear and awe engendered by the regimented Hitler Youth movement.[1336] Wood continued to argue for a focus on health.

In October this call for a 'Fitter Britain' featured in the King's Speech, with Wood expected to bring in legislation for "organised facilities for physical training".[1337]   Although the country might be sceptical that this would happen, the National Government was determined that it should - though even some Conservative MPs, Duncan Sandys (1908-1987) for example, criticised such a campaign when the distressed areas were neglected.[1338]   It may have been partly to counter such views that Edward VIII (accompanied by Wood and Ernest Brown) visited parts of South Wales that November. As Titmuss, a prominent commentator like Graves, soon pointed out, "The inauguration of the Government's nationwide fitness campaign does little more than imply the existence of ill-health and inefficiency in our midst today."[1339] Having made this apparent, it became even more critical that the programme should reduce it.

[1335] An example of the former was the report in the *Liverpool Daily Post* (23rd October 1936, KW21 61/3) linking that autumn's Ministry of Health report and its focus on public health rather than just administration: "It will doubtless run hand-in-hand with the 'fitter Britain' campaign which was started by Mr Neville Chamberlain's remarks at Margate."

[1336] Zweiniger-Bargielowska, op cit, p280

[1337] *Bournemouth Echo* 14th October 1936, KW21 61/7
Also, *Sunday Despatch* 11th October 1936, KW21 72/1 report of the King's Speech included a cartoon captioned "Taxpayers who now have their 1937 assessments must agree with Neville Chamberlain on how to keep fit".

[1338] *Oxford Mail* 24th October 1936, KW21 82/9
Duncan Sandys was a Conservative MP for nearly forty years, Winston Churchill's son-in-law from 1935 to 1960 until divorced and a close ally of Anthony Eden.

[1339] Titmuss, 1938, op cit, p xxiv

It was believed that an advertising campaign would be financed by the insurance companies and approved societies, for whom a 0.25% contribution from profits would fund a campaign close to £0.5m and should provide an exceptional return on their investment.[1340] Meanwhile the *Daily Telegraph* published a Fitter Britain supplement in which Wood highlighted the three million new houses built since 1919, with £300,000 currently being spent each year, the half-million slum-dwellers already in new homes and a programme that saw 6000 moving each week. Nevertheless, he concluded, "everyone will agree that there is still a great deal to be done ..." for prevention, opportunities for exercise and vigorous health, not just the absence of disease. Wood's article was entitled 'Comradeship in search of physical efficiency' in which he argued that "good comradeship and care for others" was as important to overall well-being as looking after yourself.[1341]

The following month the *Municipal Journal* published what it described as a 'Special Message' from Wood, alongside a report on the week-long Public Health Congress that he was to open at the Royal Agricultural Hall in London:

Of late years we have made progress in public health which would have astonished our forefathers, but it is an honourable tradition of English social reform that it never stands still. From protecting the health of the community by providing adequate sanitary services we have passed on in the present century to making public provision for maintaining and restoring the health of the individual. We are now on the threshold of a further development - the planned co-ordination of every effort, whether public or voluntary, in an ordered and positive pattern which will make available the means of a healthy life in a healthy environment throughout all the seven ages of man. Advance on these lines is only possible with the full support of advanced public opinion. Fortunately, we are assured of that support, as has been shown by the remarkable response to Mr Chamberlain's inspiring call for a 'Fitter Britain'. ...[1342]

[1340] *Advertisers' Review* 22nd October 1936, KW21 82/1

[1341] CPA CRD 1/60/6 Physical Training Oct 1936 to Aug 1938

Item 36: *Daily Telegraph* Fitter Britain supplement 7th December 1936

[1342] *Municipal Journal* 13th November 1936, KW21 102/12

In September 1937 the *Times* published a forty-page special issue 'The Nation's Health', alongside the national health campaign which Neville Chamberlain (now Prime Minister) inaugurated that day, broadcasting from an evening reception over which Wood presided and with Arthur Greenwood and Percy Harris among the representatives from other parties.[1343] The TUC had given its backing and the accompanying Physical Training and Recreation Act 1937 has been described as the "most direct piece of interventionist legislation in the recreational field".[1344] On 26th October 1937 the *Times* special issue was re-printed as a 212-page book, covering all aspects of health in seven sections ranging from food to mental health. At 2s 6d (and 6d postage) it was hardly a populist tract, but that would not have been the audience the *Times* was seeking to reach. Wood's article opened with a statement of the approach he took and which he was expecting the Ministry of Health to foster: "Good health is pursued as both an end and a means. As an end, because physical well-being is its own reward. As a means to other ends, because …" health is required to partake of and enjoy other pleasures in life.[1345] Lord Aberdare, the Chairman of the National Advisory Council on Physical Training and Recreation for England and Wales, wrote of the capital grants available for new projects under the Act, particularly community centres, village halls and other local schemes, while others contributed articles on subjects as varied as pubs, playing fields, occupational health and voluntary hospitals. (The critical importance of community centres within new housing estates had been recognised a year earlier when Wood had approved a meeting between Ministry of Health officials, the National Council of Social Service and certain MPs "to foster the provision of community centres on these estates".[1346])

Joseph Ball had previously alerted Neville Chamberlain to Wood's impatience "…to get on and [described him as] apprehensive lest the tide should go back", to which Chamberlain

---

[1343] Zweiniger-Bargielowska, op cit, pp319 & 320
King George VI endorsed it in a February 1938 broadcast.
[1344] Stephen G Jones, "State intervention in sport and leisure in Britain between the wars", *Journal of Contemporary History*, 1987, 22, pp163-182
[1345] *Times*, 'The Nation's Health', 1937, p10
[1346] *Times* 11th July 1936, KW21 4/7
Community centres on housing estates featured in the parliamentary debate the following week on Ministry of Health estimates. *Times* 18th July 1936, KW21 20/6; *Morning Advertiser* 21st July 1936, KW21 15/4

replied that "I cannot help thinking that Sir Kingsley is unduly apprehensive about missing the tide for I see no danger of its going back for a long time to come".[1347] The programme was now finally underway, with Wood soon praising the "voluntary clubs and societies where the [contribution of individual] efforts can be co-ordinated in a spirit of friendly rivalry".[1348] The impact was evident before long:

- by the end of 1938 the Treasury had increased the money available (mainly capital grants for developments in Special Areas) from the original £2.4m to £4m, with nearly 800 projects sponsored[1349]

- in June 1939 84.5% of 20,000 militiamen were classed as Grade 1 "completely fit" (under the Military Training Act of 1939 which required six months conscription) and 9% fit apart from "minor disabilities"[1350]

- evidence from WWII recruitment of major "improvements in public health in the space of a generation", though major regional differences did remain.[1351]

The *Daily Mail* had accused Wood of playing "Napoleonically before the colossal canvas of the nation's health"[1352] but another paper the *Daily Despatch* showed him as less motivated by self-aggrandisement than driven by belief when it reported that

> What a worker Sir Kingsley Wood is! I was looking through a list of his engagements today, and found that in the course of four weeks he will make twenty-three public speeches on all kinds of topics.
>
> Tuberculosis, waterworks, obstetrics, health insurance, housing, public health, public baths, and town planning are just a selection from the list of subjects on which he is expected to speak with authority, wit and wisdom.

[1347] CPA, CRD 1/60/6 Item 33 including Ball and Chamberlain exchange of letters 26th, 27th and 29th October 1936

[1348] As it happened in a message to the annual dinner of Tunbridge Wells and District Physical Culture Club.
Health and Strength editorial 26th February 1938, p293 in Zweiniger-Bargielowska, op cit, p212

[1349] Zweiniger-Bargielowska, op cit, p325

[1350] *Times* 20th June 1939 and Zweiniger-Bargielowska, op cit, p331

[1351] Zweiniger-Bargielowska, op cit, p332

[1352] *Daily Mail* 10th November 1936, KW21 94/1 (Percy Cater's column 'The House As I See It')

It was Mr Arthur Greenwood, I believe, who said that the Ministry of Health is the Department which looks after you before birth, during life and after death.[1353]

Nowhere would this be more evident than in the house-building and slum clearance programmes and the overcrowding initiative Wood instituted.

Housing and Slum Clearance

Despite successive government initiatives since the First World War, and those of many local authorities such as London County Council and Manchester City Council, housing remained a major problem. There was not enough of it and much was of such poor quality that it impaired the health of the occupants and blighted the lives of neighbourhoods. As the Registrar-General identified in his 1935 report, houses were crowded together into towns, people were crowded together into houses too small for them, poverty aggravated both standards of living and environment in towns, and smoke "robbed the towns of sunshine".[1354] Or, as the Labour Research Department (LRD) judged that year, despite a million new houses built with State assistance between 1919 and 1931, and another three quarters of a million without, the housing shortage had worsened because, like slums themselves, it was a symptom of poverty with people unable to afford more space. In the LRD's view the housing required was of three types: structurally separate dwellings for families, more rooms for over-crowded families and new houses for slum and semi-slum dwellers.[1355] There were various estimates of the numbers required,[1356] but the Government's Five Year Plan restricted the subsidy available to replacing 300,000 slum houses (and flats in central areas under the 1935 Housing Act), yet this was less than a third of ED Simon's estimate of 1m. Furthermore, 300,000 was the proposed figure

---

[1353] *Daily Despatch* 13th October 1936, KW21 54/11
[1354] Women's Group on Public Welfare, 'Our Towns: A Close-Up', 2nd ed., 1944, p xv
[1355] Dick Hale, 'The National Government and Housing', 1935, pp1-3
[1356] Including by the *Architects Journal*, in the Amulree and Dudley reports and by ED Simon. The latter estimated the catch-up at 1m homes to meet the first two shortages and 1m houses to rent at 7s per week inclusive, with 120,000 houses per year thereafter in order to maintain the replacement number required. Hale, op cit, p4

rather than the number that would actually be achieved and there was always a gap between the two.[1357]

Wood had been alarmed at housing conditions in the East End since his earliest days, and this was one of the major factors that propelled him into politics in the first place. If the experience gave him the determination to do something about it, his time on the London County Council and at the Ministry of Health between 1919 and 1929 had enabled him to develop the expertise required. By appointing him as Minister, Baldwin was putting housing at the forefront of the Government's priorities - the reconstruction at home that the 1935 manifesto had promised to complement the pursuit of peace abroad,

> ... a practical programme put forward by Ministers who have the burden of responsibility upon them; it is not a programme drafted by private individuals who have no prospect of [putting] their plans into effect.[1358]

It was not Wood's publicity skills that the country needed to awaken it to the problem of slums for these were evident to all, but the energy and organisation he had shown at the Post Office.[1359]

One of Wood's first tasks as Minister of Health on 26th July 1935 was to lead the Commons through the many amendments that the House of Lords had proposed to the existing Housing Bill.[1360] There were few clauses that the Lords had left untouched but they had paid particular attention to the overcrowding provisions.[1361] In

---

[1357] Ibid, pp6-7
In the five years to 1935 only 41,000 houses had been cleared out, and at this rate of 8,200 pa it would take until 1972 to eradicate 300,000 slums, by which time another 1.6m would have appeared.
[1358] The latter was a dig at Lloyd George, both his Council of Action and his advice at the 1931 General Election to vote against National Government candidates.
CPA CRD 1/7/21 Cabinet Emergency Business Committee 1935 - Questions of Policy 1-57 item 1: CRD observations on circular from the Council of Action on Peace and Reconstruction
[1359] *Methodist Recorder* 13th June 1935, KW19 401/1
[1360] Hilton Young, the previous Minister, had discussed it with Collin Brooks the month before he introduced it in Parliament. Crowson, 1998, op cit, p68 - Brooks' diary entry for 7th December 1934
[1361] Hansard 26th July 1935, vol. 304, cols. 2181-2220; *Walthamstow Guardian* 2nd August 1935, KW19 458/7

most instances Wood recommended acceptance for it was only with the Act in force that overcrowding could be more effectively tackled and slum clearance speeded up. In Wood's view accepting the Lords amendments was a small price to pay for this national benefit. He visited the Manchester slums a few days later and, after the Housing Act had become law on the last day of the parliamentary session, those in Birmingham at the end of October.[1362] Exploiting the Chamberlain connection, the Leader of the Labour Group on Birmingham City Council had mischievously challenged Wood to say publicly that the Ministry of Health was dissatisfied with progress there,[1363] a gambit to which he did not succumb. Only the day before, as if to indicate that all those animated by a concern for human welfare shared the objective, he had called at the centenary dinner of the Association of Municipal Corporations for the abolition of slums, pointing out that the Prince of Wales, their guest of honour, backed this as well.[1364] For Wood slum clearance and the Housing (Overcrowding) Act was an example of religious faith in action,[1365] a renewal of the environmental campaigns of the previous century, with one-fifth of 280,000 slum homes already gone, 300,000 houses under construction and complete abolition within five years a real possibility.[1366] He had told the Commons on 19th December 1935 that 58,000 houses had been demolished in the five years since the 1930 Act compared to only 14,000 in the twelve years before that (since the Armistice).[1367] But by January 1936 Wood claimed slum clearance was proceeding at 80,000 houses per year[1368] - though this seems to have counted both the houses demolished and those built to replace them for in July that year Wood's figures were 21,125 slums demolished in the half-year

---

[1362] *Daily Express* 31st July 1935, KW19 436/3 carried a picture of Wood watching masked men fumigating the Collyhurst slums in Manchester as part of that clearance.

[1363] *Birmingham Gazette* 21st October 1935, KW20 2/3 reported his visit to Birmingham slum clearance and housing sites; as did KW20 13/2, with a picture of Wood talking to the residents under the heading 'Health Minister Visits Slums - for First-hand Information'.

[1364] *Times* 23rd October 1935, KW20 16/9

[1365] A point that Shakespeare also made (op cit, pp157-158).

[1366] CPA CRD 220/80 *'Politics in Review'*, vol. 2, opening article to quarter 3 pp3-7

[1367] Hansard 19th December 1935, vol. 307, col. 1948

[1368] Shakespeare recorded in his memoirs that 60,000 pa was achieved (op cit, p158).

to 31st March and 20,782 new homes built to replace them.[1369] Nevertheless, the programme was considerably faster than previously.

The Housing Act added a legal standard for overcrowding for the first time, required local authorities to survey overcrowding in their areas against this standard and set out a plan to tackle it. It was up to Wood to set the deadline ("appointed day") by which each local authority had to submit their plan to the Ministry. Wood required local authorities to have inspected working-class houses and ascertained overcrowding by 1st April 1936; to report to the Ministry the number of new houses to abate overcrowding by 1st June 1936; and to submit proposals for the provision of new houses by 1st August 1936. These were final dates so local authorities could get on faster than this if they were able.[1370] By 1st January 1937 fresh overcrowding would be an offence for about three-quarters of authorities.[1371]

Some local authorities responded more rapidly than others of course, with smaller authorities (particularly Urban District Councils and Rural District Councils) apprehensive that they did not have the expertise to meet this timetable. When the Conservative MP for Wallsend Irene Ward (1895-1950) asked Wood about this he requested further information for he doubted that 1st January 1937 was an unrealistic deadline for those authorities set it.[1372] Sixty-four local authorities out of 1536 failed to meet Wood's deadline of 1st June 1936 for reports on overcrowding, only 4% but embarrassingly including the Prime Minister's constituency of Bewdley. Even though "Time was extended [and the] number of defaulters dropped to a dozen, Bewdley's lips were still sealed," as the *Daily Express* put it. Overall, however, the newspaper accepted that the Ministry's report was "voluminous" and that Wood had the "satisfaction of finding that Woolwich has the lowest percentage of overcrowding in London".[1373]

[1369] CPA Pub 146/3 *The Elector* January 1935 - December 1938, January 1936, p2 and July 1936, p1
[1370] *Daily Herald*, 20th November 1935, KW20 33/13
[1371] CPA 12-page pamphlet (reprinted from '*Politics in Review*' April-June 1936) 'Our Social Services', August 1936; Hansard 16th July 1936, vol. 314, col. 2288 Wood said in Committee on Ministry of Health Supply that 1st January would be the "appointed day for bringing the overcrowding code into operation in this country" for most authorities.
[1372] Hansard 13th July 1936, vol. 314, cols. 1658-1659
[1373] *Daily Express* 31st July 1936, KW21 20/3

Wood described the overcrowding report as "a social document of the first importance" but it was also bound to be treated as a political one too, with both left and right finding facts to support their views. So, for example, the conservative *Morning Post* reported 'Overcrowding less than 4 per cent; Two Black Spots', with 470 families of 6-10 units occupying one room only.[1374] This was accurate but, as the *Daily Herald* pointed out, 3.8% equated to 341,554 overcrowded dwellings out of the 8.9m inspected.[1375] This in turn meant that well over a million people were affected, but the real sting in the tail came from the *Daily Mirror*, for babies had not been counted at all: "A child under ten is only half a person and a baby simply doesn't count" as it put it.[1376]

The overall report also concealed huge differences between authorities. Some 1200 had less than 2% overcrowding and it was these that had been given the target date of 1st January 1937. Among the 36 authorities set 1st April 1937 were West Ham with 5746 overcrowded dwellings (8.4%) and Berwick-on-Tweed with 630 (18.3%), while another 200 local authorities had yet to be given any date at all, including those where overcrowding was most severe.[1377]

Yet for all the reservations, and these included the least appetising aspects of local government bureaucracy with people trampled on to massage the figures,[1378] it would be difficult to disagree with the judgement that

> The session of Parliament which has just ended has discussed and passed measures such as the Education and Midwives Bills, the effects of which will be far-reaching, while

---

[1374] *Morning Post* 31st July 1936, KW21 22/14; An adult = 1 unit, child under 10 = ½ unit
Also, Burnett, op cit, p303
[1375] *Daily Herald* 31st July 1936, KW21 22/6
[1376] *Daily Mirror* 31st July 1936, KW21 23/8
[1377] *Manchester Guardian* 2nd October 1936, KW21 46/2; also *Municipal Journal and Public Works Engineer* 9th October 1936, KW21 66/1
[1378] For example, an open letter from 'Ben Blunt' to Wood, headed 'Muzzle the Meddlers', reporting the cranky ruses some local authorities were taking to reduce overcrowding, such as writing to a householder to say that his two oldest children had to sleep elsewhere (*NA* 21st November 1936, KW21 89/9).

a big step in the Government's war against slums has been the Ministry of Health's report on overcrowding.[1379]

Some did dispute this accolade though - for example, Attlee's 'Challenge to the Blunderers', (i.e., the Government at the start of a new session, with pictures of Simon, Inskip, Wood and Eden at the head of the article),[1380] or 'Baldwin's Bunglers', setting out what a Martian would think and naming Eden, Simon, Hore-Belisha, Ramsay MacDonald and Swinton specifically.[1381] Wood escaped lightly in the latter because of his lack of association with foreign policy as yet, but also perhaps because he had drawn attention previously to 15,000 basement babies in London (i.e., less than 10 years old) and 20,108 underground rooms,[1382] as well as to the role of housing in economic recovery and reducing unemployment.[1383]

It would not be long before some views of him might even be described as romantic, as the cartoon on the opposite page shows. Although real life rarely resembles a fairy tale, this should not be entirely surprising for, according to Shakespeare, over 270,000 new houses were built by local authorities by March 1939, enabling 1.3 million people to move "from their slum hovels and [be] re-housed in modern homes". Shakespeare illustrates this even more memorably by pointing out that, if 1.3 million people were to march past the Ministry of Health four abreast, it would take nine days for the columns to finally pass.[1384]

In December 1936 the *Times* reported a record number of houses completed in the year to 30th September, 339,500 or ten thousand more than the previous record.[1385] One recent author captured the mood of upheaval and renewal that this represented:

Indeed, it was a social revolution: between 1919 and 1937 twelve million people - almost 30% of the British population were re-housed. 'Removals on so large a scale involving so high a proportion of the population have never taken place

---

[1379] *Sunday Graphic and Sunday News* 2nd August 1936, KW21 23/1

[1380] *Daily Express* 30th October 1936, KW21 89/6

[1381] *Saturday Review* 31st October 1936, KW21 90/1

[1382] *News Chronicle* 10th February 1936, KW20 84/2

[1383] In his review of the Ministry of Health in the Committee on Supply. *The Architect and Building News* and *Municipal Journal* both 24th July 1936, KW21 12/3 & 4

[1384] Shakespeare, op cit, p159

[1385] *Times* 30th December 1936

before in the whole course of our history,' as [Wood], the Minister of Health remarked in 1937.[1386]

A CHANCE FOR CINDERELLA.
FIRST UGLY SISTER (to Second Ditto): "The minx! I suppose we'll lose her now!"

News of the World 17th January 1937, KW21 126/9
Wood as Prince Charming giving 'Housing and Health' slipper to 'Slum Dweller' Cinderella while the Ugly Sisters, 'Overcrowding' and 'Unhealthy Conditions', look on: "The minx! [one says]. I suppose we'll lose her now."

The *Times* report added that Wood had recently fixed 1st July 1937 as the appointed day for another 159 authorities to bring the overcrowding provisions into effect. These included ten London authorities, three in Wales (including Merthyr Tydfil) and eight major towns in England (from Birkenhead to Norwich and from Sunderland to Stoke-on-Trent). This left 59 authorities still to be set a date, including thirteen in London, ten county boroughs and twelve in Wales. In more than 96% of authorities, however, overcrowding would be tackled from January, April or July 1937, from which date "any new cases of overcrowding ... must be

---

[1386] Juliet Gardiner, 'The Thirties: An Intimate History', 2010, p272

reported to the local authority by either the occupier or the landlord".[1387]

Other advantages accrued to tenants, for example slum residents in Gildersome took advantage of the right to petition the Minister of Health for protection from slum landlords and an authority that still allowed "blocks of hovels ... condemned by public health authorities as unfit for habitation".[1388]   Or, conversely, in November 1936 when the residents of Portland Town (at the back of Lord's cricket ground in London), including seven churches and social organisations, considered petitioning Wood to avoid the area being re-developed. The residents argued that it was "a democratic oasis" in St John's Wood and some people who had already moved out to the LCC Becontree estate in Dagenham could not afford transport to continue their jobs.[1389]   By April 1937 they had 1836 signatures on a petition they then presented to Wood.[1390]

[1387] *Times* 30th December 1936

[1388] This right had existed for six years since the previous 1930 Housing Act but had been little publicised by local authorities. *John Bull* 12th September 1936, KW21 44/13

[1389] *Evening News* 21st November 1936, KW21 88/1
There are clearly parallels with re-development in Stockton and McGonigle's conclusions but also with housing benefit changes in London in the current century.

[1390] *Times* 29th April 1937, KW22 22/3

Vignettes

Edward VIII visit to South Wales and abdication

On 10th December 1936 the Speaker read to the Commons King Edward VIII's brief message announcing his "final and irrevocable decision … to renounce the throne" and expressing the hope that his brother the Duke of York would swiftly succeed him.[1391] The Prime Minister Stanley Baldwin then explained the recent chronology of events behind the King's decision, opening with the observation that

> No more grave message has ever been received by Parliament and no more difficult, I may almost say repugnant, task has ever been imposed upon a Prime Minister

and closing with "let us rally behind the new King".[1392] The House was then suspended for an hour and a half at the request of Attlee, the Leader of the Opposition, so that MPs might have time to come to terms with the announcement. When the House resumed, Attlee's formal speech and that of the Leader of the Liberals, Archibald Sinclair (1890-1970), were followed by a few others over the next fifty minutes, but in reality there was little that could meaningfully be said before the Abdication Bill was considered formally the following day.

It would not have been a surprise to the Cabinet, nor to MPs in the know or advising him, that the King was under pressure to decide between the throne and Mrs Simpson, but the timing of the denouement must have been a shock for many. Outside parliament, the press had been muzzled, or chose to muzzle itself in line with the standards of the time,[1393] so that the public had been kept in the dark until the last few days about the King's affair with the twice-divorced Mrs Simpson and the agonising dilemma he

---

[1391] Hansard 10th December 1936, vol. 318, cols. 2175-2176
Illustrated London News undated but December 1936, KW21 119/1: picture of Speaker reading Edward VIII's decision to abdicate.
[1392] Hansard 10th December 1936, vol. 318, cols. 2176-2186
Illustrated London News 12th December 1936, KW21 115/1: picture of Baldwin speech
[1393] Apart from the small circulation *Cavalcade*: Crowson, 1998, op cit, p175 - Brooks' diary entry for 22nd October 1936

faced. The *Daily Sketch* anticipated events on the day itself under the headline 'The King's Decision': the lobbies were buzzing that it would be abdication, but there was an overwhelming regret and "sadness that ... a man called to the highest destiny of this world is unable to fulfil that ..." because of a conflict with his private life.[1394] But it was very late to be still preparing, or at least softening up, the public, many of whom were predisposed to view any monarch sympathetically but in the case of Edward VIII had reasons to regard him affectionately. Not least, as the House of Windsor website puts it, were his

> ... regional visits (including [to] areas hit by economic depression) and other official engagements. These visits and his official tours overseas, together with his good war record and genuine care for the underprivileged, had made him popular.[1395]

Though the cartoonist David Low says that in reality this public affection was only "skin-deep" and "could be turned on and off ... according to an official steer".[1396]

Uppermost in the public mind, and of particular relevance to Wood's story, was the two-day visit Edward VIII had paid to the depressed areas of South Wales only three weeks earlier. The Ministers accompanying the King, or to put it another way his official minders, were the Minister of Labour Ernest Brown and Kingsley Wood. Their programme was:

18th November - Llantwit Major to Penrhiwceiber, including Merthyr Tydfil

19th November - Llantarnam to Rhymney, including Pontypool and Abertillery.[1397]

That this royal visit has remained in the memory eighty years later might be due to the evocative pictures that resulted,[1398] the contrast

---

[1394] *Daily Sketch* 10th December 1936, KW21 105/6 (a)

It was alongside this article that the paper carried 'Romances of the King's Advisers' KW21 105/6 (b) referred to earlier in Ch15.

[1395] House of Windsor part of www.royal.gov.uk

[1396] Low, op cit, p290

[1397] *Daily Express* 5th November 1936, KW21 80/4

[1398] Many of which are in the University of Kent archive, for example: KW21 97/1-14 and 98/1-7, especially *The Sphere* and *Illustrated London News* both 28th November 1936, 98/2 & 98/3 ; *Weekly Illustrated* 28th November 1936, KW21 100/1, with the cover showing the King and his two

between the opulence of the monarchy and the distressed areas through which the King progressed, or some of the views he expressed on being confronted by the horror in which many of his subjects lived. As Chips Channon recorded in his diary at the time, they were "two dreadfully sad days in the distressed areas".[1399] Later observers such as Alan Clark have concurred that it was depressing, which it was metaphorically as well as literally, though the overall programme had been designed to highlight some of the more positive initiatives as well: for example, a visit to the Land Settlement Society's co-operative farm for 70 miners at Boverton.[1400]

THE TRAGEDY OF A FORGOTTEN TOWN: 6,000 WORKED HERE—NOW 50 PULL IT DOWN

KW21 104/1 *Weekly Illustrated* undated
King Edward VIII visiting Dowlais

The King was said to have criticised the National Government for "'playing too much to the Opposition' as he put it",[1401] a sentiment that was at odds with the evidence confronting

---

Cabinet Ministers 'in the Distressed Areas'; *News Chronicle* 19th November 1936, KW21 101/1 including their Dowlais and Merthyr visits.
[1399] Robert Rhodes James (ed.), 1967, op cit, p80
[1400] Blakeway, op cit, p307
[1401] Robert Rhodes James (ed.), 1967, op cit, p80

him - not least when he visited the abandoned iron and steel works at Dowlais near Merthyr. But Collin Brooks' diary offers a different view for he noted the widespread attention paid to Edward VIII's "outspoken demand that 'Works [such as at Dowlais] brought these men here - something ought to be done to find them work'". Brooks thought this a sign that the King might "yet dominate the politicians".[1402] As the picture on the previous page shows, and the caption states, "the tragedy of a forgotten town" was all too apparent.

Baldwin had been aware several months earlier of the crisis that was brewing. His speech to the Commons identified October 1936 as the date at which he first became concerned at stories in the American press, meeting with the King on the 20th of that month to make him aware of the risks.[1403] Baldwin had been indisposed in August and September, having been told to rest for the sake of his health, yet as early as July he had instructed the Cabinet "to hold themselves in readiness for an emergency summons at short notice should circumstances arise" and had himself cancelled his annual holiday to Aix-les-Bains,[1404] a most singular and unusual step for a man accustomed to recuperating in the same place in France nearly every year. After the Hoare-Laval pact the previous December following Mussolini's invasion of Abyssinia, the German re-occupation of the Rhineland in March and the budget disclosure debacle of June and the resignation of JH Thomas, it might be expected that Baldwin would have every incentive to fulfil his long-planned intention to resign and to do so at the end of that parliamentary session.[1405] But this would be to misread Baldwin's motivation, that is to say an overwhelming sense of duty and public service, and to confuse his lethargic style and approach with apathy and self-interest. Aware of the country's vulnerability in the face of German aggression, a position to which he had partly

---

[1402] Crowson, 1998, op cit, p180 - Brooks diary entry for 18th November 1936

[1403] Hansard 10th December 1936, vol. 318, cols. 2177-2178

[1404] *Daily Mail* 30th July 1936, KW21 20/5

[1405] Some papers had expected Baldwin to remain in office until after Edward VIII's Coronation but had not thought this certain as he was clearly exhausted. E.g., *Liverpool Daily Post* 4th July 1936, KW21 1/2
Shay, op cit, pp86-87 asserts that it was the foreign policy threats, including the country's rearmament deficiencies, as well as his ill-health that led Baldwin to delay his resignation. It might be assumed, however, that these would be reasons to confirm it earlier than otherwise intended.

contributed,[1406] and of the constitutional crisis that was emerging, Baldwin may have judged it his duty, even from his sick-bed, to see matters through. Neville Chamberlain was the heir apparent, and indeed he had everyday control while Baldwin was ill, but it was the latter's skills that would be needed most by the country at this time.[1407]

Nor would Baldwin want to resign his third premiership at such a low point, not only because his enemies (Churchill, for example) would have characterised him as the rat leaving a sinking ship. Rather he would prefer to hand over the post to his successor when the country was in a more positive position. To cancel his Aix-les-Bains holiday Baldwin must have had more than an inkling of the King's predicament and the ferment it would throw the country into (over and above the foreign events that were of widespread concern in any case), even if at the time the British press did not. As it turned out, his astute and adroit handling of the abdication crisis was to prove exactly that, providing another illustration of the consummate one-nation skills he had shown previously during the General Strike and the 1931 financial crisis. As Shay put it, this enabled him to stand down on a high in June 1937. For Channon, Baldwin "was a master power-broker. King Edward, naïve and infatuated, was no match for this avuncular but ruthless politician".[1408]

Ten days before the King's decision was conveyed to the Commons the Crystal Palace had burnt down on 30th November and the fire was seen all over London. Originally built in Hyde Park to house the Great Exhibition of 1851 that Prince Albert had been instrumental in planning, the fire now appears symbolic of his great

---

[1406] Though much less than many historians allege.
It is sometimes said that Baldwin put party political advantage before rearmament, but the evidence is, to say the least, mixed. For example, Roskill, op cit, p89 asserts that Baldwin was not particularly perturbed at the time of the East Fulham by-election on 25th October 1933 won by Labour and that this was not the chief cause of slow re-armament in the 1930s. On the other hand, Baldwin had himself told the Commons in his "appalling frankness" speech of 12th November 1936 how he had not dared re-arm after the result of the East Fulham by-election without a fresh electoral mandate. Robert Rhodes James (ed.), 1967, op cit, p79
[1407] Chamberlain thought otherwise, misjudging his premier's ability to handle the crisis and hoping it would be an opportunity to replace him. Robert Rhodes James (ed.), 1967, op cit, p299
[1408] Shay, op cit, p87; Robert Rhodes James, 1967, op cit, p299

grandson's prospects as King even if it was not recognised as such at the time. For Collin Brooks it was the end of "that strange symbol of the Victorian assurance of peace and plenty."[1409] This too would soon be a potent image.

[1409] Crowson, 1998, op cit, p181 - Brooks' diary entry for 30th November 1936

Appeasement and fascism

As early as July 1934 Baldwin had felt it necessary to warn the Conservative Party that it should not be seduced by the supposed attractions of Fascism. Mussolini might have got the Italian trains to run on time, Hitler might be rejuvenating the German economy while the British one was still in the doldrums, and Conservative disillusion with the National Government might make the apparent return of German self-confidence superficially appealing, but below the surface lay threats to individual liberty that could destabilise Britain and western society as a whole. The rise of Communism was anathema to many and might prove even more threatening. One did not need to share Baldwin's religious beliefs to appreciate that fundamental values such as equality and tolerance, indeed the humanitarian philosophy itself, were at risk from totalitarian regimes.[1410]

But recognising this also gave rise to very real dilemmas less than twenty years after the First World War. Firstly, a belief in the League of Nations and its ability to conciliate in disputes between countries was rapidly waning,[1411] but secondly, the alternative to diplomacy was to forgo peaceful solutions and resort to 'might is right'. Most people of all political persuasions in the 1930s would do almost anything to avoid a repeat of the suffering and horrors of the First World War. Baldwin and Chamberlain were themselves illustrative of those who, having lived through it, consequently hated war and would try to avoid it at any cost - even if others judged their actions as unacceptable appeasement.[1412]

The dilemmas only became deeper as the impotence of the League of Nations increased and the totalitarian regimes imposed their will on their neighbours. Indicating the desire for peace, if not the means by which to sustain it, Reverend Dick Sheppard's Peace Pledge Union was established in May 1936 with more than 100,000 members initially, including celebrities as diverse as Aldous Huxley,

---

[1410] Philip Williamson, "Christian Conservatives and the totalitarian challenge 1933-1940", *English Historical Review*, 2000, vol. 115, pp607-642

[1411] CPA Pub 146/3 *The Elector* January 1935 - December 1938, June 1936, p1: Britain was still a loyal supporter of the League of Nations Baldwin said, but collective security depended on the USA joining and Germany and Japan being induced to re-join.

[1412] Blakeway, op cit, p173

Bertrand Russell, George Lansbury, AA Milne and Siegfried Sassoon.[1413]

Psychologists describe thorny dilemmas where two (or more) attitudes and behaviours are out of line or in conflict with another, as cognitive dissonance, the term Leon Festinger first coined more than fifty years ago.[1414] Extreme cases, where the dissonance and conflict is at its strongest, might precipitate a nervous breakdown for individuals or mental health problems. For nation states, if diplomacy does not resolve the equivalent political dissonance, countries either fail and are taken over or they fight back. The latter would be the least favoured option for those whose memory stretched back a generation, as those of many senior politicians did, and who were conscious that an air war would result in even greater slaughter and civilian misery.

The diagram on the following page[1415] attempts to distil the 'threads of political dissonance' that faced western politicians in the 1930s, threatened by a growing and increasingly active totalitarian menace, but whose experience and beliefs made them keen to preserve peace if they could. The dissonance revolves round the incompatibility between: religious faith (primarily but not exclusively Christianity, for other religions would take a similar view and pacifism would require it), attempts to secure peace through appeasement, though increasingly this became a goad rather than

---

[1413] Ibid, pp171 & 183

[1414] Leon Festinger, 'A Theory of Cognitive Dissonance', 1957

[1415] Some of the sources for the diagram are:

[1] Sumner Welles, 'The Time for Decision', 1944, p13

[2, 4] Brian Bond, 'Chief of Staff: The Diaries of Lt Gen Sir Henry Pownall 1933-1940', 1972, pp81 & 92

[6, 11] Philip Williamson, "Christian Conservatives and the totalitarian challenge 1933-1940", *English Historical Review*, 2000, vol. 115, pp 634 & 638

[7] Herbert Morrison, 'An Autobiography', 1940, p165

[8] Stafford Cripps p112 in Bertrand Russell, Vernon Bartlett, GDH Cole, Stafford Cripps, Herbert Morrison and Harold Laski, 'Dare We Look Ahead?', 1938

[9] CPA Pub 146/2 *Elector* July 1934

[10] Tom Stannage, 'Baldwin Thwarts the Opposition: The British General Election of 1935', 1980, p171

THE THREADS OF POLITICAL DISSONANCE IN THE 1930s

appeasement

- guilt over 1919 Versailles treaty and trampling over Germany
- little attempt to build up democratic mechanisms in Germany in the 1920s or support adequately the few that emerged [1]
- France intransigent yet "not run risk of war" [2]
- Germany re-occupied Rhineland March 1936
- Britain not ready for war in 1930s
- expectation of civilian slaughter in air war
- Hoare-Laval pact "a reward for proved aggressor" [4]
- Austrian/Czech "endorsement" of German ambitions (Anschluss, Sudetenland)
- belief in League of Nations abandoned after 1936 [6]
- non-intervention in Spain [7]
- Peace Ballot: 95% of 11.6m signatories for League of Nations; 91% for international disarmament

POTENTIAL POLITICAL DISSONANCE

Christianity

- **not** pacifism but memory of WWI carnage and anxiety to avoid repeat of total war
- ILP was pacifist as Ramsay MacDonald had been in WWI; PM to 1935 he favoured US while others in the National Government looked to Empire and/or the League of Nations

Political beliefs/values/attitudes

- for Conservatives this would include Communism greater threat than Fascism initially; compounded by Lloyd George warning in 1933 that if Nazism overthrown in Germany it would be replaced by Communism [8]; but Baldwin July 1934 warning to Conservatives [9]
- by November 1935 Baldwin condemning totalitarianism of both left and right [10]
- unemployment/economic depression/ inequality
- Special Areas
- economic planning (i.e., spiritual/moral as well as material re-armament)

rearmament

principle from 1934 → speeded up from 1938

how to pay for it?

risk/affordability ratio shifted by Kristallnacht pogrom, Prague occupation, Anschluss [11]

a barrier to Hitler;[1416] the risk of replacing Nazism with another form of totalitarianism in Communism and the implications of this in a depressed economy where many workers felt betrayed by the market economy and capitalist classes, and had lost all hope; and the financial consequences of rearmament in terms of the commercial exports on which the country depended. To put it crudely, though this was the Treasury line in the 1930s, "more money for guns meant less money for butter"; or, less crudely, reduced exports as labour and industry were re-directed and more imports of the raw materials required for armaments rather than for the well-being of the population. Removing appeasement would resolve the dissonance, for political ideology was more malleable and all religions could justify war in the final analysis (as they often had).

The dissonance is labelled 'potential' because some politicians with a maverick reputation who were not practising Christians (Churchill, for example)[1417] would find it easier to be anti-appeasement.[1418] This was especially true when they were relegated to the sidelines and had no direct or immediate responsibility for the well-being of other people. And, in Churchill's case of course, he had a long history of preferring fight to flight and a predisposition to belligerence regardless of the evidence. His alleged involvement in Tonypandy, as well as his actual record during Gallipoli and the General Strike, are just some of the better known. Like Lloyd George he was ultimately a victorious war leader, and like Lloyd George his legacy as a peacetime politician was much more mixed, but unlike Lloyd George, he also wrote the history.

Geoffrey Francis Fisher (1887-1972), archbishop of Canterbury, said of Churchill that

... he had a very real religion, but it was a religion of the Englishman. He had a very real belief in Providence; but it

---

[1416] JB Priestley judged in his Postscripts broadcast of 23rd June 1940 that "You might as well try to come to an amicable settlement with a pack of ravening wolves" as with the Nazis. JB Priestley 'Postscripts', 1940, p15
[1417] John D Fair, personal communications, 23rd to 28th April 2016 compares Churchill's spiritual beliefs to those of Harold Temperley for they had "basically disavowed Christian beliefs and practices but [their] attitudes and behaviour exhibited a strong residue effect". Williamson, 2000, op cit refers to Churchill's faith in a "Churchillian deity".
[1418] Williamson, 2000, op cit, pp607-642

was God as the God with a special care for the values of the British people. There was nothing obscure about this; it was utterly sincere, but not really at all linked on to the particular beliefs which constitute the Christian faith and the life which rests on it.[1419]

Contemporaries, including Conservative colleagues, had other reasons to suspect Churchill's motives too, for his disloyalty over India was fresh in their mind and he damaged his career by openly believing that Edward VIII should remain King and marry the woman he loved.[1420] Indeed, the prospect of Churchill forming a "King's Party" had prompted Baldwin to act, securing assurances from Attlee and Sinclair that they would not form an alternative government and "putting pressure on Churchill to do the same".[1421] Baldwin "did not trust Churchill for a moment [and] remained suspicious that he would challenge the government on the issues".[1422] An unusually abrasive Baldwin is supposed to have told Thomas Jones in May 1936:

> When Winston was born lots of fairies swooped down on his cradle gifts - imagination, eloquence, industry, ability, and then came a fairy who said 'No one person has a right to so many gifts', picked him up and gave him such a shake and twist that with all these gifts he was denied judgement and wisdom.[1423]

[1419] Edward Carpenter, 'Cantuar: The Archbishops in Their Office', 1971, p489, quoting in turn from William Purcell, 'Fisher of Lambeth: A Portrait from Life', 1969, p110
Many thanks to Peter Catterall, personal communication, 5th October 2016 for drawing this quotation to my attention.
[1420] Hansard 10th December 1936, vol. 318, cols. 2189-2191 when Churchill said "As I have been looking at this matter, as is well known, from an angle different from that of most hon. Members, I thought it my duty to place this fact also upon record.
"... I should have been ashamed if, in my independent and unofficial position, I had not cast about for every lawful means, even the most forlorn, to keep him on the Throne of his fathers ..."
[1421] Middlemas and Barnes, op cit, pp1002 & 1008, for example.
[1422] Blakeway, op cit, p315
Elsewhere, Blakeway claims that not only was Churchill an ally of the King (favouring a morganatic marriage and the 'Cornwall Plan'), but he saw it as an opportunity to replace Baldwin (p312).
[1423] Conversation 22nd May 1936, cited by Blakeway, op cit, p10

The *Spectator* reported in December 1936 that Churchill had "defeated himself by his own extravagance", his oratorical flourishes exceeding his grasp of the issues.

Another reason for labelling the dissonance 'potential' reflects the three-way distinction Crowson[1424] draws between those who practised appeasement because they were pacifists themselves, those who were attracted to the fascist and Nazi ideals, even regimes, and those who advocated it for strategic reasons to avoid bolshevism, the end of Empire or to delay war (if it could not be avoided altogether) while Britain built up its offensive and defensive resources. Examples of all types are not hard to find and some are identified in the above diagram. Not all of these groups would experience appeasement as anything other than consonant with their other beliefs and behaviours. But those who might find it dissonant would be those who believed in the supremacy of Britain and its Empire yet thought the fascist approach attractive if not superior. This could only be rationalised by putting the 'might is right' belief ahead of all other human and political considerations (including life and democracy). For example, the diarist Harold Nicolson records that "The feeling in the House is 'terribly pro-German', which means afraid of war."[1425] A few months later Nicolson could not conceal his disgust that his fellow MP Channon had fallen under the influence of Ribbentrop, their host at the Berlin Olympics.[1426]

This was the social and democratic context in which, on the one hand, Mosley's Blackshirts felt able to display their muscles, notably in the immigrant communities of the East End, and, on the other, the establishment that looked to Nancy Astor and her 'Cliveden set' could parade its totalitarian sympathies.

To give just one example of the Fascist agitation in October 1936 and the resulting public disorder, the *Daily Herald* reported that, at a Fascist meeting at Hampstead Town Hall, trouble started during a speech attacking the Jews by William Joyce, director of propaganda for the British Union of Fascists. When heckling did not stop him, hand-to-hand fighting broke out and the Fascists ejected ten men and two women protesters from the meeting. Later four

---

Also, *Spectator* 4th December 1936

[1424] NJ Crowson, 'Facing Fascism: The Conservative Party and the European Dictators 1935-1940', 1997, p3

[1425] Harold Nicolson, 'Diaries and Letters vol. I 1930-1939, 1966, p254 - 23rd March 1936

[1426] Ibid, p273 - 20th September 1936

people were arrested and charged (two with using insulting words and behaviour, one with assaulting a police officer, and another with obstructing a police officer).[1427] The reactions included a London Labour Party deputation to the Home Secretary John Simon, who said that the Government was giving the matter careful consideration but he was not yet in a position to anticipate the announcement.[1428] Simon's response was considered feeble for

> Conservatives, who have as strong a fear of the Fascist menace as have orthodox Labour members, think he should have taken responsibility for stopping the marches in the East End instead of leaving it to a police chief.[1429]

According to one newspaper, a decision on whether to ban Blackshirt demonstrations was a "most ticklish problem" for Baldwin, especially as he had always promised freedom of speech,[1430] while another argued, somewhat disingenuously, that the Government had two other pressing dilemmas to resolve as well.[1431] Wood responded more decisively in a speech at Greenwich, as the *Daily Herald* report acknowledged:

> Parliament will have to consider whether, in the interests of the country as a whole, it will permit the continuance of the disorder and disgraceful occasions which have taken place.

He concluded that, if they were to have democratic government in the country, it meant liberty not licence.

Nancy Astor hosted one of the key social and political salons of the time at her country house Cliveden in Buckinghamshire, and one of the attractions in the 1930s was its support for appeasement. The house is now a very expensive hotel, but unusually the inter-

---

[1427] *Daily Herald* 23rd October 1936, KW21 77/5
[1428] The deputation over disorder arising from Fascist marches in the East End included Harold Clay, Chairman, Herbert Morrison MP, Dr Mallon, Warden of Toynbee Hall and Dr Salter MP. Wood and Simon's PS were also present. *Times* 21st October 1936, KW21 69/2
[1429] *Sunday Mercury* 7th March 1937, KW22 14/1
[1430] *Cavalcade* 24th October 1936, KW21 74/3
[1431] *News Chronicle* 19th October 1936, KW21 79/3: The other two being a new Secretary of State for Scotland and "new speeding up of the re-armament programme".

war visitor books still exist.[1432]   Many famous people spent long weekends there, some more often than others. In the early years they included Neville Chamberlain, George Bernard Shaw, Brendan Bracken and others. Thomas Jones and Geoffrey Dawson, the editor of the *Times*, were frequent visitors, as were Halifax, John Buchan, Duff and Diana Cooper, and other grandees of the Conservative party. It was at Cliveden that Bob Boothby and Dorothy Macmillan continued their affair, for Harold Macmillan was rarely if ever there. There are also some unexpected names, such as the Russian ambassador Ivan Maisky, and the Labour politicians Wedgwood Benn and Ellen Wilkinson - the latter to work with Nancy Astor on women's rights, as her biographer Matt Perry has explained.[1433]

Although Lloyd George was there once (in February 1922), some people never were. Foremost among these were Baldwin, Churchill and Wood.[1434]   One can think of various social and political reasons why Baldwin and Churchill would not be invited or, if they were, would refuse. That Kingsley Wood was never there either appears to contradict the story often put around by others that this was one demonstration of his appeasement tendencies. According to Maisky, for example,

> In October, the 'Cliveden Set' proved especially lively and active. It is grouped around Lady Astor's salon and it has the *Times* and the *Observer* as its mouthpieces. ...
> Lady Astor's group has a powerful representation in Cabinet: the majority of the 'old men', including Hoare, Simon, Halifax, **Wood** [emphasis added], and Hailsham. Hoare plays the most active role amongst the 'Cliveden' ministers.
> ...
> The 'old men's' programme roughly boils down to the following ...[including] A deal with Germany and Italy [and] the Cliveden Conspiracy in which Hoare plays the leading

---

[1432] In the University of Reading Special Collections where all those between October 1919 and July 1941 were examined in March 2015.
[1433] Personal communication, 27th March 2015
[1434] Although Middlemas and Barnes, op cit, pp822 & 824 assert that Baldwin was at Cliveden at the start of June 1935 this is a mis-reading of Thomas Jones' diary.

role. Halifax and **Wood** [emphasis added] are active participants.[1435]

One of the attractions of studying the past is that it contains different sorts of evidence, often appearing to point in different directions. Maisky's is one sort, the Cliveden visitor books another. Both are first-hand (which is more than can be said for much of the internet or those writers who rely on repeating secondary sources), but one is based on hearsay only. Personally, I would have been delighted to uncover evidence that validated the prevailing view of Wood as an unthinking appeaser in the 1930s. His absence from the Cliveden visitor books does not prove otherwise, but they do suggest that the story was more complicated.

[1435] Gabriel Gorodetsky, 'The Maisky Diaries: Red Ambassador to the Court of St James 1932-1943', 2015, p93: 1st December 1937

Water and worse (Croydon typhoid outbreak)

Though science, sanitation and public hygiene had advanced a long way from the mid-nineteenth century, when cholera, dysentery, typhoid and other water-borne diseases were commonplace even in London, rural areas with intermittent water supply, often drawn from wells and rivers, were still prone to such calamities in the 1930s. However, it could happen in urban areas as well if treatment engineers were insufficiently trained or overworked and, in the case of the Croydon typhoid outbreak in autumn 1937, the main cause was the Borough Council's attempt to cut costs by cutting corners. Nine people died in the outbreak and Wood set up an inquiry to establish what had gone wrong and the lessons to be learned for public health and by local government, as he informed the House of Commons that November:

> ... [after] the two assessors [hold] an informal meeting this afternoon, ... I hope to be able to announce the date of the opening of the inquiry tomorrow or the next day. ... the time of the officers of the Croydon Corporation is at present very fully occupied with urgent executive duties in dealing with the outbreak, and I am sure it will be generally recognised that the performance of these duties must be a first call for the present. ... As I have already stated, all possible effective steps have been taken by the Corporation, acting in collaboration with officers of my Department, to safeguard the purity of the water supply, and I am glad to have this opportunity of giving an assurance that, on the advice available to me, the public need have no further fear of infection from that source. ... I have no doubt that members of the public will be given the fullest opportunity of tendering all relevant evidence that may be in their possession.[1436]

The inquiry reported the following February, uncovering how the fatalities and widespread sickness suffered by many people were due to bureaucratic bungle as much as human error, "an indictment not of a faulty system but of a total absence of system",

---

[1436] Hansard, 25th November 1937, vol. 329, cols. 1401-1402; *Daily Telegraph* and *Times* 26th November 1937, KW23 69/4 & 70/9
Also, Bill Luckin, 'Death and Survival in Urban Britain: Disease, Pollution and Environment, 1800-1950', 2015, p107

as a *Times* leading article described it.[1437] The newspaper reported the findings in detail the same day, including the questionable evidence Croydon Council had sometimes submitted in an attempt to mitigate the absence of proper controls and their lamentable performance. Water was an essential service that the public depended on and water quality was vital to health and well-being. Despite this, Croydon had attempted to get by without a water engineer of sufficient status and authority within the corporation. They were alone among London boroughs in this and Wood was equally alarmed, writing formally to Croydon admonishing them for the mistakes that had proved so costly to human life and health, and instructing them in the steps required to tackle the issues and recover public and Ministry confidence in the service.[1438]

Ellen Wilkinson was one of many MPs who had been appalled by the authority's cavalier approach. The consequences extended as far as a fifteen year-old Jarrow constituent who had been knocked down by a car in Croydon in October 1937 and taken to a local hospital. Demonstrating just how pervasive, dreadful and perhaps long-lasting the outbreak had been, even after the inquiry had started and any risk to public health had supposedly passed, she put Wood on the spot by pointing out that "[Her constituent] ... contracted typhoid while [at Mayday Hospital, Thornton Heath], [was then] transferred to the borough council hospital at Croydon, [and] died on 20th January, 1938." She asked whether this "transfer occurred during the typhoid inquiry?" In other words, after the infected water had been isolated or purified and any further risk of disease supposedly eliminated (as Wood had been advised and had told the Commons). Wood assured Wilkinson that "I have communicated with the town council on the matter and I will send ... the particulars I have received".[1439]

A few months later Wood became Minister of Air, and the Croydon typhoid inquiry seems not to have been considered formally in parliament, perhaps because of the timing, perhaps because of Wood's swift and comprehensive executive action, and perhaps because several residents would pursue claims against

---

[1437] Wood had received the report on 9th February 1938 and would publish it, as Robert Bernays (1902-1945) his recently appointed parliamentary secretary at the Ministry, told the Commons in a written answer. Hansard, 9th February 1938, vol. 331, cols. 1062-1063W
Times 15th February 1938
[1438] *Times* 25th February 1938 (also, KW23 147/10)
[1439] Hansard, 24th February 1938, vol. 332, col. 569W

Croydon through the High Court towards the end of 1938. The authority had been negligent, not just unfortunate, and the Commons may not have felt it necessary nor feasible to discuss the matter further.

The Croydon outbreak was unusual in that it took place in a relatively affluent area on the fringes of London. Such hazards were more common elsewhere in the country and not just in the north or distressed areas. Given that this occurred only eighty years ago, it is salutary to reflect how far the country has come in a relatively short time. Today we might worry about inadequate power supply to keep the lights on 24/7 or slow broadband speeds in rural areas. Eighty years ago some homes not only had no electricity at all but might still get their water from a well in the garden. If they wanted it hot, they had to boil it. Boiling water, often on an open fire, would in effect have to be continuous and was standard practice to be sure of avoiding infection as well. It was not only for reasons of cost and temperance that tea had come to replace beer as the drink of choice.

One illustration of the different expectations and standards that then applied are apparent from a particularly chilling report from Kent at the start of 1938 when a man's body was still stuck in the well at his house a month after he had fallen to his death there. Kent County Council and Swale District Council had been arguing most of that time about which of them was responsible for getting the body out, for neither authority had the power to spend money in such circumstances and were each trying to shuffle the costs on to the other. Fortunately, if perhaps belatedly, Kingsley Wood intervened as Minister of Health, making it clear to both authorities that he would permit either to spend as much as was required as long as it happened urgently as a matter of public decency.[1440]

[1440] *East Kent Gazette* 15th January 1938, KW23 120/1

17.   MINISTER OF AIR 1938-1940

I can put a girdle round the earth in an aeroplane, and tomorrow the aeroplanes may destroy London, Paris, Berlin, Vienna, bringing our world down in flames.[1441]

Storm Jameson

In March 1939 Churchill was still in the political shadows, if no longer in the Conservative party wilderness that he had occupied for much of the 1930s, but he had yet to be re-instated in the Government until Chamberlain re-appointed him to the Admiralty in September 1939. Yet he and Wood had already established a working relationship of sorts, one that largely involved accusation and rebuttal as Churchill criticised Britain's lack of preparedness for war and Wood responded as any Minister would. On 14th March 1939, for example, Churchill had his private secretary draw Wood's attention[1442] to an article on "Hitler's aerial triumph" in *Readers Digest.*[1443] Churchill's anxiety was that, though some of the claims in the article were clearly exaggerated, there was enough in it to disquiet him and he thought Wood should also be aware. Many of the figures cited in the article are indeed wildly misleading but are also indicative of the defeatist expectations at the time, particularly in America where the forecast for Europe's future was grim. The article claimed that "Hitler was not bluffing at Munich. He had irresistible power", and that Germany was building 1000 planes per month, five times the British rate and nearly fourteen times the French one. "The disparity steadily grows greater" it asserted, adding that this was the case for factories and pilots as well. In other words, "Germany, supreme in the air, is supreme over Europe".[1444]

Wood's private secretary replied later that month, thanking Churchill for forwarding the article and informing him that he would

---

[1441] In chapter "The defence of freedom", p154 in 'Civil Journey', 1939
[1442] Churchill College archives, Churchill Papers, CHAR 2/371 A-B, Public and Political: General: Defence, 6th November 1936 to 20th January 1942, item 2
[1443] Marc A Rose, *Readers Digest*, vol. 4, no. 203, March 1939, pp6-10 condensed from his original in 'The Forum', a US publication.
[1444] Ibid, pp6, 7 & 10

be bringing it to Wood's attention.[1445] If he did so, there is no record of Wood's response. Possibly Wood was disappointed that his meeting with Churchill at the Ministry of Air a month earlier, when Wood and his colleagues had taken Churchill through the production graphs[1446] had had only a limited impact on his appreciation of the position. This was not the first time that Churchill had been ready to believe German propaganda, putting unwarranted, and ultimately unhelpful, pressure on his party chiefs who had to spend time clarifying the position rather than dealing with other matters. In June 1938, for example, only a month after Wood became Minister of Air, Churchill had admonished him about the lack of progress on air defence.[1447]

This frequent contact, building on their long-standing connections in the Party (and, of course, Professor Lindemann's advice), may have helped their relationship to blossom. And while Wood must have found Churchill suspect on figures, he would have been one of the first to agree with him on the implications for morale. In the long run this would be as significant as numerical superiority.

There had been press speculation that when Baldwin relinquished the premiership in favour of Neville Chamberlain, and John Simon was promoted in turn to the post of Chancellor, it would be Wood who stepped up as Home Secretary. However, the newspapers hedged their bets by acknowledging that this was not certain and in the event the most significant promotion was Hoare's when it was he who became Home Secretary. Hoare had begun his recovery at the Admiralty under Baldwin after the craven pact

---

[1445] Churchill College archives, Churchill Papers, CHAR 2/371 A-B, Public and Political: General: Defence, 6th November 1936 to 20th January 1942, item 33

[1446] Ibid, items 25 & 26 ahead of their meeting on 9th February 1939. Wood had asked Air Marshal Sir Wilfrid Freeman (1888-1953), responsible since 1937 for Production and by 1938 Air Member for Development and Production, to be available, as well as his PPS (also known to Churchill). Shortly after Wood's death, Freeman recalled appreciatively that Wood had left him alone to get on with the job. In Sebastian Richie, 'Industry and Air Power: The Expansion of British Aircraft Production', 1997, p51 Freeman's section became Beaverbrook's Ministry of Aircraft Production after May 1940, with Freeman attempting to resign from it twice, eventually returning to the Air Ministry in November 1940.

[1447] Roskill, op cit, p325 - see Appendix: 1930s Chronologies, June 1938 rearmament item

with Laval that capped the Abyssinian debacle in December 1935 and the resulting public outrage had forced his resignation as Foreign Secretary. His return to one of the most senior posts in the Government represented in effect his total rehabilitation and, with Swinton remaining at Air, Wood continued at Health for another year until May 1938.[1448] Hoare's replacement at the Admiralty was Duff Cooper, with Hore-Belisha moving to War in his stead, thereby benefitting from the high profile he had generated at Transport and, initially at least, cementing his carefully garnered reputation as the man to watch. Not everybody was taken in though, for Patrick Gower had commented as early as January 1935 that Wood and Hore-Belisha were

> The only two [in the Government] with any sense of the theatre about 'em [but while] Wood boosts his Department and is content with the reflected glory, young Belisha boosts himself [and] that's a mistake.[1449]

Eden remained as Foreign Secretary and Inskip continued as the Minister responsible for co-ordinating defence.

Chamberlain may have thought that, by promoting Simon and rehabilitating Hoare, he was signalling that it was he, not the Party or the public, who had the strongest will and the final say in such matters.[1450] On the other hand, he may just have been demonstrating the insensitivity to others' views for which he was already well-known.[1451] One Conservative backbencher, Ronald Cartland (1907-1940), is supposed to have said that

---

[1448] There was even uncertainty that Simon would be appointed Chancellor when his mishandling of the Fascist marches had resulted in many Conservative MPs lambasting his feeble conduct. *Sunday Mercury* 7th March 1937, KW22 14/1

[1449] Crowson, 1998, op cit, p71 - Brooks diary entry for 6th January 1935

[1450] Paul Addison, 'The Road to 1945: British Politics and the Second World War', 1994 (orig. 1975), pp61-62

[1451] Robert Rhodes James (ed.), 1967, op cit, p175 reports Channon contrasting an "affectionate and sensitive" Chamberlain in private life with his "aloof, arrogant, obstinate and limited" public persona. Channon thought he should have remained a "first-class municipal administrator", a similar jibe to the one had Churchill had levelled at Chamberlain ten years earlier.

... they now had a Fuhrer in the Conservative Party. The Prime Minister was getting more and more dictatorial. It was astonishing how the bulk of the Party followed him blindly.[1452]

What Chamberlain was doing though, almost certainly deliberately, with the sideways move of Duff Cooper, the continuation of Eden, Inskip and Swinton in their posts, and even more so with the Simon and Hoare appointments, was sending to Hitler and Mussolini a signal that British policy would remain reactive and unthreatening. More of the same in other words for, even if the overall competence of the Cabinet had been increased, this was administrative rather than strategic capacity. Britain would respond if necessary and if provoked, but the Government's over-riding priority would be to preserve a peaceful status quo. In effect, it was the Treasury view that held sway: economic recovery should not be imperilled by over-hasty rearmament for this was not sound policy, either financially or politically.

British Rearmament in the 1930s

The Appendix sets out the 1930s Chronologies in terms of economic and political events in Britain, events abroad and the significant steps that resulted in rearmament overall and for the RAF specifically. Some might arrange the Appendix in this order, but for the purposes of Wood's story it is the RAF schemes that are most significant and the table is therefore organised in reverse (as it were). It should also be pointed out that, though there are relatively few entries in the economic events column, this does not mean that this was an insignificant part of British thinking. On the contrary, what it demonstrates above all else is that the Treasury were set on a course in 1931, when Chamberlain first became Chancellor of the Exchequer in the National Government, from which they deviated only when the evidence became overwhelming that national defence was more important than trade. Interestingly, and perhaps counter-intuitively, it was the Austrian Anschluss in March 1938, not Munich six months later, that forced the normal trade principle to be revoked. This had been instituted two years earlier as a brake to discourage rearmament at the expense of trade. But it had been

---

[1452] Ben Pimlott (ed.), 'The Political Diary of Hugh Dalton 1918-1940, 1945-1960', 1986, p225 - 7th April 1938

the Government's stance in effect since March 1932, when Hitler's rise was apparent even before he took power and Japan had invaded Manchuria. It was at this point that the international situation was sufficiently alarming for the automatic roll forward of the Ten Year rule[1453] to be revoked.[1454] As Peden points out,[1455] rearmament was insurance against the risk of war; but the pace and scale of rearmament would be self-defeating if it antagonised or provoked, turning potential opponents into actual ones, and in peacetime it was the Government's responsibility, and arguably the Treasury's duty, to balance affordability against the likelihood of war in deciding spend. Too much would be a problem for trade, too little perhaps the last problem an independent country would have. But, in "... revoking the [Ten Year] rule the Cabinet acknowledged the worsening of the world situation without making a commitment to deal with it", as Shay puts it. Chamberlain's view had prevailed at Cabinet that finance should come first, with rearmament subordinate to affordability - in other words, "The services had won the right to plan, but not to spend".[1456] This framed the Cabinet's thinking and set the tone for their debate over the next five years. It was soon reinforced by Lloyd George's warning that if Nazism was overthrown in Germany it would be replaced by Communism,[1457] the outcome that many Conservatives feared most and as it resonated with them emotionally they were hardly likely to challenge intellectually.[1458]

[1453] In other words, the country could plan on the basis that it would not have to fight a major war in the next ten years. This had seemed sensible when the Ten Year rule was first adopted as a one-off in the early 1920s for faith in the diplomatic sway of the League of Nations was then absolute and the countries defeated in the First World War represented no threat. When Chancellor in the late 1920s, Churchill had persuaded the Government to adopt an annual automatic roll-forward of the principle. Middlemas and Barnes, op cit, p760 describe Churchill's insistence in 1928 that it be "reinforced and put on the sliding scale".

[1454] It was at this point too (according to RJ Minney, 'The Private Papers of Hore-Belisha', 1960, p155) that the Government finally recognised that they might have to equip an Army large enough to send to the Continent.

[1455] George Peden, 'British Re-armament and the Treasury:1932-1939', 1979, p64

[1456] Robert Paul Shay, 'British Re-armament in the Thirties', 1977, pp24 & 27

[1457] Cripps, op cit, p112

[1458] This was the time of the show trials in the Soviet Union so it should be clear that, had they been known about in the west, Stalin was not doing

Two years later in March 1934 the Cabinet considered the results of this service planning when the report of the Defence Requirements Committee (DRC) came before them.[1459]   It was subsequently remitted to the Ministerial Disarmament Committee in May, chaired by Simon as both MacDonald and Baldwin were attending the Parliamentary Privileges Committee that Churchill had sought in his campaign against the India Bill.[1460]   Subsequently, Hankey (the author of the DRC report) visited the Dominions of South Africa, Australia, New Zealand and Canada that summer to advise them on British rearmament and encourage them to spend more on defence, but he received a mixed reception with the Canadians least interested in collective security, not least because it might have "unforeseen and awkward consequences", both globally and for them as neighbours of an isolationist USA.[1461]   The Government was conscious of the risks and, as Ramsay MacDonald explained to the Commons as a way of deflecting a question about the implications and outcome of Hankey's trip, Hankey had travelled clandestinely, supposedly for personal reasons to South Africa on his way to Australia and New Zealand at their invitation, and then returned by way of Canada to complete a round-the-world holiday.[1462]   This mixed reception in the Empire was echoed at the top of the British government by the differences between the line that Chamberlain and the Treasury followed, Baldwin's anxiety about the electoral impact of rearmament and MacDonald's increasing ill-health, which even had he been fully fit would have been compounded by his preference for the American view.

It was perhaps foreseeable, therefore, that the steps towards British rearmament taken during the remainder of 1934 (as the Appendix shows) should be both modest and tentative, but they were at least a start. Shadow factories were established that could be turned over to manufacture technical goods and equipment once

---

Communism's reputation any good. But the establishment was animated by an instinctive dislike anyway.

[1459] Roskill, op cit, p107

[1460] Churchill had accused Hoare of a breach of Parliamentary privilege, an accusation rejected as unfounded by the Commons in June. See Roskill, op cit, p107 fn3 for further detail; also, Middlemas and Barnes, op cit, p711.

[1461] Roskill, op cit, pp122 & 137

[1462] Hansard, 13th November 1934, vol. 293, col. 1763

war broke out.[1463] Initiated by Lord Weir, they became reality in 1935 when the scare took hold that the Germans had already attained air parity. In June Baldwin suggested a defence loan, a proposal Chamberlain then opposed, arguing it was unfair that succeeding generations should repay the debts of previous ones.[1464] In July Baldwin pointed out that defence now started at the Rhine not Dover,[1465] but as Pownall noted in his diary, the Chancellor of the Exchequer continued to be "strangely obtuse in strategical questions, even ignorant".[1466] Such was Chamberlain's short-sighted parsimony in Pownall's view that he automatically took against building more battleships because of the expense, whereas America conceived of them as a way of relieving unemployment.

The economy or defence choice re-surfaced at the Committee for Imperial Defence (CID) in November 1934 when the Prime Minister was quite explicit about the horns of the dilemma on which the Government felt itself impaled: a return to prosperity and a healthy economy or more spending on sufficient defence, which in the final analysis might not be needed and in the meantime would have interfered with, even prevented, the economic objective. Shay describes the Government trying to have the best of both worlds by "seeking to create the image of power without investing in its more costly substance".[1467] In March 1935 a Defence White Paper was issued, arguing that rearmament was necessary in view of the deteriorating world situation and especially the failure of the disarmament conference at Geneva, but it was watered down by the Cabinet in case it affronted Germany - which it did anyway.

Baldwin and MacDonald swapped places in June, Baldwin now Prime Minister for the third time (in name no longer just in

---

[1463] Shay, op cit, pp93-94
Roskill, op cit, pp195-196 adds that they were built and run by Rootes, Humber, Daimler, Standard and Austin. By October 1937 they were operating at full capacity whereas a year earlier the sites had been green fields.
[1464] Shay, op cit, p42
This statement was repeated verbatim by the Cameron Conservative government to justify austerity. By March 1937, when he introduced the Defence Loans Act, even Chamberlain had realised the position was no longer sustainable. Without the loan there might be no future generation to worry about.
[1465] Hansard, 30th July 1934, vol. 292, col. 2339
[1466] Bond, op cit, pp49-50 - Pownall diary entry for 20th July 1934
[1467] Shay, op cit, p46

effect), but the Government's constrained and conflicted approach to rearmament continued for the remainder of 1935.[1468] Italy's attack on Abyssinia in October provided an opportunity to change direction, and indeed Ernest Bevin did implore the Labour conference to support sanctions against Italy. When the Labour leader Lansbury dissented, Bevin precipitated his resignation by accusing him of "hawking [his] conscience round from body to body asking to be told what to do with it". Lansbury was replaced by Attlee, who in turn was expected to be leader only temporarily, but the obvious alternative Arthur Henderson died two weeks later, Baldwin called an election for 14th November and such was the mutual antipathy between Bevin and Morrison that neither would challenge Attlee for fear that the other might replace him.[1469]

A neutered and toothless League of Nations was in no position to impose sanctions and the Government chose the politically expedient option of deferring the decision until after the election.

Three days before the November election, and exactly seventeen years after the Armistice that ended the First World War, the Cabinet did consider what was termed the 'Ideal Scheme' of rearmament. Over and above an annual defence spend of £124m, this would have expanded both air reserves and the navy but would have cost a further £418m in the four years to 1940. Once again political and economic issues prevailed over national security, with "ideal" being judged unaffordable and therefore unrealistic.[1470] But nor did the Government want rearmament to be a major issue at the election for, even if one in ten people were still unemployed, the message was that the National Government had rescued the country from the worst of the depression and the prospect of prosperity now beckoned. Rearmament would threaten this.

Although the Conservatives lost 70 seats at the election, they were still the largest party by some distance with 387 seats. Labour had increased its MPs by nearly 100 from 59 to 154, but were still confronted by a National Government that could count on

---

[1468] Londonderry announced Air expansion scheme C in May and was replaced by Cunliffe-Lister a fortnight later, with anxieties soon surfacing in the Commons that this might generate excess profits for the manufacturers. Addison was particularly scathing given his experience at Munitions in the First World War. Shay, op cit, pp53, 105-109
[1469] Morrison, op cit, pp160-162
[1470] Shay, op cit, p56

at least 428 votes.[1471] Shortly after the election it became apparent that the Foreign Secretary Hoare had agreed with his French counterpart Laval that sanctions would not be imposed on Italy over Abyssinia and, when this became public knowledge and the outcry mounted, a tacitly complicit Government disowned him in order to preserve themselves, claiming that he had taken this step on his own initiative. Hoare had to resign.

The Government began to build up rearmament reserves from early 1936 so that, should war break out, there was a margin to tide the country over while industry geared up for full war production. But the Cabinet was clear that this was not to impede civil or export trade,[1472] nor restrict social services,[1473] and, as Peden points out, this rule applied from the February 1936 Cabinet until it was revoked in March 1938.[1474] When Germany re-occupied the Rhineland in March 1936, the point at which many agree firm action might have deterred Hitler,[1475] France and Britain did nothing. It did prompt Baldwin to stress in the Commons the following day (in a debate he had instigated on the Government's defence proposals) the need for industry and Government to co-operate,[1476] but the appointment of Thomas Inskip as Minister for the Co-ordination of Defence was a signal that a full-blown Ministry of Defence was not thought necessary[1477] - and avoided appointing Churchill, who had wanted the post but whose opposition over India had put him beyond the pale.[1478] The impact of rearmament on the April budget was clear, Chamberlain increasing income tax by 3d and some other indirect taxes also rising (for example, tea by 2d), with the RAF the priority given public anxiety over bombing and the potential for a "knock-out blow".[1479] It was his disclosure of this budget that forced JH Thomas to resign, but of more significance was Labour's

---

[1471] Including 33 Liberal National and 8 National Labour

[1472] Shay, op cit, p99

[1473] Peden, op cit, p89

[1474] Ibid, p153

[1475] Bond, op cit, p95
This breached both the Versailles and Locarno treaties, and Hitler's generals had sought to dissuade him from this provocation.

[1476] Hansard, 9th March 1936, vol. 309, cols. 1827-1841; Shay, op cit, p98

[1477] Shay, op cit, p73

[1478] Roskill, op cit, p207

[1479] Shay, op cit, pp78-79, 90
The RAF was to receive an additional £10m and the Navy and Army £10m between them.

dispute as to whether an additional £20m on top of the existing £34m spend on rearmament was necessary, while so little was spent on the distressed areas.[1480]

Air defence, particularly anti-aircraft guns, was the Defence Policy and Requirements Committee (DPRC, a sub-committee of CID) priority by November 1936 and a balance of payments deficit became apparent in December as trade was diverted away from export markets.[1481] The Treasury had rationed defence services spend to £1500m in 1937 as war was not yet certain and in the hope that some rearmament would assist diplomacy to prevail without weakening the economy. Yet already the impact on "normal" trade was starting to become evident.

The Spanish Civil War was the next opportunity for decisive intervention but the French and British governments dared not do so in case it angered "the insurgents and their Axis allies".[1482] In addition to the Defence Loans Act in March 1937,[1483] Chamberlain's budget introduced a National Defence Contributions tax on the increase in profits above £2000 made by businesses.[1484] Initially, the tax was to be graduated and calculated against the return on capital, but this was seen as too socialist, penalising success in effect, and following Conservative opposition in the budget debate on 27th April,[1485] Chamberlain as Prime Minister dropped it on 1st June in favour of "a simpler tax upon the profits of industry ... to produce not less than £25m".[1486] It was reintroduced as a 5% tax on profits.[1487]

In February 1938, the month before the Anschluss, Inskip produced his second report. Between this and September 1939, as the situation deteriorated and war became more likely, the perspective changed from the Treasury's "re-armament being rationed by finance" to the Cabinet view that "financial policy [should be] reviewed in light of the needs of rearmament".[1488] When

---

[1480] Hansard, 21st, 22nd and 23rd April 1936, vol. 311, cols. 60, 159, 322ff

[1481] Peden, op cit, pp126-127, 80

[1482] Morrison, op cit, p165

[1483] The third reading was passed on 4th March by 241 votes to 117, the Lords did not amend it and it was added to the statute book on 19th March 1937. Hansard, vol. 321, cols. 561-684, 2269, 2468

[1484] Hansard, 20th April 1937, vol. 322, cols. 1616-1620

[1485] Hansard, 27th April 1937, vol. 323, cols. 178, 235-303

[1486] Hansard, 1st June 1937, vol. 324, col. 927

[1487] Peden, op cit, p87; Shay, op cit, pp147-156

[1488] Ibid, p92

Britain's ambassador to Berlin Nevile Henderson met Hitler on 3rd March 1938 it became clear that Hitler was uncompromising about "getting into the German fold the German minorities [in Europe] outside Germany".[1489]   Hitler was prepared to leave aside Germany's wish to recover the non-European colonies it had lost at Versailles, but this determination within Europe would provide the overarching justification - and cover - for his actions in Austria and Czechoslovakia.   The British Cabinet asked industry to make rearmament the priority,[1490] agreeing the RAF requirements (Scheme L) that April.   Pownall was exasperated about this, recording that the Cabinet gave Swinton whatever he asked for, even more than their allocation, while the Army and Navy were cut further.[1491] Inskip had supported Air rather than the Treasury and eventually Chamberlain and the Cabinet agreed that the country ought to buy up everything the aircraft industry could produce over the next couple of years so as to negotiate from a position of strength.   According to Shay, Chamberlain had realised that the Treasury limit was not absolute and adhering to it might prove more dangerous than exceeding it.[1492]

At Cabinet at the start of July 1939 Wood asked the Treasury's Richard Hopkins (1880-1955), then Second Secretary, whether Britain's finances were "still sufficiently sound to permit her to conduct a war". Hopkins said that they were at that moment but were becoming weaker every day.   Perhaps therefore, as Shay suggests, the optimum moment for declaring war came with the fall of Poland when decreasing financial strength and increasing rearmament were relatively balanced.   That is to say, the country did not dare see its reserves further depleted as the economic damage would not be offset by further rearmament. In other words, the risk/reward ratio had then tilted sufficiently to trigger the declaration that came on 3rd September.[1493]

Expansion of the RAF

As the Appendix shows, and the biographer of Air Marshal 'Peter' Portal (1893-1971) put it,

---

[1489] Bond, op cit, p137 - Pownall diary entry for 7th March 1938
[1490] National Archives Cab 23/93: Cabinet minutes p73; Peden, op cit, p93
[1491] Bond, op cit, p141 - Pownall diary entry for 4th April 1938
[1492] Shay, op cit, pp212 & 216
[1493] Ibid, p280

> Between mid-1934 and October 1938 [RAF] Expansion
> Scheme succeeded Expansion Scheme with bewildering
> rapidity - thirteen in all ... and one scheme was never
> anything like fully implemented before another was
> concocted ...[1494]

Furthermore, despite Chamberlain's assertion at Cabinet in June
1934 that "defence of these islands" was the overwhelming priority
for the next five years,[1495] until Wood became Air Minister in May
1938 expansion schemes had emphasised the offensive role of
bombers. This was as true of the first, as it would be of later ones,
for Scheme A in July 1934 had proposed 43 bomber to 28 fighter
squadrons (which, added to overseas numbers, amounted to 1252
aircraft in total in 111 squadrons).[1496] It would be another four years
before Wood persuaded the Cabinet to adopt Scheme M in October
1938, re-aligning the ratio of fighters to bombers, in other words of
defence to offence. Arguably, had this not happened, the Battle of
Britain might not have been won at all and had the German
bombing attacks not been deterred, the war in Europe might have
been concluded before the end of 1940 to Britain's detriment. After
the fall of France and the evacuation of the BEF from Dunkirk,
Britain did indeed stand alone and the threat of invasion by the
Germans was a very real prospect that summer.

But Wood's predecessor Swinton[1497] had taken one difficult
decision in 1935 that was to prove of huge significance, sticking to it
in the face of substantial opposition. Industry was then struggling to
keep up with even the limited expansion the Air Ministry required
and one way of narrowing the gap was to build more old-fashioned
and obsolescent aircraft types that would make the numbers look
better in the short-term even if they proved hopeless in battle.
Fortunately, Swinton held to a preference for quality over quantity,

---

[1494] Denis Richards, 'Portal of Hungerford', 1977
Air Marshal Sir Charles Portal, known as 'Peter', was a close colleague of
Wood and a regular visitor to Ickworth House near Bury St Edmunds. The
Visitors book for the latter was examined in October 2015.
John Slessor, 'The Central Blue: Recollections and Reflections', 1956
includes on p185 a summary of the expansion schemes.
[1495] Shay, op cit, p91 who cites the Cabinet record Cab. 16/111, DCM(32),
120.
[1496] Basil Collier, op cit, p28
[1497] Who as Philip Cunliffe-Lister replaced Londonderry at Air in May 1935;
he became Lord Swinton that November.

even though this was unpopular with both manufacturers and the electorate.[1498] The former were more concerned with their balance sheets while the public would only be placated by a larger number of planes.[1499] But as well as the delay in deliveries that Swinton's insistence on more modern types inevitably caused, the manufacturers also griped that the Air Ministry demanded minor modifications while planes were being built, delaying deliveries further. In the end Swinton resigned in the face of criticism in Parliament and the press,[1500] though Chamberlain may have been close to sacking him anyway after Labour had castigated the Air Ministry in a debate in Parliament. Swinton's colleague Lord Weir resigned in protest at what in effect was a "dismissal".[1501] Three days after this, on 17th May, Wood became Air Minister.

[1498] That this decision took some time to work through is shown by reports in May 1938 of RAF mass formation flights over all parts of the country, including London. The *Daily Sketch* illustrated their report with a picture of Harrow bombers (24th May 1938, KW23 207/1). The Bomber Command website explains that "A total of 100 Harrows were built (all in 1937) and they served with ... Bomber Squadrons between January 1937 and December 1939". "An interim, expansion-period bomber" the Harrow had been transferred to transport duties by the start of the war.
www.raf.mod.uk/history/bombercommandheavybombersavroaldershot.cfm

[1499] Peden, op cit, p154

[1500] Ibid, p155
When Churchill challenged Wood at the War Cabinet on 12th January 1940 as to whether the RAF had overhauled the Germans as promised with regard to the number of planes, Wood replied on the 15th that quality was more important and by concentrating on numbers the Germans might have sacrificed this. Martin Gilbert, 'Winston Churchill - vol. 6: Finest Hour 1939-1941', 1983, pp131, 134-135
Also, John Ferris, "Catching the wave: The RAF pursues a RMA 1918-1939", pp159-178: "as the Air Minister, Kingsley Wood, said in 1939, massive and rapid expansion from a small base had made the Luftwaffe larger than the RAF but also 'likely to show the defects of its rapid growth when a heavy strain was put upon it'" (p173) (in Talbot C Imlay and Monica Duffy Toft (eds.), 'Fog of Peace and War Planning: Military and Strategic Planning Under Uncertainty', 2006).

[1501] Shay, op cit, pp218 & 219; 12th May debate in Parliament after Anschluss and the start of the Czechoslovakian crisis.
According to Cecil King's diary, Dowding told him that it was Nuffield and Kingsley Wood who ousted Swinton. In Cecil H King (ed. William Armstrong), 'With Malice Toward None', 1970, p223 - 15th June 1943 diary entry.

Wood, though knowing nothing about airplanes, turned out to be a quick learner and an excellent administrator. He set about re-organising the production of aircraft, combining firms into a number of 'production' groups and limiting the types of aircraft in production. Wood's efforts would be seen in the mounting production figures in the spring of 1939.[1502]

In the early 1930s Swinton's star had been as high as Wood's in the Conservative firmament, indeed as Philip Cunliffe-Lister he had been one of four Conservatives in the August 1931 National Government Cabinet (along with Baldwin, Chamberlain and Hoare), but those days had gone. It was now Wood, Chamberlain's "tried and trusted colleague" as Shay describes him,[1503] who was tasked to speed up production and restore public confidence, a job that would have been more difficult for Swinton in the Lords. Donald Banks, Wood's colleague from the Post Office, advised him that the quickest way to do this was for Lord Nuffield to build fighters.[1504] Wood took his advice and persuaded Nuffield to build a shadow factory at Birmingham,[1505] demanding more funds from the Treasury as a consequence.[1506] That Wood persuaded Nuffield was even more remarkable for "From the day in 1936 when Lord Nuffield ... left Lord Swinton with the parting 'God help you in

---

[1502] Zara Steiner, 'The Triumph of the Dark: European International History 1933-1939', 2011, p606

In the first six months of 1939 3753 aircraft were produced compared to 1045 in the same period in 1938, more than three times as many. Steiner, op cit, p699

[1503] Shay, op cit, p221

[1504] Banks, op cit, p7; another contemporary Philip Gibbs, 'Ordeal in England', p150 came to the same conclusion, though the historian Robert Rhodes James, op cit, p178 judged that "Chamberlain had got rid of the energetic Secretary for Air, Lord Swinton, and appointed a convenient nonentity Kingsley Wood in his place."

Banks records that, "without losing a moment, [Wood] transferred from the Ministry of Health with his faithful PPS, Sir Edward Campbell."

[1505] CG Grey, 'A History of the Air Ministry', 1940, p278; also, *Daily Mail* 30th May and 2nd June 1938, KW23 178/5 & 215/1

Austin also built a plane factory at the Longbridge site (Fairey Battles initially), opened by Wood as Minister of Air. The University of Kent collection includes at KW26 an album of photographs from his Longbridge visit on 22nd July 1938. See www.kent.ac.uk/library/specialcollections/other/kingsley-wood/index.html

[1506] Shay, op cit, pp222-224

case of war', the breach had never been completely healed",[1507] and Nuffield had closed an aero-rotors factory three years before as Air Ministry support had not been forthcoming. Brooks recorded in his diary that the Ministry had "turned down flat" Nuffield's offer to build aeroplane engines and, furious at being told in effect that his help was not wanted, he in turned charged them with discourtesy, denouncing the shadow scheme.[1508]

Despite these unpromising portents, Nuffield had responded favourably to Wood and for this and other reasons, monthly production increased from 80 planes in 1938 to 546 in April 1940.[1509] A further factor in the decision to replace Swinton may have been that, despite the development of radar making fighter defence more realistic, Swinton's Air Ministry had continued to argue for an expanding bomber programme, on the basis that the best deterrence was for Germany (and any enemy) to see the country's offensive force as equivalent to, or greater than, their own. As Britain could not afford both, this meant the fighter programme was depleted. As he would soon show, Wood was more prepared to focus on fighters.[1510]

Although a casual glance at Low's cartoon for the *Evening Standard* in May 1938 (on the following page) might indicate that the newly-appointed Air Minister was hopelessly out of his depth, there is another way of reading it. Wood is putting on his flying gloves as if he means business, with Thomas Inskip the Minister for defence co-ordination right behind him. Wood is confronted by a Churchill-shaped windsock, labelled 'Winston Gale Telltale', while Wood and his co-pilot may be about to get into the 'flying wheelbarrow' rather than the planes behind, one of which bears the same name - a biplane whose performance would be far short of a

---

[1507] *East Anglian Daily Times* 21st May 1938, KW23 180/3
[1508] Crowson, 1998, op cit, pp175-176 - Brooks diary entry for 22nd October 1936
[1509] www.birminghamhistory.net/category/1960-1969/
John Ferris notes that difficulties with Supermarine's production of Spitfires led to it being brought together with the financial and managerial skills of Vickers and Nuffield in a new plant at Castle Bromwich. "Achieving air ascendancy: challenge and response in British strategic air defence, 1915-1940", p44 in Sebastian Cox and Peter Gray, 'Air Power History: Turning Points from Kitty Hawk to Kosovo', 2002
Also, Wood's entry in Keith Laybourn (ed.), 'British Political Leaders: A Biographical Dictionary', 2001, pp334-335
[1510] Shay, op cit, p172

1930s combat aircraft. Behind those, however, is a sleek, modern and quality fighter and perhaps it is this that they will opt for - as indeed they did.

David Low, *Evening Standard* 19th May 1938

In mid-October 1938 Wood had written to Chamberlain refuting an attack on the Air Ministry's competence, pointing out that in 1932/33 "all development work on the larger types of aircraft had been discontinued in deference" to Treasury and Foreign Office views, while the latter attempted to negotiate a disarmament treaty. Similarly, financial restrictions curtailed expansion schemes in 1934 and 1935 to light bombers rather than the heavier ones the Ministry preferred. But, Wood pointed out, as aircraft design was revolutionised by the late 1930s, the early lead enjoyed by the Germans meant that much of their production before 1938 would be obsolescent.[1511]

Ten days later Wood put before the Cabinet his assessment of 'Relative Air Strengths and Proposals for the Improvement of the Country's Position'.[1512] The fifteen page document covered sixty-five paragraphs of closely reasoned argument, with a further two-

---

[1511] National Archives PREM 1/252 14th October 1938; Peden, op cit, p154
[1512] National Archives CAB 24/279/18 25th October 1938

page appendix on potential German aircraft industry expansion. Wood argued for accelerated production (pp6-7, paras 18-24), covered the necessity for additional aircraft (pp7-9, paras 25-37), tackled the development and organisational arrangements he proposed for air strength (pp9-13, paras 39-54) and the issue of overseas squadrons (p13, para 55). Without a doubt his most significant conclusion was that fighter strength be increased by 25% from 640 to 800 by 1939 (p12, para 48).[1513] As the number of bombers would remain as in Scheme L at 1360, the ratio of fighters to bombers would then be 1:1.7 rather than 1:2 heralding a recognition that defence through fighters needed to precede offence by bombers. Wood acknowledged that the costs would be "truly formidable, but no more so than the menace with which we are confronted" (pp13-14, para 56). His conclusions occupied nine paragraphs (pp14-15, paras 57-65), of which the last harked back to the commitments Chamberlain had given the Commons the previous March. These were to protect Britain, its trade routes and overseas territories, and to help defend the country's allies. Wood did not pretend that parity with Germany would be achieved but he did argue that the expansion he proposed would enable the RAF to fulfil these promises. No longer could it be claimed that Britain had "not taken a sufficiently long range view and [had] under-estimated both the capacity and intentions of Germany", the accusation that had been levelled at previous expansion programmes.[1514]

Although Wood was no doubt able to convince the Cabinet partly because of the doubts that surfaced almost before the ink

---

[1513] Orders were to be placed immediately for 1850 fighters, 1750 bombers and 2400 other planes so that by 1941 and 1942 there was a delivery programme of 12,000 aircraft, but it was the increase of twelve fighter squadrons that would prove critical.

Also, Collier, op cit, pp67-68: 50 squadrons, 800 fighters in Scheme M, compared to 38 squadrons and 608 in Scheme L and speeded up the fighter force to spring 1939; Peden op cit, p134: Chamberlain and Wood accepted Hopkins' argument that concentrating on fighters and going slow on bombers would alleviate strain on the economy; Peden, op cit, p133 and Richards, op cit, p123: after Munich the fighter timetable was changed to April 1940 and the bomber one to 1942, though the numbers proposed for each remained the same.

[1514] As Wood had explained to the Cabinet, according to Martin Gilbert, 'Winston Churchill - vol. 5: 1922-1939', 1976, pxix

was dry on the Munich Agreement the month before, the Head of the Civil Service Horace Wilson (1882-1972)[1515] had told him that

> the RAF would not be allowed to increase its production 'to a level equal to the estimated German capacity' because Germany would 'take it as a signal that we have decided at once to sabotage the Munich agreement'.[1516]

Wilson had worked closely with Chamberlain on appeasement and subsequently fell foul of Churchill in July 1941 who doubted his commitment and wrote to Wood advocating his dismissal.

Wood took two other decisions at Air that were to prove vital to the future course of events. The first of these came in April 1939 when the imminent retirements of Air Marshals Bowhill (1880-1960) and Hugh Dowding (at Coastal and Fighter Commands respectively) were postponed. Both had been due to retire in summer 1939 but, for example, Dowding (1882-1970) had his service extended, first by nine months, then by another three and was about to be given another short extension when the Battle of Britain started.[1517] Dowding eventually retired in November 1940, by which point Archibald Sinclair had succeeded Wood at Air and Portal was Chief of the Air Staff (CAS),[1518] and in May 1941 Bowhill

---

[1515] Wilson had negotiated direct on Chamberlain's behalf with the Society of British Aircraft Constructors (SBAC) to reach an agreement on fair prices. The negotiations started in 1936 without Swinton's knowledge and the agreement was signed off more than two years later in Wood's first month as Air Minister. SBAC did at least negotiate collectively, whereas the motor manufacturers had to be approached individually. Shay, op cit, pp111-120, 124, 205

[1516] Lynne Olson, 'Troublesome Young Men: The Churchill Conspiracy of 1940', 2007, p186
The Munich Agreement was signed after three meetings between Chamberlain and Hitler on 15th, 22nd and 29th September 1938 at Berchtesgarden, Godesberg and Munich respectively.
According to Colville, op cit, pxii: "... after the signing of the Munich Agreement Neville Chamberlain assured us that there would be peace in our time; and he really believed it," but p18: Chamberlain had "an ingenuous faith in the Munich Agreement" believing Hitler was sincere when he signed it "but changed his mind a few days later".
[1517] Richards, op cit, p129
[1518] Cyril Newall had been Wood's CAS throughout 1938 to 1940. After Wood left Air murmurings against Newall became more explicit with a friend of Beaverbrook's identifying him as the RAF's weak link in the Battle

was moved to Canada to oversee the establishment of Ferry Command.

The second came in September 1939, after war had been declared but at the start of what would prove a lengthy hiatus. This was the establishment of the Empire Air Training Scheme which Wood and his deputy Balfour were fundamental to initiating. It has been described in many other places so does not need labouring here,[1519] but without the pilots trained in Canada, New Zealand and Australia, as well as the contributions of other nationalities, particularly perhaps the Polish, it would not have been sufficient to have enough planes. There also had to be an adequate supply of pilots to meet round the clock requirements, but also to provide relief and replace those who had flown the required number of sorties or whom injury, death or exhaustion had removed from the front line. It was estimated that about 20,000 trained pilots a year would be required and, while Britain might eventually have forty flying training schools, another fifty would be required in the Commonwealth, with all the advanced training to be done in Canada. The agreement was signed in Ottawa on 17th December 1939 and by 1942 it was producing 11,000 pilots a year (and another 17,000 aircrew).

Furthermore, demonstrating his belief in the power of publicity, Wood had appealed in June 1938 for 31,000 recruits to the RAF. By the following January nearly 27,000 pilots, airmen and boys had joined since April, increasing to over 35,000 in the year to April 1939.[1520]

Apart from the strategic direction that Wood provided (and the contributions of thousands of others), there were a number of other factors that enabled Britain and its allies to mount an effective

---

of Britain. Although Newall received the support of Churchill and Sinclair initially, when he then fell foul of Beaverbrook and the Ministry of Aircraft Production, his days were numbered. Wood is not mentioned in Sebastian Richie, "A political intrigue against the Chief of the Air Staff: The downfall of Air Chief Marshal Sir Cyril Newall", *War and Society*, 1998, 16, pp83-104 n987, perhaps because the intrigue against Newall took place mainly after May 1940.

[1519] For example: Richards, op cit, pp133-136; Balfour, op cit, pp114-117; and Alfred Critchley, 'Critch! The Memoirs of Brigadier AC Critchley', 1961, pp188 ff on air crew training.

[1520] CPA CRD 1/78/2 Points for Propaganda No. 111 1st February 1939; *Times* 31st January 1939; CPA CRD 1/78/2 Points for Propaganda No. 120 5th April 1939.

air campaign in the 1940 period. The early development of radar (by Watson-Watt with Dowding's support)[1521] was fundamental to the Battle of Britain, as was the Anglo-French strategy Wood and Balfour agreed with their counterparts on 3rd September 1939 of "not provoking German air attack until Allied air forces were stronger".[1522] This was a strategic decision not appeasement for the sake of it or because of fear, and the same distinctions should be drawn in the 1930s as well. Some chose appeasement because of the attractions of totalitarian regimes, some preferred it to war and some thought it the only realistic strategic option at the time. Britain could not have won a war in the late 1930s, so if diplomacy proved ineffectual delay was vital. Yet appeasement is often treated as if the connotations were automatically negative and the causation was the same in every case. Gilbert and Gott are particularly prone to this naïve and unipolar approach: for example, "failed to achieve the needed air parity with Germany. Machines were not lacking. Will-power was."[1523] Other writers are more sophisticated. For example, Middlemas and Barnes state that for Baldwin

> Deterrence and appeasement were ... not alternatives but sides of the same coin. Effective defence was both safeguard and deterrent; the search for a settlement was at once the hope of peace and the moral courage of the British nation.[1524]

Similarly, others described appeasement in the 1930s as "a Christian and compassionate policy", hence its support by churches;[1525] judged that (a) it "does not merit the obloquy into which it fell", (b) "no political leader in this generation [including Churchill] entirely escapes blame for the neglect to re-arm in time" with Labour opposing all rearmament until 1937, (c) the benefits of an additional year before the war as result of Munich, and (d) a clear demonstration that Britain had done all it could to avoid war.

[1521] Collier, op cit, p36
[1522] Richards, op cit, pp137 and 138
[1523] Gilbert and Gott, op cit, p12
The "machines" were presumably machine tools, rather than planes themselves, but it was much more complex (economic stability, prosperity and conciliation - i.e., appeasement) than this suggests.
[1524] Middlemas and Barnes, op cit, p793
[1525] Ball, 2013, op cit, p85

In a *Sunday Times* article in March 1939 Lord Kemsley concluded there was "nothing to regret [in appeasement] and much of which may be proud" for it gave Britain a moral strength even if it failed to deflect Germany.[1526] As another historian has put it,

> [t]he country, in fact, was faced with an astonishing paradox. The Conservatives were in favour of armaments on the understanding that they would not be used, and the Labour opposition were in favour of using armaments on the understanding that they were not to be provided.[1527]

As Shay points out, if another "more independent, dynamic" Prime Minister than Chamberlain had been in post, rearmament might, and could, have been a priority much earlier. But would the Conservative party have accepted them? And, as Chamberlain was the best administrator anyway, rearmament under another Prime Minister might have been much more chaotic.[1528] It is worth noting in this respect that in September 1939 Churchill wrote to Wood proposing the removal of balloons and anti-aircraft guns from London to protect aircraft factories at, for example, Coventry, Derby and Bristol. On the face of it this suggestion had some obvious merit, but would have proved disastrous had Wood complied. Fortunately, he did not and Churchill, still at the Admiralty, was not yet able to order him to do so.[1529] Wood had told his adopted daughter the year before "to get out of London as there was only one anti-aircraft gun to defend London".[1530] This was parental anxiety and exaggeration but things were not greatly improved on the outbreak of war, with Collier's history of home defence, for example, painting a bleak picture. David Low writes of defenceless London, waiting for "AA guns that didn't come".[1531] Similarly, in April 1939 Hore-Belisha had been challenged by Horace Wilson about the number of searchlights covering London. He explained that he had 96 with the crews living nearby but that this would not

---

[1526] Hadley, op cit, pp150, 152, 153, 154-157
[1527] William R Rock, 'Appeasement on Trial', 1966, p323
[1528] Shay, op cit, pp293-294
[1529] Churchill College archives, Churchill Papers, CHAR 19/2C/314 18th September 1939 and CHAR 19/2A/40 19th September 1939 for Wood's judicious reply.
[1530] Robin Brothers, personal communication 28th November 2014
[1531] Low, op cit, p332

help Wood's planes as they were intended for the anti-aircraft guns.[1532]

There were other factors in the air campaign as well, not least apparently haphazard and unsustained bombing by the Luftwaffe. With the exception of the London docks and some other major objectives, it was rare for the same targets to be selected repeatedly and pulverised continually. Collier makes the point that it was as if the German planners considered a single visit to have achieved their purpose, while repeated follow-ups on the same factory and transport targets would have been devastating - to morale as well as to production. For example, horrendous though the raid on Coventry was on 14th November 1940, the German failure to follow-up on subsequent nights, switching to London and Southampton instead, was inexplicable and meant that factories and the city itself were functioning again within a few days.[1533] The same was true of airfields put out of action at the start of the Battle of Britain but then attention switched elsewhere.

Just as Wood had opened post offices, hospitals and housing schemes in his previous posts, so his official duties now included opening airports, which could be commercial in the short-term but then mothballed or used as airfields on the outbreak of war. These are said to have included Cambridge 1937 [sic],[1534] Manchester June 1938, Luton[1535] and the new Exeter terminal in July 1938,[1536] and Derby in June 1939. In July 1938 he helped establish the Civil Air Guard[1537] and the Spitfire Ladies.[1538] In August 1938 Beaverbrook passed on to him, at one of those points when his and Wood's relations were on an even keel, a commendation from the US Commission on civil aviation, adding

---

[1532] Churchill College archives, HOBE 1/5 Hore-Belisha 1938 diary, pp64-65 - entry for Wednesday 12th April 1939
[1533] Collier, op cit, pp263-265; Alan Pollock play 'One Night in November', 2008
[1534] http://myntransportblog.com/2014/06/15/marshall-buses-cambridge-since-1909-england-uk
[1535] www.lutontoday.co.uk/.../flying-heroine-amy-johnson-helped-luton-airport- take-off-1-6293191; *also, KW23 157/1-14*
[1536] http://www.exetermemories.co.uk/em/_scrapbook/1930s.php
[1537] *Belfast Whig and Belfast Post* 25th July 1938, KW23 263/1
[1538] www.lady.co.uk/people/8838-the-spitfire-ladies The Civil Air Guard had been set up to help the RAF and during the war delivered planes from factories to airfields.

I am delighted in the immense public approval that you win in every direction. It is entirely in accordance with my belief. In other words, you are a Derby winner, and I have put some money on the result of the race.[1539]

In 1939 Wood visited Kidbrooke as part of a recruitment drive for 5,000 men over 35 to join the Balloon Service and on another of his trips to see things for himself, Wood's plane crash-landed at Kirkby-in-Furness in Cumbria on the way to Belfast in June 1939. Wood was unhurt but, according to Grey, most of the party were "damaged" and Edward Campbell, Wood's PPS, "damaged his head and broke his wrist".[1540] The History of Kirkby Group has published a fuller version in Volume 13 of 'Kirkby Fragments' describing this

... Kirkby Moor forced aircraft landing a few weeks before the outbreak of war which involved Air Minister Sir Kingsley Wood.
... [He] spent the night as the guest of the ... Kirkby vicarage and returned to London by train in the morning.
The air crew and passenger ... Sir Christopher Courtney were detained in Ulverston with minor injuries.
Over the next few days an RAF team from Chester dismantled the plane and took it away, but not before sightseers came out from Ulverston and Kirkby to view the wreckage.[1541]

Various British Pathe films testify to Wood's constant shuttling around the country to open new facilities and boost morale throughout Britain.[1542] If his schedule at the Ministry of Health had been hectic, his time at Air was even more so. Slums and health

---

[1539] Parliamentary archives, BBK/C/330, Beaverbrook letter to Wood 8th August 1938
[1540] Grey, op cit, p302
[1541] http://www.nwemail.co.uk/memories/how-villagers-coped-with-six-years-of-war-1.1140013
[1542] Examples in 1938 are the Empire Air Day in May, a visit from the French Air Ministry to London in June, Wood's reciprocal trip that December to Paris, in which he took in the Aeronautical Exhibition as well as meeting his French colleagues, and opening a memorial at RAF Mildenhall in August to commemorate George V's review. He also inspected aircraft research facilities and the RAF in training.

provided one sort of urgency but this was now even more literally a matter of life and death in which every moment was vital. Wood spread himself and his energies across all aspects: for example, from liaising regularly with Dalton to ensure Labour were kept fully briefed,[1543] supporting Hore-Belisha and others who argued for a Ministry of Supply in early 1939,[1544] baling out Balfour who had exceeded his brief in buying planes in America without authority[1545] and arguing strongly at the CID Sub-Committee against an air force restricted to the "zone of the Armies" as if they would be fighting WWI all over again.[1546] In October 1939 the Air Ministry asked the War Office to return two out of the four Hurricane squadrons supporting the BEF in France, promising two (old-fashioned) Gladiator squadrons instead if, but only if, the Germans attacked anywhere in France.[1547] Conversely, but with the same intent of putting defence of Britain first, Wood resisted Chamberlain's desire to fight Russia in Finland and the Prime Minister's proposal to send 100 planes.[1548] Wood thought this too risky and the overall enterprise came to nought only when Sweden refused passage to the troops that would have been sent to Finland.[1549]

Yet this was not enough to satisfy his critics with both Hore-Belisha and Bracken claiming that Wood had been too unassertive

---

[1543] Pimlott, op cit, p269 when Dalton agreed to liaise with Wood (and Ronald Cross, the Minister for Economic Warfare); pp295, 298, 302-304, 313-314 & 321 reporting their meetings in 1939 and 1940. Taken from Dalton, 1957, op cit, pp272-274.

[1544] Churchill College archives, HOBE 1/5; Bond, op cit, p184 - Pownall diary entry for 23rd January 1939; Shay, op cit, p265

[1545] Balfour, op cit, pp101 & 103: Wood "was a splendid little man ..." who rescued Balfour by convincing the Commons. The aftermath included Churchill and Beaverbrook eventually apologising for their opposition to Balfour's unauthorised purchase. Wood had considered the matter closed for the Treasury within days, though he had lodged a mild complaint to preserve the formalities. Balfour, op cit, pp138-145; also Parliamentary archives, BBK/D/527

[1546] Bond, op cit, p181 - Pownall diary entry for 9th January 1939: this "was nonsense and a sheer waste of time for busy men to consider".

[1547] Bond, op cit, pp242 & 244 - Pownall diary entries for 5th & 12th October 1939 doubting this promise would be kept, especially if England were attacked at the same time.

[1548] Vincent, op cit, pp612-613 - Crawford diary entry for 23rd January 1940

[1549] Healey, op cit, p99 described Chamberlain's desire to fight Russia as well as Germany "insanity".

at Air in the face of the high Tory and military establishments.[1550] On the other hand he had got things done without antagonising them, whereas the military might have been trained to obey orders but that did not prevent their whispering against Hore-Belisha becoming too deafening even for Chamberlain. The RAF had no reason to revenge themselves on their Minister unlike the Army. Wood presented the Air estimates in the Commons on 7th March 1940,[1551] when the otherwise obscure Conservative Edward Keeling (1888-1954) thought Wood was "not on top of the job and never has been. Keeling would like a three-party secret meeting upstairs, where Wood could be cross-examined".[1552] Wood did talk to the Supply Committee, but there were no 'man hunts' as Wood had expected there would be.[1553]

In April 1940 an exhausted Wood, "tired and ill ... left for one of the sinecure Cabinet offices", the non-Departmental post of Lord Privy Seal, exchanging with Hoare.[1554] But, within five weeks, his health restored, the new Prime Minister Churchill appointed him Chancellor of the Exchequer. Wood's contribution had been one of the reasons for the effective air war that would soon begin, and Air Vice-Marshal PB Joubert de la Ferte commanding No 11 Fighter Group commented that "Sir Kingsley Wood showed himself to be an able and forceful leader and it was a loss to the RAF ..." especially as the Chancellor of the Exchequer's "occupation in war-time must be rather like that of King John and the Jews in the Tower - 'Pay or I pull out your teeth'."[1555]

[1550] In their interviews for William Crozier, 'Off the Record: Political Interviews 1933-1943', 1973, pp 130 & 151
[1551] Notable both for Wood's presentation and for the issues he raised regarding problems of air defence and evacuation during this quiet "phoney war" period. Hansard, 7th March 1940, vol. 358, cols. 595-704
[1552] Pimlott (ed), op cit, pp 321-322 - Dalton diary entry for Thursday 7th March 1940
[1553] Ibid, p322 - Dalton diary entry for Thursday 14th March 1940
[1554] Balfour, op cit, p119
Balfour adds that Hoare was "pleasant personally [but] the most unpleasant administrator", the latter a distinct contrast to Wood.
[1555] Sir Philip Joubert de la Ferte, 'The Third Service: The Story Behind the RAF', 1955, p120

Vignettes

Cabinet Camaraderie

Despite the over-riding threat from Germany and its allies, this did not necessarily bring senior politicians together in every circumstance for they held widely different views and recognised that crises provided opportunities as well for the ambitious.[1556] Apart from the obvious distinction between former "appeasers" (Simon and Hoare, for example) and those who would have preferred war sooner (such as Churchill and Hore-Belisha), Chamberlain's War Cabinet in September 1939 was divided in other ways. The Prime Minister himself had been a hero at the time of Munich but his stock had fallen far from that high point by the time war was declared. His Foreign Secretary Halifax continued to hanker for accommodation with Germany provided Britain was allowed to retain its Empire. The other three members, Hankey, Wood and Chatfield, held the ring. In the wider Cabinet Anthony Eden (1897-1977) had resigned as Foreign Secretary in February 1938 when Chamberlain had countermanded Eden's support for Roosevelt's offer of an international conference[1557] without telling him. Eden was now at the Dominions Office and

> ... still loathes the Prime Minister whom he regards as obstinate, opinionated, rather mean, and completely ignorant of the main issues involved. ... He feels that Kingsley Wood ... is a help since he is truthful.[1558]

[1556] There was much jockeying for position in the early years of Churchill's Cabinet too, with for example Bevin and Beaverbrook at odds, and in 1942 both Cripps and Beaverbrook aspiring to replace Churchill. Addison, 1994, op cit, p62 also makes the point that this is often inevitable in politics. There was also much criticism of Churchill's overbearing manner. For example, Jon Schneer, 'Ministers At War: Churchill and His War Cabinet', 2015, pp108-112. Laski was often scathing about Churchill's "18th century outlook, his undemocratic temper, his prejudiced anti-Socialism" (Martin, op cit, p154).

[1557] To try and disengage Mussolini and Italy from Germany's influence over the Spanish Civil War - one reason for the absence of sanctions on Italy after it invaded Abyssinia.

[1558] Harold Nicolson, 'Diaries and Letters - vol. II: 1939-1945', 1967, pp55-56 - 6th January 1940

Alliances were forged on the basis of mutual interests as well, and Wood and Hore-Belisha,[1559] two of the armed service Ministers, enjoyed a close relationship across the Cabinet table. One of the files in the Churchill College archives consists almost entirely of notes that Hore-Belisha and Wood passed between each other at Cabinet. One of the items that stands out is Wood's note on the reverse of an exchange between them over the French Chief of Staff Gamelin. Wood's warning, presumably to Hore-Belisha as the note ended up in his possession, was

If Hitler is Mahomet it is no use telling Mahomedans that Mahomet is a swine. Say his advisers are swine not Mahomet. [1560]

When Chamberlain decided in early January 1940 that Hore-Belisha had upset too many senior officers in the Army and had to be moved from the War Office, offering him the Board of Trade instead, Hore-Belisha refused. Despite Wood's strenuous efforts to get him to change his mind, Hore-Belisha left the Cabinet.[1561]

[1559] Secretary of State for War (i.e., the Army) May 1937 - January 1940
[1560] Churchill College archives, HOBE 5/38 item 4
Schneer, op cit, p10 comments that "Note passing appears to have been common parlance" in Chamberlain's War Cabinet.
[1561] Churchill College archives, HOBE 1/7 Hore-Belisha 1939-1940 diary, pp93,99, 100, 102 - entries for 4th - 16th January 1940

Guy la Chambre and General Sikorski

Two of Wood's most important links in this period were with his French counterpart Guy la Chambre before the war and then with General Wladyslaw Sikorski once it had been declared.

Guy la Chambre (1898-1975) was French Minister of Air from January 1938 to March 1940, serving three Prime Ministers in that time. He and Wood met formally on 4th April 1939[1562] at the Air Ministry in London (Hore-Belisha, Newall the CAS and others were present) to thrash out the problems of French aircraft production and to see how Britain could help.[1563] The meeting lasted virtually all day and at the end Wood and la Chambre agreed on eight points. The most significant were:
- Britain's offer to supply planes for operational and training purposes on a commercial basis would be considered by France: 50 Battles now, 150 more in six months for combat and 75 Tiger Moths and 50 Magisters now for training. This would obviate the need for France to place orders in the US.
- plans for common standards and specifications (instruments, fuel, raw materials, as well as planes as a whole, even factories) to be considered and agreed between Britain and France
- joint use of the existing British production arrangements in Canada, rather than a separate French factory there, would be discussed further.

Given that the meeting considered other ways in which France might be prepared to benefit from Britain's experience, or to put it another way give up their autonomy, it may not be surprising that this rankled with la Chambre. The following November, at a lunch the French Prime Minister Daladier (1884-1970)[1564] hosted for Hore-Belisha, la Chambre was very critical of his relationship with the British Air Ministry and the lack of information he had received.[1565] This might have been of a piece with the criticisms

---

[1562] A previous meeting had taken place in Paris in December 1938 and General Vuillemin, the Chief of the French Air Staff, had visited in May 1938 (*Times* 30th May 1938, KW23 178/6).
[1563] Churchill College archives, FROB 1/9
[1564] Daladier had signed the Munich Agreement along with Chamberlain.
[1565] Churchill College archives, HOBE 1/7 Hore-Belisha 1939-1940 diary pp79-80 - entry for 20th November 1939
According to Francois Duchene, 'Jean Monnet: The First Statesman of Interdependence', 1944, pp65-69, Monnet was one of those working in the

that Paul Reynaud (1878-1966), then French Finance Minister (premier from March 1940) was making at the same time, for in his view British strategy was to see French resources exhausted first.[1566]

Some of the information that la Chambre had been given, and which he referred to, seems to have been misleading, perhaps deliberately so - though he may have just been badly briefed or was taking the opportunity to be mischievous. In the event, however, little of this was of relevance once France fell the following June.

General Wladyslaw Sikorski (1881-1943)
Little more than a fortnight after German troops entered Prague, Britain unilaterally guaranteed on 31st March 1939 that it would come to Poland's aid if it was attacked.[1567] Both Britain and France made similar guarantees to Greece and Romania a fortnight later. In both instances this was an attempt to demonstrate that the Czechoslovakian disgrace would not recur.[1568] The month after Munich the Kristallnacht pogrom[1569] had brought home, if this was needed, the relentless nature of Nazi brutality and the abject failure of appeasement to stop Hitler, but defeatist articles soon followed in the *Times* and *Evening Standard* to which Raczynski, then Polish Ambassador in London, and others objected.[1570]

Germany and Russia signed a non-aggression treaty in August 1939 and on 1st September Germany invaded Poland. Chamberlain then tried to put off the decision to honour the guarantee Britain had given Poland less than six months earlier, but

---

group around la Chambre, "the vigorous young Air Minister", and was to approach Roosevelt about US planes to help Daladier close the air gap after Munich. Duchene may ascribe more influence and significance to Monnet at this point in his career than was actually the case.

[1566] Talbot Charles Imlay, "A re-assessment of Anglo-French strategy during the phoney war, 1939-1940", *English Historical Review*, 2004, 119, pp333-372 (p345)

[1567] Count Edward Raczynski, 'In Allied London', 1962, p12

[1568] Poland had issued its own ultimatum to Czechoslovakia over Teschen on 30th September 1938 even as the Munich Agreement sought to impose a three-month moratorium over Polish and Hungarian claims against territory then inside Czechoslovakia. This was another element of that country's dismemberment.

[1569] Williamson, op cit, p638; Bond, op cit, p169

[1570] Raczynski, op cit, p13

it was Wood who "in particular tried to draw attention to the delay in issuing an ultimatum" to Germany.[1571]

Not to be outdone, the Soviets soon attacked their traditional enemy from the east.[1572] Poland could not long survive these twin thrusts and in little more than a month the country's military resistance had been crushed.[1573] Sikorski escaped at the end of the month for Paris where he led a re-grouped Polish army in France.[1574] A Polish government in exile was then formed in Paris with Sikorski as Prime Minister and Commander-in-Chief of those Polish forces that had either escaped or were already elsewhere but had vowed to re-take the country.[1575] August Zaleski (1883-1972), the Minister for Foreign Affairs, made it clear that the one purpose of the government was to work alongside their allies to win the war and liberate Poland,[1576] and he visited London later that month for discussions with the British government. By the end of October the Polish government had agreed with the French to move out of Paris but that Sikorski's headquarters would remain there.

General Sikorski was in London for three days in mid-November and met Wood on the 15th.[1577] The programme for Sikorski's visit is in the Polish Institute/Sikorski Museum,[1578] as is the record of his discussions with several British Ministers. Most of these records exist in both English and Polish, but the discussion with Wood had not been translated until the Director did so in November 2014.[1579]

[1571] Anita Prazmowska, 'Britain, Poland and the Eastern Front, 1939', 1987, p180

[1572] Dalton, 1957, op cit, pp274-277 describes in detail the discussions during September between Raczynski, the Air Ministry and Wood, and between Dalton and Wood in their liaison meetings, about support to Poland.

[1573] The Katyn massacre in spring 1940 was to be but one such that occurred during the twin German and Soviet occupations of Poland.

[1574] *Times* 29th September 1939

[1575] *Times* 2nd and 3rd October 1939; Raczynski, op cit, p43
The President was the civilian lawyer Wladyslaw Raczkiewicz after the French had objected to the first choice.

[1576] *Times* 9th October 1939
Zaleski would be succeeded as Foreign Minister by Raczynski from July 1941 to July 1943.

[1577] Raczynski, op cit, p46 says they met in mid-September but there is no other evidence for this.

[1578] Polish Institute/Sikorski Museum (PISM) A.12.49/WB/14

[1579] PISM A.11E/175

They discussed civilian staff[1580] and the incorporation of LOT airlines into British ones for the duration of the war, but the substantive points Sikorski raised about airmen were:
- the organisation of Polish squadrons in England
- the oaths Polish airmen would be required to swear. Sikorski "emphasised that the Polish soldier wherever he [fights], fights [for] the cause of Poland and [this must be included]. While [there may be] formal reasons [why] English oaths are required, [a] formula would have to be found [that meets both requirements]".[1581]
- "pensions for the orphans and widows of fallen airmen"
- "the importance of retaining the Polish (eagle) badge [the]... symbol [under which] ... our airmen fought in Poland."
In reply, Wood promised "to look at these matters positively and [did] not see any problem with having them accepted", though it would be for the Treasury to decide on the issue of pensions for orphans and widows. He assured Sikorski that he could rely on the "utmost support". An item in the Imperial War Museum collections shows Wood meeting newly arrived Polish Air Officers at the Eastchurch receiving centre in Kent.[1582] This was two months after his meeting with Sikorski so it should be clear that their discussion was entirely practical rather than theoretical.

After the fall of France the Polish government in exile moved to London. On 5th August 1940 Wood was present at the signing (by Churchill and Halifax for Britain, Sikorski and Zaleski for Poland) in the Cabinet Room at 10 Downing Street of the military agreement re-establishing a Polish state in London.[1583] In November Sikorski and Wood met again to try to resolve the issue of Polish bullion held by the French in Dakar.[1584] When Sikorski sought to raise this with Churchill two months later, Churchill said that he was not prepared

---

My thanks to Dr Andrzej Suchcitz for his generosity in this.
[1580] In other words, the "involvement of civilian personnel [in] the aviation industry [so that] good staff, mainly engineers, designers and mechanics, ... could be used to rebuild the Polish aviation industry after the war".
[1581] There is a reference in Raczynski, op cit to a Polish airman who refused to swear the English oath and was barred from flying before the authorities eventually relented.
[1582] On 27th January 1940
www.iwm.org.uk/collections/item/object/205207514
[1583] Raczynski, op cit, p60
[1584] On 21st November 1940 PISM Polskie Dokumenty Dyplomatyczne 1941, p9

to discuss it as it was a matter for Wood as Chancellor.[1585]   The gold seems not to have been retrieved, or not at this stage anyway, and perhaps partly for this reason in July 1941 Churchill and Dalton, the Minister for Economic Warfare, authorised Wood to pay a credit of £600,000 to the Polish Military account that had been agreed a year earlier.[1586]

After Operation Barbarossa, the German invasion of Russia in June 1941, Poland and Russia soon agreed on 29th July 1941 to fight alongside each other against Germany. It was in order to see how this agreement was working that Sikorski and his British government liaison Victor Cazalet (1896-1943) undertook a two month visit at the end of 1941.[1587]   Between 31st October and 6th January 1942 they flew to Malta to talk to General Gort, to Cairo and General Auchinleck, to the Polish Brigade stationed in Tobruk, to the Polish General Anders in Teheran before visiting Russia itself, firstly Cripps and Vyshinsky and then on to Moscow where Sikorski met Stalin.   There were 2m Polish exiles in camps in Russia, though an agreement limited the Polish army to 30,000 men there.[1588]

It was on another visit in 1943, this time of six weeks to raise Polish morale in the Middle East, that their plane crashed on 4th July when taking off from Gibraltar to return to London. Sikorski, Cazalet and others on board were killed. Given the timing many thought then, and many still do, that this was sabotage rather than an accident. Sikorski received a state funeral in London on 15th July and was buried in Newark.[1589]   Sikorski and Wood were born the same year and died within three months of each other, and since one judgement of Sikorski was that he had "a decided gift for getting things done",[1590] an assessment that many applied equally to Wood, there were clearly other similarities too. Both were a significant loss at the time but with Russia and the US now fighting alongside countries such as Britain and Poland the outcome was inevitable even if the timing was as yet uncertain.

[1585] On 19th February 1941 PISM Polskie Dokumenty Dyplomatyczne 1941, p87

[1586] On 5th July 1941, referring to the agreement signed 3rd June 1940. PISM PRM 39A/28

[1587] Victor Cazalet, 'With Sikorski to Russia', 1942
Cazalet restricted the print run to 300 copies for private circulation.

[1588] Waszak, op cit, p46

[1589] Ibid, pp81, 83 and 85

[1590] Raczynski, op cit, p150

18.   THE 1940 CRISES

At the start of 1939 Chamberlain forecast "I think 1939 will be a more tranquil year than 1938".[1591]   This was the hope of the German people too for, as the popular author Philip Gibbs wrote to the *Times* at the end of February, "every German one meets … expresses an anxious desire for friendship with England and for avoidance of war".[1592]   But these aspirations were unfulfilled, for even before the tipping point of Poland, German aggression towards its neighbours continued.   In March 1939 the remaining parts of Czechoslovakia were occupied by German forces,[1593] and in April an emboldened Italy invaded Albania.   The Liberal leader Archibald Sinclair had referred in the Commons to Chamberlain's disastrous foreign policy though "I have never doubted his sincerity, nor his devotion to the pursuit of peace …"[1594] But this had been of no avail with Chamberlain's obsession now looking naïve, and in September the invasion of Poland finally triggered the declaration of war.

From the outset Britain and France agreed three strategic objectives through their Supreme War Council: not to undertake any land offensive in the west other than a "token advance … to offer some comfort to Poland", but to pursue the war at sea vigorously and to keep Italy neutral if possible.[1595]   Britain was still in command of the seas (though less so as German submarines threatened), but Chamberlain was concerned in particular about the weakness of the French air force, especially given the lesson of Poland that a powerful air force could "paralyse the operations of land forces",[1596] and was anxious that an army of fifty-five divisions would draw resources away from a strong RAF that he felt should still have "absolute priority".   That he was eventually persuaded to raise an army as large as this was in order to demonstrate to France that they would not be left to shoulder the burden of land defence on

---

[1591] CPA CRD 1/78/2 Points for Propaganda No. 107 4th January 1939
[1592] *Times* 28th February 1939; CPA CRD 1/78/2 Points for Propaganda No. 115 1st March 1939
[1593] These were Bohemia and Moravia, the Sudetenland having been annexed in September 1938 (the Munich agreement) and Slovakia having declared itself pro-Axis.
[1594] CPA CRD 1/78/2 Points for Propaganda No. 112 8th February 1939
[1595] David Dilks, "The Twilight war and the fall of France: Chamberlain and Churchill in 1940", *Transactions of the Royal Historical Society*, 1978, 28, pp61-86 (p64)
[1596] Chamberlain to Churchill 16th September 1939

their own or, as David Dilks put it more poignantly, to reassure the French that they would not be asked "to pay almost the whole of the blood tax on land".[1597]

Based on experience in the First World War emergency regulations were introduced but there was increasingly a mixture of Government diktat and voluntary effort.[1598] Evacuation provided an early demonstration of the latter combination, for even before the war started about two million people had privately moved themselves to safer areas between June and September 1939 and another 1.5m were officially evacuated in the first three days of September.[1599] The official evacuation from cities at risk of bombing covered children of school age and mothers with young children. Rates of official evacuation varied considerably: from more than 60% of school children in Manchester, Newcastle and Liverpool to 15% in Sheffield and 8% in Rotherham; and for mothers and young children from 35% in London to 24% in Liverpool and 6% in Rotherham. There were no clear reasons for these variations, either in the families themselves or amongst the planning authorities and their preparedness. The rural reception areas also varied hugely but there was a groundswell of complaint and amazement at the condition of the evacuees. When the war failed to materialise, the majority of them returned to their homes where they felt more comfortable and part of a community, perhaps reasoning that, if things changed, it would be better for the family to die together rather than apart.[1600] It was subsequently decided that, after the daily lives of between one-quarter and one-third of the population (those evacuated and those left behind) had been turned upside down for no good reason, mothers would be excluded from any subsequent evacuations and even unaccompanied children would only be moved out of the urban areas when air raids had actually started.[1601]

Norway Campaign

According to Imlay, the French became increasingly disillusioned with the long war strategy they and Britain had agreed initially,

---

[1597] Dilks, 1978, op cit, p67

[1598] JM Lee, 'The Churchill Coalition 1940-1945', 1980, p28

[1599] Titmuss, 1950, op cit, pp101 and 102

[1600] Ibid, pp103, 104, 105, 114-132

[1601] Ibid, pp137 and 142

thinking that they should pursue an early knock-out blow if they were ever to defeat Germany before their own resources ran out and Germany became too strong to defeat.[1602] By contrast, the British reasoned that time was on their side and, in Chamberlain's case, the hope (if not the expectation) remained that at some point the German people would overthrow the Nazi regime. As Olivia Cockett put it in her wartime diary,

> We have deliberately refrained from bombing over Germany, though we ran big risks with the leaflets. I think our Government have been sweating on the top line on fostering a revolution in Germany but now they realise they have overestimated the unrest, and anyway the actual people have no means to make a revolution.[1603]

A staple that is regurgitated uncritically across the internet is the remark attributed to Wood that "the RAF … should not bomb munitions dumps in the Black Forest", usually with the addition that this was private property. This distorts his concern, shared by many others (including the French) at this early stage of the war, that Germany should not be bombed too heavily lest they took revenge on France. What James Cecil, the 4th Marquess of Salisbury, heard Wood tell Amery **two days after the start of the war** in early September 1939 was a refusal to bomb the Black Forest or even the Essen munition works. This reinforced Cecil's contempt for the Chamberlain government but it also adhered to the cautious approach agreed with France.[1604]

Although this might never have proved the knock-out blow they sought, however, the French planned to cut off the main German supply of Swedish iron ore shipped from Narvik in northern Norway. Their objective was shared by Churchill who, back at the Admiralty, was in charge of the strongest part of the British war machine and was in any case temperamentally unsuited to a waiting game. An additional rationale for this action after the fall of

---

[1602] Imlay, op cit, p343
France had other reasons for this change, including concerns over the Soviet Union's intentions and anxiety about Britain's contribution (with only ten army Divisions on the Continent, few fighter planes and obsolescent bombers).
[1603] Malcolmson (ed.), op cit, p33 - Cockett 19th October 1939 diary entry
[1604] Kenneth Rose, 'The Later Cecils', 1975, p105

Finland may have been to demonstrate that Britain was capable of more than just reacting to German aggression.[1605]

Lord Salisbury, the fourth marquess James Cecil, set up a Watching Committee of twenty-eight MPs and peers in March 1940 to keep a check on Chamberlain for, ever since the Munich agreement unravelled, there were significant doubts that he would be able to prosecute an effective war. Indeed, one of their number Wolmer had described Munich as no more than "a short pause in the Napoleonic career of Herr Hitler".[1606] On 15th April British troops landed in Norway, and while the Watching Committee would have been pleased that this action indicated Britain was showing some initiative at last, they also warned Chamberlain that should this turn into military defeat, they would be forced to challenge the government. When Norway did prove a debacle, with the troops neither properly equipped nor supported, the crisis of confidence threatened by Salisbury was precipitated.[1607]

Even while the expedition was at the planning stage Lieutenant-General Henry Pownall was scathing:

- the Narvik scheme "has apparently been hatching for the last six weeks in the War Office, I understand that it is the child of those master strategists Winston and Ironside"
- "Of all the hare-brained projects I have heard this is the most foolish and its inception smacks all too alarmingly of Gallipoli ..." (9th February 1940)
- "The perils of amateur strategy are all with us again" after the project, initially discarded, was revived (4th April 1940)[1608]

Pownall predicted the worst:

> Great as are [Churchill's] uses he is also a real danger, always tempted by the objective, never counting his resources to see if the objective is attainable. And he is unlucky ... a bad and dangerous failing ... (30th April 1940)

[1605] Dilks, 1978, op cit, p74
[1606] Larry L Witherell, "Lord Salisbury's 'Watching Committee' and the fall of Neville Chamberlain", *English Historical Review*, 2001, 116, pp1134-1166 (p1138)
[1607] Ibid, p1154
[1608] Bond, op cit, pp280, 282 & 296 - Pownall diary entries

and yet he expected that Churchill, despite being "probably more to blame than anyone for the various muddles ... (and certainly for the general mix-up in affairs generally), seems likely to emerge with increased powers" (5th May 1940).[1609]

Other contemporary observers concluded that Churchill was either "the main contributor" to the Norwegian disaster or one of them,[1610] with Channon concurring that it "was Churchill's adventure, and poor Chamberlain blamed for it".[1611] Several historians have also judged that Churchill was largely to blame: for example, Dilks claimed Churchill had "greater responsibility than any other Minister for the failures of the campaign";[1612] the Norway debacle might have succeeded if Churchill had executed the plan properly and "The public perception of [Churchill's] value as a war leader ... was based more on his imagined than his proven ability".[1613]

Although he was not culpable, Wood did not escape entirely:

> A long Cabinet till 1.30. [Norway] situation bad, and a long discussion as to what Kingsley Wood should say to the Press. He is a chicken-hearted little mutton-head ...[1614]

[1609] Ibid, pp 304 & 306
Chief of Staff of the BEF, Pownall recorded on 20th May 1940 after Churchill had become Prime Minister that the Cabinet ordered the BEF to retire south-west to Amiens (i.e., retreat in face of a German onslaught) judging it "A scandalous (i.e., Winstonian) thing to do and in fact quite impossible to carry out ..." Bond, op cit, p323
[1610] Basil Liddell Hart, "The military strategist" in AJP Taylor (ed.), 'Churchill Revised: A Critical Assessment', New York, Dial Press, 1969 quoted in Colin F Baxter, "Churchill: Military strategist?", *Military Affairs*, 1983, 47, pp7-10; also Addison, op cit, pp87-92.
[1611] Robert Rhodes James (ed.), 1967, op cit, pp251-252 - Channon diary entry for 11th May 1940
Addison, op cit, p78 points out that 57% of the public approved of Chamberlain as Prime Minister in April 1940.
[1612] Dilks, 1978, op cit, p79
[1613] John D Fair, "The Norwegian campaign and Churchill's rise to power in 1940: A study of perception and attribution", *International History Review*, 1987, 9, pp410-437 (pp417 & 426)
[1614] David Dilks (ed.), 'The Diaries of Sir Alexander Cadogan OM 1938-1945', 1971, p272 - Cadogan diary entry for 22nd April 1940
Also Robert Rhodes James notes that Eden did not disagree with Cadogan's assessment in 'Anthony Eden', 1986, p226.

Cadogan's diary entry, and Eden's acceptance of his dismissive remark, requires some explanation. By this point Wood had become Lord Privy Seal and John Reith, who had left the BBC in 1938 to revive Imperial Airways at Wood's request,[1615] was now Minister of Information.[1616] Wood took a special interest in the Ministry of Information, and he and Reith had several talks between 11th and 14th April about the absence of any information on Norway - even after they had been to see Churchill.[1617] Although Wood and Reith had been instructed to hold a press conference about Norway, they agreed that they would not as neither of them knew anything.[1618] It was this to which Cadogan referred in his diary and Reith's recollections cast a somewhat different light on it.

However, Wood could not escape his previous responsibilities at Air completely for, on the day the troops were re-embarked from Namsos, the partisan observer Cadogan alleged that

> To my mind [the] *whole* thing turns on air production, which seems to be awful. Probably Kingsley's fault. He has the air, now, of a dog that's stolen the ham off the sideboard.[1619]

Withdrawal from Norway was clearly the right decision given the German blitzkrieg through Holland, Belgium and France a week later but this did not lessen the humiliation that Parliament felt.

[1615] Reith and Wood had resolved their differences by January 1938 when Wood suggested that Reith "ought not to stay much longer in the BBC". Reith, op cit, p301
In March 1938 Cadman, part of the Bridgeman inquiry team at the Post Office, reported on Imperial Airways and in May, once Wood was Air Minister, Chamberlain's adviser Horace Wilson was authorised by Wood and Chamberlain "to instruct [Reith] to go to Imperial Airways [as Chair] - tomorrow if possible." Reith, op cit, pp311-312; *Times* 15th June 1938, KW23 219/4 As he had to sever all links with the BBC, Reith claims that he did so only reluctantly, agreeing to become full-time executive chairman. Reith, op cit, p314
[1616] Reith had been appointed Minister of Information on 11th January 1940 and, after visiting Churchill at the Admiralty, called on Wood next. Wood was "very cordial; said he had wanted [Reith] to be in the Government from the beginning of the war". Reith, op cit, pp356 & 357
Reith became MP for Southampton on 1st February 1940.
[1617] Reith, op cit, pp374 & 375
[1618] Ibid, p377
[1619] Dilks, 1971, op cit, p276 - Cadogan diary entry for 2nd May 1940

Norway Debate

On Thursday 2nd May 1940 Chamberlain made an interim statement in the Commons but as "certain operations", as he described them, (i.e., troop evacuations) were still in progress and "we must do nothing which might jeopardise the lives of those engaged in them", a full debate would have to await their completion. The Prime Minister hoped that this would be the following week and that he and Churchill would be able to say more then.[1620] Sinclair asked for an assurance that the debate would last for more than one day so that all Members who wished to speak had "ample opportunity" to do so.

The following Tuesday 7th May Chamberlain opened the debate by speaking for an hour. He confirmed that, since his interim statement, the last troops had been evacuated from Namsos and rather than present a blow-by-blow account of the campaign he intended to give the House "a picture of the situation and ... consider certain criticisms" of the Government's actions, for "No doubt the news of our withdrawal ... created a profound shock".[1621] Not just in the Commons and the country, but "All over the world", as one MP interjected.

Although the Hansard record gives the impression that Chamberlain was listened to in silence, this was because the Speaker had made it clear early on that he would not allow members to keep interrupting the Prime Minister's speech. In an attempt to mollify those critics who sought a different kind of Cabinet, Chamberlain concluded by saying that not only was Churchill Chairman of the Cabinet's Military Co-ordinating Committee (a step that had been announced a month earlier when Chatfield retired) but he would now oversee the Chiefs of Staff Committee as well, giving him "a special responsibility for the supervision of military operations day by day ... [so] that when policy is decided upon it is followed up with promptness and energy". He would remain First Lord of the Admiralty.

Chamberlain was followed by Attlee.[1622] In Harold Nicolson's view, both speeches were "feeble" whereas the next by Sinclair was "a good one".[1623] Harold Nicolson's diary contains the

---

[1620] Hansard, 2nd May 1940, vol. 360, cols. 906-913
[1621] Hansard, 7th May 1940, vol. 360, cols. 1073-1086
[1622] Ibid, cols. 1086-1094
[1623] Ibid, cols. 1094-1106

most extensive of all contemporary reports of the debate, describing the "absolutely devastating attack" that followed from Admiral Sir Roger Keyes (1872-1945) on "the naval conduct of the Narvik episode and the Naval General Staff". Even Attlee described Keyes as "unusually lucid".[1624] Nicolson continued

> The House listens in breathless silence when he tells how the Naval General Staff had assured him that the naval action at Trondheim was easy but unnecessary owing to the success of the military. There is a great gasp of astonishment. It is by far the most dramatic speech I have ever heard, and when Keyes sits down there is thunderous applause.
> Thereafter ... all the more able Conservatives have been driven into the ranks of the rebels. A further terrific attack is delivered by [Leo] Amery, who ends up by quoting from Cromwell, 'In the name of God, go!'[1625]

There were another three hours of speeches after Amery's on 7th May before the House adjourned at 11.30pm. These are rarely reported but several commentators thought Chamberlain had survived that day.

At the opening of the following day's session the Speaker announced the death of George Lansbury and Chamberlain's tribute to him included

> In his later years [his] intense hatred of war became more and more the leading feature of his political creed. ... He ... was deeply loved by all who knew him best, on account of his passionate devotion to the cause of the poor and helpless and his unselfish and kindly nature ... one who loved his fellow man.[1626]

After Attlee and Sinclair had added their praise, Herbert Morrison opened the second day of the Norway debate for Labour. It was his

---

[1624] Attlee, 1954, op cit, p112
[1625] Nicolson, 1967, op cit, p77 - 7th May 1940
Hansard, 7th May 1940, vol. 360, cols. 1124-1130 for Keyes' speech and cols. 1140-1150 for Amery's
[1626] Hansard, 8th May 1940, vol. 360, col. 1234

394

criticisms that provoked Chamberlain to intervene fifty minutes later, accepting the

> ... primary responsibility for the actions of the Government, and my colleagues will not be slow to accept their responsibility too ... But [the occasion] is grave, not because of any personal consideration ... but because ... this is a time of national danger, and we are facing a relentless enemy who must be fought by the united action of this country. It may well be that it is a duty to criticise the Government. I do not seek to evade criticism, but I say this to my friends in the House - and I have friends in the House. No Government can prosecute a war efficiently unless it has public and parliamentary support. I accept the challenge. I welcome it indeed. At least we shall see who is with us and who is against us, and I call on my friends to support us in the Lobby tonight.[1627]

The last sentence was unfortunate for it suggested that some might put party advantage above the national interest. For Attlee, Chamberlain's "appeal to 'his friends' was ill-judged and annoyed the House".[1628] Nicolson does not mention it but it is often cited as a key reason why the outcome was so disastrous for Chamberlain. Yet there were still more than six hours of debate before the vote at 11pm and substantive speeches were to be made by Lloyd George and Cripps among others,[1629] before Churchill re-appeared in the House just after 9.30pm in time to wind up for the Government at 10.15pm.

Nicolson thought Churchill had "an almost impossible task. On the one hand he has to defend the Services; on the other, he has to be loyal to the Prime Minister".[1630] Indeed, according to Dalton, Churchill had been overheard saying to Wood as they left

[1627] Ibid, cols. 1265-1266
[1628] Attlee, 1954, op cit, p112
[1629] Hansard, 8th May 1940, vol. 360, cols. 1277-1283 for Lloyd George's speech and cols. 1289-1298 for Cripps'.
According to one Cripps biographer, his "intervention figured among the 'hardest hits' of the debate in press comment, which noted that 'in his precise and damaging way' he mounted a case for greater initiative in the war effort which was taken up in subsequent speeches". In Peter Clarke, 'The Cripps Version: The Life of Sir Stafford Cripps', 2002, p172
[1630] Nicolson, 1967, op cit, p79 - 8th May 1940

the Chamber earlier in the day "This is all making it damned difficult for me tonight".[1631] Yet although Nicolson

> ... felt that it would be impossible to do all this ... without losing some of his own prestige, ... he manages with extraordinary force of personality to do both ...
> Up to the last moment the House had really behaved with moderation, and one had the sense that there really was a united will to win the war. During the last twenty minutes, however, passions rose, and when the Division came there was a great tensity [sic] in the air. Some 44 of us, including many of the young Service Members, vote against the Government and some 30 abstain. This leaves the Government with a majority of only 81 instead of a possible 213, and the figures are greeted with a terrific demonstration[1632] ...

However, this suggests that it was the second half of Churchill's speech that (at least in part) inflamed passions and there were certainly several interruptions from Keyes, Morrison, AV Alexander, Vernon Bartlett and Arthur Greenwood among others. AV Alexander had been First Lord of the Admiralty in the 1929-1931 Labour government, and therefore one of Churchill's predecessors, and he had asked the House earlier where Churchill was: "Is the First Lord coming? Where is he? One wonders whether to go on [with my speech], in these circumstances."[1633] All five voted against the Government, though only three were Labour MPs - as did Nicolson himself. Derrick Gunston (PPS to Wood in 1926-1929 and to Chamberlain 1931-1936, who had resigned because he could stand Chamberlain's policies no longer), Bob Boothby, Quintin Hogg, Harold Macmillan, Mavis Tate, Earl Winterton and Viscount Wolmer were some of the other Conservatives who did so.

The overall vote was 281 to 200,[1634] so about 130 did not vote, either because they were absent or abstained. This huge reduction in the Government's usual majority made Chamberlain

---

[1631] Pimlott (ed), op cit, p342-343 - Dalton diary entry for 8th May 1940
[1632] Nicolson, 1967, op cit, p79 - 8th May 1940
[1633] Hansard, 8th May 1940, vol. 360, col. 1340
[1634] Ibid, col. 1362

consider his position for, as Nicolson and Blythe report, there were calls for his resignation even as he left the Chamber.[1635]

Chamberlain Resignation

Although Chamberlain's initial reaction was that he should resign, he felt differently the following day. His natural resilience was stiffened by news of the German invasion of Holland and Belgium and he argued that this was not the time to focus on internal matters. Channon reports that "various statesmen were sent for", including Wood, and that the Labour leaders Attlee and Greenwood were asked directly by Chamberlain whether they would serve under him.[1636] Dalton recorded that Chamberlain "seems determined himself to stick on ... but is offering to get rid of Simon, Hoare, and, if need be, Kingsley Wood, if this will propitiate critics. It will not."[1637] Olson also concluded that Chamberlain was trying to placate the Tories who had voted against him the previous day, but might now be having second thoughts, by offering "to get rid of [these] arch-appeasers in his cabinet ... if the members would agree to support his staying on".[1638]

It was Wood who told Chamberlain that he should not think of doing so[1639] and that it was time to resign. The *Times* journalist Colin Coote described this as "like being bitten by a gramophone", by which he no doubt meant that Wood as 'His Master's Voice' had turned on Chamberlain.[1640] A conventional reading of their relationship might lead to this conclusion but Wood was nobody's poodle. Chamberlain may have been shocked that someone with whom he had worked so closely should be advocating his resignation, but the denigration of Wood this implies is misleading. He was the protégé of others as well as Chamberlain, but ultimately

---

[1635] Blythe, op cit, p276

[1636] Robert Rhodes James (ed.), 1967, op cit, p248 - Channon diary entry for 9th May 1940

[1637] Dalton, 1957, op cit, p308; Pimlott (ed), op cit, p342-343 - Dalton diary entry for 9th May 1940; David Dutton, 'Simon: A Political Biography of Sir John Simon', 1992, p293

[1638] Olson, op cit, p307

[1639] Blythe, op cit, p277

[1640] Colin Coote, 'Editorial: The Memoirs of Colin R Coote', 1965, p293 Coote was subsequently editor of the *Daily Telegraph* from 1942. Also cited in Angus Calder, 'The People's War: Britain 1939-1945', 1969, p84

he was his own man. Indeed, one of their first interactions in the Commons had been a vociferous dispute over the Rent Restrictions Bill in 1923.[1641]

Gilbert and Gott concluded that it was the "the kiss of Judas":

> Kingsley Wood told Chamberlain that he would have to resign. The invasion of the Low Countries made a coalition necessary. If Labour would not serve under him, Chamberlain must go. Kingsley Wood was emphatic. Chamberlain had always trusted him and accepted his advice. .... Chamberlain had expected greater loyalty from so old and proven a friend.[1642]

When Churchill appointed Wood his Chancellor of the Exchequer the following day, Maurice Cowling used similar words in describing Wood then as the "indispensable Judas".[1643]

Attlee and Greenwood told Chamberlain that they would not serve under him but they would join a national government. The question was who would lead it, Churchill or Halifax.

> Then there came a wholly unexpected ally for Churchill in Kingsley Wood. Bracken was also hard at work, with his unique press contacts, especially with Beaverbrook.[1644]

Bob Boothby takes up the story himself:

> Then, suddenly, we found an ally in Sir Kingsley Wood ... who had for many years been Neville Chamberlain's closest political friend and ally. He came out in favour of Churchill. ... When ... on the morning of 10th May Chamberlain asked Churchill to see him with Halifax, both Wood and Brendan Bracken advised him to remain silent. After a long pause, Halifax said that he felt that as a peer his position out of the House of Commons would make it difficult for him to discharge the duties of Prime Minister in war. 'It was clear,'

[1641] Gault, 2014, op cit, p193
[1642] Gilbert and Gott, op cit, pp339
[1643] Maurice Cowling, 'The Impact of Hitler: British Politics and British policy 1933-1940', 1975, p385
[1644] Robert Rhodes James, 'Bob Boothby: A Portrait', 1991, p247

wrote Churchill ... 'that the duty would fall upon me - had in fact fallen upon me'.[1645]

In effect Halifax had calculated that he would at best only be an honorary Prime Minister while Churchill ran the war anyway.[1646] Chamberlain advised the King to appoint Churchill as his successor.

The Labour Party conference was then meeting at Bournemouth and Attlee and Greenwood rushed down to secure Party endorsement. Attlee put two questions to them,[1647] with the Party voting overwhelmingly in support of joining a coalition government under a new Prime Minister (by 2.413m votes to 0.17m).

Boothby identified six men who had made Churchill Prime Minister, with Wood at the top of the list,[1648] while Middlemas judged that Wood's move from Chamberlain to Churchill "indicated a movement of party and popular opinion that the leaders could not ignore".[1649]   For Addison, "The new firm of Churchill and Wood became the main Conservative axis in the new Coalition".[1650]   As Laski put it, Churchill "was a more militant enemy of labour and all it

---

[1645] Bob Boothby, 'Boothby: Recollections Of A Rebel', 1978, p144; also, Olson, op cit, p309; AJP Taylor, 'Beaverbrook', 1972, p409n
Schneer, op cit, p32 refers to a lunch with Churchill and Eden at which Wood warned Churchill that Chamberlain favoured Halifax and would ask Churchill to support him. If that should happen: 'Don't agree and don't say anything'."
Alan Clark, 'The Tories: Conservatives and the Nation State 1922-1997', 1998, pp172-173 bases his account of this lunch at the Carlton Grill on the verbatim record in Eden's diary: "To his amazement Eden heard Wood reveal that the Prime Minister intended to ambush Churchill and secure his endorsement of Halifax's candidature, adding the far from loyal advice: 'Don't agree and don't say anything'."
Also, Henry Pelling, 'Winston Churchill', 2nd ed., 1989 (orig. 1974), p435; Charles E Lysaght, 'Brendan Bracken', 1979, pp173-174: Churchill "fresh from a lunch where Wood had urged him to make plain that he thought he should succeed" Chamberlain rather than Halifax.
[1646] Schneer, op cit, p30
[1647] Attlee, 1954, op cit, p113; Dalton, 1957, op cit, pp309-312
[1648] Boothby, op cit, p144
The other five were Lloyd George, Clement Davies, Leo Amery, Brendan Bracken and Halifax himself.
[1649] Middlemas, 1979, op cit, p270n
[1650] Addison, 1994, op cit, pp101-102

stood for than Chamberlain. But Hitler had ironed out the past."[1651] Equally ironically, "the crisis of confidence in the conduct of war which provoked the revolt was about the defence of Norway for which Churchill ... was directly responsible."[1652] Churchill's appointment as Prime Minister was

> against the wishes of the King, the Queen, the staff at Number 10 Downing Street, and a substantial number of Ministers and back-benchers in the Conservative Party.[1653]

Critically though, it was not just Labour and MPs who had lost faith in Chamberlain as a war leader, with Churchill (like Lloyd George a generation before) seen as the man of destiny the country needed then. The characteristics that had often proved a liability in peacetime were exactly what might be required of a war leader. For Sheila Lawlor "reaction and bombast were transformed into patriotism and resolution".[1654] Furthermore, as Lee points out,

> The new regime brought the formal parliamentary basis for popular consent into line with feelings in the country precisely because it had the guarantee of Labour's consultations at Bournemouth and the assurances conveyed in the Conservative Party through Kingsley Wood.

and

> ... it seems clear that Wood did play an important part in swinging party opinion against Chamberlain and in giving Churchill the impression he had sufficient party backing in the country in spite of the mistrust which he still induced in the 'professionals'.[1655]

Addison adds that "the main force behind Churchill was that obscure and owlish-looking figure, Kingsley Wood, the Lord Privy Seal".[1656]

[1651] Martin, op cit, p141
[1652] Lee, op cit, p16
[1653] Clark, op cit, p175
[1654] Sheila Lawlor, 'Churchill and the Politics of War, 1940-1941', 1994, pp43-44
[1655] Lee, op cit, pp31 & 32
[1656] Addison, op cit, p101

Dunkirk Evacuation

In the face of the German onslaught in France the BEF were retreating by the 21st May. By the 28th the Cabinet had decided that they should withdraw to the coast, which meant Dunkirk as Boulogne had already been captured and Calais was surrounded. Evacuation began almost immediately, continuing to 3rd June, and although they had to leave behind much of their equipment and all the transport and heavy armaments, over 300,000 Allied (French and British) troops were rescued.[1657] Churchill made a statement in the Commons on Tuesday 4th June, drawing attention to the fact that the number evacuated were more than ten times as many as the estimate a week earlier, but that nevertheless more than 30,000 had been killed or wounded or were missing. So, while there was much reason to be thankful for the "escape of our Army", this "must not blind us to the fact that what has happened in France and Belgium is a colossal military disaster". Invasion of Britain was a likely next step.[1658]

On Friday 7th June Wood wrote to Beaverbrook, now Minister of Aircraft Production which had previously been just one part of Wood's Air Ministry but had now been separated from the remainder (under Sinclair). Wood asked Beaverbrook to "say something this weekend" about Wood's term of office at Air. The following day he received a typed sheet highlighting five of his achievements: (1) production increased fivefold; (2) labour force increased; (3) capacity developed in Canada, Australia and New Zealand; (4) large scale contracts negotiated in US; and (5) Empire Air Training Scheme conceived and inaugurated.[1659] Wood replied on Monday 10th June "My dear Max, Very many thanks. I am indebted to you."[1660]

On the face of it this was a very strange request but Wood had his reasons for making it. Although Beaverbrook was a close and influential friend of Churchill, it is hard to believe that Wood felt at all vulnerable in that respect. He had played a prominent part in

---

[1657] Bond, op cit, pp346 & 359 - Pownall diary entries
[1658] Hansard, 4th June 1940, vol. 361, cols. 787-793
For Briggs, 1961, op cit, p191: Dunkirk was "the year of greatest national danger", but also the year that made the post-war welfare state possible "when values changed as well as mood".
[1659] Parliamentary archives , BBK/C/330, Correspondence between Wood and Beaverbrook 1931-1940
[1660] Parliamentary archives , BBK/D/336, 10th June 1940 Wood reply

Churchill's elevation to Prime Minister and had been "rewarded"[1661] with the Treasury only a month earlier. The RAF had been less significant than the Navy at Dunkirk, but it could hardly be otherwise given that they were operating at the limits of their range. In any case Churchill had gone out of his way in his parliamentary statement to highlight their role, inflicting losses on the German air force of four to one. However, many of the soldiers on the beaches had not witnessed the air force play any part at all in their protection and were openly talking about it. Nicolson recorded that "the men who have come back from the front feel that Wood and Inskip let them down and must go".[1662] Even if there was no press comment, repetition of innuendo and rumour might soon have a deleterious effect on morale. Beaverbrook's statement would provide a helpful counterweight to that, perhaps thwarting any lasting impact on Wood's prospects.

But, in addition, Beaverbrook was the proprietor of the *Evening Standard* as well as the *Express* stable of papers and Wood may have known (from other sources if not from Beaverbrook himself) that three of his journalists were then preparing a damning indictment of those they thought responsible for Britain's calamities. Wood could not have been certain, but may have suspected, that he was named among them. Michael Foot was the lead author and publication would soon appear under the pseudonym Cato as 'Guilty Men'.[1663] Approaching Beaverbrook in these circumstances might have been foolhardy, and was certainly cheeky, but on the other hand Beaverbrook may have known little of the content at this stage. Wood's background would predispose him to bank as much credit as he could, building up insurance as well as to withstand any negative views that Dunkirk itself might have generated among the troops. Beaverbrook was a trump card in this situation.

[1661] Pelling, op cit, p441 uses this word.

[1662] Nicolson, 1967, op cit, p94 - 6th June 1940

[1663] See Foot's DNB entry for more detail. This includes: "Foot's friend Aneurin Bevan introduced him to the right-wing Canadian newspaper magnate Lord Beaverbrook. These two unlikely associates hit it off at once. Foot claimed to see Beaverbrook, an appeaser and champion of empire, as a fellow radical. Beaverbrook was charmed by Foot's iconoclasm and literacy. He soon made Foot assistant editor of his London newspaper, the *Evening Standard*, and Foot's columns were prominent in the paper when the Second World War broke out ... In 1942 he was to become the *Standard*'s editor."

Fall of France

In 1944 the French journalist André Géraud published 'The Gravediggers of France' under the pseudonym Pertinax. This traced in forensic detail the political and military arrogance and errors that contributed to the fall of France in June 1940. It pulled few punches and, perhaps for that reason alone, was published only in America. Géraud argued that the French army was untrained, unprepared, poorly equipped and had put too much reliance on the Maginot Line. Their air force was even less well-equipped, almost nothing had been learned from the defeat of Poland and little use had been made of the eight month lull between September 1939 and April 1940.[1664] On 16th May 1940 the French Prime Minister Reynaud appealed to Churchill for ten squadrons of RAF fighter aircraft to be sent to France but Britain, already concerned that France was a lost cause, sent very little as it would weaken the defence of London and the planes might be lost altogether.[1665] To have acquiesced would also have been at odds with the decision the Air Ministry had reached previously when they recalled four Hurricane squadrons supporting the BEF. Dunkirk a fortnight later confirmed for Britain not only that they had been correct to refuse Reynaud, but that London was as much at risk as Paris. Nor did the proposals put forward by the French Commander-in-Chief Maxime Weygand (1867-1965) cause the British to change their mind. Weygand, Chief of Staff to Marshal Foch in World War I, had retired in 1935 but had been brought back as Commander-in-Chief on May 20th even as the French were being over-run. Now in his seventies he was unable to reverse the situation and on 12th June, two days after the French government evacuated Paris, advised them to capitulate. The Germans entered Paris on the 13th. On 16th June Pownall wrote in his diary "no need to record the German advance, the capture of Paris, the entry of Italy into the war (that typical stab in the back by the descendants of the Borgias)".[1666] Britain and the Empire were fighting alone.

[1664] Pertinax, 'The Gravediggers of France', 1944, pp27 & 29
[1665] Ibid, p200
[1666] Bond, op cit, p360

Churchill Cabinet

In his final days as Prime Minister, and after Chatfield's retirement, Chamberlain had operated a War Cabinet of eight which, in addition to himself as Prime Minister and Halifax as Foreign Secretary, included the three Service Ministers (Churchill, Stanley and Hoare),[1667] the Chancellor of the Exchequer (Simon), the Lord Privy Seal (Wood) and the Minister without Portfolio (Hankey). Salisbury's Watching Committee had advocated a Cabinet similar to Lloyd George's in the First World War where the members were freed from Departmental briefs to focus on the war, but neither Chamberlain nor Churchill agreed with this, the latter because it might weaken his own position as war supremo and because he believed that Ministerial colleagues should be responsible for their own Departments.

Churchill's initial War Cabinet was reduced in size to five, with only Halifax retaining the post he had held previously. Chamberlain remained, now as Lord President, while Churchill was his own Minister of Defence as well as Prime Minister. The other two were the Labour leaders Attlee as Lord Privy Seal and Greenwood as Minister without Portfolio. The Chancellor of the Exchequer Wood was not included at this point and nor were the Service Ministers.[1668] Although Salisbury may have had some success in preventing Chamberlain from returning to the Treasury or being Leader of the House,[1669] it is much more likely that Chamberlain no longer wanted a substantive post after the mauling he had received. Yet he was still Party leader and in any case Churchill wanted to retain him for personal as well as political reasons.[1670] Churchill tried to persuade Lloyd George to return to government and, though this never happened, the press campaign against Chamberlain stopped overnight in June 1940 when Churchill made his approach to Lloyd George conditional on this.[1671]

In the wider Cabinet the same post-holders remained at Education (Herwald Ramsbotham), the Home Office (John Anderson) and the Board of Trade (Andrew Duncan) among the

---

[1667] Chamberlain had sacked Hore-Belisha in January 1940, replacing him with Stanley, and Wood and Hoare had exchanged posts in April 1940.
[1668] AV Alexander had returned to the Admiralty, Eden was at War and Sinclair at Air, with Beaverbrook as Minister of Aircraft Production.
[1669] Witherell, op cit, p1163
[1670] Dilks, 1978, op cit, p79
[1671] Ibid, p83

major offices of State, while the Pensions Minister, the Postmaster-General and the Attorney-General stayed the same among the minor ones. But most of the Ministers had changed, partly to make it evident that this was a coalition government with the Trade Unionist Ernest Bevin (1881-1951) becoming Minister of Labour and National Service before a constituency was found for him the following month (Central Wandsworth) and Herbert Morrison at Supply. Only Hoare was sacked, while Simon, another of the appeasers but perhaps crucially also a Liberal, remained as Lord Chancellor.

The criticisms of Churchill's government started almost immediately. Some were dismayed that three of the four "men of Munich" were still in senior positions,[1672] by which they meant Chamberlain, Halifax and Wood. Others that Simon, another "guilty man", remained. It was

> ... a severe disappointment to the Conservative dissidents, who felt, with good cause, that those who had put Churchill in Downing Street could reasonably expect some reward", while "Boothby, Lloyd George and many others were dismayed that so many of the appeasers remained in the Cabinet, particularly Chamberlain, Sir 'Snake' Simon, Halifax and Kingsley Wood.[1673]

Colville also noted "a great deal of feeling in the country against Chamberlain and the 'Men of Munich' and a demand for their removal from office. This Churchill would never countenance unless he considered them incompetent; and he does not."[1674]

The *Economist* was particularly critical of the "downright bad appointment" of Wood as Chancellor of the Exchequer. It argued that not only was the Treasury crucial, both because of the importance of financial policy but because of its "dominating position in the whole mechanism of Government". Wood was judged not to have either the energy or the grasp required. It went further:

[1672] Ann Chisholm and Michael Davie, 'Beaverbrook: A Life', 1992, p376
[1673] Middlemas, 1979, op cit, pp248 & 256
[1674] Colville, op cit, p164 - diary entry 17th July 1940
Also, Lysaght, op cit, p181: Bracken "railed against the survival in the War Cabinet of erstwhile appeasers ... 'Little Joe', he declared, referring to Wood, 'oiled his way in by flattery'".

That the post should have been given to a man who is not known to have any qualifications of technical competence or personal character for it and has always been a ringleader of the 'Better-Notters' is a disaster ... This appointment may be the price that had to be paid for the continued support of that section of the Conservative Party which until last week formed the Government. If so, the price is too heavy.[1675]

The financial journalist Nicholas Davenport also had a poor opinion of Wood, but for a different reason:

On behalf of capital, Sir Kingsley Wood, who had impressed nobody at the Air Ministry was shuffled to the front post of Chancellor.[1676]

Wood went on to confound this perception that he was in the pocket of the wealthy and big business.

Nevertheless, on 12th June 1940 Churchill's PPS Brendan Bracken wrote to an exasperated Bob Boothby, one of the Conservative dissidents

This is, of course, a stop-press government. It contains many glaring misfits. But most of the key jobs are in the hands of the right men. And when this whizzing crisis is over, I dare say some improvements can be made.

Cato 'Guilty Men'

The book 'Guilty Men' was published by Gollancz in early July 1940.[1677] The choice of author pseudonym might refer to Cato the Censor who a century before Cicero was the "self-appointed guardian of traditional Roman values", but more likely to the better known contemporary of Julius Caesar and Cicero who has become "a byword for virtue and truthfulness".[1678] In addition, and Foot would have been aware of this further connection, there was the

[1675] *Economist* 18th May 1940, p890; also Olson, op cit, p326
[1676] Nicholas Davenport, 'Vested Interests or Common Pool?', 1942, pp73-74
[1677] "Cato", 'Guilty Men', 1940
[1678] Anthony Everitt, 'Cicero: A Turbulent Life', 2001, pp23 & 103

Cato Street conspiracy of 1820 that aimed to murder the Cabinet as they sat down to dinner.

The 'Guilty Men' book has been accorded a significant place in the historical literature, even to the extent that it is now included as a theme on the Oxford Dictionary of National Biography website, but its reception on publication may have been more muted. Not surprisingly, perhaps, the book was not reviewed in the *Times*, the establishment paper that had taken a pro-appeasement line in the 1930s. Indeed, the only mention of it in the paper is in an advertisement for Jarrolds London bookshop on 7th December 1940: "If there were GUILTY MEN in England, there were guiltier men in France. Read **GUILTY FRENCHMEN**". The latter was not only bolder but in considerably larger type as well.[1679] Both the timing and the link to France were significant, for an assumed superiority to the French was a long-standing bolster of British esteem. The *Manchester Guardian* got as far as including it in its list of books received on 12th July 1940, and on 4th August an advert in the *Observer* trumpeted that the book had been through thirteen impressions in four weeks and that Smiths had banned it. By 1st September this had become eighteen editions in seven weeks and 94,000 copies, and a week later it had passed the 100,000 mark, allowing it to be called "world famous" (though the American edition would not be published until 20th September). But neither paper reviewed it. To the extent that it reached public attention this was despite efforts to avoid this, for even the *Daily Express* that Beaverbrook owned as well as the *Evening Standard* did not mention it.

The book traced the political errors and military misfortunes that led to Dunkirk back to the 1920s. Foot and his colleagues highlighted the six years 1924-1929, followed by the eight years 1929-1937, when either Baldwin or Ramsay MacDonald had been Prime Minister: they "took over a great empire, supreme in arms and secure in liberty. They conducted it to the edge of national annihilation."[1680] Chapter 3 added Simon to this "regime of little men", Chapter 5 Hoare and Chapter 7 Chamberlain. At this stage, "Cato" claimed, the entire country was relieved that for the "apple-

---

[1679] On 30th November 1940 Jarrolds' advertisement in the *Times Literary Supplement* went further: "If there were *Guilty Men* in this country, the guilt was doubled in France. Here is the inner story of France's betrayal by her political and military leaders: a highly dramatic, up-to-the-minute and very important document containing some astonishing revelations."
[1680] "Cato", op cit, p19

blossom of Bewdley was to be substituted the hardware of Birmingham",[1681] as Chamberlain replaced Baldwin in 1937. Eventually, there were fifteen men of Munich (as the American advertising put it) and while they were all included in Chapter 8, the one that focussed on this event, Wood did not reappear until Chapter 22, 'An Epitaph'. He was castigated for his 7th March 1940 statement that he was "satisfied" with the progress made since Baldwin had promised air parity with Germany in November 1934.[1682] This sounds rather like "being damned if you do and damned if you don't", but the book went on to criticise other claims Wood had made at the time, including that planes were being delivered faster to Britain and France (combined) than to Germany, and while the Tories applauded him others "refused to believe" such assertions.

This was not universally the position, however, for the Liberal Geoffrey Shakespeare recorded that

> Of all the schemes planned by the 'guilty men' in peace-time in preparation for war, [the Empire Air Training Scheme], initiated by Sir Kingsley Wood, acting for the British Government, in co-operation with the Dominion Governments, proved the most fruitful and decisive.[1683]

Compared to some of Cato's accusations, those against Wood were relatively modest in any case but they had a prominence due to their topicality (the troops' anger over the apparent absence of air cover at Dunkirk) and Wood's long association with the three principal "villains", the Prime Ministers MacDonald, Baldwin and Chamberlain. However, it would be impossible to be a senior political figure in the 1920s and 1930s without such links. Even Churchill, though he was not of course identified as one of the fifteen guilty men, had been responsible for some of the actions that Cato argued enfeebled the country.

On 8th July 1940 the *News Chronicle* not only reported on the book's thesis but announced the results of a Gallup poll that had been commissioned alongside the article: 75% of those questioned thought Chamberlain, Simon, Halifax and Wood should leave the

---

[1681] Ibid, p43
[1682] Ibid, p111
[1683] Shakespeare, op cit, p281

government.[1684]   These mimicked the criticisms that had been levelled at Churchill's Cabinet from other quarters (as above). Had Churchill faltered at this point then it would have been fatal (both for him as war leader and for the country), for he was not then the hero and saviour that he was to become.   Isaiah Berlin argues that Churchill's "bland and phlegmatic" stoicism enabled people to armour themselves rather than becoming downhearted and to act as heroes (e.g., in the imminent Battle of Britain that August).[1685]

Baldwin was the subject of severe criticism by many others, including George Orwell:

> ... until a time came when stuffed shirts like Eden or Halifax could stand out as men of exceptional talent.   As for Baldwin, one could not even dignify him with the name of stuffed shirt. He was simply a hole in the air. [1686]

Orwell singled out Baldwin's mishandling of domestic policy in the 1920s and foreign policy between 1931 and 1939, describing the latter as "One of the wonders of the world". Even if one accepts Orwell's critique, it might be argued that anybody who was Prime Minister three times during these years was bound to be criticised for the events of his times. And there was much on the credit side, not least his handling of the General Strike in 1926 and the abdication of Edward VIII ten years later. Or, as Harold Nicolson was to put it on Baldwin's death,

> Poor old Baldwin. He was a man of little imagination and less vision, but he certainly had a gift for dealing with awkward situations. Generally his method was to evade them. But when he was forced to tackle them ... he did it very well. He was an agreeable, companionable man. He was really far more simple than he seemed. Or rather his simplicity appeared so naïve that many thought it was put on for effect: I did not think so. He enjoyed life and had certain excellent principles.[1687]

[1684] Pelling, op cit, p451

[1685] Isaiah Berlin, 'Mr Churchill in 1940', 1949, p26

[1686] George Orwell, 'The Lion and the Unicorn: Socialism and the English Genius', 1982 (orig. 1941), p56

[1687] Harold Nicolson, 'Diaries and Letters - vol. III: 1945-1962', 1968, p119 - 14th December 1947

Similarly, when there was a "renewed outburst of [public] indignation against Baldwin [in the middle of the war] for lack of military preparedness", Ernest Bevin let him know he was furious that Baldwin was being "made a scapegoat for a national failure, for which no one could escape responsibility". Orwell and Bevin may have had similar political views, but their different perspectives and understanding reflected the gap between a commentator on the outside (dependent on orientation as much as information to arrive at a judgement) and one involved on a day to day basis seeing things from the inside.[1688]

Chamberlain's Death

Orwell was also critical of Chamberlain, coining the memorable phrase "Tossed to and fro between their income and their principles ...", people like Chamberlain could only "make the worst of both worlds".[1689] Even the devoted Colville recorded in his diaries the view of Colonel Jacob that Chamberlain

> had a heavy load of responsibility for our present state of unpreparedness, although his work for peace could not be overestimated. As Chancellor of the Exchequer, and afterwards Prime Minister, he had starved the fighting forces and refused seriously to consider their expansion, because he believed in - and staked all on - the maintenance of peace. Had war never broken out, as it appeared to many good judges that it might not, Chamberlain would have rightly been thought a superman; but as events have turned out he cannot escape a large measure of blame for what we now call short-sightedness.[1690]

Just as Chamberlain had been overwhelmingly hailed when he returned from Munich[1691] so was he enthusiastically condemned

---

[1688] Alan Bullock, 'The Life and Times of Ernest Bevin: vol. 2 - Minister of Labour 1940-1945', 1967, p113

[1689] Orwell, 1982 op cit, p60

[1690] Colville, op cit, p157 - 11th July 1940 diary entry

[1691] When Churchill returned from America in January 1942 just after the US declaration of war following Pearl Harbour the month before, he received a rapturous reception in Parliament. Harold Nicolson had missed it so asked Randolph Churchill what he had thought of it: "Nothing like the

soon after. As Lord President he chaired the Committee that co-ordinated the work of five other committees addressing production, economic, food and home policy, and civil defence, resolving any issues before securing where necessary their subsequent consideration by the Cabinet or the War Cabinet.[1692] The other members of the Committee were Attlee, Greenwood, Wood and Anderson (1882-1958). This left Churchill free to focus on the war with Chamberlain acting in effect as the home Prime Minister.

Chamberlain soon became gravely ill and though he attempted to keep working was unable to do so, dying on 9th November 1940. Wood succeeded him as Chairman of the Conservative Research Department[1693] while Churchill became Party leader. When Chamberlain's death was reported to the Executive Committee of the Conservative Party, the Chairman Eugene Ramsden "voiced the feeling of deep sorrow with which the news of his passing has been received in every section of the Party organisation".[1694] At Chamberlain's funeral in Westminster Abbey on 11th November, there were ten pall-bearers,[1695] four of whom were in the War Cabinet: Churchill, Attlee, Halifax and Wood (who had been added on 3rd October 1940 when Chamberlain resigned - as had Anderson and Bevin - with the inclusion of Beaverbrook pre-dating this).[1696] Even the grudging Scotsman Reith, never one to lavish praise if he could help it, described Chamberlain as "a man of

---

reception Chamberlain got when he returned from Munich ...," he said. Nicolson, 1967, op cit, p206 - 20th January 1942

[1692] National Archives, Lord President's Committee minutes for meeting 1, 11th June 1940, CAB 71/1

[1693] John Ramsden, 'The Making of Conservative Party Policy: The Conservative Research Department Since 1929', 1980, p95
The CRD did little during wartime and according to Ramsden the position of Chairman was never properly filled after Wood's own death.

[1694] CPA NUA 4/2/1

[1695] *Times* 15th November 1940

[1696] Schneer, op cit, p88 claims that Wood was promoted to the War Cabinet after Chamberlain's death but since this had happened more than a month before Chamberlain died, it is clearly incorrect (just one of the errors in Schneer's book). Wood may have been added to compensate for Chamberlain's absence, maintaining the party balance when the War Cabinet was increased to eight.
Anderson had become Lord President on Chamberlain's resignation on 3rd October 1940, replacing him in the War Cabinet as well.

honour, integrity, devotion".[1697] When he was complimented on his obituary oration, Churchill replied that it

> was not an insuperable task, since I admired many of Neville's great qualities. But I pray to God in his infinite mercy that I shall not have to deliver a similar oration on Baldwin. That indeed would be difficult to do.[1698]

How to Pay for the War?

A different sort of problem but an equally pressing one confronting the British Government in 1940 was how to pay for the war now that it had become real. The First World War had been funded largely through borrowing, with all the difficulties that had arisen subsequently. In addition to the impact of reparations on Germany after Versailles, Britain had reneged on its debts to America in 1934 and the Johnson Act had been passed to prevent further monies being lent until this had been repaid.[1699] Drawing on reserves was the obvious alternative for the country but both gold and foreign exchange were already depleted and were fast becoming more so. Both these factors led the country to seek a third strategy which would include, but be more than, increased taxation, the first attempt at which was Simon's inconclusive and tepid budget of 23rd April 1940.[1700] In an attempt to bridge a gap between existing income (£1133m) and anticipated expenditure (£2667m) of £1534m in 1940/41, Simon proposed to raise £101m through a combination of direct and indirect taxation leaving £1432m to be found through borrowing, further use of reserves, additional War Loans (one recently having raised £100m), additional saving and, possibly, a

---

[1697] Reith, op cit, p412

[1698] Nicolson, 1967, op cit, p129 - 22nd November 1940

[1699] Shay, op cit, p279; Brian McKercher in 'Transition of Power: Britain's Loss of Global Pre-eminence to the USA, 1930-1945', 1999, pp175-176 confirms that the Johnson Act made it illegal for foreign powers that had defaulted on their debts to borrow in the US. However, despite Roosevelt stating in November 1933 that he would not consider Britain in default, Britain was subsequently caught by the Johnson Act when US legal authorities ruled that token payments were illegal. Britain refused to pay anything in June 1934 and "all of the debtor powers, except Finland, followed its lead". The debt structure agreed at Lausanne had collapsed (also pp221 & 272).

[1700] Hansard, 23rd April 1940, vol. 360, cols. 51-88

purchase tax and Keynes' scheme of "deferred earnings" (i.e., forced deduction from wages to be repaid after the war).[1701] Much was therefore left unresolved.

A little over two weeks later Simon was relieved of the problem of squaring this financial circle and it fell to the new Chancellor of the Exchequer Wood instead. One of Wood's first steps, following the precedent he had established at the Post Office and the Ministry of Health, was to establish a Consultative Council to advise him. He appointed seven people (including Keynes) and refused either to increase its size or re-balance the membership between "orthodox and progressive financial opinion", arguing that people had been chosen for their "wide variety of knowledge and experience".[1702] He chaired it himself and its discussions were confidential.[1703] The other members included a director of Guest, Keen & Nettlefold; the President of the British Bankers' Association; the Chairman of Commercial Union; and a Director of the Co-operative Wholesale Society. At the same time Lord Catto became Wood's Financial Adviser.[1704]

The following chapter concerns this climax of Wood's career in detail, but his first budget was presented exactly three months after Simon's on 23rd July 1940.[1705] It was described as a supplementary budget but was in reality an emergency one for even though Simon's April budget had only just passed into law[1706] it was already clear that such was the increased spend on the war that it was more likely that the total expenditure for the year would be £3467m (i.e., £800m more than Simon had assumed). The task facing Wood therefore was to raise £2200m. Money spent overseas could take advantage of resources held in those countries, while a better paid workforce would contribute more in tax and would have less on which to spend their money in any case. Diverting this "excess of incomes to the State", either through

---

[1701] John Maynard Keynes, 'How to Pay for the War: A Radical Plan for the Chancellor of the Exchequer', 1940; Richard Toye, "Keynes, the Labour movement and 'How to Pay for the War'", *Twentieth Century British History*, 1999, 10, pp255-281
[1702] Hansard, 9th July 1940, vol. 362, col. 1079
[1703] Hansard, 16th July 1940, vol. 363, col. 31
[1704] DE Moggridge (ed.), 'Collected Writings of John Maynard Keynes - vol. XXII: Activities 1939-1945: Internal War Finance', 1978, pp189-190
[1705] Hansard, 23rd July 1940, vol. 363, cols. 637-657
[1706] Wood had piloted this Finance Bill through Parliament from its second reading on 29th May 1940. Hansard, vol. 361, cols. 559-568

taxation or by the public lending their savings to the nation, would also lessen the likelihood of price rises and inflation. Further increases in taxation were proposed but part of the remaining difference was to be bridged by a new form of Purchase Tax (instead of Simon's initial and tentative proposal). The "purchase tax will be a big jump too" like the rise in prices.[1707]

Wood had concluded that "the problem of financing this war is in the main the problem of directing spending power from all sections of the population into the hands of the State".[1708] An apparently intractable financial problem was to be addressed in large measure, therefore, by a psychological response that built on the economic solution, reinforcing the cooperative nature of the country's struggle, to make everybody aware that their contribution was vital and they were all in it together.

Rationing would soon be accepted, if not welcomed, for similarly egalitarian reasons. As the veteran MP Dennis Skinner described it in 2014

> The war also introduced the great leveller that was rationing. I can't think of a fairer system in my lifetime for distributing food and necessities. It was a practical form of socialism. From sweets to clothes we were for the first time guaranteed a share. Some capitalists exploited it - those with money were able to buy extras. But the black market was mostly a city curse. In rural areas there was a true spirit of camaraderie.[1709]

Similarly, Roodhouse (like Ina Zweiniger-Bargielowska before him) contrasts a high level of compliant acquiescence with rationing during the war but a reduction as victory came in sight and especially afterwards as it became more uncertain that austerity was having the same effects on all. Roodhouse explains, as did Skinner, that "Limited evasion during wartime is taken to indicate

---

[1707] Malcolmson (ed.), op cit, p149 - Cockett 20th August 1940 diary entry
[1708] Hansard, 23rd July 1940, vol. 363, col. 656
[1709] Dennis Skinner, 'Sailing Close to the Wind', 2014, p23
Orwell saw beyond the surface though: "Even the rationing system is so arranged that it hits the poor all the time, while people with over £2000 a year are practically unaffected by it. Everywhere privilege is squandering goodwill." Orwell, 1982 op cit, p84

high levels of social solidarity and strong support for the coalition government".[1710]

This was not uniform and varied according to people's understanding of war prospects. Similarly, the press took a different line in 1940 to subsequently. In November 1940 Joseph Ball told the editor Collin Brooks that his newspaper should lay off Churchill and "be kindly to Kingsley Wood. Eden he agrees can be slated."[1711] That Eden should be the straw man or sacrificial lamb that took pressure off Churchill and Wood, of course, was of a piece with their and Ball's links to Chamberlain as opposed to Eden's continuing dislike of him. Most strikingly, however, Ball's intervention took place less than a fortnight after Chamberlain's death. In effect, he was continuing to influence perceptions (if not events) from beyond the grave.[1712]

[1710] Mark Roodhouse, 'Black Market Britain: 1939-1955', 2013, p16
[1711] Crowson, 1998, op cit, p279 - diary entry for 20th November 1940
At this stage Collin Brooks edited *Truth*, known for its Neville Chamberlain support being in effect the CRD and Conservative Party newspaper.
[1712] "Even with Chamberlain on his deathbed, Ball pledged his undying devotion to the Chamberlainite cause ...", according to Cockett (1989, op cit, pp10-11). A pledge Ball seems to have kept.

19.   AN INNOVATIVE CHANCELLOR OF THE EXCHEQUER

People in Britain were confronted by the daily reality of war from the second half of 1940; both those faced with German bombing on a regular basis and those who even in rural areas would have been tortured by the likelihood of a German invasion.   The official histories written by Collier, Titmuss and others sometimes do capture the perils of people's daily life but not always.   There were in addition the records compiled by Mass Observation since 1937 and the Ministry of Information's daily intelligence reports between 18th May and 27th September 1940.[1713]   Both the latter sought to highlight everyday experience and assess morale, but there are many other personal sources, particularly diaries and memoirs of the period.   These are now legion, so only a few will be cited here: for example, JB Priestley contrasting England's summer with the threat of German parachutists and invasion;[1714] or Doreen Idle's description of the first air raid on West Ham on Saturday 7th September 1940, "Black Saturday" as Ritchie Calder called it.[1715]

> Now there is another muffled roar, like the blowing of a Bessemer blast furnace, and a fountain of flames, crested by a plume of sparks as vivid as the fire-belch of a Roman Candle, leaps to the high heavens; another building has been clean-gutted.[1716]

> Woolwich in the last weeks of 1940 was like Dante's Purgatory, with more than a smattering of the Inferno. Damage littered the streets ....
> At dawn the barrage balloons looked like a swarm of silver bees, fiery with light.   After sunset the air raids began with warnings from the sirens like a chorus of sea beasts moaning in the fog ...[1717]

Some might feel helpless in the face of such overwhelming power, but it clearly evoked a determination not to be defeated in many

---

[1713] Paul Addison and Jeremy A Crang (eds.), 'Listening to Britain: Home Intelligence Reports on Britain's Finest Hour, May to September 1940', 2011

[1714] Priestley Postscripts broadcast of 23rd June 1940

[1715] Idle, op cit, p49; Ritchie Calder, 'Carry on London', 1941, p28

[1716] Calder, op cit, p17

[1717] Denis Healey, op cit, p49

others. In Kent, while the Battle of Britain was being fought overhead in September 1940, only ninety-five expectant mothers agreed to be evacuated under the emergency maternity scheme. Two months later the number had reduced to forty.[1718] And there is almost always an upside: for example, donations flooded in from the public for aircraft, and these gifts might have been added to general Treasury funds had Wood not ensured that they were sent direct to the Ministry of Supply in response to Beaverbrook's request that he "devise some method of meeting the law on the subject so that monies meant for aircraft are spent on aircraft";[1719] the blackout and regulations prohibiting large gatherings might have curtailed the leisure and pleasures of some, but must have increased those of others; and a river service was established from Westminster to Woolwich in August 1940 to take pressure off buses during the blitz.[1720]

The Chancellor's Task

In peacetime it is often the case that the Treasury is the dominant department in government, deciding not only which priorities are affordable but frequently what those priorities should be. An effective Chancellor can have as much influence over their Prime Minister as over other Cabinet colleagues and departmental Ministers. In wartime, however, the country's priority is unambiguous: to maintain an independent sovereignty, firstly by not surrendering and then ideally by forcing the enemy to do so instead. The War Cabinet and the country's allies are supreme, but for a country fighting alone, as Britain (and the Empire) was in 1940, it is even more the Prime Minister who is *primus inter pares* - particularly if, like Churchill, he is also the Defence Minister. The war may be carried to the enemy in due course, and ideally their defeat secured, but it is up to the Chancellor to identify the resources that will enable this defensive war to be fought in the first

---

[1718] Sheila Ferguson and Hilde Fitzgerald, 'Studies in the Social Services', 1954, p39
They add that there were record attendances at Tunbridge Wells child welfare centres because of evacuees (p120).
[1719] Parliamentary archives, BBK/D/336, 25th August 1940 letter from Beaverbrook to Wood and Wood's reply 2nd September 1940. Wood was required to ensure that the gifts were detailed in the Appropriation Accounts, but these would not appear until about March 1942.
[1720] Reith, op cit, p401

place. Securing the wherewithal to translate defence into offence is an even more challenging conundrum. As McKercher put it,

> ... whilst a solitary Britain and its dominion allies could defend their position against Germany in the summer of 1940 and, after September, against Italy in North Africa, there was little chance that it could launch an offensive capable of defeating the two European Axis Powers. Indeed, as ... [the] Chancellor of the Exchequer, reminded his colleagues during this difficult time, all the government could hope to do was to finance a defensive strategy not an offensive one.[1721]

The Chancellor's first task was the fiscal equivalent of fire-watching: trying to prevent the flames taking hold but, if they did, having the right means in the right place to put them out as soon as possible.

On the other hand, in wartime nobody is casting about for policy developments that will attract more voters than they antagonise, or finding ways to present an ideology as if it were the only realistic and humane option. The purpose is clear, and it is a common one shared by all, for everybody's survival depends on it being achieved. This does not mean that the Chancellor's task is easy, far from it, but it does have the critical advantage that nobody is in any doubt about the over-riding objective. As Ritchie Calder described individual actions in the blitz, people did things to help because "they thought they ought to" not because it was demanded of them or they were ordered to.[1722] The Chancellor's role, the help he had to provide, was to find the money that was needed, and, in his 1998 book on the Chancellors, Roy Jenkins' brief summary of Wood's time at the Treasury is very positive[1723] for, as Winch put it,

> At all stages [of tackling the war priorities], equity of sacrifice and the minimisation of the difficulties and burdens of the post-war period have to be kept in view.[1724]

[1721] McKercher, op cit, p291

[1722] Calder, op cit

[1723] Roy Jenkins, 'The Chancellors', 1998, pp393-400

[1724] Donald Winch, 'Economics and Policy: A Historical Study', 1969, p256

Personal Style and Public Psychology

For the consequences of this shared purpose to be viewed positively, and morale maintained, everybody must appreciate that others are making similar sacrifices (equality) and that liberty, as well as being a goal in itself, will eventually result in an improved standard of life and better prospects (compared to what went before, if not necessarily immediately). The Chancellor might not have the dominant role, but he will have a fundamental one in demonstrating this common purpose in practice. Taxes can be a public good, but this is not a given. It depends firstly on how and to whom they are applied, for they are capable of being levied inappropriately and inequitably, and secondly what element they comprise in the total package. The overall amount to be raised can be reduced by limiting public spend and in wartime this largely means domestic and non-military programmes. There are four main ways[1725] by which governments can raise funds: taxing current income (direct and/or indirect, individual and/or corporate); taxing capital or unearned income (through, for example, stamp or death duties); borrowing, in effect mortgaging or taxing future income; and compulsory and/or voluntary saving. The balance between these elements will be part of assessing whether the overall package is thought by the public to be fair and just, as will their analysis of the reductions in spend to reduce the overall amount required. As Sir Percy Harris, the Liberal MP who had known Wood since their days together on the LCC, characterised it in the debate that followed Wood's 1941 budget "... our people are prepared equally to face these colossal burdens, provided always that everybody shares and shares alike".[1726]

In his analysis Lee furnished a helpful distinction between the first years of Churchill's Coalition when the government was focussed on "the major macroeconomic choice of allocating resources between civilian and military users. [In other words,] how much could civilian consumption be cut to make available the necessary material for the armed forces?" and the second half when the key "geopolitical question [was] of balancing British interests in Europe with those in the Far East."[1727] The Chancellor

---

[1725] There are several others for in theory people, property, goods and services can be taxed regardless of whether they move or not.

[1726] Hansard, 7th April 1941, vol. 370, col. 1343

[1727] Lee, op cit, p25

of the Exchequer was fundamental to the first question, virtually redundant in the second. This might be part of the explanation for why Wood was brought into the War Cabinet from October 1940 but then dropped in February 1942. Political balance would be another justification but America's entry into the war in December 1941, with the additional financial as well as military resources this entailed, was unlikely to have been coincidental.

Wood's co-operative and consensual approach was in tune with this public and non-partisan psychology and perhaps most importantly of all he was generally trusted - not an attribute that can be automatically applied to every Chancellor, and certainly not one that was readily associated with his immediate predecessors in the post (Simon, Chamberlain, Snowden or Churchill). As Cecil King put it, Wood "is capable and energetic ... tactful, doesn't rub people up the wrong way".[1728] And, while some might have thought him personally ambitious, this was neither a widespread view nor, even among those who espoused it, was it considered as blatant and defining as it had been with, say, Lloyd George. Some argued that if anything happened to Churchill during the war "the official Conservative view might be for Kingsley Wood" to replace him,[1729] but there were others ahead of him in the queue as well as those who believed themselves the better choice even during Churchill's tenure (Beaverbrook,[1730] Cripps and Beveridge to name but three).[1731] Wood had none of this self-deluding vanity and would have been well aware that a meteoric rise could easily be followed by a plunge to earth. On the whole, his style and approach was in tune with the country's requirements and he had already shown in several Cabinet offices that he delivered what the public wanted and often what they needed: as PMG as well as at Health, for example, and at the latter in the Ministry led by Addison after World War I, in the reforming one led by Chamberlain in the 1920s or as the Minister himself in the 1930s. When news of Wood's unexpected death in September 1943 reached Washington, his

---

[1728] King, op cit, pp50-51 - diary entry for 7th June 1940

[1729] George M Thompson, 'Vote of Censure', 1968, p114

[1730] Churchill called Beaverbrook "a magician". Reith records that one of Churchill's colleagues "remarked that the magician's chief stock-in-trade was illusion".

[1731] Churchill out-manoeuvred all three in time: Beaverbrook was sent abroad; Cripps was made Leader of the House, a position which exposed his flaws, after being brought back from Russia; Beveridge was ignored, even if his Report could not be.

economic adviser John Maynard Keynes who had worked closely with the Chancellor for almost three and a half years by then, stood up at the lunch he was attending as part of his negotiations with the Americans, and paid Wood the following exceptional tribute:

> No matter how ... apparently incomprehensible an economic proposition seemed to him to be, he ... had the gift of converting it ... into a platitude intelligible to the merest child. This is a great political gift, not to be despised ...[1732]

Indeed it is, but as well as this testimony to his political and psychological skills, it also implies that he understood economics and the implications better than have many others who have occupied the post. Being able to put complex ideas in simple terms so that others can understand them is rare indeed.

As a Chancellor of the Exchequer in the 1970s has explained, a degree in economics is of no help to a Chancellor as it can only be

> a general recollection of what he was taught at least twenty years before, by academics who had studied the economy at least twenty years earlier still. Economics is not a science. It is a branch of social psychology, which makes the absurd assumption that you can understand how people behave when they are making, buying and selling things, without studying the society in which they live, and all the other ways in which they spend their time.[1733]

Wood appreciated that he needed advice from those with an academic background in the discipline, as well as from people who understood the business and public perspectives, but he had obtained much at first hand in his various posts and in running a law firm since the first decade of the century, enabling him to assess and sift the advice he was given.

[1732] Cited by Robert Skidelsky in 'John Maynard Keynes: vol. III, Fighting for Britain 1837-1946', 2000, p144 from Milo Keynes (ed.), 'Lydia Lopokova', 1983, pp171-172 and Lionel Robbins' recollection as told to Isaiah Berlin.
[1733] Healey, op cit, p377

Links to Churchill

Churchill and Wood recognised the complementary deficiencies in each other that made them more powerful in combination. Like Lloyd George, Churchill was the maverick who took no prisoners, and he too appreciated the critical contribution that Wood's competence and conscientious attention to detail supplied. To characterise their differences in an extreme fashion: Churchill acted first on the basis of instinct and sought the justification and rationale second, whereas Wood thought ahead on the basis of evidence. One had trained as a journalist whose military career also predisposed him to activity and ideally action. Wood on the other hand had a lawyer's mind and acted only when he was sure it was required and could withstand critical scrutiny, with the consequences thought through. Churchill's charisma took him a long way, but its effectiveness depended on the skills of a Wood or an Anderson whose legwork had secured the bases. There was little point in being a strategist if you did not have the political and military tacticians who could deliver the strategy in practice. Every Commander-in-Chief requires his generals and corps commanders; every leader requires his administrators. Without this support and balance the strategist would soon be found out.

Churchill and Wood had long established a mutual understanding and, although they had disagreed over many matters as colleagues, this rarely, and never substantially, impaired a sustained working relationship from which there were benefits to be gained for them both.

Many accounts give the impression that Churchill appointed Wood his Chancellor of the Exchequer in May 1940 primarily, if not entirely, as a reward for helping him replace Chamberlain as Prime Minister. That Wood was influential, both with Chamberlain and in Churchill's handling of Halifax, is not in doubt, but there is also material in the archives that indicates Churchill had long been thinking of such a step:

- Wood's ambition to be Chancellor had been apparent to Churchill as early as March 1936,[1734] when he expected Chamberlain to appoint Wood to this post as soon as he became Prime Minister;

[1734] Gilbert, 1976, op cit, p709 - 3rd March 1936
Similarly, Reith, op cit, p251 judged that Wood "was running [Chamberlain] for next Prime Minister with himself as Chancellor of the Exchequer".

- six weeks later, when Churchill was among those advocating for a Ministry of Supply to co-ordinate the service priorities and speed up rearmament across them, he told Hankey that Wood was his nominee for the role;[1735]
- in April 1940 Churchill wrote to Chamberlain proposing that he appoint Wood as Economic Minister.[1736] Churchill hoped that this would enable Wood to "have the general direction and concerting" of departments such as Food, Agriculture, Transport and Shipping, a "closely-related group at the centre of our affairs" and the "counterpart of the Co-ordinating Committee of Service Ministers".[1737]

In other words, Churchill had judged that Wood's skills were best deployed in a co-ordinating, and ideally economic, role for some time before he appointed him Chancellor himself.

Their complementary natures and roles can be illustrated by the following exchange that took place a year later when Churchill proposed adding a Minister of Economics to his War Cabinet. He discussed this with his Chancellor on the 20th June 1941 and the following day Wood replied:

Further reflections on our conversation last night:-
1. An addition to the War Cabinet of the kind discussed would feed the controversy now being engineered again on its whole composition (see *Daily Mail* and other papers this morning).
2. Such an addition would receive little or no support.
3. The presence of both the Chancellor of the Exchequer and a Minister of Economics in the War Cabinet could not be justified.
4. It is in any event doubtful if there is now any demand for the creation of such an Office. I have seen little or no criticism of financial and economic matters except on wages, which is directed to the Minister of Labour.[1738]

[1735] Ibid, p723 - 19th April 1936

[1736] Churchill was then at the Admiralty and Wood had just stood down as Minister of Air as a result of exhaustion. Chamberlain retained him in the Cabinet as Lord Privy Seal. He was Chairman of the Home and Food Policy Committee in this post, if only for a month.

[1737] Churchill College archives, CHAR19/2B/176-178 1st April 1940

[1738] Churchill College archives, CHAR20/34/7 21st June 1941

Churchill must have accepted Wood's argument for no such post was created let alone added to the War Cabinet while Wood was Chancellor, not even in the eighteen months after Wood had relinquished a place in the War Cabinet himself.

In addition, it is instructive that, in Martin Gilbert's multi-volume biography of Churchill, there are twenty-five index entries for Wood in volume 5, covering the years 1922 to 1939, but only one pre-dates 1936 and all but three are from or after 1938 when Wood was Minister of Air. Churchill's preoccupations in these years were in harmony with Wood's Ministerial responsibilities. In the three years 1939 to 1941 covered by Gilbert's volume 6, Wood is indexed forty-five times. More than half pre-date Wood's appointment as Chancellor but all of them require sub-categorisation by issue, as was not necessary (or at any rate not adopted by Gilbert) in volume 5. Wood was then not just a Conservative Minister to whom Churchill could appeal for information or harry as he thought fit, but a Cabinet colleague and in the first years of the war one of the closest. By contrast there are only two mentions of Wood in volume 7, subtitled 'Road to Victory: 1941-1945'. This might mean that Churchill was focussed on prosecuting the war and his Chancellor, having done the needful in terms of the 1941 budget or Lend-Lease for example, was no longer a high profile part of this military and international priority. This was of course true, but the converse would be that Churchill was uninterested in domestic matters that he knew he could leave to others. In addition, he was profoundly disinterested in social reconstruction which he thought a potential distraction from a war that had still to be won. Wood had shown himself to be competent and trusted, and like Attlee, Anderson, Bevin and others, could be relied on to deliver. He was one of those who could be left to get on with it; and Churchill did.

War Damage

The Chamberlain government had originally intended that the outcome of air raids be kept secret, but this soon proved misguided because in the absence of official information people had no option but to rely on rumours that were depressing morale. The best way to counter this was to provide factual information on injuries and damage and in February 1940 Wood, then Minister of Air, and Anderson, the Minister responsible for Home Defence and Home Security, asked the Cabinet to rescind their previous decision as secrecy was no longer practicable and indeed was turning out to be self-defeating.[1739]

The following September, now as Chancellor, Wood raised the issue of private insurance schemes against personal injury in air raids. Individual responsibility continued to be welcomed, but some companies were taking policies out on behalf of all their employees and were then able to set this against Excess Profits Tax (which Wood had raised to 100% for all firms).[1740] They would therefore pay less tax to the Exchequer as a result, and Wood argued that, apart from the serious financial implications for the country, the social impact could also prove significant. Some people would be covered by company schemes whereas others were not, yet it would be far better, he argued, for the State compensation scheme to be the only one, so that unnecessary divisions were avoided and everybody was treated the same. Wood asked for Cabinet approval to stop such schemes by telling underwriters they were not in the national interest and by issuing the necessary Defence Regulation. It is hard to see this as anything but social equality in action, even though a major element of Wood's motivation was undoubtedly the financial one.

Within a fortnight he brought to the Cabinet a four page report on compensation for war damage,[1741] summarising the scheme the Lord President's Committee had eventually agreed at their seventeenth meeting the day before, having previously discussed it at their fifteenth and sixteenth meetings on 25th and 26th September.[1742] Attlee and Greenwood had been unable to support it then until Wood offered to modify it for the Cabinet meeting, a point he acknowledged in the report: In order to "meet [their] suggestions ... (and also [those of] my Consultative Council at the Treasury), I have introduced" the requirement that property owners pay during the war.

Previously, householders were to receive compensation after the war, provided they were eligible, on the basis of any

---

[1739] National Archives, CAB 67/4/41 7th February 1940

[1740] National Archives, CAB 67/8/39 20th September 1940
Wood's report on raising EPT to 100% for all undertakings (not just the 'controlled' ones Simon had proposed) had been agreed by the Cabinet on 28th May 1940 so that Wood could confirm it at the second reading of the Finance Bill the following day (CAB 66/8/6).

[1741] National Archives, CAB 67/8/51 1st October 1940

[1742] National Archives, Lord President's Committee minutes 1940-1946 CAB 71/1

resources then available for this purpose (rather than for national reconstruction, payment of war pensions, repaying "the much-increased national debt", and so forth). In other words, people whose homes were bombed in, for example, 1940 would not know until after the war ended whether they would be compensated at all and if so by how much. On the other hand, and this had been the nub of Attlee and Greenwood's concerns, there was "the problem of reconciling the interests of the general community, many of whom would suffer war losses in other ways, with those of" property-owners. Or, to put it another way, there was a risk that the latter would be compensated for their losses while others, whose loss had been as least as significant, were not. Consequently, Wood had been persuaded that property-owners "to be assured of full compensation for their losses ... must themselves substantially contribute towards the cost", with contributions collected during the war (though these would not be premiums as in "a real insurance scheme" as there was no way of actuarially assessing risk). Total damage would result in compensation at pre-war value, while partial damage would be paid on the basis of estimated repair costs. Both would be retrospective and the scheme was to run initially to 31st August 1941 (i.e., covering the first two years of the war) with a 3% charge levied on the capital value of all property. This was expected to raise about £200m (the equivalent of about £6bn today) and, if that sum proved insufficient, "the State will meet the deficiency up to an amount equal to the proceeds of the 3%". A supplementary levy would be raised if even more was required, with this amount met in equal parts by the State and that levy.

Some organisations had been advertising insurance against war damage to property and belongings and Wood was asked about this in the House, as he was about progress on the State scheme. He pointed out that there were already conditions on such adverts as a result of an Act the previous year and referred to the statement the Prime Minister would make later on the scheme the Government was proposing.[1743] Churchill's assessment was of the war situation as a whole and he opened by referring to Hitler's declaration a month before (on 4th September) that he would turn "his rage and malice on to the civil population of our great cities and particularly London". This "ruthless and indiscriminate attack upon the easiest of all targets, namely, the ... built up areas" had indeed

---

[1743] Hansard, 8th October 1940, vol. 365, cols. 253-254; the Restriction of Advertisement (War Risks Insurance) Act 1939.

been launched, and while the use of shelters had reduced loss of life, the damage to property had been immense - though perhaps not as great as had been anticipated before the war. Churchill continued:

> The Chancellor of the Exchequer ... has virtually completed the preparation of a Bill for nation-wide compulsory insurance against damage to property from the enemy's fire [thereby spreading the risk across all classes, rich and poor]. Immediate needs of food and shelter are already provided for, so is loss of life and limb ... but why should we have the whole value of the buildings of this country simultaneously and universally discounted and discredited by the shadow of a sporadic sky vulture? Such a course would be financially improvident and also fiscally inane [sic].[1744]

Churchill confirmed the conclusions the Cabinet had reached, adding that a retrospective scheme would also be introduced for all forms of "moveable property, such as industrial plant, machinery, household effects ...", before underlining the immediate steps that would continue to be taken when "any district is smitten by bombs, which are flung about at utter random" and referring to the German invasion that was still a threat but less so than it had been that summer as the weather deteriorated. This must have provided considerable reassurance for people who, though they could not be protected from the random and indiscriminate vagaries of German bombing, would be returned as soon as possible to the position they were in before - provided they survived. This must have helped people to see beyond immediate threats to themselves and towards the overall objective for the nation.

Towards the end of October, as the War Damages Bill headed for discussion in parliament,[1745] and possibly as a result of a specific bombing raid in either London or his constituency in Birmingham, Leo Amery suggested that the scheme should be operated by the private sector. Wood had robust reasons for rejecting this option, as he replied in early November:

[1744] Hansard, 8th October 1940, vol. 365, cols. 294-295
[1745] Wood opened the second reading on 17th December and the Bill received its third reading on 26th February 1941. Hansard, vol. 367, cols. 1125-1190, 1243-1299; vol. 369, cols. 541-577

My dear Leo,

Thank you for your letter of 26th October in which you suggest that claims under the Government's new compensation scheme might be settled by the Insurance Companies. Whilst we are naturally very anxious to reduce as much as possible the formidable administrative problems which the scheme presents, I do not think that we could hand over the management of a national compulsory insurance scheme involving the settlement of claims amounting, possibly, to hundreds of millions of pounds to the Insurance Companies. Moreover the amounts payable on the claims will in some cases depend on decisions of Government policy and therefore could not be entrusted to the individual Companies or their agents.

As regards your more general proposal for linking the new scheme with existing fire insurance policies, we gave such a suggestion the most thorough examination but felt obliged to reject it in the end. Apart from any more detailed points, it would not be satisfactory to base a compulsory and universal Government scheme on fire insurance values which are entirely at the option of the insured.

...

Yours ever[1746]

On 2nd October 1940 Reith, who had been replaced after only three months at the Ministry of Information in May 1940 (by the equally lacklustre Duff Cooper) and shuffled to the Ministry of Transport instead, was eased into the Lords and moved again, this time to the Ministry of Works where he was responsible for post-war rebuilding and repairing bombed buildings.[1747] Although their relationship at the BBC may have been chequered, he and Wood were clearly unable to avoid each other.

Excess Profits Tax

Criticism soon mounted against an EPT of 100% for, it was argued, this discouraged companies from taking risks.[1748] On 8th January

---

[1746] Churchill College archives, AMEL 3/8 Wood letter to Amery 4th November 1940

[1747] Reith, op cit, pp403-404

[1748] For example, Daunton, 2002, op cit, p184

1941 Leo Amery suggested to Wood that some might be a loan rather than it all being taxed - compulsory borrowing in effect that would be returned after the war. Wood replied

> The particular suggestion you mention has been before me and my advisers for some time and I can certainly assure you that it will not be overlooked in the consideration which we are giving to the whole problem.[1749]

The upshot was that in his 1941 budget the Treasury still collected EPT at 100% but Wood confirmed that 20% was to be converted into deferred credits for repayment after the war. Bevin, whom Wood had asked for his views, was prepared to accept that this proportion be handed back to firms only if five conditions were met, including that it not be used for the issue of bonus shares.[1750] Wood reiterated this caveat in his budget speech, making it clear the purposes that would be permitted in order to aid reconstruction.[1751]

1941 Budget

A recent article in *Twentieth Century British History* addressed the development of financial policy in the Churchill Coalition's first year and the role that Kingsley Wood played in influencing Treasury and government thinking in the run-up to the 1941 budget.[1752] The article stressed Wood's search for fairness and consensus, even going so far as to suggest that Wood provided "a useful wartime test case" of Harrison's key distinction between those who followed public opinion in the hunt for an acceptable consensus (the direct approach) and those who shaped public opinion towards consensus (the indirect approach).[1753] The 1941 budget was of the latter

---

[1749] Churchill College archives, AMEL 2/1/33 Wood reply to Amery 9th January 1941

[1750] Churchill College archives, BEVN 3/3 Bevin reply to Wood 27th January 1941
Bevin had also argued that the national interest should prevail and in any case some "of these great undertakings, particularly aircraft, should be taken over by the State during the war".

[1751] Hansard, 7th April 1941, vol. 370, col. 1318

[1752] Robert Crowcroft, "Financial policy, coalition and Sir Kingsley Wood, 1940-1", *Twentieth Century British History*, 2015, 26, pp74-96

[1753] Ibid, p78

variety, though some historians appear to conclude that an infinitely malleable Wood allowed himself to follow rather than shape the public view. If this was the case, why employ a radical economist such as Keynes as your adviser and deliberately seek the views of independent thinkers including Treasury officials with expertise and opinions of their own?

Even if the weight of historical assessment portrays Wood as a "yes man", this would be a novel interpretation of Keynes. Furthermore, if Keynes did not think his views were being listened to, even though they might not be implemented subsequently as practical politics in every instance, it is unlikely that he would have worked for Wood for long. Crowcroft concedes that "though the inspiration came from Keynes, Wood harnessed the economist rather than allow him to dictate policy".[1754] But it would be possible to go further than this: for example, it is clear from Keynes' 'Collected Writings' that he regarded himself as the employee and Wood as his boss, not that this would stop any brilliant policy-maker, and certainly not an economic genius like Keynes, from pushing at an open door as well as at the margins if he could. This is what Wood would have wanted and respected, and why he had sought Keynes' help in the first place. It was also of course why Keynes was prepared to give it, for patriotism only went so far, as he had demonstrated for more than twenty years, from the Versailles treaty in 1919 and the return to the gold standard when Churchill was Chancellor in 1925. In a contest between patriotism and independent thought, Keynes and all people of principle would unreservedly choose the latter.

Skidelsky judged Wood's 1941 budget one of the three "achievements with which [Keynes'] ... is chiefly associated" in the last ten years of his life (1937 to 1946).[1755] Skidelsky further explained that

> Kingsley Wood's budget was far from being a copy of 'How to Pay for the War'. [For example, Keynes had proposed that] 15% of domestic government spending ... be financed by compulsory saving; [whereas] in the upshot it was under

---

Crowcroft's reference is to Brian Harrison, "The rise, fall and rise of political consensus in Britain since 1940", *History*, 1999, 84, pp301-324
[1754] Crowcroft, op cit, p91
[1755] Skidelsky, 2000, op cit, pxxxii
The other two being the Full Employment White Paper and the creation of the International Monetary Fund (IMF).

3 per cent. This reflects both the delay in implementing [Keynes'] scheme ... and the agitation to minimise the amount of repayable taxes, whether from fear of post-war inflation or from fear that the rich would be enabled to 'live off capital'.

The social contract struck in ... Wood's budget was different from the one Keynes had sought. In the original *Times* articles the reward for increased effort was simply to be postponed. There was no explicit attention to the wages problem. In the revised and expanded pamphlet, 'How to Pay for the War', wage moderation was to be secured by family allowances and an 'iron ration' of subsidised necessities. With deferred pay marginalised,[1756] and family allowances postponed, the 1941 budget sought to win consent for taxing working-class earnings by punitive taxation of the wealthy ..., price-fixing and universal rationing. The Chancellor bought Keynes' technique, but the philosophy of the budget was socialist rather than Keynesian.[1757]

In his 1960 autobiography Herbert Morrison took the view that

[Wood's] period at the Exchequer will be remembered for his Post-War Credit scheme. I never thought much of the idea, feeling that the British people were ready to pay up in order to avoid having their throats cut by the Nazi Gestapo and storm troopers, and not to expect some of their money back when the war was won. I believed also that it was an unfair burden on some future Chancellor of the Exchequer to create a debt which, by the war's end, reached £800 million. The discreditable flavour of the whole business is hardly the fault of chancellors since the end of the war, and the non-essential sugaring of the tax pill in wartime has long since been forgotten because of the nasty taste for people with credits still outstanding.[1758]

[1756] "Marginalised" in the sense that 3% is one-fifth of 15%, but it was still more than £100m per annum, and £800m by the end of the war. £100m in 1941 is the equivalent of more than £3bn today.

[1757] Skidelsky, 2000, op cit, p87

[1758] Morrison, op cit, p204

Morrison's final point refers to the fact that, whereas EPT post-war credits were paid promptly at the end of the war, the individual credits built up

Yet, if "deferred pay" was likely to discourage voluntary saving (as Simon and his Treasury advisers had argued), Wood's acceptance of it was in marked contrast to his concern in 1911 that the introduction of National Insurance would undermine thrift. Wood's July 1940 budget did not mention deferred pay or national income analysis, for these concepts only surfaced in the 1941 budget. He had clearly come a long way.

In addition, the symbolism of Wood's initiative was huge, whatever Morrison thought then and Skidelsky today. In effect, Wood had given people hope and something to look forward to rather than just fear and something to avoid (as Morrison's approach would). In current terminology, this is the difference between positive psychology and the politics of fear.

Paul Addison does not baulk at describing the 1941 budget as Keynesian, for that was certainly the impact even if some of the intent was amended by the detail. Nor does Pimlott, arguing that Wood's "pioneering Keynesian budget" was perhaps the most important of the four "foundation stones" of wartime consensus.[1759] Addison's excellent description is worth quoting at length for its clear focus on the wood rather than the trees:

> In wartime the main method of economic planning was by the use of physical controls: the fixing of import quotas and the allocation of raw materials to industry, the rationing of consumer goods, the compulsory shrinking ... of less essential industries, and the direction of man- and woman-power. Physical planning culminated with the introduction of the first manpower budget in December 1942. ... But there remained a financial dimension which it was also vital to plan. In this respect the over-riding aim was to prevent inflation, with the industrial strife and angry queues ... at the shops which must follow.
>
> ... [The] government was influenced by [Keynes' 'How to Pay for the War'] approach and employed the budget to damp down demand. But they had no means of measuring the amount by which demand had to be reduced. Inflation

---

were not paid until women were aged 55 and men aged 60. Not all had been repaid by the late 1980s. BEV Sabine, 'British Budgets in Peace and War 1932-1945', 1970, p201

[1759] In Ben Pimlott, Dennis Kavanagh and Peter Morris, "Is the 'post-war consensus' a myth?", *Contemporary Record*, 1989, 2:6, pp12-15

resulted from the gap between effective money demand and the value of goods and services. Excess demand could be removed partly by voluntary savings: the remainder had to be taken away compulsorily through taxation. But what was the size of the gap? Only an estimate of the future level of demand and savings, taking account of the taxation and spending of the government, could provide the answer. In the winter of 1940-1941 Keynes, and two of his disciples in the economic offices of the Cabinet ..., pioneered the first official statistics of national income and expenditure. Before [this national income accounting] Chancellors of the Exchequer had dealt exclusively in the figures of government revenue and outgoings. The new statistics were a little hazardous, but they transformed the budget into the key regulator of the market economy. The budget introduced by Kingsley Wood ... was a triumph for the Keynesians ... The methods of forecasting and regulating aggregate demand ... [became] permanent. When the war ended, and physical controls were gradually abandoned, they would plainly become the chief instrument of economic management. They also opened up the vista of maintaining demand at the level necessary to prevent mass unemployment.[1760]

In the view of another historian,

[1760] Addison, op cit, pp170-171

Similarly, Simon Clarke, 'Keynesianism, Monetarism and the Crisis of the State', 1988, p246: "The 1941 Kingsley Wood budget was the first Keynesian budget. However, it was not Keynesian in the sense of using fiscal policy to regulate the market economy, for the economy was regulated by the pervasive system of controls. It was Keynesian in the more limited sense of applying Keynesian principles of public finance to the formulation of the budget."

Also Roger Middleton, 'Towards the Managed Economy: Keynes, the Treasury and the Fiscal Policy Debate of the 1930s', 1985: Keynes' theory of effective demand found "eventual acceptance and expression by the Treasury in Kingsley Wood's 1941 budget and the 1944 Employment Policy White Paper" (p4); and WK Hancock and MM Gowing, 'British War Economy', 1949, p328: the April 1941 budget increased income tax again and introduced Keynes' deferred pay/savings through post-war credits.

If one had to select a single point of time from which it could be said that henceforth a guiding principle of budgetary policy in this country should be the adjustment of aggregate demand to aggregate supply, the choice would almost certainly be ... Wood's Budget of 1941, with its explicit references to the need to judge proposals for tax increases in the light of the prospective inflationary gap.[1761]

There is a risk that the clarity of Addison's analysis, or of Prest's assessment, might lead to the conclusion that this approach was inevitable and the outcome relatively effortless. This was far from the case. The 1941 budget had been months in the planning precisely because after the interim/supplementary budget of July 1940 Wood and his advisers were aware that they had to be more innovative in 1941 if the gap was to be closed, and funding for the war found, permanently. The radical nature of the budget reflected (a) a shift in the role of the State, i.e., a fresh view of the national economy, and (b) committed "the government to an unknown and unlimited liability until normal economic conditions resumed", the task in wartime.[1762] "More of the same" was not an option. In October 1940 Wood and his advisers, Keynes, Catto (1879-1959)[1763] and Stamp (1880-1941),[1764] together with Hopkins and Phillips (1884-1943) from the Treasury, held a strategy meeting to consider the possibilities, with Wood pressing them to propose alternatives. Catto's and Stamp's suggestions fell fairly early, as did Keynes' surcharge proposals. What survived was forced saving in the form of post-war credits, along with changes to income tax schedules and rates. Keynes' record of this debate makes it

---

[1761] AR Prest, "Sense and nonsense in budgetary policy", *Economic Journal*, 1968, 78, pp1-18 (p2)

[1762] Crowcroft, op cit, p88

[1763] Thomas Catto succeeded Montagu Norman as Governor of the Bank of England in 1944. See his DNB entry for further details. Norman had chosen Catto to be Wood's financial adviser according to David Kynaston, 'The City of London, vol. III: Illusions of Gold 1914-1945', 1999, p472.

[1764] Josiah Stamp and Wood had known each other for many years, both through the Methodist church and Kent. For example, both Wood and Stamp opposed a Methodist Union in 1926 -1927 (*Times* 13th January 1927, KW16 259/2 reports a meeting at the Kingsway Hall at which Wood was present and Stamp was among those who sent messages opposing Methodist Union). Stamp was killed in an air raid at his home in Shortlands Kent. See his DNB entry for further details.

abundantly clear that it was Wood who "decided" this by February 1941,[1765] so determining the financial strategy that would be followed in the budget.[1766] Crowcroft added

> Significantly, [Wood had] explicitly ordered that the 'psychological' implications of each scheme be weighed in detail alongside the 'financial', building a political consensus for the implications.[1767]

For Daunton "The 1941 budget marked the limit of reliance on direct taxes ...",[1768] the view taken at the time as the cartoon on the following page shows. How Wood managed to convince Churchill and the Cabinet that income tax be raised from 8s 6d to 10/- in the £ Sabine describes as a political mystery,[1769] concluding that it must have been the justification for also extending it down the income scale. This argument is the same as Crowcroft's about equity and fairness.[1770]

The politically aware Olivia Cockett was conscious of the severe, and frequently unanticipated, impact on many people who had no liability to income tax before this:

> I am troubled about the reaction in November, when so many workers will <u>have</u> to pay income tax for the first time. There will be very bitter resentment, and it will be a fearful shock. A <u>lot</u> of poster propaganda, showing how income tax helps, is vitally necessary - and soon so that people do not

---

[1765] Moggridge, 1978 ('CW JMK: vol. XXII'), op cit, pp254-255
Keynes' extensive description of the 1941 budget and its development occupies the whole of Chapter IV, pp195-354.
[1766] Crowcroft, op cit, pp90-91
[1767] Ibid, p89
[1768] Daunton, 2002, op cit, p185
[1769] Sabine, op cit, p199
[1770] *Primrose League Gazette* May 1941 explained "In his most drastic Budget the Chancellor imposed no new commodity or indirect taxes, confining himself to income tax." (p6)
The rate increased from 8s 6d to 10s in £; for earned income from 5s to 6s 6d in £; relief for married persons reduced from £170 to £140 and for single persons from £100 to £80; relief for earned income 1/10th instead of 1/16th.
Middlemas, op cit, p279 contrasted 100% EPT and 10s income tax with the First World War funded through debt.

have this sudden cutting down of their pay packets without <u>any</u> word of thanks or explanation from Authority.[1771]

© Solo Syndication/Associated Newspapers Ltd.
Dear me, we seem to have reached the limit
Leslie Illingworth, *Daily Mail* 2 October 1941

Wood's budget speech covered thirty-six columns in Hansard and took over two hours to deliver "without even a sip of

---

[1771] Malcolmson (ed.), op cit, p199 - Olivia Cockett 10th September 1941 diary entry
The editor Malcolmson explains that "The budget of 1941 raised the rates of income tax and significantly reduced the number of earners exempt from tax. ... A total of some four million new taxpayers were created."

water".[1772]   The opposition responses and the remainder of that day's debate occupied fifty columns.[1773]   The first to speak was Lees-Smith, the MP for Keighley and a previous PMG, whose initial remarks sum up the importance of the budget in opening a new chapter in the country's financial story:

> This year the right hon. Gentleman has broken the record. He broke a record with his last Budget, and he has broken it again this year. He has presented a Budget relating to the largest expenditure in the history of the nation and imposing taxation reaching the highest peak that has yet been achieved.   The right hon. Gentleman explained his proposals and generally carried through his task in such a disarming manner that it was, at times, difficult to realise the magnitude of the figures with which he was dealing.   He is Chancellor of the Exchequer at a time when bold measures are needed, and the present Budget will not be criticised on the ground of timidity as other Budgets have been in the past.   The right hon. Gentleman has included in it many novel features which will make our Debates this year of a great deal more than usual interest.
> As far as the actual figures of expenditure are concerned, the higher they are the more the nation will welcome them, because they mean equipment for carrying on the war. When we have the same equipment as the Germans, so that we can meet them on equal terms, as man to man - on that day the end of the war will be in sight.   Undoubtedly, the largest features of the Budget, and in a way the most novel, are those contained in the new scheme of Income Tax which the right hon. Gentleman explained.[1774]

He was followed by the Liberal Sir Percy Harris, whose congratulations to Wood were

> There was no embroidery or attempt at oratory. He took the Committee into his confidence and made us a plain, common sense, business statement. It is not an easy or an

---

[1772] Sabine, op cit, p187
[1773] Hansard, 7th April 1941, vol. 370, cols. 1297-1332 & 1335-1384 The proposals are set out in cols. 1332-1335.
[1774] Ibid, col. 1335

attractive task for a Chancellor of the Exchequer in war-time. He can offer no hope of lightening the burden of the taxpayer ... He can only give a gloomy foreboding of having to add new and fresh taxes. I think that my right hon. Friend showed courage in following a simple and straightforward method in raising the necessary money.[1775]

These were repeated by other MPs on all sides of the House. The Conservative MP for Chislehurst thought that Campbell, Wood's PPS, "must have been giving him some good practice in the [cricket] nets",[1776] while the Labour MP for Stoke added

The Chancellor of the Exchequer had a very difficult task to-day, made more difficult because in the past we have not faced up to the seriousness of the financial situation. I join with those who have congratulated him on the clear statement which he made ... The Chancellor of the Exchequer said, 'We must have regard to the post-war reconstruction and social advance which we all desire to achieve'. He went on to say, 'The housing difficulty of the last post-war period was largely due to interest payments'. That was significant, coming from the right hon. Gentleman.[1777]

In the view of Alfred Barnes, the Labour Co-op MP for East Ham South and Wood's adversary from Woolwich, "This is the first Budget which I think begins to reflect some understanding of the financial consequence of a totalitarian war". The main dissenting note came from those who were concerned about the impact after the war, either in terms of the affordability of reconstruction or its nature and the risk of returning to the pre-war position where the entrenched establishment preserved the status quo. As the Communist MP Willie Gallacher put it, "the same old Tory measures of the same old system of society".[1778]

Wood's presentation of the budget, as well as its contents, demonstrates his analytical, psychological and down-to-earth skills at their best. The debate on the second and third days underlined

---

[1775] Ibid, col. 1340
[1776] Ibid, col. 1344
[1777] Ibid, col. 1349
[1778] Ibid, cols. 1379-1384

this, as did the consideration of the Finance Bill subsequently.[1779] For example, the opening speech on day 2 from Frederick Pethick-Lawrence judged that the budget passed his three tests of facing the facts, delivering the goods, and doing so fairly. It was rightly regarded as a watershed, "the greatest financial revolution we have gone through" as one MP said. Wood referred to it as his stabilisation budget for "finance [is] a vital factor in the war effort" and it had achieved the requirements.[1780]

It also belies the historical record that Wood was a poor speaker in the Commons. Wood had not sought consensus for its own sake as the only option open to him, but rather his innovative approach resulted in consensus because people could see the sense in it. As Colville recorded in his diary,

> Budget: income tax ten shillings in the pound. Nobody seems to mind. Brendan [Bracken] says the House and the Country take a masochistic pleasure in it, like flagellating friars.[1781]

Two other judgements should also be mentioned. In October 1942 an *Economist* article "The burden of taxation", commented that

> ... the present burden of taxation is very much heavier, on all classes of income, than ever before.
> The other main conclusion is that the British system of taxation has been getting noticeably more equitable. The test of an equitable taxation system is, of course, whether it is progressive ... From £200 a year (or a little more) upwards, the present tax curve is progressive and in the upper reaches it is confiscatory. Whatever else may be its defects, substantial equity has been achieved. This is not the least of the social triumphs of the war, and it is one that should be retained when the war is over.[1782]

[1779] Sabine, op cit, pp187-198

[1780] Ibid, pp199 & 201 Sabine describes the subsequent 1942 budget as a return to financial orthodoxy.

[1781] Colville, op cit, p321 - 7th April 1941

[1782] *Economist* 24th October 1942, pp504-505 reviewing Professor Findlay Shirras and Dr L Rostas 'The Burden of the British Taxation', NIESR Studies No. 2, undated, 240pp on the impact of total taxation across different incomes (i.e., not just income tax).

The second was that of Keynes himself a week after the budget:

> ... Sir Richard Hopkins and Sir Horace Wilson, as well as the Chancellor, have been extraordinarily good to me and open-minded and ready to be persuaded; and Lord Catto has been a great help all through. Indeed we were a wonderfully united team.[1783]

To which one should add that the team was Wood's: he had not inherited it (as he had Treasury officials such as Hopkins and Wilson), he had created it. Some historians have judged his budget incremental.[1784] There are two possible reactions to this: to the extent that increments imply small steps and gradualness the 1941 budget is striking for its discontinuity, a step-change from all those that had gone before; the other is that, if this is the unbiased historical judgement seventy-five years on, Wood must have been even more subtle than he has been given credit for. In other words, the budget "extended the purpose of budgetary policy", no longer just cash surplus for the coming year but instead "a comprehensive survey of the national economy," a national accounting framework.[1785]

Lend-Lease Article VII

In August 1943, about seven weeks before he died, Wood drafted a reply for Churchill to use when explaining what Lend-Lease had meant originally and what it came to mean once the USA was a combatant in the war after the Japanese attack on Pearl Harbour in December 1941.

> It started as a means by which the United States, still neutral, gave us arms because they deemed our defence vital to their own defence - these words are drawn from the Lend-Lease Act; now that they are in the war it has developed into one aspect of the general principle of the pooling of resources; under it, we both give and receive, in

---

[1783] Moggridge, 1978 ('CW JMK: vol. XXII'), op cit, pp353-354: Keynes' letter to his mother 14th April 1941.

[1784] Crowcroft, op cit, p95 for example.

[1785] Pimlott, 1985, op cit, p467

order to ensure that the resources of the United Nations [sic] shall be distributed in the most efficient way.[1786]

Wood was using the term "United Nations" to refer to Britain and its allies. As Winterton had made clear in opening a Commons debate on post-war economic policy six months earlier, this meant specifically the United States, USSR, China and the Dominions.[1787]

Wood's bland statement might be taken to indicate that the Lend-Lease negotiations between Britain and America had proceeded smoothly throughout. But there were factions in the US government just as there were in the British one, with clear differences between the apparently positive intent of President Roosevelt (1882-1945) and the less benign State Department led by Cordell Hull (1871-1955). The latter thought help to Britain should result in a "consideration" that in the absence of a post-dated cheque would enable America to recoup their assistance in the long-term. This would become enshrined in Article VII of the Lend-Lease Act, but there would be many twists and turns to the story before this was crystallised in a form accepted by both sides.

One of the starkest differences between Britain and America had been evident for some time for, once the main proponent of free trade, Britain had moved between the wars towards Imperial Preference (i.e., favouring trade with the Empire as enshrined in the Ottawa Agreement 1932). By contrast, Hull's State Department had moved the US towards freer trade.[1788] The State Department wanted Britain to relinquish Imperial Preference in return (i.e., as a "consideration") for Lend-Lease, arguing that they ought to jettison such trade "discriminations", as it was to be described in a July 1941 draft. Wood, Leo Amery and Arthur Greenwood, among others, were against this and at their prompting Churchill offered to abolish "harmful" discriminations in trade after the war. Needless to say, this did not go far enough to satisfy Cordell Hull.

Another critical distinction, as Roosevelt's appointee as Ambassador to Britain the anglophile John Winant (1889-1947) was

---

[1786] Churchill College archives, CHAR20/93B/149 2nd August 1943
He added "We shall shortly be taking steps which will, I hope, make this matter more fully understood", suggesting that Churchill defer his reply until the White Paper on Mutual Aid was published the following week.
[1787] Hansard, 2nd February 1943, vol. 386, col. 774
[1788] Alan P Dobson, "'A mess of pottage for your economic birthright?' The 1941-42 wheat negotiations and Anglo-American economic diplomacy", *Historical Journal*, 1985, 28, pp739-750 (p739)

aware, was between a country already at war with Germany and the non-combatant US that at that stage viewed Lend-Lease primarily as a business transaction.

The forerunner of Lend-Lease in September 1940 was a deal to exchange old US destroyers (replacing those Britain had lost off Norway and Dunkirk and the loss of the French navy) for bases in the western hemisphere. Britain already paid for weapons to strengthen its land defences from US surplus stocks and these were carried to Britain in both US and allied ships.[1789] Although the American people largely accepted that they would provide "All aid short of war", this was a "cash and carry" arrangement and neither they nor the US Congress thought it should be free. The US Treasury Secretary Henry Morgenthau (1891-1967) also took this line and indeed the US Treasury starting-point was that Britain should not have gold and dollar reserves, or securities held abroad, while receiving assistance from the US for nothing. Keynes and Frederick Phillips, the man despatched to Washington to conduct negotiations initially, had agreed after a policy meeting with Wood and others at the end of October 1940 that it was not unreasonable to retain £175m (5% of total spend) as a contingency, roughly the amount of dollar securities that Britain had left.[1790] Otherwise Britain would become a client state, completely dependent on America, and if all its gold and US investments were liquidated, unable to meet its many responsibilities elsewhere.[1791]

Roosevelt announced in December 1940, first in a press conference and then in one of his "fireside chats" to the nation after Christmas, that a formal programme called Lend-Lease would begin in 1941. Under this programme

---

[1789] Hancock and Gowing, op cit, p227

[1790] DE Moggridge (ed.), 'The Collected Writings of John Maynard Keynes - vol. XXIII: Activities 1940-1943: External War Finance', 1979, pp12 & 27-28

This account deliberately simplifies three sets of negotiations: the liquidation of British assets in the US, a loan arranged through Jesse Jones at the US Department of Trade and the Lend-Lease discussion. Phillips was responsible for the first and Keynes was sent to Washington to conduct the third himself.

Skidelsky, 2000, op cit, pp126-131, 133 & 226 provides a succinct record of Article VII negotiations.

[1791] Moggridge, 1979 ('CW JMK: vol. XXIII'), op cit, p45

materials necessary for 'the defence of the US' could go to Britain, if the President thought this the most efficient way of using them, subject to acknowledgement by some consideration subsequently negotiated.[1792]

This was to Britain's advantage in that it would be sent the materials first, without any requirement to pay for them immediately; to its disadvantage in that Roosevelt made the State Department responsible for the negotiation of the "consideration" and once Lend-Lease was under way (especially before the Bill became law on 11th March) Morgenthau might be better placed to argue that the liquidation of Britain's assets overseas would help pay for what it had already received in the interim.[1793]

The different interpretations within the US government led Keynes to write a lengthy memo for Wood at the end of January 1941 setting out the practical details and covering both the old (destroyers for bases) arrangement and the issue of interim finance.[1794] Harry Hopkins (1890-1946), the first head of the Lend-Lease programme in 1941 (and later Roosevelt's adviser and assistant), was in Britain in January 1941 to assess the country's resolve on Roosevelt's behalf and Keynes had discussed his concerns with him before briefing Wood. It was clear that Roosevelt's less demanding expectation of the "consideration" would not necessarily be the one that prevailed in the US, especially as there was no guarantee that Roosevelt would be allowed to run for a fourth term in 1944 and, even if he was, that he

---

[1792] Ibid, p29
Lee, op cit, p37 describes the shift from cash and carry to lend-lease as President Roosevelt "was able to move Congress from allowing supplies in November 1939 on a 'cash and carry basis' to accepting the principle of lend-lease in March 1941. The British purchasers changed from paying in cash and carrying in their own ships to simply taking delivery and leaving the bills to accumulate."
[1793] Moggridge, 1979 ('CW JMK: vol. XXIII'), op cit, p45
The Bill had started its passage through Congress on 10th January 1941, becoming law as HR1776 (a significant date in US and British history). Meanwhile, Canada carried on supplying Britain regardless of its ability to pay. Hancock and Gowing, op cit, pp233-235
[1794] Moggridge, 1979 ('CW JMK: vol. XXIII'), op cit, pp41-44

would necessarily win.[1795] Sooner or later Britain would have to deal with a different US President and should therefore ensure as soon as possible that the interpretation of the "consideration" was agreed by all parties.

Keynes was then sent to America in May 1941 to oversee the negotiations himself, bolstering Phillips rather than replacing him. Keynes thought Morgenthau, one of the first people he met, "not merely tiresome but an ass", for "if we were to acquiesce in his policy [of liquidating British assets], we should be laying up [a] great store of trouble for everyone concerned". Keynes suspected Morgenthau's motives which might be partly to placate opposition in Congress but might also be "connected with his future power to impose his will on us".[1796] Keynes was not prepared to be bullied and, once this became clear, he and Morgenthau eventually established a productive working relationship.

By June 1941 the "consideration" for Lend-Lease was the remaining outstanding issue, as Keynes briefed Wood in a long letter in mid-June. The US Treasury and State Departments had been batting a draft back and forth between them, and Keynes's letter included a first draft he had compiled "for my own purposes", envisaging co-operation on post-war economic policy and including "a declaration of common purpose".[1797] He asked Wood to cable back any reservations,[1798] and after consulting Churchill, Wood replied a week later that the Cabinet would have to formulate Britain's position and the Dominions and India would have to be involved as aspects affected them.[1799] Finally, on 28th July the US produced a draft which included the term "discrimination" in Article VII on the "consideration", a word that Keynes disliked intensely as

---

[1795] Roosevelt had won a third term (1941-1944), the first US President to do so. After his Presidency the previously unwritten rule that Presidents not serve more than two terms became part of the US Constitution.
[1796] Moggridge, 1979 ('CW JMK: vol. XXIII'), op cit, p46
Keynes' subsequent assessment of Morgenthau is on pp87-91.
[1797] LS Pressnell with Sheila V Hopkins, "A canard out of time? Churchill, the War Cabinet, and the Atlantic Charter, August 1941", *Review of International Studies*, 1988, 14, pp223-235 (p224)
[1798] Moggridge, 1979 ('CW JMK: vol. XXIII'), op cit, pp133-140 21st June 1941
[1799] Ibid
Also, Skidelsky, 2000, op cit, p128: Wood pointed out the fundamental issues raised by heads of agreement and warned Keynes off any further concessions.

it would probably preclude Imperial Preference.[1800] "The lunatic proposals of Mr Hull", was Keynes' reaction according to Skidelsky.[1801] Returning to London at the end of July, Keynes proposed three options for dealing with the American draft: changing the wording, a separate explanatory document agreeing how Article VII was to be interpreted or an Anglo-American conference to discuss it (though the latter had previously been discouraged by London).[1802]

During August 1941, as part of the Atlantic Charter Roosevelt and Churchill were negotiating, a similar issue arose. In this instance, Wood proposed replacing discrimination with the phrase "with due respect for their existing obligations" (as had Churchill), adding "within the limits of their governing economic conditions".[1803] Keynes told Catto and Hopkins "The revised formula suggested by the Chancellor certainly would not commit us to abandoning the system of Imperial Preference in principle", only to working "to the best of our ability ... [to reduce] such special arrangements as much as possible".[1804]

Once America declared war in December 1941, Lend-Lease became understood on both sides as mutual aid, with Roosevelt's position even stronger than it had been previously and US State Department attitudes less rigid. On 17th January 1942 Wood submitted a comprehensive four page, fourteen paragraph memo to the War Cabinet setting out the up-to-date position.[1805] The salient paragraphs were:

1. Article VII as drafted included the "declaration on our part that we shall work towards the eventual abolition of Imperial Preference". This was unnecessary now, would be controversial in the Dominions, and would provoke opposition in parliament and the country, even though it was only the "eventual" and "ultimate" aim.
2. Imperial Preference should be removed from the list. The US were unlikely to object as it was not a sticking-point in agreeing the Atlantic Charter.

[1800] Moggridge, 1979 ('CW JMK: vol. XXIII'), op cit, pp171-177
[1801] Skidelsky, 2000, op cit, p130
[1802] Moggridge, 1979 ('CW JMK: vol. XXIII'), op cit, pp194-196
[1803] Pressnell with Hopkins, op cit, pp227 & 228
[1804] Moggridge, 1979 ('CW JMK: vol. XXIII'), op cit, p204
[1805] Churchill College archives, AMEL 1/6/9 WP (42) 25 for War Cabinet 17th January 1942

3. In any case Imperial Preference was of practical value to the UK, especially as "the proper balancing of our external trade may well prove to be one of our most formidable post-war problems".

4. It would be dangerous, therefore, to rule out Imperial Preference now for the following reasons:

   5. UK exports to the Empire were half of the total of £470m, while the US only accounts for £20m, and the bulk of those to Europe had been prevented by the war;

   6. UK was no longer a manufacturing economy as it had been in the nineteenth century; therefore need to maintain "invisible exports" to pay for the imports the country needs;

   7. "unrestricted world competition" after the war would not be good for the UK and Imperial Preference might prove "indispensable to restoration of our national economy" (e.g., cotton industry);

   8. nor is reduction in US tariff as *quid pro quo* useful: in the immediate aftermath all markets likely to favour sellers, whereas in the longer term all countries would benefit from reduction in US tariff;

   9. Imperial Preference also critical to welfare of colonies in East Africa, West Indies, Mauritius and Fiji; this is not the time to remove it especially as the public increasingly conscious of these wider welfare issues; it "would spell ruin for many of [these Colonies]";

   10. importance of political solidarity of Commonwealth, both of itself and in promoting world peace; and

   11. US tariffs favour Puerto Rico.

Everybody wants to reduce tariffs, but preference may be different and whereas the US has a federal structure it is Imperial Preference that provides the Commonwealth with its economic ties.

12. Post-war Europe may well see small nations banding together in this sort of preference structure (i.e., economic block) and we should welcome this as the best means to preserve peace.[1806]

13 Other non-Imperial Preference aspects of Article VII were also of concern, as telegrams from Halifax (Britain's Ambassador in the US) had already shown: "... after the war [the country will need] measures to safeguard our economic position unless and until better arrangements can be devised".

[1806] This was to prove a far-sighted prediction; even if, by a slight majority, Britain would vote to leave the EU after 40 years in 2016.

Consequently, Britain should not sign this Agreement unless and until an interpretive document is forthcoming.

14. **Matters have changed greatly since July 1941 when the Agreement was drafted** [emphasis added]. It now looks odd and out-of-date as US also involved in all-out war and, therefore, a reciprocal agreement would now be more appropriate.

So, if Britain was to sign the Agreement, it should be accompanied by a note of interpretation setting out agreed US/UK understanding of Article VII. On 6th February the Cabinet decided to send the telegram Eden had drafted two days earlier, let the Dominion governments know the action Britain was taking and make it clear to the President that

> the point to which we attached most importance was that we should not be asked to give any undertaking in regard to our system of Imperial Preference in exchange for benefits under the Lend-Lease Act.[1807]

The necessary assurance was then provided by Roosevelt and the Lend-Lease Agreement signed on 23rd February 1942.[1808]

In August 1942 Wood reported to the Cabinet on Lend-Lease operations, noting that this worked both ways.[1809] Britain had paid the US £1000m "for a very large proportion of arms and other commodities ... and we [also] furnish aid to the US", for example, supplies and services at no charge to the American troops based in Britain and the Empire. By the time of his financial statement the following April Britain's spending in the US had risen by 50% to £1500m (£1.5bn then, the equivalent of £45bn today) since the outbreak of war, and the reciprocal principle of Lend-Lease

---

[1807] National Archives, CAB 65/25/14 and CAB 65/25/17 set out further Cabinet discussions on 2nd and 6th February 1942.
The latter includes Wood's endorsement of Eden's 4th February 1942 WP(42)62 alternative draft reply to Halifax after consultation with Wood. This included in para 2: "Present wording of Article VII must inevitably provoke awkward questions [re Imperial Preference and general post-war economic difficulties] to which satisfactory answers will be difficult ..."
[1808] Skidelsky, 2000, op cit,p133; Dobson, op cit, p749; David Reynolds, 'The Creation of the Anglo-American Alliance1937-1941: A Study in Competitive Co-operation', 1981, pp270, 272, 279
[1809] National Archives CAB 66/28/16 28th August 1942

extended beyond Britain's support to the US to Russia, China and certain allies in Europe.

> The supplies which we are contributing in this way to the common task have increased greatly in the last year. The whole conception of the plan does not and is not intended to lend itself to close accounting. The American people have never put the dollar sign in the help they have given us, and we are not putting the pound sign in the help we give back to them or give to others.[1810]

Consequently, though Wood had told the Cabinet in August 1942 that he expected to provide parliament with the specifics, he never did so either in April 1943 when answering oral questions or two months later when replying to the same questioner in writing.[1811] On the latter occasion Richard Stokes (1897-1957), Labour MP for Ipswich, had asked, as the US government was keeping a detailed tally, how Wood

> proposed to deal with any claim made against this country at the end of the war, in view of the fact that no similar strict account is being kept of any supplies or services rendered by this country to the United States?,

to which Wood responded that

> Our position will not, in my judgment, be prejudiced by the fact that we do not keep a strict monetary account of the value of supplies and services rendered by this country to the United States. I explained in my Budget Speech why we do not do so.

Wood's successor Anderson took the same stance when Stokes pursued the issue with him later in the year.[1812] In view of

---

[1810] Hansard, 12th April 1943, vol. 388, col. 938
It should be noted for comparison purposes that by this point Britain was spending £15m per day on the war, three times what it had been in 1940. (col. 943)
[1811] Hansard, 8th April 1943, vol. 388, cols. 806-807 and 3rd June 1943, vol. 390, col. 384
[1812] Hansard, 26th October 1943 vol. 393, cols. 43-44 and 2nd November 1943, vol. 393, col. 523

this, it is worth noting that Britain finally paid off its Lend-Lease debts to the US in December 2006.[1813]

In July 1943 Wood, Eden and Dalton (by then President of the Board of Trade) proposed the start of discussions with the US on the full range of items covered in Article VII ("principally monetary policy, international investment ... and commercial policy"). While it would be necessary for multilateral discussions on specific issues in due course (e.g., commercial policy), they argued that there would be advantages in agreeing an overall programme with the US first. Frederick Phillips had started some preliminary discussions but was now ill (and would be dead within the month) and in any case a delegation led by Eden's PS at the Foreign Office (Richard Law, Conservative MP for South West Hull) "would emphasise the formal and comprehensive nature" of Britain's approach.[1814] The British Ambassador Halifax was to be asked to alert Cordell Hull at the US State Department to the initiative. Wood and his Cabinet colleagues were already looking to shape the post-war world.

Family Allowances

In World War I Wood had been vice-chair of the London committee administering separation allowances to women whose husbands were in the services.[1815] As Burnett noted, the separation allowance system was one of the main factors in improving living standards during this period (along with "the virtual disappearance of unemployment, [and] employment of married women at relatively well-paid work").[1816] Wood had introduced the Widows', Orphans' and Old Age Contributory Pensions Act in 1925 and several other initiatives designed to reduce poverty and improve people's well-being. These can be traced as far back as the early 1900s when he fought many cases as a lawyer for workmen's compensation, in addition to other examples from his time as Minister of Health.

[1813] Hansard (HC Deb 6s.), 28th February 2002, vol. 380, Ruth Kelly answer to Bob Spink (1439w to 1441w) covering all World War II debts of which Lend-Lease was $586m (£145m at 1945 exchange rates), the total being repaid in 50 annual instalments from 1950 (but with six deferrals). All World War II debts owed to the UK had either been repaid or settlements agreed.
[1814] National Archives, CAB 66/39/29 22nd July 1943
[1815] Gault, 2014, op cit, p102
[1816] Burnett, op cit, p282

There can, therefore, be little doubt about Wood's principles and reforming zeal but as Chancellor of the Exchequer he had to temper these by other considerations. One of the key differences between a government minister and a campaigner is that the latter has no other duty than to pursue the cause they are fighting for as far as they can. As Minister of Health Wood might have helped to push the case for family allowances; as a wartime Chancellor of the Exchequer he had to be more circumspect. In September 1940 he and Attlee clashed over a proposed rise in family allowances for service personnel.[1817] Wood had recommended an increase of one shilling per week for a wife and each child from 1st November 1940, at a cost of £3m per annum for each 1m men.[1818] Attlee thought it should be trebled.

Agitation for a general system of family allowances to lift families out of poverty and promote equal citizenship, liberating women from dependence on their husbands, had started in the early years of the twentieth century (Mabel Atkinson in 1914 and Mary Stocks and Eleanor Rathbone in 1917, for example), but this was controversial for though it had developed out of the women's and socialist movements it also generated Labour and trade union opposition in case it enabled employers to depress wages In the absence of a state scheme, some companies started their own, such as Bulmer's in 1938 and Rowntree's in 1940, but the national issue gathered pace in 1941. Wood was asked in February 1941 whether he was considering family allowances generally, to which his PS Crookshank responded by saying that the issue was too controversial to be dealt with by oral questions. Eleanor Rathbone added the supplementary:

Is the Minister aware that nearly every economist in the country has been pressing for a long time for family allowances as a means of preventing malnutrition without precipitating inflation? Will not the Government at last pay attention to this long-neglected subject?[1819]

The Family Endowment Society persuaded the Bishop of Winchester to raise it in the Lords in March and though he received

---

[1817] Crowcroft, op cit, p82
National Archives, CAB 65, WM(40), 251 17th September 1940
[1818] National Archives, CAB 67/8/36 12th September 1940
[1819] Hansard, 26th February 1941, vol. 369, col. 527

support from Viscount Samuel and Lord Stamp he withdrew the motion in the face of government opposition.[1820] A fortnight later Seebohm Rowntree characterised as a mockery Wood's failure to find extra money "to prevent a cruel deterioration in the standard of health of the poorest section of the population".[1821] Lord Wolmer added his support a week later, concluding that

> I submit that if Sir Kingsley Wood can give no better reason for inaction than has so far been adduced he will lay himself open to the charge of shirking the issue, which is so serious that public opinion in present circumstances will not accept such an attitude.[1822]

A specific proposal was put to Wood in parliament later that month, along the lines suggested by Rowntree, but he was no more forthcoming.[1823] On 16th April a deputation of MPs went to see him,[1824] and although this did not incline him to say more the next time it arose in the Commons,[1825] Rathbone confronted him the following week with a motion signed by 150 MPs and asking him to prepare an estimate for a national scheme that paid 5s per week to every child under 15. Wood confirmed that such an estimate was being made.[1826] On 29th May she asked him whether the estimate was yet available and although Wood replied that such a scheme would cost £130m per annum before offsetting savings (of which there were expected to be many), he was not yet ready to make this available as he was still investigating the ramifications.[1827] Rathbone pressed Wood again a fortnight later, receiving a longer reply this time but not getting any nearer the answer she

---

[1820] Hansard (118 HL Deb 5s), 5th March 1941, vol. 118, cols. 563-593; *Times*, 6th March 1941

[1821] Letter to the *Times*, 17th March 1941

[1822] Letter to the *Times*, 25th March 1941

[1823] Hansard, 27th March 1941, vol. 370, col. 702
This was to pay 5s per week from the third child on to parents whose income was below the Income Tax limit. If new money was not forthcoming, the cost of £12m per annum should be met by reducing certain food subsidies.

[1824] Susan Pedersen, 'Family, Dependence. and the Origins of the Welfare State: Britain and France, 1914-1945', 1993, pp330-331

[1825] Hansard, 13th May 1941, vol. 371, col. 1076

[1826] Hansard, 20th May 1941, vol. 371, cols. 1395-1396

[1827] Hansard, 29th May 1941, vol. 371, cols. 1991-1992

sought.[1828]   A Labour party conference had debated family allowances at the beginning of June but without committing itself, for while there was much support there continued to be opposition from the trade unions who believed this would depress wages.[1829] This remained the nub of the problem for Wood for, subject to another deputation on the 16th, he argued not only about the pressure on finances but that such a scheme required a "much greater measure of agreement ... than at present existed," not only among the political parties:

> The trade unions were by no means agreed upon the desirability of such a scheme, and it would be undesirable to introduce a scheme of this kind unless it received [their] wholehearted support ...[1830]

But the trade unions were coming under pressure to change their stance, Leo Amery noting in September 1941 that the issue was to be remitted back to the Labour Party again. He had little doubt that the TUC would now agree provided that the money came from Wood and the Treasury, adding that there was no stronger means than family allowances for stabilising wages, especially as prices rise.[1831] Once the TUC General Council did so, though not unanimously, in March 1942 the way was clear for a State scheme and on 7th May 1942 Wood's White Paper was published.[1832] Rathbone was furious that this had come too late to influence financial discussions for 1942/43, accusing Wood of delaying matters deliberately. He responded that this did not prevent her discussing the issue if she wished.[1833] The Commons debated it extensively on 23rd June and Wood acknowledged in his response that the arguments for such a scheme were very powerful. There remained certain policy issues to resolve, including whether family allowances should be contributory or non-contributory,[1834] and the

---

[1828] Hansard, 12th June 1941, vol. 372, cols. 363-364

[1829] *Times* 5th June 1941

[1830] *Times* 17th June 1941; also, Pedersen, op cit, p330; Susan Pedersen, 'Eleanor Rathbone and the Politics of Conscience', 2004, p362

[1831] Churchill College archives, AMEL 2/1/33 Amery letter to Wood 10th September 1941

[1832] 'Family Allowances: Memo by the Chancellor of the Exchequer' Cmd 6354 May 1942

[1833] Hansard, 7th May 1942, vol. 379, col. 1406

[1834] CPA PUB 189/34 Speakers' Notes July 1942 - Dec 1943

TUC General Council would not reach a final decision on their support until the following September.[1835] There was no vote at the end of the debate and the motion required the government to consider immediately a national scheme of allowances, but, as Wood had pointed out, the Beveridge Committee were also considering such an initiative and the government would have to respond both to the views expressed in the debate and to those in the Beveridge Report in the autumn. It would be remiss to do otherwise.[1836] Pedersen may well be correct in arguing that Wood was "playing for time", but it is hard to see how the government could have pre-empted Beveridge and she is surely incorrect to say that this "was purely a delaying tactic for Beveridge was known to be strongly in favour".[1837] Firstly, Beveridge could only propose - it would be up to parliament and government to decide; secondly, Beveridge would presumably want his scheme to be considered, and costed, as a whole; and thirdly, would Beveridge have found it acceptable for elements of his proposals to be implemented piecemeal and in ways that he did not necessarily intend? Furthermore, early implementation of one element might ensure that others could not be implemented at all. That Wood did resist the introduction of such a scheme in wartime is not in doubt, but this was based entirely on financial considerations and procedural arguments rather than on principle.

Beveridge Report

The publication of the Beveridge Report, and Wood's initial reaction as the Chancellor of the Exchequer (rather than as a campaigner for improved living conditions and social reform) is referred to briefly in the Primrose League vignette above. The report also needs to be considered in the context of other events of its time.

Malta had experienced 2000 air raid alerts by early April 1942 and the *Times* reported that the Germans were trying "to let hell loose" on the island. A letter in the paper the same day suggested King George VI should recognise their heroic resistance to German and Italian bombing by presenting a suitable commemorative standard.[1838] This prompted Leo Amery to propose

---

[1835] Hansard, 23rd June 1942, vol. 380, cols. 1853-1944
[1836] Ibid, col. 1941
[1837] Pedersen, 2004, op cit, p363
[1838] *Times* 10th April 1942

to the King's private secretary Sir Alexander Hardinge that this banner should be accompanied by a VC for the island. Hardinge replied to say that something similar had been planned for some time and they were only waiting for the most suitable moment to make the announcement. Hardinge thought the moment had now arrived and he expected it to be announced in the press shortly.[1839] The following day 15th April 1942 Malta was awarded the George Cross.

In November 1942 Britain paid tribute to Russian resistance with a party at the Russian Embassy in London. The Ambassador Ivan Maisky recorded in his diary that Wood was there, "answering posers set by poker-faced Jan Masaryk", the Foreign Minister of Czechoslovakia.[1840] Two months later the siege of Leningrad was lifted and Bevin wrote to Maisky to congratulate the Russian people, agreeing to Maisky's request that his letter be published in the press as Leningrad was particularly symbolic for workers everywhere.[1841] At the end of the month the Germans capitulated at Stalingrad.

Arthur Greenwood had been in charge of reconstruction policy since early 1941, shunted there by Churchill to keep him occupied and out of the way, and in February 1942 he was sacked. Greenwood was removed from the War Cabinet at the same time as Beaverbrook and Wood, and according to Thomas Jones, who had worked for both Lloyd George and Baldwin in the Cabinet Office, Beaverbrook, Wood and Greenwood were "pushed out - the country will be delighted."[1842] Churchill's terse and matter of fact letter to Wood informed him that he had "not been able to include the Chancellor of the Exchequer", but "you will always have to come when your affairs are involved".[1843] Predictably, Cadogan was surprised that Wood had remained in the overall Cabinet: "Kingsley had crept in again! How?".[1844]

In March 1942 the paymaster-general William Jowitt took over the reconstruction committee, working to the same terms of

---

[1839] Churchill College archives, AMEL 2/1/34: Amery letter 10th April and Hardinge reply 14th April 1942
[1840] George Bilainkin, 'Maisky, Ten Years Ambassador', 1944, p387 Maisky diary 7th November 1942
[1841] Churchill College archives, BEVN 3/3: Bevin letter 20th January and Maisky reply 22nd January 1943
[1842] In 'A Diary With Letters 1931-1950', 1954, p497 - 19th February 1942
[1843] Churchill College archives, CHAR 20/66/38 and 20/53A/56 Churchill to Wood 19th February 1942
[1844] Dilks, 1971, op cit, p437 - Monday 23rd February 1942

reference as had Greenwood to consider both social reconstruction at home and the reconstruction of Europe and the world after the war was over. As Jowitt explained to Amery, the fact that the Empire was not specifically mentioned did not mean that they would be excluded from either consideration or consultation.[1845] Wood was among the seven members of Jowitt's committee. As it turned out, it would be the Beveridge Report and the 1944 Education Act that were to be the foundations of the post-war welfare state in Britain but neither had been generated through the reconstruction committee. Bevin had thought he was side-lining Beveridge by getting him to inquire into social services in June 1941 and Churchill warned Butler (1902-1982) to avoid comprehensive reform when appointing him President of the Board of Education a month later in July 1941.[1846] Beveridge's report, 'Social Insurance and Allied Services', was published in December 1942 and was to prove as significant as had the resistance of Malta and Russia. In his biography of Bevin, Alan Bullock noted that the moment for the Government to give proper consideration to post-war reconstruction had arrived.[1847]

While the Beveridge report has been described as

universal in cover, comprehensive in provision and - through the subsistence principle - adequate in amount to then deliver the long-standing radical dream of a 'national minimum',

with family allowances, the NHS and full employment underpinning the new social security system, the same author on the next page refers to it as really just "a completion of what was begun in 1911".[1848] The cost of pensions was the major problem.[1849]

[1845] Churchill College archives, AMEL 2/1/34: Amery letter 23rd March and Jowitt reply 30th March 1942
[1846] Butler joined the reconstruction committee in November 1943 after Wood's death.
[1847] Bullock, op cit, p220
[1848] John MacNicol, 'The Politics of Retirement in Britain, 1878-1948', 1998, pp287 & 288; Gault, 2014, op cit, pp44-53 for the introduction of National Insurance in 1911.
[1849] MacNicol, op cit, p353 points out the three key issues faced by Beveridge with regard to pensions: universality to avoid the necessity for a means test but with the consequence that it would then be paid to those who didn't need support; subsistence, thereby justifying insurance

Wood and Beveridge had first clashed in January 1942 when Wood insisted that the departmental representatives on Beveridge's Social Insurance Committee should be advisers only so that the Government should not be committed in advance. Beveridge rejected Wood's subsequent suggestion that he add other non-departmental representatives to the Committee and so was left to sign the report himself.[1850]   Once the report was published, and rather than being content to advise the government, Beveridge lobbied for the proposals. This attempt "to steal the limelight from Cabinet ministers" was entirely predictable in terms of Beveridge's arrogance and conceit, but as Attlee put it "Always a mistake to think yourself larger than you are".[1851]

Although the *New Statesman* reported that "One can imagine Sir Kingsley Wood, as he read the report, heaving a sigh of deep relief at the smallness of the bill he will need to meet ...",[1852] in fact both Wood and Keynes were concerned at the huge financial implications. As Beveridge's biographer puts it:

> The Chancellor of the Exchequer, Kingsley Wood was doubtful whether the necessary resources would be available in the post-war economic climate; and he was sceptical about the willingness of the public to countenance extra taxation, once released from the constraints of war.[1853]

Indeed, Wood had advised Churchill in mid-November 1942 that it was "an impracticable financial commitment".[1854]   Alan Clark confirms that

---

contributions and not requiring tax funding; retirement condition so that workers had to retire and had enough to live on rather than continuing to work for reduced wages to supplement an inadequate pension.
[1850] Beveridge, 1953, op cit, pp298-299
This is slightly different from Middlemas, 1979, op cit, p273: Wood "insisted Beveridge alone should sign it, exonerating the civil servants from responsibility for its commitments".
[1851] Francis Williams, 'A Prime Minister Remembers', 1961, p57
[1852] *New Statesman* 5th December 1942, pp367-368
[1853] Jose Harris, 'William Beveridge: A Biography', 1977, pp244-245
Wood made this point in the debate on the Beveridge Report when arguing that other priorities such as housing, education and (perhaps) civil aviation should be considered at the same time. Hansard, 17th February 1943, vol. 386, col. 1829
[1854] Cited in Addison, op cit, p220: 17th November 1942 PREM 4/89/2

Wood had written to Churchill in advance of publication on 17th November 1942 arguing that the scheme involved a huge pay-out to those with savings and resources, who did not need it. This was wasteful ...[1855]

King's diary entry for 21st November 1942 quotes Cripps' secretary as predicting the report would be "cut up in pieces and some parts will be adopted". King continued:

[Wood] is already mobilising the Treasury against it. Kingsley Wood [according to Cripps' secretary] is gaining in influence - partly as the result of some discreet little hunches. I cannot take this ridiculous little puppet seriously, but so low is the standard of realism in the Tory party and the House generally, that they really think he might matter.[1856]

Yet Keynes was also concerned, promising to support the report if the additional burden could be reduced to £100m pa for the first five years[1857] and working with Beveridge to reduce the costs by removing the first child from the family allowance proposals.[1858] In a memo to Jowitt's Committee on 1st January 1943 Wood repeatedly stressed "the uncertainty of Beveridge's long-term financial commitments".[1859]

The Cabinet considered the report for the first time on 14th January when, according to Addison, Wood "had produced another wrecking paper".[1860] There was to be a separate debate on the Beveridge report[1861] and this was keenly anticipated with Pethick-Lawrence and two Liberal MPs referring to it in a debate on economic policy at the beginning of February.[1862] The day before the Beveridge parliamentary debate Churchill proposed to the War Cabinet how he thought the report should be handled. Firstly, he judged it an essential part of post-war reconstruction and argued for

---

[1855] Clark, op cit, pp244-245

[1856] King, op cit, pp199-200

[1857] Beveridge, op cit, pp308-310

[1858] Skidelsky, 2000, op cit, pp267-273

[1859] Cited in MacNicol, op cit, p390: PRO CAB 123/45

[1860] Addison, op cit, p221: CAB(8)43

[1861] Promised by Jowitt on the day the report was published, Hansard, 1st December 1942, vol. 385, col. 1077.

[1862] Hansard, 2nd February 1943, vol. 386, cols. 780-781, 791, 834

it to be treated as an integral whole and not just what remained after the unworkable and unacceptable elements had been removed. Secondly, a commission should be charged with honing the proposals ready for the legislation required but without any commitment to implementation or the costs involved as such decisions would depend on post-war circumstances and the government then in power. The task of the current government, already in its eighth year, was to prepare the ground in readiness but not to fetter the response of whatever government was in power after the war.[1863] This was the line that Wood took when he spoke on the second of the three days of debate.

He opened by reminding the House that

> ... a great proportion of my work has been devoted to the health and insurance side of our country's social services. No one need be in any doubt as to where my sympathies and my hopes lie. I hope at any rate that our national affairs will be such that it will permit us to put many of the principles and ideas ... into operation, as well as others ... such as housing and education. That is where I, personally, stand as regards these proposals.[1864]

He then quoted from a speech Greenwood had made when Minister of Health fourteen years before in 1929, concurring that "generous hearts do not foot bills"[1865] and pointing out that Beveridge himself had acknowledged in that week's *Observer* that when the war was over the country would not "at once be able to afford almost anything". Wood continued

> In asking the House to consider, not unsympathetically, the proposals before us today, it is right and proper and only fair to the country and our people that the financial aspect should be carefully considered and weighed. While I agree that finance should not be our master but rather our servant, that servant must be fairly and properly treated and certainly

---

[1863] Churchill College archives, CHAR23/11 WP(43)65 15th February 1943
[1864] Hansard, 17th February 1943, vol. 386, col. 1825
[1865] Ibid, col. 1827
It had been Greenwood who had opened the debate on 16th February. Hansard, 16th February 1943, vol. 386, cols. 1615-1628

should not be so dealt with that he breaks or collapses in the course of his work.[1866]

Although the costs of the war were still rising and it was not known precisely when it might end, the eventual outcome was not in doubt by this stage. Wood confirmed that negotiations would begin on family allowances and the comprehensive medical service immediately after the debate.[1867] However, it was the government's intention to deal with the proposals as a whole thereby assessing the overall costs.[1868]

Addison described Wood's speech as "inept",[1869] Harris thought it an "unhelpful" contribution[1870] and Violet Bonham Carter judged it "disastrous".[1871] Strangely though, Jim Griffiths, who would implement much of the Beveridge report as Minister of National Insurance in 1946, does not mention Wood at all, blaming Anderson's speech instead.[1872] At the start of the third day's debate Griffiths proposed an amendment so that the motion read

this House expresses its dissatisfaction with the now declared policy of HMG towards [the Beveridge Report] and urges the reconsideration of that policy with a view to the early implementation of the plan.[1873]

Many historians have judged that Morrison rescued the position for the government when winding up the debate.[1874] Although Greenwood now associated himself with the amendment, his original motion was agreed by 335 votes to 119, welcoming the

---

[1866] Hansard, 17th February 1943, vol. 386, cols. 1827-1828

[1867] Ibid, col. 1832

[1868] By contrast, in June 1943 RA Butler was clear that full implementation of the Education Act would take a generation given the huge capital and revenue implications. Consequently, he was preferred by the Treasury to Beveridge (RA Butler, 'The Art of the Possible', 1971, p117).

[1869] Addison, op cit, pp224-225

[1870] Harris, op cit, p167

[1871] Mark Pottle (ed.), 'Champion Redoubtable: The Diaries and Letters of Violet Bonham Carter 1914-1945', 1998, p255 - 18th February 1943 diary entry: "Wood's speech had a disastrous effect and the Labour Party and our people are in revolt".

[1872] James Griffiths, 'Pages from Memory', 1969, pp70-71

[1873] Hansard, 18th February 1943, vol. 386, col. 1965

[1874] Ibid, cols. 2030-2050

report "as a comprehensive review ... and as a valuable aid in determining ... the Government's policy of post-war reconstruction". Beveridge acknowledged that, though Morrison's speech might have "put a better face on their policy",[1875] the government was "in no way committed to the plan; [for] it was open to reconsideration on financial grounds".[1876] Yet there was little doubt about intent, for the Conservative Party conference and Central Council annual meeting on 20th and 21st May 1943 considered five motions on the Beveridge report, all supportive.[1877]

PAYE

Although deduction at source became more common during the war, this was not the same as tax deductions in line with current earnings, the holy grail of tax collection. For the most part income tax was paid six months in arrears, causing problems both for workers whose wages fluctuated and for the Treasury who had to borrow to cover the collection lag. As Wood had said at the start of his 1942 budget, "What I need is cash and cash out of current income".[1878] To change the system of tax collection during wartime would be a massive undertaking, which Keynes put no higher than a possibility, however desirable it might be: "The question of whether any change is possible is under consideration".[1879] Yet the work did go ahead and after months of consultations with employers and workers Wood was to introduce the PAYE White Paper in Parliament on the afternoon of 21st September.[1880] He collapsed and died that morning and it fell to his successor Anderson to see it into effect from 6th April 1944.

[1875] Foot, op cit, pp190-191 described Anderson and Wood as cautious while Morrison accepted all the principles (bar one).
[1876] Beveridge, op cit, p324
[1877] CPA NUA 4/2/1
[1878] Sabine, op cit, p241
Lee, op cit, p20 ascribes the same words to Wood's July 1940 budget. This is not correct, an error Lee compounds by stating that this 1940 budget introduced PAYE, which it did not.
[1879] Moggridge, 1979 ('CW JMK: vol. XXIII'), op cit, p224
[1880] CPA PUB 189/34 Speakers' Notes July 1942 - Dec 1943 PAYE, Cmnd 6469, Sept 1943; Income Tax (Employment) Act 1943; Anderson House of Commons speeches 14th October and 2nd November 1943
Sabine, op cit, pp242-243 sets out the huge implementation initiative that was required before all Schedule E taxpayers were included.

Although there had been "acrimonious interchanges" between Wood and Bevin over wages,[1881] not only was the necessary finance found for the war, but this was thought to have been done as equitably as possible, inflation had been minimised, thereby stabilising the standard of living,[1882] and the problems that would have arisen if borrowing had been the main source were avoided. Sabine concludes that Wood

> had been a successful Chancellor , and his success had come not from any inherent financial skill, but because he was willing to hear advice, to judge its merits and to act upon it. His appreciation of the realities of war finance was unsurpassed by the financial ministers of any of the belligerent countries ... [1883]

This returns us to the opening of this chapter, for Sabine's comments confirm those arrived at independently there. As notably, the economist Lionel Robbins pointed out that when John Anderson succeeded Wood as Chancellor on 24th September 1943 "the main features of the war economy had been settled".[1884] Robbins had been advising Anderson since late 1940 but Robbins' loyalty to his old boss is excessive when he claims that Anderson was responsible. As Lord President in those years Anderson had played a significant part, but no more significant than others such as Bevin or Attlee. It is Wood who should receive the credit as Chancellor of the Exchequer for the three and a half years from May 1940 to September 1943 when democracy was in real peril.

Russia, the USA, the Dominions and other countries played a huge part, of course, as did the leadership that came from people like Smuts, Sikorski, Mackenzie King and de Gaulle, as well as from Churchill, Stalin and Roosevelt, but had Wood and his Treasury team not met the financial challenges in 1940/41 the outcome might have been very different.

To put it another way: a stool with three legs will always stand firm, one with four legs can only do so on a level floor and one with two legs is no use at all. If leadership and morale were

---

[1881] Moggridge, 1979 ('CW JMK: vol. XXIII'), op cit, p223

[1882] Hancock and Gowing, op cit, pp335 & 339; also, Davenport, op cit, p107

[1883] Sabine, op cit, p242

[1884] Lord Robbins, 'Autobiography of An Economist', 1971, p174

two of the legs, the third was finance. In the absence of any of these, neither military defence initially nor offence in later years would have been possible. Wood deserves appropriate recognition and acknowledgement for his contribution.

20.   CONCLUSION

Wood is rarely remembered today, more than seventy years after his death and this is perhaps the fate that awaits all politicians other than the most scandalous or the most prominent Prime Ministers. But dying in the middle of the Second World War, opposing early implementation of the Beveridge report, being closely associated with Neville Chamberlain for much of your career and being labelled one of the 'Guilty Men' over Dunkirk and appeasement would all be compelling reasons for Wood to slip from the public memory faster than most. He was neither bad enough nor so exceptional that he would be readily recalled. On the other hand, Madame Tussaud's judged him sufficiently eminent in 1938 to add him to their waxworks[1885] and, just as Chamberlain has been re-evaluated in recent years, so Wood's long record of public service should not be obliterated. He too may be overdue reconsideration. Issues of motivation are critical for, if Chamberlain was naïve over Munich, or Baldwin misguided over re-armament, there can be little doubt that they believed that what they were doing was entirely justified at the time. The majority of their contemporaries of all political persuasions and none agreed with them then and, while hindsight has cast the outcome of their decisions in a different light, by definition they could not have known at the time the information that has become available subsequently. Additionally, there are many aspects of Wood's story that remain relevant today, such as housing, benefits, the power of advertising, information about people's rights, equality and one-nation Toryism.

Winston Churchill provides an interesting counterpoint, for few people have been more distrusted and disliked than he was in the 1930s. It was only the exceptional circumstances of 1940 that gave him a second chance to recover his reputation and even then it was only the wholly unexpected events of 1941 that enabled him to do so.

Agnes, Lady Wood, said that her husband "was very tired when he arrived home on Monday evening [20th September], and during the night was taken ill and complained of pain".[1886] His neighbour and fellow Athenaeum Club member the physician Sir Stanley Woodwark, who was with him when he died, certified the cause of death as angina pectoris (not the same as a heart attack

---

[1885] *Bystander* 6th July 1938, KW23 246/1
[1886] *Times* 22nd September 1943 p4

and not usually fatal). His private funeral service took place at Wesley's Chapel on the morning of Friday 24th September for forty relatives and friends and he was afterwards cremated at Golders Green. People from many areas of his life were there, including his personal secretary Miss McCarthy who had been with him for the twenty-five years since he had entered parliament,[1887] but the only politicians to attend were his constituency chairman Halse and agent Markham from Woolwich, his PPS Edward Campbell and the Lord Chancellor Viscount Simon, Wood's predecessor as Chancellor of the Exchequer and a ministerial colleague for twelve years. The latter had been the last of five peers paying tribute to Wood in the House of Lords on the Wednesday, singling out two of Wood's characteristics: "his invariable energy of mind. He was never slack or indifferent about any piece of public work" and his "happy knack ... of promoting and maintaining a level of good humour and pleasantness", no matter how controversial the issue, so that "he hardly made an enemy". Simon added that this was not the usual platitude but in Wood's case a genuine assessment and helped explain why the Lords had set aside their usual custom to mark "the passing of this distinguished Commoner".[1888]

Nearly 250 people attended his memorial service at St Margaret's Church, Westminster that afternoon[1889] and only a few were Conservative MPs fulfilling a duty. Some people who had worked for Wood long before made sure others attended on their behalf if they could not do so themselves. The King was represented, while the Duke of Norfolk, Earl Baldwin and twenty-five other peers attended. Twenty-six ministers, including most of the War Cabinet (Attlee, Eden and Bevin, for example), led by Mr and Mrs Churchill were present, as were nine of the most senior civil servants from the Treasury, Cabinet Office and the Ministry of Information. Among the fifty-eight other MPs the best known Labour member was Wood's old sparring partner Arthur Greenwood, while Hugh Dalton and Stafford Cripps were represented. The diverse group of Liberals included Dingle Foot,

---

[1887] A report in the *Sunday Mercury* seven years before about Whitehall secretaries ('Our Famous Men Value ... Women Who Keep Silent'), included Miss McCarthy "who has championed Kingsley Wood through eighteen years of his career" (12th January 1936, KW20 78/1).
[1888] Hansard (HL Deb 5s), 22nd September 1943, vol. 129, cols. 64-66 Also, *Times* 23rd September 1943
[1889] The *Times* listed over 240 on Saturday 25th, adding another six it had omitted on Monday 27th September 1943.

Percy Harris and William Jowitt. There were four Ambassadors (Belgium, Holland, Poland and the USA) and two High Commissioners (Canada and Australia). Montagu Norman from the Bank of England was there as was the Chairman of the Stock Exchange. People from the Primrose League, insurance, Freemasons, the Post Office and the Health and Air Ministries were present, as were another seventy-three from aspects of Wood's career as varied as the Balloon Command that covered Woolwich, journalism, the Inland Revenue staff federation, magistrates and boxing. His sister Dorothy Weaver and his daughter Marjorie Brothers were not and had not been at the funeral either. His aunt Lady Graham Wood who had attended the funeral in the morning did not remain for the memorial service, while Dorothy's husband (Wood's brother-in-law) Edward Weaver only managed the latter.

One way of assessing a politician's legacy is to ask who benefitted and who did not from their actions. In Wood's case, women certainly did as on the whole did the sick and the elderly. The prospect of real social reform was always considered particularly important to women who, thinking of their children in particular, might be encouraged thereby to vote Conservative.[1890] The position is less clear with regards to children themselves and men of working age, though many of those who were badly housed and impoverished did so. Similarly, local government and health services were improved by his interventions. The wealthy did not obviously benefit, though the sacrifices they were asked to make during the war through higher and, in some cases, punitive taxation were judged appropriate and fair. As Donald Winch put it, the success of British war finance in the Second World War "can ... be judged by the fact that 'those responsible for organising Britain's war effort were never forced to feel that financial policy was important'".[1891] This is similar to the conclusion of the previous chapter.

In marked contrast to the *Economist* opinion that Wood's appointment as Chancellor was inappropriate given his lack of qualifications or known expertise, the *Daily Sketch* judged his appointment as Minister of Air "a good one, just because he is not an expert already". The newspaper concluded that the job of any Departmental Minister is to capitalise on the expertise of civil

---

[1890] For example, Jarvis, op cit, p149
[1891] Winch, op cit, p257

servants but not to get captured ("possessed") by them.[1892] Perhaps significantly, the article was entitled 'The Man Who Gets Things Done'.

Another test is what was said about you in the days and weeks following your death and by whom. Few are disposed to speak ill of the dead but for most if there's nothing good to say, best to say nothing at all. In Wood's case plaudits were received from political colleagues both in this country and abroad.

On the day of Wood's death Churchill and Pethick-Lawrence followed the customary Commons formula of mentioning it in passing ahead of the formal tributes the following day, but Wood's adversary Stokes, who knew he would not get another chance, did not want to let the opportunity pass without referring to the "courtesy and good humour" with which Wood answered his questions (about three every week) and who "had the regard of every Member of this House".[1893] Churchill's fulsome tribute on Wednesday 22nd was followed by five others, and all six referred to having lost a friend.[1894] As late as the following February, Churchill was telling Barrington Ward (then editor of the *Times*) that he missed Wood as a barometer of Conservative party feeling.[1895]

Perhaps even more critical are what your opponents say. In Wood's case these ranged from Paul Einzig, a journalist on the *Financial News* who often clashed with him:

> There was indeed very little love lost between us. Yet, as I was to discover later, I did not know when I was well off. It was only after his death, when he was succeeded by Anderson, that I came to realise belatedly what a nice little man Kingsley Wood had really been.[1896]

to the Liberal (later National Liberal) Geoffrey Shakespeare:

> One must regret that Sir Kingsley Wood is no longer there to counter his opposite number, Herbert Morrison. The Conservative Party, I believe, have not yet realised what a loss they suffered by his death. He buzzed like a mosquito

---

[1892] *Daily Sketch* 18th May 1938, KW23 197/2

[1893] Hansard, 21st September 1943, vol. 392, col. 167

[1894] Hansard, 22nd September 1943, vol. 392, cols. 211-219; *Times* 23rd September 1943

[1895] Addison, op cit, pp235-236

[1896] Paul Einzig, 'In the Centre of Things', 1960, p240

along the Socialist front bench from 1929 to 1931 and bit the Government so often that it became infected and enfeebled.[1897] Lord Woolton, perhaps, with his genius for estimating the undercurrents of public opinion will fill the gap which [Wood's] death has left, but he is in the Lords.[1898]

to that "opposite number", Labour's Herbert Morrison:

The Chancellor of the Exchequer, Sir Kingsley Wood, **had not been too successful as Secretary of State for Air under Chamberlain** [emphasis added], but he had been a notable success in the Post Office in the thirties. He had 'glamorized' the GPO very ably, and had undoubtedly modernized its public relations. He was an experienced politician, a lively debater and one of the controversialists of the Tory party; a strong anti-socialist, despite his work on behalf of all the nationalised postal, telegraph and telephone services. Like all Tory PMGs, he was proud of the nationalised Post Office.[1899]

to the Liberal Percy Harris:

I knew him long before he achieved success. I was on the LCC with him for some years, though he made no particular mark there. He first caught the public attention by his criticism of L[loyd] G[eorge]'s Health Insurance Act. Then he achieved nuisance value by putting inconvenient questions to ministers during the Labour Government. Neville Chamberlain took him up and he became his loyal understudy at the Ministry of Health. He was in turn Minister of Health and Secretary of State for Air, but no one considered he possessed outstanding abilities: his success consisted in his always being calm and imperturbable. Nothing would put him out and however strong the attack might be upon his policy, he would nod and smile and look quite unconcerned. When he was made Chancellor of the

---

[1897] Arthur Greenwood had similarly described Wood as "a benign mosquito" in 1936 (see Chapter 16 above). The mosquito analogy clearly stuck, though Shakespeare thought Wood had stung Labour repeatedly.
[1898] Shakespeare, op cit, p126
[1899] Morrison, op cit, p203

Exchequer by Churchill at a time of the highest expenditure on record, everyone was surprised. He had the reputation of knowing nothing about finance and I don't think he pretended to. ... But he was clever enough to choose first-class advisers and had the wisdom to be guided by them. He was a good listener and though he would not lightly make a concession, he had a way of bringing his critics together in his private room and meeting them half-way.
He was a general favourite and essentially a House of Commons man, and the tributes paid to him on his death were quite genuine and sincere.[1900]

The *Times* on 22nd September carried a news report of his death, referring to his "native shrewdness, great personal popularity, energy in administration, long experience in both national and municipal politics, and a thorough understanding of current political values", as well as his "capacity for hard work". A longer obituary a few pages later was accompanied by two appreciations, the first of which by the engineer Sir Ernest Lemon who had worked for him at Aircraft Production and was on the Air Council started:

Sir Kingsley Wood has gone but his work for the nation will live. Perhaps this country hardly realises the value of his work as Secretary of State for Air, but I, who was closely associated with him from 1938 to 1940, can confidently assert that much is owed to him for our victory in the Battle of Britain.[1901]

The notes for Churchill's speech in parliament highlighted the Empire Training Scheme, which the Air Ministry described as "another debt we owe", as well as the information Sir Richard Hopkins had provided about Wood's time at the Treasury. Hopkins mentioned his innovative "recasting of the form and general presentation of the Budget and of the Nation's accounts", "the War Damage Acts ... a monument to his name", savings, Income Tax,

[1900] Harris, op cit, p152
[1901] *Times* 22nd September 1943 pp5 & 8 There was also an item on p9 in 'City Notes'.
KW23 227/1-12 includes Lemon's appointment as Director-General of Production at the Air Ministry

foreign exchange and dealings with the US Treasury. In addition, Wood

> ... had the courage to impose disagreeable burdens and the persuasiveness to secure their ready acceptance.
> ... secured his loans at rates of interest so low as vastly to mitigate their burden upon posterity.
> and
> ... originated the policy of the stabilisation of the cost of living which has contributed so much to the welfare of the community in time of war.[1902]

In addition, Hopkins thought PAYE "will always be associated with his name".

The second appreciation alongside the *Times* obituary was by "RA" (presumably Ralph Assheton, Financial Secretary to the Treasury). It focussed on Wood's qualities, rather than on his specific achievements:

> Perhaps only those who worked closely with him appreciated to the full his qualities ... The most outstanding among these was his friendliness, which he showed to all with whom he came in contact. ...
> He had a great faculty for inspiring loyalty among his staff; he trusted them, and he knew that they trusted him. ... He had the power of drawing out from those whom he consulted a candid expression of their views, and though it was always he who took the decision, he never took it without seeking the best advice he could obtain.

Agnes received so many letters of condolence that she was unable to reply to them all personally (as she announced in the *Times* on 2nd October). Churchill received more than thirty telegrams, from the Prime Minister of Australia (John Curtin) and Henry Morgenthau for example,[1903] all of which he forwarded on to Agnes as well as writing himself from Chequers on 2nd October. Morgenthau wrote that Wood's

---

[1902] National Archives, PREM 4/7/12
[1903] Both in National Archives, PREM 4/7/12

sincere friendliness and co-operative spirit have done so much to advance the common cause of our two countries. We in the US, who know of his great abilities as well as fine integrity and personal charm, join with you in mourning of his departure.

John Curtin wrote:

My colleagues and I [in the Australian government] regret exceedingly to learn of the sudden death of Sir Kingsley Wood. He rendered highly distinguished service to his Country during a period of great national danger and his passing will be a grievous loss to your Government and to the Nation.

Attlee had also received some telegrams that he sent on.
Not every comment was positive of course, with his fellow Conservative MP Cuthbert Headlam particularly grudging,[1904] but most were. Churchill concluded his Commons speech by saying that Wood

... was a good party man ... because these are the qualifications of a good party man - you must know how to put your party before yourself, and you must know the occasions when to put nation before party. In this he fully qualified.[1905]

"RA" judged in his assessment that

Much of [Wood's] work will only be appreciated when history comes to be written ... His loss to the country, to his colleagues, and to his party is heavy.

However, the very last word should come from Kingsley Wood himself. Halfway between Cabinet consideration of the Beveridge report in January 1943 and the Commons debate on it that February, parliament undertook a full consideration of post-war economic policy on 2nd and 3rd February 1943. This was little more than a year after the USA had entered the war, eighteen months

---

[1904] Ball, 1999, op cit, p378
[1905] Hansard, 22nd September 1943, vol. 392, col. 215

after the USSR had allied itself with the west against the Axis and still with two and a half years of the war to go. It may be a revelation to many, therefore, that so much time was given so early to considerations of post-war reconstruction, especially when the Prime Minister himself was mostly disinterested and certainly concerned by what he thought potential distractions from winning the war.

The debate, sponsored by MPs from all parties, was opened by the Conservative MP Earl Winterton. His motion,

> That this House urges upon the Government the essential need so to direct their economic and financial policy as to ensure that employment, industry and commerce may be increased and developed after the war to the greatest possible extent, and for that purpose to co-operate to the full with other members of the United Nations.[1906]

was agreed without a vote after two days of debate.

Not surprisingly, the Chancellor of the Exchequer made a major contribution,[1907] one small section of which sums up his motivation and might well serve as his epitaph:

> In any consideration of our economic future, we must rightly have regard to the conditions of our people, their health, the conditions of their homes, their families, their security against want and unemployment, and above all, we must see to it that opportunities are afforded to them to strike out for themselves and so to enjoy for themselves and their children the fruits of their own efforts. Every civilised country must, to the utmost of its capacity, have all [these] vital things ... as being so necessary and requisite for the life of the workers ... among its first and most dominant objectives.[1908]

With many politicians this might be no more than the fine phrases that go with the territory today. In the middle of WWII, however, posturing was soon exposed as shallow and unhelpful; it was action that counted. Kingsley Wood believed in these objectives and

---

[1906] Hansard, 2nd February 1943, vol. 386, col. 770
[1907] Ibid, cols. 812-827
[1908] Ibid, cols. 822-823

sought to deliver them in a wide range of legal, political and government roles over forty years.

Appendix: 1931-1940 Chronologies

rM	D	RAF schemes	Re-armament	Events abroad	UK events	
					political	economic
931 Oct	27				General Election	
932 Mar	23			Japan invades Manchuria	Ten Year rule revoked	
933					Lloyd George warning	
an	30			Hitler becomes German Chancellor		
Oct	14			Germany leaves League of Nations		
934 Mar	7		Cabinet. considers DRC report			
Apr			'shadow' factories start			
un			Chamberlain "prioritises" defence at Cabinet			
Jul		Scheme A by March 1939		murder of Austrian Chancellor Dollfuss in abortive Nazi putsch	Baldwin warning against Fascism in *Elector*	
ov	1				London municipal elections	
ov	22				economy v defence dilemma	
935				German air parity scare		
Mar	4		Defence White Paper			
ay	21	Scheme C by March 1937				

YrM	D	RAF schemes	Re-armament	Events abroad	UK events	
					political	economic
May	29	expansion announced			excess profits concerns	
Jun		Cunliffe-Lister (Swinton) decision re quality rather than quantity			Baldwin/ MacDonald swap	
Jul	1		Baldwin establishes DPRC Sub-Comm of CID			
Oct	3			Italy attacks Abyssinia	Labour conference - Bevin seeks sanctions against Italy	
Nov	11		'Ideal Scheme'			
Nov	14				General Election	
Nov		Scheme F by March 1939				
Dec	8			Hoare-Laval pact		
Dec	12				Cabinet furore over Hoare-Laval pact	
Dec	18				Cabinet, after which Hoare resigns	
1936 Feb			reserves margin build-up; trade rule remains			normal trade principle instigated
Mar	8			Germany re-occupies Rhineland		
Mar	9				Defence debate	
Mar			Cabinet: rearmament not to restrict soc services		Inskip appointed	

YrM	D	RAF schemes	Re-armament	Events abroad	UK events political	economic
Apr	21				Chamberlain budget statement	RAF priority in budget
May						Budget disclosure inquiry
Jun	11					JH Thomas & Butt resign
		Austin/ SBAC negotiations			Baldwin delays resignation	
Nov		Scheme H	Air Defence DPRC priority			
Dec					industry diverted from export markets; Edward VIII abdication	
1937 Jan		Scheme H by March 1939				
				Spanish Civil War starts		
Feb	24	Cabinet and Treasury agree Scheme H unaffordable				
		30 new airfields begun 1937-1939				
Mar			Cripps speech against making armaments			Defence Loans Act
Apr						National Defence Contributions tax in budget
Jun					PM: Baldwin resigned, Chamberlain replaced	

YrM	D	RAF schemes	Re-armament	Events abroad	UK events political	economic
Oct		Scheme J by June 1941				
Dec			Inskip memo re increasing fighter strength			
1938 Jan		Scheme K by March 1941				
Feb			Inskip 2nd report			
Mar	3			Nevile Henderson/ Hitler meeting		
Mar			Rearmament now Government priority	Austria ("Anschluss")	Cabinet still wary of TU reactions to dilution	normal trade principle revoked
Apr	4	Scheme L by March 1940	Cabinet agrees RAF requirements			
May	12				Air Ministry debate re failure to deliver expansion	
May	14				Swinton resigns; Wood replaces	
May	31	SBAC agreement signed				
Jun			Churchill critical re lack of Air Defence progress		Reith Chair of Imperial Airways	
Sep				Czech-oslovakia crisis	Exchange Equalisation Account	
Sep	30			Munich agreement		
Oct	14	Wood memo to Chamberlain				

rM	D	RAF schemes	Re-armament	Events abroad	UK events	
					political	economic
Oct	25	Wood Scheme M proposals to Cabinet				
Nov				Kristallnacht pogrom		
939 Feb	13			end of Spanish Civil War; recognition of Franco in sight		
Mar	15			German troops enter Prague		
Mar	31			British guarantee to Poland		
Apr	7			Italy invades Albania		
Apr	13			British & French guarantees to Greece & Romania		
		Retirement of coastal & fighter command Air Marshals postponed				
May					Cripps expelled from Labour party	
Aug	23			Nazi-Soviet Pact signed		
Sep	1			Germany invades Poland		
Sep	3	War preparation meeting including Wood & Balfour			British ultimatum expires & WWII begins	
Sep	23	Empire Air Training Scheme				

YrM	D	RAF schemes	Re-armament	Events abroad	UK events political	economic
Nov				Soviet attack on Finland		
1940 Mar	12			Treaty of Moscow agreeing Finland peace		
Apr	9			Germany invades Norway and Denmark		
		Joubert comment on KW				
May	7-8				Norway debate	
	9			Germany invades Low Countries		
	10				PM: Chamberlain resigned, Churchill replaced	
May	21			Dunkirk evacuation of BEF		
Jun	14			Germans enter Paris		

PARTICIPANTS/CAST OF CHARACTERS[1909]

Christopher Addison   1869-1951
Lib → Labour (Lab); MP for Hoxton 1910-1918, Shoreditch 1918-1922,
Swindon 1929-1931, 1934-1935; Baron Addison 1937; Viscount Addison
1945
Cabinet posts 1916-1921, 1929-1931, 1945, 1947, 1948-1949, 1951

Max Aitken   1879-1964
Unionist (C); MP for Ashton under Lyne 1910-1916; Baron Beaverbrook
1917
Proprietor of *Express, Evening Standard* and other newspapers
Cabinet posts 1918, 1940-1941, 1942, 1943-1945

A V Alexander   1885-1965
Secretary of the Co-operative Congress 1920
Co-op; MP for Sheffield Hillsborough 1922-1931, 1935-1950; Viscount
Alexander 1950, Baron Alexander of Weston-super-Mare 1963, Earl
Alexander of Hillsborough 1963
Cabinet posts 1929-1931, 1940-1945, 1945-1951

[1909] For people appearing only in Part 1, see that book.

In alphabetical order by surname if referred to in Part 2, though no further information is included for a few minor characters who had little impact on Wood's story. It could not be found for Marguerite Eveleigh-de-Moleyns, FG Markham or Robert Williamson.

Law is not identified separately where this preceded a political career - then as now this profession was often a stepping-stone to politics. Otherwise, a brief description of employment / vocation / activity is given unless politician only.

Ministerial posts outside the Cabinet are omitted.

Cabinet posts refer to those identified as such at the time. Therefore, Attorney-General is included but Solicitor-General is not (e.g., Carson 1900-1905). President of the Board of Education is usually included but President of the Board of Trade is not always (though the latter post was held by Churchill 1908-1910 and Lloyd George before him). The Postmaster-General (PMG) was not in the Cabinet until 1933 when Wood was added while in this post.

Information after Wood's death in 1943 is included to ensure entries are not partial or misleading.

The following are not included: army and navy ranks; military decorations (other than VC); foreign honours, Baronet, Privy Councillor, Justice of the Peace, Knighthood, or positions as president (usually honorary), Lord Lieutenant and in the Primrose League. They are in the text if relevant. University Chancellor is included but Rector (often an honorary position, especially in Scotland) is not.

Leo Amery   1873-1955
Journalist, including *Times* 1899-1909
Conservative (C); MP for South Birmingham 1911-1918, Birmingham
Sparkbrook 1918-1945
Cabinet posts 1922-1923, 1924-1929, 1940
Served in First World War

John Anderson   1882-1958
Civil servant; Governor of Bengal 1932-1937
Independent MP for Scottish Universities 1938-1950; Viscount Waverley
1952
Cabinet posts 1939-1945

HH Asquith   1852-1928
Lib; MP for East Fife 1886-1918, Paisley 1920-1924; Earl of Oxford and
Asquith 1925
Cabinet posts 1892-1895, 1905-1908
Prime Minister 1908-1916

Nancy Astor   1879-1964
C; MP for Plymouth Sutton 1919-1945

Clement Attlee   1883-1967
Lab; MP for Limehouse 1922-1950, West Walthamstow 1950-1955; Earl
Attlee 1955
Cabinet posts 1940-1945
Prime Minister 1945-1951

John Baird   1874-1941
C; MP for Rugby 1910-1922, Ayr Burghs 1922-1925; Baron Stonehaven
1925, Viscount Stonehaven 1938
Cabinet posts 1922-1924
Governor-General of Australia 1925-1930; Conservative Party chairman
1931-1936

Lord Balcarres, David Lindsay   1871-1940
Unionist (C); MP for Chorley Lancashire 1895-1913; 10th Earl of Balcarres
and 27th Earl of Crawford 1913
Cabinet posts 1916, 1922

Lucy Baldwin   1869-1945
Campaigner, including for improved maternity care

Stanley Baldwin   1867-1947
C; MP for Bewdley 1908-1937; Earl Baldwin 1937
Cabinet posts 1921-1922, 1931-1935

Prime Minister 1923-1924, 1924-1929, 1935-1937; Leader of the Conservatives 1923-1937; Chancellor of St Andrews University 1929-1947 and Cambridge University 1930-1947

AJ Balfour   1848-1930
C; MP for Hertford 1874-1886, Manchester East 1886-1905, City of London 1906-1922; Earl Balfour 1922
Cabinet posts 1886-1892, 1895-1902 & 1915-1922
Prime Minister 1902-1905. Leader of the Unionists (Conservatives) 1891-1902, 1906-1911

Harold Balfour   1897-1988
C; MP for Thanet 1929-1945; 1st Baron Inchrye 1945

Joseph Ball   1885-1961
Intelligence officer 1914-1927, 1940-1942
Director of Publicity, Conservative Party 1927-1930; Director, Conservative Research Department 1930-1939
Businessman from 1945

Donald Banks   1891-1975
first Director-General of the Post Office 1934-1936, Permanent Secretary, Ministry of Air 1936-1938, Under-Secretary of Air 1938-1939; Director-General of Petroleum Warfare 1940-1945
Served in First World War

William Barefoot   1872-1941
Lab; Woolwich Council member for 33 years
Mayor of Woolwich 1925-1927

Ernest Barker   1874-1960
University professor; Principal of King's College, London 1920-1927

Alfred Barnes   1887-1974
Lab; MP for East Ham South 1922-1931, 1935-1955
Cabinet post 1946-1951

Vernon Bartlett   1894-1983
Journalist and broadcaster
Director of London office of League of Nations 1922-1932
Served in First World War 1914-1915

Joseph Batey   1867-1949
Miner from 1879 and Miners' agent from 1915
Lab; MP for Spennymoor 1922-1942

Ernest Benn 1875-1954
Chairman Benn Brothers 1922-1941, Ernest Benn 1924-1945, UK
Provident Institution 1934-1949. Founder and editor of *The Independent*

William Wedgwood Benn 1877-1960
Lib → Lab; Lib MP for St George's Tower Hamlets 1910-1918, Leith 1918-
1927, Lab MP for Aberdeen North 1928, 1929-1931, Gorton 1937-1941;
Viscount Stansgate 1942
Cabinet posts 1929, 1945-1946
Served in First World War 1914-1918, RAF during Second World War from
1939

Henry Betterton 1872-1949
C; MP for Rushcliffe, Nottinghamshire 1918-1934; Baron Rushcliffe 1935
Cabinet post 1931-1934
Chairman of Unemployment Assistance Board 1934-1941

William Beveridge 1879-1963
Civil servant 1908-1915; Director of London School of Economics 1919-
1937
Lib; MP for Berwick-on-Tweed 1944-1945; Baron Beveridge 1946
Chairman Aycliffe Development Corporation

Ernest Bevin 1881-1951
General Secretary, Transport and General Workers' Union 1922-1940
Lab; MP for Central Wandsworth 1940-1950; Woolwich East 1950-1951
Cabinet posts 1940-1945, 1945-1951

Noel Pemberton Billing 1881-1948
Aviator, founder and editor of *Aerocraft* 1908-1910, constructor of flying
boats, playwright and inventor
Independent; MP for East Hertfordshire 1916-1921
Founder and President of "Vigilantes" society
Served in Boer War 1899-1901 and First World War 1914-1916

John Blaker 1854-1926
Mayor of Brighton 1895-1898

Henry Bolton 1874-1953
Blaydon Councillor 1919-1937 (Chairman in 1926 and four other times),
Durham County Council 1937/8-1945

Margaret Bondfield 1873-1953
Trade unionist and campaigner for shop assistants and women's interests
Chairman of Trades Union Congress 1923
Lab; MP for Northampton 1923-1924, Wallsend 1926-1931

Participants/Cast of characters

Cabinet post 1929-1931

Charles Booth   1840-1916
Social investigator and social reformer, particularly employment, Poor Law and old age pensions
Chairman of Booth Steamship Co.

Bob Boothby   1900-1986
C; MP for East Aberdeen and Kincardine 1924-1950, Aberdeenshire East 1950-1958; Baron Boothby 1958

Alfred Bossom   1881-1965
Architect
C; LCC 1927-1934; MP for Maidstone 1931-1959; Baron Bossom 1960

Horatio Bottomley   1860-1933
Bankrupt, swindler and newspaper owner/editor including *The Sun* 1902-1904, *John Bull* 1906-1921
Lib → Independent; Lib MP for Hackney South 1906-1910, Independent MP for Hackney South 1910-1912, 1918-1922

Frederick Bowhill   1880-1960
Director of Organisation, Air Ministry 1929-1931, Air Vice-Marshal defence of Great Britain 1931, member of the Air Council 1933, Head of Coastal Command 1937-1941, set up Ferry Command in Canada 1941, Commander-in-Chief Transport Command 1943-1945
Served in First World War 1914-1918

Brendan Bracken   1901-1958
Publisher; Chairman *Financial News* 1926-1945, *Financial Times* 1945-1958
C; MP for Paddington North 1929-1945, Bournemouth 1945-1950, Bournemouth East and Christchurch 1950-1952; Viscount Bracken 1952
Cabinet posts 1941-1945

Frank Briant   1865-1934
Civil servant
Lib; LCC 1905-1919, 1931-1934; MP for North Lambeth 1918-1929, 1931-1934
Chairman of Lambeth Board of Guardians 1910-1925, Old Age Pensions Committee for London 1914-1915

WC Bridgeman   1864-1935
C; MP for Oswestry Shropshire 1906-1929; Viscount Bridgeman 1929
Cabinet posts 1922-1929

Edmund Brocklebank   1882-1949
C; MP for Nottingham East 1924-1929, Liverpool Fairfield 1931-1945

Fenner Brockway   1888-1988
Journalist
Lab; MP for East Leyton 1929-1931, Eton and Slough 1950-1964; Baron
Brockway 1964

Ernest Brown   1881-1962
Lib; MP for Rugby 1923-1924, Leith 1927-1945
Cabinet posts 1935-1940, 1940-1945
President of the Baptist Union 1948-1949
Served in First World War 1914-1918

W J Brown   1894-1960
Lab → Indep; MP for Wolverhampton West 1929-1931, Independent MP
for Rugby 1942-1950

George Buchanan   1890-1955
Lab; MP for the Gorbals, Glasgow 1922-1948
Chairman, National Assistance Board 1948-1953

R A Butler   1902-1982
C; MP for Saffron Walden 1929-1965; Baron Butler of Saffron Walden
1965
Cabinet posts 1941-1945, 1951-1964
Chancellor of Sheffield University 1960-1978 and Essex University 1962-
1982

John Cadman   1877-1941
Mining engineer, Professor of Mining at Birmingham University 1908
Chairman, Anglo-Persian Oil Company 1927-1941; Lord Cadman 1937

Alexander Cadogan   1884-1968
Diplomat; Permanent Under-Secretary, Foreign Office 1938-1945; first UK
representative to the United Nations 1945-1950
Government director of the Suez Canal Company 1951-1957; Chairman of
the BBC 1952-1957

Edward Taswell Campbell   1879-1945
C; MP for North West Camberwell 1924-1929, Bromley 1930-1945
PPS to Kingsley Wood 1931-1943

Gordon Campbell, VC   1886-1953
Naval officer; National; MP for Burnley 1931-1935
Served in First World War 1914-1918; Victoria Cross 1917

Edward Carson   1854-1935
Unionist; MP for Dublin University 1892-1918, Duncairn Belfast 1918-1921; Baron Carson 1921
Cabinet posts 1915, 1916-1918
Leader of the Irish Unionist party in the House of Commons 1911-1921

Ronald Cartland   1907-1940
Unionist (C); MP for King's Norton, Birmingham 1935-1940

Thomas Catto   1879-1959
Banker and company director; Baron Catto 1936
Governor of the Bank of England 1944-1949

Victor Cazalet   1896-1943
C; MP for Chippenham, Gloucestershire 1924-1943
British liaison officer with General Sikorski and Polish Forces 1940-1943

Austen Chamberlain   1863-1937
C; MP for East Worcestershire 1892-1914, West Birmingham 1914-1937
Cabinet posts 1902-1905, 1915-1922, 1924-1929, 1931
Leader of the Unionists (Conservatives) 1921-1922

Neville Chamberlain   1869-1940
C; Birmingham City Council 1911-1916; MP for Ladywood Birmingham 1918-1929, Edgbaston Birmingham 1929-1940
Cabinet posts 1923-1924, 1924-1929, 1931-1937
Prime Minister 1937-May 1940. Leader of the Conservatives 1937-Oct 1940

Henry "Chips" Channon   1897-1958
Diarist
C; MP for Southend-on-Sea 1935-1950, Southend-on-Sea West 1950-1958

Charlie Chaplin   1889-1977
Film actor and director

Samuel Chapman   1859-1947
Company director
C; MP for Edinburgh South 1922-1945

Winston Churchill   1874-1965
C → Lib → C; C MP for Oldham 1900-1906, Lib MP for North-West Manchester 1906-1908, Dundee 1908-1922, C MP for Epping 1924-1945, Woodford 1945-1964

Cabinet posts 1908-1915, 1917-1922, 1924-1929, 1939-1940 Prime
Minister 1940-1945, 1951-1955. Leader of the Conservatives Oct 1940-
1955
Served in Boer War and First World War 1916

Alan Clark   1928-1999
Writer and diarist
C; MP for Plymouth Sutton 1974-1992, Kensington and Chelsea 1997-
1999

JR Clynes   1869-1949
Trade Unionist, founder of Piecers' Union, District organiser for National
Union of Gasworkers and Secretary Oldham Trades Council 1894-1912
President of the National Union of General and Municipal Workers 1912-
1937
Lab; MP for Manchester North-East 1906-1918, Manchester Platting 1918-
1931, 1935-1945
Cabinet posts 1924, 1929-1931
Chairman of the Labour Party in the House of Commons 1921-1922

John Colville   1915-1987
Civil servant 1937-1955 (Private Secretary to Chamberlain, Churchill and
Attlee)
Chairman Eucalyptus Pulp Mills, Director of National and Grindlay,
Ottoman and Coutts banks
In RAF during Second World War 1941-1944

Joseph Compton   1881-1937
Lab; Manchester City Council 1919-1925; MP for Manchester Gorton
1923-1931, 1935-1937

Martin Connolly   1874-1945
Lab; Newcastle-upon-Tyne City Council; MP for Newcastle East 1924-
1929

Martin Conway   1856-1937
Art historian, mountaineer and Director-General of the Imperial War
Museum
Unionist (C); MP for Combined Universities 1918-1931; Lord Conway of
Allington 1931

AJ (Arthur James) **Cook**   1883-1931
Miner, miners' agent 1919 and General Secretary Miners' Federation of
Great Britain 1924-1931

Diana Cooper   1892-1986   Actress and writer

Duff Cooper   1890-1954
C; MP for Oldham 1924-1929, St George's Westminster 1931-1945
British Ambassador to France 1944-1947; Viscount Norwich 1952
Cabinet posts 1935-1938, 1940-1943
Served in First World War 1917-1918

Stafford Cripps   1889-1952
Lab; MP for Bristol East 1931-1950
British Ambassador to the Soviet Union 1940-1942
Cabinet posts 1942-1945, 1945-1950

Will Crooks   1852-1921
Lab; LCC 1892-1910; MP for Woolwich 1903-1910, 1910-1918, Woolwich
East 1918-1921
Chairman of Poplar Board of Guardians 1898-1906

Harry Crookshank   1893-1961
C; MP for Gainsborough, Lincolnshire from 1924-1956

Philip Cunliffe-Lister   1884-1972
C; MP for Hendon 1918-1935; Viscount Swinton 1935, Earl Swinton 1955
Cabinet posts 1922-1923, 1924-1929, 1931-1938, 1951-1955
Served in First World War 1914-1916

George Curzon   1859-1925
C; MP for Southport Lancashire 1886-1898; Baron Curzon (I) 1898, Earl
Curzon of Kedleston 1911, Marquis Curzon of Kedleston 1921
Cabinet posts 1915-1925
Viceroy of India 1898-1905
Chancellor of Oxford University 1907-1925

Edouard Daladier   1884-1970
French Prime Minister 1933, 1934, 1938-1940; Served in First World War

Hugh Dalton   1887-1962
Lab; MP for Peckham 1924-1929, Bishop Auckland 1929-1931, 1935-
1959; Baron Dalton 1960
Cabinet posts 1942-1945, 1945-1947, 1948-1951

Henry Dalziel   1868-1935
Lib; MP for Kirkcaldy 1892-1921; Baron Dalziel of Kirkcaldy 1921
Owner of *Reynolds' Newspaper* (1914-1922) and *Pall Mall Gazette* (1917-
1922)

JCC Davidson   1889-1970
C; MP for Hemel Hempstead 1920-1923, 1924-1937; Viscount Davidson 1937
Conservative Party Chairman 1926-1930

William Davison   1872-1953
C; MP for Kensington South 1918-1945; 1st Baron Broughshane 1945

Harry Day   1880-1939
Lab; LCC 1931-1935; MP for Southwark 1924-1931, 1935-1939

Joseph Devlin   1872-1934
Independent; MP for North Kilkenny 1902-1906, West Belfast 1910-1918, Falls division of Belfast 1918-1922, Fermanagh and Tyrone 1929-1934

Benjamin Disraeli   1804-1881
Novelist
C; MP for Maidstone 1837-1841, Shrewsbury 1841-1847, Buckinghamshire 1847-1876; Earl of Beaconsfield 1876
Cabinet posts 1852, 1858-1859, 1866-1868
Prime Minister 1868, 1874-1880

Hugh Dowding   1882-1970
Director of Training, Air Ministry 1926-1931, Air Vice-Marshal 1929, member of the Air Council 1930-1936, Air Marshal 1933, Head of Fighter Command 1936-1940, Air Chief Marshal 1937; Baron Dowding 1943
Served in First World War 1914-1918

Arthur Conan Doyle   1859-1930
Doctor, writer and war reporter in the Boer and First World Wars

Will Dyson   1880-1938
Cartoonist

Anthony Eden   1897-1977
C; MP for Warwick and Leamington 1923-1957; Earl of Avon 1961
Cabinet posts 1935-1938, 1939-1940, 1940-1945, 1951-1955
Prime Minister 1955-1957
Chancellor of Birmingham University 1945-1973
Served in First World War 1915-1918

Walter Elliot   1888-1958
C; MP for Lanark 1918-1923, Kelvingrove, Glasgow 1924-1945
Cabinet posts 1932-1940

Geoffrey Francis Fisher   1887-1972
Bishop of London 1939-1945, Archbishop of Canterbury 1945-1961; Baron
Fisher of Lambeth 1961

Warren Fisher   1879-1948
Permanent Secretary to the Treasury and Head of the Civil Service 1919-
1939

Dingle Foot   1905-1978
Writer
Lib → Lab; Lib MP for Dundee 1931-1945, Lab MP for Ipswich from 1957-
1970

Michael Foot   1913-2010
Journalist and writer
Lab; MP for Devonport 1945-1955, Ebbw Vale 1960-1983 and Blaenau
Gwent 1983-1992
Labour Party leader 1980-1983

David Lloyd George   1863-1945
Lib; MP for Carnarvon 1890-1945; Earl Lloyd-George of Dwyfor 1945
Cabinet posts 1906-1915, 1915-1916
Prime Minister 1916-1922
Order of Merit 1919

Patrick Gower   1887-1964
Chief Publicity Officer, Conservative Party 1929-1939

William Graham   1887-1932
Lab; MP for Central Edinburgh 1918-1931
Cabinet post 1929-1931

Arthur Greenwood   1880-1954
Economics lecturer 1913-1914
Civil servant during the First World War, then Joint Secretary of the
Whitley Committee and Secretary of joint Labour Party - TUC Research
Department
Lab; MP for Nelson and Colne 1922-1931, Wakefield 1932-1954
Cabinet posts 1929, 1940-1942
Deputy Leader of the Parliamentary Labour Party 1942
Head of Labour Party Research Department 1927-1943

John Gretton   1867-1947
Chairman of the brewers Bass
C; MP for South Derbyshire 1895-1906, Rutland 1907-1918, Burton-upon-
Trent 1918-1943

Jim Griffiths   1890-1975
Lab; MP for Llanelli 1936-1970
Cabinet posts 1950-1951, 1964-1966

Edward Grigg   1879-1955
Journalist
Lib → C; Lib MP for Oldham 1922-1925, C MP for Altrincham 1933-1945;
Baron Altrincham 1945
Governor of Kenya 1925-1930
Served in First World War

Leslie Haden Guest   1877-1960
Doctor
Lab; MP for North Southwark 1923-1927, Islington 1937-1950; Baron
Haden-Guest 1950
Served in Boer War 1902; Red Cross and RAMC First and Second World
Wars

Derrick Gunston   1891-1985
C; MP for Thornbury, Gloucestershire 1924-1945
PPS to Kingsley Wood 1926-1929
Served in First World War

Maurice Hankey   1877-1963
Civil servant and Cabinet Secretary 1920-1938
Baron Hankey 1939
Cabinet post 1939-1942

Wal Hannington   1896-1966
Trade unionist, shop steward, national organiser National Unemployed
Workers' (Committee) Movement 1921 and Amalgamated Engineering
Union (AEU) 1942; Founder member of the Communist Party of Great
Britain 1920

Percy Harris   1876-1952
Lib; LCC 1907-1934, 1946-1952; MP for Market Harborough,
Leicestershire 1916-1918, Bethnal Green 1922-1945

Clarence Hatry   1888-1965
Insurance broker and company promoter

Cuthbert Headlam   1876-1964
Clerk in the House of Lords 1897-1924
C; Durham County Council 1931-1939; MP for Barnard Castle 1924-1929,
1931-1935, Newcastle North 1940-1951
Served in First World War 1915-1918

Arthur Henderson   1863-1935
Lab; MP for Barnard Castle 1903-1918, Widnes 1919-1922, Newcastle
East 1923-1924, Burnley 1924-1933, Claycross Derbyshire 1933-1935
Cabinet posts 1916, 1924, 1929
Chairman of the Labour Party in the House of Commons 1908-1910, 1914
(Father of Arthur Henderson (1893-1968), Baron Rowley from 1966)

Gordon Hewart   1870-1943
Journalist and lawyer
Lib; MP for Leicester 1913-1918, Leicester East 1918-1922; Baron Hewart
of Bury 1922, Viscount Hewart 1940
Cabinet post 1921-1922
Lord Chief Justice 1922-1940

George Hicks   1879-1954
National organiser 1912 and General Secretary 1919 of Operative
Bricklayers' Society, General Secretary of the Amalgamated Union of
Building Trade Operatives 1921-1940; Chairman of TUC 1926-1927
Lab; MP for Woolwich East 1931-1950

Edward Hilton Young   1879-1960
Lib → C; Lib MP for Norwich 1918-1923, 1924-1926, C MP for Sevenoaks
1929-1935; Lord Kennet 1935
Cabinet post 1931-1935.

Samuel Hoare   1880-1959
C; LCC 1907-1910; MP for Chelsea 1910-1944; Viscount Templewood
1944
Cabinet posts 1922-1924, 1924-1929, 1931-1935, 1935, 1936, 1937,
1939-1940
Chancellor of Reading University 1937-1959
Ambassador to Spain 1940-1944

Douglas Hogg   1872-1950
C; MP for Marylebone 1922-1928; Baron Hailsham 1928
Cabinet posts 1922-1924, 1924-1928, 1931-1935

Herbert Hoover   1874-1964
31st President of the USA 1929-1933

Harry Hopkins   1890-1946
New Deal relief programmes in 1930s; US Presidential link to Churchill
and Stalin during Second World War; Administrator of Lend-Lease

Richard Hopkins   1880-1955
Civil servant and Permanent Secretary to the Treasury 1942-1945

Leslie Hore-Belisha 1893-1957
Lib → Indep → C; Lib MP for Plymouth Devonport 1923-1942, Indep MP
for Plymouth Devonport 1942-1945; Baron Hore-Belisha 1954
Cabinet posts 1936, 1937-1940
Served in First World War 1914-1918

J F Horrabin 1884-1962
Journalist, artist and editor of *Plebs Magazine* 1914-1932
Lab; MP for Peterborough 1929-1931
Served in First World War 1917-1918

Cordell Hull 1871-1955
US Secretary of State 1933-1944

Gerald Hurst 1877-1957
C; MP for Manchester Moss Side 1918-1923, 1924-1935
County Court judge 1938-1952
Served in First World War 1914-1918

Robert Hutchison 1873-1950
Lib; MP for Kirkcaldy Burghs 1922-1923, Montrose 1924-1932; 1st Baron
Hutchison of Montrose 1932

Leslie Illingworth 1902-1979
Cartoonist

Thomas Inskip 1876-1947
C; MP for Bristol Central 1918-1929, MP for Fareham, Hampshire 1931-
1939; Viscount Caldecote of Bristol 1939
Cabinet posts 1928-1929, 1932-1936, 1936-1939, 1939-1940
Lord Chief Justice 1940-1946

Thomas Johnston 1881-1965
Clerk, writer and editor of *Forward* 1906-1933
 Lab; MP for West Stirlingshire 1922-1924, Dundee 1924-1929, West
Stirlingshire 1929-1931, 1935-1945
Cabinet posts 1931, 1941-1945

Frederick Jowett 1864-1944
Trade unionist
Lab; MP for West Bradford 1906-1918, East Bradford 1922-1924, 1929-
1931
Cabinet post 1924

William Jowitt   1885-1957
Lib → Lab; Lib MP for Hartlepool 1922-1924, Preston 1929, Lab MP for
Preston 1929-1931, Ashton under Lyne 1939-1945
Cabinet posts 1931, 1945

William Joynson-Hicks   1865-1932
C; MP for North-West Manchester 1908-1910, Brentford 1911-1918,
Twickenham 1918-1929; Viscount Brentford 1929
Cabinet posts 1923-1924, 1924-1929

Edward Keeling   1888-1954
Civil servant and businessman
C; MP for Twickenham 1935-1954
Served in First World War 1915-1918

Joseph Kenworthy   1886-1953
Lib → Lab; Lib MP for Hull 1919-1926, Lab MP for Hull 1926-1931; 10th
Baron Strabolgi 1934

Roger Keyes   1872-1945
Naval officer, Director of Plans, Admiralty 1917-1919, Deputy Chief of
Naval Staff 1921-1925
C; MP for Portsmouth North 1934-1943; Baron Keyes 1943
Served in First World War 1914-1918

John Maynard Keynes   1883-1946
Economist; Fellow and Bursar, King's College, Cambridge
Editor *Economic Journal* 1911-1944. Baron Keynes 1942

David Kirkwood   1872-1955
Trade Unionist, Amalgamated Engineering Union 1892-1949
Lab; MP for Dumbarton Burghs 1922-1950, Dumbarton East 1950-1951;
Baron Kirkwood 1951

Guy la Chambre   1898-1975
French Minister of Air 1938-1940

George Lansbury   1859-1940
Lab; MP for Bromley and Bow 1910-1912, 1922-1940
Cabinet posts 1929-1931
Leader of the Labour Party 1931-1935
Editor-proprietor of *Daily Herald* 1912-1922, *Lansbury's Labour Weekly*
1925-1927

Harold Laski   1893-1950
Writer and political theorist

Andrew Bonar Law   1858-1923
C; MP for Glasgow Blackfriars 1900-1906, Dulwich 1906-1910, Bootle
1911-1918, Glasgow Central 1918-1923;
Cabinet posts 1915-1922
Prime Minister 1922-1923. Leader of the Unionists (Conservatives) 1911-
1921

Susan Lawrence   1871-1947
C → Lab; C LCC 1910-1912, Lab LCC 1913-1928; Lab MP for East Ham
1923-1924, 1926-1931

William Lawther   1889-1976
Miner from 1901
Lab; Durham County Council 1925-1929; MP for Barnard Castle 1929-
1931
Miners' agent and trade union official from 1933; TUC General Council
1935-1954; President of the Miners Federation of Great Britain 1939-1945;
first President of the NUM 1945-1954

Hastings (Bertie) Lees-Smith   1878-1941
Lib → Lab; Lib MP for Northampton 1910-1918, Lab MP for Keighley
1922-1923, 1924-1931, 1935-1941
Cabinet post 1931
Served in First World War 1915-1918

John Scott Lidgett 1854-1953
Wesleyan Minister; Editor *Methodist Times*
Lib; LCC 1905-1928

Abraham Lincoln   1809-1865
16th President of the USA 1861-1865

George Lloyd   1879-1941
Unionist (Lib) → C; Unionist (Lib) → C MP for West Staffordshire 1910-
1918; C MP for Eastbourne 1924-1925; Baron Lloyd of Dolobran 1925
Governor of Bombay 1918-1923, High Commissioner of Egypt and Sudan
1925-1929
Served in First World War 1914-1918

David Low   1891-1963
Cartoonist

James Lowther   1855-1949
C; MP for Rutland 1883-1885, Penrith, Cumberland 1886-1921;
1st Viscount Ullswater 1921
Speaker of the House of Commons 1905-1921

Malcolm MacDonald   1901-1981
Lab; LCC 1927-1930; MP for Bassetlaw, Nottinghamshire 1929-1935,
Ross and Cromarty 1936-1945
Cabinet posts 1935-1940
High Commissioner to Canada 1941-1945, India 1955-1960
Governor-General of Malay States, Singapore and Borneo 1946-1948,
Commissioner-General for South-East Asia 1948-1954; Governor-General
of Kenya 1963-1964 and High Commissioner after independence 1964-
1965
Chancellor of University of Malaya 1949-1961 and Durham University
1970-1981

Ramsay MacDonald   1866-1937
Lab; LCC 1901-1904; MP for Leicester 1906-1918, Aberavon Glamorgan
1922-1929, Seaham Durham 1929-1935, Scottish Universities 1936-1937
Cabinet posts 1935-1937
Prime Minister 1924, 1929-1935
Labour Party Secretary 1900-1912, Chairman 1912-1914.

Donald Maclean   1864-1932
Lib; MP for Bath 1906-1910, Peebles and Selkirk 1910-1918, Peebles and
South Midlothian 1918-1922, North Cornwall 1929-1932
Cabinet posts 1931-1932

Harold Macmillan   1894-1986
C; MP for Stockton-on-Tees 1924-1929 and 1931-1945, Bromley 1945-
1964; Earl Stockton 1984
Cabinet posts 1945, 1951-1957
Prime Minister 1957-1963
Chancellor of Oxford University 1960-1986
Served in First World War

Arthur MacNalty   1880-1969
Medical practitioner; specialist in chest diseases and TB
Chief Medical Officer, Ministry of Health 1935-1940
Author, including the official medical history of the Second World War

Frederick Macquisten   1870-1940
C; MP for Springburn Glasgow 1918-1922, Argyll 1924-1940

Ivan Maisky   1884-1975
Diplomat
USSR Ambassador to Finland 1929-1932, Britain 1932-1943; Deputy
Foreign Minister 1943-1946

George Marks 1858-1938
Engineer and senior partner of an international engineering company
Lord Marks of Woolwich 1929

Frederick Marquis 1883-1964
Businessman; Baron Woolton of Liverpool 1939, Viscount Woolton 1953, 1st Earl Woolton 1955
Cabinet post(s) 1940-1945, 1951-1955
Conservative Party Central Office Chairman 1946-1955
Chancellor of the University of Manchester 1944-1964

Arthur Marsden 1883-1960
C; MP for North Battersea 1931-1935, Chertsey 1937-1950

CFG Masterman 1874-1927
Journalist
Lib; MP for West Ham North 1906-1911, Bethnal Green South-West 1911-1914
Cabinet post 1914-1915
Chairman of National Insurance Commission 1911

Reginald McKenna 1863-1943
Lib; MP for North Monmouthshire 1895-1918
Cabinet posts 1907-1908, 1908-1911, 1911-1915, 1915-1916
Director of the London City and Midland Bank 1917-1919, Chairman of the Midland Bank 1919-1943

Ronald McNeill 1861-1934
Journalist
C; MP for Canterbury 1911-1927; Baron Cushendun 1927
Cabinet post 1927-1929

J J McShane 1882-1972
Lab; MP for Walsall 1929-1931

Bertram Mills 1873-1938
Circus impresario and owner

William Mitchell-Thomson 1877-1938
C; MP for Lanarkshire North-West 1906-1910, North Down 1910-1918, Glasgow Maryhill 1918-1922, Croydon South 1923-1932; Lord Selsdon 1932

Alfred Mond 1868-1930
Lib →C; Lib MP for Chester 1906, Swansea Town 1910-1918, Swansea West 1918-1922, Carmarthen 1924-1926; C MP for Carmarthen 1926-1928; 1st Baron Melchett 1928

Cabinet posts 1916-1922
Director of International Nickel Company of Canada
Chairman Imperial Chemical Industries, Brunner Mond, Finance Company
of GB and America, and Westminster Bank

John Moore-Brabazon   1884-1964
C; MP for Chatham 1918-1929, Wallasey 1931-1942; Lord Brabazon of
Tara 1942
Cabinet post 1941-1942
Served in First World War 1914-1918

Robert Morant   1863-1920
Civil servant 1895-1920 Chairman of Insurance Commission 1912-1919

Henry Morgenthau   1891-1967
Farmer; US Treasury Secretary 1934-1945

Owen (Temple-) Morris   1896-1985
C; MP for Cardiff East 1931-1942
judge 1942-1969

Herbert Morrison   1888-1965
Secretary, London Labour Party 1915-?
ILP → Lab; LCC 1922-1940; MP for South Hackney 1923-1924, 1929-
1931, 1935-1950, South Lewisham 1950-1959; Baron Morrison of
Lambeth 1959.
Cabinet posts 1940-1945, 1945-1951

WS Morrison   1893-1961
C; MP for Cirencester and Tewkesbury 1929-1959; Viscount Dunrossil
1959
Cabinet posts 1936-1940
Speaker of the House of Commons 1951-1959
Governor-General of Australia 1959-1961
Served in First World War 1914-1918

Oswald Mosley   1896-1980
Unionist → Independent → Lab; U MP for Harrow 1918-1920, Indep MP
for Harrow 1920-1924, Lab MP for Smethwick 1926-1930
Founder and leader of New Party then British Union of Fascists

(George) Evelyn Pemberton Murray   1880-1947
Civil servant and Secretary of the Post Office 1914-1934

George Herbert Murray   1849-1936
Civil servant and Secretary of the Post Office 1897-1903

Cyril Newall   1886-1963
Head of Operations and Intelligence, Air Ministry 1926-1931, Air Vice-Marshal 1930, member of the Air Council 1935, Air Marshal 1935, Chief of the Air Staff 1937-1940, Air Chief Marshal 1938
Governor-General of New Zealand 1941-1946; Baron Newall 1946
Served in First World War 1914-1918

George Newman   1870-1948
Doctor and public health physician
Chief Medical Officer at Board of Education 1907-1935, Local Government Board 1919, Ministry of Health 1919-1935

Harold Nicolson   1886-1968
Diplomat, journalist and diarist
Lab; MP for Leicester West 1935-1945

TP O'Connor   1848-1929
Nationalist (N); MP for Galway 1880-1885, Liverpool Scotland 1885-1929
Editor of many newspapers including *Star*, *Sun*, *TP's Weekly* and *TP's Journal*

William Ormsby-Gore   1885-1964
Unionist (C); MP for Denbigh 1910-1918, Stafford 1918-1938; 4th Baron Harlech 1938-1964
Cabinet posts 1931-1936, 1936-1938
Director of the Midland Bank 1944-1952, Chairman Midland Bank 1952-1957; Chairman of the Bank of British West Africa 1951-1961
Pro-Chancellor of University of Wales 1945-1957
Served in First World War 1914-1917

John Boyd Orr   1880-1971
Nutritionist
Director of Aberdeen University Institute of Nutrition 1913-1923, Rowett Institute 1923-1945
Independent MP for Scottish Universities 1945-1946
first Director-General of UN Food and Agriculture Organisation 1945-1948
Chancellor of the University of Glasgow 1946-1971; Baron Boyd Orr 1949

John Pennefather   1856-1933
Cotton merchant
C; MP for Liverpool Kirkdale 1915-1929

Frederick Pethick Lawrence   1871-1961
Owner 1901 and editor *The Echo* 1902-1905; editor *Labour Record and Review* 1905-1907; joint editor *Votes for Women* 1907-1914
Campaigner for women's suffrage alongside wife Emmeline (1867-1954)

Lab; MP for Leicester West 1923-1931, Edinburgh East 1935-1945; Baron Pethick-Lawrence 1945
Cabinet post 1945-1947

Frederick Phillips   1884-1943
Civil servant, Under-Secretary to the Treasury 1932-1939, Third Secretary 1939-1942, Joint Second Secretary 1942-1943
Head of Treasury mission to USA 1940-1943

Alan Pitt-Robbins   1888-1967
Journalist from 1904; editorial staff of *Times* 1909-1953, including parliamentary correspondent 1928-1938, Home News editor 1938-1953
Institute of Journalists 1920-1951; Secretary of General Council of the Press 1954-1960

William Plender   1861-1946
Accountant; Senior partner at Deloitte 1904; Institute of Chartered Accountants 1903-1946
Baron Plender 1931

Charles 'Peter' Portal   1893-1971
Director of Operations, Air Ministry 1937-1939, member of the Air Council 1939, Commander-in-Chief of Bomber Command 1940, Chief of the Air Staff 1940-1945
Baron Portal of Hungerford 1945; Viscount Portal 1946
Company director and Controller of atomic energy production 1946-1951

Assheton Pownall   1877-1953
C; MP for Lewisham East 1918-1945
Brother of Henry Pownall

Henry Pownall   1887-1961
Director of Military Operations and Intelligence, War Office, 1938; Chief of Staff of the British Expeditionary Force 1939-1940, i.e., at Dunkirk
Chief Commissioner of St John Ambulance Brigade 1947, Chancellor of the Order of St John 1951; Chairman of Friary Meux
Brother of Assheton Pownall; Churchill's military consultant on 'History of the Second World War'; Served in First World War 1914-1918

Harry Preston   1860-1936
Hotel proprietor in Brighton: Royal York 1901 to 1929 and Royal Albion from 1913

Eleanor Rathbone   1872-1946
Indep; Liverpool City Council 1909-1935; MP for Combined English Universities 1929-1946

John Reith   1889-1971
General Manager then Director-General of BBC 1922-1938
MP (National) for Southampton 1940; Baron Reith 1940
Cabinet posts 1940-1942
Chairman Imperial Airways, British Overseas Airways Corporation, Hemel
Hempstead Development Corporation, Colonial Development Corporation,
State Building Society. Director of Phoenix Assurance
Served in First World War 1914-1915

Paul Reynaud   1878-1966
French Finance Minister 1930, 1938-1940, Minister of Colonies 1931-
1932, Minister of Justice 1932, 1938, Prime Minister 1940
Served in First World War 1914-1918

Robert Richardson   1862-1943
Miner
Lab; Durham County Council 1901-1925; MP for Houghton-le-Spring,
County Durham 1918-1931

George Riddell   1865-1934
Baron Riddell 1920
Chairman *News of the World*, Newspaper Proprietors' Association, George
Newnes and C. Arthur Pearson

Arthur Robinson   1874-1950
Civil servant; Permanent Secretary Air Ministry 1917-1920, Ministry of
Health 1920-1935, Ministry of Supply 1939-1940; Company director

Franklin D Roosevelt   1882-1945
32nd President of the USA 1933-1945

Seebohm Rowntree   1871-1954
Quaker, chronicler of poverty in York, welfare sociologist and advocate of
enlightened business management

Lord Salisbury, James Cecil   1861-1947
C; MP for Darwen Lancashire 1885-1892, Rochester Kent 1893-1903;
Viscount Cranborne 1868-1903, 4th Marquess of Salisbury 1903
Colonel in Boer War

David Salomons   1851-1925
and
Vera Salomons   1888-1969
Daughter of the above, from whom she inherited Broomhill Bank, the home
of Sir Kingsley and Lady Agnes Wood from 1928-1943

Alfred Salter   1873-1945
Doctor
Lab; LCC 1905-1910; MP for West Bermondsey 1922-1923, 1924-1945

Arthur Salter   1881-1975
Civil servant 1904-1930 and author
Indep →C; Indep. MP for Oxford University 1937-1950, C MP for Ormskirk
1951-1953; Baron Salter of Kidlington 1953
Cabinet posts 1945, 1951-1953

Herbert Samuel   1870-1963
Lib; MP for Cleveland 1902-1918, Darwen 1929-1933; Baron Samuel of
Carmel and Toxteth 1937
Cabinet posts 1909-1915, 1915-1916, 1931-1932
first High Commissioner of Palestine 1920-1925

William (WS) Sanders   1871-1941
Secretary of Fabian Society 1914-1920
Lab; MP for North Battersea 1929-1931, 1935-1940
Captain in First World War

Duncan Sandys   1908-1987
Diplomat
C; MP for Norwood 1935-1945, Streatham 1950-1974; Baron Duncan-
Sandys 1974

Lord Selborne, William Waldegrave Palmer   1859-1942
Lib → Lib Unionists; MP for Petersfield 1885-1892, Edinburgh 1892-1895;
Viscount Wolmer 1882, 2nd Earl of Selborne 1895
Cabinet posts 1900-1905, 1915-1916

Geoffrey Shakespeare   1893-1980
Civil servant 1921-1922 and journalist
Lib; MP for Wellingborough, Northamptonshire 1922-1923, Norwich 1929-
1945

Drummond Shiels   1881-1953
Physician
Lab; Edinburgh Town Council 1924; MP for Edinburgh East 1924-1931
Served in First World War

Manny Shinwell   1884-1986
Tailor
Lab; MP for Linlithgow 1922-1924, 1928-1931, Seaham Harbour
(Easington) 1935-1970; Baron Shinwell 1970
Cabinet posts 1945-1947, 1950-1951

Labour Party Chairman 1947-1948; Chairman of the Labour Party in the House of Commons 1964-1967

Alfred Short   1882-1938
Lab; MP for Wednesbury 1918-1931, Doncaster 1935-1938

Wladyslaw Sikorski   1881-1943
Chief of the Polish general staff 1921-1922, 1939-1943
Prime Minister of Poland 1922-1923; Prime Minister of Polish government in exile 1939-1943
Cabinet post 1924-1925
Served in First World War

Ernest Simon   1879-1960
Lib → Lab; Manchester City Council 1912-1925, Lord Mayor of Manchester 1921-1922; MP for Withington Manchester 1923-1924, 1929-1931; Baron Wythenshawe 1947
Chairman of BBC 1947-1952

John Simon   1873-1954
Lib; MP for Walthamstow 1906-1918, Spen Valley Yorkshire 1922-1940; Viscount Simon 1940
Cabinet posts 1913-1915, 1915-1916, 1931-1935, 1935-1937, 1937-1940, 1940-1945
Leader of Liberal National Party in House of Commons 1931-1940
Served in First World War 1917-1918

Archibald Sinclair   1890-1970
Lib; MP for Caithness and Sutherland 1922-1945; Viscount Thurso 1952
Cabinet posts 1931-1932, 1940-1945
Served in First World War

FE Smith   1872-1930
C; MP for Walton Liverpool 1906-1918, West Derby Liverpool 1918-1919; Lord Birkenhead 1919
Cabinet posts 1915-1922, 1924-1928

Henry Snell   1865-1944
Lab; MP for Woolwich East 1922-1931; Baron Snell of Plumstead 1931

Philip Snowden   1864-1937
Civil servant
Lab; MP for Blackburn 1906-1918, Colne Valley 1922-1931; Viscount Snowden 1931
Cabinet posts 1924, 1929-1931

Daniel Somerville   1879-1938
C; MP for Barrow-in-Furness 1922-1924, Willesden 1929-1938

Victor Spencer   1864-1934
Viscount Churchill of Wychwood 1902

Josiah Stamp   1880-1941
Civil servant 1896; Company director; Director of the Bank of England
1928; Baron Stamp of Shortlands 1938

Edward George Villiers Stanley   1865-1948
C; MP for West Houghton, Lancashire 1892-1906; Baron Stanley of
Preston 1896, 17th Earl of Derby 1908
Lord Mayor of Liverpool 1911; Chancellor of Liverpool University 1908-
1948
Ambassador to France 1918-1920
Cabinet posts 1903-1906, 1916-1918, 1922-1924

Oliver Stanley   1896-1950
C; MP for Westmorland 1924-1945, Bristol West 1945-1950
Cabinet posts 1934-1935, 1935-1937, 1937-1940, 1942-1945
Served in First World War 1915-1918

Arthur Steel-Maitland   1876-1935
C; MP for East Birmingham 1910-1918, Erdington, Birmingham 1918-
1929, Tamworth 1929-1935
first Conservative Party chairman 1911
Managing director of Rio Tinto Zinc 1919-1924
Cabinet post 1924-1929

James Stewart   1863-1931
Hairdresser and businessman
Lab; Glasgow Town Council 1909-1922; MP for Glasgow St Rollox 1922-
1931

Richard Stokes   1897-1957
Engineer; Managing director and chairman of Ransome and Rapier
Lab; MP for Ipswich 1938-1957
Cabinet post 1951
Served in First World War 1916-1918

Hannan Swaffer   1879-1962
Journalist, including *Daily Mail*, *Daily Mirror*, *Daily Sketch* and *Daily Herald*;
editor *The People* 1924; author

Stephen Tallents 1884-1958
Civil servant 1909
first Post Office Public Relations officer 1933-1935; Controller of Public
Relations, then of overseas services BBC 1935-1941; first Public Relations
officer, Ministry of Town and Country Planning 1943-1946
Served in First World War 1914-1915

Mavis Tate 1893-1947
C; West Willesden 1931-1935, Frome, Somerset 1935-1945

JH Thomas 1874-1949
Secretary Amalgamated Society of Railway Servants 1906-1910, General
Secretary National Union of Railwaymen (NUR) 1916-1931
Lab; MP for Derby 1910-1936
Cabinet posts 1924, 1929-1931, 1931-1935, 1935-1936
Chairman of TUC 1919-1920

Trevelyan Thomson 1875-1928
Businessman
Lib; Middlesbrough County Borough Council 1904-1928; MP for
Middlesbrough West 1918-1928
Served in First World War 1917-1918

Will Thorne 1857-1946
General Secretary, National Union of Gasworkers and General Labourers
1889-1934
Lab; MP for West Ham 1906-1918, Plaistow 1918-1945

Robert Topping 1877-1952
Principal Conservative Party agent and Director-General of the
Conservative Party 1927-1945

George Tryon 1871-1940
C; MP for Brighton 1910-1940; Baron Tryon from 1940

Charles Stewart Henry Vane-Tempest-Stewart 1878-1949
C; MP for Maidstone 1906-1915; 7th Marquis of Londonderry 1915
Minister of Education in Northern Ireland 1921-1926
Cabinet post 1931-1935

Lord Ventry, Arthur Eveleigh de Moleyns 1898-1987
Author and airship pilot
7th Lord Ventry 1936
Served in First World War 1917-1918 and Second World War 1939-1945

John Tudor Walters 1868-1933
Lib; MP for Sheffield Brightside 1906-1922, Penryn and Falmouth Cornwall 1929-1931; Chairman of London Housing Board

Irene Ward 1895-1980
C; MP for Wallsend 1931-1945, Tynemouth 1950-1974; Baroness Ward of North Tyneside 1974

Ronald Waterhouse 1878-1942
Principal private secretary to the Prime Minister1922-1928
Served in Boer War, First World War 1914-1918 and Second World War 1940

Beatrice Webb 1858-1943
Public servant, social reformer and activist (including for women, Fabian Society and Labour party)

Josiah Wedgwood 1872-1943
Lab; Staffordshire County Council 1910-1918; MP for Newcastle-under-Lyme, Staffordshire 1906-1942; 1st Baron Wedgwood 1942
Cabinet post 1924
Served in Boer War 1900-1901 and First World War 1914-1916

Andrew Weir 1865-1955
Shipowner from 1885 and owner of Andrew Weir Shipping; Baron Inverforth 1919
Cabinet post 1919-1921
Chairman of Anglo-Burma Burma Rice Company, Wilmer Grain Company and United Baltic Corporation. Director of Lloyds Bank

HG Wells 1866-1946
Shop assistant, teacher, writer, social commentator and visionary

John Wesley 1703-1791
Founder of Methodism

Maxime Weygand 1867-1965
French Chief of Staff to Marshal Foch in WW I, retired 1935, Commander-in-Chief 1940

John Wheatley 1869-1930
Lab; MP for Shettleston Glasgow 1922-1930
Cabinet post 1924

William Whiteley 1881-1955
Lab; MP for Blaydon 1922-1931, 1935-1955

Labour chief whip 1942-1955

John Whitley   1866-1935
Lib; MP for Halifax 1900-1928
Speaker of the House of Commons 1921-1928
BBC Chairman 1930-1935

Ellen Wilkinson   1891-1947
Novelist and journalist; Trade unionist and campaigner for women's
suffrage and shop assistants
Lab; Manchester City Council 1923-1926; MP for Middlesbrough East
1924-1931, Jarrow 1935-1947
Cabinet post 1945-1947

Horace Wilson   1882-1972
Personal adviser to Baldwin and then Chamberlain from 1935; Permanent
Secretary to the Treasury and Head of the Civil Service 1939-1942

John Winant   1889-1947
Governor of New Hampshire 1925-1927, 1931-1935; US Ambassador to
Britain 1941-1946
Order of Merit 1947
Served in First World War 1917-1918

Earl Winterton (I),[1910] **Edward Turnour**   1883-1962
C; MP for Horsham Sussex 1904-1918, Horsham and Worthing 1918-
1945, Horsham 1945-1951
Cabinet post 1938; Served in First World War

Lord Wolmer, Roundell Cecil Palmer   1887-1971
C; MP for Newtown, Lancashire 1910-1918, Aldershot 1918-1940;
Viscount Wolmer 1895, Baron Wolmer 1940, 3rd Earl of Selborne 1942
Director of Boots 1936-1963
Cabinet post 1942-1945
Served in First World War 1914-1918

Edward Wood (Halifax)   1881-1959
C; MP for Ripon 1910-1925; Baron Irwin 1926, Viscount Halifax 1934, Earl
Halifax 1944
Cabinet posts 1922-1923, 1924-1925, 1935-1940
Viceroy of India 1926-1931, Ambassador to USA 1941-1946
Chancellor of Oxford University 1933-1959 and Sheffield University 1946-
1959
Served in First World War 1916-1917

[1910] (I) = in the Irish peerage

Kingsley Wood's family:

Agnes Fawcett 1877-1955 Wife	
Marjorie Henry 1903-1989 Adopted daughter	Francis Brothers 1900-1972 Son-in-law
Arthur Wood 1853/4-1919 Father and Wesleyan Minister	Harriet Siddons Howard 1857?-? Mother
Dorothy Wood/Weaver 1884-1966 Sister	Edward Weaver Brother-in-law and Wesleyan Minister
Thomas Smith Wood c1813-1858 Grandfather and Wesleyan Minister	Edward Graham Wood 1854-1930 Uncle
Henry Frederick Fawcett 1850/1-1929 Father-in-law	Elizabeth Burridge 1852?-? Mother-in-law
Mary Thurston Sister-in-law	HP Thurston Sister-in-law's husband

Alfred Woodgate 1860-1943
Civil servant; Chairman of the West Ham Board of Guardians 1926-1929

Stanley Woodwark 1879-1945
Physician

Laming Worthington-Evans 1868-1931
Solicitor from 1890 until retired in 1910
C; MP for Colchester 1910-1929, St George's Westminster 1929-1931
Cabinet posts 1919-1922, 1923-1924, 1924-1929

August Zaleski 1883-1972
Polish Ambassador to Greece 1919-1926; Polish Minister for Foreign
Affairs 1926-?

Grigori Zinoviev 1883-1936
Chairman of the Comintern (Third International) 1919-1926

Sources
Biographical Dictionary of the Former Soviet Union 1992
Dictionnaire De Biographie Francaise 1989
Dictionnaire Des Parlementaries Francais 1889-1940
Dod's Parliamentary Companion 1895-1986
Oxford Dictionary of National Biography 2004
Polish Biographical Dictionary 1992
Polski Słownik Biograficzny 1996/97
Who Was Who 1916-1990 (vols. II to VIII)

BIBLIOGRAPHY

Primary Sources

Books and Other Contemporary Documents

Attlee, Clement, "Post Office reform", *New Statesman and Athenaeum*, 7th November 1931, pp565-566

Baldwin Papers vol. 15, 223-235; vol. 21, 246-251; vol. 22, 21-43, 69-72; vol. 23, 5, 6-9, 10, 16, 17-23

Blaydon Benzol Works 30th April to 13th May 1926

Blaydon Council 10th May 1926

'Britain's Industrial Future, being the Report of the Liberal Industrial Inquiry 1928' (the Liberal Yellow Book), London, Ernest Benn, 1928

BBC archives:

Board of Governors Minutes 1932 - 86, 102, 114, 115 & 123; 1933 - 21, 27, 31 & 44; 1934 - 29, 36, 38 & 46; 1935 - 15 & 75

Director-General Reports to Board of Governors 24th May 1933 & September 1933

Letter to Donald Banks 26th April 1935

R4/69/1, 14th August & 26th November 1934; 3rd January, 12th, 15th, 17th & 26th April 1935

R4/70/1, 30th April & 2nd May 1935

R4/70/2, 2nd January 1936

RCont1, 2nd January 1933

RCont1, 6th June 1934

TV 16/214/1, 31st January 1935

British Gazette 13th May 1926

Central Council of Economic Leagues (CCEL) Strike Bulletins 1-7, 4th-11th May 1926

Churchill College archives:

Amery Papers,

AMEL 1/6/9 WP (42) 25, Wood memo on Lend-Lease Article VII for War Cabinet 17th January 1942

AMEL 2/1/33, Wood reply to Amery 9th January 1941; Amery letter to Wood 10th September 1941

AMEL 2/1/34, Amery letter 10th April and Hardinge reply 14th April 1942; Amery letter 23rd March and Jowitt reply 30th March 1942

AMEL 3/8, Wood letter to Amery 4th November 1940

Bevin Papers,

BEVN 3/3, Bevin reply to Wood 27th January 1941; Bevin letter 20th January and Maisky reply 22nd January 1943

Churchill Papers,

CHAR 2/371 A-B, Public and Political: General: Defence, 6th November 1936 to 20th January 1942

CHAR 19/2C/314, 18th September 1939 Churchill letter and CHAR 19/2A/40, 19th September 1939 Wood reply

CHAR 19/2B/176-178, 1st April 1940 Churchill letter to Neville Chamberlain

CHAR 20/34/7, 21st June 1941 Wood letter to Churchill

CHAR 20/66/38 and 20/53A/56, Churchill letter to Wood 19th February 1942

CHAR 20/93B/149, 2nd August 1943 Wood draft for Churchill on Lend-Lease

CHAR 23/11 WP (43) 65, 15th February 1943 Churchill proposal re Beveridge report in Commons debate

FROB 1/9

Hore-Belisha Papers,

HOBE 1/5, Hore-Belisha 1938 &1939 diaries

HOBE 1/7, Hore-Belisha 1939-1940 diary

HOBE 5/38

Cliveden Visitors books October 1919 - July 1941, University of Reading Special Collections

Conservative Party Archive, Bodleian Library, Oxford:

Annual Conference minutes 1930, 1932-1937

Cabinet Conservative Committee 1934-1935

Cabinet Emergency Business Committee 1935

Central Council Minutes 24th February 1931

Committee Against Malnutrition (CAN) Bulletins 9 (July 1935) & 12 (January 1936)

The Elector June 1924-December 1934, January 1935-December 1938

Electoral Reform 1935-1938: Brooke note on proportional representation 17th December 1935

Executive Committee Minutes 1922-1931, 1931-1937, 1938-1948

General Election 1935 Correspondence

Gleanings and Memoranda, vol. LXXI, January - June 1930

Health and physique of the nation – General, July 1934 and Physical training, March 1935

Liberal, Labour and National Government manifestoes (for 1935 General Election)

'Man in the Street', February 1925

Ministry of Health note 28th October 1935

Miscellaneous candidate material for 1935 General Election

Monthly NPB Statements March 1935-Nov 1938

Monthly NPB Statements to Kingsley Wood

National Publicity Bureau pamphlet, 'A Better Way to Better Times', July 1935

National Union Executive Minute Book pp468-470

Opposition misrepresentations

Organisation of Conservative Research Department 1930-1939

Physical Condition of Potential Recruits for Regular Army 1933

Physical Training Oct 1936 to Aug 1938

Points for Propaganda January to July 1939

Politics in Review, 1935, vol. 2, opening article to quarter 3; April-June 1936

Popular Illustrated, no. 1, May/June 1935

Reports of the Executive Committee to the Central Council

Speakers' Notes, July 1942-Dec 1943

George, David Lloyd, Lord Lothian and Rowntree, Seebohm, 'How to Tackle Unemployment: The Liberal Plans as Laid Before the Government and Nation', London, The Press Printers, 1930

Hansard (H. C. Deb. 5 s.):

8th October 1924, vol. 177, cols.581-704

to

2nd November 1943, vol. 393, col. 523

Hansard (118 HL Deb, 5s.):

5th March 1941, vol. 118, cols. 563-593

22nd September 1943, vol. 129, cols. 64-66

Hansard (H. C. Deb. 6 s.):

28th February 2002, vol. 380, 1439w to 1441w

House of Commons Command Papers:

Bridgeman Committee of Enquiry on the Post Office, 'Report', 1932, Cmd 4149

'British Broadcasting Corporation Sixth Annual Report 1932', 1933, Cmd 4277

Budget Disclosure Inquiry, 'Report of the Tribunal Appointed Under the Tribunals of Inquiry (Evidence) Act, 1921', 1936, Cmd 5184

'Certain Legislation respecting Religion in force in the Union of Soviet Socialist Republics', 1929-30, Cmd 3641

'Conference on Electoral Reform. Letter from Viscount Ullswater to the Prime Minister', 1930, Cmd 3636

'Family Allowances: Memo by the Chancellor of the Exchequer', May 1942, Cmd 6354

'First Report of the Royal Commission on Unemployment Insurance', 1931, Cmd 3872

Ministry of Health:

Fifteenth Annual Report of the Ministry of Health 1933-34, 1934, Cmd 4664

Sixteenth Annual Report of the Ministry of Health 1934-35, 1935, Cmd 4978

'Report of an Inquiry into the Effects of Existing Economic Circumstances on the Health of the Community in the County Borough of Sunderland and Certain Districts of County Durham', 1935, Cmd 4886

'Report of an Investigation into Maternal Mortality', 1937, Cmd 5422

'Preliminary Conference with a View to Concerted Economic Action. Commercial Convention and Protocol, Protocol Regarding Future Negotiations, and Final Act', 1930, Cmd 3539

'Report of the Broadcasting Committee 1935', 1936, Cmd 5091

'Report of Committee on National Expenditure', 1931, Cmd 3920

Ickworth House, Bury St Edmunds Visitors book

National Archives:

CAB 23/93 Cabinet minutes March 1938

CAB 65/25/14 Lend-Lease Article VII 2nd February 1942

CAB 65/25/17 Lend-Lease Article VII 6th February 1942

CAB 65, WM(40), 251 re family allowances for service personnel 17th September 1940

CAB 66/28/16 Wood report on Lend-Lease operations 28th August 1942

CAB 66/39/29 re Article VII discussions with USA 22nd July 1943

CAB 67/4/41 Wood and Anderson report on air raids 7th February 1940

CAB 67/8/36 re family allowances for service personnel 12th September 1940

CAB 67/8/39 Wood report on private insurance schemes 20th September 1940

CAB 67/8/51 Wood report on compensation for war damage 1st October 1940

CAB 71/1 Lord President's Committee minutes 1940-1946

CAB 24/279/18 Minister of Air report, 'Relative Air Strengths and Proposals for the Improvement of the Country's Position', 25th October 1938

PREM 1/252 14th October 1938

PREM 4/7/12

Northumberland Coal Owners' Association Minutes 30th April 1926, 18th May 1926, pp126-128; pp136-138

Northumberland Miners Union:

4th May 1926, Minute 2; Annual Council 15th May; 17th May 1926, Minute 1; 25th May 1926, Minute 11; 10th July 1926, Minute 10

Strike Bulletin 4th May 1926, pp1-4

Parliamentary archives:

BBK/C/330 Correspondence between Wood and Beaverbrook 1931-1940

BBK/D/336 10th June 1940 Wood reply; 25th August 1940 Beaverbrook letter and 2nd September 1940 Wood reply; 5th January Beaverbrook letter and 7th January 1941 Wood reply

BBK/D/527 re Harold Balfour

LG/G/19/22 item 5 27th December 1933

Polish Institute/Sikorski Museum (PISM):

A.11E/175 Sikorski/Wood meeting 15th November 1939

A.12.49/WB/14 Sikorski visit to London November 1939

Polskie Dokumenty Dyplomatyczne 1941

Sikorski/Wood meeting 21st November 1940

Churchill/Sikorski 19th February 1941
PRM 39A/28 5th July 1941
Post Office establishment book, 1935
Public Health Act 1935-36
Westminster Rate books 1935-1943
Lord Wolmer, 'Post Office Reform: Its Importance and Practicability', London, Ivor Nicolson and Watson, 1932
Woolwich and Eltham Searchlight December 1934 & January 1935
Woolwich West Conservative & Unionist Association, Greenwich Heritage Centre 1930 item 5 (but undated); 5th June 1931 item 10
The Workers' Chronicle Nos. 1, 4, 8, 12 & 14, 6th,7th 8th, 11th & 14th May 1926

Diaries and Memoirs

J Allison, North Walbottle miner reminiscences, Tyne and Wear Archives and Museums DX201/2
Ball, Stuart (ed.),
'Parliament and Politics in the Age of Baldwin and MacDonald: The Headlam Diaries 1923-1935', London, The Historians' Press, 1992
'Parliament and Politics in the Age of Churchill and Attlee: The Headlam Diaries 1935-1951', Cambridge, Cambridge University Press, 1999
Bond, Brian (ed.), 'Chief of Staff: The Diaries of Lt Gen Sir Henry Pownall, vol. 1: 1933-1940', London, Leo Cooper, 1972
Dilks, David (ed.), 'The Diaries of Sir Alexander Cadogan OM 1938-1945', London, Cassell, 1971
Ruth Dodds, Tyne and Wear Archives and Museums DF.DOD
James, Robert Rhodes,
'Chips: The Diaries of Sir Henry Channon', London, Weidenfeld & Nicolson, 1967
'Memoirs of a Conservative: JCC Davidson's Memoirs and Papers 1910-1937', London, Weidenfeld & Nicolson, 1969
Thomas Jones, 'A Diary with Letters 1931-1950', London, Oxford University Press, 1954
Cecil H King (ed. William Armstrong), 'With Malice Toward None', London, Sidgwick & Jackson, 1970
Malcolmson, Robert (ed.), 'Love and War in London: The Mass Observation Wartime Diary of Olivia Cockett', Stroud, The History Press, 2008
Middlemas, Keith (ed.), 'Thomas Jones: Whitehall Diary vol. II 1926-1930', London, Oxford University Press, 1969
Mylett, Andrew (ed.), 'Arnold Bennett: The *Evening Standard* Years "Books and Persons 1926-1931"', London, Chatto & Windus, 1974
Harold Nicolson,
'Diaries and Letters - vol. I: 1930-1939', London, Collins, 1966

'Diaries and Letters - vol. II: 1939-1945', London, Collins, 1967

'Diaries and Letters - vol. III: 1945-1962', London, Collins, 1968

Self, Robert (ed.),

'The Neville Chamberlain Diary Letters: vol. II 1921-1927', London, Ashgate, 2000

'The Neville Chamberlain Diary Letters: vol. III 1928-1933', London, Ashgate, 2002

Stevenson, Frances, 'Lloyd George: A Diary', London, Hutchinson, 1971

Vincent, John (ed.), 'The Crawford Papers: The Journal of David Lindsay 27th Earl of Crawford and 10th Earl of Balcarres 1871-1940 during the years 1892-1940', Manchester, Manchester University Press, 1984

Williamson, Philip (ed.), 'The Modernisation of Conservative Politics: The Diaries and Letters of William Bridgeman 1904-1935', London, The Historians' Press, 1988

Newspapers - generally, but not always, University of Kent archives. In the latter case identified in the text as KW... However, if not listed below, then either undated or unattributed in that press cuttings archive.

Aberdeen Journal 30th August 1934;

Bath Chronicle and Herald 18th September 1936

Beckenham Journal 24th October 1936

Belfast Whig and Belfast Post 25th July 1938

Birmingham Daily Mail 22nd November 1929; 14th February & 1st November 1935

Birmingham Gazette 14th March & 21st October 1935

Birmingham Post 27th February, 4th March & 1st July 1931; 23rd September 1933

Blaydon Courier 22nd May 1926; 13th March 1953

Bournemouth Echo 14th October 1936

Brighton Gazette 28th March 1925

Bristol Times & Mirror 5th September 1931

Brixton Free Press 8th March 1929

Burton Daily Mail 7th & 14th February 1929

Bystander 14th September 1932; 26th June & 2nd October 1934; 6th July 1938

Cambridge Daily News 21st April 1934

Citizen 13th September 1935

Cork Examiner 15th July 1929

Courier 8th July 1938

Crystal Palace Advertiser 23rd November 1928

Daily Chronicle 26th November 1925; 9th October 1928

Daily Dispatch [Despatch] 13th June 1935; 13th October 1936

Daily Express 3rd November 1924, 28th December 1925; 21st January, 21st February, 6th November, 3rd & 19th December 1930; 27th February & 11th June 1931; 10th February 1932; 22nd July & 21st December 1933;

5th November & 18th December 1934; 22nd May, 31st July & 27th September 1935; 17th & 31st July, 30th October & 5th November 1936

Daily Graphic 28th January 1925; 12th May 1926

Daily Herald undated but November 1926; 23rd January, 23rd May & 11th December 1929; 31st March & 7th July 1930; 23rd & 29th January, 13th February, 1st July & 31st December 1931; 13th February 1932; 6th January, 16th August & 21st December 1933; 23rd April, 5th & 26th October, 29th December 1934; 14th January, 14th February, 7th & 11th March, 11th July, 5th August & 29th October 1935; 31st July & 23rd October 1936; 14th April 1937; 31st October 1938

Daily Independent 21st December 1934

Daily Mail 8th May 1926; 15th December 1928; undated but November 1929; 1st April 1930; 27th January & 28th August 1931; 8th January, 16th February & 8th July 1932; 23rd February 1933; 17th & 28th February & 1st May 1934; 19th November 1935; 9th, 30th & 31st July, 10th November 1936; 5th November 1937; 30th May & 2nd June 1938

Daily Mirror 29th December 1925; 10th November 1926; 4th January 1927; 2nd June 1928; 24th January 1929; 11th December 1930; 20th February 1934; 31st July 1936

Daily News 27th December 1925; 9th August 1926; 14th December 1928; 8th December 1929; 12th November 1934

Daily Sketch 8th January 1925; 1st April 1927; 17th December 1928; 1st November 1934; 10th December 1936; 18th & 24th May 1938

Daily Telegraph 17th August 1922; 10th June 1924; 28th January & 27th March 1925; 3rd June & 27th July 1926; 16th July 1929; 15th October 1930; 13th February, 29th August & 2nd November 1931; 21st July, 22nd August & 21st December 1933; 20th February & 21st December 1934; 29th October 1935; 3rd September & 7th December 1936; 26th November 1937; 24th May 1938

Daily Worker 31st October 1935; 9th October 1936;

Derby Evening Telegraph 25th October 1935

Durham Chronicle 31st July 1936

East Anglian Daily Times 21st May 1938

East Anglian Times 24th February 1931

Eastern Daily Express undated but November 1929; undated but 1930

East Kent Gazette 15th January 1938

Edinburgh Evening News 22nd December 1934

Evening Chronicle 10th May 1926

Evening News 25th November & 30th December 1925; 9th November 1926; 24th October 1928; 14th November & 10th December 1930; 23rd January & 17th March 1931; 21st July 1933; 21st November 1936

Evening Standard 13th January, 6th August & 9th November 1926; 23rd October, 13th November & 14th December 1928; 14th February 1929; 14th November & 17th December 1930; 17th March & 31st July 1931; 28th September, 31st October, 20th & 24th December 1934; 2nd March 1935;

21st September & 23rd December 1936; 17th & 19th May & 20th June 1938

Evening Star 26th June 1930; 9th February 1934

Financial News 15th December 1928

Financial Times undated but 1929; 6th January 1930; 9th March 1931

Forward 8th August 1936

Glasgow Evening Citizen 24th February 1931

Glasgow Herald 7th December 1926; 11th March & 13th June 1931

Glasgow News 27th December 1934

The Graphic 7th December 1929

Gloucestershire Echo 26th September 1928

Guardian 10th April 1931

Hertfordshire Hemel Hempstead Gazette 22nd February 1936

Islington Gazette 31st January 1934

Jewish Chronicle 5th May 1933

John Bull 26th October 1935; 12th September 1936

The Journal 6th November 1982

Kent and West Sussex Courier 21st October 1955

Kentish Independent October 1926; 12th April 1929; 21st March, 15th August, 24th & 31st October, 14th November 1930; 23rd January, 6th March, 3rd April, 12th June, 3rd & 22nd July, 7th & 21st August, undated but September 1931; 14th December 1934; 1st November 1935

Kentish Mail 21st August 1931

Kentish Mercury 23rd May 1925; October 1926; 12th April 1929; 3rd & 31st October, 21st November, 12th December 1930; 28th August & 18th September 1931; 29th September 1933; 9th November 1934

Kent Messenger 14th & 21st September 1935

Launceston Examiner 11th June 1888

Leeds Mercury 8th May 1926; 22nd July 1933; 2nd April 1937

Leicester Evening Mail 13th June 1934

Leicester Mail 6th April 1929

Lewisham Borough News undated but 1929

Lincoln & Stamford Independent 31st July 1931

Liverpool Daily Post 29th October 1935; 4th July, 24th August & 23rd October 1936

Liverpool Mercury 30th July 1931

Liverpool Post 28th January 1925; 24th October 1928; 4th March & 30th July 1931

Lloyd's Sunday News 14th February 1926

Manchester Evening News 13th February 1925

Manchester Guardian 3rd January 1925; 24th April & 31st October 1930; 24th February & 30th July 1931; 18th & 25th July 1933; 20th February, 6th October, 10th & 14th November 1934; 25th July & 2nd October 1936

Melbourne Argus 18th November 1946

Methodist Recorder 27th September & 20th December 1934; 13th June & 1st November 1935

Methodist Times and Leader 14th October 1935
Mirror [sic] 20th August 1934
Morning Advertiser 21st July 1936
Morning Post 28th January 1925; 13th January 1926; 4th October 1928; 12th July & 4th November 1930; 4th,12th & 17th March 1931; 28th September, 14th November, 20th & 31st December 1934; 23rd February, 18th & 28th March 1935; 31st July, 19th August & 27th November 1936
Newcastle Chronicle 22nd May 1926
Newcastle Daily Journal 13th July 1923; 4th & 8th May 1926
Newcastle Daily Journal 17th May & 2nd July 1926; 7th March 1929
Newcastle Evening Chronicle 13th, 14th & 18th May 1926
New Leader undated but May 1926; 3rd May 1929
News Chronicle 13th & 27th February & 15th April & 12th December 1931; 23rd February 1933; 10th May & 28th December 1934; 10th February, 22nd July, 19th October & 19th November 1936
News of the World July 1926
News World [sic] 16th August 1936
Northampton Echo 11th March 1931
Northampton Evening Telegraph 20th November 1929
North Devon Journal 2nd August 1937
North Eastern Daily Gazette 6th August 1930
Northern Daily Telegraph 23rd January 1931
Northern Echo 3rd & 17th May 1926; 14th September 1927; 29th July 1936
Northern Whig 24th August 1934
North London Recorder 3rd May 1929
North Mail 4th, 13th, 14th, 17th & undated May 1926
North Mail and Newcastle Chronicle 20th & 21st May 1926; 15th November 1930
North Star 17th May & 2nd July 1926; 7th March 1929
North Wales Observer 1st November 1934
Nottingham Evening Post 27th February 1931
Nottingham Guardian 4th March 1931
Nottingham Journal 15th October 1930
Observer 26th July 1931; 16th May 1937
Oxford Mail 24th October 1936
Pearson's Weekly 20th January 1934
People 10th May 1931; 30th July 1933; 30th September 1934; 2nd August 1936
Peterborough Standard 31st July 1931
Portsmouth Evening News 16th October 1930
Punch 11th December 1929; 10th & 17th December 1930; 5th August 1931; 13th March 1935; 21st April 1937
Reynolds 27th December 1925; 13th May 1928; 30th December 1934
Saturday Review 23rd February 1930; 27th October 1934; 30th March 1935; 31st October 1936
Scotsman 30th July 1931

Sheffield Independent 24th February 1931
Sheffield Telegraph 4th March 1931
Shields Daily News 14th & 19th May 1926
Sidcup Times 31st October 1930; 12th June 1931; 4th August 1933
South Eastern Mercury 9th June & 18th August 1931
The Sphere 4th August 1928; 28th November 1936
Star 27th March 1925; 24th October 1928; 5th & 25th November 1929; 13th
    May & 10th November 1930; 4th, 11th & 24th March, 26th June & 17th July
    1931; 31st October & 21st December 1934; 17th July & 25th September
    1936
Sunday Chronicle 13th December 1931; 6th March 1932
Sunday Dispatch 4th November 1934; 26th April, 2nd August & 11th October
    1936
Sunday Express 20th January & 23rd June 1929; 21st July 1935
Sunday Graphic and Sunday News 4th March 1934; 2nd August 1936
Sunday Herald 2nd January 1927
Sunday Mercury 12th January 1936; 7th March 1937
Sunday Pictorial 10th July 1938
Sunday Referee 14th March & 7th April 1935; 14th February 1937; 22nd May
    1938
Sunday Times 28th October 1928; 19th July 1936
Sussex Daily News 30th December 1925; 4th January 1926; 17th November
    1927; 3rd January 1928; 1st May 1935
Sydney Morning Herald 17th June 1924
Times 13th January 1919; 30th August 1921; 12th November 1924; 25th
    March 1925; 4th June, 22nd July, 14th, 17th & 20th August 1926; 13th
    January 1927; 2nd January & 4th October 1928; 19th February, 1st June,
    19th & 24th July 1929; 10th April, 20th June, 1st & 4th July, 2nd & 3rd
    October, 24th, 26th, 28th & 29th November & 10th December 1930; 12th,
    13th & 27th February, 3rd, 4th & 5th March, 16th April, 6th May, 9th, 11th,
    12th & 16th June, 1st, 2nd, 17th & 30th July, 1st, 3rd, 4th, 12th & 25th August,
    19th & 29th October, 12th December 1931; 4th January, 23rd August & 3rd
    September 1932; 23rd February, & 11th September 1933; 11th & 18th
    December 1934; 15th January, 28th March, 8th June, 5th September,
    12th, 23rd, 25th & 29th October, 1st, 16th & 19th November 1935; 11th, 17th,
    18th, 25th & 28th July, 22nd September, 3rd, 21st & 24th October, 30th
    December 1936; 18th February, 29th April & 26th November 1937; 15th &
    25th February, 30th May & 15th June 1938; 31st January, 28th February,
    4th & 22nd April, 20th June, 29th September, 2nd, 3rd & 9th October 1939;
    15th November 1940; 17th & 25th March, 5th & 17th June 1941; 10th April
    1942; 22nd, 23rd, 25th & 27th September 1943
Tit-Bits 28th September 1935
Toronto Evening Telegram 2nd November 1935
Truth 5th August 1931; 18th September 1935
Walthamstow Guardian 2nd August 1935
Weekly Despatch 22nd October 1922; 3rd June 1928

Western Daily Press 9th May 1929; 26th June 1931
Western Mail and South Wales News 2nd April 1937
Western Morning Press 11th December 1934
Western News and Mercury 26th February 1931
Westminster Gazette 22nd November 1924
Winnipeg Tribune 25th November 1931
Woman's Leader and Common Cause 6th December 1929
Woolwich Gazette 16th June 1931
Woolwich Pioneer 3rd July 1925
World's Press News 13th December 1934; 21st March & 24th June 1935
Yorkshire Evening Express 26th June 1930
Yorkshire Evening News 16th August 1927; 29th April 1938; undated but 1929
Yorkshire Herald undated but September 1933
Yorkshire Observer 5th November 1926
Yorkshire Post 1st May 1922; 8th May & 4th June 1926; 27th February 1931; 27th September & 21st December 1933; 2nd August 1937

Periodicals and Specialist Publications

Advertisers' Review 22nd October 1936
Architect and Building News 24th July 1936
British Medical Journal 1st December 1928; 22nd Februaary 1936; 30th July 1938
Cavalcade 24th October 1936
Economist 1st June 1935; 18th May 1940; 24th October 1942
Engineer 9th October 1936
GK's Weekly 13th August 1936
Good Housekeeping July 1934
Health and Strength 26th February 1938
Home and Empire September 1935
Illustrated London News 28th November & 12th December 1936
Insurance Record August 1929
Labour Leader March 1927
Labour Monthly June 1926
Listener 22nd February 1933; 3rd & 31st January, & June 1934
Mother and Child October 1935
Municipal Journal 29th November 1935; 24th July, 9th October & 13th November 1936
Nash's Magazine June 1935
National Review January 1935
Nature 19th September 1936
New Statesman and Nation 15th June 1935; 5th December 1942
The Passing Show 3rd December 1932; 5th October 1935
Popular Wireless 11th November 1933; 13th January & 5th May 1934
The Post 16th July 1933; 15th June 1935

Post Office magazine July & August 1934

Primrose League Gazette June, October, November & December 1935; October 1936; April, May, June, October & November 1938; January, July, October & December 1939; January & June 1940; May 1941; January & May 1942; January, May & October 1943

Publisher's Circular 23rd March 1929

Queen 20th December 1933

Radio Times 30th December 1932

St Martins le Grand October 1932

School Governor Review undated but 1936

Spectator 10th December 1928; 28th July 1933; 4th December 1936

Supervisory 15th July 1932; 1st September 1933

Tatler 1st December 1937

Times Literary Supplement 30th November 1940

Today's Cinema undated but 1937

The Week-End Review, April 1933

Weekly Illustrated 28th November 1936

Secondary Sources

Books

Addison, Paul, 'The Road to 1945: British Politics and the Second World War', London, Pimlico, 1994 (orig. 1975)

Addison, Paul and Crang, Jeremy A (eds.), 'Listening to Britain: Home Intelligence Reports on Britain's Finest Hour, May to September 1940', London, Vintage Books, 2011

Armstrong, Keith and Beynon, Hugh (eds.), 'Hello, Are You Working? Memoirs of the Thirties in the North-East of England', Whitley Bay, Strong Words, 1977

Attlee, Clement, 'As It Happened', London, Heinemann, 1954

Balfour, Harold, 'Wings Over Westminster', London, Hutchinson, 1973

Ball, Stuart,
'Baldwin and the Conservative Party: The Crisis of 1929-1931', London, Yale University Press, 1988
'Portrait of a Party: The Conservative Party in Britain 1918-1945', Oxford, Oxford University Press, 2013

Ball, Stuart (ed.), 'Conservative Politics in National and Imperial Crisis: Letters from Britain to the Viceroy of India 1926-31', Farnham, Ashgate, 2014

Ball, Stuart and Holliday, Ian (eds.), 'Mass Conservatism: The Conservatives and the Public since the 1880s', London, Frank Cass, 2002

Banks, Donald, 'Flame Over Britain: A Personal Narrative of Petroleum Warfare', London, Sampson Low, Marston, 1946

Bentley, Michael (ed.), 'Public and Private Doctrine: Essays in British History presented to Maurice Cowling', Cambridge, Cambridge University Press, 1993

Berlin, Isaiah, 'Mr Churchill in 1940', London, John Murray, 1949

Beveridge, William,
'Causes and Cures of Unemployment', London, Longmans, 1931
'Power and Influence', London, Hodder & Stoughton, 1953

Bilainkin, George, 'Maisky, Ten Years Ambassador', London, Allen & Unwin, 1944

Blakeway, Denys, 'The Last Dance - 1936: The Year of Change', London, John Murray, 2010

Blythe, Ronald, 'The Age of Illusion: England in the Twenties and Thirties 1919-1940', London, Hamish Hamilton, 1963

Bondfield, Margaret, 'A Life's Work', London, Hutchinson, 1949

Boothby, Robert, 'Boothby: Recollections Of A Rebel', London, Hutchinson, 1978

Bossom, Alfred, 'Some Reminiscences', Maidstone, Kent Messenger, 1959

Brabazon, John (Lord Brabazon of Tara), 'The Brabazon Story', London, Heinemann, 1956

Branson, Noreen and Heinemann, Margot, 'Britain in the Nineteen Thirties', London, Weidenfeld & Nicolson, 1971

Briggs, Asa,
'A Study of the Work of Seebohm Rowntree 1871-1954', London, Longmans, 1961
'Governing the BBC', London, BBC, 1979
'The History of Broadcasting in the UK: Vol. II –The Golden Age of Wireless, 1927-1939', Oxford, Oxford University Press, 1995

Bullock, Alan,
'Ernest Bevin: A Biography', London, Politico's Publishing, 2002
'The Life and Times of Ernest Bevin: vol. 2 - Minister of Labour 1940-1945', London, Heinemann, 1967

Burnett, John, 'Plenty and Want: A Social History of Diet in England from 1815 to the Present Day', London, Scolar Press, 1979 (orig. 1966)

Burns, Emile, 'The General Strike May 1926: Trades Councils in Action', London, Labour Research Department, 1926

Butler, RA, 'The Art of the Possible', London, Hamish Hamilton, 1971

Calder, Angus, 'The People's War: Britain 1939-1945', London, Jonathan Cape, 1969

Calder, Ritchie, 'Carry on London', London, English Universities Press, 1941

Campbell, Gordon, 'Number Thirteen', London, Hodder & Stoughton, 1932

Campbell-Smith, Duncan, 'Masters of the Post: The Authorised History of the Royal Mail', London, Allen Lane, 2011

Carder, Tim, 'The Encyclopaedia of Brighton', East Sussex, East Sussex County Libraries, 1990

Carlton, David, 'MacDonald versus Henderson: The Foreign Policy of the Second Labour Government', London, Macmillan, 1970

Carpenter, Edward, 'Cantuar: The Archbishops in Their Office', London, Cassell, 1971

"Cato", 'Guilty Men', London, Gollancz, 1940

Cazalet, Victor, 'With Sikorski to Russia', London, Curwen Press, 1942

Chester, Lewis, Fay, Stephen and Young, Hugo, 'The Zinoviev Letter', London, Heinemann, 1967

Chisholm, Ann and Davie, Michael, 'Beaverbrook: A Life', London, Hutchinson, 1992

Clark, Alan, 'The Tories: Conservatives and the Nation State 1922-1997', London, Weidenfeld & Nicolson, 1998

Clarke, Peter, 'The Cripps Version: The Life of Sir Stafford Cripps', London, Allen Lane, 2002

Clarke, Simon, 'Keynesianism, Monetarism and the Crisis of the State', Aldershot, Edward Elgar, 1988

Cockett, Richard, 'Twilight of *Truth*: Chamberlain, Appeasement and the Manipulation of the Press', London, Weidenfeld & Nicolson, 1989

Cole, GDH, 'The Simple Case for Socialism', London, Gollancz, 1935

Cole, GDH and Cole, Margaret, 'The Condition of Britain', London, Gollancz, 1937

Collier, Basil, 'The Defence of the United Kingdom', London, HMSO, 1957

Colville, John, 'The Fringes of Power: Downing Street Diaries 1939-1945', London, Hodder & Stoughton, 1985

Conway, Martin, 'Episodes in a Varied Life', London, Country Life, 1932

Cooke, Alistair, 'A Gift from the Churchills: The Primrose League 1883-2004', London, Carlton Club, 2010

Cooper, Diana, 'The Light of Common Day', London, Rupert Hart-Davis, 1959

Coote, Colin,
'A Companion of Honour: The Story of Walter Elliot', London, Collins, 1965
'Editorial: The Memoirs of Colin R Coote', London, Eyre and Spottiswoode, 1965

Cowell, FR, 'The Athenaeum: Club and Social Life in London, 1824-1974', London, Heinemann, 1975

Cowling, Maurice, 'The Impact of Hitler: British Politics and British Policy 1933-1940', London, Cambridge University Press, 1975

Cox, Sebastian and Gray, Peter, 'Air Power History: Turning Points from Kitty Hawk to Kosovo', London, Frank Cass, 2002

Critchley, Alfred, 'Critch! The Memoirs of Brigadier AC Critchley', London, Hutchinson, 1961

Cronin, AJ, 'The Citadel', London, Gollancz, 1937

Crook, Wilfrid Harris, 'The General Strike: A Study of Labor's Tragic Weapon in Theory and Practice', Chapel Hill, University of North Carolina Press, 1931

Crowson, NJ, 'Facing Fascism: The Conservative Party and the European Dictators 1935-1940', London, Routledge, 1997

Crowson, NJ (ed.), 'Fleet Street, Press Barons and Politics: The Journals of Collin Brooks, 1932-1940', Camden Fifth Series vol. 11 for the Royal Historical Society, 1998

Crowther, MA, 'The Workhouse System 1834-1929', London, Batsford, 1981

Crozier, William, 'Off the Record: Political Interviews 1933-1943', London, Hutchinson,1973

Dalton, Hugh, 'The Fateful Years: Memoirs 1931-1945', London, Frederick Muller, 1957

Daunton, Martin,
'Just Taxes: The Politics of Taxation in Britain, 1914-1979', Cambridge, Cambridge University Press, 2002
'Royal Mail: The Post Office Since 1840', London, Athlone Press, 1985

Davenport, Nicholas, 'Vested Interests or Common Pool?', London, Gollancz, 1942

Davies, AJ, 'We, The Nation: The Conservative Party and the Pursuit of Power', London, Little Brown, 1995

Davison, Jack, 'Northumberland Miners 1919-1939', Newcastle, Co-operative Press, 1973

Day, J Wentworth, 'Lady Houston DBE: The Woman Who Won the War', London, Allan Wingate, 1958

Dilks, David, 'Neville Chamberlain - Vol. 1: Pioneering and Reform, 1896-1929', Cambridge, Cambridge University Press, 1984

Duchene, Francois, 'Jean Monnet: The First Statesman of Interdependence', London, Norton, 1944

Dutton, David, 'Simon: A Political Biography of Sir John Simon', London, Aurum Press, 1992

Einzig, Paul, 'In the Centre of Things', London, Hutchinson, 1960

Evans, Joan, 'The Conways: A History of Three Generations', London, Museum Press, 1966

Everitt, Anthony, 'Cicero: A Turbulent Life', London, John Murray, 2001

Ewing, KD and Gearty, CA, 'The Struggle for Civil Liberties: Political Freedom and the Rule of Law in Britain, 1914-1945', Oxford, Oxford University Press, 2000

Feiling, Keith, 'Life of Neville Chamberlain', London, Macmillan, 1946

Ferguson, Sheila and Fitzgerald, Hilde, 'Studies in the Social Services', London, HMSO, 1954

Festinger, Leon, 'A Theory of Cognitive Dissonance', Evanston, Illinois, Row Peterson, 1957

Foot, Dingle, 'British Political Crises', London, William Kimber, 1976

Ford, Herbert, 'Pitcairn Island as a Port of Call', McFarland, 2012

Francis, Martin and Zweiniger-Bargielowska, Ina (eds.), 'The Conservatives and British Society, 1880-1990', Cardiff, University of Wales Press, 1996

Fraser, W Hamish, 'A History of British Trade Unionism 1700-1998', Basingstoke, Macmillan, 1999

Fyfe, Hamilton, 'Behind the Scenes of the Great Strike', London, Labour Publishing Co. (Whitefriars Press), 1926

Galbraith, JK, 'The Great Crash 1929', London, Hamish Hamilton, 1929

Gardiner, Juliet, 'The Thirties: An Intimate History', London, Harper Press, 2010

Gault, Hugh,
'1809: Between Hope and History', Cambridge, Gretton Books, 2009
'Making the Heavens Hum: Kingsley Wood and the Art of the Possible 1881-1924', Cambridge, Gretton Books, 2014

Géraud, André (Pertinax), 'The Gravediggers of France', New York, Doubleday, 1944

Gibbs, Philip, 'Ordeal in England', London, Heinemann, 1938

Gilbert, Bentley, 'British Social Policy 1914-1939', London, Batsford, 1970

Gilbert, Martin,
    'Winston Churchill - vol. 5: 1922-1939', London, Heinemann, 1976
    'Winston Churchill - vol. 6: 1939-1941', London, Heinemann, 1983
    'Winston Churchill, vol.6 [sic]: The Prophet of Truth', Boston, Houghton Mifflin, 1977

Gilbert, Martin and Gott, Richard, 'The Appeasers', London, Weidenfeld & Nicolson, 1963

Glasgow, George, 'General Strikes and Road Transport', London, Geoffrey Bles, 1926

Gorodetsky, Gabriel, 'The Maisky Diaries: Red Ambassador to the Court of St James 1932-1943', London, Yale University Press, 2015

Grant, Mariel, 'Propaganda and the Role of the State in Inter-War Britain', Oxford, Clarendon Press, 1994

Grant, Thomas, 'Jeremy Hutchinson's Case Histories', London, John Murray, 2015

Graves, Robert and Hodge, Alan, 'The Long Week-End: A Social History of Great Britain 1918-1939', London, Hutchinson, 1985 (orig. 1940)

Greenwood, Arthur, 'The Labour Outlook', London, Chapman and Hall, 1929

Greenwood, Walter,
    'How the Other Man Lives', London, Labour Book Service, undated but 1938/39
    'Love on the Dole', London, Vintage 1993 (orig. 1933)

Grey, CG, 'A History of the Air Ministry', London, Allen and Unwin, 1940

Griffiths, James, 'Pages from Memory', London, Dent, 1969

Guest, Leslie Haden, 'Where is Labour Going? A Political Pamphlet', London, Jonathan Cape, 1927

Hadley, WW, 'Munich: Before and After', London, Cassell, 1944

Hale, Dick, 'The National Government and Housing', London, Labour Research Department, 1935

Hancock, WK and Gowing, MM, 'British War Economy', London, HMSO, 1949

Hannington, Wal, 'The Problem of the Distressed Areas', London, Gollancz, 1937

Harris, Jose, 'William Beveridge: A Biography', Oxford, Clarendon, 1977

Harris, Percy, 'Forty Years In and Out of Parliament', London, Andrew Melrose, 1946

Haws, Duncan, 'Merchant Fleets 10: Shaw, Savill and Albion', Burwash, TCL Publications, 1987

Healey, Denis, 'The Time of My Life', London, Penguin, 1990 (orig. 1989)

Herbert, S Mervyn, 'Britain's Health', London, Penguin, 1939

Hibbert, Christopher, 'Disraeli: A Personal History', London, HarperCollins, 2004

Holtby, Winifred, 'South Riding', London, Ebury Publishing (BBC Books), 2011 (orig. 1935)

Hughes, Michael, 'Cartoons from the General Strike', London, Evelyn Adams and Mackay, 1968

Hutt, Allen, 'The Condition of the Working Class in Britain', London, Martin Lawrence, 1933

Idle, E Doreen, 'War Over West Ham: A Study of Community Adjustment', London, Faber and Faber, 1943

Imlay, Talbot C and Toft, Monica Duffy (eds.), 'Fog of Peace and War Planning: Military and Strategic Planning Under Uncertainty', London, Routledge, 2006

James, Robert Rhodes,
'Anthony Eden', London, Weidenfeld & Nicolson, 1986
'Bob Boothby: A Portrait', London, Hodder & Stoughton, 1991

Jameson, Storm, 'Civil Journey', London, Cassell, 1939

Jenkins, Roy,
'The Chancellors', London, Macmillan, 1998
'Mr Attlee: An Interim Biography', London, Heinemann, 1948

Johnston, James, 'A Hundred Commoners', London, Herbert Joseph, 1931

Johnston, Thomas, 'Memories', London, Collins, 1952

Joubert de la Ferte, Philip, 'The Third Service: The Story Behind the RAF', London, Thames and Hudson, 1955

Kenworthy, Joseph,
'Narvik and After: A Study of the Scandinavian Campaign', London, Hutchinson, 1940
'Sailors, Statesmen and Others - An Autobiography', London, Rich and Cowan, 1933

Keynes, John Maynard,
'The Economic Consequences of Mr Churchill', London, Hogarth Press, 1925
'How to Pay for the War: A Radical Plan for the Chancellor of the Exchequer', London, Macmillan, 1940

Keynes, John Maynard and Henderson, Hubert, 'Can Lloyd George Do It? An Examination of the Liberal Pledge', London, The Nation and Athenaeum, 1929

Keynes, Milo (ed.), 'Lydia Lopokova', London, Weidenfeld & Nicolson, 1983

Kingsford, Peter, 'The Hunger Marchers in Britain 1920-1939', London, Lawrence and Wishart, 1982

Koss, Stephen, 'Fleet Street Radical: AG Gardiner and the *Daily News*', London, Allen Lane, 1973

Kynaston, David, 'The City of London, vol. III: Illusions of Gold 1914-1945', London, Chatto & Windus, 1999

Labour Research Department, 'Why It Happened: Capitalism in Crisis', London, Marshalsea Press, 1934

Lawlor, Sheila, 'Churchill and the Politics of War, 1940-1941', Cambridge, Cambridge University Press, 1994

Laybourn, Keith, 'British Political Leaders: A Biographical Dictionary', Oxford, ABC-CLIO, 2001

Lee, JM, 'The Churchill Coalition 1940-1945', London, Batsford, 1980

Lewis, Jane, 'The Politics of Motherhood: Child and Maternal Welfare in England, 1900-1939', London, Croom Helm, 1980

Low, David, 'Low's Autobiography', London, Michael Joseph, 1956

Luckin, Bill, 'Death and Survival in Urban Britain: Disease, Pollution and Environment, 1800-1950', London, IB Tauris, 2015

Lysaght, Charles E., 'Brendan Bracken', London, Allen Lane, 1979

Macintyre, Stuart, 'Little Moscows: Communism and Working-Class Militancy in Inter-War Britain', London, Croom Helm, 1980

Macleod, Iain, 'Neville Chamberlain', London, Muller, 1961

Macmillan, Harold, The Middle Way: A Study of the Problem of Economic and Social Progress in a Free and Democratic Society', London, Macmillan, 1938

MacNalty Arthur (ed.), 'The Civilian Health and Medical Services, vol. I', London, HMSO, 1953

MacNicol, John, 'The Politics of Retirement in Britain, 1878-1948', Cambridge, Cambridge University Press, 1998

Martin, Kingsley, 'Harold Laski (1893-1950): A Biographic Memoir', London, Gollancz, 1953

Mason, Anthony, 'The General Strike in the North East', Hull, University of Hull, 1970

McCarrison, Robert, 'Nutrition and National Health', London, Royal Society of Arts, 1936

McGonigle, GCM and Kirby, J, 'Poverty and Public Health', London, Gollancz, 1936

McKercher, Brian, 'Transition of Power: Britain's Loss of Global Pre-eminence to the USA, 1930-1945', Cambridge, Cambridge University Press, 1999

Middlemas, Keith, 'Politics in Industrial Society: The Experience of the British System since 1911', London, Andre Deutsch, 1979

Middlemas, Keith and Barnes, John, 'Baldwin: A Biography', London, Weidenfeld & Nicolson, 1969

Middleton, Roger, 'Towards the Managed Economy: Keynes, the Treasury and the Fiscal Policy Debate of the 1930s', London, Methuen, 1985

Minney, RJ, 'The Private Papers of Hore-Belisha', London, Collins, 1960

Moggridge, DE (ed.),

'Collected Writings of John Maynard Keynes - vol. XXII: Activities 1939-1945: Internal War Finance', London, Macmillan/Cambridge University Press for the Royal Economic Society, 1978

'The Collected Writings of John Maynard Keynes - vol. XXIII: Activities 1940-1943: External War Finance', London, Macmillan/Cambridge University Press for the Royal Economic Society, 1979

Morrison, Herbert, 'An Autobiography', London, Odhams, 1960

Mowat, Charles Loch, 'Britain Between the Wars 1918-1940', London, Methuen, 1955

Muckle, William, 'No Regrets', Newcastle, People's Publications, 1981

Muir, Ramsay, 'The Record of the National Government', London, George Allen & Unwin, 1936

Nicholson, AP, 'The Real Men in Public Life: Forces and Factors in the State', London, Collins, 1928

Olson, Lynne, 'Troublesome Young Men: The Churchill Conspiracy of 1940', London, Bloomsbury, 2007

Orr, John Boyd,
'As I Recall', London, Macgibbon & Kee, 1966
'Food, Health and Income: Report on a Survey of Adequacy of Diet in Relation to Income', London, Macmillan, 1936

Orwell, George,
'A Clergyman's Daughter', London, Penguin, 1935
'The Lion and the Unicorn: Socialism and the English Genius', London, Penguin, 1982 (orig. 1941)

Peden, George, 'British Re-armament and the Treasury: 1932-1939', Edinburgh, Scottish Academic Press, 1979

Pedersen, Susan,
'Eleanor Rathbone and the Politics of Conscience', London, Yale University Press, 2004
'Family, Dependence. and the Origins of the Welfare State: Britain and France, 1914-1945', Cambridge, Cambridge University Press, 1993

Pelling, Henry, 'Winston Churchill', 2nd edition, London, Macmillan, 1989 (orig. 1974)

Perkins, Anne, 'A Very British Strike 3 May-12 May 1926', London, Macmillan, 2006

Perry, Matt, '"Red Ellen" Wilkinson: Her Ideas, Movements and World', Manchester, Manchester University Press, 2014

Pertinax (André Géraud), 'The Gravediggers of France', New York, Doubleday, 1944

Pethick-Lawrence, Frederick, 'Fate Has Been Kind', London, Hutchinson, 1942

Phillips, GA, 'The General Strike: The Politics of Industrial Conflict', London, Weidenfeld & Nicolson, 1976

Pimlott, Ben (ed.), 'The Political Diary of Hugh Dalton 1918-1940, 1945-1960', London, Cape, 1986

Political and Economic Planning (PEP),
'Report on the British Health Services', London, PEP, 1937
'Report on the British Social Services', London, PEP, 1937

Postgate, RW, Wilkinson, Ellen and Horrabin, JF, 'A Workers' History of the Great Strike', London, The Plebs League, 1927

Pottle, Mark (ed.), 'Champion Redoubtable: The Diaries and Letters of Violet Bonham Carter 1914-1945', London, Weidenfeld & Nicolson, 1998

Prazmowska, Anita, 'Britain, Poland and the Eastern Front, 1939', Cambridge, Cambridge University Press, 1987

Preston, Harry,
'Leaves From My Unwritten Diary', London, Hutchinson, 1936
'Memories', London, Constable, 1928

Priestley, JB, 'Postscripts', London, Heinemann, 1940

Purcell, William, 'Fisher of Lambeth: A Portrait from Life', London, Hodder & Stoughton, 1969

Raczynski, Edward, 'In Allied London', London, Weidenfeld & Nicolson, 1962

Ramsden, John, 'The Making of Conservative Party Policy: The Conservative Research Department Since 1929', London, Longman, 1980

Reith, John, 'Into the Wind', London, Hodder & Stoughton, 1949

Reynolds, David 'The Creation of the Anglo-American Alliance1937-1941: A Study in Competitive Co-operation', London, Europa Publications, 1981

Richards, Denis, 'Portal of Hungerford', London, Heinemann, 1977

Richie, Sebastian, 'Industry and Air Power: The Expansion of British Air-craft Production', London, Frank Cass, 1997

Robbins, Lionel, 'Autobiography of An Economist', London, Macmillan, 1971

Robinson, Howard, 'Britain's Post Office: A History of Developments from the Beginnings to the Present Day', London, Oxford University Press, 1953

Rock, William R, 'Appeasement on Trial', Hamden, Conn., Archon, 1966

Roodhouse, Mark, 'Black Market Britain: 1939-1955', Oxford, Oxford University Press, 2013

Rose, Kenneth, 'The Later Cecils', London, Weidenfeld and Nicolson, 1975

Roskill, Stephen, 'Hankey: Man of Secrets - vol. III 1931-1963', London, Collins, 1974

Russell, Bertrand, Bartlett, Vernon, Cole, GDH, Cripps, Stafford, Morrison, Herbert and Laski, Harold, 'Dare We Look Ahead?', London, George Allen & Unwin, 1938

Sabine, BEV, 'British Budgets in Peace and War 1932-1945', London, George Allen & Unwin, 1970

Salter, Arthur, 'Memoirs of a Public Servant', London, Faber and Faber, 1961

Saunders, Anne (ed.), 'London County Council Bomb Damage Maps 1939-1945', London Topographical Society and London Metropolitan Archives, 2005

Schneer, Jon, 'Ministers At War: Churchill and His War Cabinet', London, One World, 2015

Self, Robert, 'Neville Chamberlain: A Biography', Aldershot, Ashgate, 2006

Shakespeare, Geoffrey, 'Let Candles Be Brought In', London, Macdonald, 1949

Shay, Robert Paul, 'British Re-armament in the Thirties', Princeton NJ, Princeton University Press, 1977

Simon, John,
'Retrospect: The Memoirs of the Rt Hon Viscount Simon', London, Hutchinson, 1952
'Three Speeches on the General Strike', London, Macmillan, 1926

Skelton, Noel, 'Constructive Conservatism', London, William Blackwood and Sons, 1924

Skidelsky, Robert,
'Britain Since 1900: A Success Story?', London, Vintage Books, 2014
'John Maynard Keynes: vol. III, Fighting for Britain 1837-1946', London, Macmillan, 2000
'Politicians and the Slump: The Labour Government of 1929-1931', London, Macmillan, 1967

Skinner, Dennis, 'Sailing Close to the Wind', London, Quercus, 2014

Slessor, John, 'The Central Blue: Recollections and Reflections', London, Cassell, 1956

Smart, Nick, 'The National Government 1931-1940', London, Macmillan, 1999

Smith, FE (Earl of Birkenhead), 'Contemporary Personalities', London, Cassell, 1924

Snell, Henry, 'Men, Movements and Myself', London, JM Dent & Sons, 1936

Stannage, Tom, 'Baldwin Thwarts the Opposition: The British General Election of 1935', London, Croom Helm, 1980

Steiner, Zara, 'The Triumph of the Dark: European International History 1933-1939', Oxford, Oxford University Press, 2011

Symons, Julian, 'The General Strike: A Historical Portrait', London, Readers Union/Cresset Press, 1959

Tayar, Graham (ed.), 'Personality and Power: Studies in Political Achievement', London, BBC, 1971

Taylor, AJP,
'Beaverbrook', London, Hamish Hamilton, 1972

'English History 1914-1945', Oxford, Oxford University Press, 1965

Taylor, AJP (ed.), 'Churchill Revised: A Critical Assessment', New York, Dial Press, 1969

Thomas, JH, 'My Story', London, Hutchinson, 1937

Thompson, George M, 'Vote of Censure', London, Secker and Warburg, 1968

Times, 'The Nation's Health', London, *Times*, 1937

Tinniswood, Adrian, 'The Long Weekend: Life in the English Country House Between the Wars', London, Jonathan Cape, 2016

Titmuss, Richard,
'Poverty and Population: A Factual Study of Contemporary Social Waste', London, Macmillan, 1938
'Problems of Social Policy', London, HMSO, 1950

Tree, Ronald, 'When the Moon Was High: Memoirs of Peace and War 1897-1942', London, Macmillan, 1975

Turberfield, Alan, 'John Scott Lidgett', Peterborough, Epworth Press, 2003

Vernon, James, 'Hunger: A Modern History', London, Harvard University Press, 2007

Waszak, Leon J, 'Agreement in Principle: The Wartime Partnership of General Wladyslaw Sikorski and Winston Churchill', New York, Peter Lang, 1996

Waugh, Evelyn, 'Scoop', London, Chapman and Hall, 1938

Welles, Sumner, 'The Time for Decision', London, Hamish Hamilton, 1944

Wilkinson, Ellen,
'Clash', London, Virago, 1989 (orig.1929)
'Peeps At Politicians', London, Philip Allan & Co., 1930
'The Town That Was Murdered', London, Gollancz, 1939

Williams, Francis,
'A Prime Minister Remembers', London, Heinemann, 1961
'Dangerous Estate: The Anatomy of Newspapers', Cambridge, Patrick Stephens, 1984 (orig. 1957)

Williamson, Philip, 'National Crisis and National Government: British Politics, the Economy and Empire, 1926-1932', Cambridge, Cambridge University Press, 1992

Winch, Donald, 'Economics and Policy: A Historical Study', London, Hodder and Stoughton, 1969

Winter, CWR, 'Queen Mary: Her Early Years Recalled', Wellingborough, Patrick Stephens, 1986

Winterton, Earl (Edward Turnour), 'Orders of the Day', London, Cassell, 1953

Women's Group on Public Welfare, 'Our Towns: A Close-Up', 2nd edition, London, Oxford University Press, 1944

Worley, Matthew, 'Oswald Mosley and the New Party', Basingstoke, Palgrave Macmillan, 2010

Wrigley, Chris (ed.), 'A History of British Industrial Relations 1914-1939', Aldershot, Gregg revivals, 1993 (orig. 1987)

Young, Ken, 'Local Politics and the Rise of Party: The London Municipal Society and the Conservative Intervention in Local Elections 1894-1963', Leicester, Leicester University Press, 1975

Youngson, AJ, 'The British Economy 1920-1957', London, George Allen & Unwin, 1960

Zweiniger-Bargielowska, Ina, 'Managing the Body: Beauty, Health and Fitness in Britain, 1880-1939', Oxford, Oxford University Press, 2010

Articles

Baxter, Colin F, "Churchill: Military strategist?", *Military Affairs*, 1983, 47, pp7-10

Beers. Laura, "A model MP? Ellen Wilkinson, gender, politics and celebrity culture in inter-war Britain", *Cultural and Social History*, 2013, 10, pp231-250

Cockett, RB, "Ball, Chamberlain and *Truth*", *Historical Journal,* 1990, 33, pp131-142

Crowcroft, Robert, "Financial policy, coalition and Sir Kingsley Wood, 1940-1", *Twentieth Century British History*, 2015, 26, pp74-96

Dilks, David, "The twilight war and the fall of France: Chamberlain and Churchill in 1940", *Transactions of the Royal Historical Society*, 1978, 28, pp61-86

Dobson, Alan P, "'A mess of pottage for your economic birthright?' The 1941-42 wheat negotiations and Anglo-American economic diplomacy", *Historical Journal*, 1985, 28, pp739-750

Fair, John D,
    "The Conservative basis for the formation of the National Government of 1931", *Journal of British Studies*, 1980, 19, pp142-164
    "The second Labour government and the politics of electoral reform", *Albion*, 1981, 13, pp276-301
    "The Norwegian campaign and Churchill's rise to power in 1940: A study of perception and attribution", *International History Review*, 1987, 9, pp410-437

Fair, John D and Hutcheson, John, "British Conservatism in the twentieth century: An emerging ideological tradition" *Albion*, 1987, 19, pp 549-578

Gibbon, IG, "Town planning: It's place in social development", *Public Administration*, 1923, 1, pp333-342

Harrison, Brian,
    "The rise, fall and rise of political consensus in Britain since 1940", *History*, 1999, 84, pp301-324

"Women in a men's house: The women MPs, 1919-1945", *Historical Journal*, 1986, 29, pp623-654

Hollins, TJ, "The Conservative Party and film propaganda between the wars", *English Historical Review*, 1981, 96, pp359-369

Imlay, Talbot Charles, "A re-assessment of Anglo-French strategy during the phoney war, 1939-1940", *English Historical Review*, 2004, 119, pp333-372

Jarvis, David, "Mrs Maggs and Betty: The Conservative appeal to women voters in the 1920s", *Twentieth Century British History*, 1994, 5, pp129-152

Jones, Stephen G, "State intervention in sport and leisure in Britain between the wars", *Journal of Contemporary History*, 1987, 22, pp163-182

Koss, Stephen, "Lloyd George and Nonconformity: The last rally", *English Historical Review*, 1974, 89, pp77-108

Loudon, Irvine, "The transformation of maternal mortality", *BMJ*, 1992, 305, pp1557-1560

McDonald, GW and Gospel, Howard F, "The Mond-Turner talks 1927-1933: A study in industrial co-operation", *Historical Journal*, 1973, 16, pp807-829

Mosley, Stephen, "A network of trust: Measuring and monitoring air pollution in British cities, 1912-1960", *Environment and History*, 2009, 15, pp273-302

Pimlott, Ben, Kavanagh, Dennis and Morris, Peter, "Is the 'post-war consensus' a myth?", *Contemporary Record*, 1989, 2:6, pp12-15

Political and Economic Planning (PEP), "The malnutrition controversy", *Planning*, 1936, No. 88, p2

Pressnell, LS with Hopkins, Sheila V, "A canard out of time? Churchill, the War Cabinet, and the Atlantic Charter, August 1941", *Review of International Studies*, 1988, 14, pp223-235

Prest, AR, "Sense and nonsense in budgetary policy", *Economic Journal*, 1968, 78, pp1-18

Reid, Alastair and Tolliday, Simon, "The General Strike 1926", *Historical Journal*, 1977, 20, pp1001-1012

Richie, Sebastian, "A political intrigue against the Chief of the Air Staff: The downfall of Air Chief Marshal Sir Cyril Newall", *War and Society*, 1998, 16, pp83-104

Robertson, DH, "A narrative of the General Strike of 1926", *Economic Journal*, 1926, 36, pp375-393

Rose, Marc A, "Hitler's aerial triumph", *Readers Digest*, March 1939, 4, no. 203, pp6-10

Ross, William A, "Local Government Board and after", *Public Administration*, 1956, 34, pp17-25

Self, Robert, "Treasury control and the Empire Marketing Board: The rise and fall of non-tariff preference in Britain, 1924-1933", *Twentieth Century British History*, 1994, 5, pp153-182

Simon, ED, "Slum clearance", *The Nineteenth Century and After*, 1930, 107, pp331-338

Toye, Richard, "Keynes, the Labour movement and 'How to Pay for the War'", *Twentieth Century British History*, 1999, 10, pp255-281

Webster, Charles, "Healthy or hungry Thirties?", *History Workshop Journal*, 1982, 13, pp110-129

Williamson, Philip, "Christian Conservatives and the totalitarian challenge 1933-1940", *English Historical Review*, 2000, 115, pp607-642

Witherell, Larry L, "Lord Salisbury's 'Watching Committee' and the fall of Neville Chamberlain", *English Historical Review*, 2001, 116, pp1134-1166

Wood, Kingsley, "Slum clearance: A reply", *The Nineteenth Century and After*, 1930, 107, pp480-483

Other

Alleynian, vol. LXXIII, No. 509, November 1945

Annual Register, 6th January 1928

'Dod's Parliamentary Companion', London, Dods, 1895-1986

Institute of Journalists, 'Grey Book', 1923, 1928-1940

Kelly's Directories for:
>London 1930 & 1945
>Westgate-on-Sea 1916/17, 1920-1927, 1928

London County Council, 'List of Streets and Places Within the Administrative County of London', 3rd edition, London, PS King & Son, 1929

'Oxford Dictionary of National Biography', Oxford, Oxford University Press, 2004

'Oxford English Dictionary', 2nd edition, Oxford, Clarendon, 1989

Alan Pollock play 'One Night in November', 2008

Post Office Directories for London 1928-1945

Radio 4 'Desert Island Discs', 20th October 2013

Vacher's Parliamentary Companion 1935 and 1936

Westgate-on-Sea Official Guide, Chamber of Commerce, 1937

'Who Was Who' for 1916-1990 (vols. II to VIII), London, A & C Black, 1929-1991

Websites

Airfields/Airports

http://myntransportblog.com/2014/06/15/marshall-buses-cambridge-since-1909-england-uk

http://www.exetermemories.co.uk/em/_scrapbook/1930s.php

www.lutontoday.co.uk/.../flying-heroine-amy-johnson-helped-luton-airport-take-off-1-6293191

Bibliography

Birmingham
www.birminghamhistory.net/category/1960-1969/

Bomber Command
www.raf.mod.uk/history/bombercommandheavybombersavroaldershot.cfm

Father Tierney
http://aodhruadh.org/facilities/father_tierney.php.

Gresford Colliery
www.wrexham.gov.uk/english/heritage/gresford_disaster/nations_
reaction.htm

History of the BBC
http://www.bbc.co.uk/historyofthebbc/research/culture/bbc-and-
gov/hashagen

Imperial War Museum
www.iwm.org.uk/collections/item/object/205207514

Kirkby
http://www.nwemail.co.uk/memories/how-villagers-coped-with-six-years-of-
war-1.1140013

Spitfire Ladies
www.lady.co.uk/people/8838-the-spitfire-ladies

University of Kent Special Collections (Kingsley Wood)
www.kent.ac.uk/library/specialcollections/other/kingsley-wood/index.html

OVERALL INDEX to Parts 1 and 2

First seven chapters (i.e. Pt1) = Pt1-; this book, chapters 8-20 (i.e. Pt2) = Pt2- followed by relevant page, footnote number.

n preface refers to the footnotes; it is followed by the note rather than the page number

People's names as referred to in the text: i.e., Viscount Cranborne or Lord Cheylesmore but George (rather than Marquis) Curzon.

Some minor references are not indexed.

Morgenthau, Henry   Pt2-442,
443, 444, n1796, 469
Morris (Temple-Morris), Owen
Pt2-254, n1074
Morrison, Herbert   Pt2-n263,
103, n517, 131, 164, 189,
220-221, 294, 316, n1428,
362, 394-395, 396, 405, 431,
n1758, 432, 459, 460, n1875,
466, 467
Morrison, WS   Pt2-199, 218
Mosley, Oswald Pt1- 196, 200,
215; Pt2-4, 110, n510, 188,
213, 348
Muckle, William   Pt2-40 *see*
General Strike
Munich *see* Chamberlain
Municipal Reform *see* London
County Council
municipal trading Pt2-118-122
Murray, Evelyn Pemberton   Pt2-
168, 169, n709, 172, 174,
178-179, n740
Murray, George Herbert   Pt2-
168, 172
Mussolini, Benito   Pt2-89, 277,
340, 343, 358, n1557

national crisis 1931 Pt2-134-166,
n575 *see* other crises
national fitness Pt2-291, 292,
311, 313, 322-329
National Government
- 1931 Pt2-n69, n235, 92,
n529, 134-135, 155-165,
n690, 168-169, 204, 209,
210, 215, 218-219, 221,
228-229, n959
- 1935 Pt2-197, 211, 243-244
see e.g. general election
1935, Kingsley Wood
National Health Week 1912 Pt1-
78-79
national insurance Pt1-44-53,
90-91, 187-192 *see* Kingsley
Wood

National Publicity Bureau *see*
Conservative Party and
Kingsley Wood
National Union of Conservative
and Unionist Associations
Pt2-n893, 215
National Union of Distributive
and Allied Workers (NUDAW)
Pt2-n113
National Union of Railwaymen
(NUR) Pt2-n113, 57
National Union of Sailors and
Firemen Pt2-n113, n190
National Unemployed Workers
Movement (NUWM) Pt2-247,
n1034, 291 *see* Hannington
Nazi/Nazism Pt2-87, 88, 323,
346, n1416, 358, 359, 383,
389, 431
New Party *see* Mosley
Newall, Cyril   Pt2-n1518, 382
Newcastle and General Strike
Pt2-26-44 *see* Distressed
(Special) Areas
Newcastle Council Pt2-40 *see*
General Strike
Newman, George   Pt2-59, 284,
n1186, 296, 304, 314
New Zealand Pt2-96, 282, 360,
373, 401
Nicolson, Harold   Pt2-348, 393-
394, 395, 396, 397, 402, 409,
n1691
Nonconformist Unionist
Association *see* home rule
(Ireland)
Northern Division see General
Strike
Northumberland Pt2-23, 26, 30,
33, 39, 44 *see* General Strike
Northumberland Coal Owners'
Association Pt2-n96, 45
Northumberland Miners Union
Pt2-26, 30, 40, 44, 45
Norway campaign Pt2-388-392,
400, 442

Poplarism Pt2-n396 *see* Poor Law

Portal, Charles 'Peter' Pt2-365, n1494, 372

Postmaster-General *see* Kingsley Wood

Post Office Pt2-n56, 17, n662, 167-211, *passim including* films and Film Unit 180, 181, savings bank 167, 174, telegrams 167, 168, 174, telephones Pt2-167, 174, 179, 185

poverty Pt1-15-16, 32, 38, 43, 44, 45, 97, 116; Pt2-39, 48, 65, 97, 134, 182, 293, 297, 300, 303, 305, 307, 308, 310, 312, 316, 318, 322, 449, 450 *see* Distressed (Special) Areas, housing, slums overcrowding

Pownall, Assheton Pt2-20, n72, n506, n527, n657

Pownall, Henry Pt2-186, 361, 365, n1547, 390, n1609, 403

Preston (town) Pt2-n235, 300

Preston, Harry Pt1-35, 142, 210, n913; Pt2-11, 12-14, n48, 102, 268, 273-274

Priestley, JB Pt2-269
- WWII broadcasts Pt2-189-190, n1416, 416

Primrose League Pt1-8, n60; Pt2-132, n587, 233, 260-264, n1090, 275, 465

Progressives *see* London County Council

protection/protectionism and tariffs Pt1-68, 210-212, 213; Pt2-7, 97, 121, 142, 162, 163, 165, 218, 446 *see* Baldwin, trade and tariffs

public health Pt2-n260, 79, 187, 254, 289, 290, n1224, 303, n1335, 352-354 *see* Distressed (Special) Areas, housing, slums, national fitness, overcrowding, physique

Public Health Act 1936 Pt2-290, 319, n1309

Queen Mary (ship) Pt1-197, n856; Pt2-280

Queen Mary (wife of George V) Pt1-42, 76, 157-158

Ramsden, Eugene Pt2-217, 411

Rathbone, Eleanor Pt2-301, 306 *see* family allowances

rating and valuation Pt2-5, 59, 68, 73-74, 76, 79, 123, 148-149

Rattenbury, JE Pt1-55, 128, n638, n639

Raw, Nathan Pt1-135-136

Redmond, John Pt1-62

rearmament Pt2-n959, 292, n1405, n1406, 346, 358-365, 374, 375, 423

Reith, John Pt1-1; Pt2-30-31, n120, 186-202, n822, n825, n1009, 392, n1615, n1616, 411, n1730, n1734, 428

rent controls/restrictions *see* housing

Reynaud, Paul Pt2-383, 403

Rhondda Pt2-311

Rhondda, Lord David Thomas Pt1-111, 113, 114, 136
- Lloyd George links Pt1-n472

Richardson, Robert Pt2-28

Riddell, George Pt1-50, 62, n287, 109, 119, 120; Pt2-132
- Lloyd George links Pt1-n19, n171

Robinson, Arthur Pt2-59, n263, 60, 61

Roosevelt, Franklin D Pt2-n828, 226, 380, n1565, n1699, 461